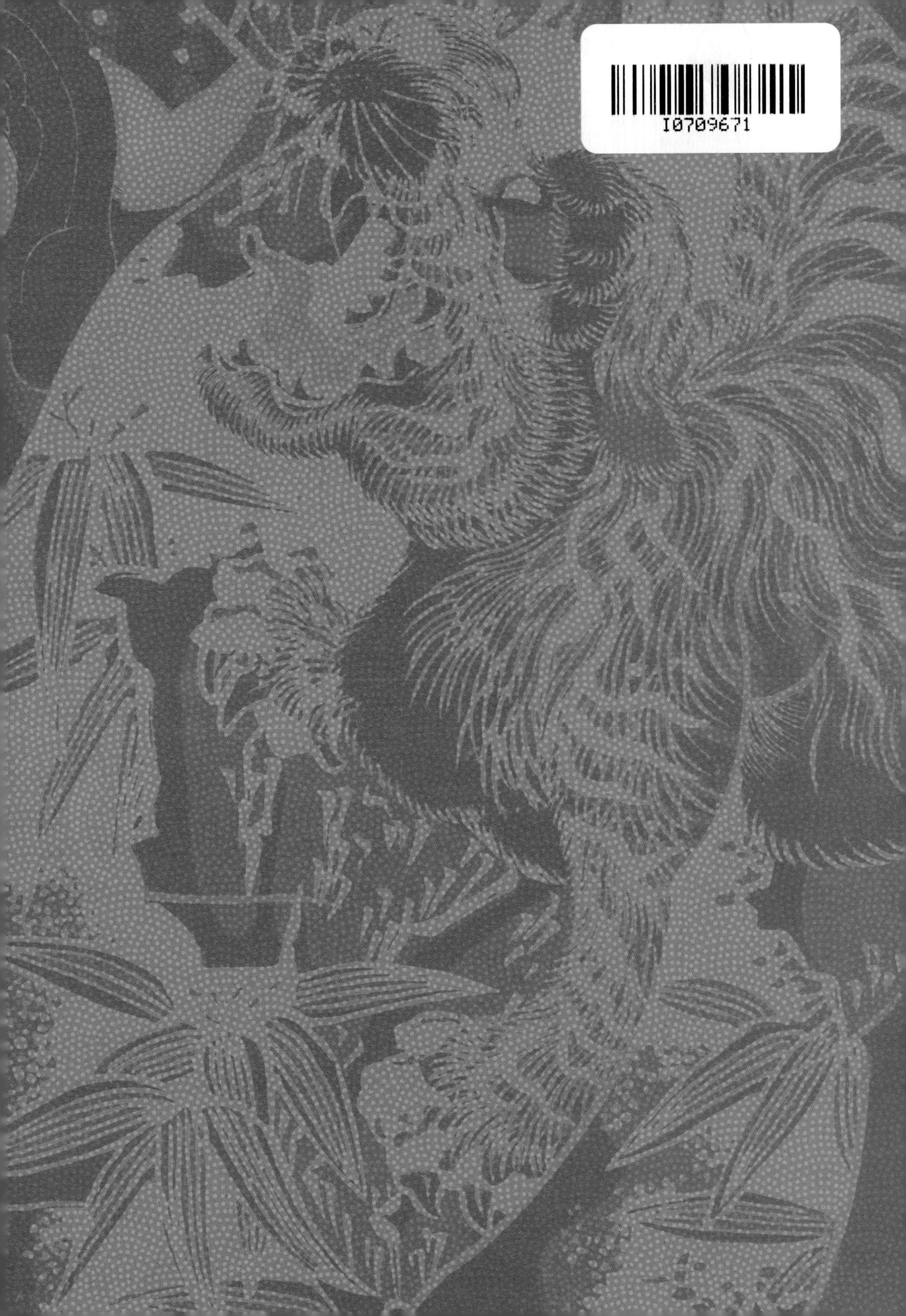

I0709671

日本の図像

刺青

TATTOO:
The Iconography of Japan

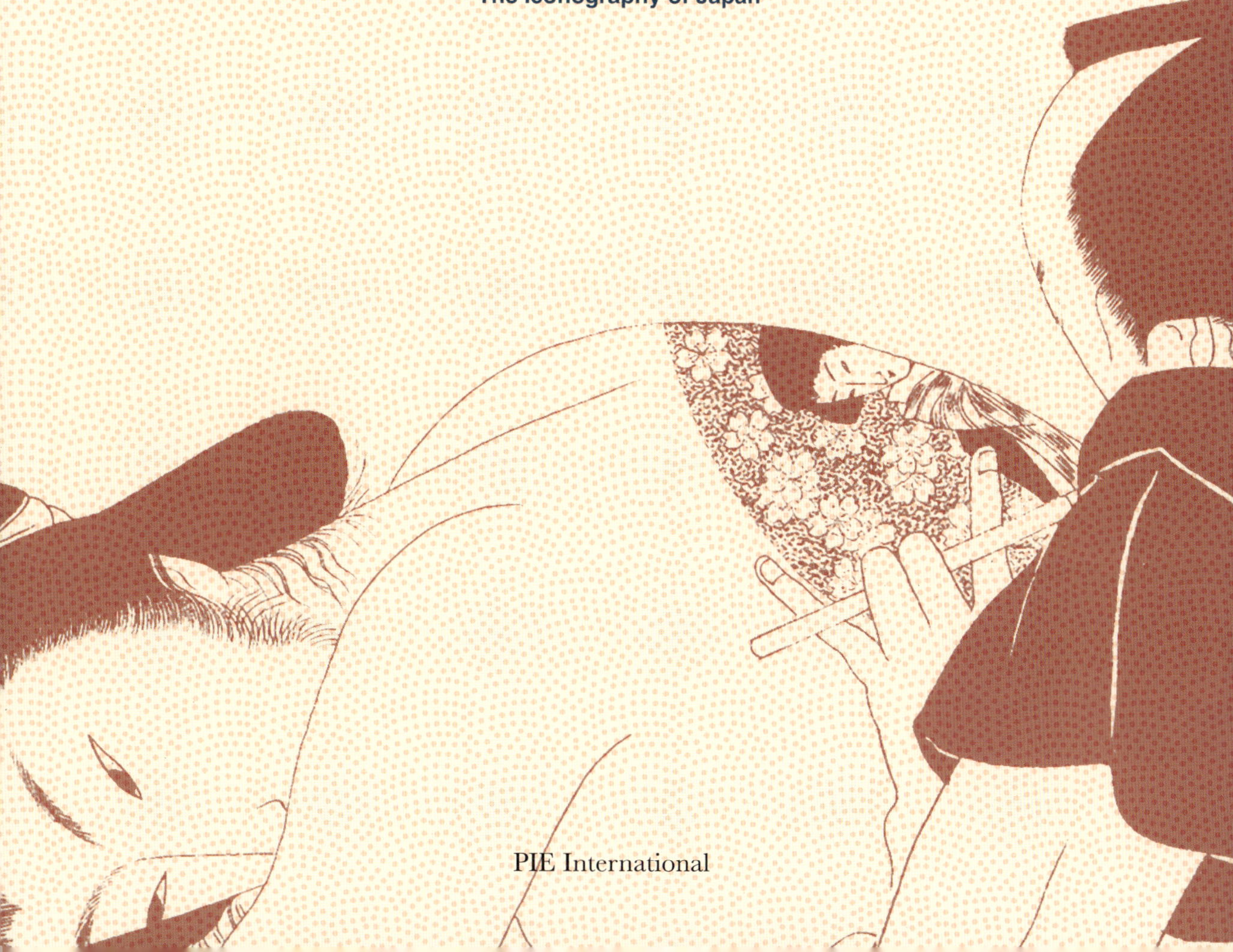

PIE International

　刺青は日本だけのものではなく、世界各地に亘る風俗である。な
かでも日本の「ほりもの」とよばれる刺青は、浮世絵にえがかれた
武者絵を参考にしたもので他国に見ることのできない見事なもので
ある。

　入墨とは墨を入れること、鋭利な道具で皮膚に傷をつけ、そこに色料をすり込
むか注入することにより文様を浮かび上がらせるものである。文身、刺青、黥な
どともよばれている。

　江戸時代には入墨という言葉は、墨刑のことで前科者の意味であり、風俗とし
ての刺青は彫物とよばれて区別されていた。

　刺青は江戸時代にはじまったもので、最初は京阪の遊里街でおこった「入れ
黒子」の風習がほりものの始まりといわれた。これは男女が手を握りあって、た
がいの親指の先にあたる位置にほくろ状の刺青をするという一種の誓であり、
「起請彫」ともよばれた。お互いにほくろを見ては相手のことを想い出そうとい

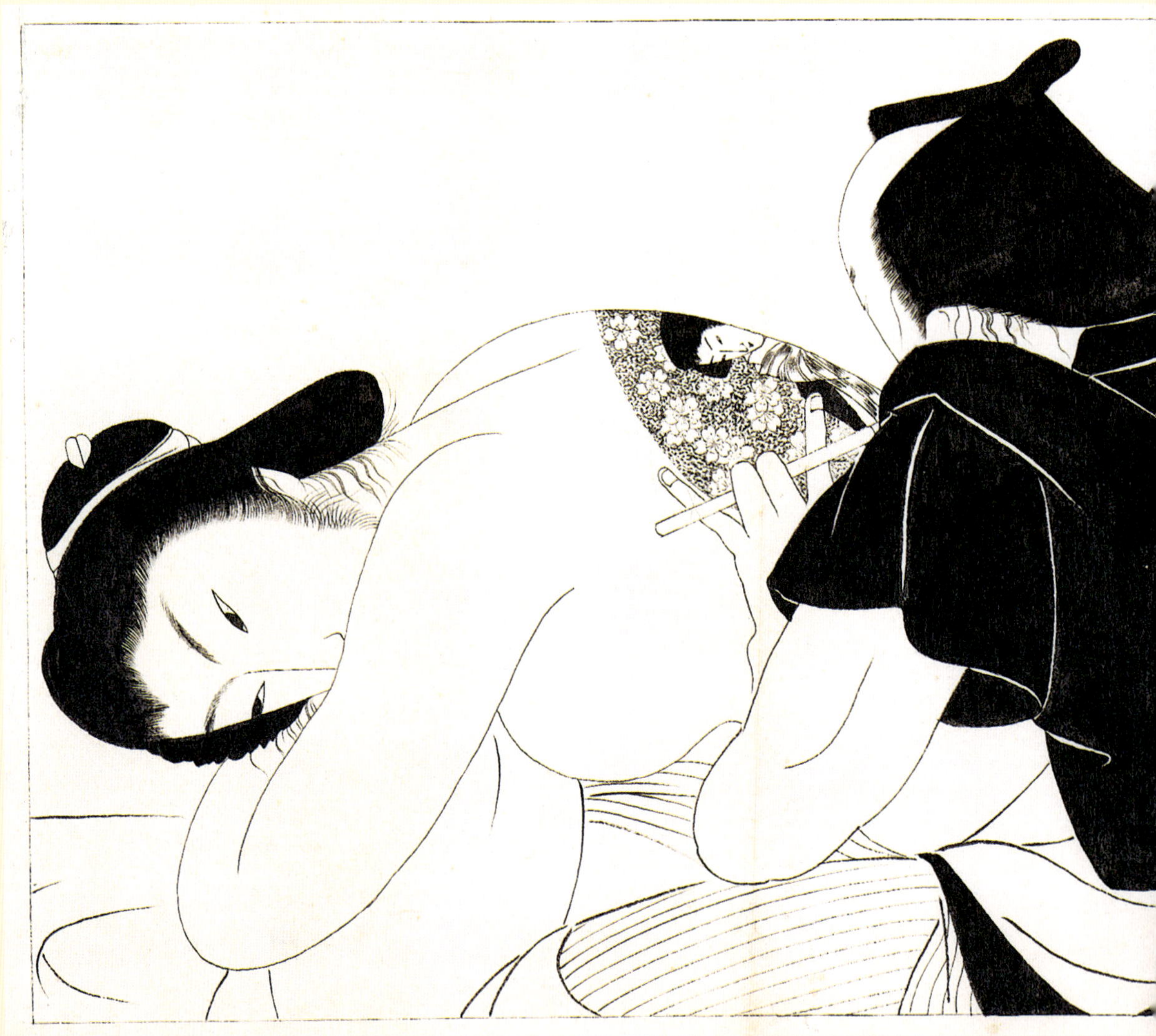

うものであった。

　そしてこの風習は江戸でも流行し、入れ黒子がさらに発展すると文字を刻むようになる。一心太助が頸筋に「一心白道」と彫ったのがそれで、また鐘弥左衛門なる侠客は背に「南無阿弥陀仏」と大きく文字を彫り、侠気を誇るものの間で流行した。

　このように最初は印や文字などが彫られていたが、やがて時代がくだり江戸の中期になると職人や勇み肌の者が粋や伊達から威勢を示すために競って彫物を施し、また絵柄も豊富となった。

　こうしたはやりを強めたのは、天保元年（1830）頃より歌川国芳が描いた武者絵、「本朝水滸伝豪傑百八人」が豪傑な錦絵として評判になってからである。その雄渾なタッチが侠気の人々の心をとらえ、そこにえがかれた登場人物の刺青を身体に彫ろうとする渡世ものたちが続出したという。国芳の一連の作品は、文化・文政年間（1804-30）には幕府の禁止になったが彫物は盛行を極めた。

　『水滸伝』のなかで江戸っ子に人気のあった登場人物は、九紋龍史進、花和尚魯智深、浪裡白跳張順などである。史進は九匹の青龍を彫ったことから九紋龍というニックネームがあり、火事場の鳶たちにとって龍は水をよぶことから縁起がいいものとされていた。また魯智深という豪傑も、背に花の刺青をしており花和尚とよばれ人気があった。

　歌舞伎界では天保4年（1833）、四代目の中村歌右衛門が中村座で上方へ帰る御名残狂言に倶利伽羅太郎になり、両方の腕へ倶利迦羅龍の刺青をしたところ、それがなかなかの評判で芝居が大入りであった。また歌右衛門は小作りな男であったため、初役で『夏祭浪花鑑』の団七九郎兵衛を演じた時、身体が小さくて見立がないことから、工夫をして全身に刺青を描いて登場した。それがまた大当たりとなり、団七九郎兵衛の役は必ず全身へ刺青を描いて登場することになった。

　西洋のタトゥーはそばに寄ってみたくなるが、日本の刺青は見るのが恐ろしくなるようなところがある。それは般若や髑髏首などのおどろおどろしい図が彫られているからという絵柄だけの問題ではなく、人間の背部に妖怪のようにじっと根をはり、睨み返しているからなのである。自分では見ることのできない部分を補って完全なものにしているからであり、見るものが妖しい戦慄を覚えるのは、背を刺青で守っているからなのだろう。

　刺青とは、自分の中に守護神を住まわせることであり、妖怪を一匹飼っておくことなのかもしれない。

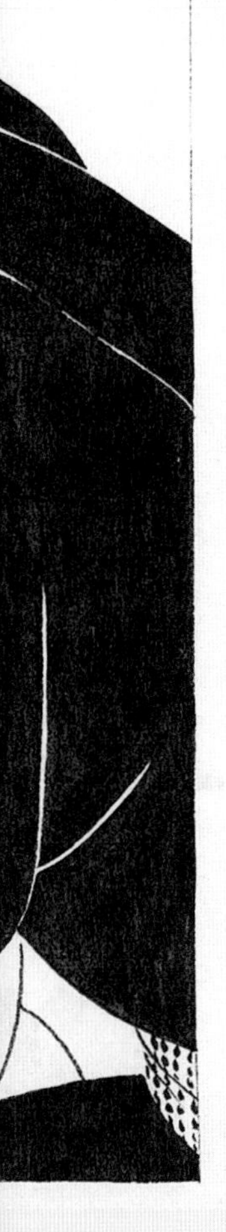

「お傳地獄挿絵原画（刺青）」小村雪岱
昭和10年・1935　埼玉県立近代美術館蔵

Introduction

Tattooing is a custom found the world over. It is not confined to Japan. But of all the various forms of tattoo, the Japanese tattoos, also called *horimono* (carved or sculpted things), that reference samurai warriors depicted in ukiyo-e are truly extraordinary and found nowhere else.

Irezumi, the most common Japanese term for tattoo, literally means to insert ink, in other words to pierce the skin with a sharp tool, creating a wound through which the pigment is inserted, creating the pattern that appears on the surface. Other terms include *bunshin*, *shisei*, and *gei*.

During the Edo period (1600-1868), the term *irezumi* was synonymous with *bokutei*, tattoos used as to identify people with criminal records. The word *horimono* was introduced to distinguish tattoos as a popular custom.

Today's *irezumi* date back to the Edo period. They are said to have begun with a custom called *irebokuro* that appeared first in the pleasure quarters of Kyoto and Osaka. Men and women would have a beauty marks tattooed where the tips of their thumbs rested when the clasped hands. These tattoos were tokens of love, signifying vows. Gazing at them evoked feelings for the other.

As this custom became popular and spread to Edo, the *irebokuro* developed further to include text. The fictional character Isshin Tasuke was described as having the phrase "single minded pure path" tattooed on his neck. The gallant Tsurigane Yazaemon was said to have the Buddhist incantation "*Namu Amida Butsu*" tattooed in large characters on his back, and doing so became fashionable among men proud of their chivalrous nature.

Thus, the first *irezumi* were symbolic marks or written characters. As time passed, by the middle of the Edo period, tattoos came to be employed competitively by craftsmen and manly men displaying their chivalry, dashing chic and courage. Visual imagery also flourished.

From around 1830, this trend was strengthened by the acclaim accorded to Utagawa Kuniyoshi's *One Hundred and Eight Heroes from the Tales of the Water Margin* series of polychrome prints, which were regarded as masterpieces. The boldness with which the artist depicted warrior virtue captivated those who saw these prints, and many working men wanted the same tattoos as the heroes depicted in them. Despite this series of Kuniyoshi's prints being banned for a time by the shogunate,

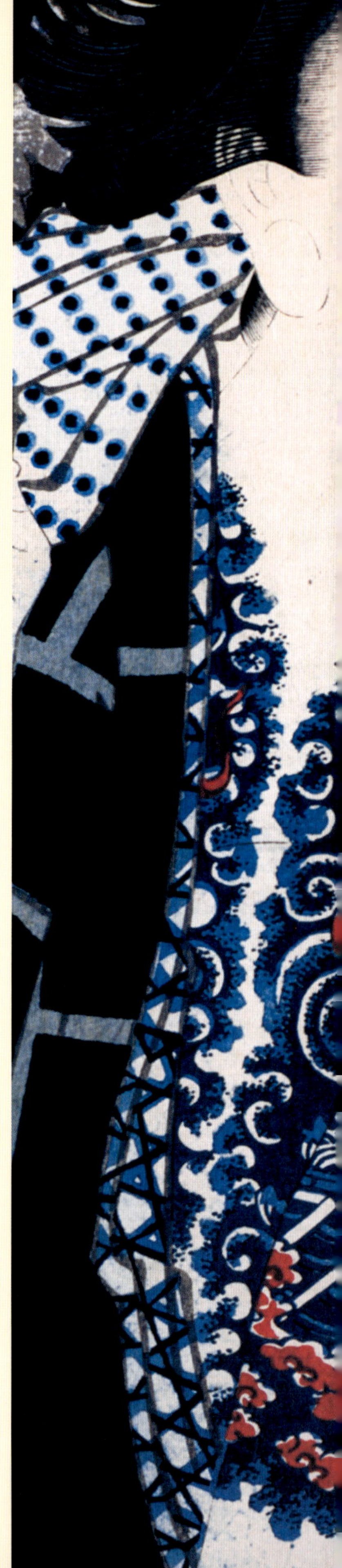

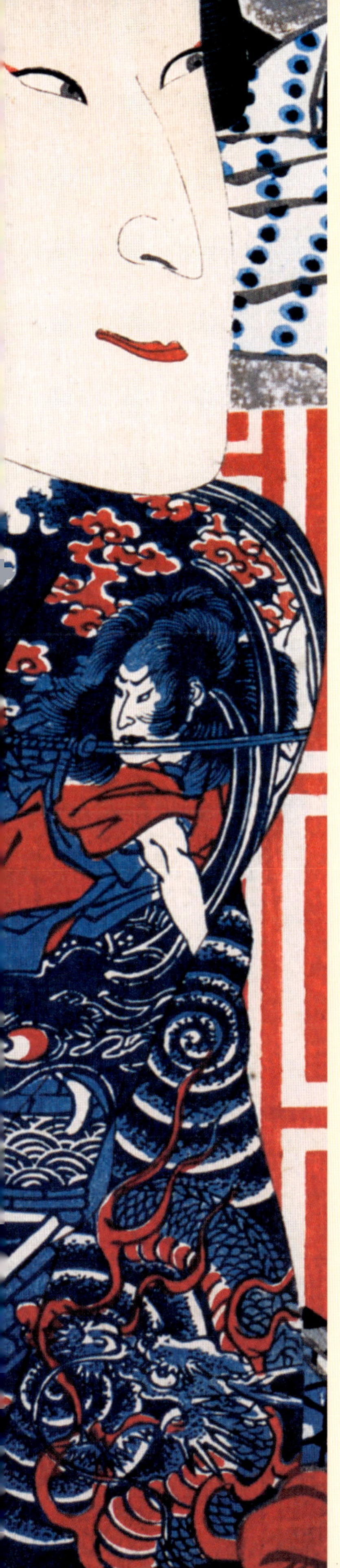

the tattoos became extremely popular.

Water Margin characters popular among Edo natives included Kumonryū Shishin (Nine-Dragon Tattoo Shi Jin), Kaosho Ro Chishin (Flowery Monk Lu Zhishen), and Rorihakucho Chojun (White Streak in the Waves Zhang Shun). Shi Jin got his nickname from the nine dragons in his tattoos. To firefighters, dragons signified the sources of the water they used to fight fires. Another popular hero, Lu Zhishen, was called "flowery monk" because he had flowers tattooed on his back.

In 1833, the Kabuki actor Nakamura Utaemon IV appeared at the Nakamuraza theater as Kurikara Taro, in his farewell performance before he returned to the Kansai. A moment that won rave reviews was when both of Kurikara Taro's arms were tattooed. In another instance, Utaemon, in his first performance, played the part of Danshichi Kurobe, a famously courageous hero, in *Natsumatsuri Naniwakagami*. Utaemon was a small man; to suit the role and enhance his performance, he was made up to appear to have tattoos over his whole body. That proved a big hit. Subsequently, whoever played the part of Danshichi Kurobe appeared with tattoos covering his whole body.

When we see a Western tattoo, we try to get closer. But peering at Japanese tattoos can be scary. The problem is not that the motifs include the demonic faces of jealous women or skulls signifying death. Placed in the middle of a human back, they appear to be staring back at us. Displayed like ghastly monsters at a person's weakest point, they send a shiver up our spines. These tattoos may be placed where they are to protect the back. Tattoos are likely placed there as guardian spirits to protect the weak self, or to feed the monster within.

Kawarazaki Gonjūrō, from the series
Isami-no-Kotobuki, Detail, Tsukioka
Yoshitoshi, 1865, Hagi Uragami Museum

第2章　刺青の文様
Chapter 2 **Tattoo Designs**

［凡　例］
○作品は原則として全図を掲載するが、部分図を掲載した場合は作品名の後に（部分）と表示した。
○図版データは、作品名、作者名、制作年、所蔵家の順に掲載している。
○制作年代は所蔵先のデータのため、不明なものは省略した。また解読不明な作品名は□で示した。

江戸のバロキスム——刺青浮世絵　谷川渥

刺青は人間の皮膚をキャンバスとする絵画である。絵画ではあるが、しかし描くとはいわない。刺青は彫る（刺る）ものだ。立体的な人体に彫るものではあるが、もとより彫刻ではない。絵でありながら彫る、ここに行為としての刺青の微妙にして本質的な特異性がある。

その彫り方は、墨や朱などの色料を一点一点刺し入れるかぎりにおいて、いわば点描法である。それは西洋絵画におけるスーラやシニャックなどの点描法と軌を一にする。とはいえ、刺青において個々の点は見えるものとはならない。色彩が皮膚に染み込んで連続するからだ。むしろ染み込ませることこそが、刺青の本質である。それは「カラー・フィールド・ペインティング」（色彩の場の絵画）の代表者のひとり、モーリス・ルイスの実践した染み込み画法に似ている。生キャンヴァスにアクリル絵具を流し込むのである。皮膚がまさしく生キャンヴァスになる。

染み込み画法に似ているとはいえ、刺青は基本的に線描的である。線描的であるとは、色面と色面の境界が線としてあらわれるということである。だからそれは、やはり染み込み画法とは明らかに異なる。ルイスの絵のように染み込ませた色彩同士が重なり合うということがない。くっきりと輪郭をたどることができる。

刺青の起源のひとつとしての「文字彫」は、もとより線描である。文字は、「筋彫り」による線描によって成立するからだ。そして線描によって文字ならぬ図柄を浮き出させる、いわゆる「ヌキ彫」が試みられることになろう。「ヌキ彫」は、いわばデッサンないしドゥローイングに相当する。

しかし、郡司正勝「刺青と役者絵」（1976 年）がいうように、「浮世絵が紙を離れて、人間の皮膚に移ったのが日本の刺青であって、それは原始的な黥とも、また入墨ともちがった、一種の芸術運動を意味している」とすれば、地肌をつぶして色面を成立させること、いわゆる「ぼかす」ことこそが、刺青の最大の眼目となるだろう。こうして「生きた錦絵」が展開されることになる。点で面をつくる。無数の点描による面の形成。この比類のない行為に、刺青に特有の情念がまつわる。

浮世絵が人間の皮膚に移ったのが日本の刺青だとしても、浮世絵と刺青とではやや異なる点がある。それは、刺青の場合にはほかならぬ色彩が比較的に限定されるということだ。

「生きた錦絵」の色彩は、いうなれば基本的に二系統しかない。青（ないし藍）と赤である。色料でいえば、墨と朱である。墨の黒色は皮膚を透して青（藍）色として現象する。他の色彩も用いることもできないわけではないが、結局それも青（藍）か赤に収斂しようとする。刺青は、端的に寒色と暖色の芸術なのである。

刺青の精神的基盤がいわゆる起請彫に発することは間違いあるまい。願い、信条、祈り、あるいはこれはおおむね遊女のあいだでだが、思う相手、約束を交わした相手の名前など、いずれにせよ「起請」すなわち神仏に誓いを立てる文字を入れるのである。起請彫は、それゆえ「文字彫」である。

18 世紀後半、宝暦（1751 〜 64）以降、明和（1764 〜 72）・安永（1772 〜 81）年間に、とりわけ江戸の侠客、博徒、鳶の者、火消人足、駕籠かきなどのあいだに、こうした起請彫、あるいはさらに小模様の威嚇彫・伊達彫とでもいうべき刺青が急に目立つようになったという。

そこに『水滸伝』ブームが起こった。『水滸伝』は明代初めの成立と推測されるが、宋の徽宗の時代、宋江ら百八人に及ぶ反骨の豪傑たちの梁山泊への結集と、その後の悲壮な運命を描いた大長篇小説である。わが国では安永・天明（1781 〜 89）・寛政（1789 〜 1801）年間に、これがさまざまなかたちで翻案脚色され、すでに歌舞伎上演されさえしたようだが、ここでまず特筆すべきは文化 3 年（1806）から刊行された馬琴訓訳・北斎画の『新編水滸画伝』であろう。挿絵の花和尚魯智深の背中に花模様の刺青が、そして九紋龍史進の全身に刺青が見られるが、これは「ヌキ彫」であって、まだいわゆる「ぼかし」を入れていない。地肌をつぶす「面」が見られないのである。

文政 10 年（1827）に板行の始まった歌川派一門の一勇斎国芳の大判錦絵『通俗水滸伝豪傑百八人之一個』のシリーズこそが、刺青浮世絵の真骨頂である。北斎に触発されもしたのであろうが、しかしその武者絵的世界は尋常ではない。画面いっぱいに広がる臨場感、歌舞伎の隈取にも似た強烈な表情、躍動する肉体の迫力とダイナミズム、そしてなによりも絢爛たる色彩の乱舞、まさにいまだ誰も見たことのない、全身彫を初めて絵画化した、文字どおり前代未聞の世界が現出した。松田修は、その著書『刺青・性・死』（1972 年）において、国芳の刺青画を「バロックの極地」と呼んでいるが、これを江戸爛熟期頽廃期幕末のバロキスムと称することができよう。そしてこのバロキスムの意匠は、まったく国芳の創意、独創になるものである。

実際、岩波文庫版『水滸伝』（吉川幸次郎・清水茂訳）全篇に目を通してみても、刺青の描写はきわめて少ないというかむしろ貧弱であることに注意しよう。「銀の皿にも似た顔して、年のほどは十八、九」の九紋龍史進の「総身には青い竜の彫りもの」とあるだけだし、「太っちょの大入道」花和尚魯智深の背中に彫りものがあるといわれるだけである。解宝には「両方の腿にほりもの、二体の飛天夜叉」、花項虎襲旺には「からだじゅう虎斑のほりもの、くびには虎の頭が大口をあけています」とやや詳しいが、あとは林冲も何濤も揚志も唐の牛公も武松も盧俊義も、そして中心人物の宋江も、刑罰として顔に「入れ墨」をされ流罪になった存在でしかない。ちなみに、宋江の入れ墨を「療治」して消す次第も書かれている。「毒薬をさしてから、あとでよい薬で療治しますと、赤い傷あとがもりあがります。今度は、上等の黄金白玉を粉末に碾いたものを、毎日擦りこみますと、おのずから消えてしまいました」と。

原作では彫りものをみずから背負う豪勇たちはわずか数人にすぎなかったが、国芳はそれを恣にほぼ三倍、十数人にまで広げた。異様な国芳ブームのなかで、天保 4 年（1833）9 月に中村座で上演された中村芝翫の「手向山紅葉御幣」では、国芳の下絵による「くりから太郎」の倶利伽羅

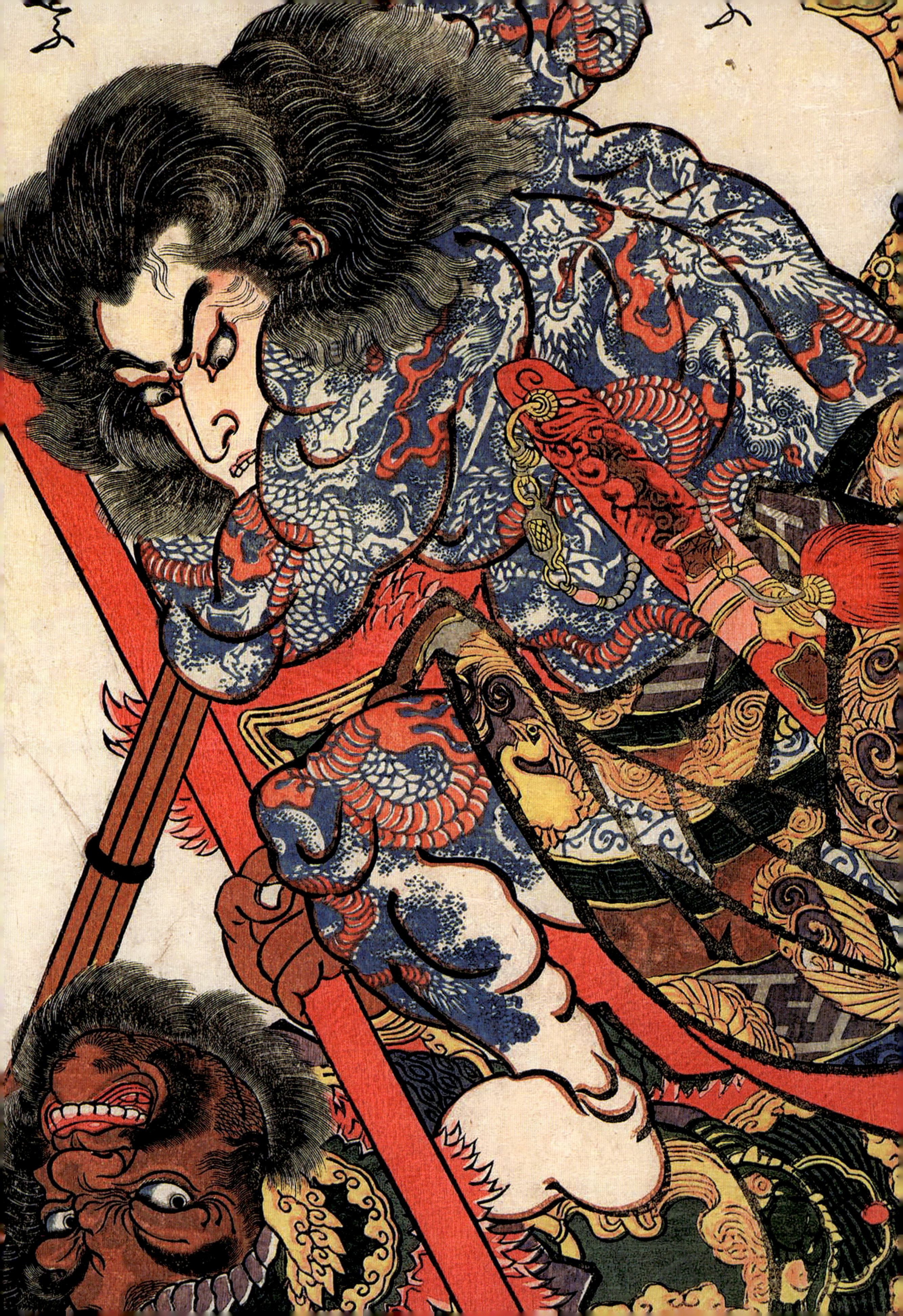

龍の刺青が評判になり大当たりをとったという。ちなみに、後世、刺青のことをたんに「くりから」といい「くりから紋々」というのは、郡司正勝の前掲論文によれば、「倶利伽羅が刺青を代表し、竜紋がその王者を占めたからで、これは流行としての水滸伝の九紋竜と、信仰としての倶利伽羅竜が合体したもの」であろうという。倶利伽羅竜王とは不動明王の化身である。

　国芳の刺青画は、歌舞伎の世界に波及したばかりではない。威嚇彫や伊達彫に現を抜かしていた侠客、博徒、火消し、鳶などが競ってその刺青画そのものをみずから背負おうとし始めた。すでに刺青を背負う英雄像を、いままた己れの肉体に彫り入れる「二重彫り」という、これまた前代未聞の行為が成立することになった。肉体にいわば画中画が成立するわけである。それは男伊達でもあり威嚇でもあったろうが、なによりも無頼の英雄像にみずからを重ね合わせようとする一種の「見立て」でもあったろう。

　ところで、国芳に関係する注目すべき小説に触れておこう。赤江瀑の『雪華葬刺し』（1975 年）だ。谷崎潤一郎『刺青』（1910 年）以来の刺青を主題にした小説のなかでも特筆すべき作品である。高木彬光に『刺青殺人事件』（1953 年）があるが、これはあくまでもアリバイ工作として刺青を利用するという推理小説であって、刺青そのものを主題化しているとはいえない。

　赤江瀑の小説は、全篇これ国芳讃ともいうべき異色作で、刺青狂いの藤江田の妻、茜が国芳の画帳からみずから選んだ彫り物の図柄は、「本朝武者鏡・橘姫」の構図である。こう描写される。「巨大な鱗身を逆巻きおどらせている龍は、獣頭を上からではなく、橘姫の下から立てて襲いかかり、咽笛近くで緋色の口を裂いている。美姫は、その龍の咽元を毅然とつかみ、朱房の芭蕉扇ではなく、抜き身の白刃を髪ふり乱した頭上にふりかぶっている」と。京都二条寺町に居を構える大和経五郎は、彫経と呼称される名人彫師だが、茜の背中にくだんの図柄を彫る際に、仰向けになった一人の若者の上に彼女をうつ伏せに寝かせる。つまり男に下から抱かれた女の背に彫りを入れるというわけである。苦痛と快楽の極みに彫りが成立する。その若者、春経の裸体前面には国芳の『通俗水滸伝豪傑百八人之一個』の「水滸伝中無双の剛力を誇る屈強な花形人物」たる「浪子燕青」の、背にはその燕青と「若い美形を競う怪傑」たる「九紋龍史進」の絵姿が彫られていた。「裸身の若者は、つまり背胸両面から、裸身の若武者に相擁されているかに見える、全身二重彫りの彫り物に飾られていた」というわけである。二重、三重の国芳幻想…。

　私はここで「隠し彫り」とか「葬刺し」という言葉を初めて知ったが、この小説は、若山富三郎の彫経、宇都宮雅代の茜、京本政樹の春経の配役で高林陽一監督によって 1982 年に『雪華葬刺し』として映画化された。原作

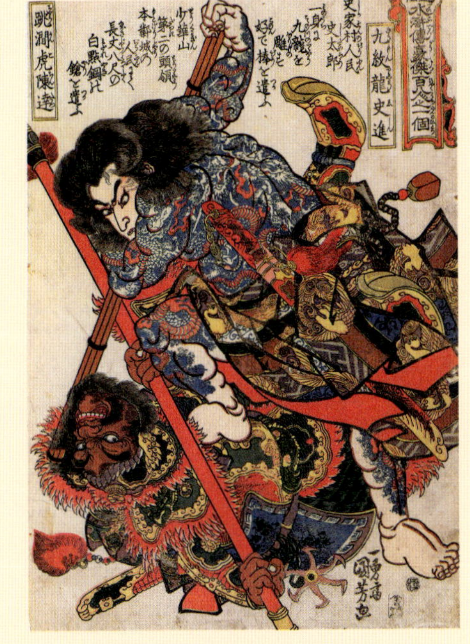

「通俗水滸傳豪傑百八人之一個
九紋龍史進・跳澗虎陳達」歌川国芳
江戸時代・19 世紀
東京国立博物館蔵
出典：ColBase（https://colbase.nich.go.jp）

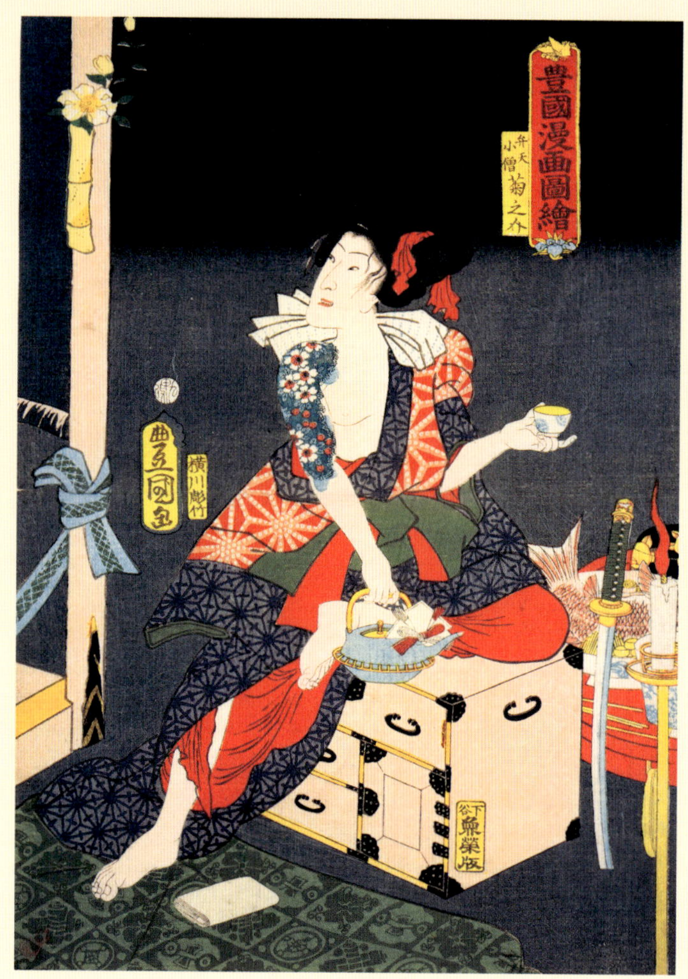

「豊国漫画図絵　弁天小僧菊之介」歌川豊国
万延元年・1860　国立国会図書館デジタルコレクション

に勝るとも劣らない見事な傑作であるとはいっておかなければならない。

　特権的に男のものであった刺青が、いつ頃から女の肌に蟠るようになったのか詳らかにしない。「白波五人男」のひとり「弁天小僧」あたりが、象徴的な転換点といえるのかもしれない。いずれにせよ、女の刺青は比較的新しい現象であろう。しかし、男であれ女であれ、本来、刺青が非日常的・異端的な「輝かしき悪の華」（郡司正勝）であることに変わりはあるまい。「悪の華」であるからこそ、それは見る者を遠ざけ、かつ惹きつける。その両義性が刺青固有の魅力につながる。

　国芳に端を発し、しかもすでに頂点を極めたといっても過言ではない刺青浮世絵は、しかしもとよりその「系譜」をたどることができないわけではない。そのおおよそは、郡司正勝監修・福田和彦編『原色浮世絵刺青版画』（芳賀書店、1977年）に収められた福田和彦の論文「刺青浮世絵師の系譜」にほぼ明らかである。

　国芳とともに初代歌川豊国門下であった一勇斎国貞（のち三代目歌川豊国）は、役者絵で名声を博したが、江戸末期の侠客、力自慢、美男、毒婦など、さまざまな実在の人物をそれぞれ歌舞伎役者に見立てた刺青画で一世を風靡した。肖像画的な半身像は国芳の武者絵的な迫力と勇壮美に欠けるが、そのスタティックにして華麗な役者見立絵には独特の存在感がある。刺青の絵画化という点で、やはり特筆すべき存在であろう。

　国芳門下の異才、これも北斎に私淑した江戸最後の浮世絵師のひとり、月岡芳年（のちに大蘇芳年）は、時代の狂気に照応したかのようなその『英名二十八衆句』と『魁題百撰相』における、いわゆる「血みどろ絵」「無惨絵」でとりわけ有名だが、わずかながら刺青画にも手を染めている。やはり国芳的なダイナミズムには欠けるが、精緻極まりない写実的な描刻には注目すべきだろう。それにしても芳年の「血みどろ絵」は、国芳の武者絵の踏襲という側面があるとはいえ、ひょっとしたら師が刺青でやったことを血でやろうとしたのではあるまいか、私にはそんなふうに思われもする。色料を皮膚の下に刺し入れて図柄を浮き出させるのが刺青だとすれば、血は皮膚を破り外に溢れ出て皮膚を染めるものだ。そうして皮膚あるいは肌・衣装・血の綾なす絢爛たる図柄を構成することになる。これが芳年に刺青画そのものが少ない理由とはいえまいか。

　落合芳幾、豊原国周、歌川芳艶、そして歌川芳虎は、いずれも江戸末期から明治にかけて活躍した歌川派の浮世絵師である。国芳、国貞、芳年の系譜を引きつつ刺青画の芸術化に貢献した彼らの作品と師兄のそれとの微妙な異動をお確かめいただきたい。

　刺青は、皮膚を徹底的に視覚的対象と化す。皮膚は、ひとえに眼差されるものとなる。触れ、あるいは触れられるという皮膚に固有の相互性は、刺青によっていわば括弧に入れられる。皮膚は、刺青によって完全に対自的かつ対他的なものとなる。対自的とは、見られている自分を意識すること、対他的とは、自分を見ている他者を意識することである。意識化された皮膚のことを、日本語では「肌」という。肌の対自性・対他性は、おのずから触れ、触れられることを含意している。刺青の対自性・対他性は、しかし、見せ、あるいは見られることに結びついている。刺青は、対自性・対他性を変質させてしまうといってもいい。触覚性と視覚性とのこの微妙な乖離こそ、おそらく刺青のエロティシズムの本質である。

　いま街に出ると、そこかしこに腕や肩や脚にタトゥーを入れた男女に出会う。刺青は気楽な人体装飾のひとつとして定着してしまったかのようだ。起請彫、あるいは伊達彫とも威嚇彫とも似て非なる、エロティシズムとも無縁なアクセサリーのようなタトゥー。松田修は、「刺青は無頼異端の徒のものである、あらねばならぬ」と書いていた。「顕在化してはならない秘儀である」と。いまや「悪の華」どころではない。時代の趨勢というべきだろうか。ともあれ、こうした嗟嘆に多少とも共感を覚えながら、比類のない江戸のバロキスム、正真正銘の刺青芸術、刺青浮世絵を眺めることにしよう。

（たにがわ あつし　美学者）

Edo Baroque: Tattooed Ukiyo-e

Tanigawa Atsushi

Tattoos are images for which human skin is the canvas. While they are images, they could not be described as painted or drawn. Tattooing is piercing (or, in Japanese, carving). Yet while tattoos are carved into three-dimensional human bodies, they are not sculpture. They are an art form created by the act of carving or piercing. That fundamental characteristic is what makes tattooing essentially different.

Tattoos are created by inserting black, scarlet or other pigments, one drop at a time, through openings made by piercing the skin, using a technique called pointillism. That practice of creating images with tiny dots of pure color is similar to the technique used in Western painting by the Pointillists Seurat and Signac. In tattoos, however, the individual dots are not visible because the colors permeate the skin and the dots connect, blending together. The essence of tattooing lies in the act of making the colors diffuse in the skin. In the way in which the colors permeate the skin, tattooing resembles Color Field painting exemplified by the art of Morris Louis, who worked by pouring acrylic paint on raw canvas. The skin is, indeed, a raw canvas.

While, however, it can be said that tattooing resembles painting techniques in which pigments spread and soak into the canvas, tattooing is fundamentally a linear art, for lines separate blocks of color. In this respect, it is clearly different from color field painting. In tattoos, colors are not overlaid and do not bleed into each other as they do in Louis's paintings. We can trace clear contour lines in tattoos.

"Text carving," one of the origins of tattooing, is essentially line drawing: fine lines are carved to represent characters. Characters are formed by lines that trace their "sinews." A further development was *nukibori*, an attempt to create designs, not texts, using lines, with no background. *Nukibori* could be said to be the tattoo equivalent of drawing or sketching.

It is virtually undeniable that the spiritual foundation from which tattooing developed was tattoos inscribing vows. These texts were wishes, convictions, prayers, or, primarily among prostitutes, names of lovers, or names of those with whom promises had been exchanged. They also includes what were truly vows, i.e. oaths sworn before gods or Buddhas. In the latter half of the eighteenth century, these vow-marks suddenly flourished as tattooed threats or expressions of dandyish style among self-styled humanitarian vigilantes, gamblers, construction workers, firefighters, and palanquin bearers.

Utagawa Ichiyusai (later Kuniyoshi), a member of the Utagawa school, began producing his *oban* size polychrome print series *One Hundred and Eight Heroes from the Tales of the Water Margin*, the epitome of tattoo ukiyo-e, in 1827. This series may have been inspired by Hokusai, but these are not images from the ordinary world of warrior prints. These images fill the picture plane with a powerful presence. The intensity of the expressions on the faces resemble *kumadori*, the stylized makeup used in Kabuki for *aragoto*, wildly vital performances. Their energetic bodies exude power and dynamism, and the colors are magnificent. They were utterly unprecedented, the first visualizations of total-body tattoos, a world unheard of in earlier times. Matsuda Osamu wrote in *Tattoos, Sex, Death* (1972) that Kuniyoshi's depictions of tattoos are "ultimate baroque." By "baroque," he implies the late Edo decadence of the closing years of the Tokugawa shogunate. This baroque design was, however, totally and uniquely Kuniyoshi's creation.

Kuniyoshi's tattoo art spread beyond the world of Kabuki. Gangsters, gamblers, fire-fighters and construction workers, who had been indulging in tattoos that were either threats or signs of stylishness, began to compete to carry that tattoo art on their own backs. A heroic figure already bearing a tattoo was being carved into his own body, in the unprecedented act of double tattooing. A painting within a painting was born on the body. It may have been a way for men to appear chic or intimidating, but above all, as a type of analogue, it likened the wearer of the tattoo to that image of a reckless hero.

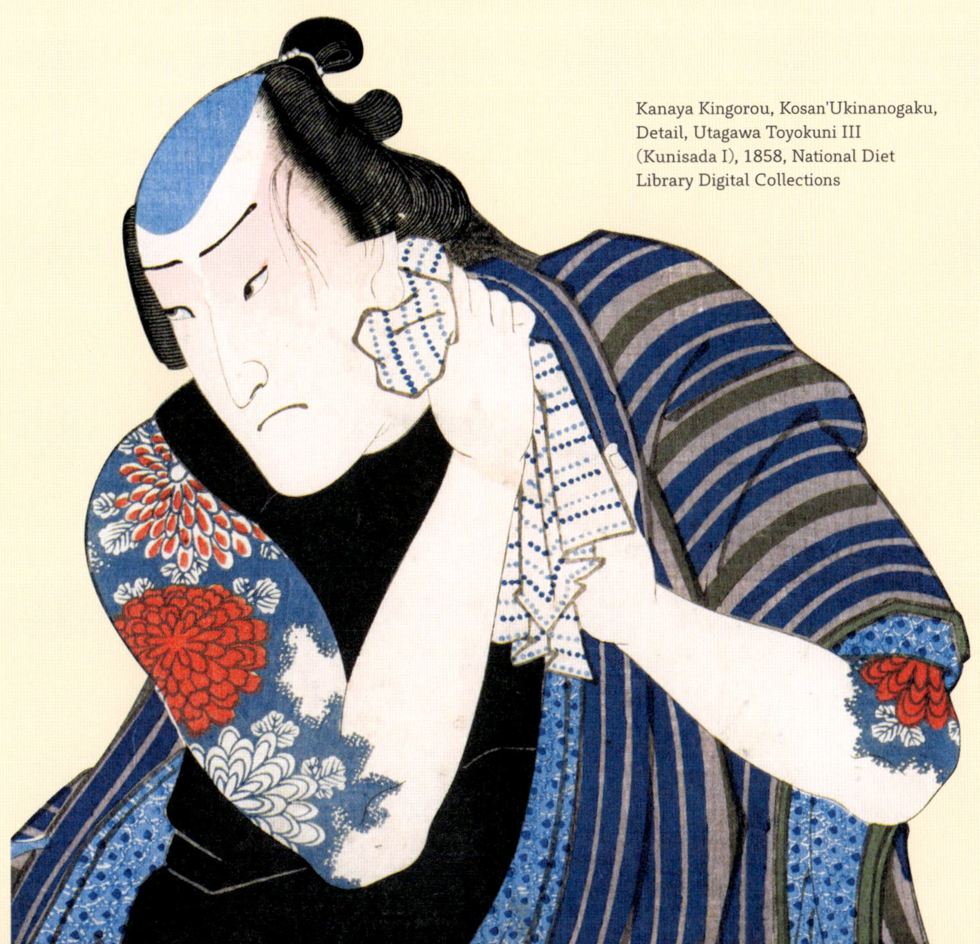

Kanaya Kingorou, Kosan'Ukinanogaku, Detail, Utagawa Toyokuni III (Kunisada I), 1858, National Diet Library Digital Collections

Like Kuniyoshi, Utagawa Kunisada (later Utagawa Toyokuni III) was a student of Utagawa Toyokuni I. He, too, became famous for his depictions of actors. It was, however, his tattoo art, likening actual vigilantes, strongmen, beautiful boys, and femmes fatale to Kabuki actors, that took the world by storm. His bust portraits lack Kuniyoshi's martial power and heroic beauty, but the static sheer gorgeousness of his actor portrait analogues have a special presence all their own. There is no denying that their depiction of tattoos is noteworthy.

Tsukioka Yoshitoshi (later Taiso Yoshitoshi), who was a talented student of Kuniyoshi and an admirer of Hokusai, was Edo's last great master of ukiyo-e. He was famous for his "bloody prints" and "cruel paintings," like those in his series *Twenty-Eight Famous Murders with Verse and Selection of One Hundred Warriors*, works that seem to embody the madness of his times. He also produced a small amount of tattoo art. Yoshitoshi's work lacks Kuniyoshi's dynamism, but the incredible realism down to the fine details deserves notice. Even so, Yoshitoshi's "bloody prints" can be seen as a continuation of Kuniyoshi's warrior prints. It may be that he used blood as his teacher used tattoos, or so it seems to me. If we see tattooing as inserting pigments beneath the skin to create a pattern that floats to the surface, blood shattering the skin and spurting out of a wound stains the surface, creating gorgeous designs on skin or clothing. Perhaps that parallelism was why Yoshitoshi produced only a few tattoo ukiyo-e.

Ochiai Yoshiiku, Toyohara Kunichiku, Utagawa Yoshitsuya, and Utagawa Yoshitora were all Utagawa-school printmakers active from late Edo to the Meiji period. Here I want to confirm the subtle differences between their contributions to the artistic transformation of tattoo art and those of their teachers and predecessors Kuniyoshi, Kunisada, and Yoshitoshi in the lineage they continued.

Now, when we go out on the town we encounter men and women with tattoos on their arms, shoulders, or legs. Tattoos have become ornaments casually applied to the body. They no longer signify vows, daring dandyism, or threats. Tattoos now also seem to be accessories unrelated to eroticism. Matsuda Osamu wrote that tattoos should be marks of heresy, signs of secrets not casually revealed. But now they are no longer Fleurs du mal. This change might be said to be a sign of the times. One can only feel sympathy with those who sigh and say that we must turn to ukiyo-e to appreciate the incomparable Edo baroque of genuine tattoo art.

Tanigawa Atsushi
Professor of Aesthetics

第1章 刺青 勇肌の美

Chapter 1
Tattoos: The Beauty of the Heroes' Skin

　中国宋代の群盗ら百八人の豪傑たちが山東省梁山泊に集まり、義を誓って活躍する通俗小説『水滸伝』が江戸時代に伝わったことを機に、天保元年（1830）頃より歌川国芳がえがいた武者絵「本朝水滸伝豪傑百八人」は、勇猛果敢に活躍する勇士の錦絵として評判になった。その雄渾なタッチが仁侠のものたちの心をとらえ、そこにえがかれた登場人物の刺青を身体に彫ろうと勇み肌の渡世ものたちが続出した。

　国芳をはじめ、江戸時代後期から明治にかけて活躍した歌川豊国・月岡芳年・落合芳幾・豊原国周・歌川芳虎・梅堂小国政・小林清親たちがえがいた刺青浮世絵の世界を紹介する。

Tattoos in Japan became popular around 1830, when Kuniyoshi Utagawa created *One Hundred and Eight Heroes from the Tales of the Water Margin*, a series of prints based on the popular Chinese novel *The Water Margin*, which tells the story of 108 brave outlaws who gathered in Shandong Province's Liangshan Marsh during the Song Dynasty in China, and swore an oath to act righteously. These polychrome prints depicted valiant and heroic warriors in a dynamic and vibrant style. The bold and powerful artwork resonated with the spirit of these noble and brave figures, inspiring many in the underworld to imitate their tattoos. This chapter introduces the world of ukiyo-e featuring tattoos, as depicted by prominent ukiyo-e artists from the late Edo to the Meiji period. Starting with Utagawa Kuniyoshi, it includes prints by other eminent artistsm including Utagawa Toyokuni, Tsukioka Yoshitoshi, Ochiai Yoshiiki, Toyohara Kunichika, Utagawa Yoshitora, Baido Kokunimasa, Utagawa Hiroshige, and Kobayashi Kiyochika, all of whom contributed to this genre.

歌川国芳
Utagawa Kuniyoshi ｜ 1797-1861

うたがわ くによし　寛政 9 年〜文久元年（1797-1861）

　江戸時代後期の浮世絵師。初代歌川豊国の門人。文政 10 年（1827）ごろから版行され始めた錦絵のシリーズ「通俗水滸伝豪傑一百八人之一個」により一躍人気を博し、武者絵の国芳とよばれた。また清新な洋風陰影法を用いた風景画にもすぐれ、「東都名所」「東海道五十三駅」などの作品がある。その性格も豪放淡泊で、多くの逸話が残されているが、天保年間（1830-1844）ごろより天保の改革をテーマとした諷刺画や諧謔味あふれる戯画を描き、戯画における第一人者としても活躍した。月岡芳年らおおくの弟子をそだてた。豊国の役者、広重の景色、国芳の武者を世に三羽烏という。

Kuniyoshi Utagawa (1797-1861)

Late Edo-period Ukiyo-e Artist. Student of Utagawa Toyokuni I. Became instantly popular when publication of his first polychrome print series *One Hundred and Eight Heroes from the Tales of the Water Margin*, began in 1827. He became known as the Warrior-painting Kuniyoshi. He also created the outstanding landscapes in *Famous Places in the Eastern Capitol and Fifty-three stations of the Tokaido Road* using recently introduced Western-style chiaroscuro. A bold but unpretentious personality, he left behind many anecdotes. During the Tenpo era (1830-44), when his works included many caricatures satirizing the Tenpo Reforms and illustrations full of wit, he was peerless in the world of humorous art. His many students included Tsukioka Yoshitoshi. Toyokuni's actors, Hiroshige's landscapes, and Kuniyoshi's warriors made these artists the triumvirate of the greatest artists of their time.

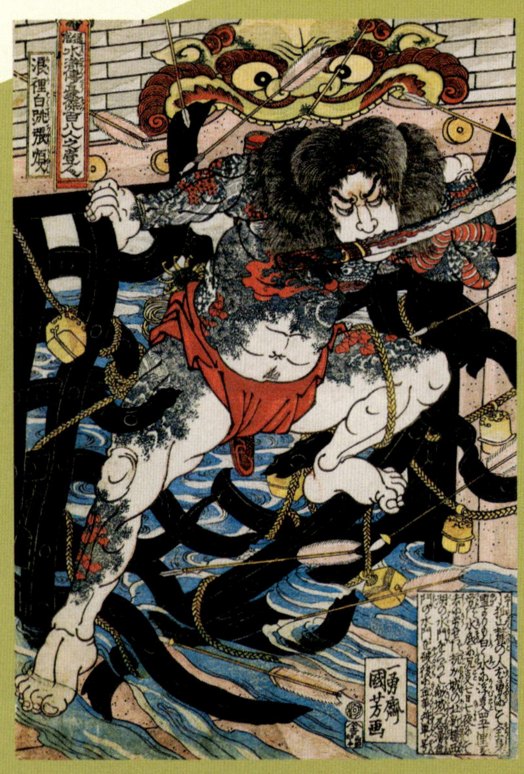

「通俗水滸傳豪傑百八人之壹人
浪裡白跳張順」（変わり図）
歌川国芳
Rōri Hakuchō Chōjun, from the series One hundred and eight Heroes of the Suikoden,
Utagawa Kuniyoshi

江戸時代・19 世紀　東京国立博物館蔵
出典：ColBase (https://colbase.nich.go.jp)
Edo period, 19th century, Tokyo National Museum

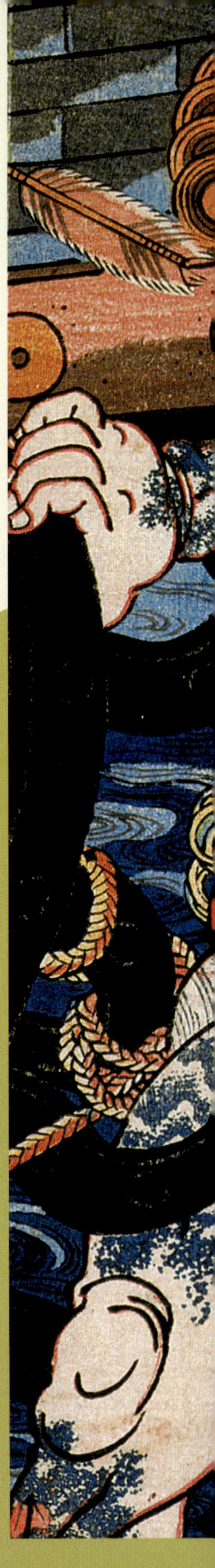

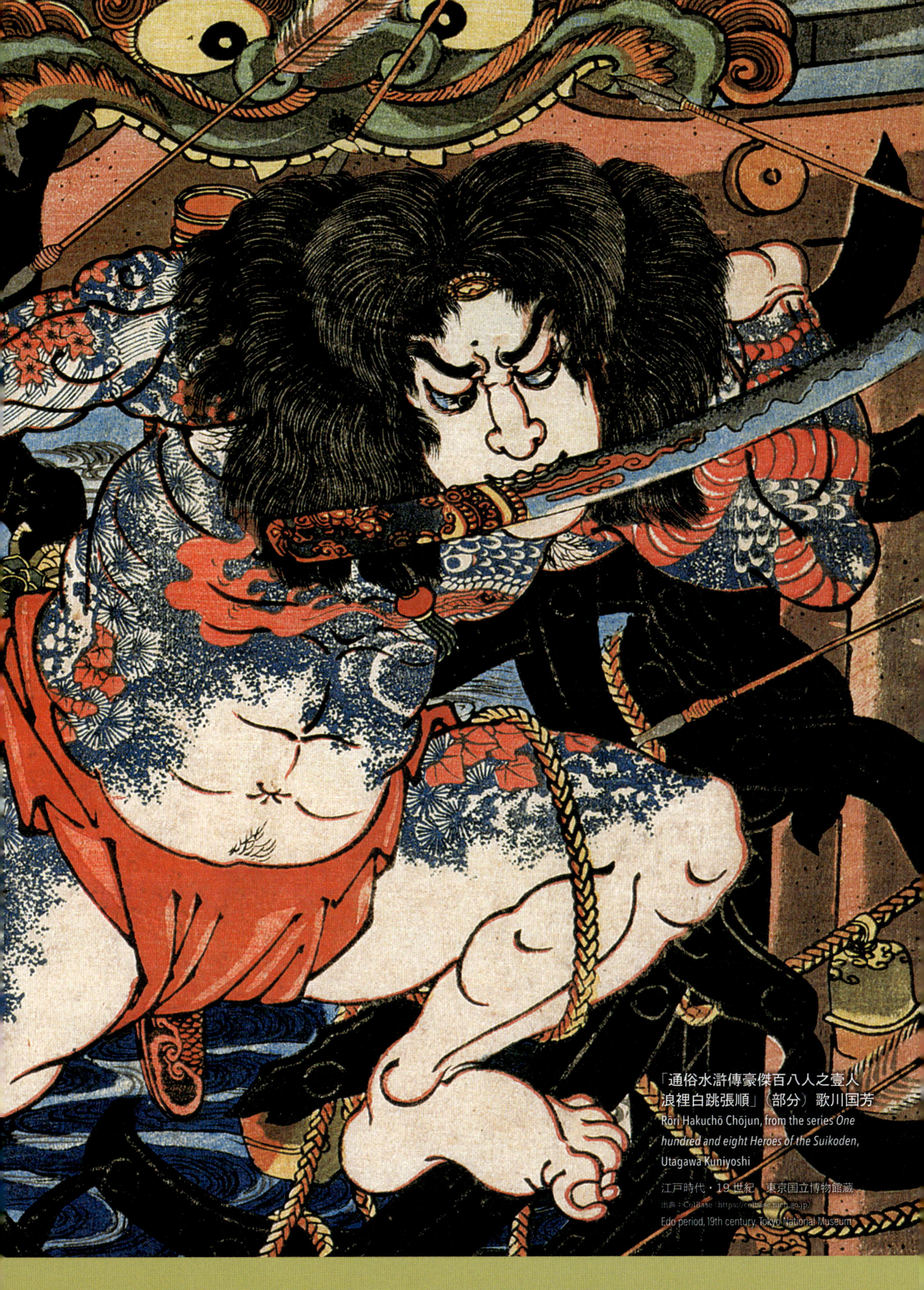

「通俗水滸傳豪傑百八人之壹人
浪裡白跳張順」〈部分〉歌川国芳
Rōri Hakuchō Chōjun, from the series *One
hundred and eight Heroes of the Suikoden*,
Utagawa Kuniyoshi

江戸時代・19 世紀　東京国立博物館蔵
出典：ColBase（https://colbase.nich.go.jp）
Edo period, 19th century, Tokyo National Museum

　　Chapter 1 | Tattoos: The Beauty of the Heroes' Skin　**Utagawa Kuniyoshi**

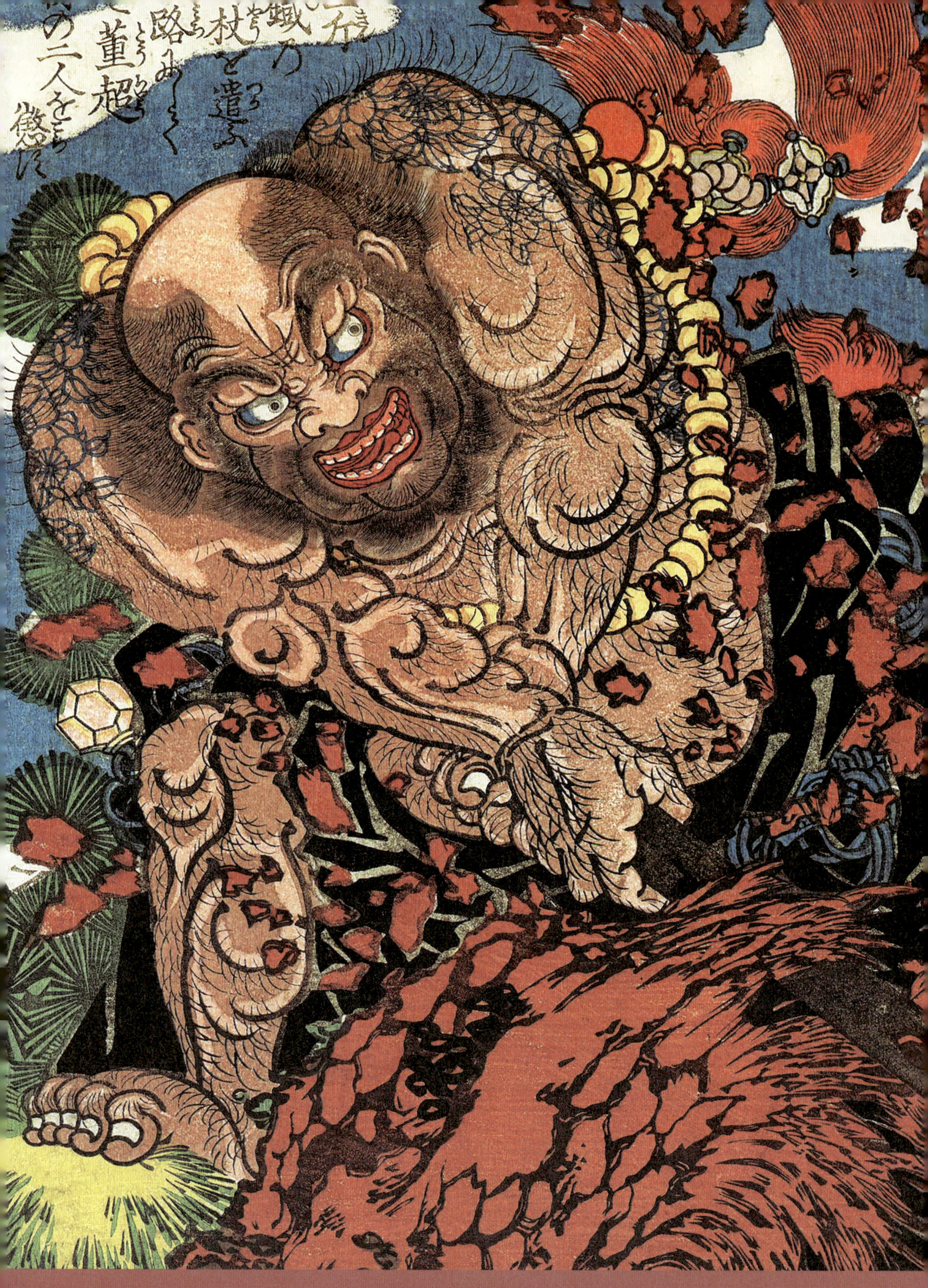
杖を遣ふ
董超
の二人を
懲らしに

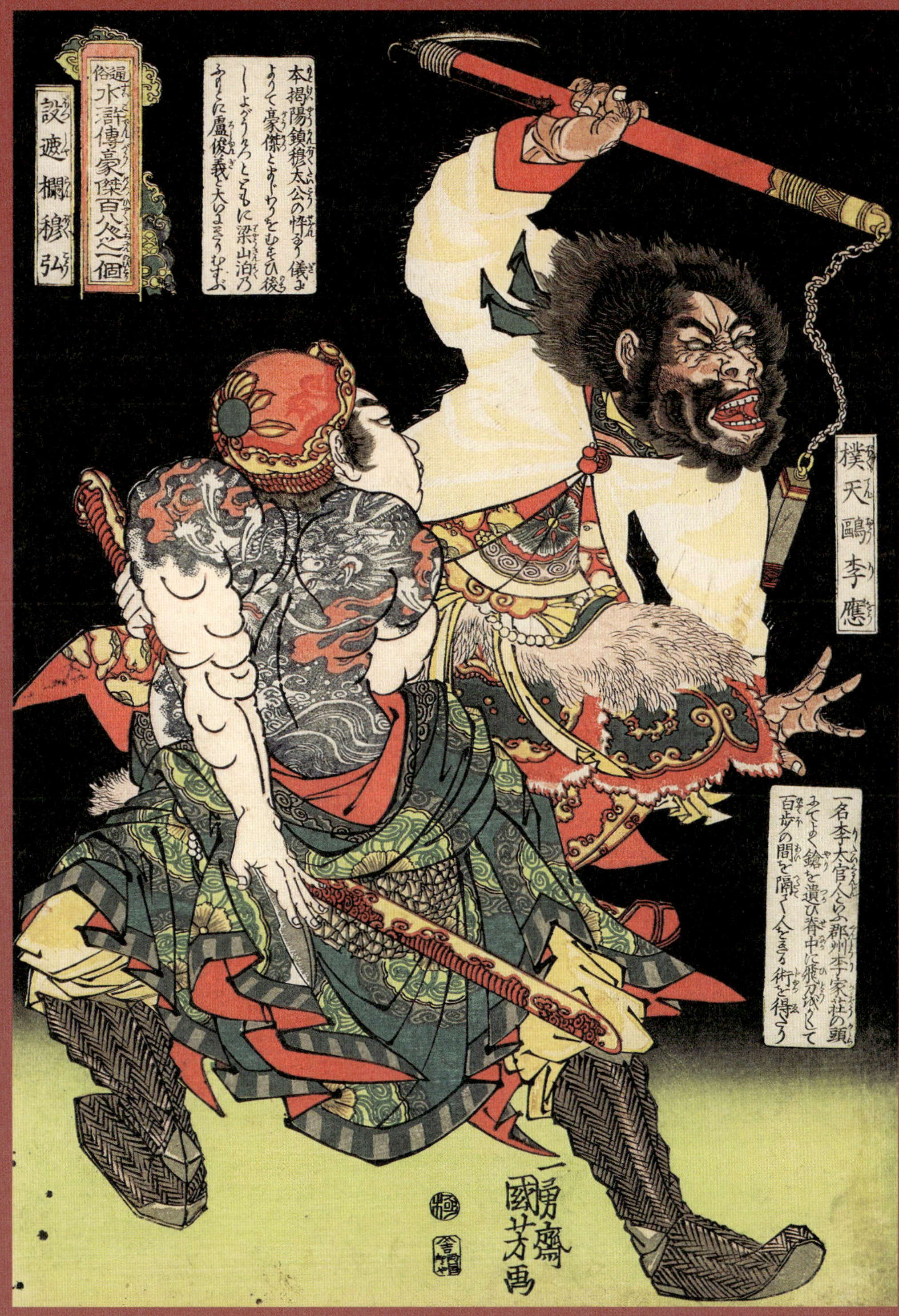

「通俗水滸傳豪傑百八人之一人
花和尚魯知深初名魯達」（部分）歌川国芳
Kaoshō Rochishin, from the series *One hundred and eight
Heroes of the Suikoden*, Detail, Utagawa Kuniyoshi

文政末期・1828-29　山口県立萩美術館・浦上記念館蔵
Edo period, 1828-29, Hagi Uragami Museum

「通俗水滸傳豪傑百八人之一個
撲天鵰李應・没遮欄穆弘」歌川国芳
Hakutenchō Rio and Bossharan Bokkō, from the series *One
hundred and eight Heroes of the Suikoden*, Utagawa Kuniyoshi

江戸時代・19 世紀　東京国立博物館蔵
出典：ColBase (https://colbase.nich.go.jp)
Edo period, 19th century, Tokyo National Museum

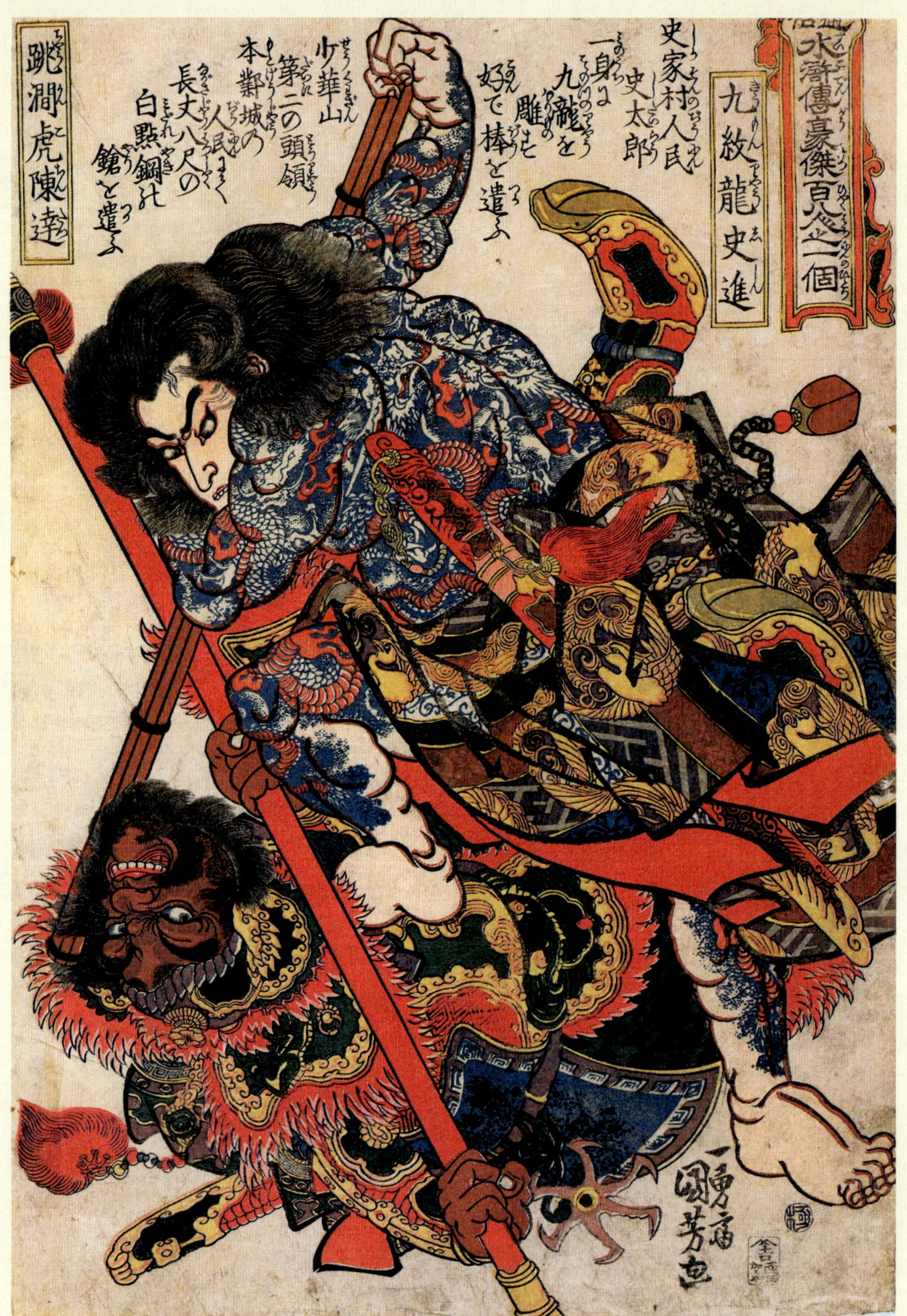

「通俗水滸傳豪傑百八人之一個
　九紋龍史進・跳澗虎陳達」歌川国芳
Kumonryū Shishin and Chokankō Chintatsu, from the
series *One hundred and eight Heroes of the Suikoden*,
Utagawa Kuniyoshi
江戸時代・19 世紀　東京国立博物館蔵
出典：ColBase (https://colbase.nich.go.jp)
Edo period, 19th century, Tokyo National Museum

「通俗水滸傳豪傑百八人之一個
　九紋龍史進」（部分）歌川国芳
Kumonryū Shishin, from the series *One
hundred and eight Heroes of the Suikoden*,
Detail, Utagawa Kuniyoshi
江戸時代・19 世紀　東京国立博物館蔵
出典：ColBase (https://colbase.nich.go.jp)
Edo period, 19th century, Tokyo National Museum

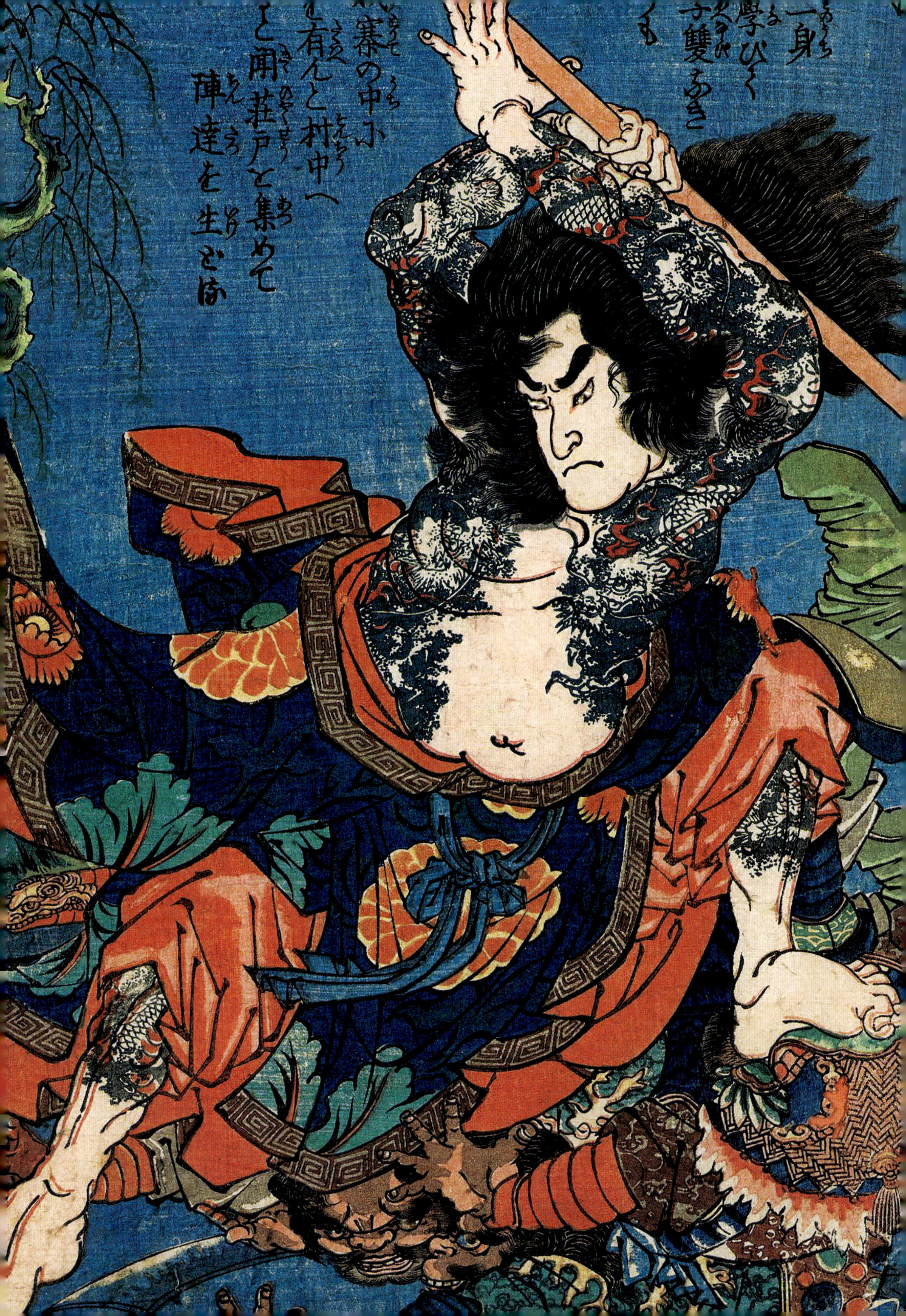

一身に
學びて
方雙ふき
も
寨の中小
有んと村中へ
と聞莊戸を集めて
陣達を生ごは

「通俗水滸傳豪傑百八人之一個
混江龍李俊」歌川国芳
Konkōryu Rishun, from the series *One hundred and
eight Heroes of the Suikoden*, Utagawa Kuniyoshi
江戸時代・19世紀　東京国立博物館蔵
出典：ColBase (https://colbase.nich.go.jp)
Edo period, 19th century, Tokyo National Museum

「通俗水滸傳豪傑百八人之一個
舩火兒張横」（部分）歌川国芳
Senkaji Chōou, from the series *One hundred and eight
Heroes of the Suikoden*, Detail, Utagawa Kuniyoshi
江戸時代・19世紀　東京国立博物館蔵
出典：ColBase (https://colbase.nich.go.jp)
Edo period, 19th century, Tokyo National Museum

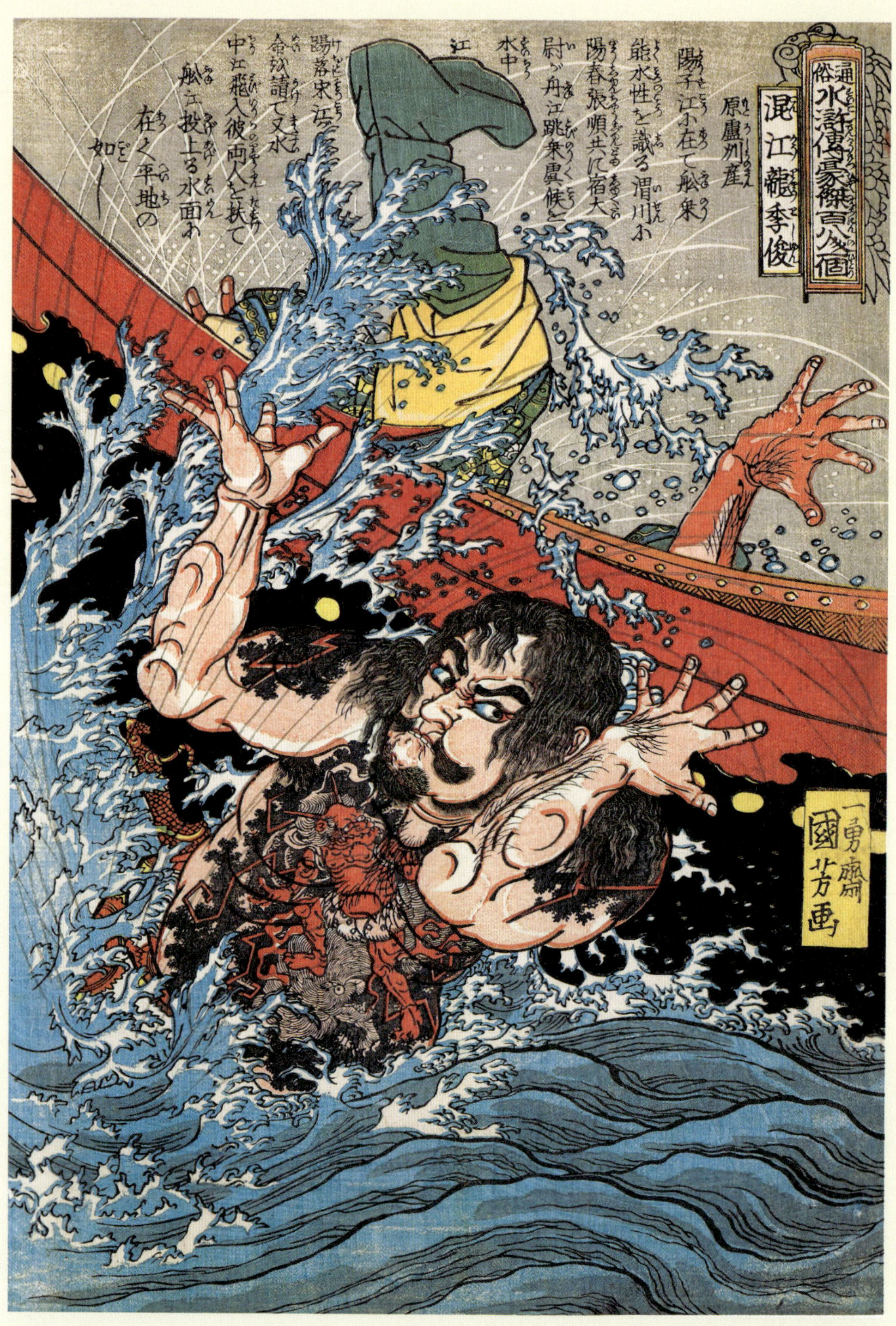

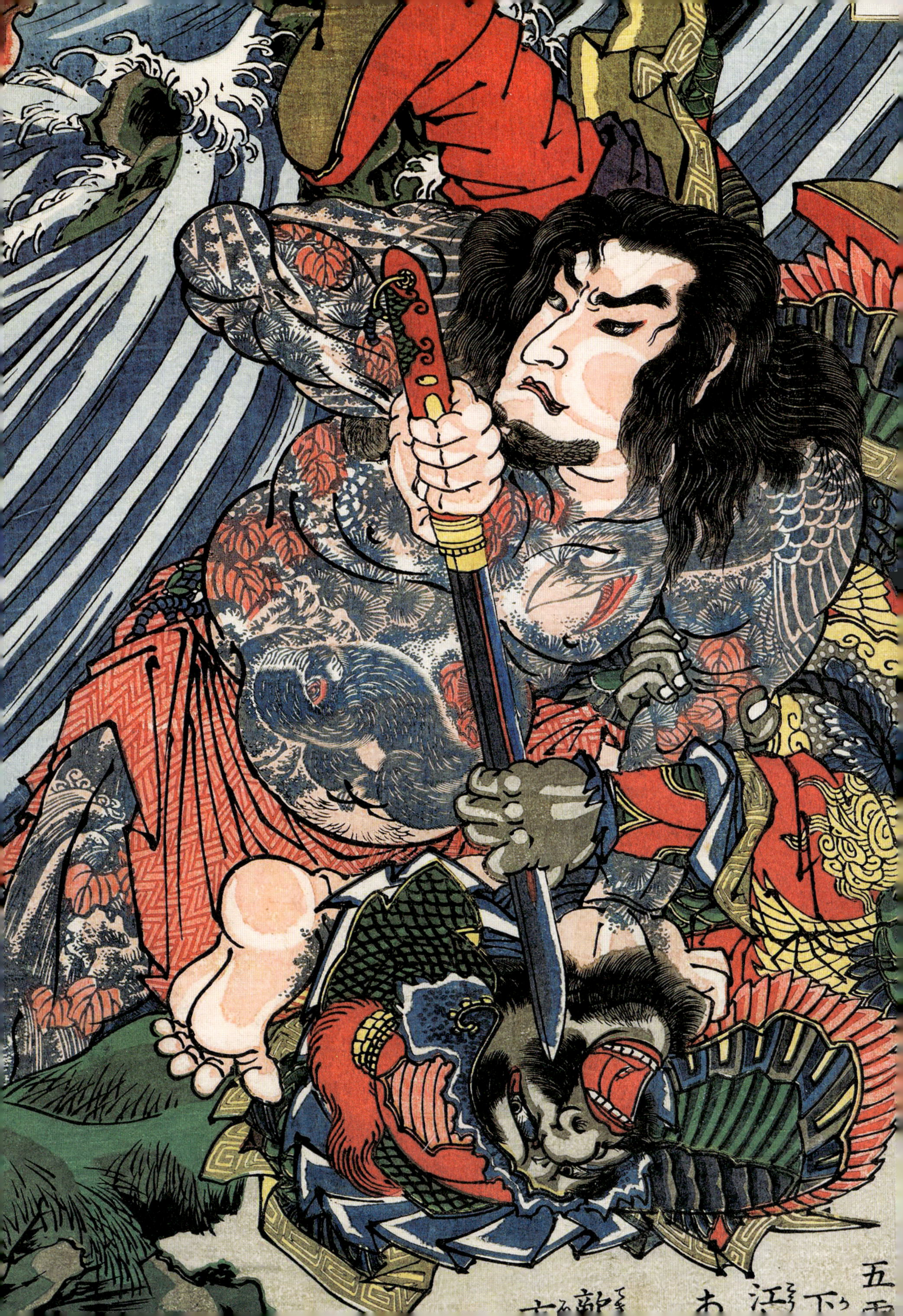

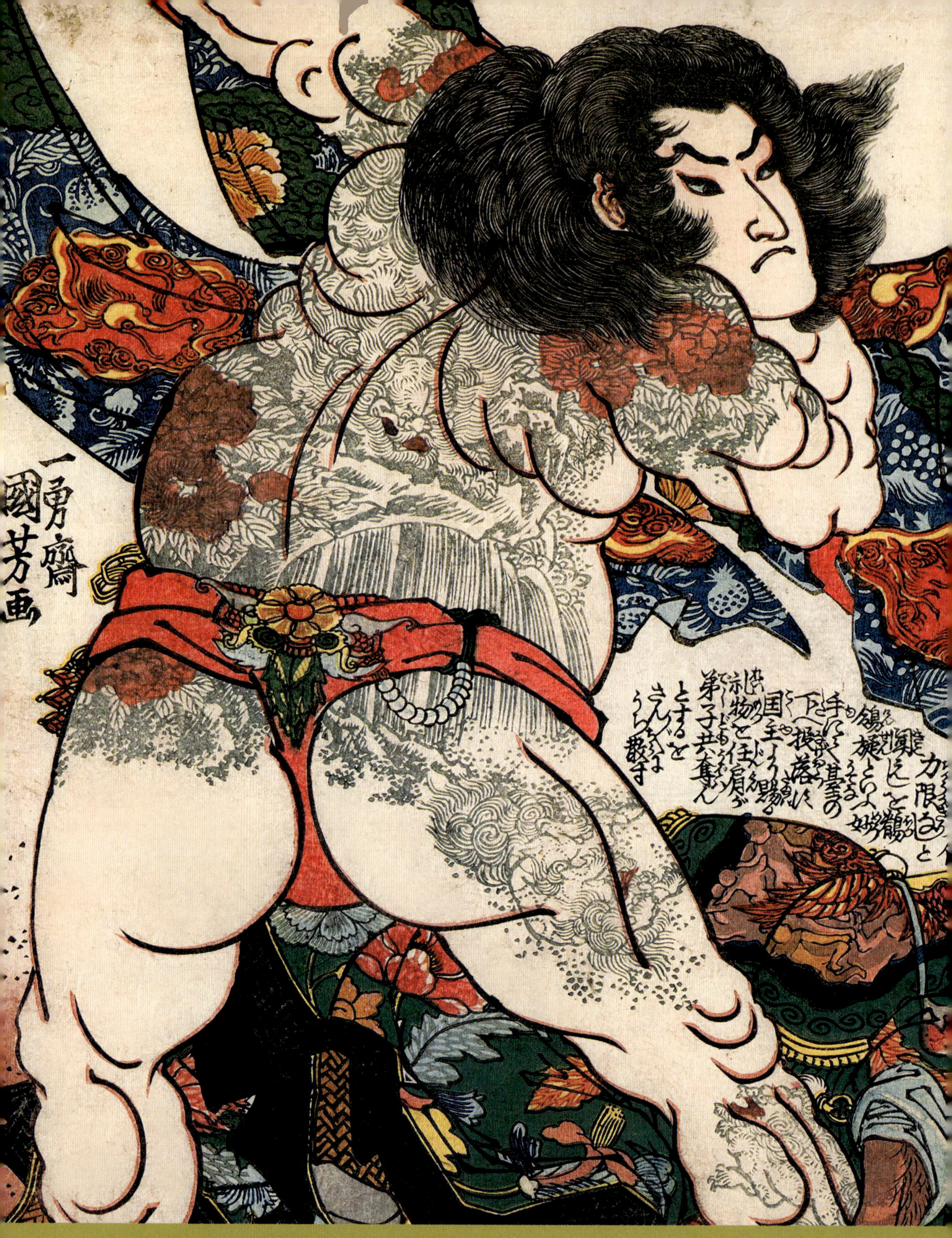

「通俗水滸傳豪傑百八人之一個　浪子燕青」（部分）歌川国芳
Roushi Ensei, from the series *One hundred and eight Heroes of the Suikoden*, Detail, Utagawa Kuniyoshi

江戸時代・19世紀　東京国立博物館蔵　出典：ColBase (https://colbase.nich.go.jp)　Edo period, 19th century, Tokyo National Museum

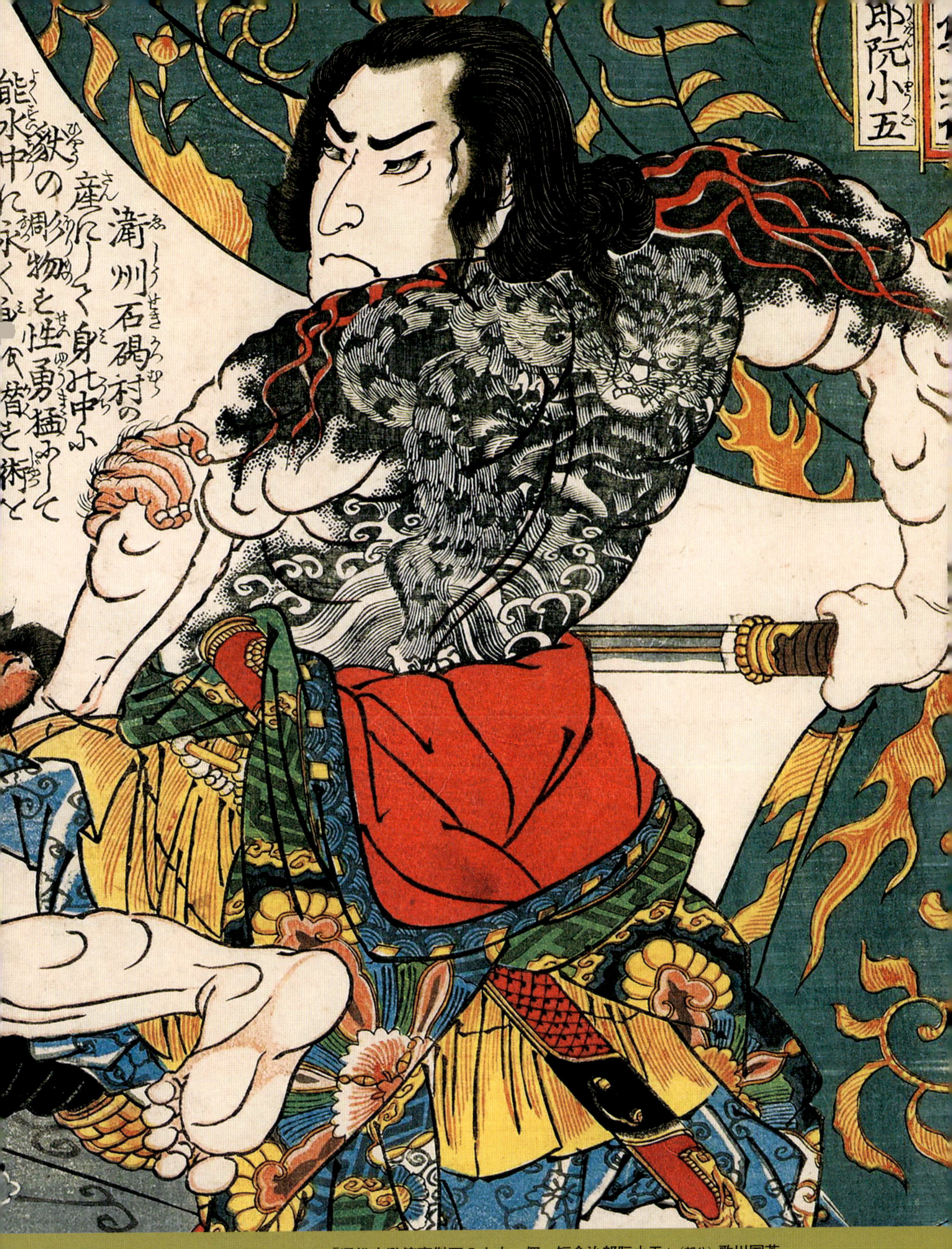

「通俗水滸傳豪傑百八人之一個　短命治郎阮小五」（部分）歌川国芳

Tanmei Jirō Gen Shōgo, from the series *One hundred and eight Heroes of the Suikoden*, Detail, Utagawa Kuniyoshi

江戸時代・19世紀　東京国立博物館蔵　出典：ColBase (https://colbase.nich.go.jp)　Edo period, 19th century, Tokyo National Museum

Chapter 1 │ Tattoos: The Beauty of the Heroes' Skin　**Utagawa Kuniyoshi**

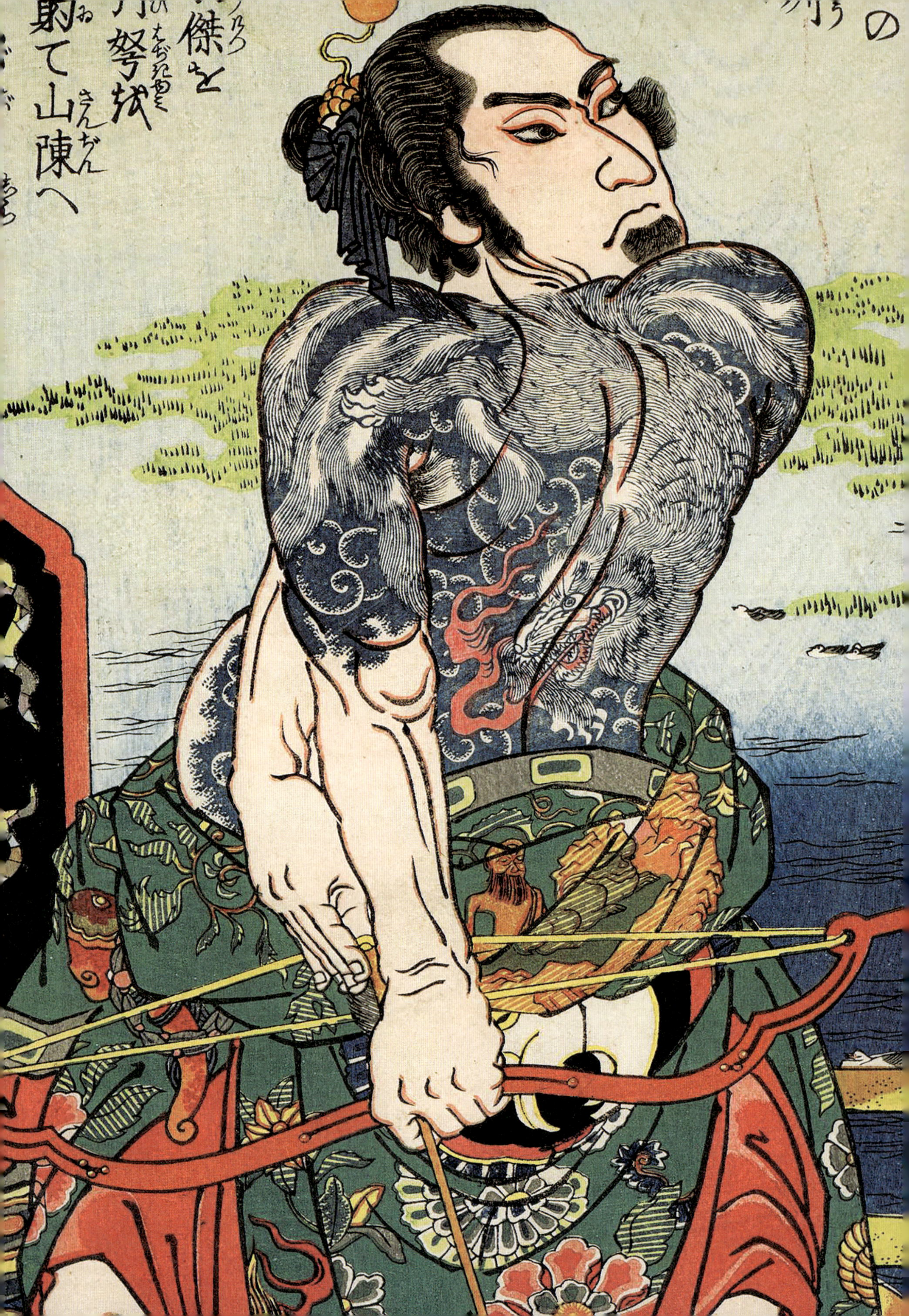

傑と小弩城射て山陳へ

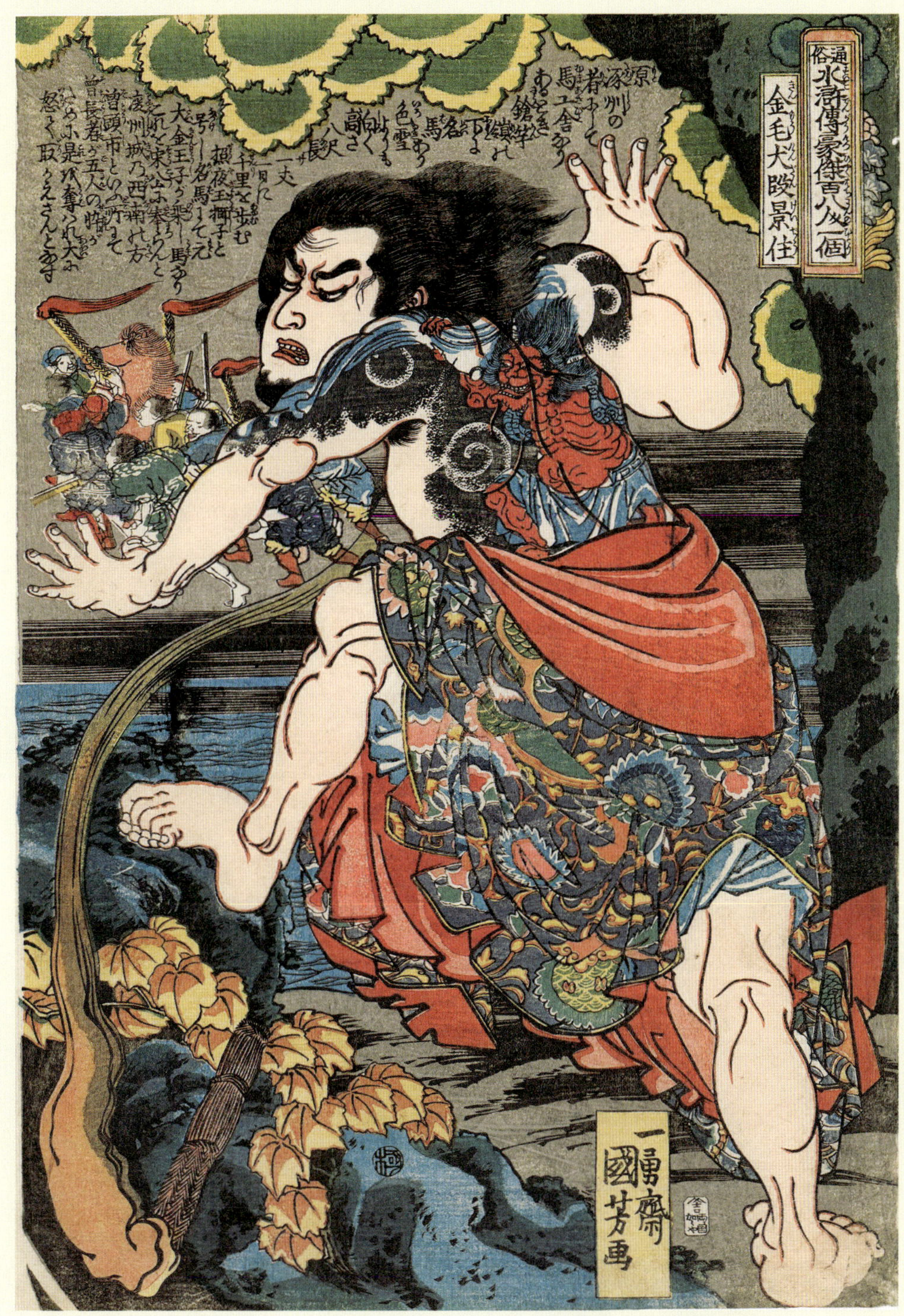

「通俗水滸傳豪傑百八人一個
金毛犬段景住」歌川国芳

Kinmōken Dan Keijū, from the series *One hundred
and eight Heroes of the Suikoden*, Utagawa Kuniyoshi

江戸時代・19 世紀　東京国立博物館蔵
出典：ColBase（https://colbase.nich.go.jp）
Edo period, 19th century, Tokyo National Museum

「通俗水滸傳豪傑百八人一個
旱地忽律朱貴」（部分）歌川国芳

Kanchi Kotsuritsu Shuki, from the series *One hundred and
eight Heroes of the Suikoden*, Detail, Utagawa Kuniyoshi

文政末期・1828-29　山口県立萩美術館・浦上記念館蔵
Edo period, 1828-29, Hagi Uragami Museum

Chapter 1 ｜ Tattoos: The Beauty of the Heroes' Skin　**Utagawa Kuniyoshi**

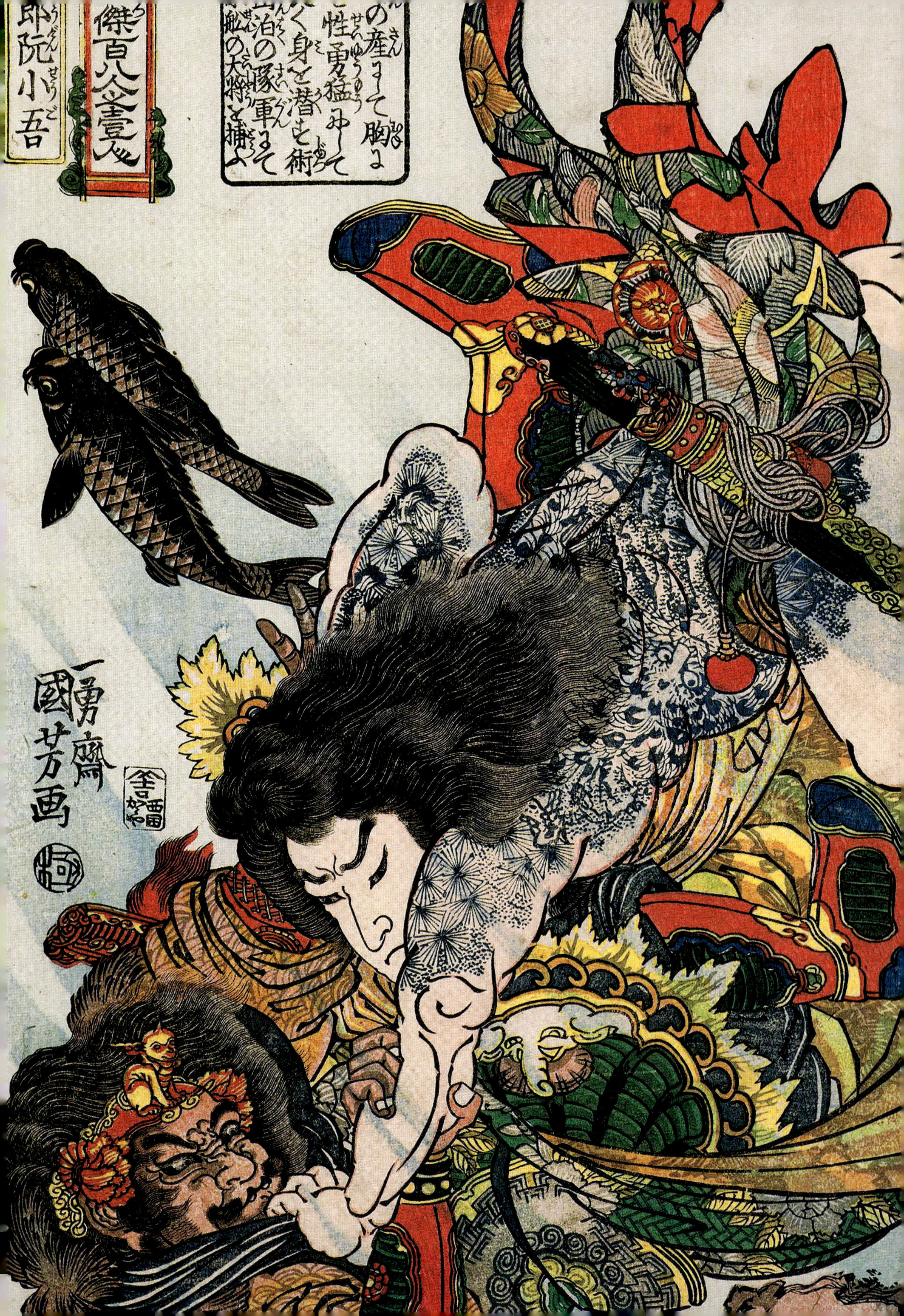
傑百人一首
阮小吾
性勇猛にして身を潜をの術よく
その産にして胸より
泊の隊軍まて
舟の大将を捕よ
一勇斎
國芳画

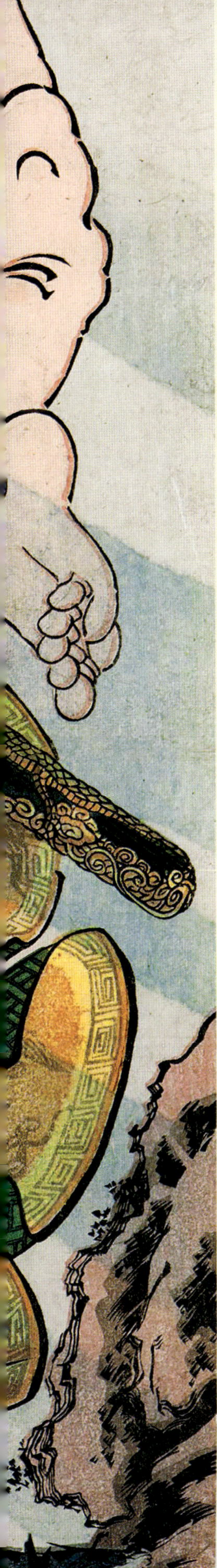

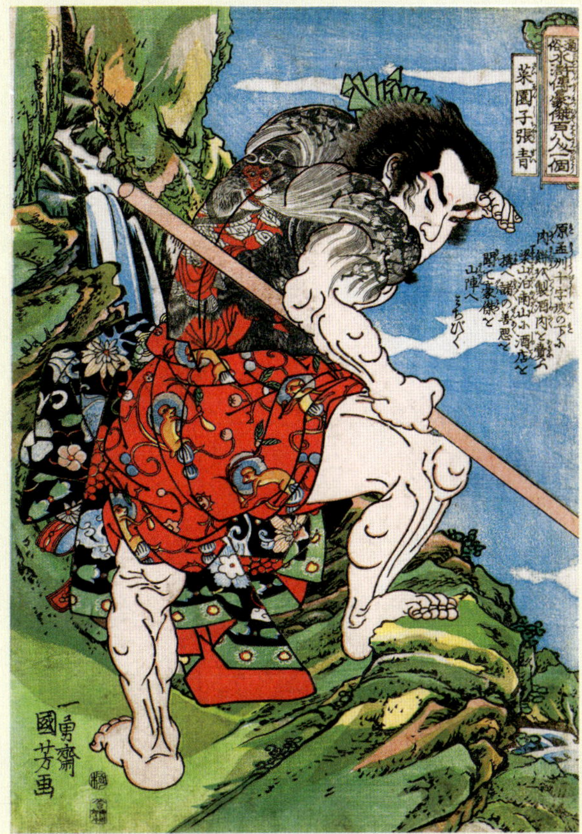

「通俗水滸傳豪傑百八人
之一個　菜園子張青」
歌川国芳
Saienshi Chousei, from the series
*One hundred and eight Heroes of
the Suikoden*, Utagawa Kuniyoshi

江戸時代・19 世紀
東京国立博物館蔵
出典：ColBase (https://colbase.nich.go.jp)
Edo period, 19th century, Tokyo National
Museum

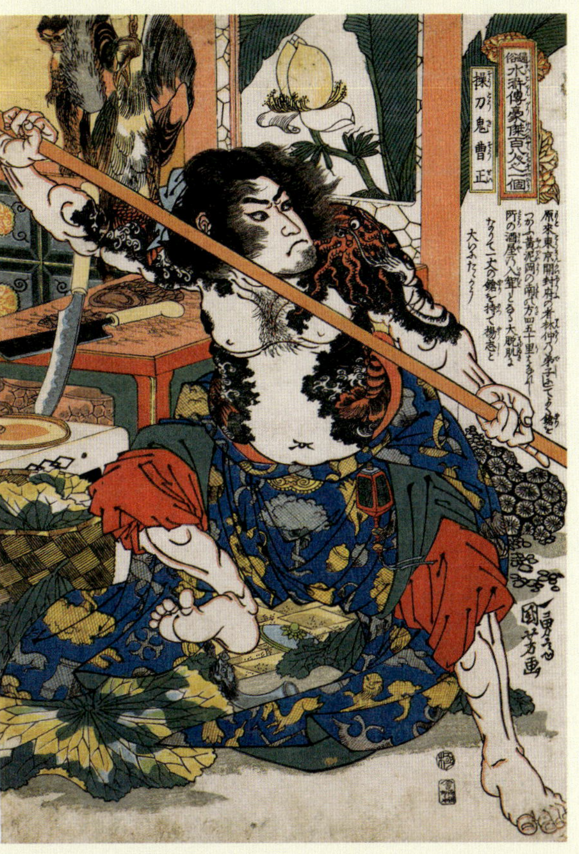

「通俗水滸傳豪傑百八人
之一個　操刀鬼曹正」
歌川国芳
Soutouki Sousei, from the series
*One hundred and eight Heroes of
the Suikoden*, Utagawa Kuniyoshi

江戸時代・19 世紀
東京国立博物館蔵
出典：ColBase (https://colbase.nich.go.jp)
Edo period, 19th century, Tokyo National
Museum

「通俗水滸傳豪傑百八人之
壹人　短冥次郎阮小吾」
（部分）歌川国芳
Tanmei Jirō Gen Shōgo, from the series
*One hundred and eight Heroes of the
Suikoden*, Detail, Utagawa Kuniyoshi

江戸時代・19 世紀
東京国立博物館蔵
出典：ColBase (https://colbase.nich.go.jp)
Edo period, 19th century, Tokyo National
Museum

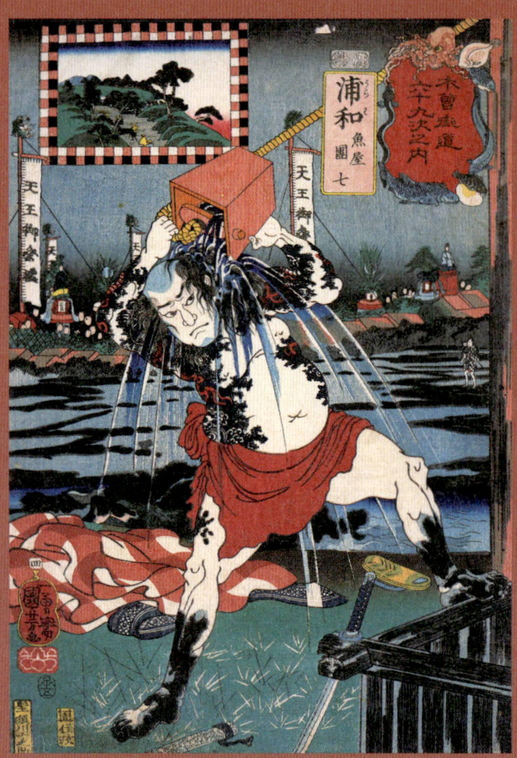

「木曾街道六十九次之内
四　浦和　魚屋團七」歌川国芳

Station IV Urawa, Sakanaya Danshichi, from
the series *The Sixty-Nine Stations of the
Kisokaidō Road*, Utagawa Kuniyoshi

嘉永 5 年・1852
東京都立中央図書館特別文庫室蔵
1852, Tokyo Metropolitan Library

「華古与見」歌川国芳

Hanagoyomi: Calender for flower plucking, Utagawa Kuniyoshi

天保 6 年・1835　国際日本文化研究センター蔵
1835, International Research Center for Japanese Studies

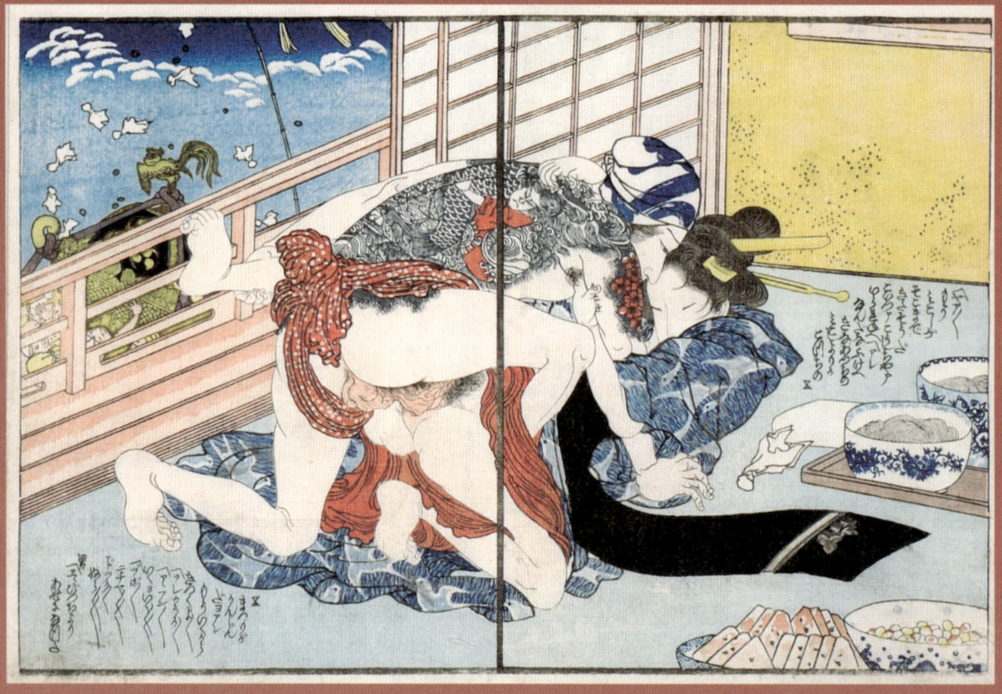

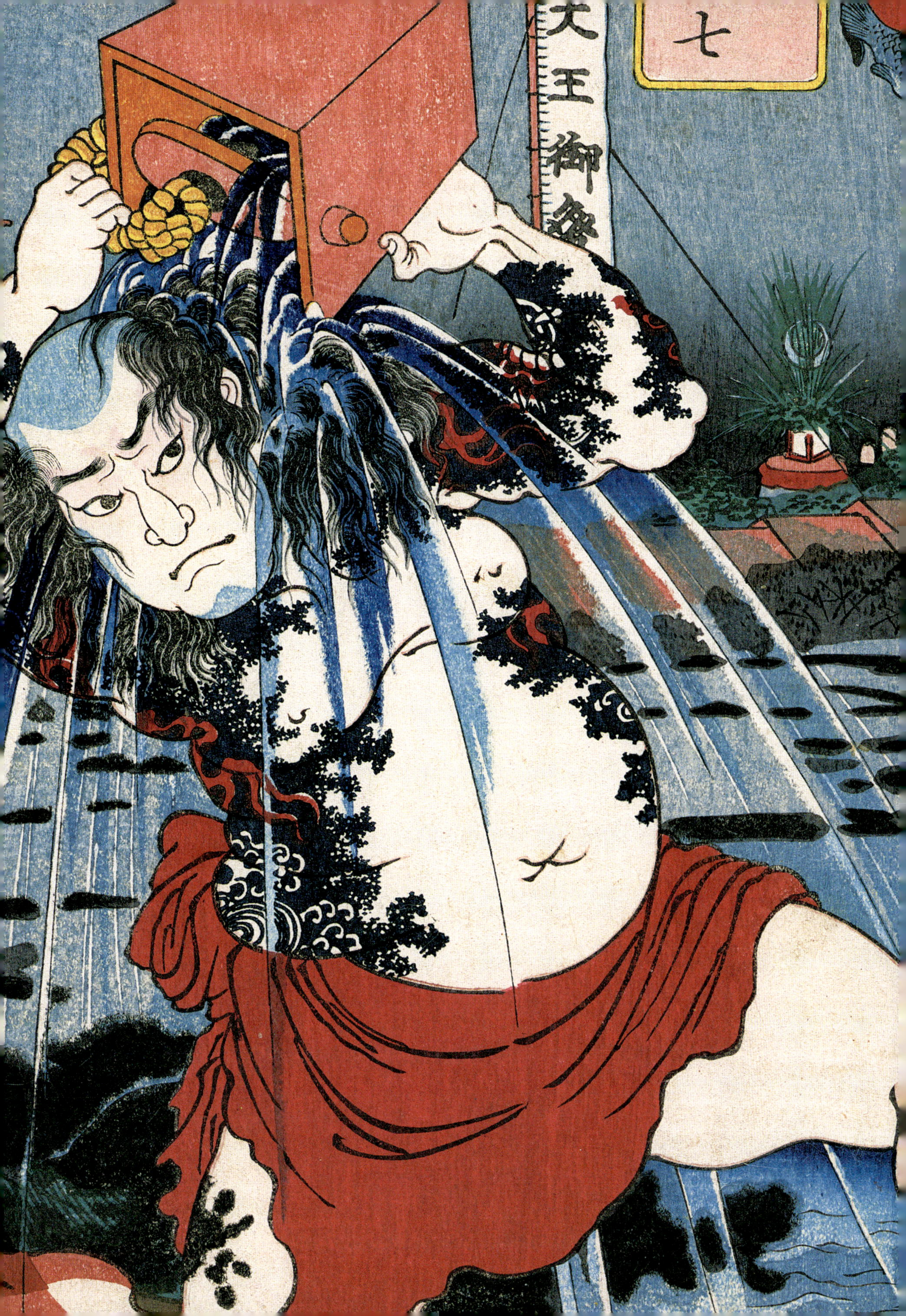

七
大王御盤

歌川豊国（3世）

うたがわとよくに（歌川国貞・1世）天明6年〜元治元年（1786-1864）

　江戸時代後期の浮世絵師。初代歌川豊国の門人。天保15年（1844）三世歌川豊国（自称二世）を襲名した。代表作となった柳亭種彦の合巻『偐紫田舎源氏』の挿絵は文政12年（1829）に始まり評判となる。役者絵や猫背猪首型の美人画、合巻挿絵などに才能を発揮した。「豊国漫画図絵」のうちに弁天小僧の絵があるが、これは豊国の創作で、趣向の面白さに注目した河竹黙阿弥が、この暗示から『青砥稿花紅彩画』（文久2年（1862）、「白浪五人男」）を書下ろしたといわれる。幕末を代表する絵師では最大の勢力を形成し、もっとも多くの作品を残した。

「豊国漫画図絵　弁天小僧
菊之介」（部分）歌川豊国
Bentenkozō Kikunosuke, from *The Heroes and
Heroines of the Popular Fiction (Toyokuni Manga
Zue)* , Detail, Utagawa Toyokuni III (Kunisada I)

万延元年・1860　国立国会図書館
デジタルコレクション
1860, National Diet Library Digital Collections

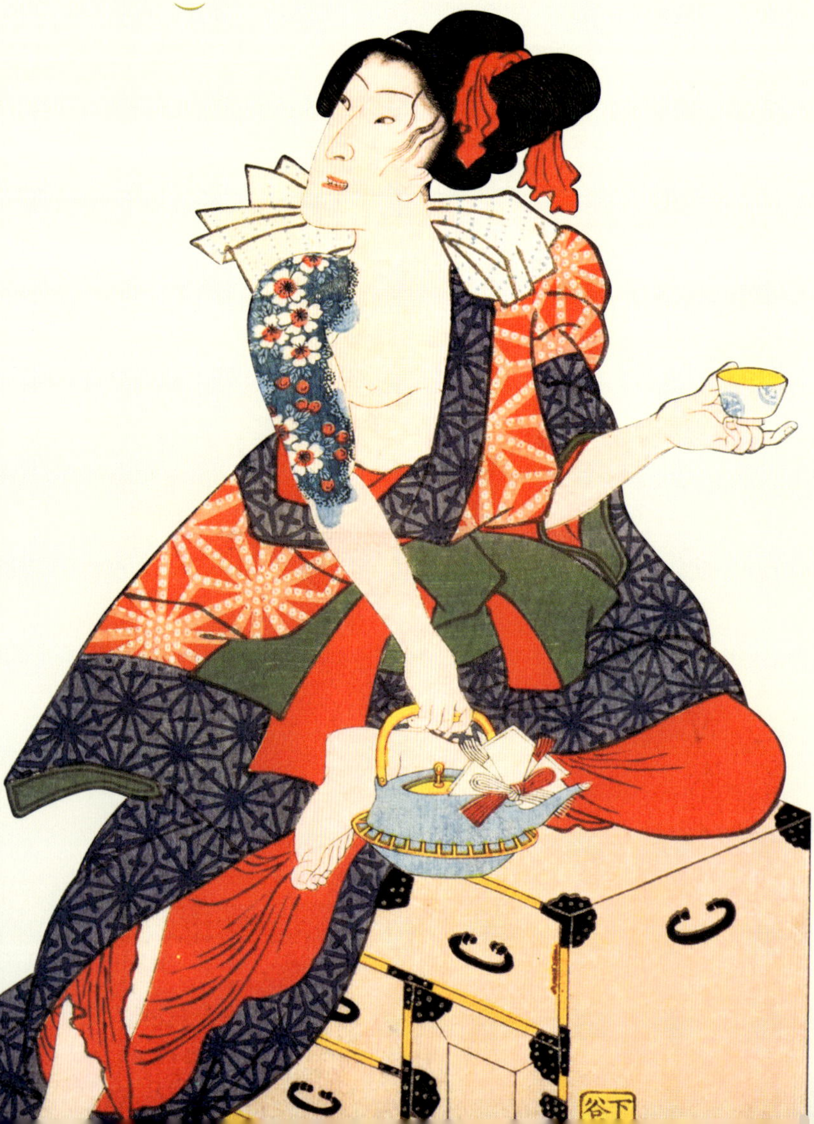

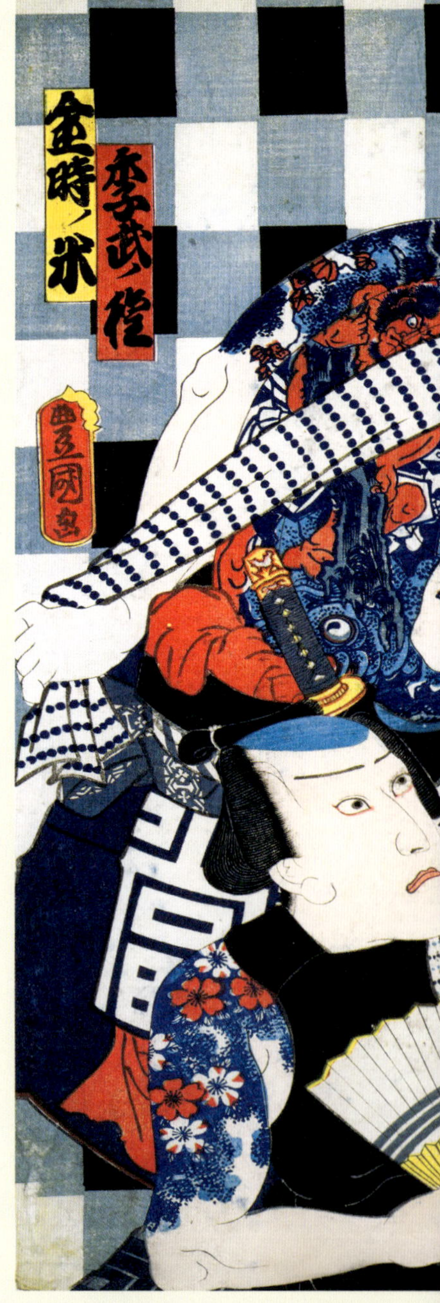

Utagawa Toyokuni III (Utagawa Kunisada I) 1786-1864

Late Edo-period Ukiyo-e Artist. A student of Utagawa Toyokuni I, he succeeded to the name Utagawa Toyokuni III (although he called himself Toyokuni II). He became famous in 1829 for the talent displayed in the illustrations he created for Ryutei Tanehiko's poetry collection *The Rustic Genji*. He displayed his talent in paintings of actors and round-shouldered beautiful women, and illustrations for popular books of revenge tales. *Toyokuni's Comic Illustrations* includes depictions of Benten Kozo. It is said that, noting that fascinating trend, Kawatake Mokuami was inspired to create his original Kabuki plays *Aoto Zoshi Hana no Nishiki-e* (1862) and *Shiranami Gonin Otoko* (Five Men of the White Waves), which were based on that picture. The leading painter of the Bakumatsu period, Toyokuni III left us by far the largest number of works.

「今四天王大山帰り　貞光ノ市・渡辺ノ福・季武ノ権・金時ノ米」『東錦絵』より歌川豊国
Ima Shitennō Ōyamagaeri, Sadamitsu no ichi, Watanabe no fuku, Kibu no gon, Kintoki no me, from the picture album Azuma Nishiki-e, Utagawa Toyokuni III (Kunisada I)

安政 5 年・1858
国立国会図書館蔵デジタルコレクション
1858, National Diet Library Digital Collections

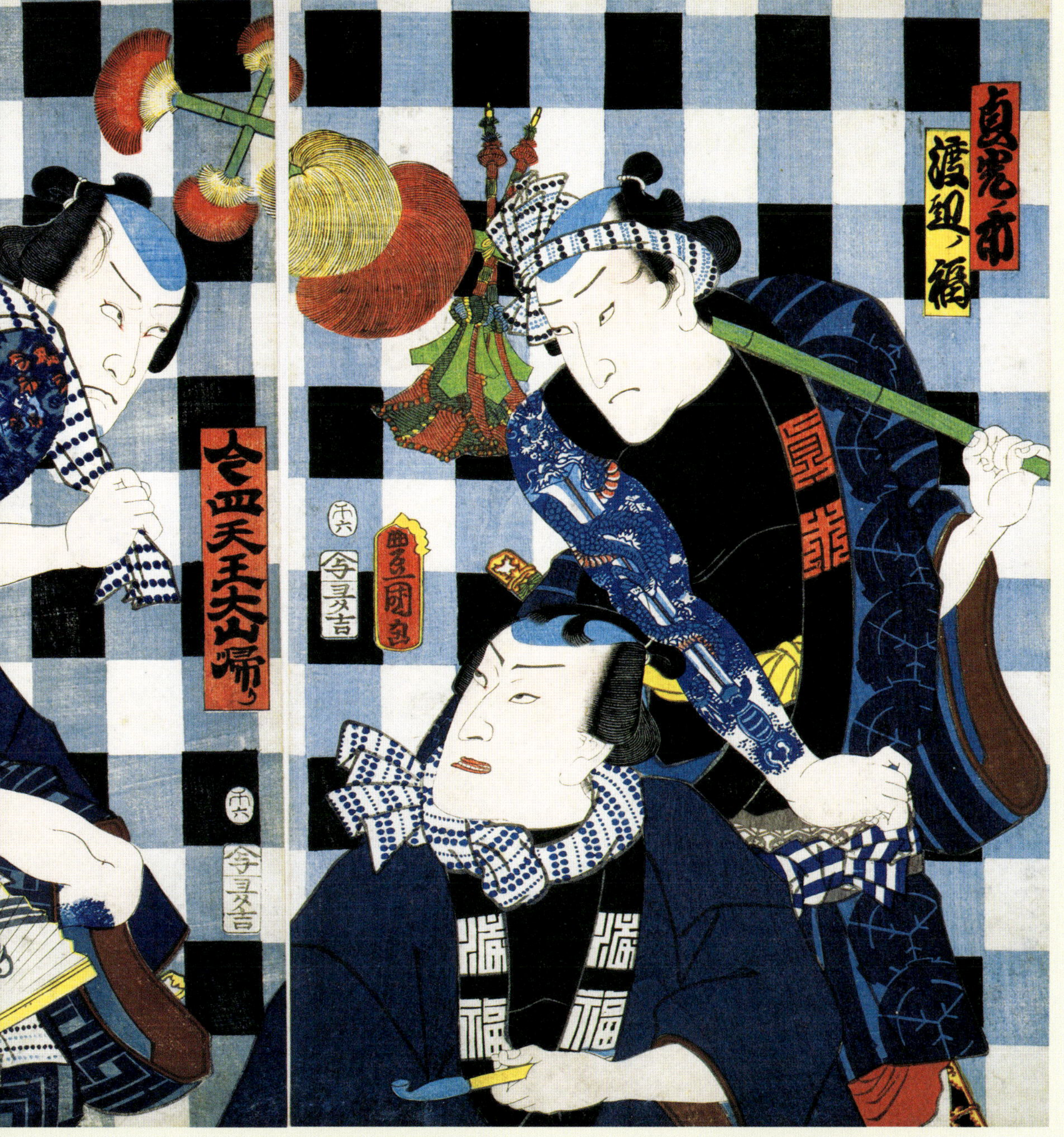

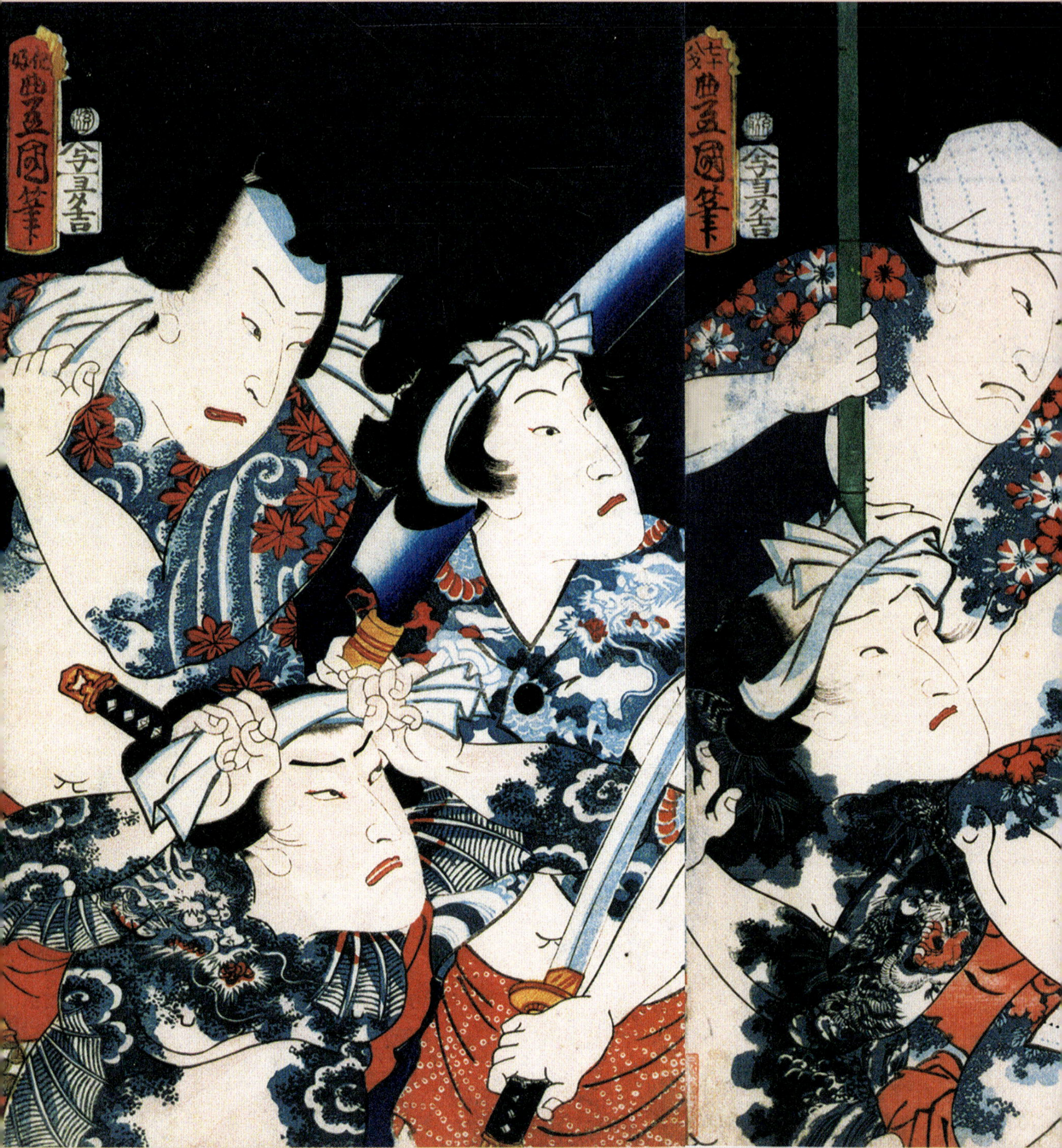

「見立十人豊国一世一代　屋久ら水滸傳」（部分）歌川豊国
Ten Imaginary Portraits, Toyokuni's Once-in-a-Lifetime Shuihuzhuan of the Stage (*Mitate jūnin Toyokuni issei ichidai yagura Suikoden*), Detail, Utagawa Toyokuni III (Kunisada I)

文久 3 年・1863　東京都立中央図書館特別文庫室蔵
1863, Tokyo Metropolitan Central Library

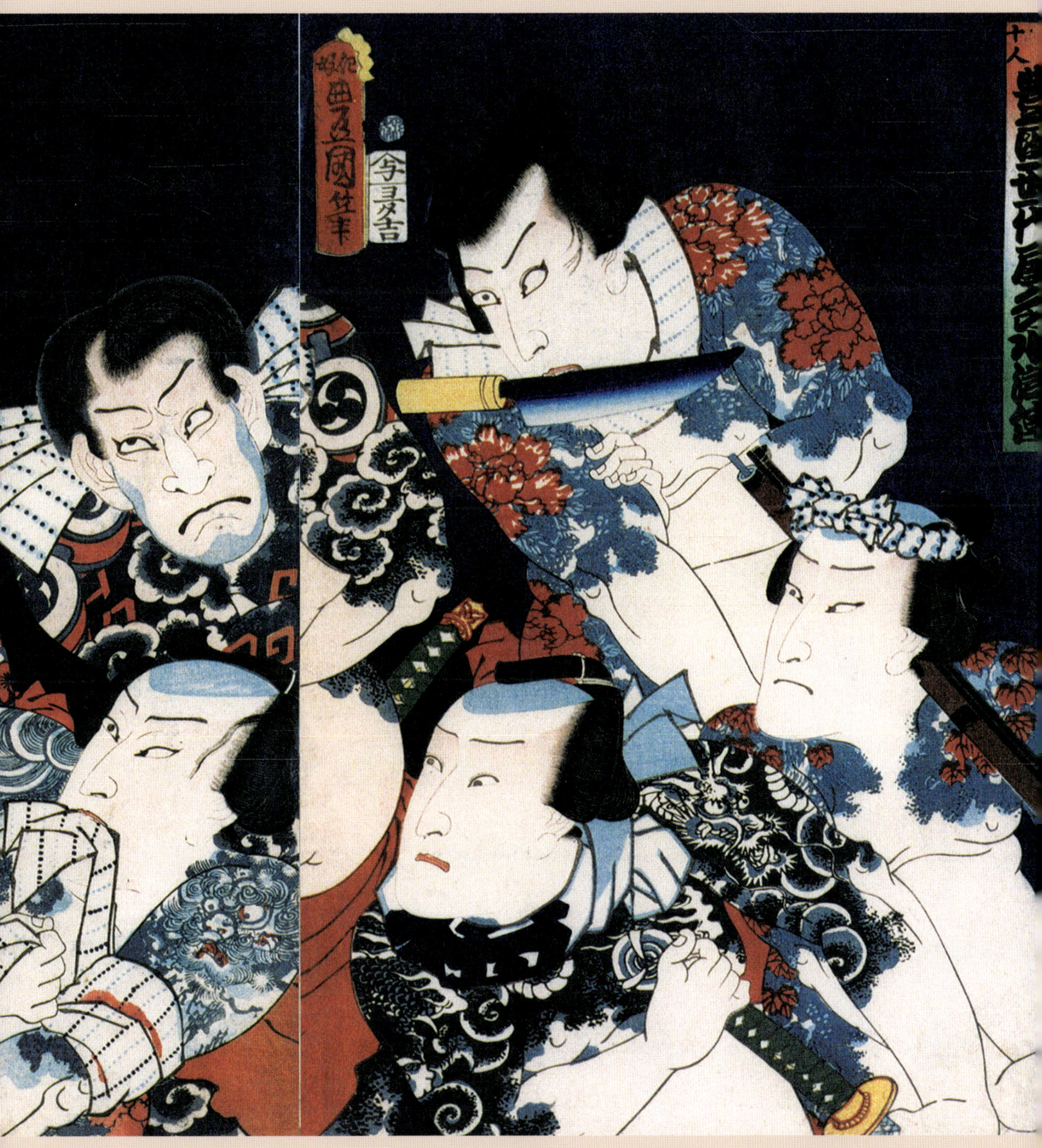

Chapter 1 | Tattoos: The Beauty of the Heroes' Skin **Utagawa Toyokuni**

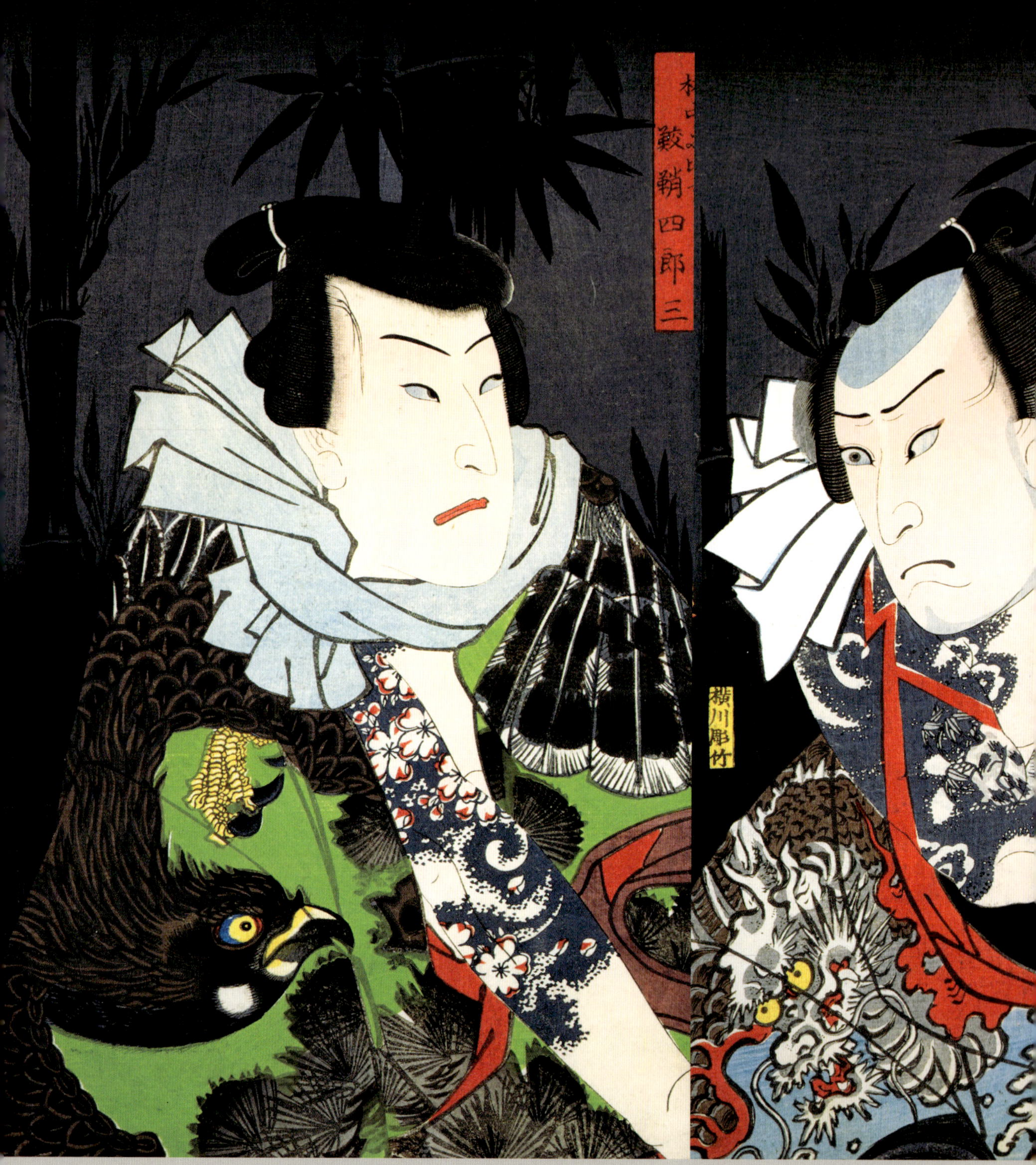

「當世好男子傳　林中に比す鮫鞘四郎三」（五代目坂東彦三郎）歌川豊国
Actors Bandō Hikosaburō V as Samezaya Shiroza, comparable to Lin Zhong (Rinchū ni hisu),
from the series *A Modern Shuihuzhuan (Tōsei suikoden)*, Utagawa Toyokuni III (Kunisada I)
安政6年・1859　国立国会図書館デジタルコレクション　1859, National Diet Library Digital Collections

「當世好男子傳　張順に比す夢の市郎兵衛」（八代目片岡仁左衛門）歌川豊国
Actors Kataoka Nizaemon VIII as Yume no Ichirobei, Comparable to Zhang Shun (Chōjun ni hisu), from the
series *A Modern Shuihuzhuan (Tōsei suikoden)*, Utagawa Toyokuni III (Kunisada I)
安政6年・1859　国立国会図書館デジタルコレクション　1859, National Diet Library Digital Collections

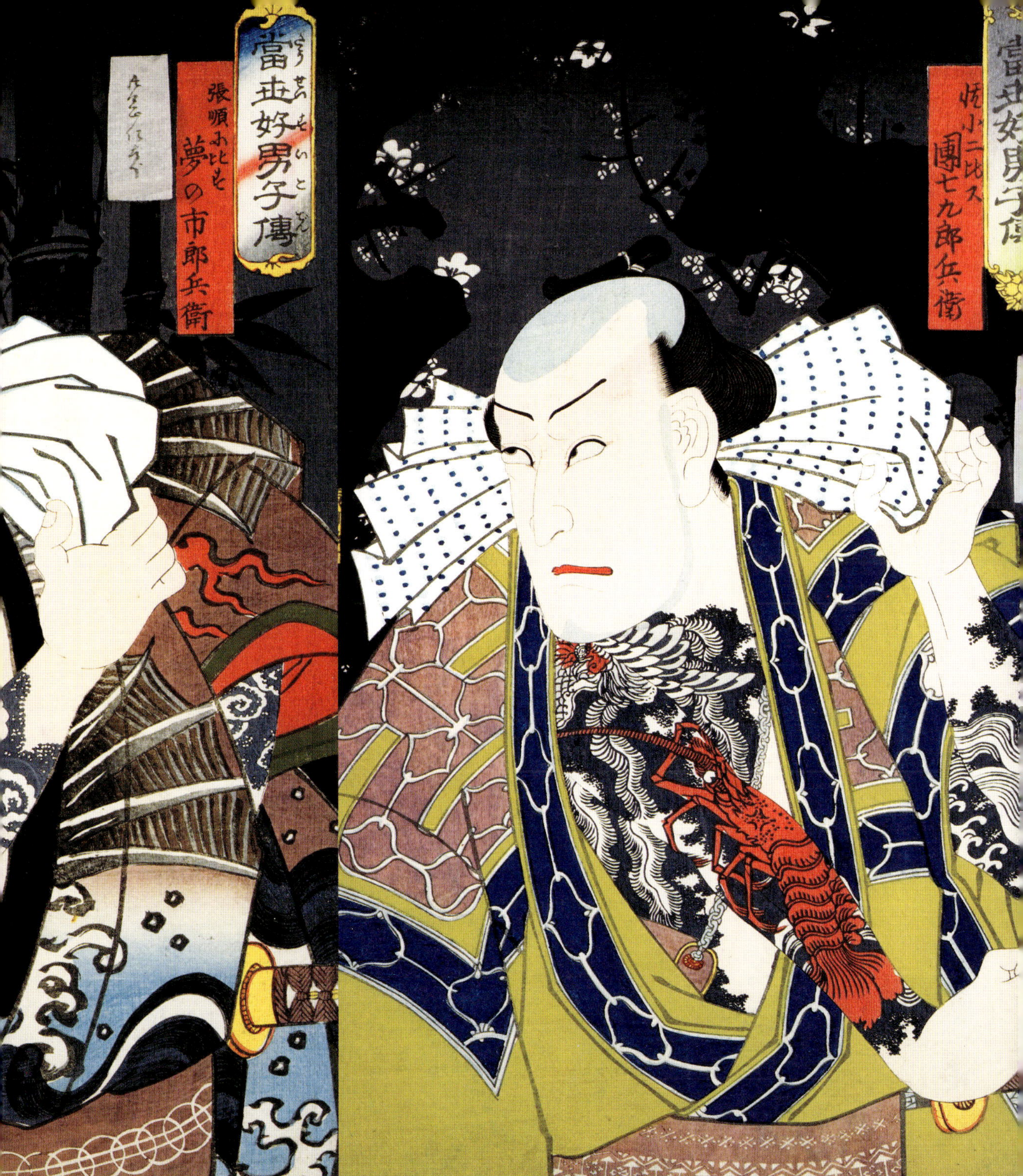

「當世好男子傳　慴小ニ比ス團七九郎兵衛」（市川小團次）歌川豊国
Actors Ichikawa Kodanji as Danshichi Kurobei, Comparable to Ruǎn Xiǎowǔ (Genshogo ni hisu), from the series *A Modern Shuihuzhuan (Tōsei suikoden)*, Utagawa Toyokuni III (Kunisada I)
安政 5 年・1858　国立国会図書館デジタルコレクション　1858, National Diet Library Digital Collections

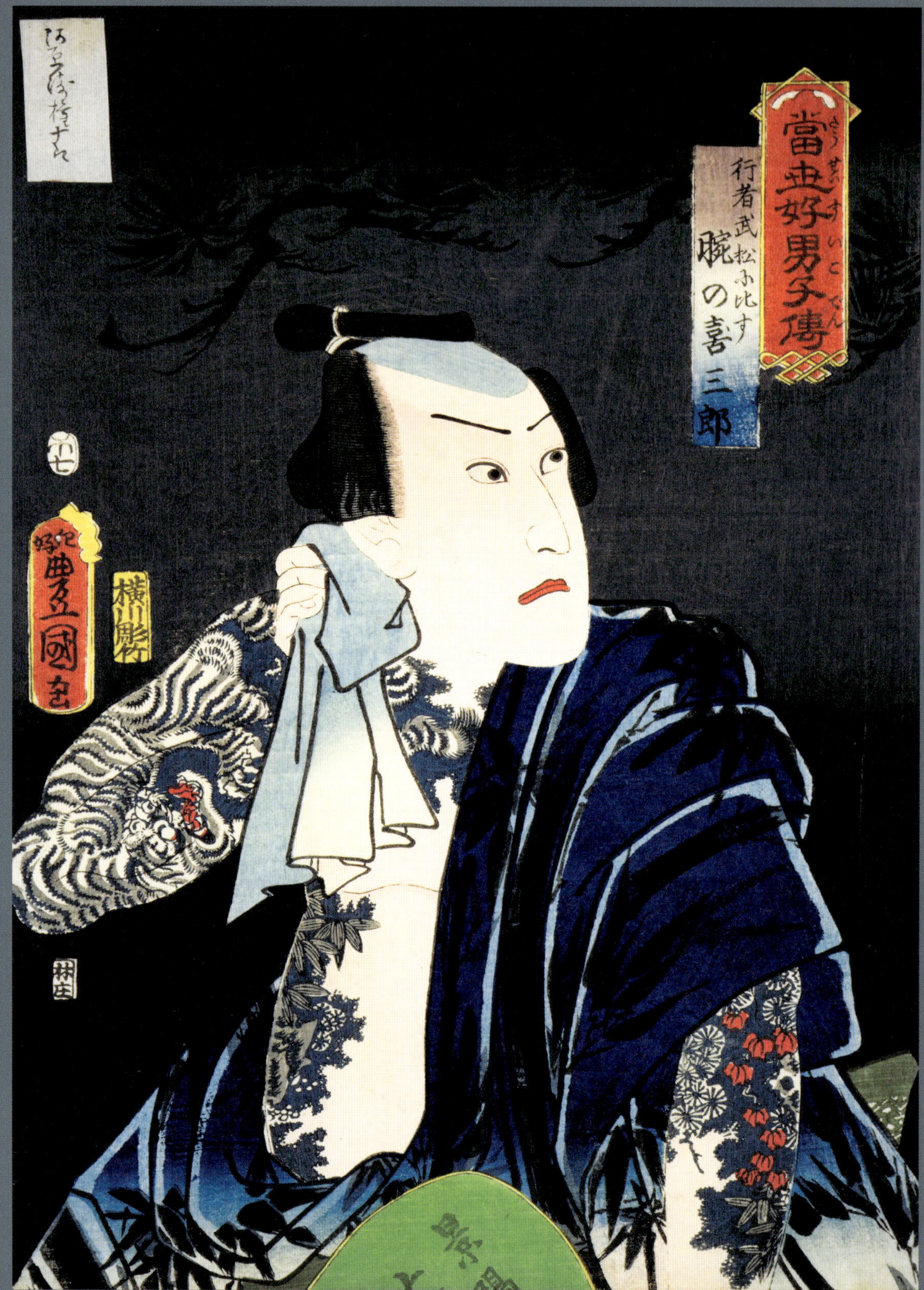

「當世好男子傳　行者武松に比す腕の袁三郎」歌川豊国
Ude no Kisaburō, comparable to Wu Song the Ascetic (Gyōjya Bushō ni hisu), from the
series *A Modern Shuihuzhuan (Tōsei suikoden)*, Utagawa Toyokuni III (Kunisada I)

安政5年・1858　国立国会図書館デジタルコレクション
1858, National Diet Library Digital Collections

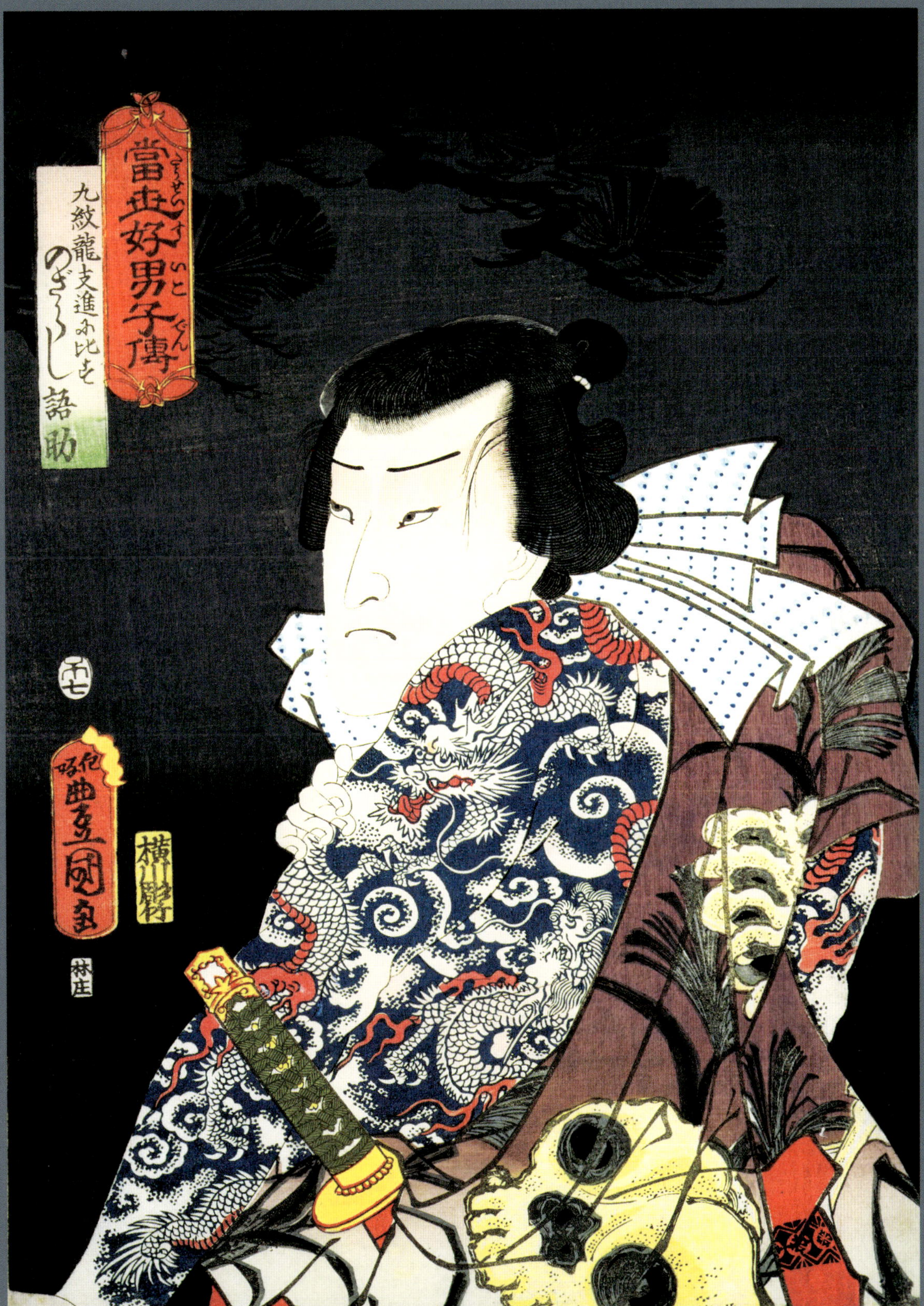

「當世好男子傳　九紋龍支進に比すのざらし語助」歌川豊国

Nozarashi Gosuke, comparable to Kumonryū Shishin, from the series *A Modern Shuihuzhuan (Tōsei suikoden)*, Utagawa Toyokuni III (Kunisada I)

安政 5 年・1858　国立国会図書館デジタルコレクション
1858, National Diet Library Digital Collections

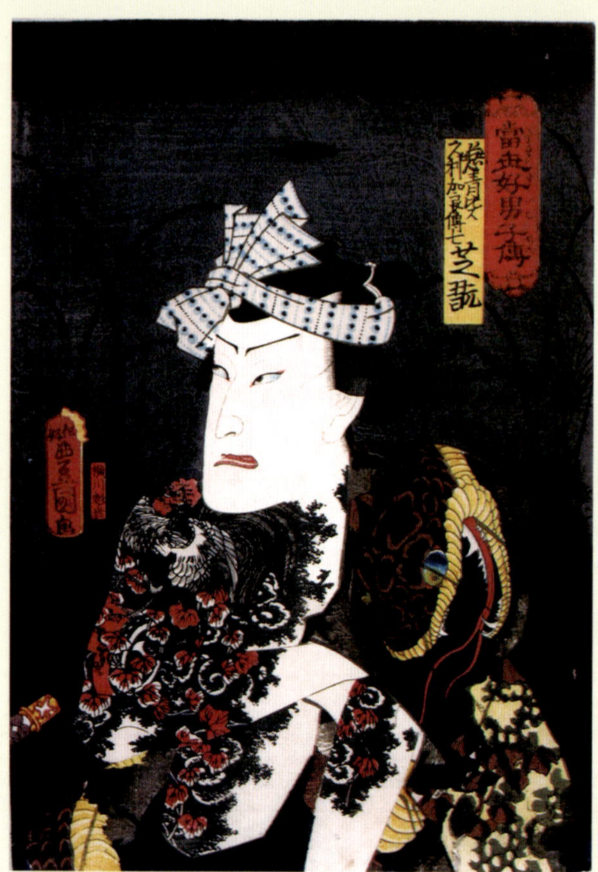

「當世好男子傳
恋青□久利加良傳七芝翫」歌川豊国
Actor Nakamura Shikan as Kurikara Denshichi, from
the series *A Modern Shuihuzhuan (Tōsei suikoden)*,
Utagawa Toyokuni III (Kunisada I)

静岡県立中央図書館蔵
Shizuoka Prefectural Central Library

「勇肌対弁慶」歌川豊国
Isamihada vs. Benkei, Utagawa Toyokuni III (Kunisada I)

万延元年・1860　静岡県立中央図書館蔵
1860, Shizuoka Prefectural Central Library

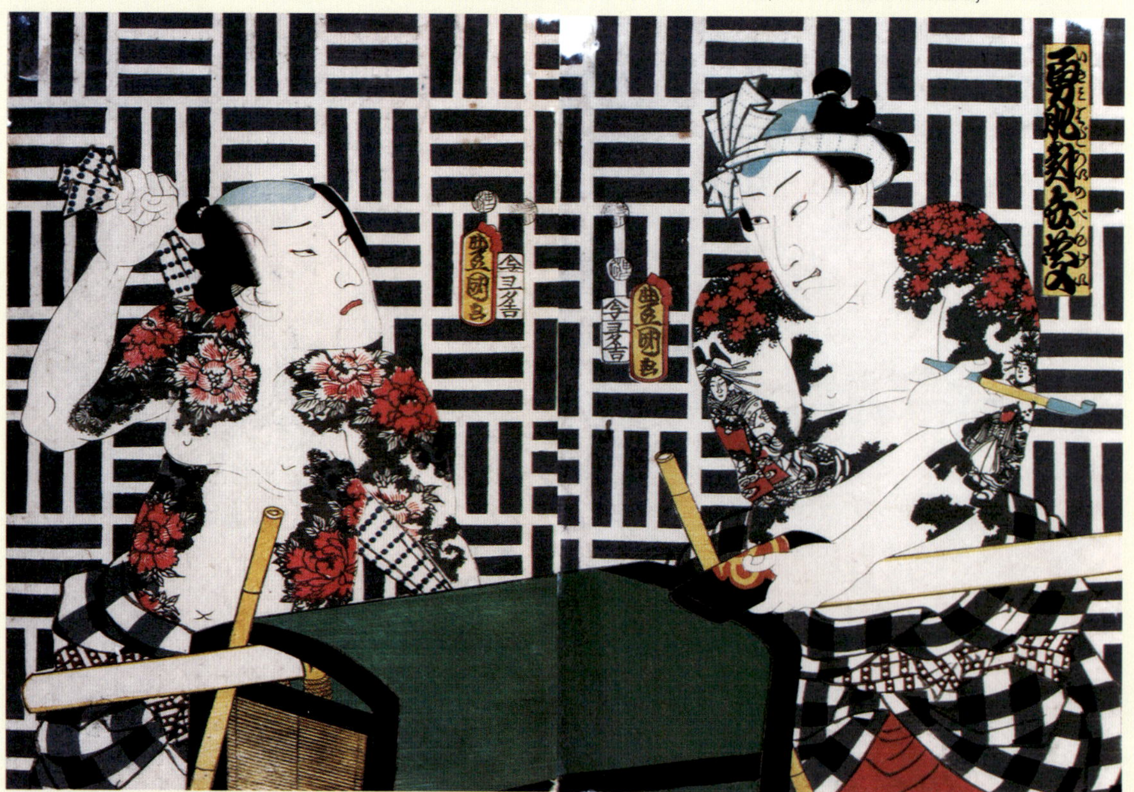

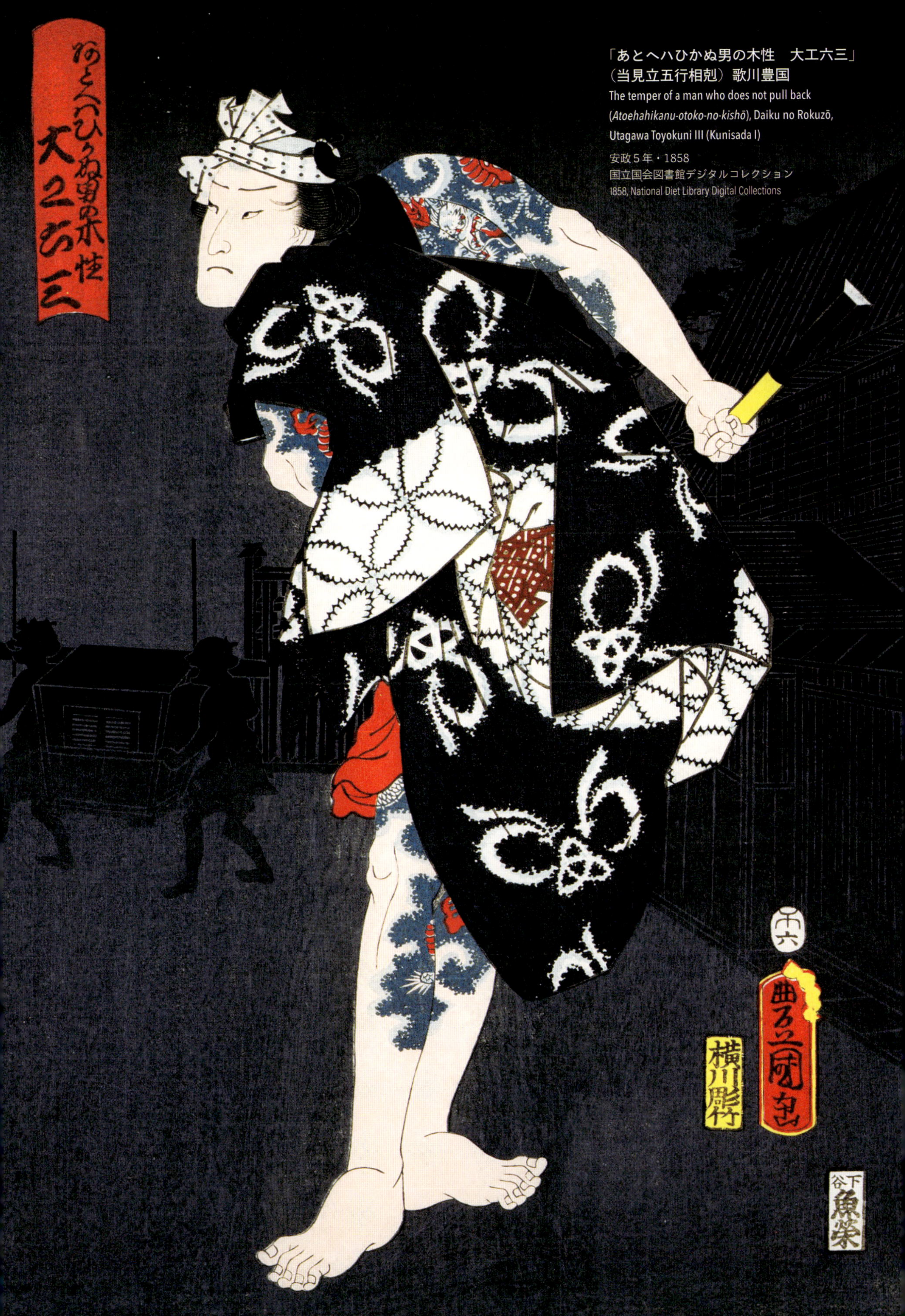

「あとへハひかぬ男の木性　大工六三」
（当見立五行相剋）歌川豊国
The temper of a man who does not pull back
(*Atoehahikanu-otoko-no-kishō*), Daiku no Rokuzō,
Utagawa Toyokuni III (Kunisada I)

安政5年・1858
国立国会図書館デジタルコレクション
1858, National Diet Library Digital Collections

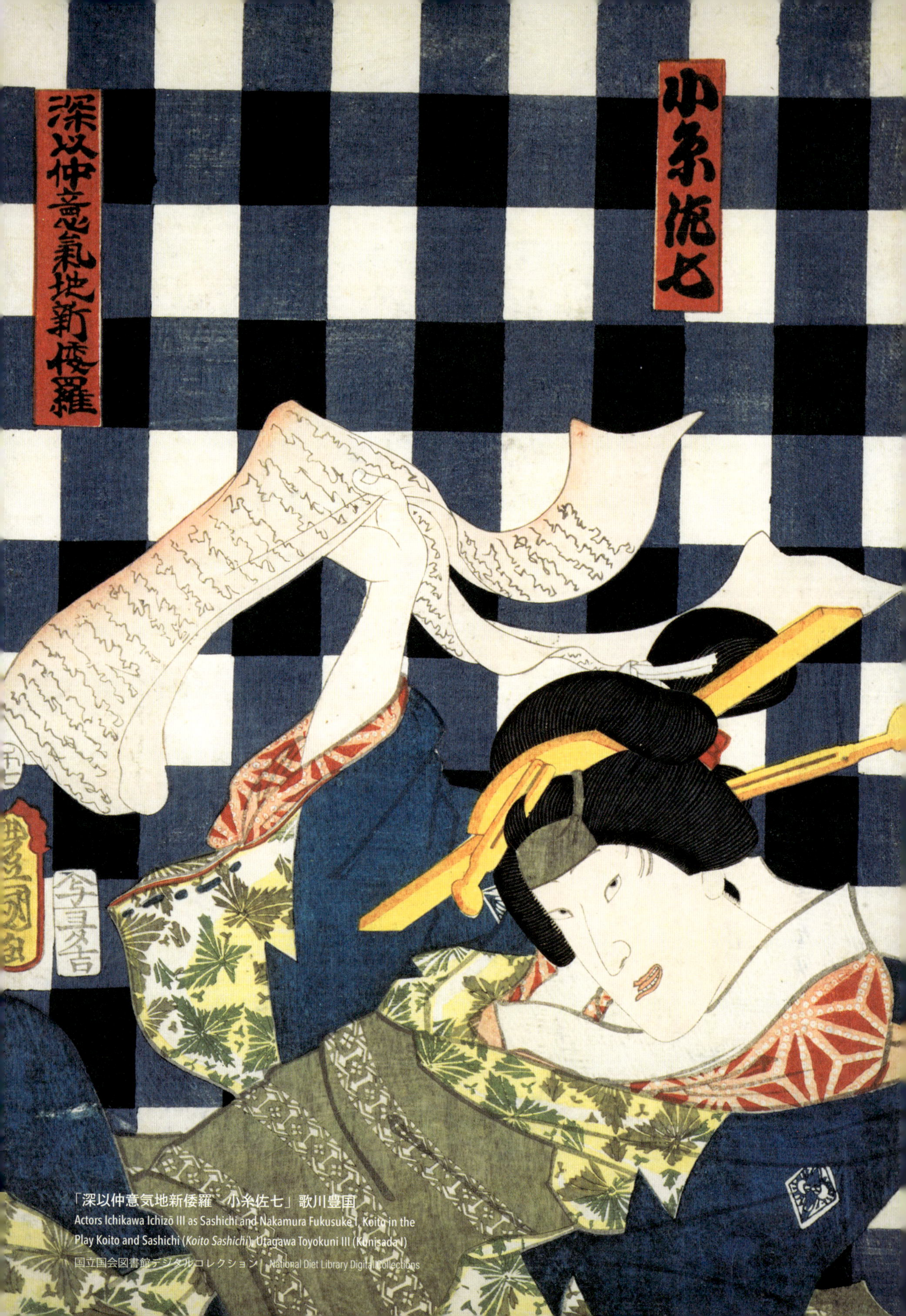

「深以仲意気地新倭羅　小糸佐七」歌川豊国
Actors Ichikawa Ichizō III as Sashichi and Nakamura Fukusuke I, Koito in the
Play Koito and Sashichi (*Koito Sashichi*), Utagawa Toyokuni III (Kunisada I)

国立国会図書館デジタルコレクション　National Diet Library Digital Collections

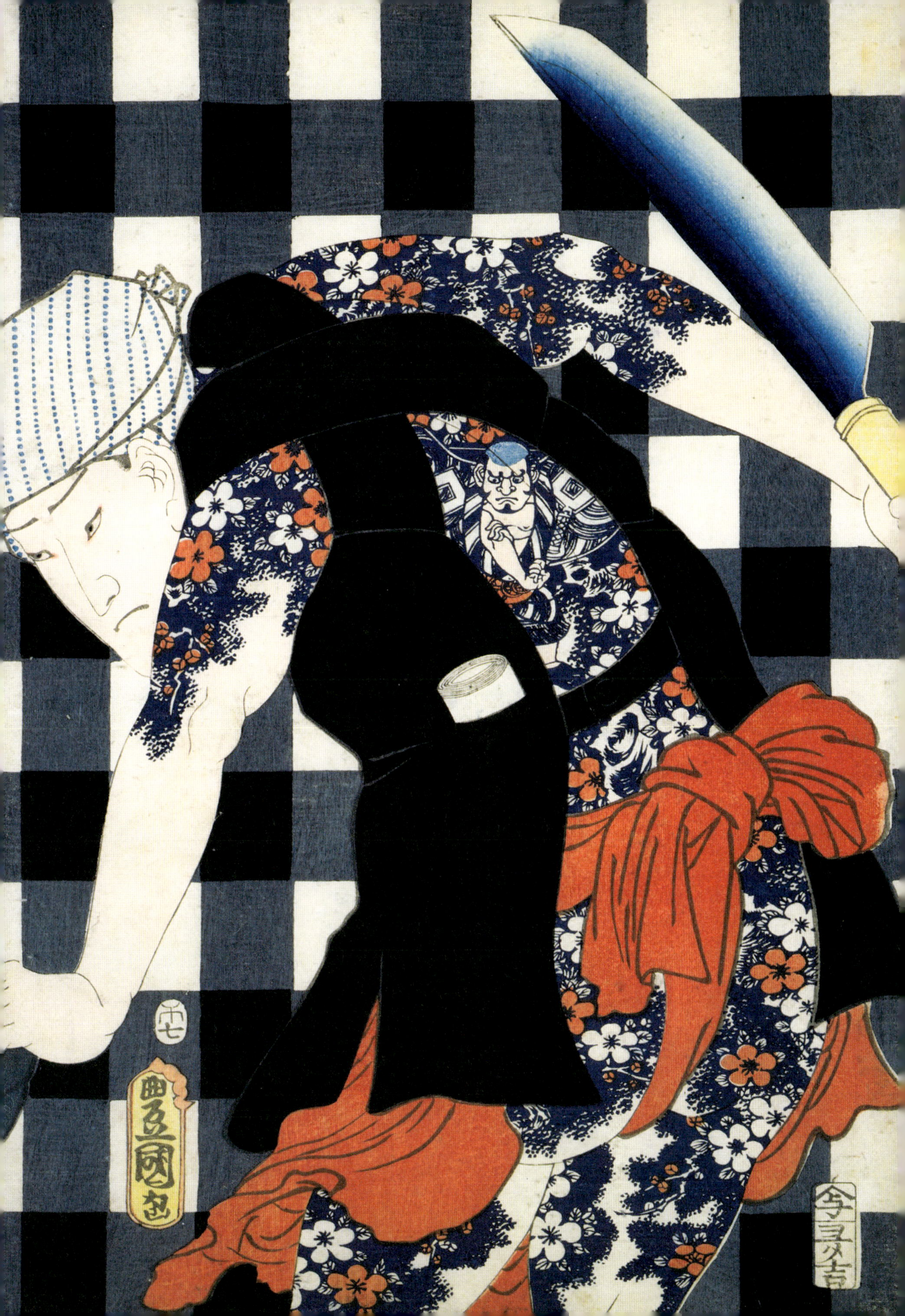

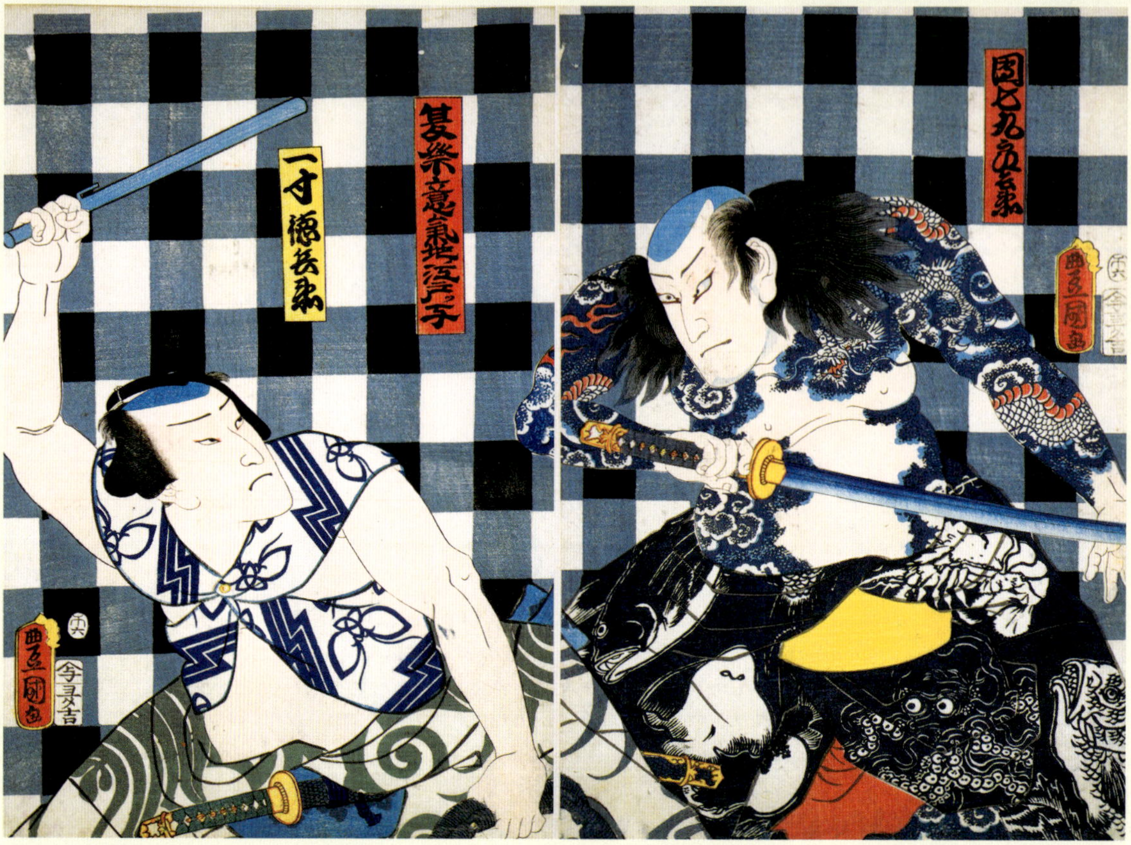

「團七九郎兵衛・夏祭意気地ノ江戸ッ子　一寸徳兵衛」歌川豊国
Danshichi Kurobei, *Natsumatsuri-Ikijino-Edokko*, Issun Tokubei, Utagawa Toyokuni III(Kunisada I)

国立国会図書館デジタルコレクション　National Diet Library Digital Collections

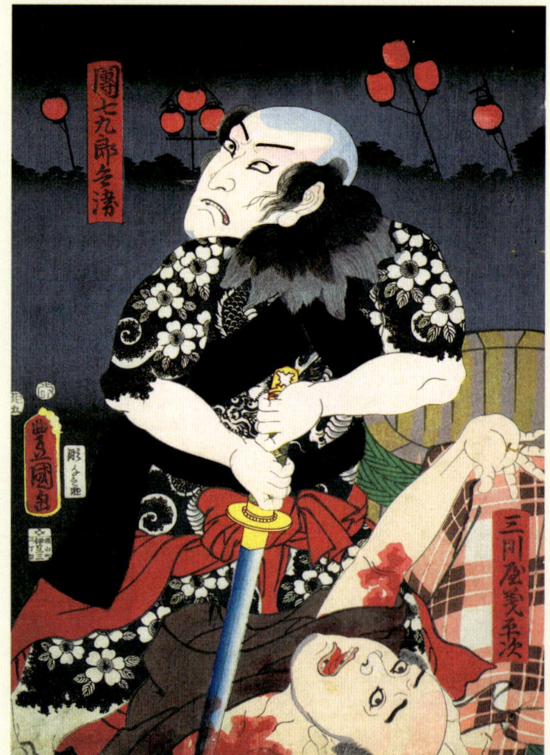

「花菖蒲男鑑」歌川豊国
Hanashōbu Otokokagami, Utagawa Toyokuni III (Kunisada I)

安政 2 年・1855　東京都立中央図書館特別文庫室蔵
1855, Tokyo Metropolitan Central Library

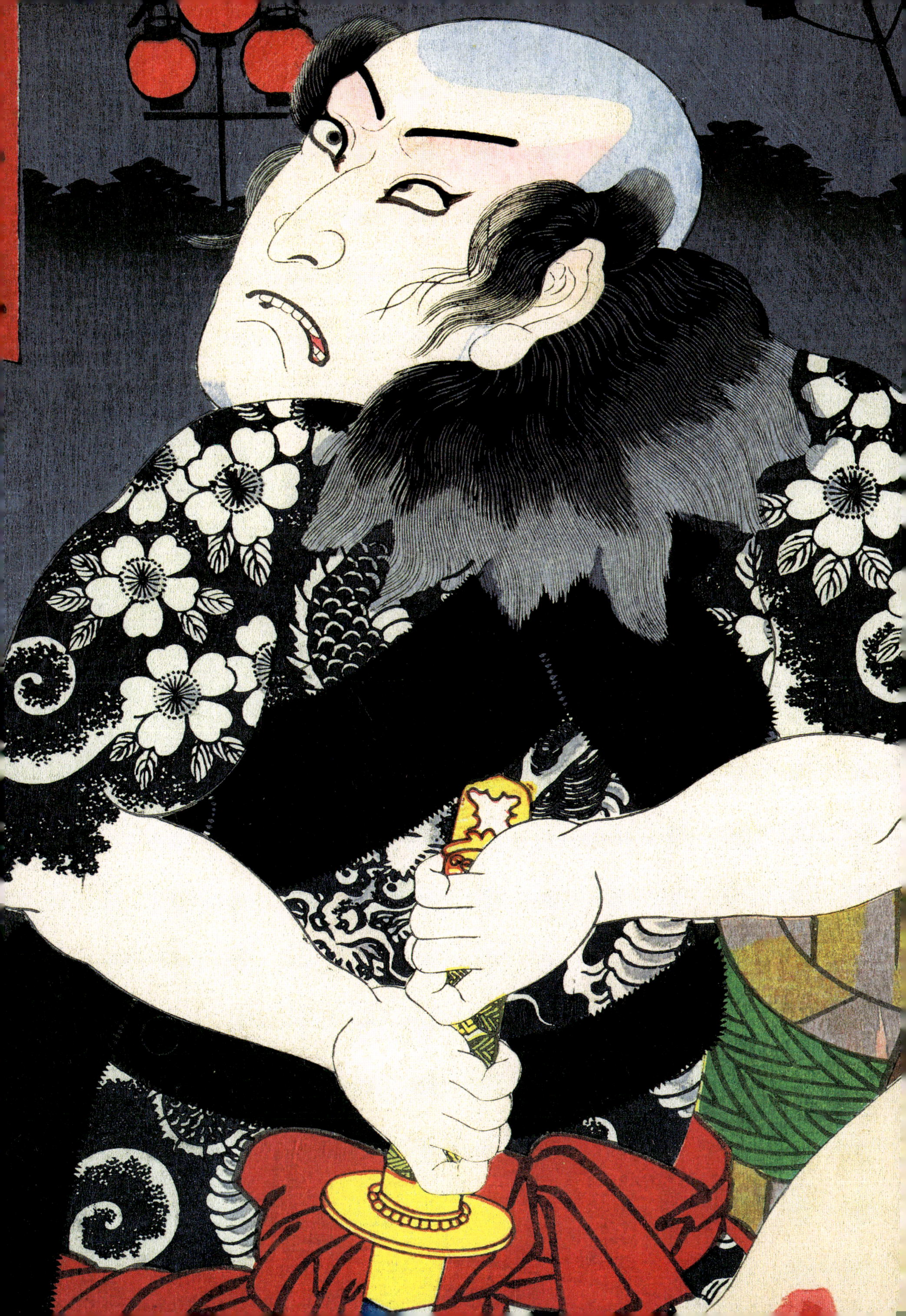

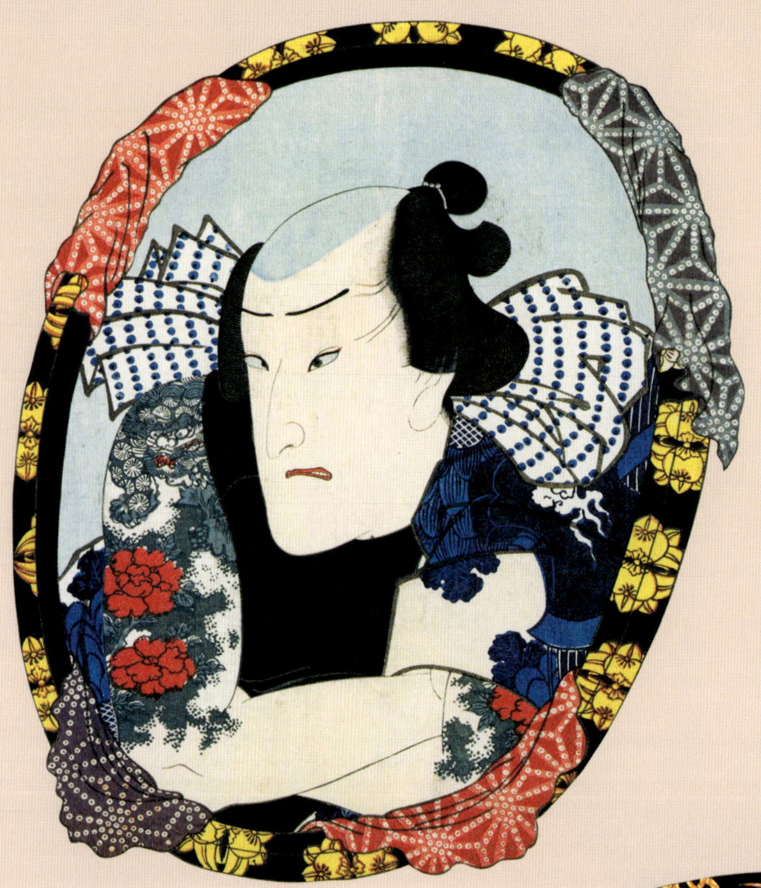

「今様押絵鏡　白瀧の佐吉」（部分）
歌川豊国
Shirataki no Sakichi, from the series *the Imayō
Oshiekagami*, Detail, Utagawa Toyokuni III (Kunisada I)

万延元年・1860
国立国会図書館デジタルコレクション
1860, National Diet Library Digital Collections

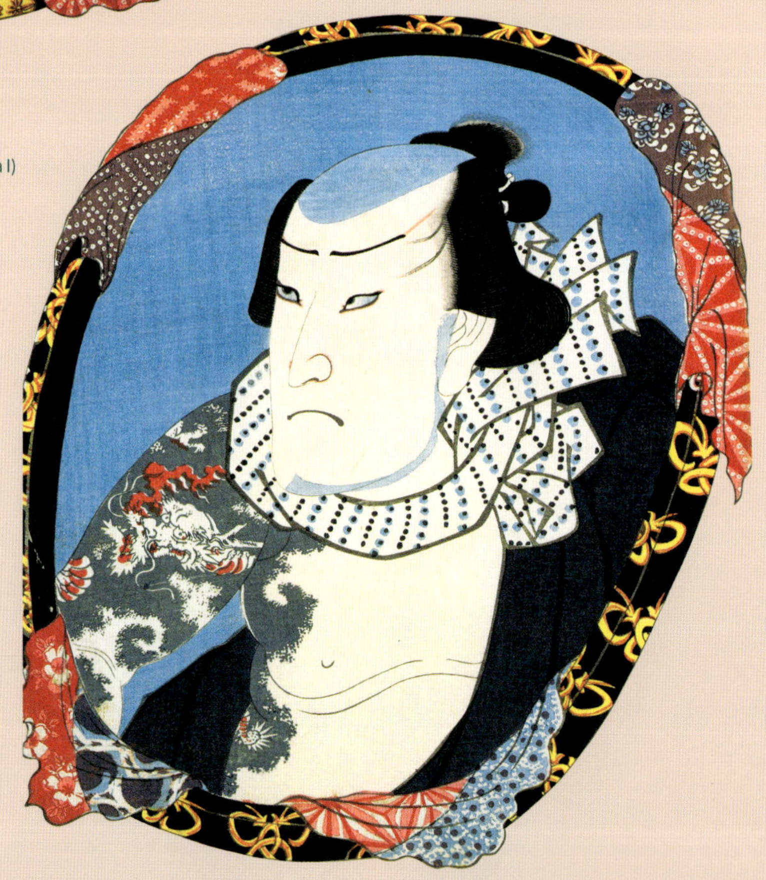

「今様押絵鏡　出来ぼしの三吉」
（部分）歌川豊国
Dekiboshi no Sankichi, from the series
the Imayō Oshiekagami, Detail, Utagawa
Toyokuni III (Kunisada I)

安政6・1859
国立国会図書館デジタルコレクション
1859, National Diet Library Digital Collections

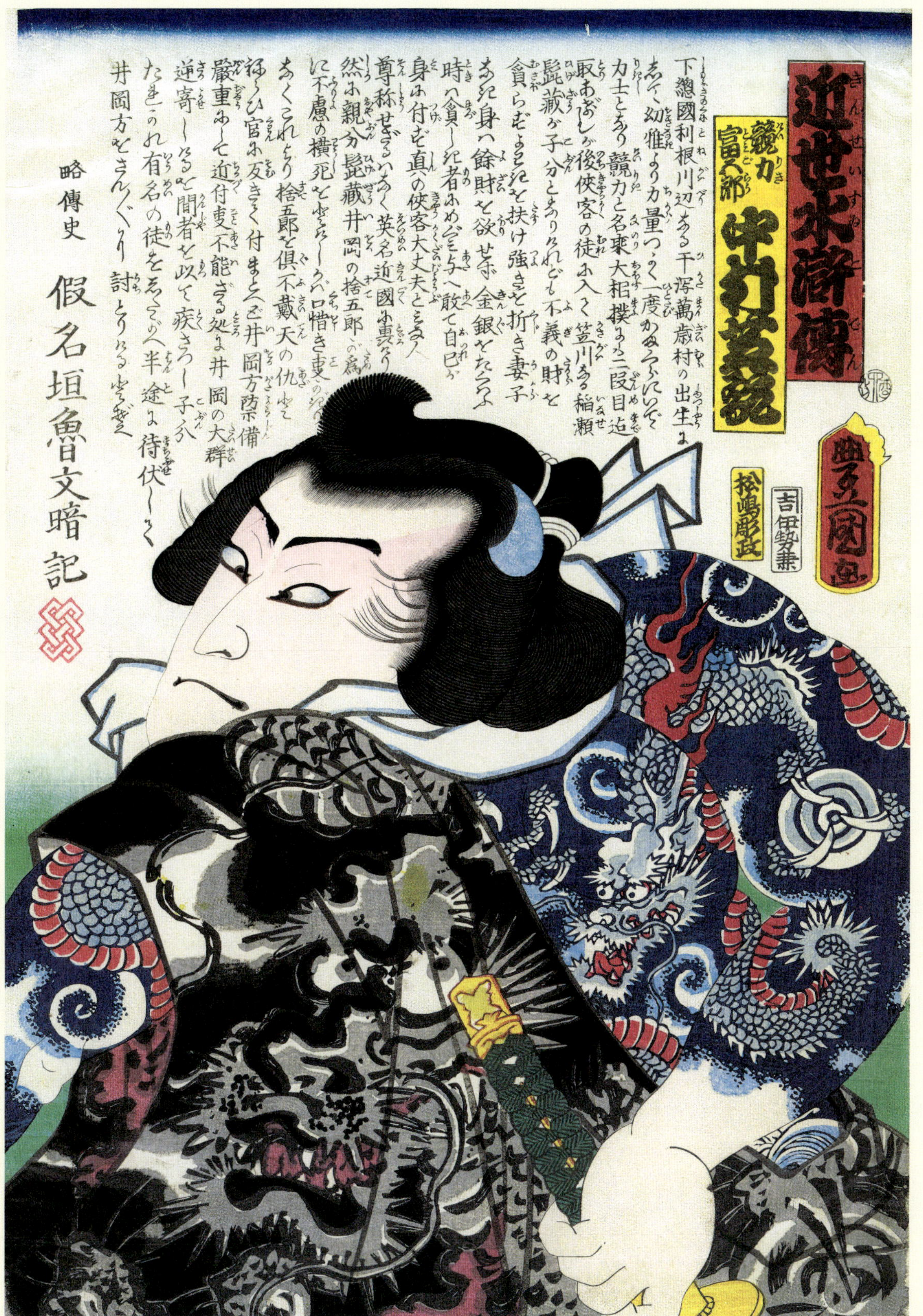

「近世水滸傳　競力富五郎　中村芝翫」歌川豊国

Actors Nakamura Shikan IV as Keiriki Tomigorō, from the series *A Modern Suikoden (Kinsei Suikoden)*, Utagawa Toyokuni III (Kunisada I)

文久元年・1861　東京都立中央図書館特別文庫室蔵
1861, Tokyo Metropolitan Central Library

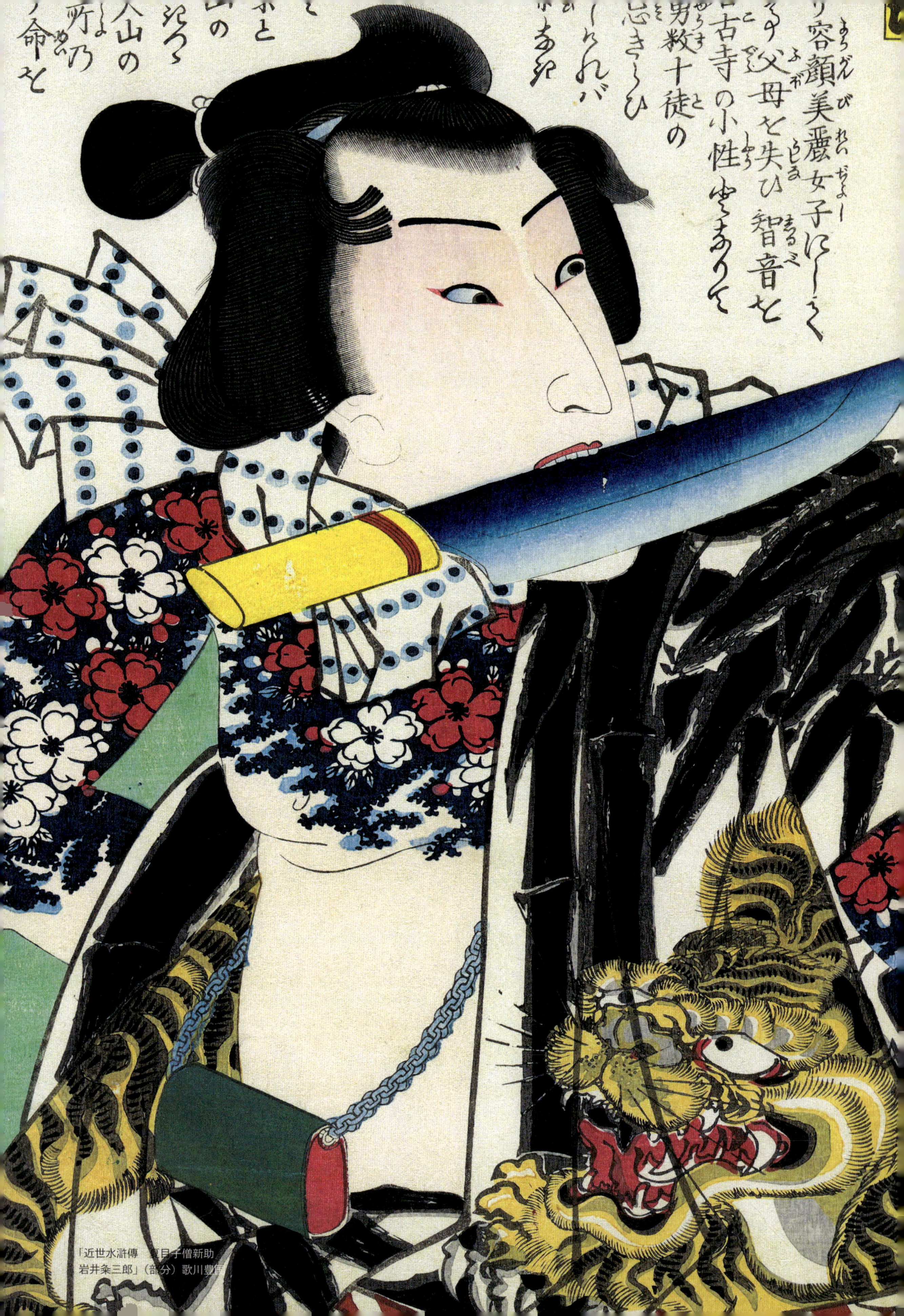

「近世水滸傳　夏目子僧新助　岩井粂三郎」（部分）歌川豊国

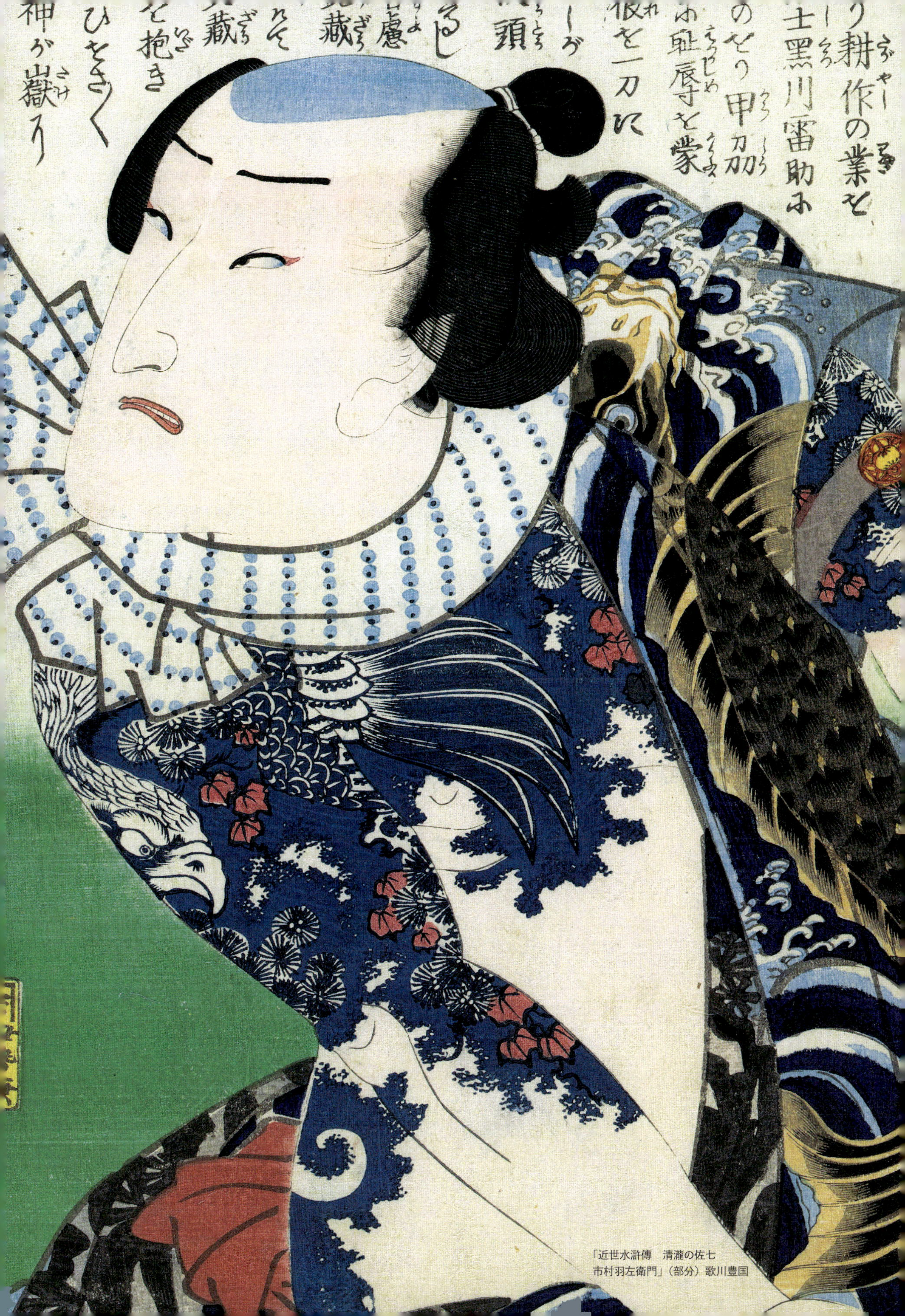

「近世水滸傳　清瀧の佐七　市村羽左衛門」（部分）歌川豊国

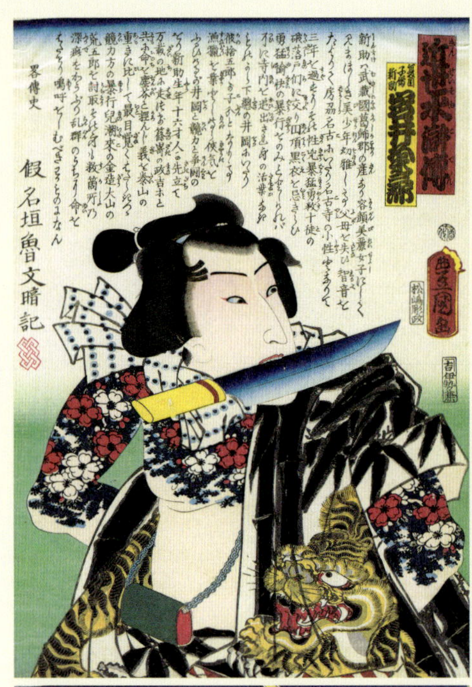

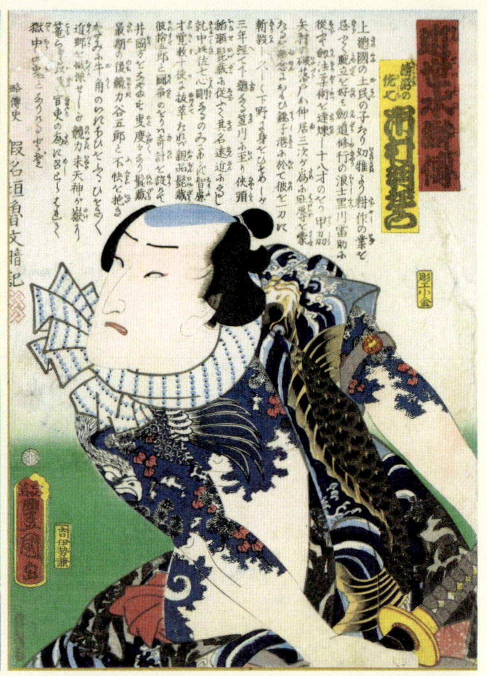

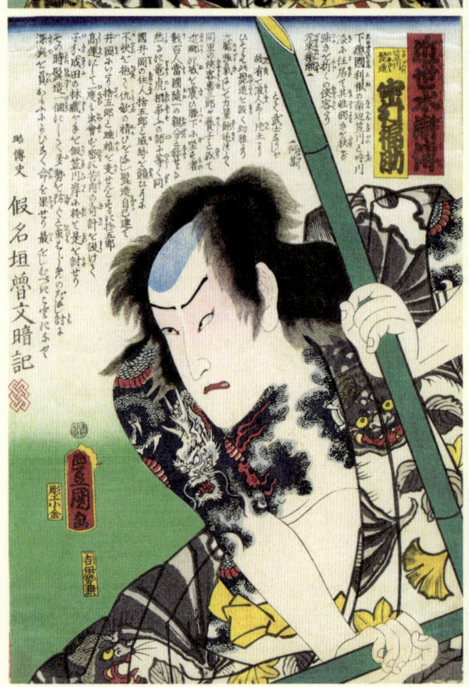

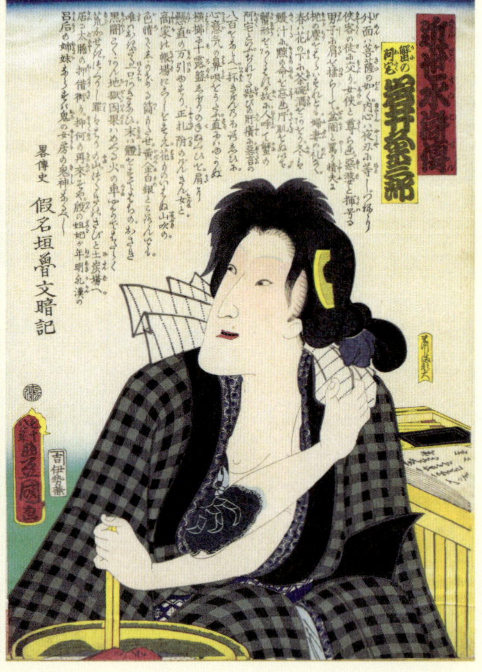

「近世水滸傳　夏目子僧新助　岩井粂三郎」歌川豊国

Actors Iwai Kumesaburō III as Natsume-kozō Shinsuke, from the series *A Modern Suikoden (Kinsei Suikoden)*, Utagawa Toyokuni III (Kunisada I)

文久元年・1861　東京都立中央図書館特別文庫室蔵
1861, Tokyo Metropolitan Central Library

「近世水滸傳　清瀧の佐七　市村羽左衛門」歌川豊国

Actors Ichimura Uzaemon XIII as Kiyotaki-no-Sashichi, from the series *A Modern Suikoden (Kinsei Suikoden)*, Utagawa Toyokuni III (Kunisada I)

嘉永 5 年・1852　東京都立中央図書館特別文庫室蔵
1852, Tokyo Metropolitan Central Library

「近世水滸傳　笠川髭造　中村福助」歌川豊国

Actors Nakamura Fukusuke II as Sasagawa Higezō, from the series *A Modern Suikoden (Kinsei Suikoden)*, Utagawa Toyokuni III (Kunisada I)

文久元年・1861　東京都立中央図書館特別文庫室蔵
1861, Tokyo Metropolitan Central Library

「近世水滸傳　蟹の阿宅　岩井粂三郎」歌川豊国

Actors Iwai Kumesaburō III as Kani-no-Otaku, from the series *A Modern Suikoden (Kinsei Suikoden)*, Utagawa Toyokuni III (Kunisada I)

文久 3 年・1863　東京都立中央図書館特別文庫室蔵
1863, Tokyo Metropolitan Central Library

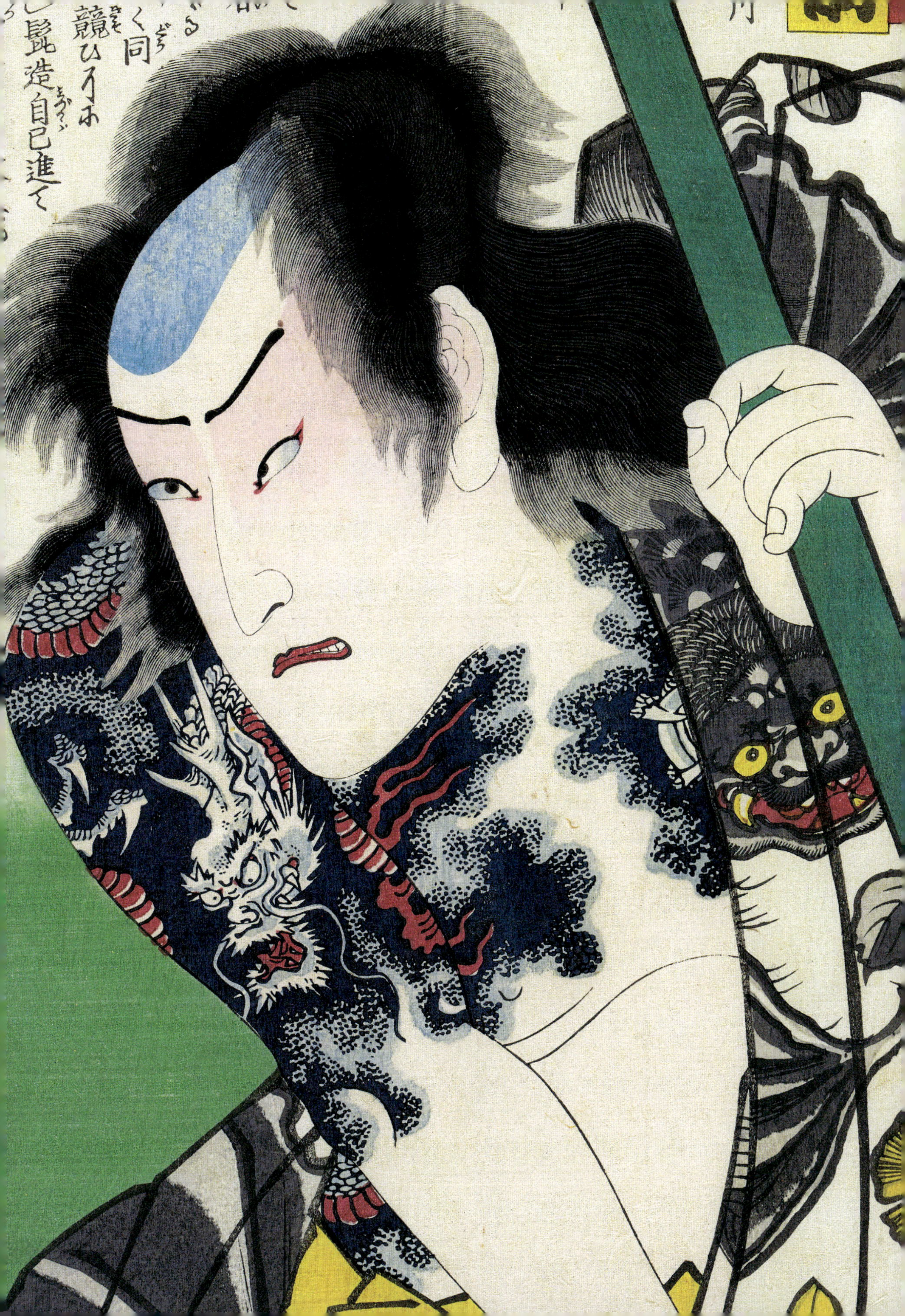

同じく
競ひ
馘造自巳進て

「梨園俠客傳　喧嘩屋五郎吉」（部分）歌川豊国
Kenkaya Gorokichi, from the series The Heroic Commoners in Kabuki
(Rien kyokaku den), Detail, Utagawa Toyokuni III (Kunisada I)
文久 3 年・1863　個人蔵（千葉市美術館寄託）
1863, Private collection (Chiba City Museum of Art)

「梨園俠客傳　しら瀧の佐吉」（部分）歌川豊国
Actors Ichimura Kakitsu IV as Shirataki no Sakichi, from the series The Heroic
Commoners in Kabuki (Rien kyokaku den), Detail, Utagawa Toyokuni III (Kunisada I)
文久 3 年・1863　個人蔵（千葉市美術館寄託）
1863, Private collection (Chiba City Museum of Art)

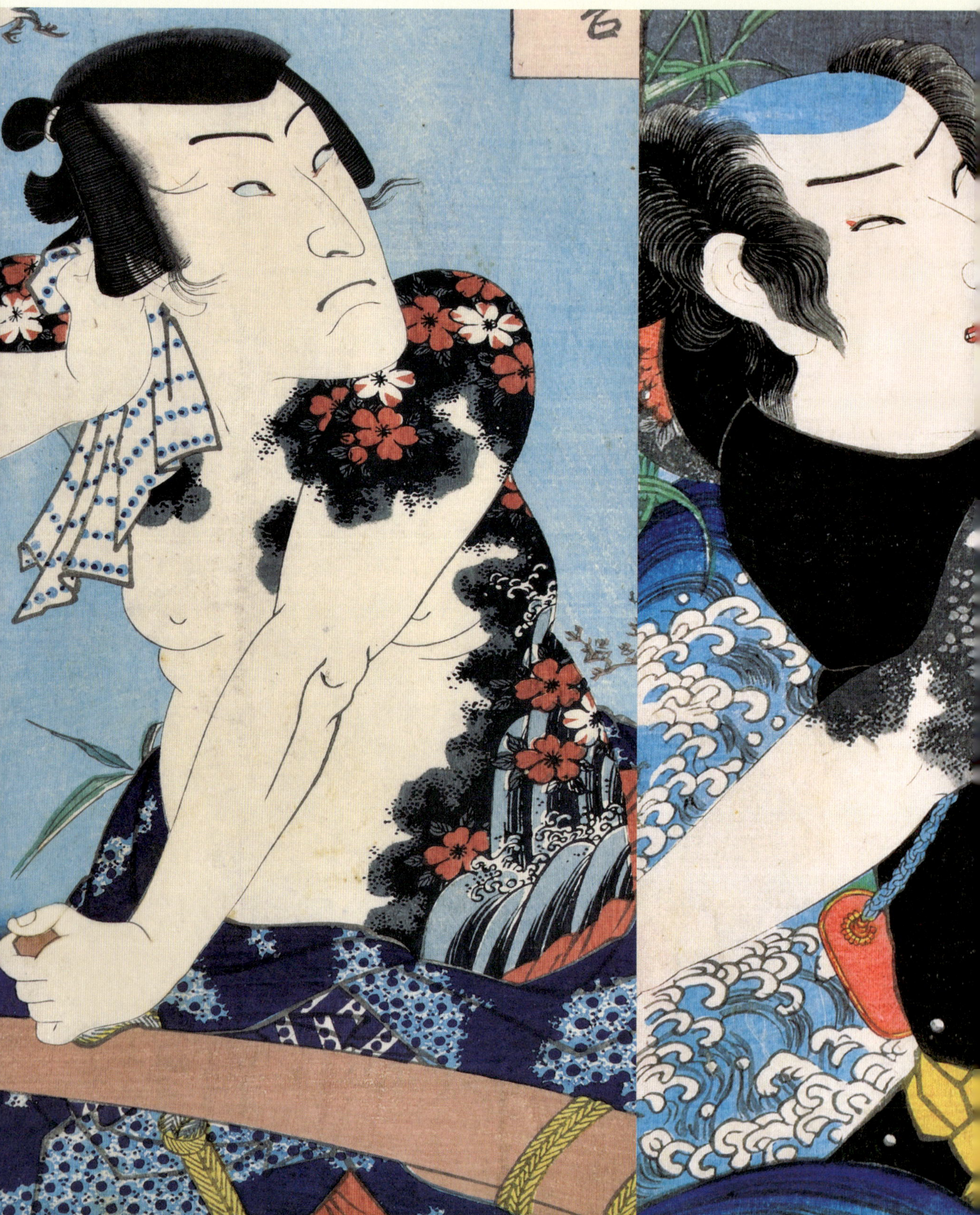

「梨園俠客傳　釣ふねのさぶ」（部分）歌川豊国
Actors Nakamura Tsuruzō as Sampu of a fishing boat, from series *The Heroic Commoners in Kabuki (Rien kyokaku den)*, Detail, Utagawa Toyokuni III (Kunisada I)
文久 3 年・1863　個人蔵（千葉市美術館寄託）
1863, Private collection (Chiba City Museum of Art)

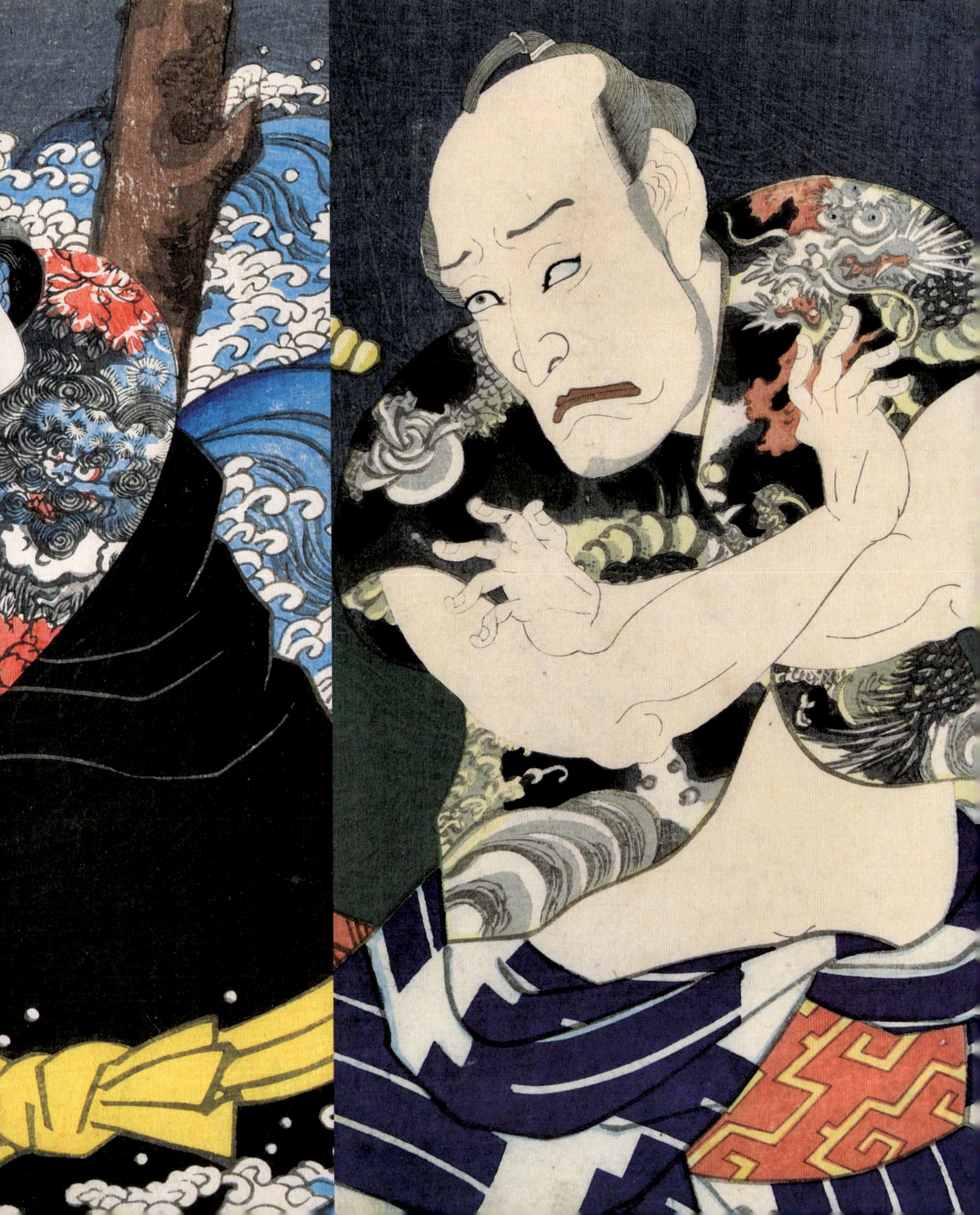

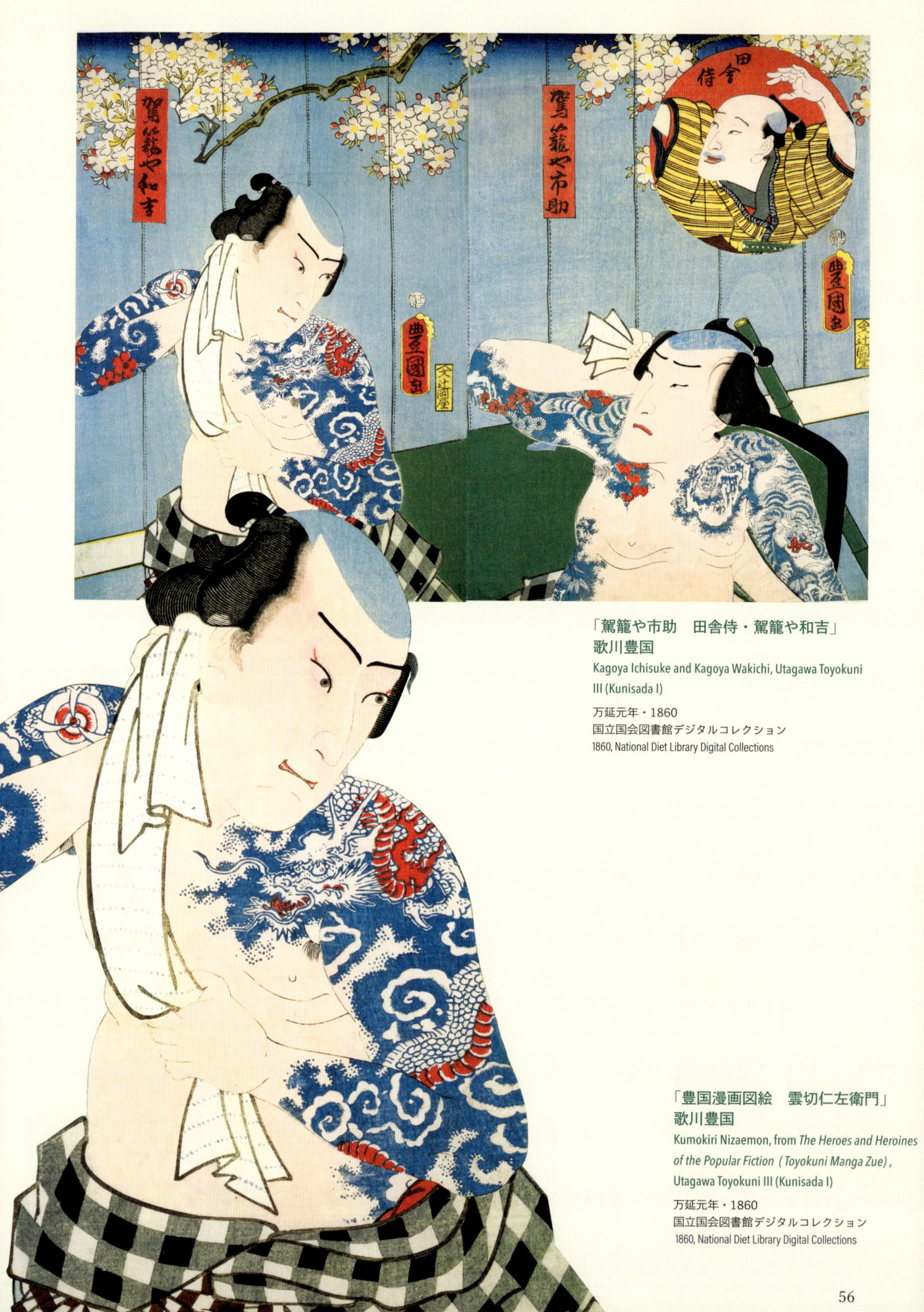

「駕籠や市助　田舎侍・駕籠や和吉」
歌川豊国
Kagoya Ichisuke and Kagoya Wakichi, Utagawa Toyokuni
III (Kunisada I)

万延元年・1860
国立国会図書館デジタルコレクション
1860, National Diet Library Digital Collections

「豊国漫画図絵　雲切仁左衛門」
歌川豊国
Kumokiri Nizaemon, from *The Heroes and Heroines
of the Popular Fiction（ Toyokuni Manga Zue）*,
Utagawa Toyokuni III (Kunisada I)

万延元年・1860
国立国会図書館デジタルコレクション
1860, National Diet Library Digital Collections

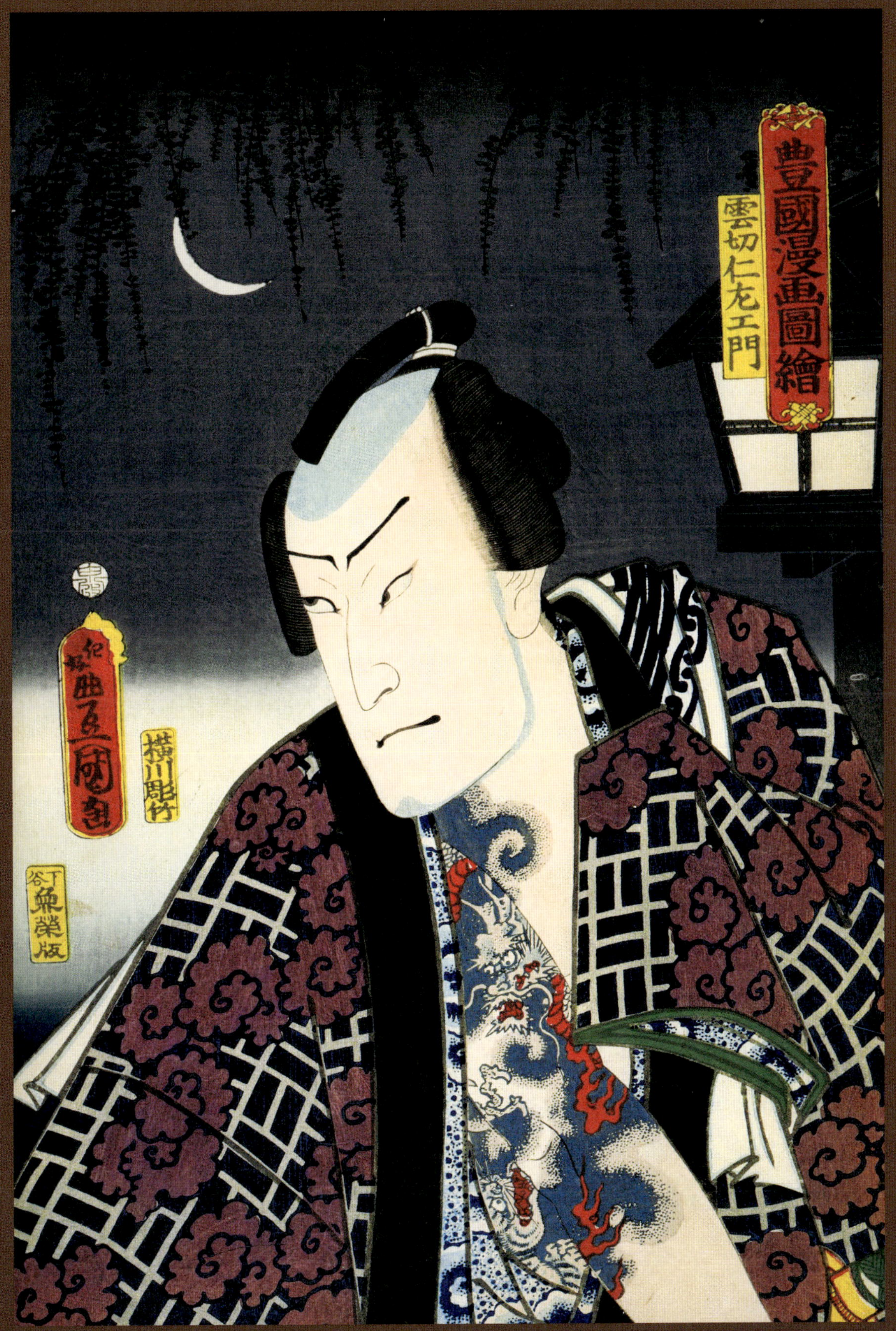

 Chapter 1 │ Tattoos: The Beauty of the Heroes' Skin Utagawa Toyokuni

月岡芳年

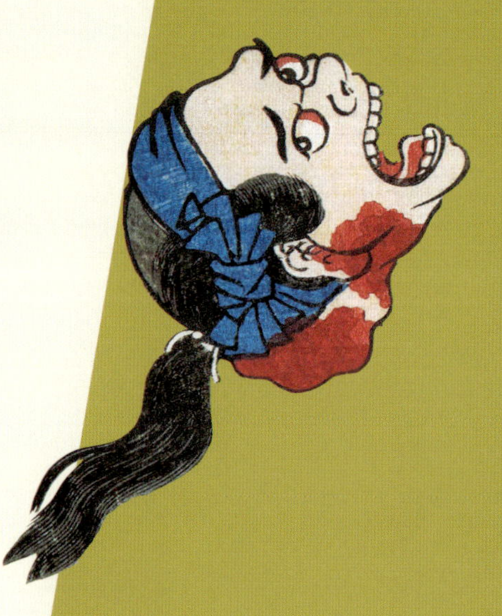

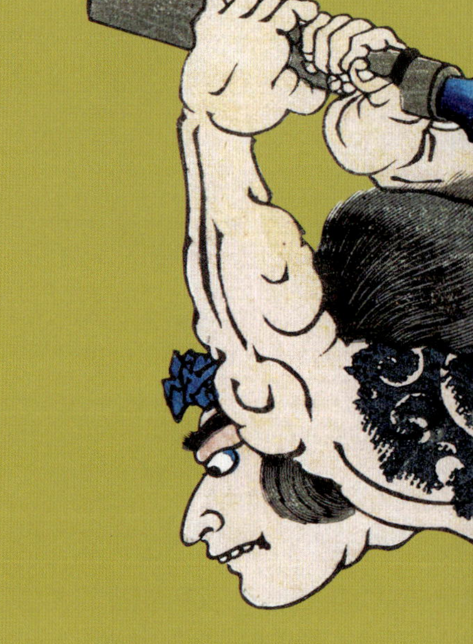

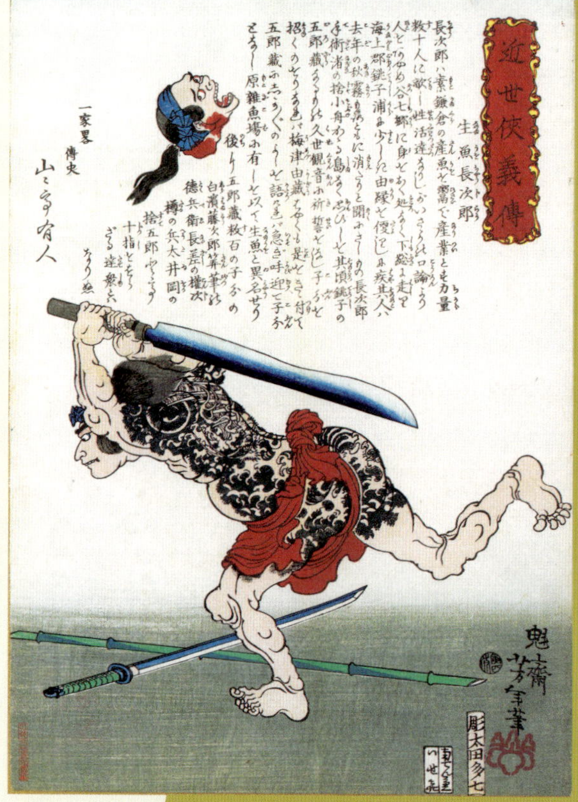

「近世俠義傳　生魚長次郎」月岡芳年
Namauo Chōjirō, from the series *A Biographies of Fine Modern Men (Kinsei Kyougiden)*, Tsukioka Yoshitoshi

慶応 2 年・1866　東京都立中央図書館特別文庫室蔵
1866, Tokyo Metropolitan Library

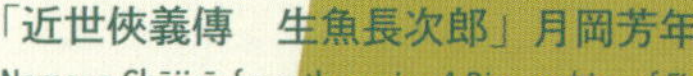

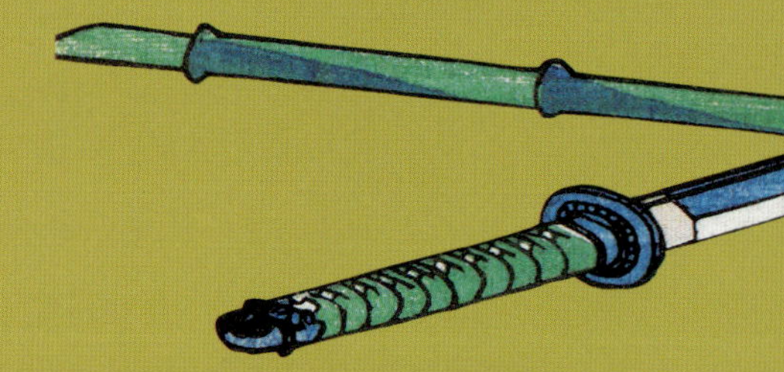

つきおか よしとし
天保 10 年〜明治 25 年（1839-1892）

　幕末から明治期の浮世絵師。月岡雪斎の養子。嘉永 3 年（1850）ごろ歌川国芳に入門し、武者絵を発表。慶応元年（1865）刊行の『和漢百物語』から特異な才能をあらわす。のち菊池容斎に私淑し、詩趣豊かな稗史画（はいし）、美人画、役者絵をえがいた。慶応 2 年（1866）に兄弟子の落合芳幾と共筆の『英名二十八衆句』の残酷絵シリーズで一躍人気絵師となる。また時事報道の分野に新生面をみいだし、『郵便報知新聞』『絵入自由新聞』『やまと新聞』などの新聞挿絵で活躍した。「月百姿」（つきひゃくし）や「風俗三十二相」などの美人画の大作も発表している。

Tsukioka Yoshitoshi 1839-1892

Ukiyo-e Artist from the Bakumatsu to the Meiji Period. The adopted son of Tsukioka Sessai, became a student of Utagawa Kuniyoshi around 1850 and produced his first warrior prints. His *One Hundred Stories of Japan and China* published in 1865 demonstrated his extraordinary talent. Subsequently, he idolized Kikuchi Yosai and produced luxuriantly lyrical paintings of scenes from popular history, beautiful women, and actors. In1866, he became an enormously popular printmaker when he and Ochiai Yoshiiku, his senior as a Kuniyoshi student, jointly produced the series of "bloody prints," the *Twenty-Eight Famous Murders with Verse*. His illustrations brought new perspectives to news stories in the *Yubin Hochi Shimbun* (Postal News), *Eiri Jiyu Shimbun* (Liberal-Illustrated News), and the *Yamato Shimbun* (Yamato News). He also produced large-format pictures of beautiful women, including the series *One Hundred Aspects of the Moon* and *Thirty-two Aspects of Customs and Manners*.

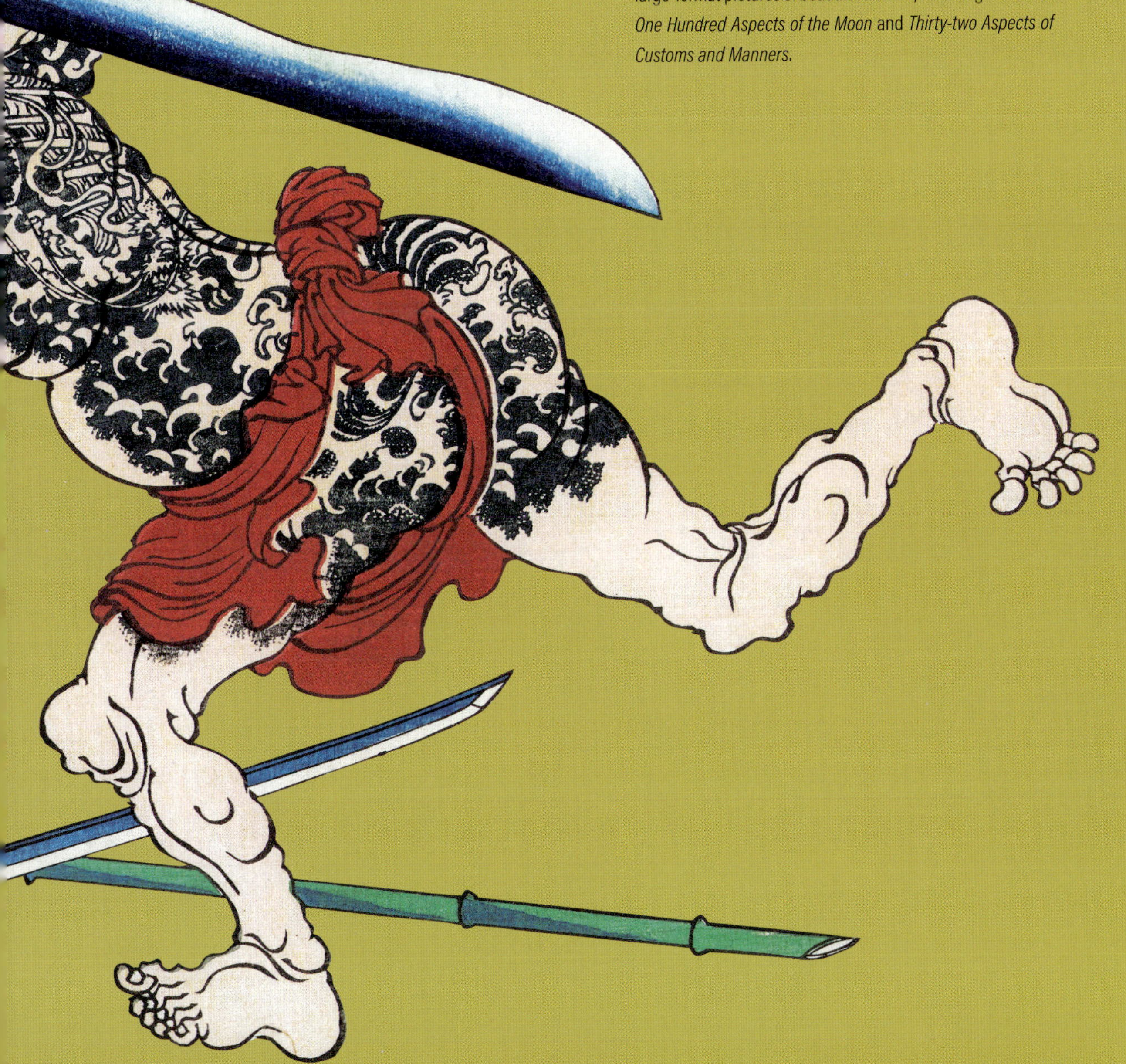

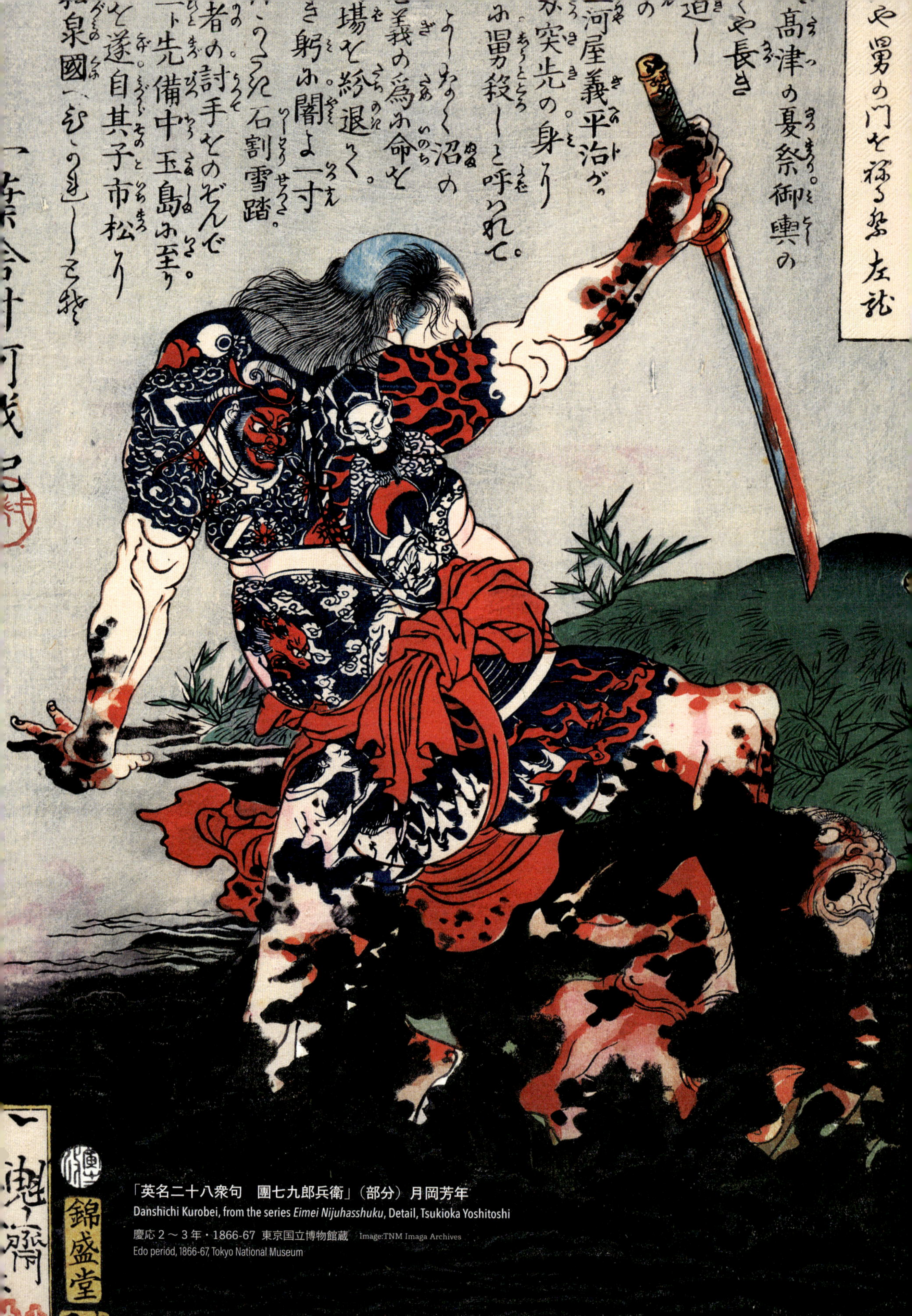

「英名二十八衆句　團七九郎兵衛」（部分）月岡芳年
Danshichi Kurobei, from the series *Eimei Nijuhasshuku*, Detail, Tsukioka Yoshitoshi
慶応2〜3年・1866-67　東京国立博物館蔵　Image:TNM Imaga Archives
Edo period, 1866-67, Tokyo National Museum

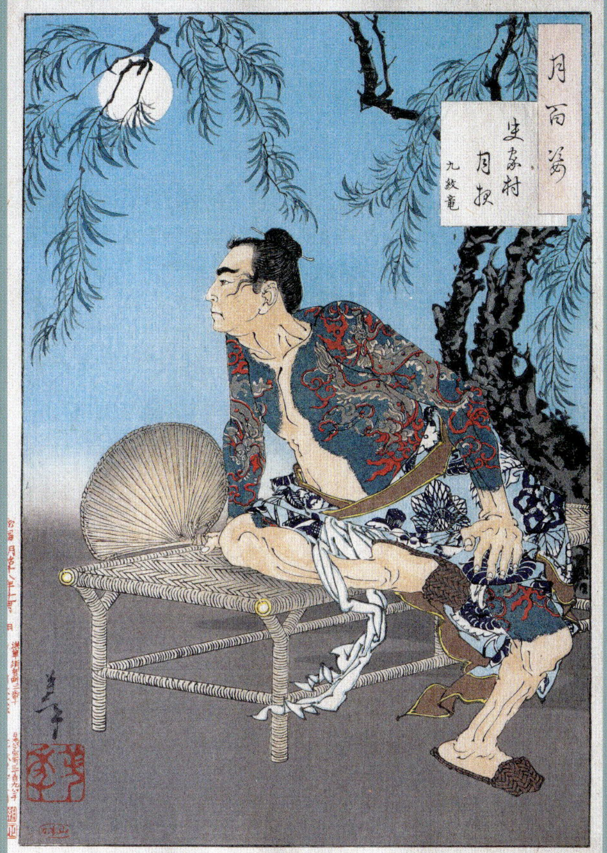

「月百姿　史家村月夜　九紋龍」
月岡芳年

Shikason Tsukiyo, Kumonryū Shishin, from the series *the One Hundred Aspects of the Moon (Tsuki Hyakushi)*, Tsukioka Yoshitoshi

明治 18 年・1885
山口県立萩美術館・浦上記念館蔵
1885, Hagi Uragami Museum

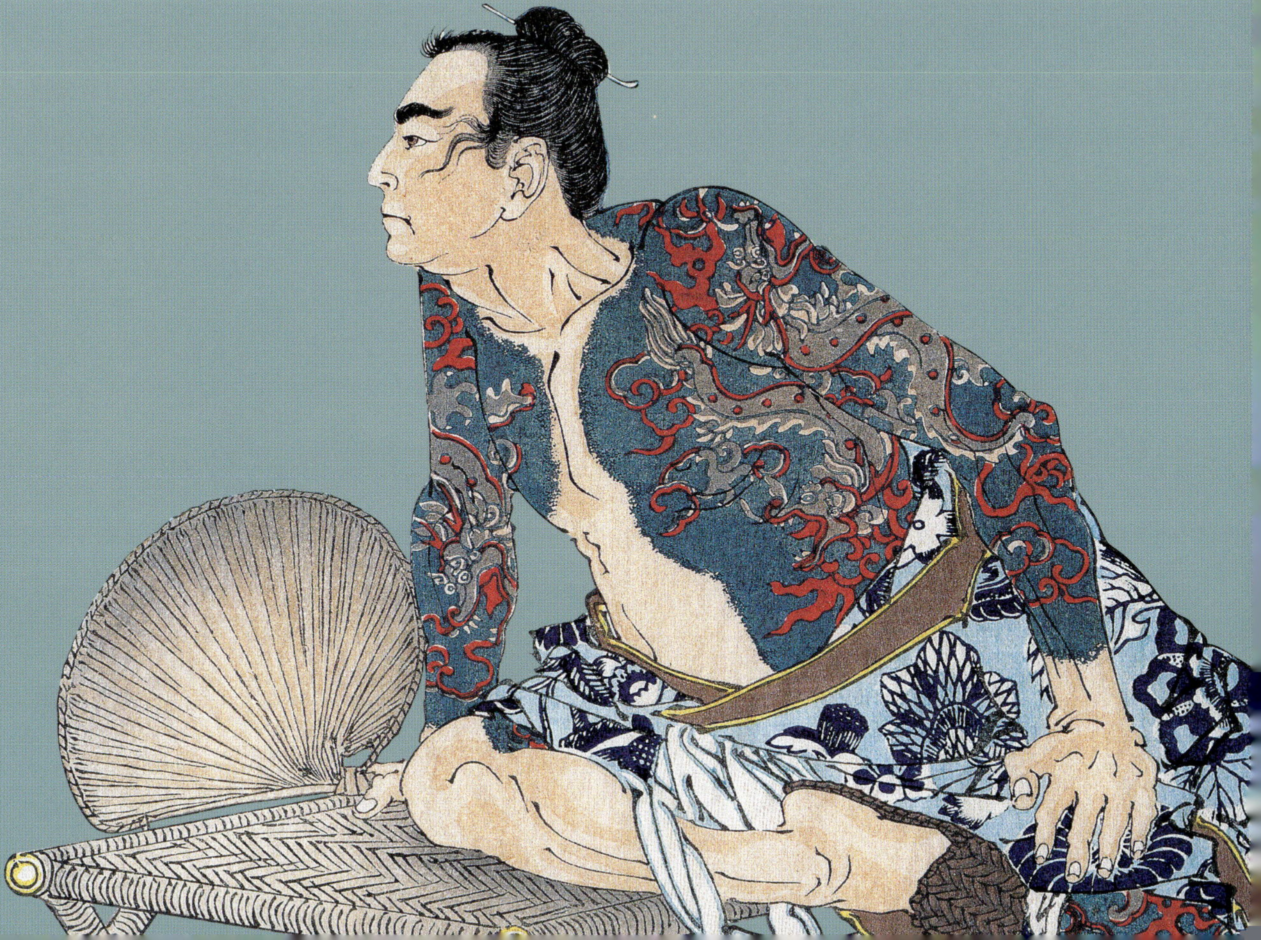

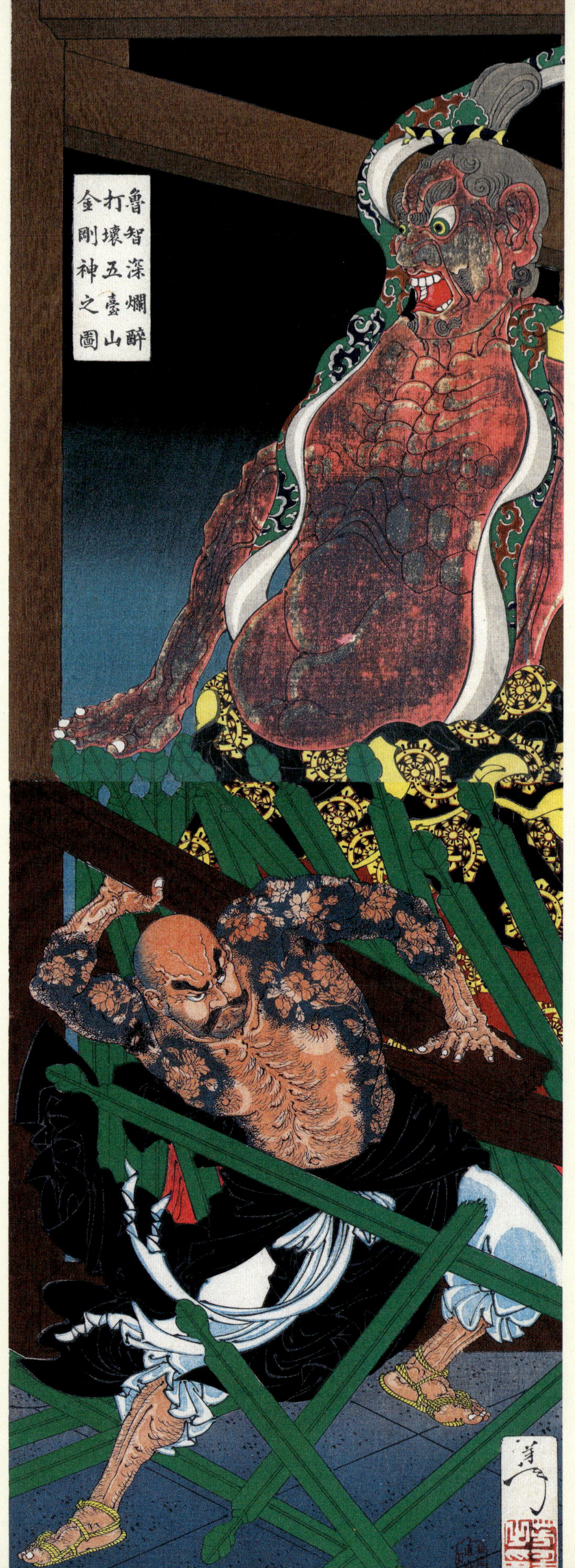

「魯智深爛酔打壊五台山
金剛神之図」月岡芳年

Rochishin-ransuidakai-godaisan-
kongoushin-no-zu, Tsukioka
Yoshitoshi

明治 20 年・1887
山口県立萩美術館・浦上記念館蔵
1887, Hagi Uragami Museum

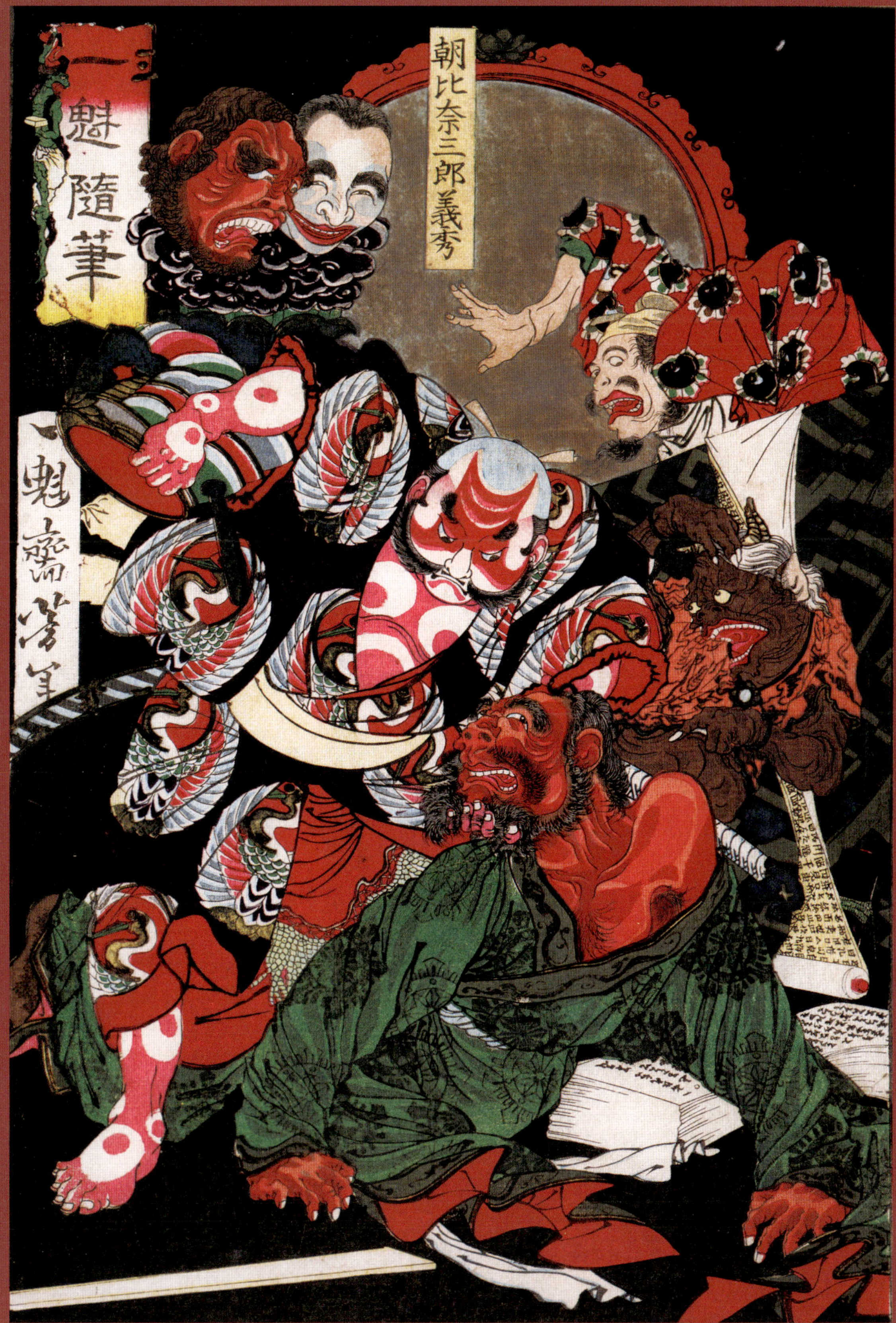

「一魁随筆　朝比奈三郎義秀」月岡芳年
Asahina Saburou Yoshihide, from the series *the Ikkaii Zuihitsu*, Tsukioka Yoshitoshi

明治 5 〜 6 年・1872-73　千葉市美術館蔵
Meiji period, 1872-73, Chiba City Museum of Art

Chapter 1 | Tattoos: The Beauty of the Heroes' Skin　**Tsukioka Yoshitoshi**

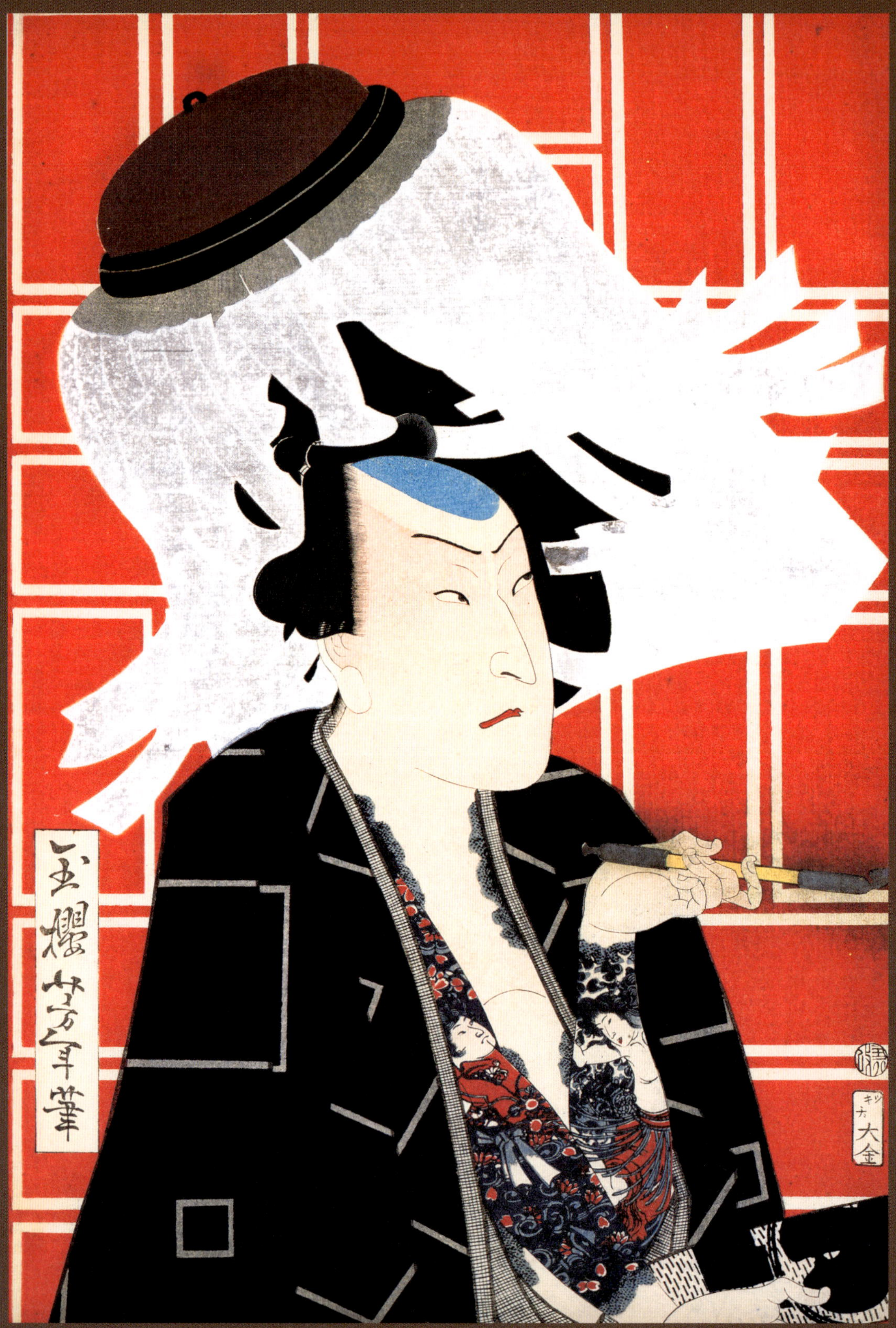

「勇の寿　二代目沢村訥升」月岡芳年
Sawamura Toshō II, from the series *Isami-no-Kotobuki*,
Tsukioka Yoshitoshi

慶応元年・1865　山口県立萩美術館・浦上記念館蔵
1865, Hagi Uragami Museum

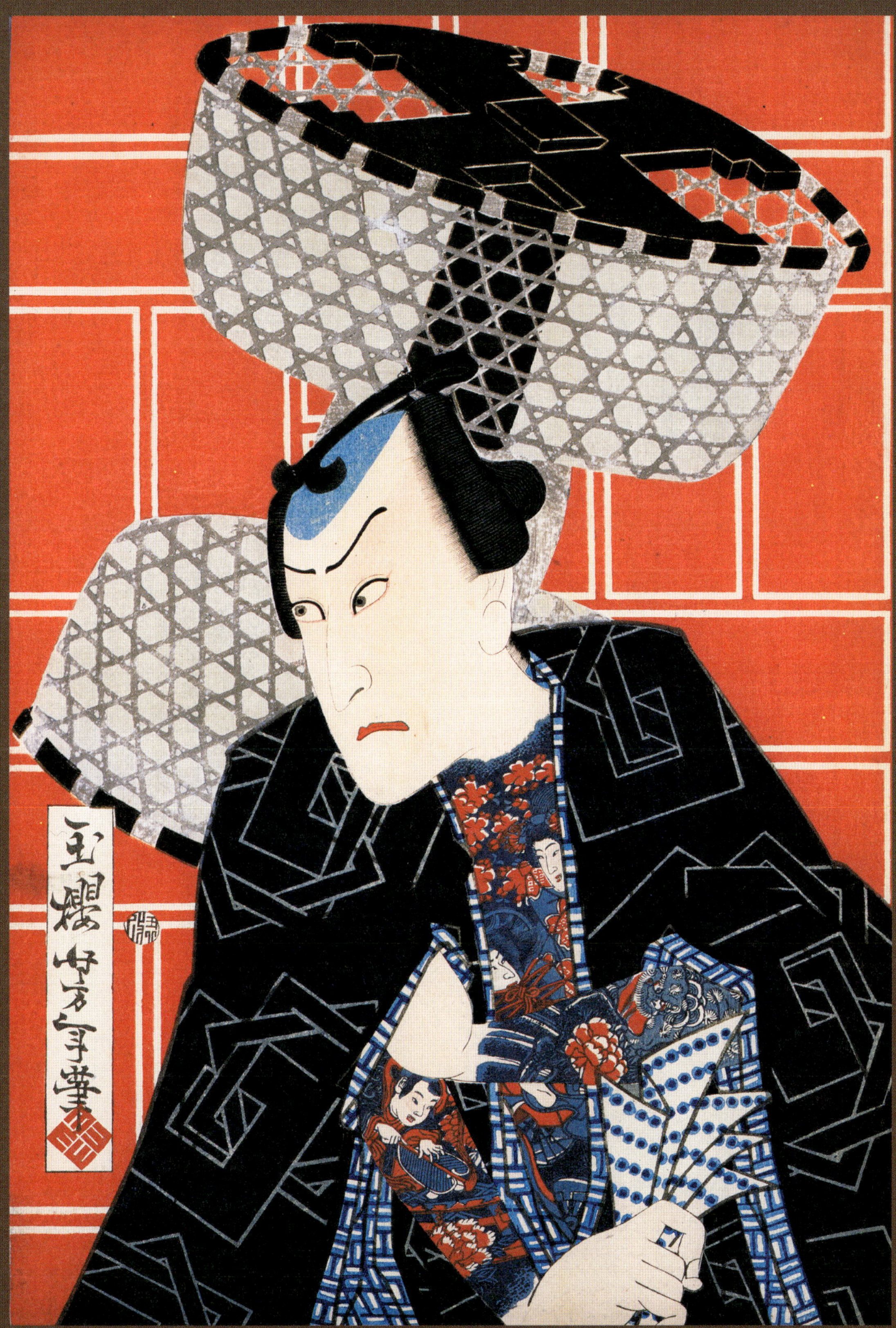

「勇の寿　河原崎権十郎」月岡芳年
Kawarazaki Gonjūrō, from the series *Isami-no-Kotobuki*,
Tsukioka Yoshitoshi

慶応元年・1865　山口県立萩美術館・浦上記念館蔵
1865, Hagi Uragami Museum

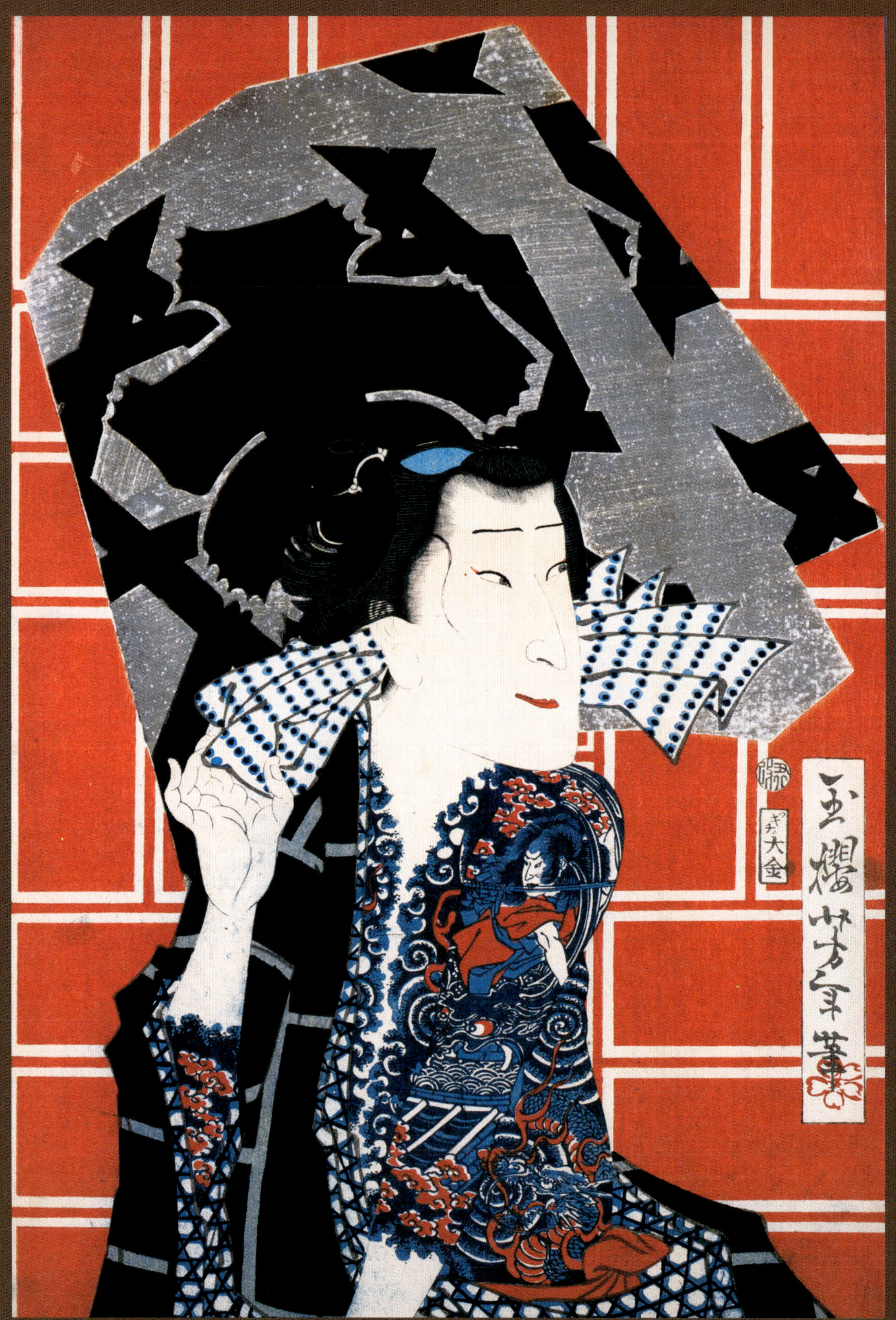

「勇の寿　沢村田之助」月岡芳年
Sawamura Tanosuke, from the series *Isami-no-Kotobuki*,
Tsukioka Yoshitoshi

慶応元年・1865　山口県立萩美術館・浦上記念館蔵
1865, Hagi Uragami Museum

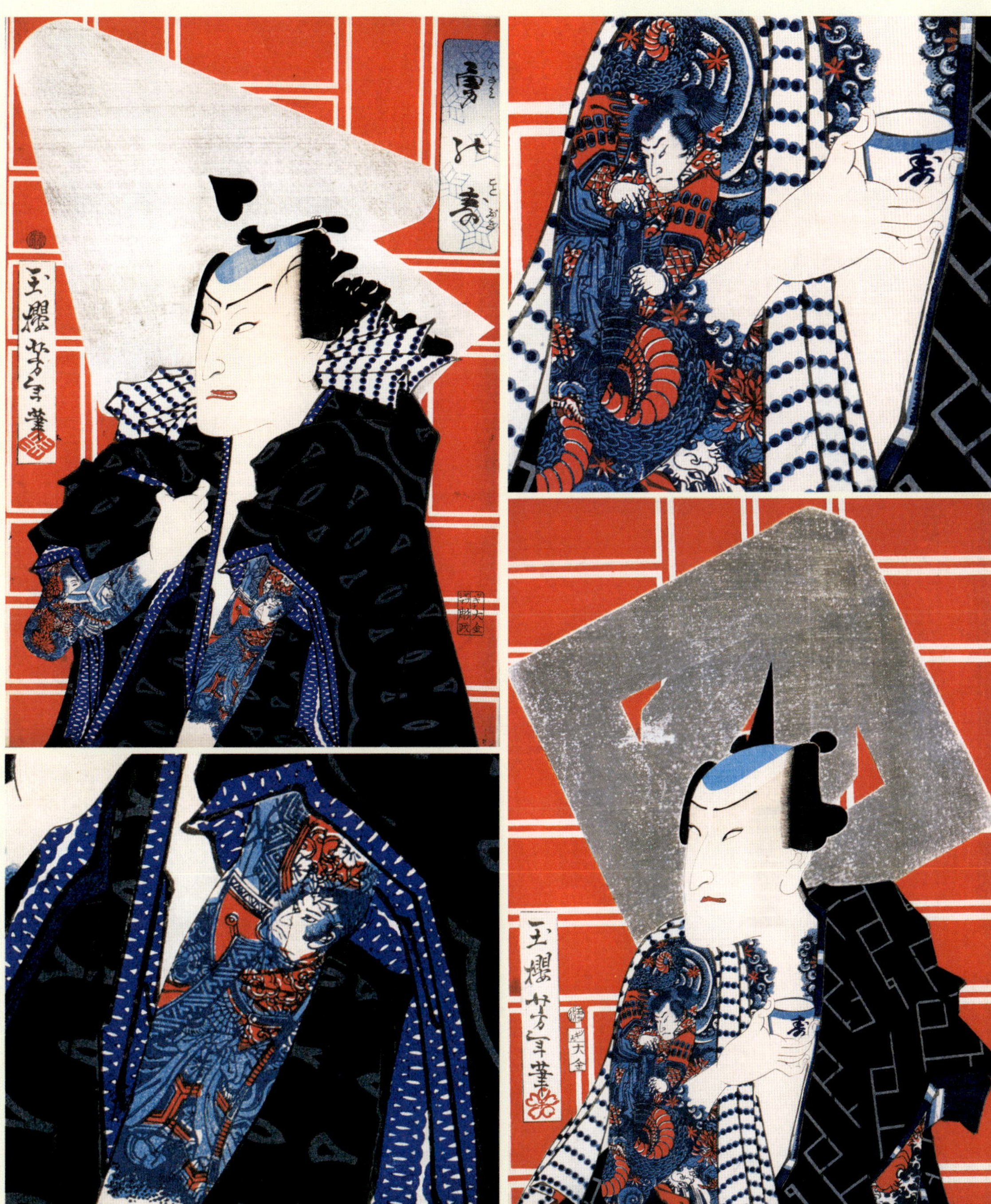

「勇の寿　四代目中村芝翫」月岡芳年
Nakamura Shikan IV, from the series *Isami-no-Kotobuki*,
Tsukioka Yoshitoshi

慶応元年・1865　山口県立萩美術館・浦上記念館蔵
1865, Hagi Uragami Museum

「勇の寿　四代目市村家橘」月岡芳年
Ichimura Kakitsu IV, from the series *Isami-no-Kotobuki*,
Tsukioka Yoshitoshi

慶応元年・1865　山口県立萩美術館・浦上記念館蔵
1865, Hagi Uragami Museum

落合芳幾

おちあい よしいく　天保 4 年～明治 37 年（1833 － 1904）

　幕末から明治期の浮世絵師。歌川国芳にまなび、同門の月岡芳年とならび称された。多方面にその才能を発揮し、美人風俗画や陰影表現を取り入れた役者似顔絵などを得意とした。幕末の世情を反映した「競細腰雪柳風呂」のような銭湯の女湯風景や、芳年と共筆の「英名二十八衆句」などの残酷絵をえがいた。明治 5 年（1872）創立の『東京日日新聞』の幹部を務めて錦絵新聞をえがき、同 8 年には『東京絵入新聞』を創刊、また雑誌「歌舞伎新報」を主宰し執筆した。

Ochiai Yoshiiku 1833-1904

Ukiyo-e Artist in Bakumatsu and Meiji. Studied under Utagawa Kuniyoshi and was acclaimed alongside his fellow student, Utagawa Yoshitoshi. A multifaceted talent, he developed as his fortes portraits of beautiful women in everyday life and the use of shading in portraits of actors. His depictions of women bathing at public baths, for example, *Slender Hips Like Willows at the Yanagiya Bathhouse*, reflect the state of everyday life in Bakumatsu Japan. He also produced "bloody prints," including the *Twenty-Eight Famous Murders with Verse* in collaboration with Tsukioka Yoshitoshi. He also provided polychrome prints for the newspaper while working in management at the *Tokyo Nichinichi Shimbun*, founded in 1872. In 1875 he founded the *Tokyo Illustrated News*, while also leading and writing for the *Kabuki Bulletin magazine*.

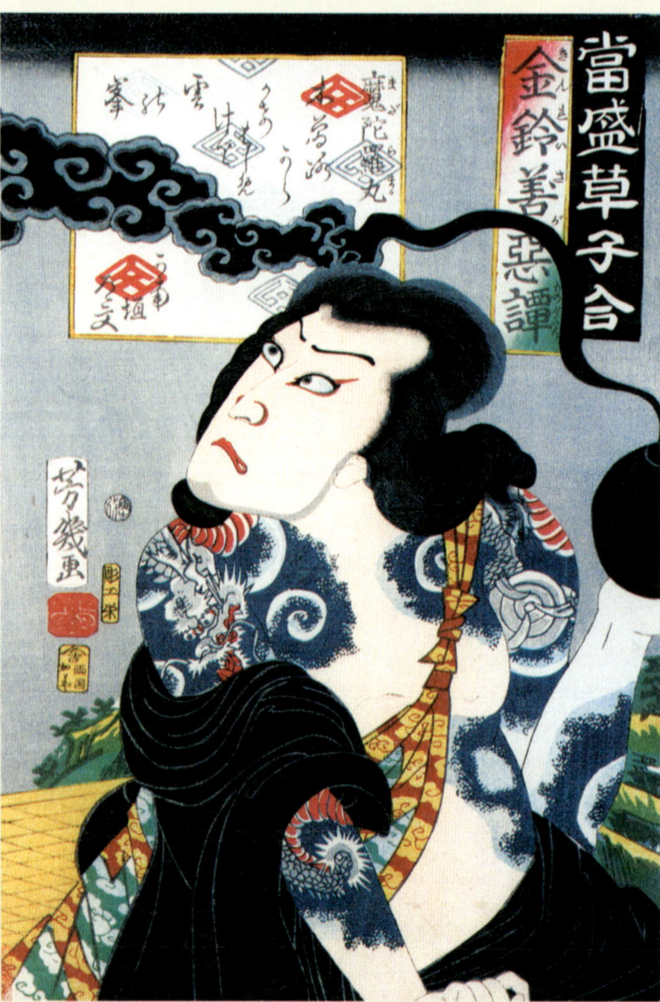

「當盛草子合　金鈴善悪譚」
「魔陀羅丸」落合芳幾
Madara Maru, *Kinrei Saga-Monogatari*
(Kinrei zen'aku monogatari), Tosei Soshi
Awase, Ochiai Yoshiiku

慶応 2 年・1866
東京都立中央図書館特別文庫室蔵
1866, Tokyo Metropolitan Library

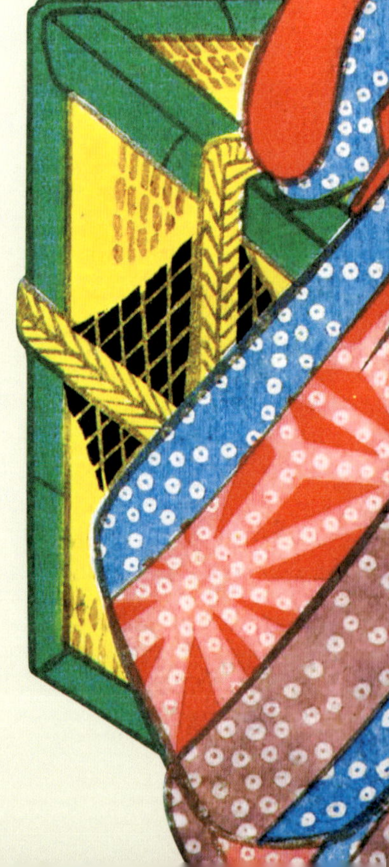

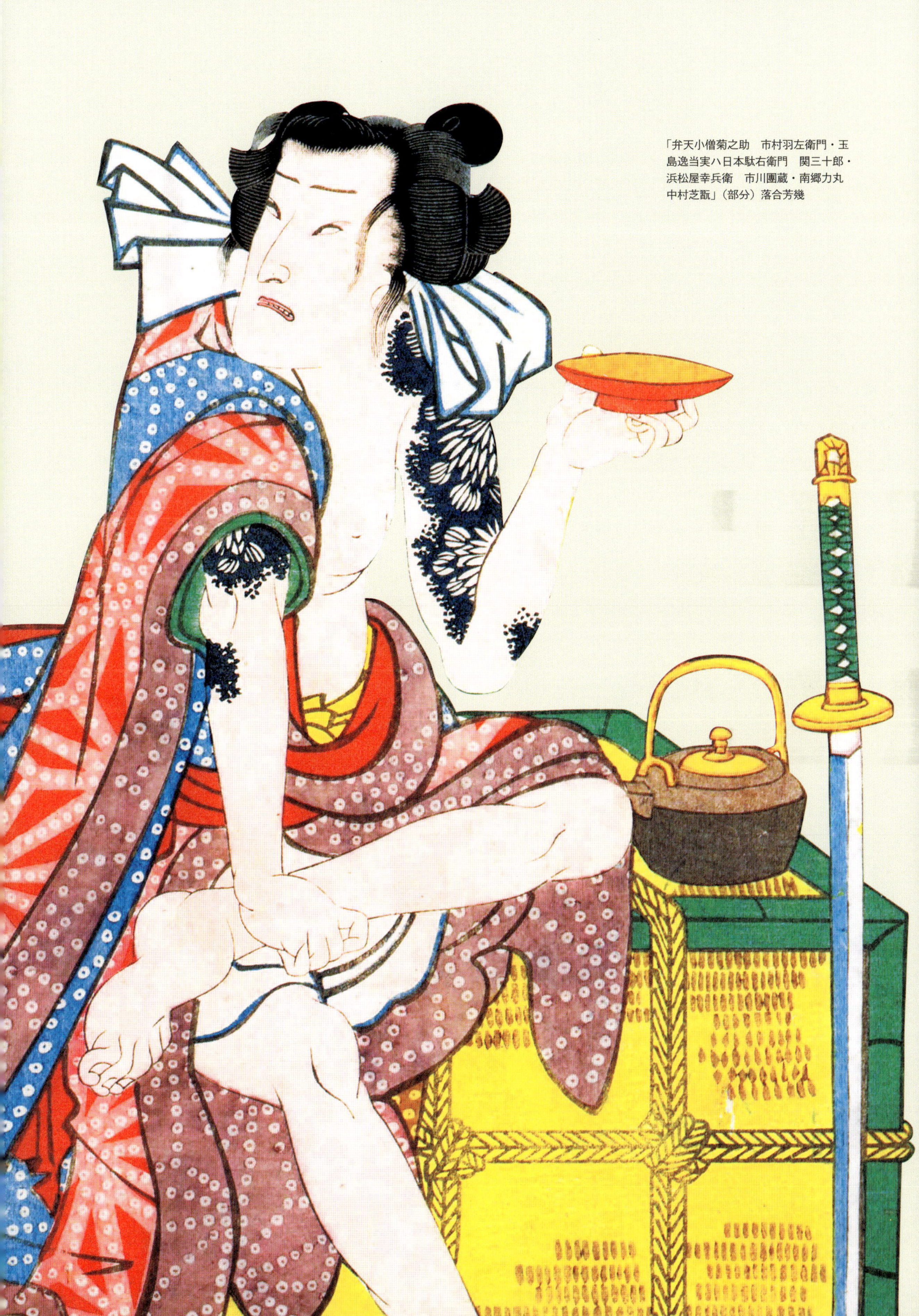

「弁天小僧菊之助　市村羽左衛門・玉
島逸当実ハ日本駄右衛門　関三十郎・
浜松屋幸兵衛　市川團蔵・南郷力丸
中村芝翫」（部分）落合芳幾

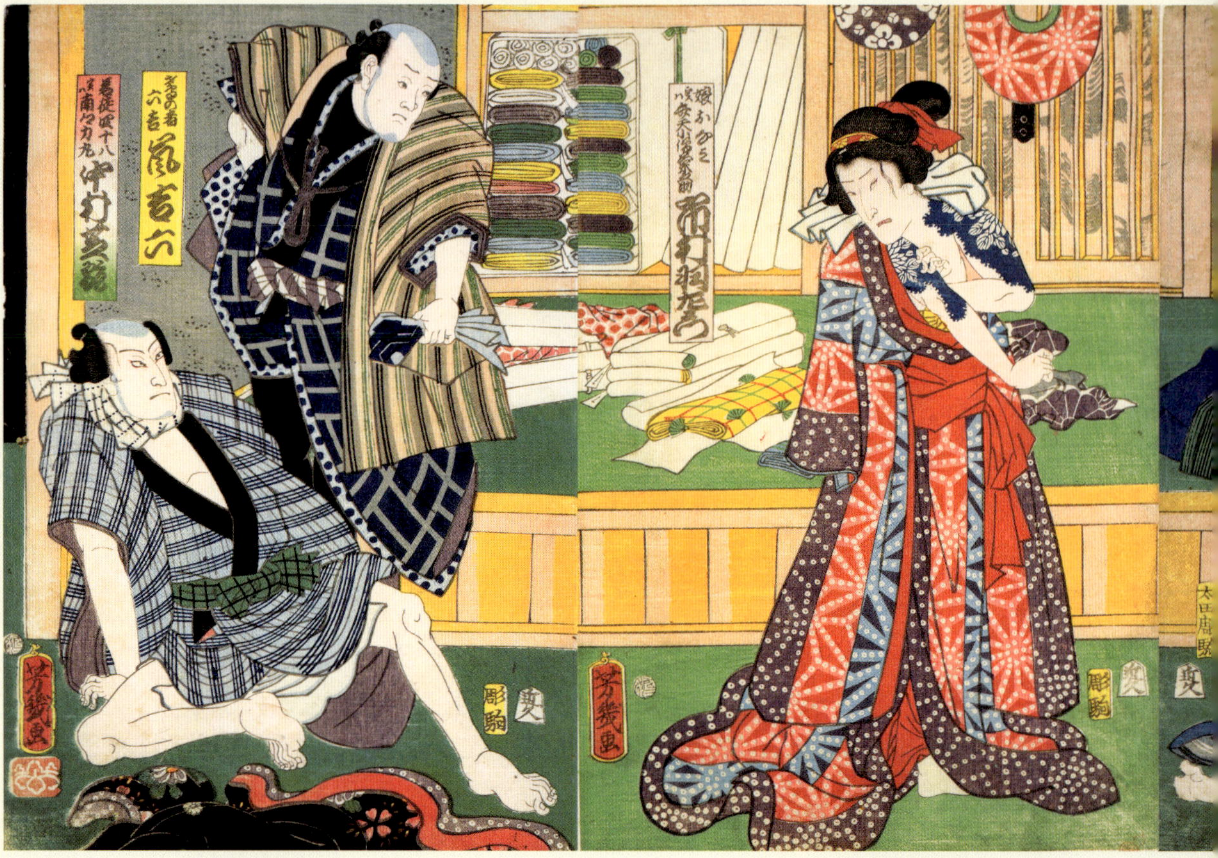

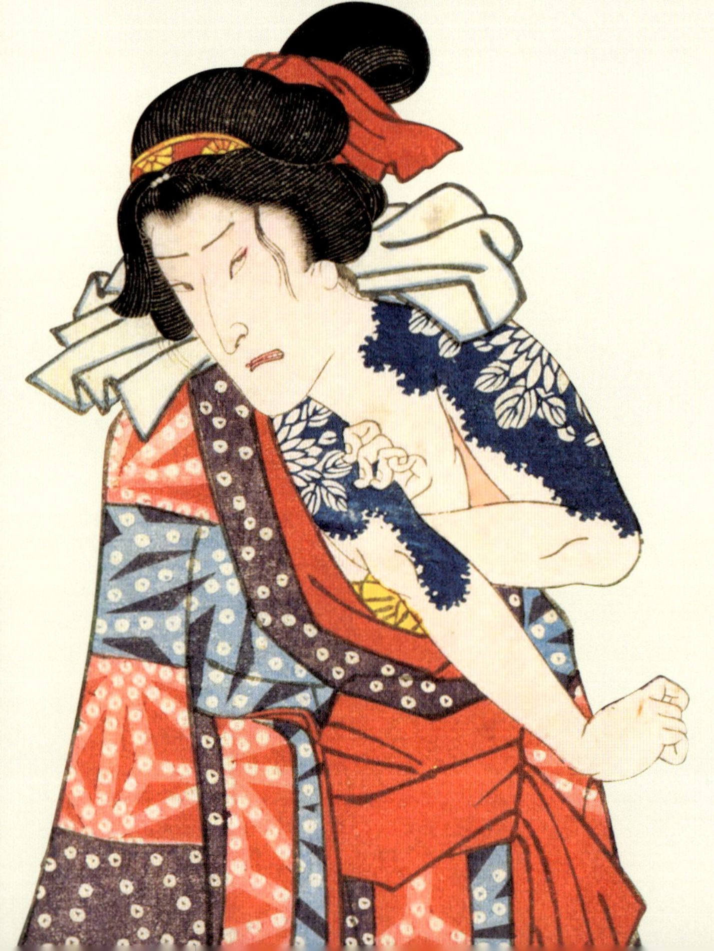

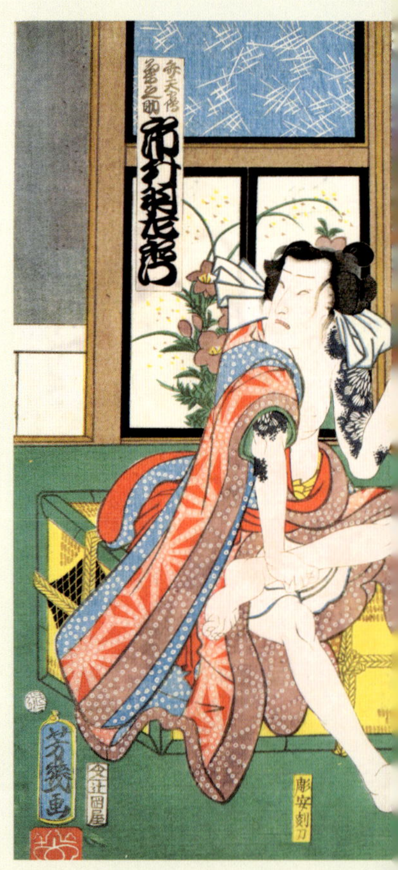

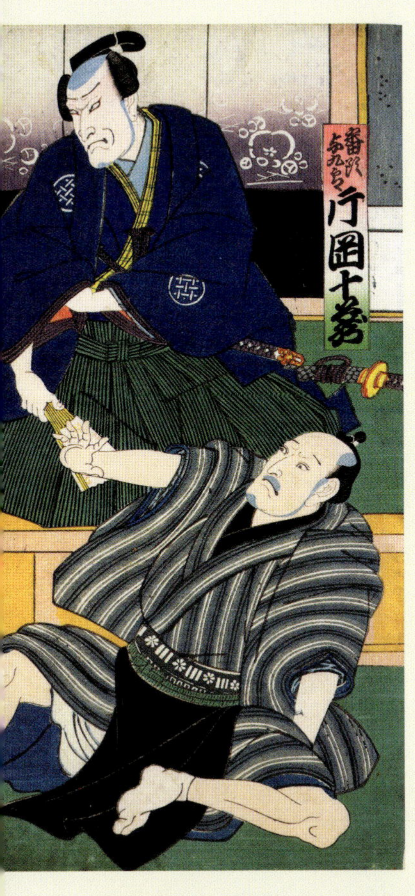

「番頭与九郎 片岡十蔵・玉嶋逸当実ハ日本駄
右衛門 関三十郎・娘おなみ実ハ弁天小僧菊
之助 市村羽左衛門・鳶の者六吉 嵐吉六・若
従四十八実ハ南郷力丸 中村芝翫」落合芳幾

Actors Kataoka Jūzō as Bantō Yokurō, Seki Sanjūrō as Nihon
Daemon, Ichimura Uzaemon as Benten Kozō Kikunosuke,
Arashi Kichiroku as Tobi no Mono Rokukichi, Nakamura Shikan
as Nangou Rikimaru, Ochiai Yoshiiku

文久 2 年・1862　国立国会図書館デジタルコレクション
1862, National Diet Library Digital Collections

「弁天小僧菊之助　市村羽左衛門・玉島逸当実ハ日
本駄右衛門　関三十郎・浜松屋幸兵衛　市川團蔵・
南郷力丸　中村芝翫」落合芳幾

Actors Ichimura Uzaemon as Benten Kozō Kikunosuke, Seki Sanjūrō as
Nihon Daemon, Ichikawa Danjūrō as Hamamatsuya Kōbei, Nakamura
Shikan as Nangou Rikimaru, Ochiai Yoshiiku

文久 2 年・1862　国立国会図書館デジタルコレクション
1862, National Diet Library Digital Collections

Chapter 1 ｜ Tattoos: The Beauty of the Heroes' Skin　**Ochiai Yoshiiku**

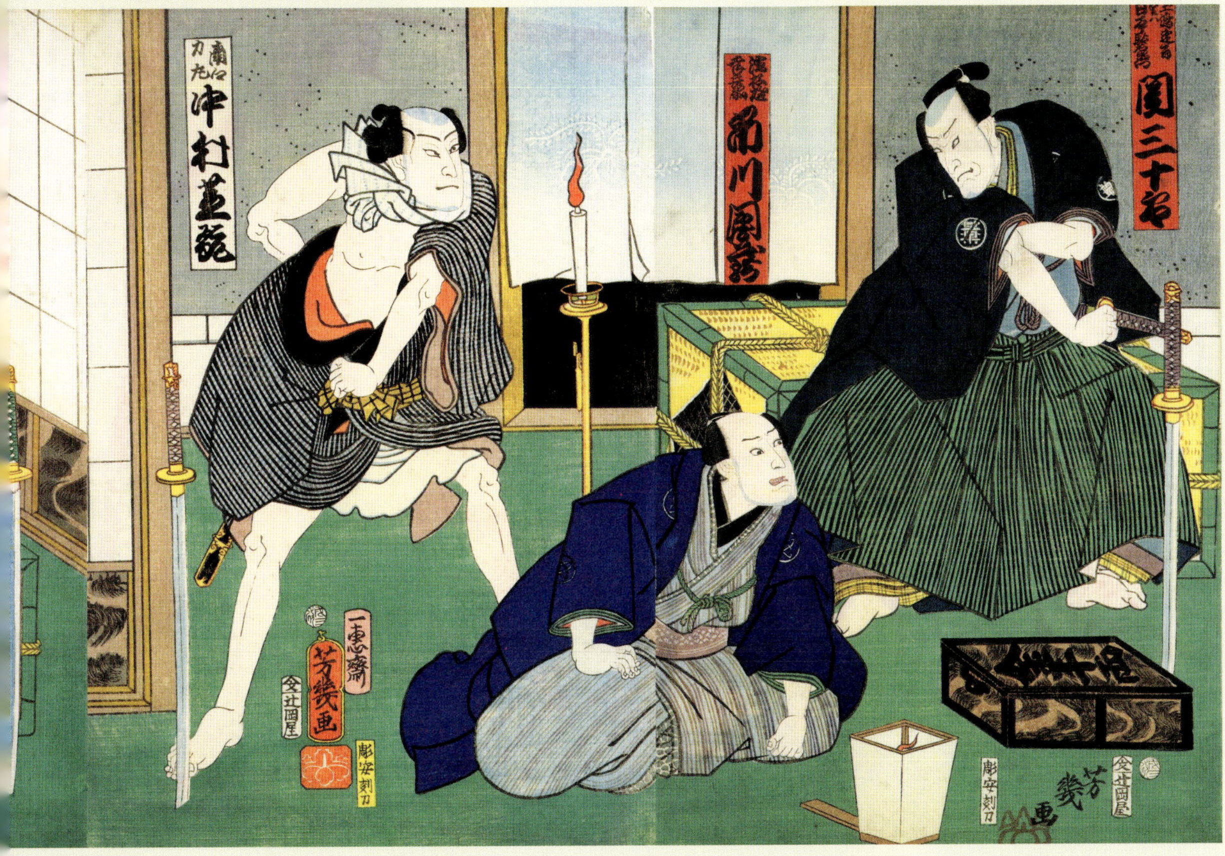

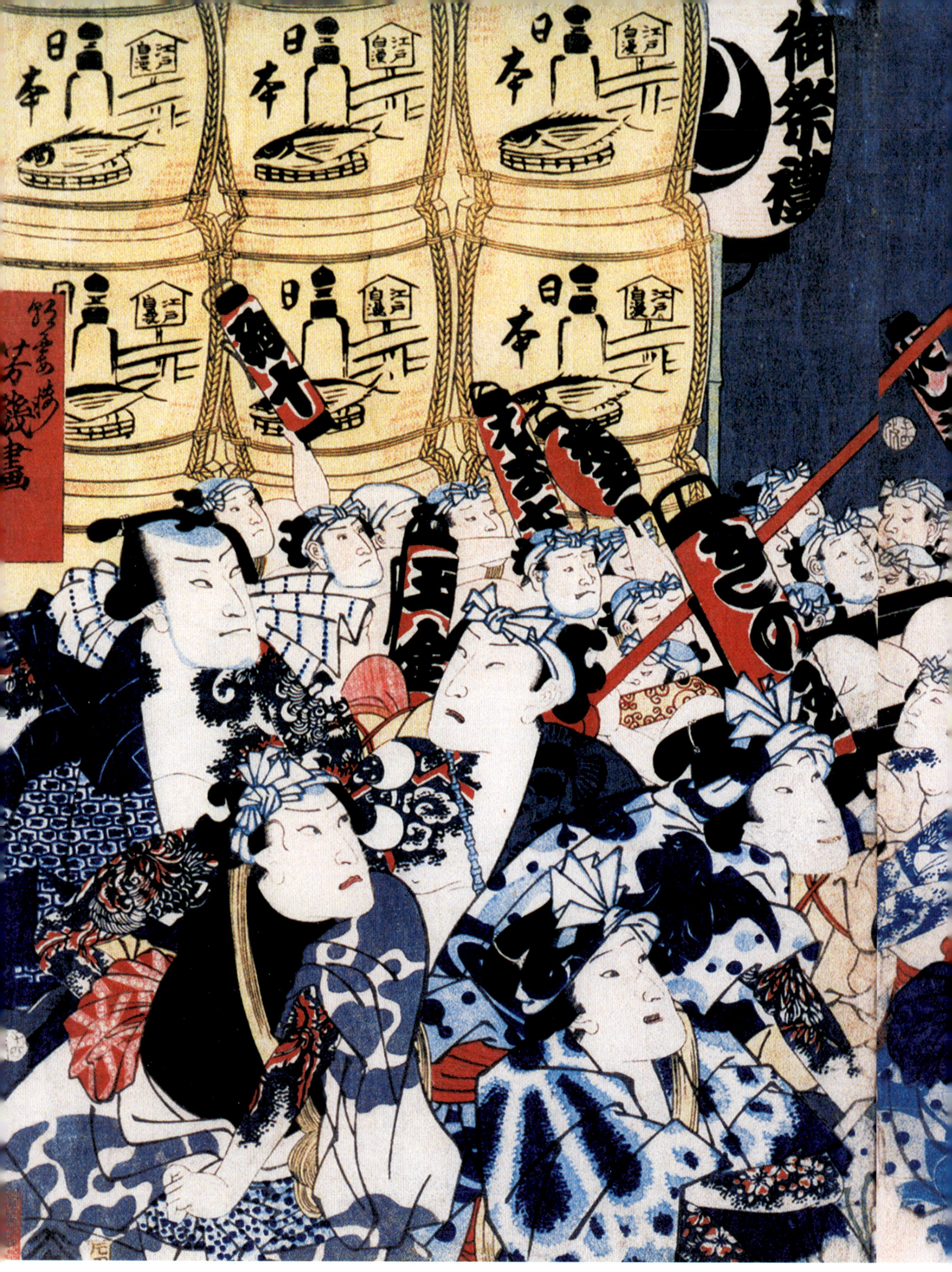

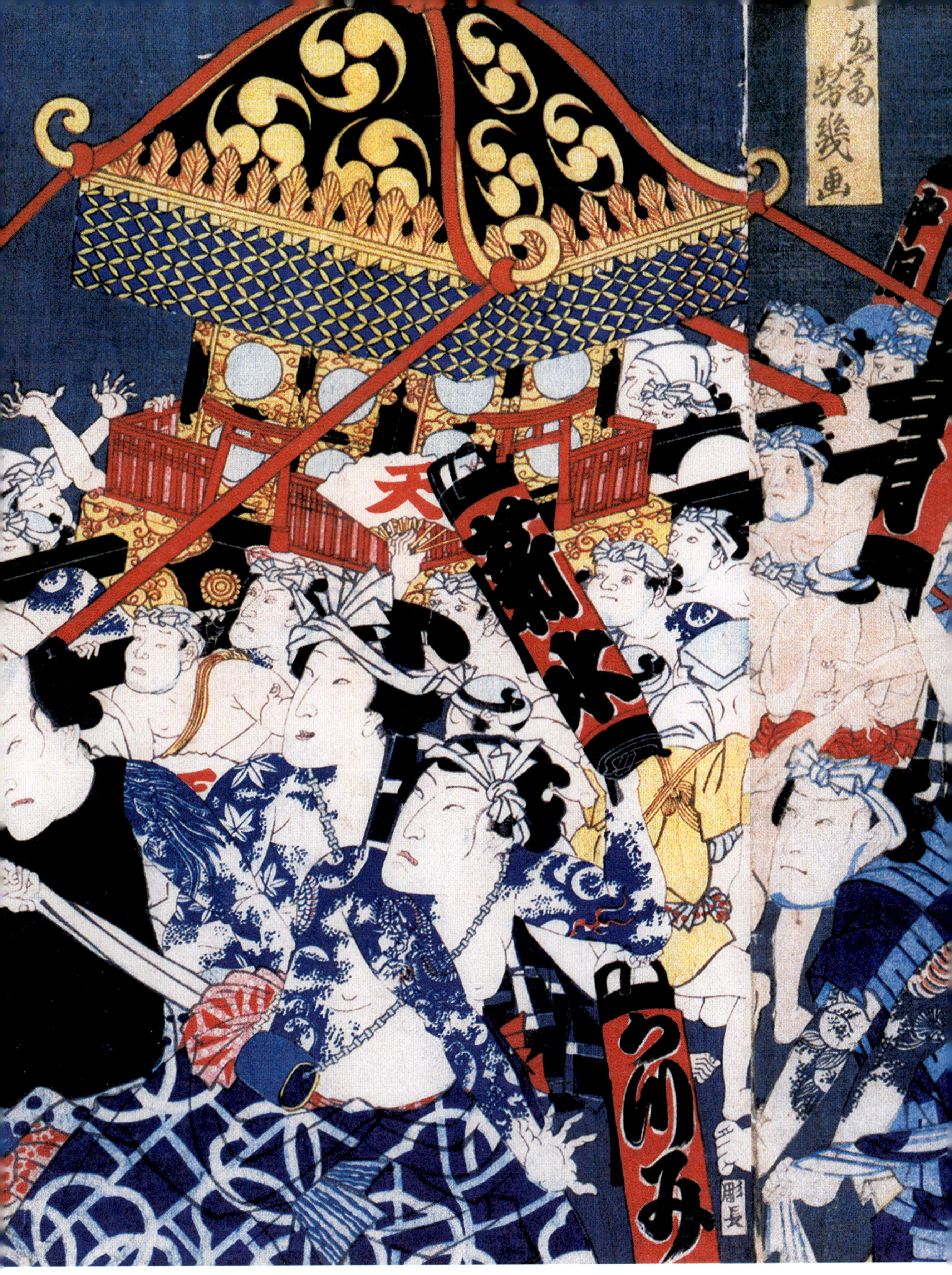

「天王御祭礼之図」（部分）落合芳幾

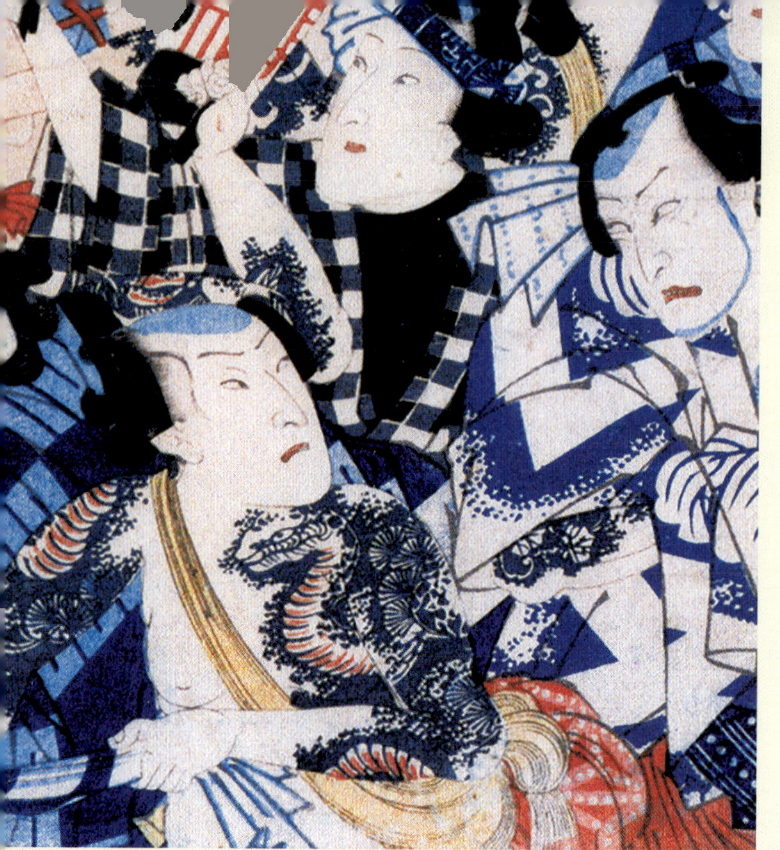

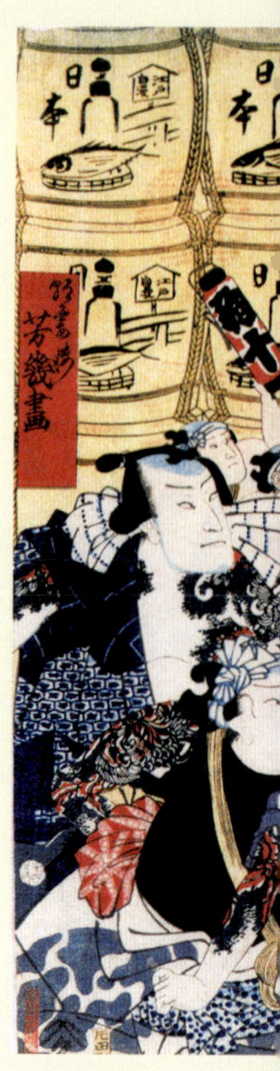

「天王御祭礼之図」落合芳幾
Illustration of the Tenno Festival (*Tennou-Gosairei-no-Zu*), Ochiai Yoshiiku

元治元年・1864
東京都立中央図書館特別文庫室蔵
1864, Tokyo Metropolitan Library

「誠忠岳王図傳」落合芳幾
Illustrated biography of King Seichung Gakko(*Seichū-Gakuō-Zuden*), Ochiai Yoshiiku

元治元年・1864　山口県立萩美術館・浦上記念館蔵
1864, Hagi Uragami Museum

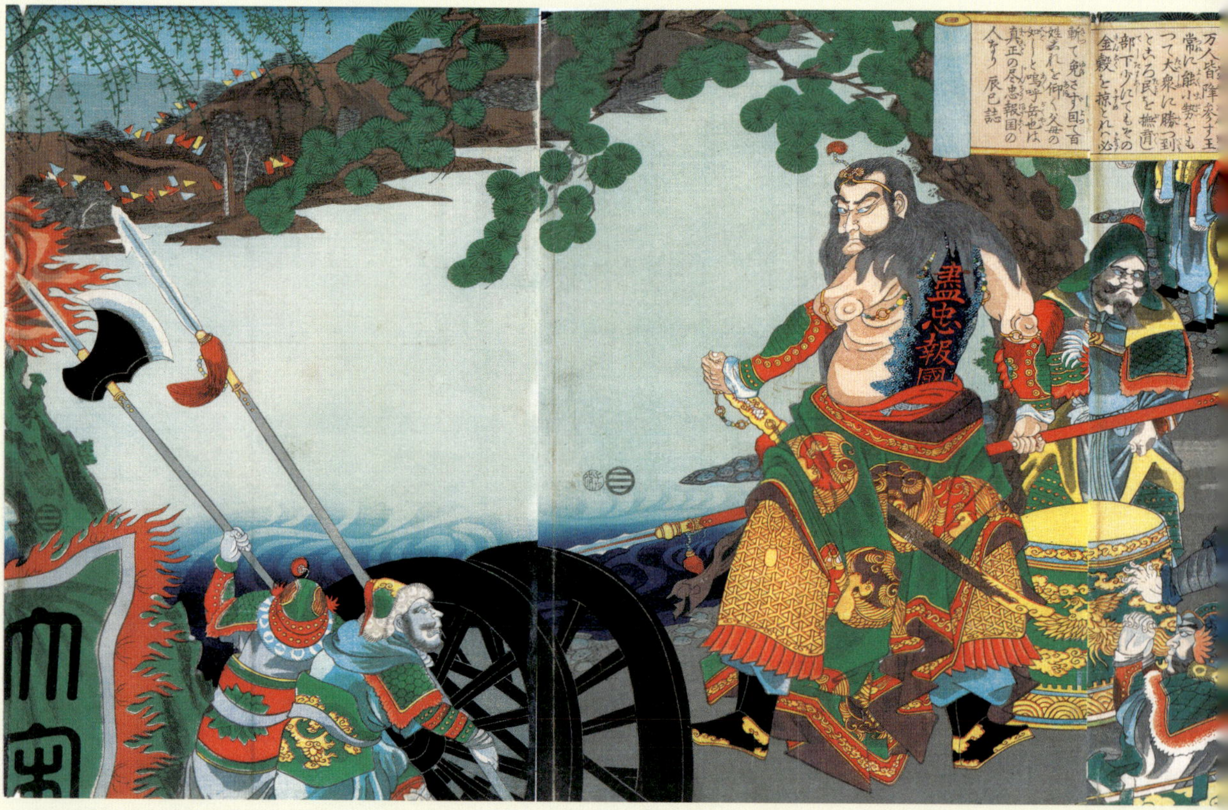

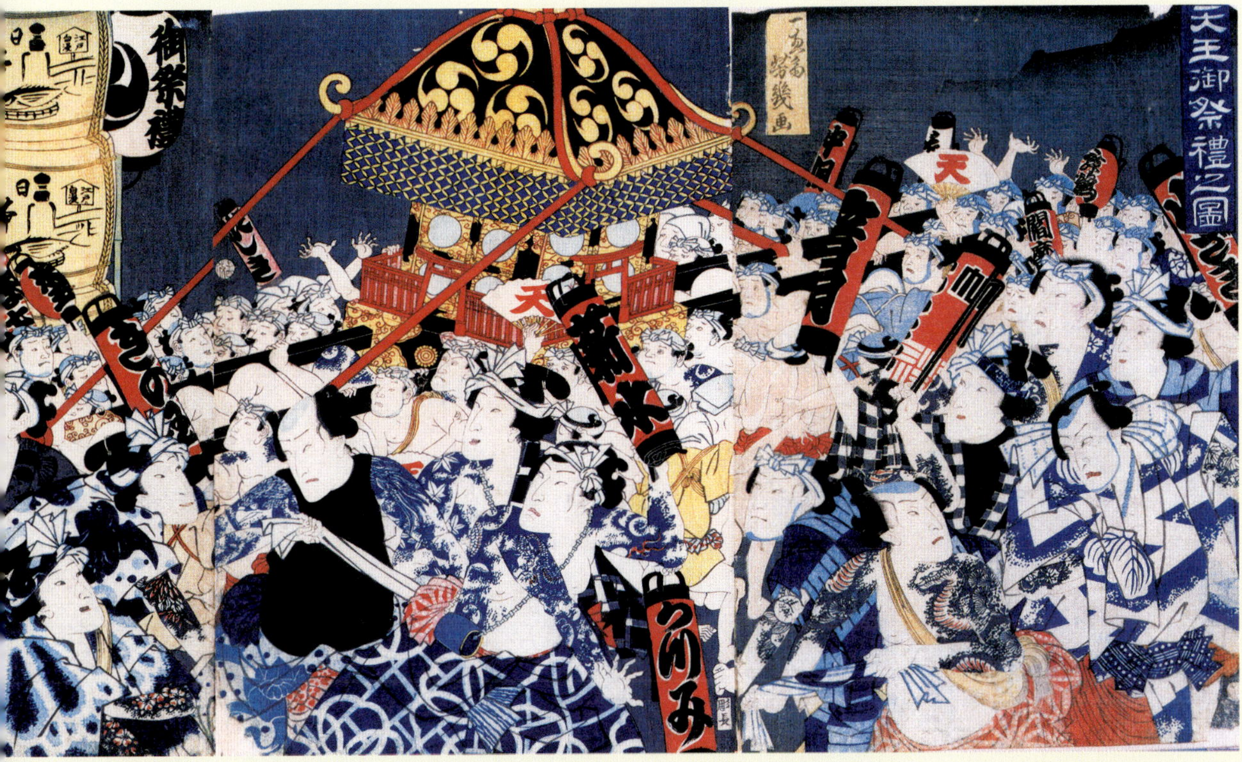

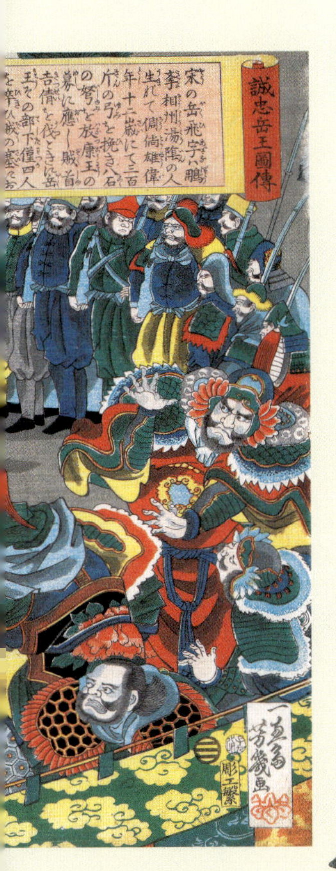

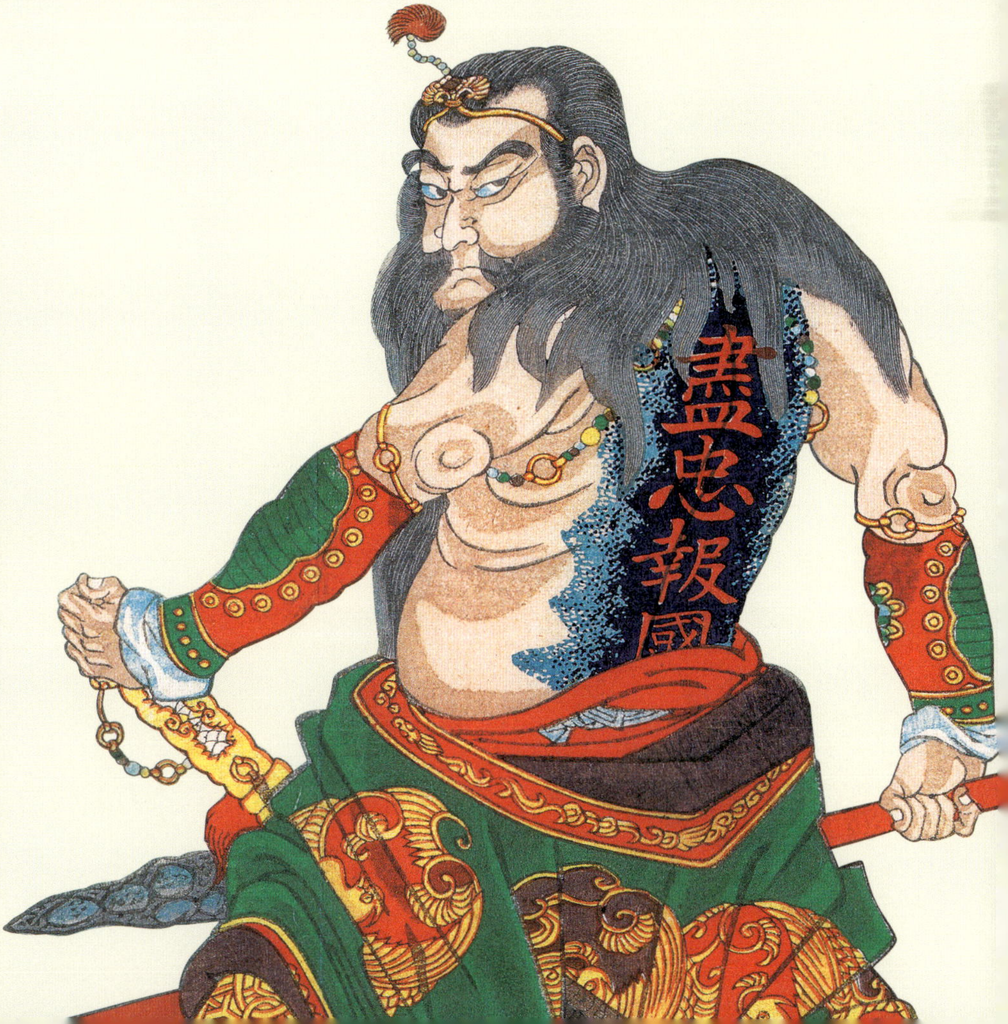

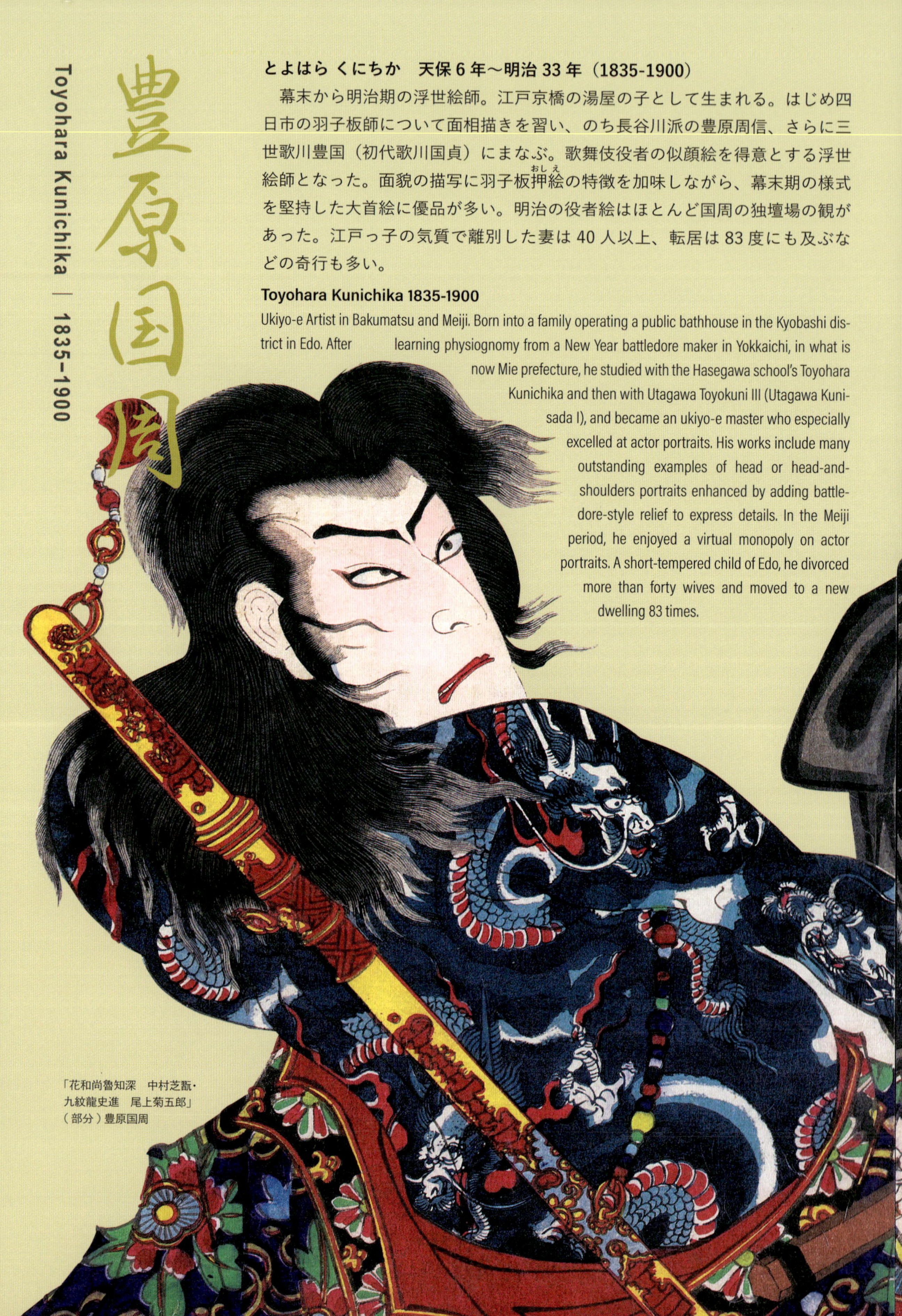

豊原国周

とよはら くにちか　天保 6 年〜明治 33 年（1835-1900）

　幕末から明治期の浮世絵師。江戸京橋の湯屋の子として生まれる。はじめ四日市の羽子板師について面相描きを習い、のち長谷川派の豊原周信、さらに三世歌川豊国（初代歌川国貞）にまなぶ。歌舞伎役者の似顔絵を得意とする浮世絵師となった。面貌の描写に羽子板押絵（おしえ）の特徴を加味しながら、幕末期の様式を堅持した大首絵に優品が多い。明治の役者絵はほとんど国周の独壇場の観があった。江戸っ子の気質で離別した妻は 40 人以上、転居は 83 度にも及ぶなどの奇行も多い。

Toyohara Kunichika 1835-1900

Ukiyo-e Artist in Bakumatsu and Meiji. Born into a family operating a public bathhouse in the Kyobashi district in Edo. After learning physiognomy from a New Year battledore maker in Yokkaichi, in what is now Mie prefecture, he studied with the Hasegawa school's Toyohara Kunichika and then with Utagawa Toyokuni III (Utagawa Kunisada I), and became an ukiyo-e master who especially excelled at actor portraits. His works include many outstanding examples of head or head-and-shoulders portraits enhanced by adding battledore-style relief to express details. In the Meiji period, he enjoyed a virtual monopoly on actor portraits. A short-tempered child of Edo, he divorced more than forty wives and moved to a new dwelling 83 times.

「花和尚魯知深　中村芝翫・
九紋龍史進　尾上菊五郎」
（部分）豊原国周

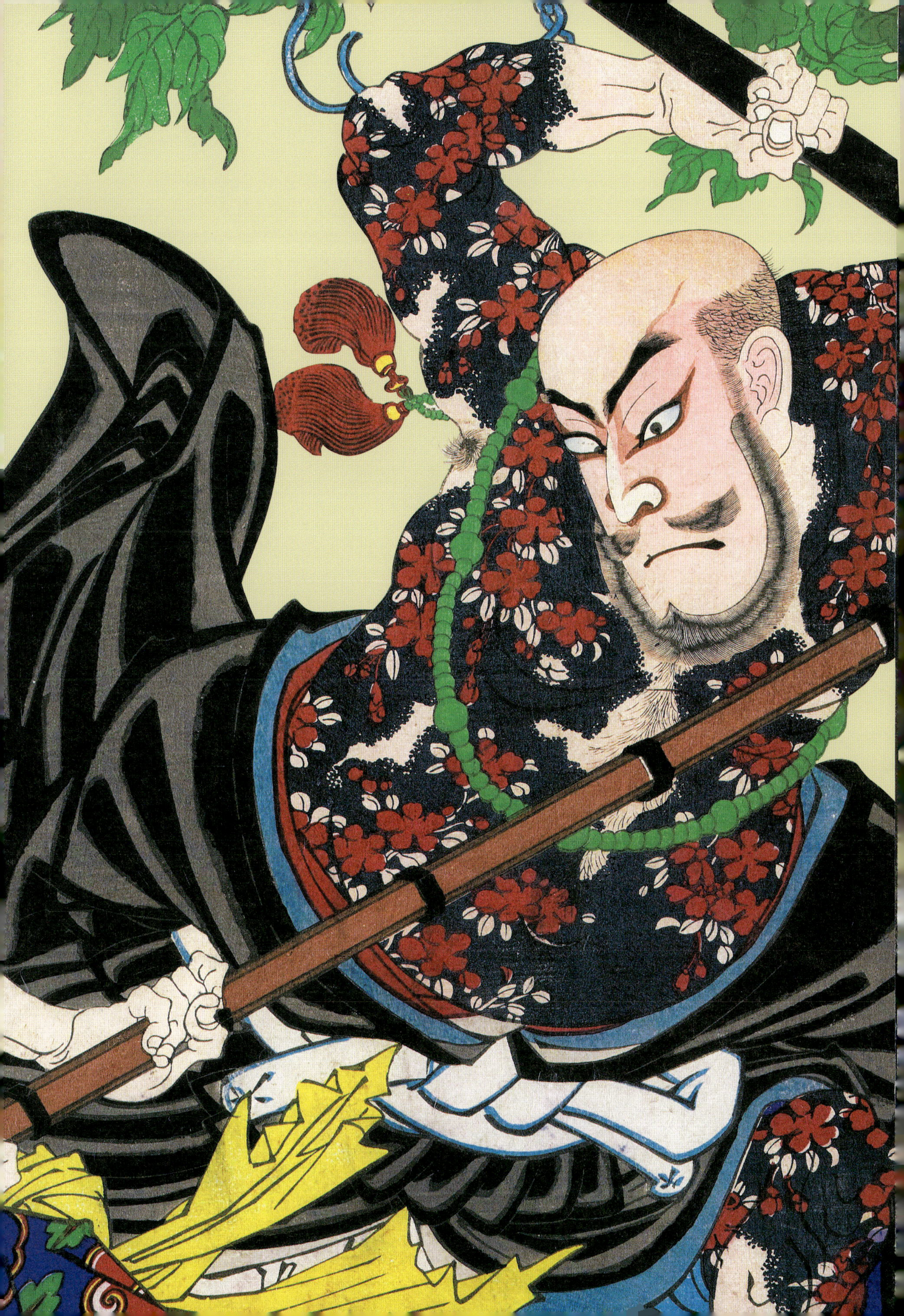

「水滸傳雪挑 夢物語廬生容画」
「花和尚魯智深　市川左團次・
九紋龍史進　市川團十郎」豊原国周
Suikoden Snow Battle *(Suikoden-Yuki-no-Danmari,*
Yumemonogatari-Rosei-no-Sugata), Actors Ichikawa
Sadanji as Kaoshō Rochishin, Ichikawa Danjūrō as
Kumonryū Shishin, Toyohara Kunichika
明治 19 年・1886
東京都立中央図書館特別文庫室蔵
1886, Tokyo Metropolitan Library

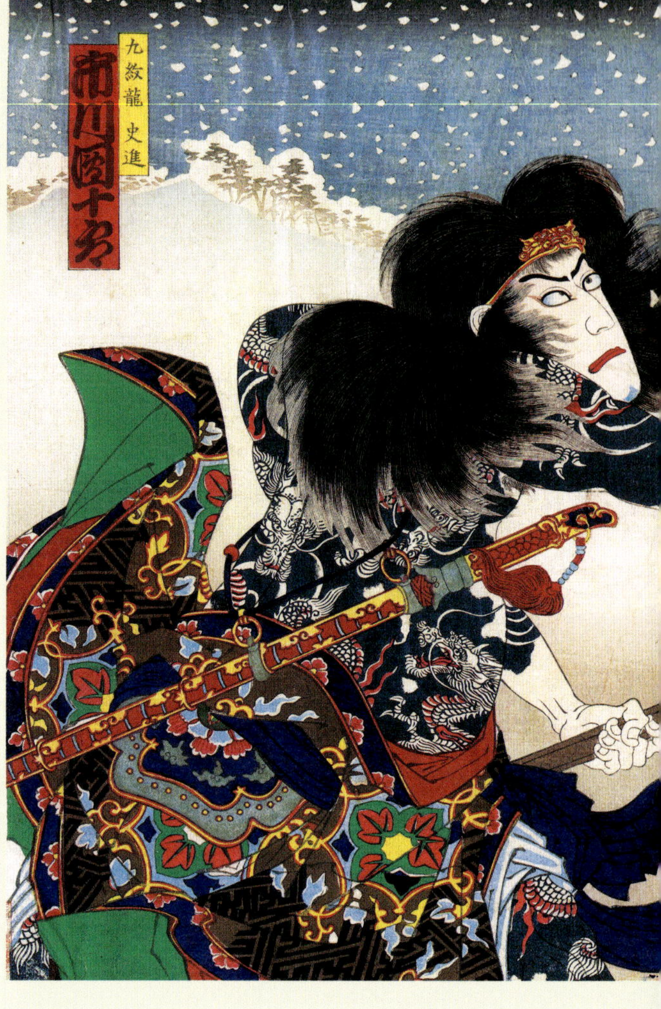

「花和尚魯知深　中村芝翫・
九紋龍史進　尾上菊五郎」豊原国周
Actors Nakamura Shikan as Kaoshō Rochishin, Onoe Kikugorō
as Kumonryū Shishin, Toyohara Kunichika
明治 16 年・1883　東京都立中央図書館特別文庫室蔵
1883 Tokyo Metropolitan Library

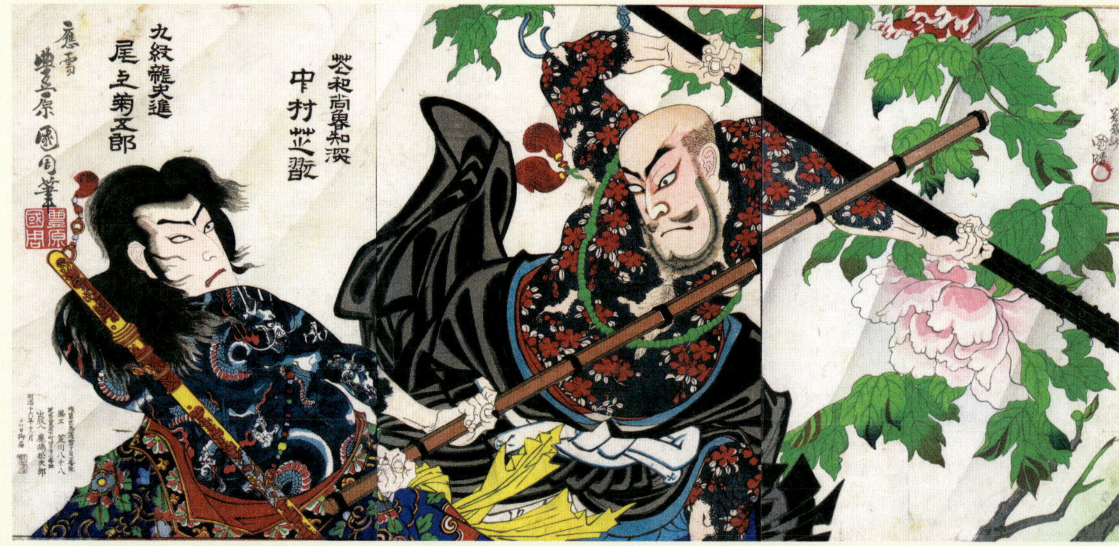

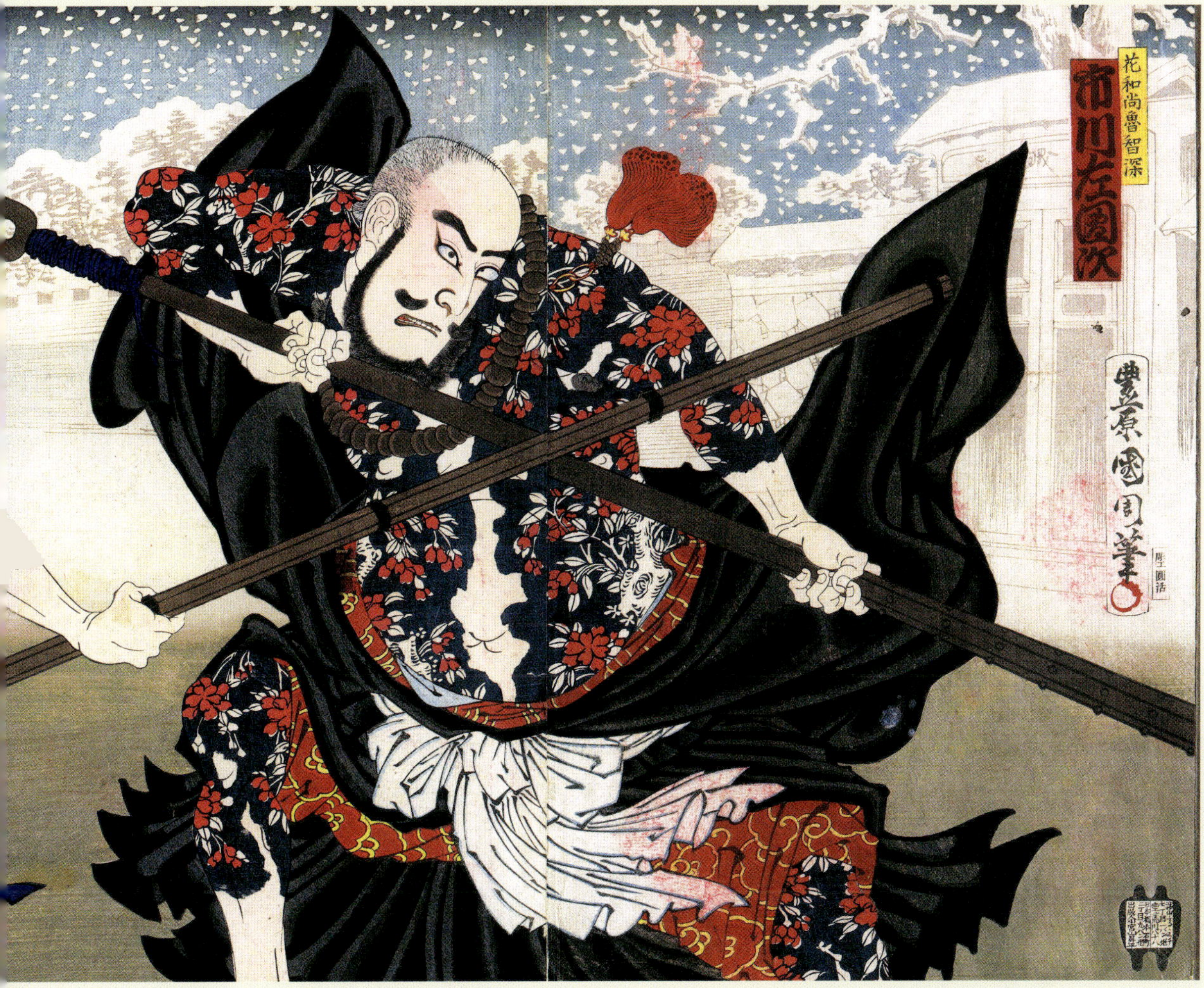

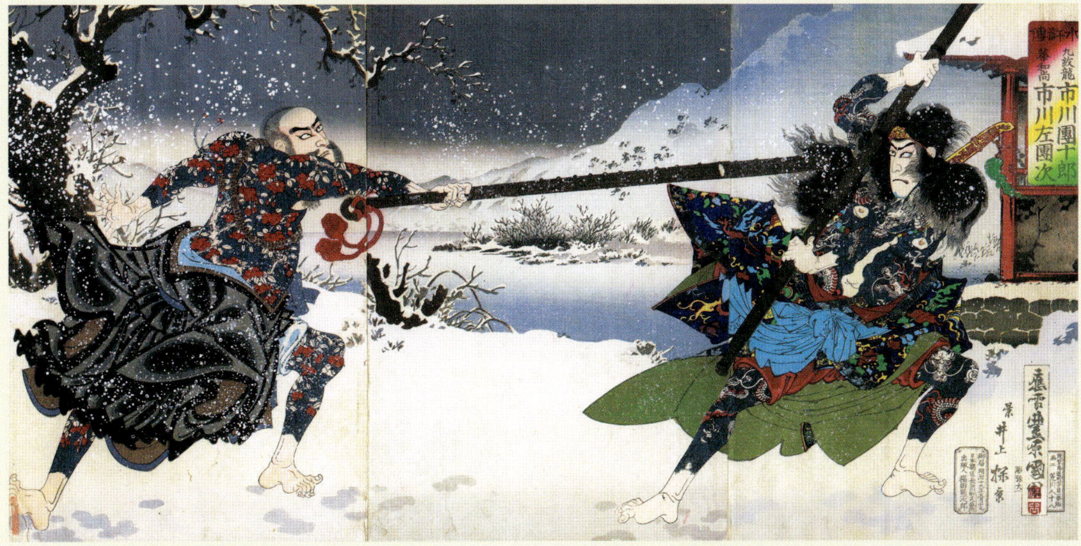

「水滸傳雪挑」豊原国周
Suikoden Snow Battle (Suikoden-Yuki-no-Danmari),Toyohara Kunichika
明治 19 年・1886　東京都立中央図書館特別文庫室蔵
1886, Tokyo Metropolitan Library

Chapter 1 ｜ Tattoos: The Beauty of the Heroes' Skin　**Toyohara Kunichika**

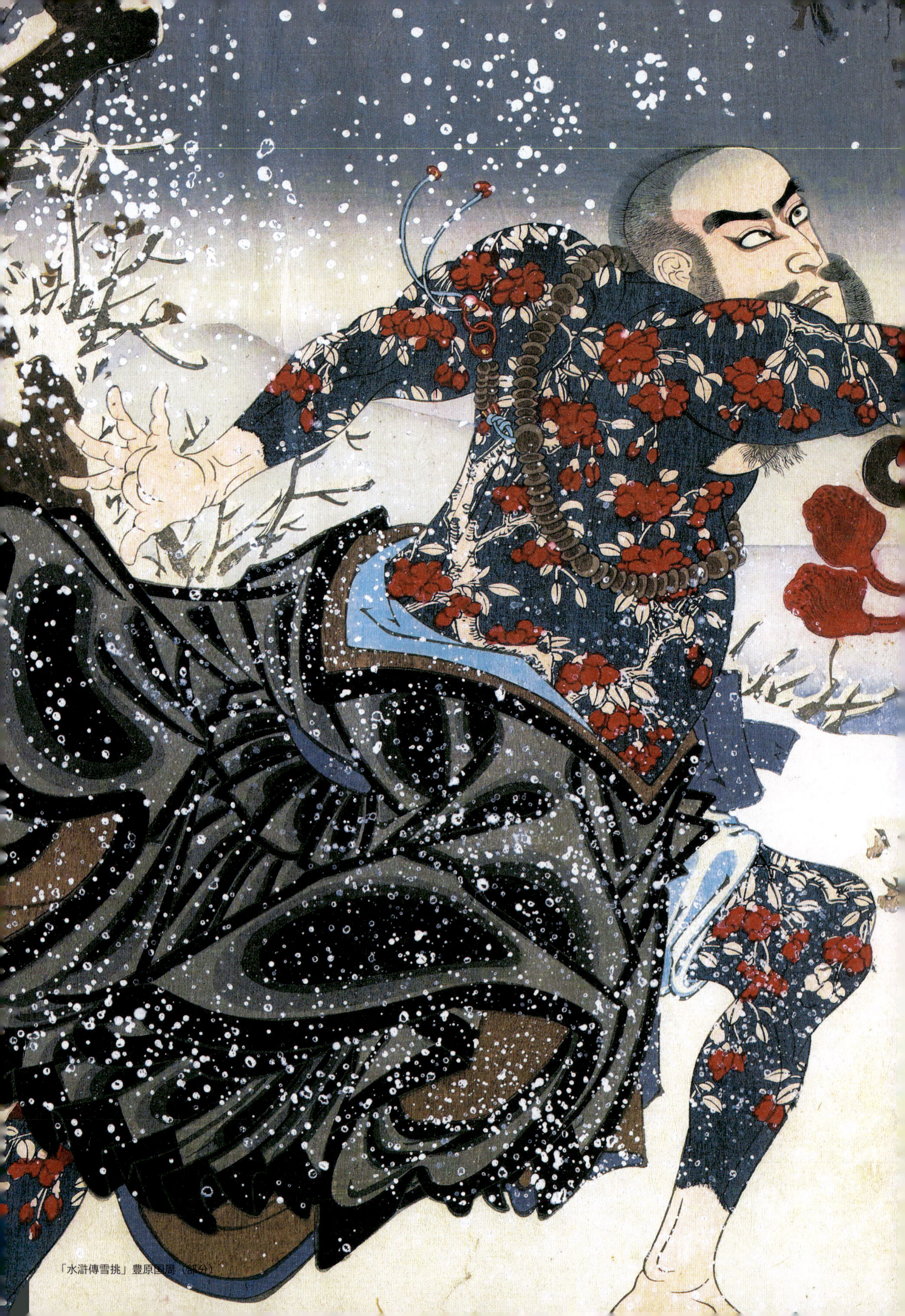

「水滸傳雪挑」豊原国周（部分）

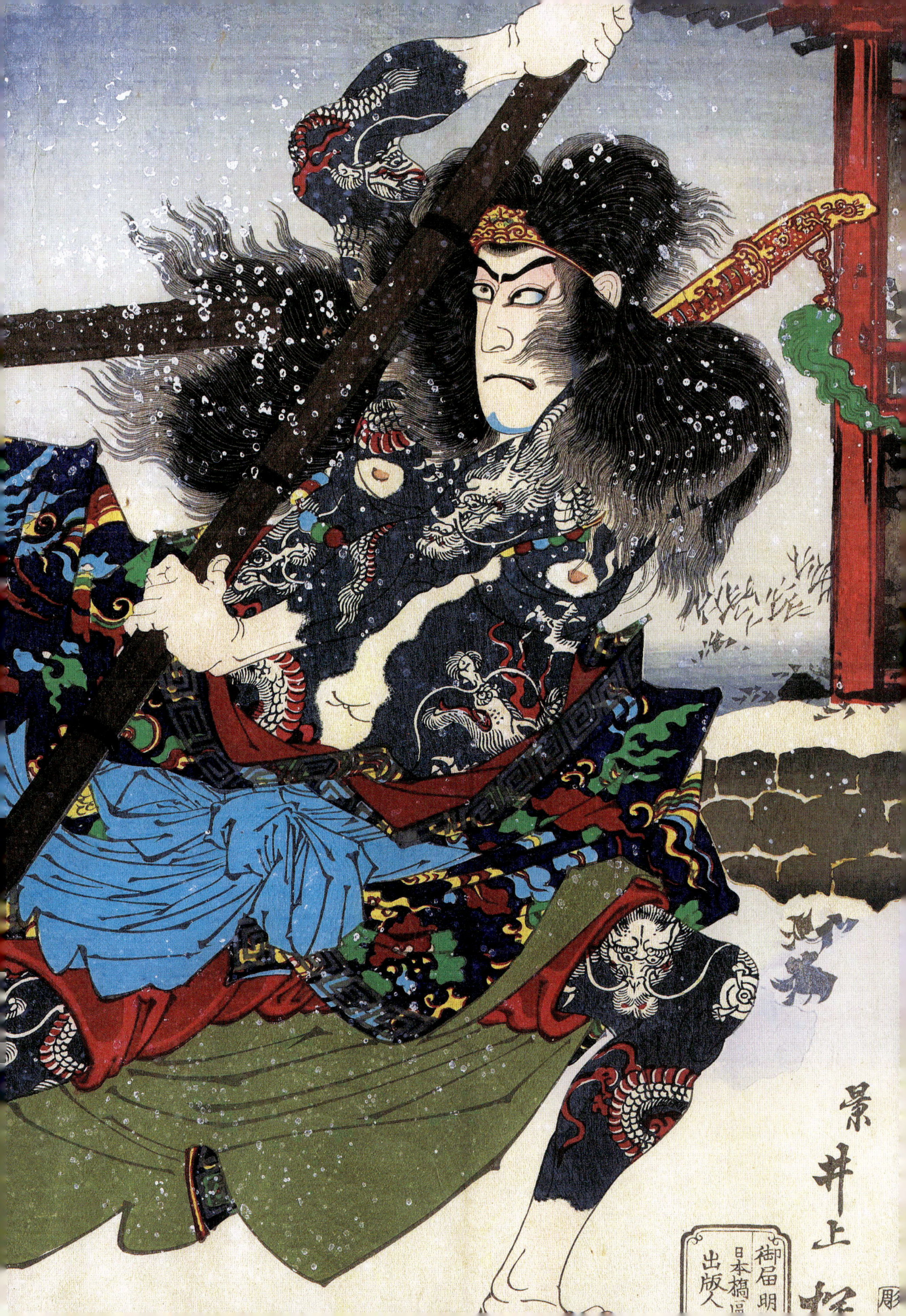
景
井上
御届明
日本橋
出版人
彫

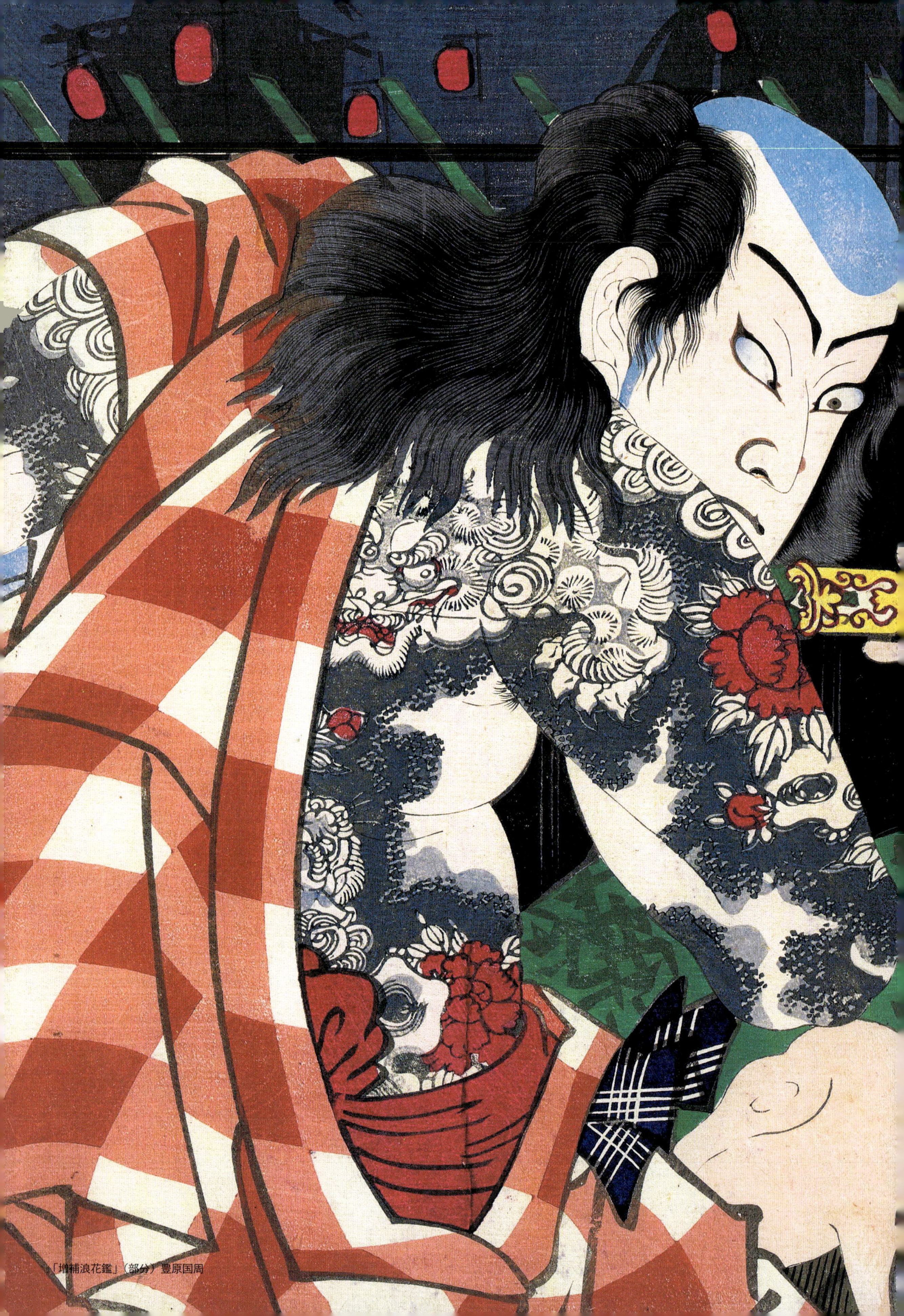

「増補浪花鑑」（部分）豊原国周

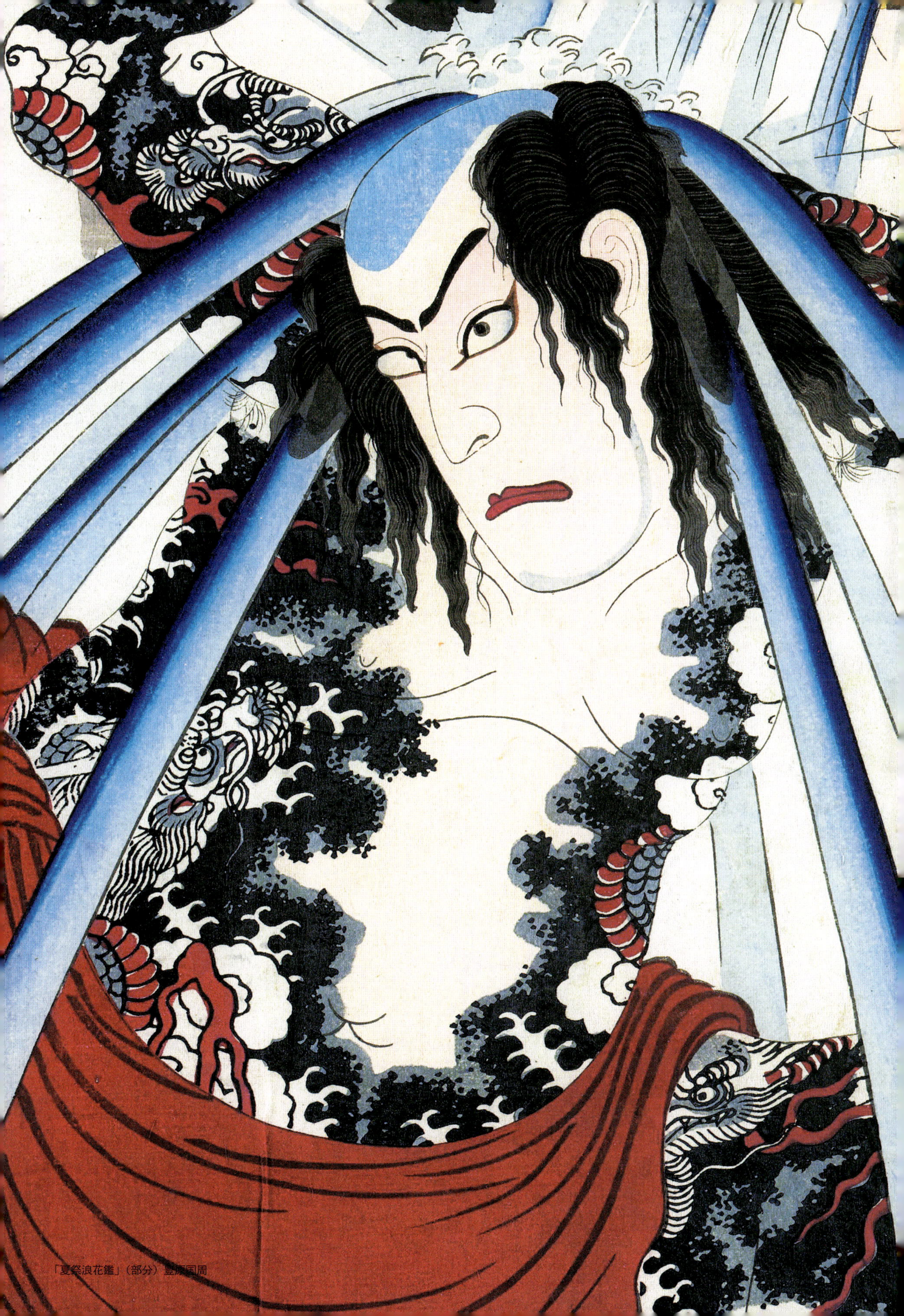

「夏祭浪花鑑」（部分）豊原国周

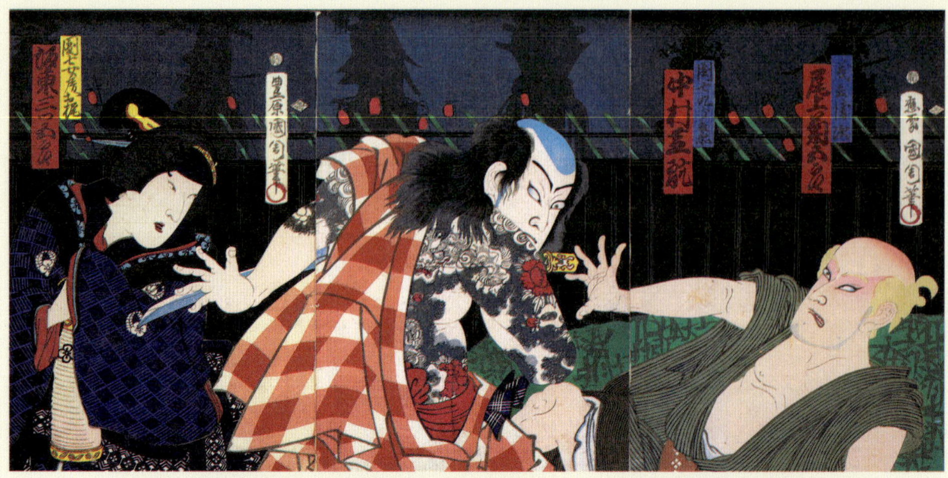

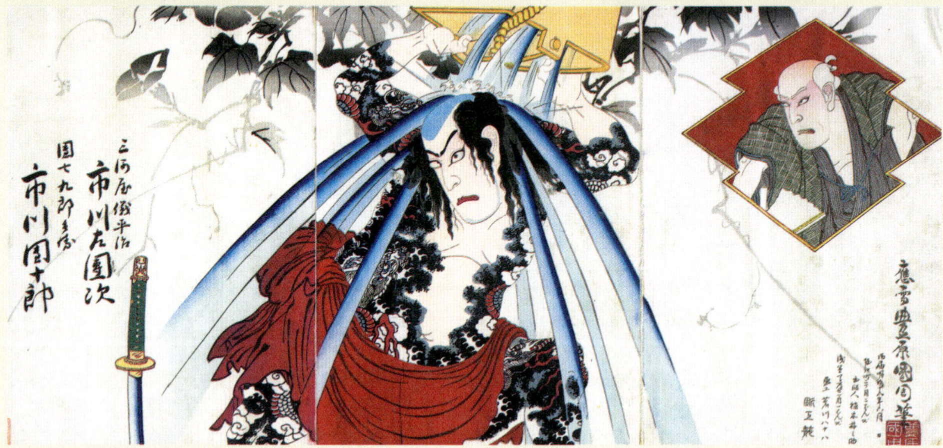

「増補浪花鑑」豊原国周
Zouho Naniwakagami, Toyohara Kunichika

明治 5 年・1872　東京都立中央図書館特別文庫室蔵
1872, Tokyo Metropolitan Library

「夏祭浪花鑑」豊原国周
Natsumatsuri Naniwakagami, Toyohara Kunichika

明治 16 年・1883　東京都立中央図書館特別文庫室蔵
1883, Tokyo Metropolitan Library

「三河屋儀平治　尾上菊五郎・
團七九郎兵衛　市川團十郎・
一寸徳兵衛　市川左團次」豊原国周
Actors Onoe Kikugorō as Mikawaya Giheiji, Ichikawa Danjūrō
as Danshichi Kurobei, Ichikawa Sadanji as Issun Tokubei,
Toyohara Kunichika

明治 16 年・1883　国立国会図書館デジタルコレクション
1883, National Diet Library Digital Collections

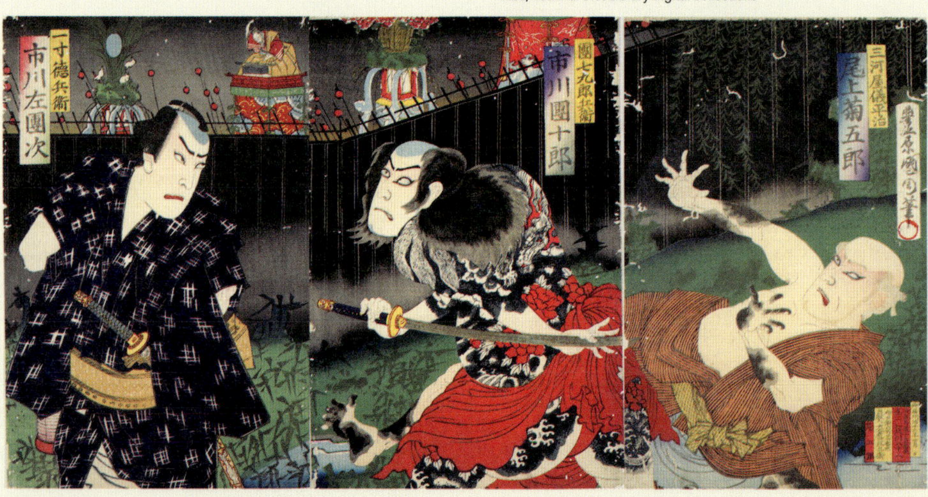

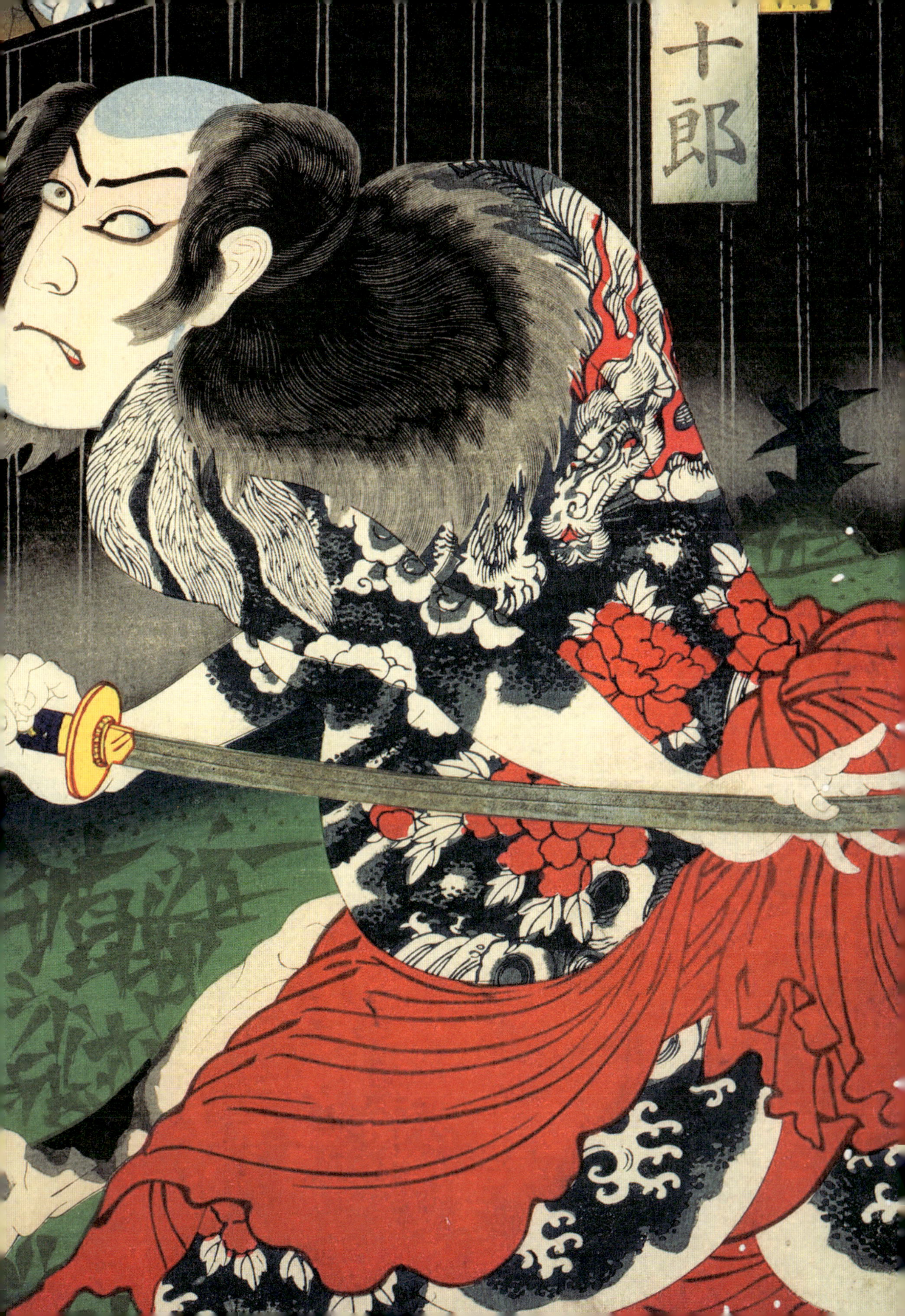

十
郎

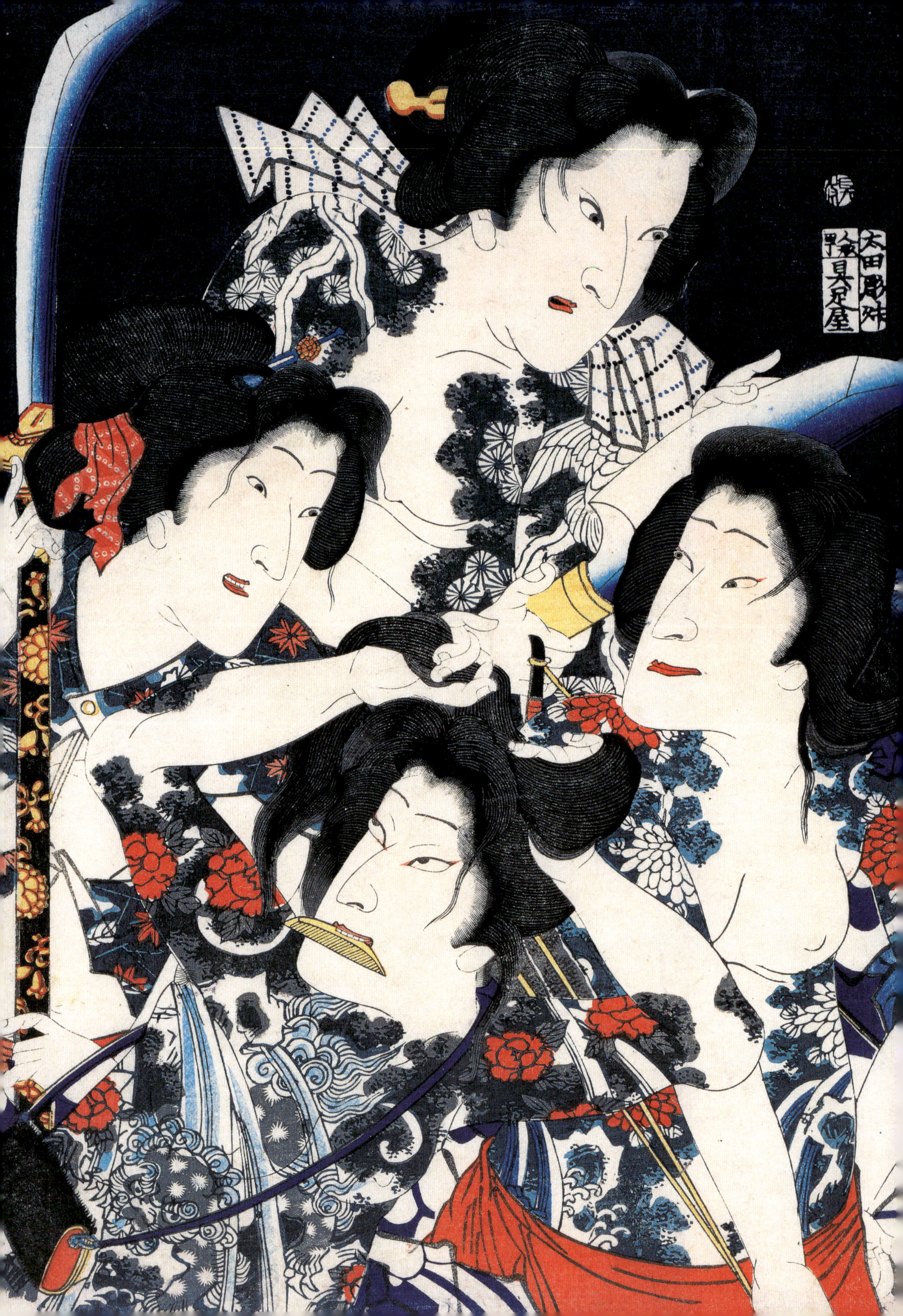

太田彫政
人形師
野具足屋

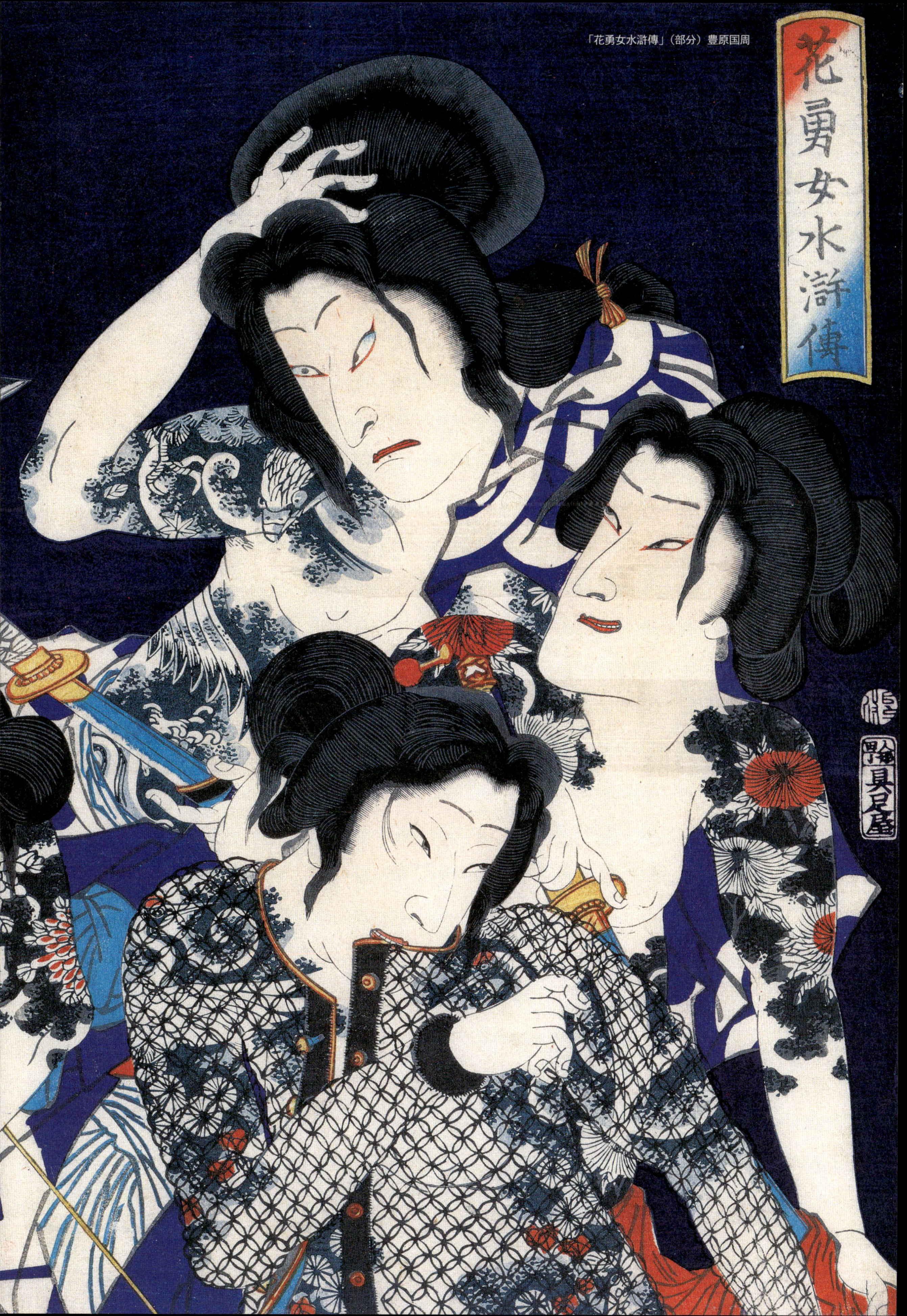

「花勇女水滸傳」（部分）豊原国周

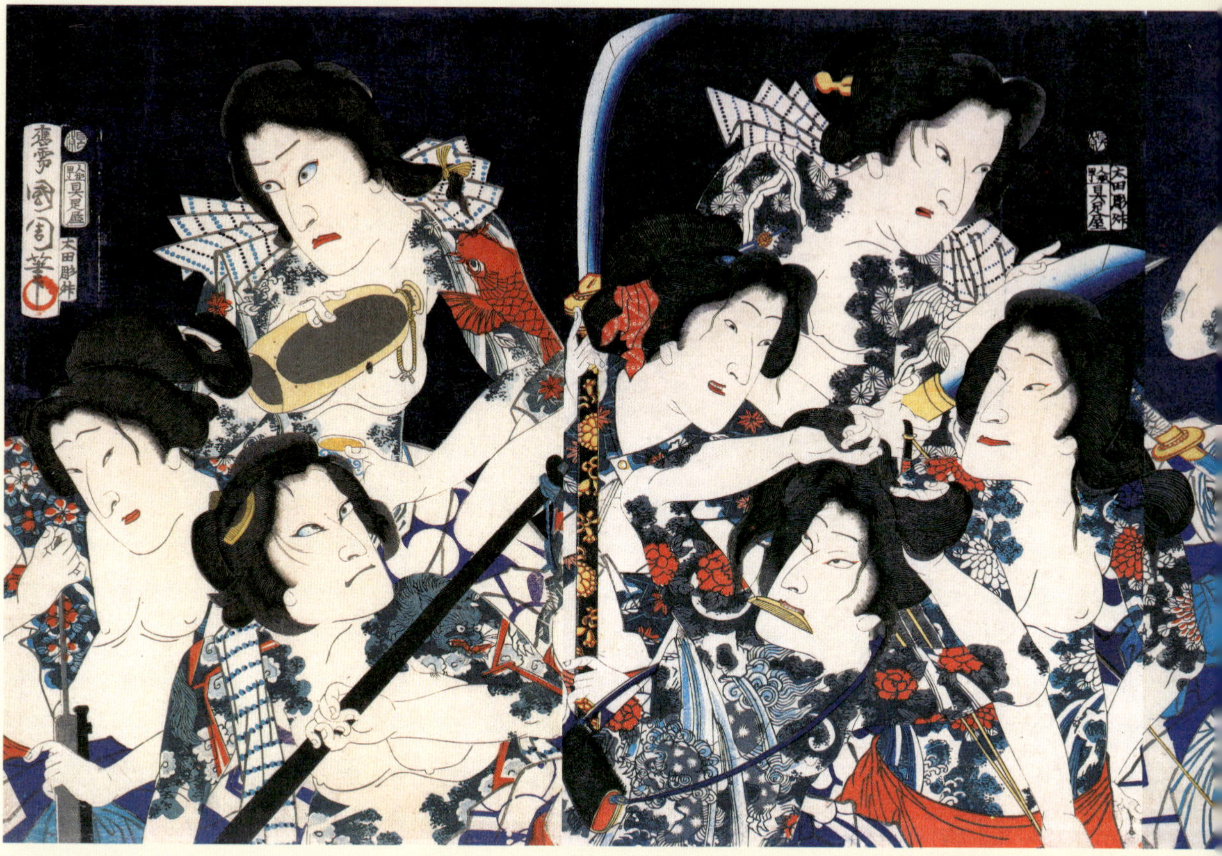
應需國周筆

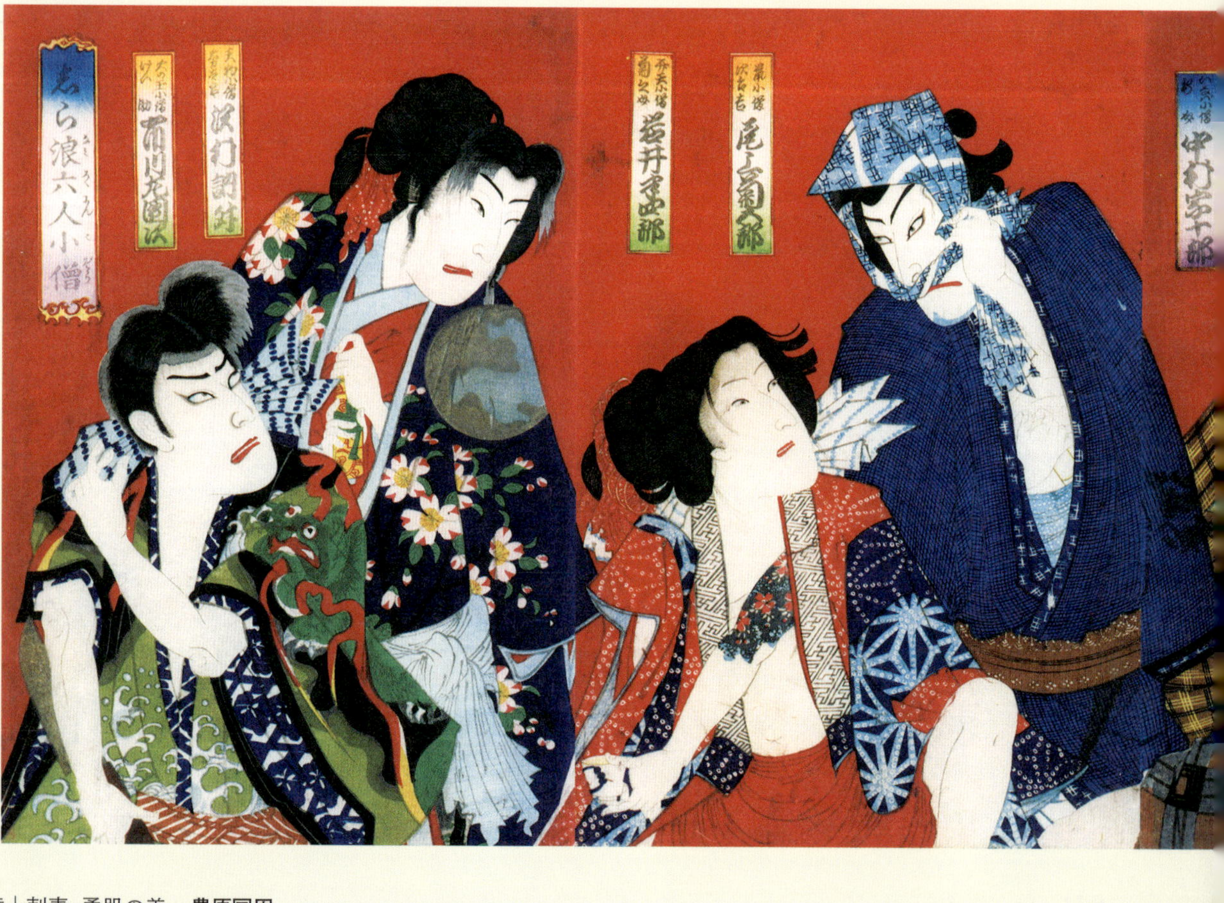
しら浪六人小僧
尾上菊五郎
中村宗十郎

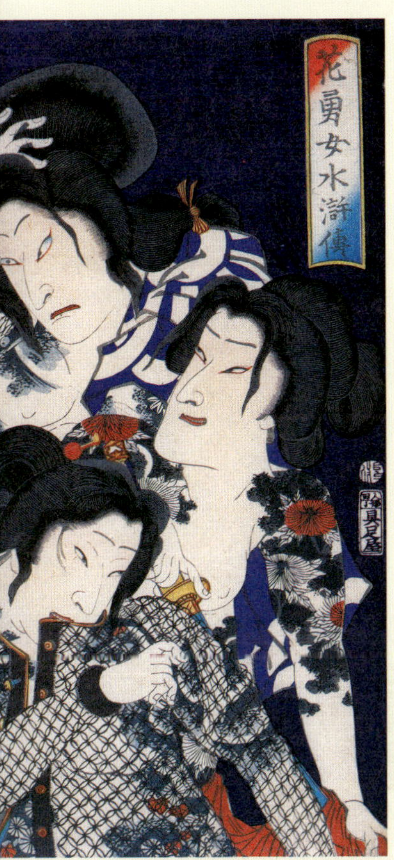

「花勇女水滸傳」豊原国周
Hanayūjo Suikoden, Toyohara Kunichika

明治 2 年・1869
山口県立萩美術館・浦上記念館蔵
1869, Hagi Uragami Museum

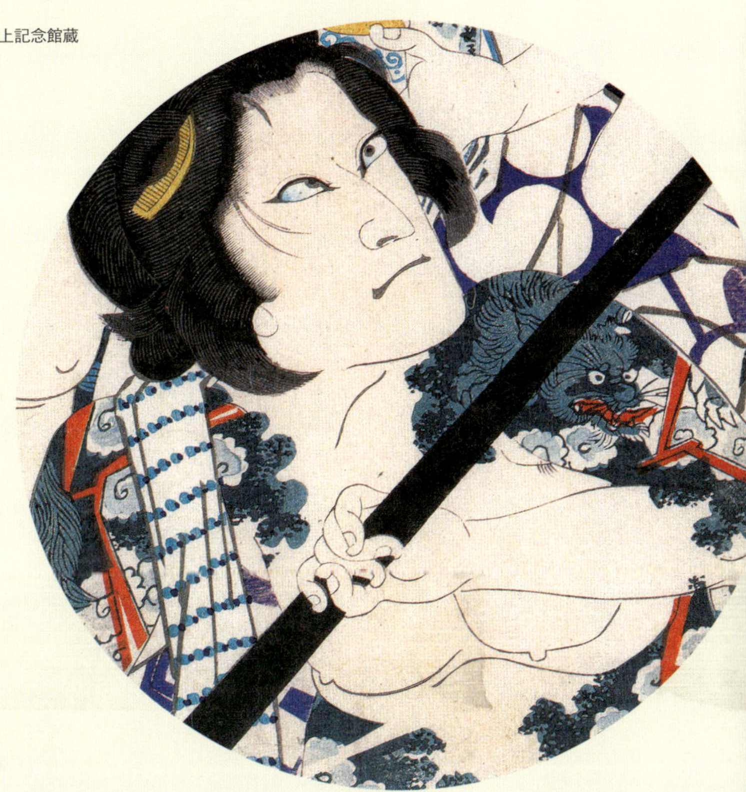

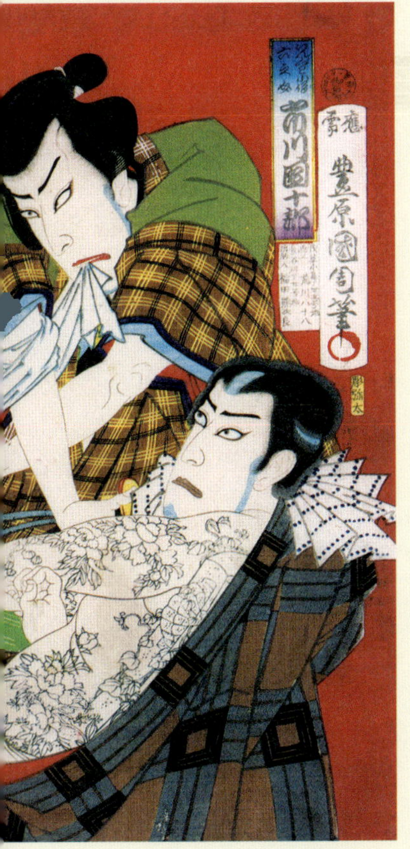

「しら浪六人小僧」「いんぐわ小僧六之介
市川團十郎・いなば小僧新介　中村宗十
郎・鼠小僧次郎吉　尾上菊五郎・弁天小
僧菊之介　岩井半四郎・天狗小僧忠力太
郎　沢村訥升・火の玉小僧けい助　市川
左團次」豊原国周
*Actors Ichikawa Danjūrō as Ingakozō-Rokunosuke,
Nakamura Sōjūrō as Inabakozō-Shinsuke, Onoe Kikugorō
as Nezumikozou-Jirokichi, Iwaihanshirou as Bentenkozō-
Kikunosuke, Sawamura Toshō as Tengukozō-Churikitarō,
Ichikawa Sadanji as Hinotamakozō-Keisuke, from the
Shiranamirokunin-Kozō, Toyohara Kunichika*

明治 11 年・1878　東京都立中央図書館特別文庫室蔵
1878, Tokyo Metropolitan Library

　Chapter 1 | Tattoos: The Beauty of the Heroes' Skin　**Toyohara Kunichika**

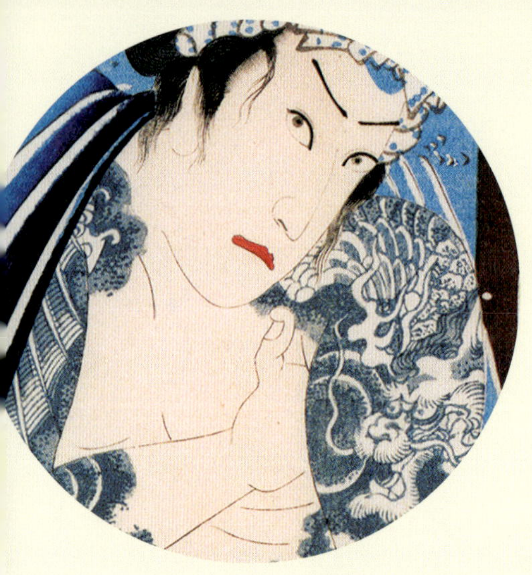

「當盛五人揃肌競」
「坂東彦三郎・沢村田之助・河原崎権十郎・
市村家橘・中村芝翫」豊原国周
Bandou Hikosaburō, Sawamura Tanosuke, Kawarazaki
Gonjurō, Ichimura Kakitsu , Nakamura Shikan, from the
Tose-Goninsoroi-Hadakurabe, Toyohara Kunichika

元治元年・1864　東京都立中央図書館特別文庫室蔵
1864, Tokyo Metropolitan Library

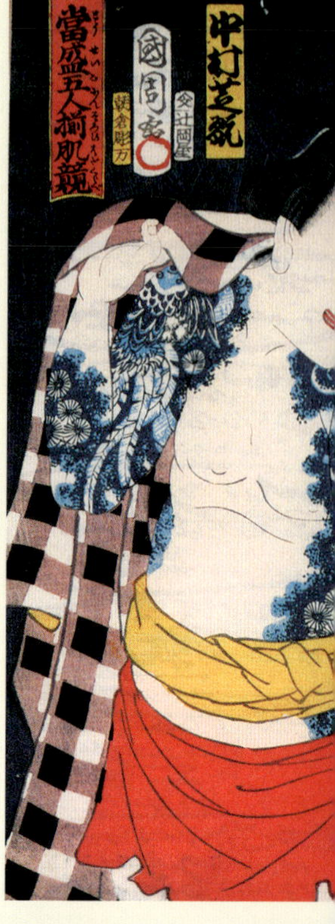

「伍俳優時世大山」「浪花の米松　市川右團次・魁の梅吉
尾上菊五郎・打出のおつち　助高屋高助・松川の蔦蔵
市川左團次・翫すゝめの福右衛門　中村芝翫」豊原国周
Actors Ichikawa Udanji as Naniwa-no-Yonematsu, Onoe Kikugorō as Kai-no-
Umekichi, Sukedakaya Takasuke as Uchide-no-Ozuchi, Ichikawa Sadanji as
Matsukawa-no-Tsutazō, Nakamura Shikan as Kanjaku-no-Fukuemon, from the
Goninzure-Tokini-Ooyama, Toyohara Kunichika

明治 15 年・1882　東京都立中央図書館特別文庫室蔵
1882, Tokyo Metropolitan Library

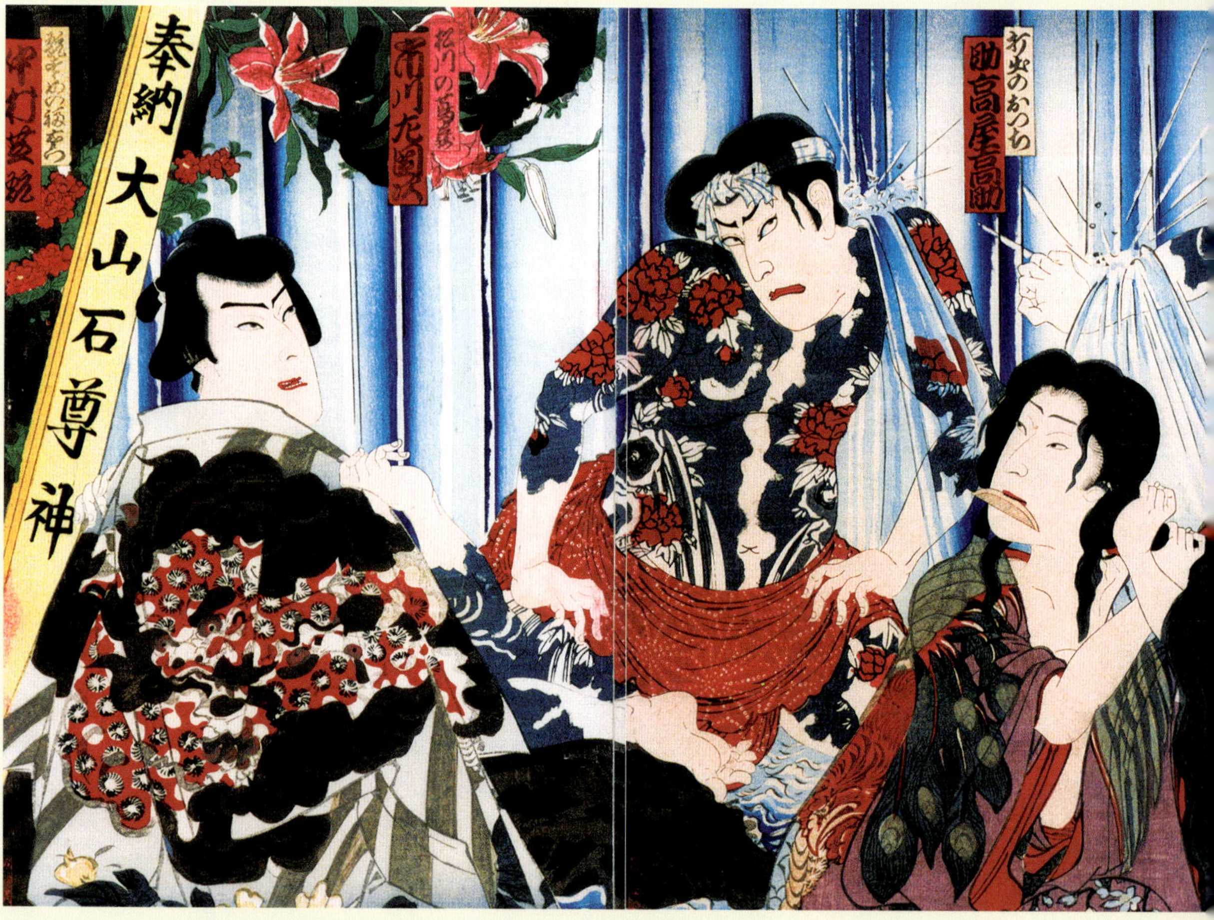

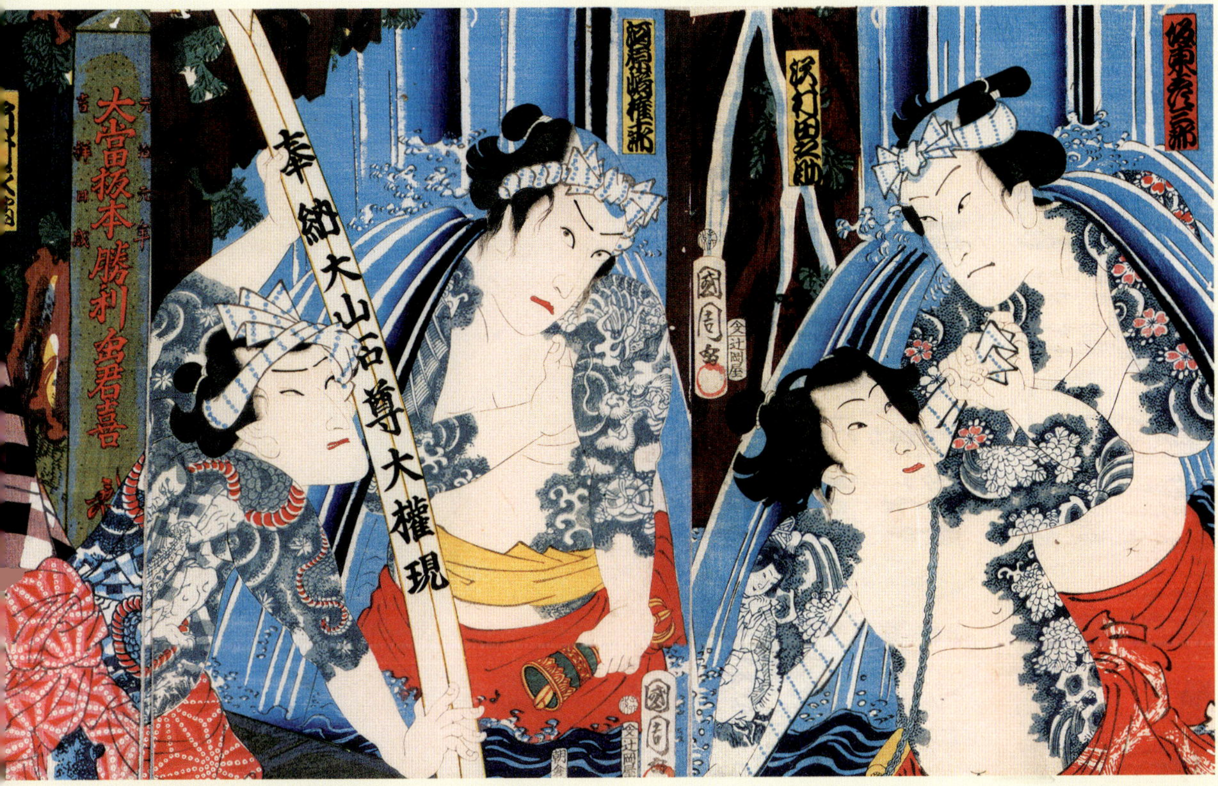

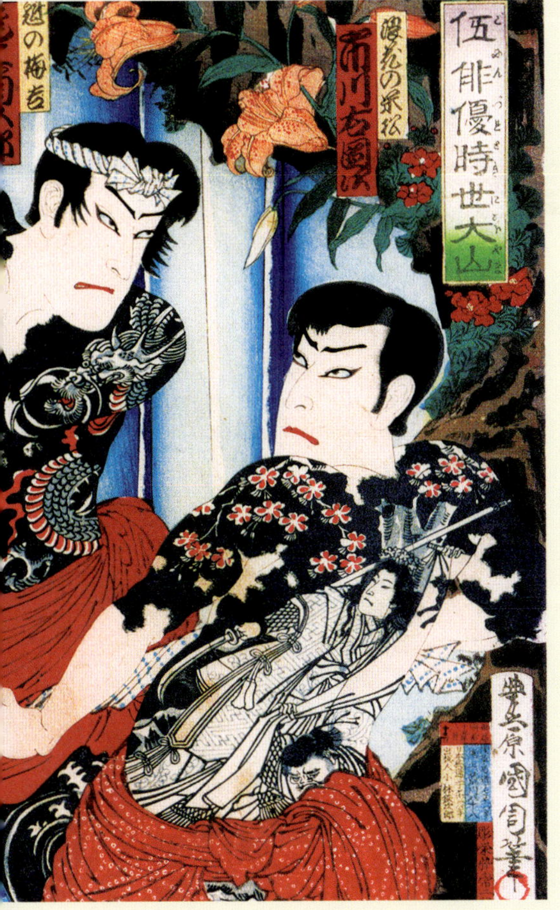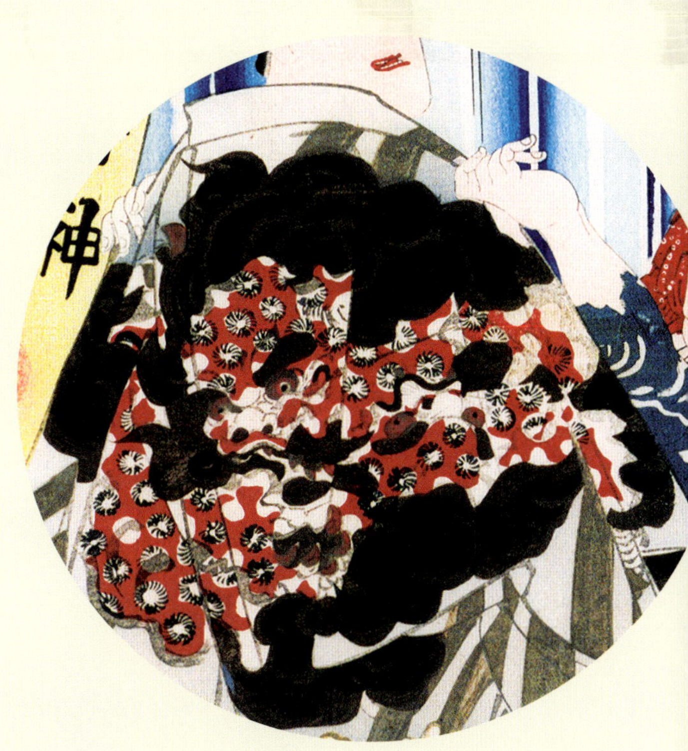

Chapter 1 | Tattoos: The Beauty of the Heroes' Skin **Toyohara Kunichika**

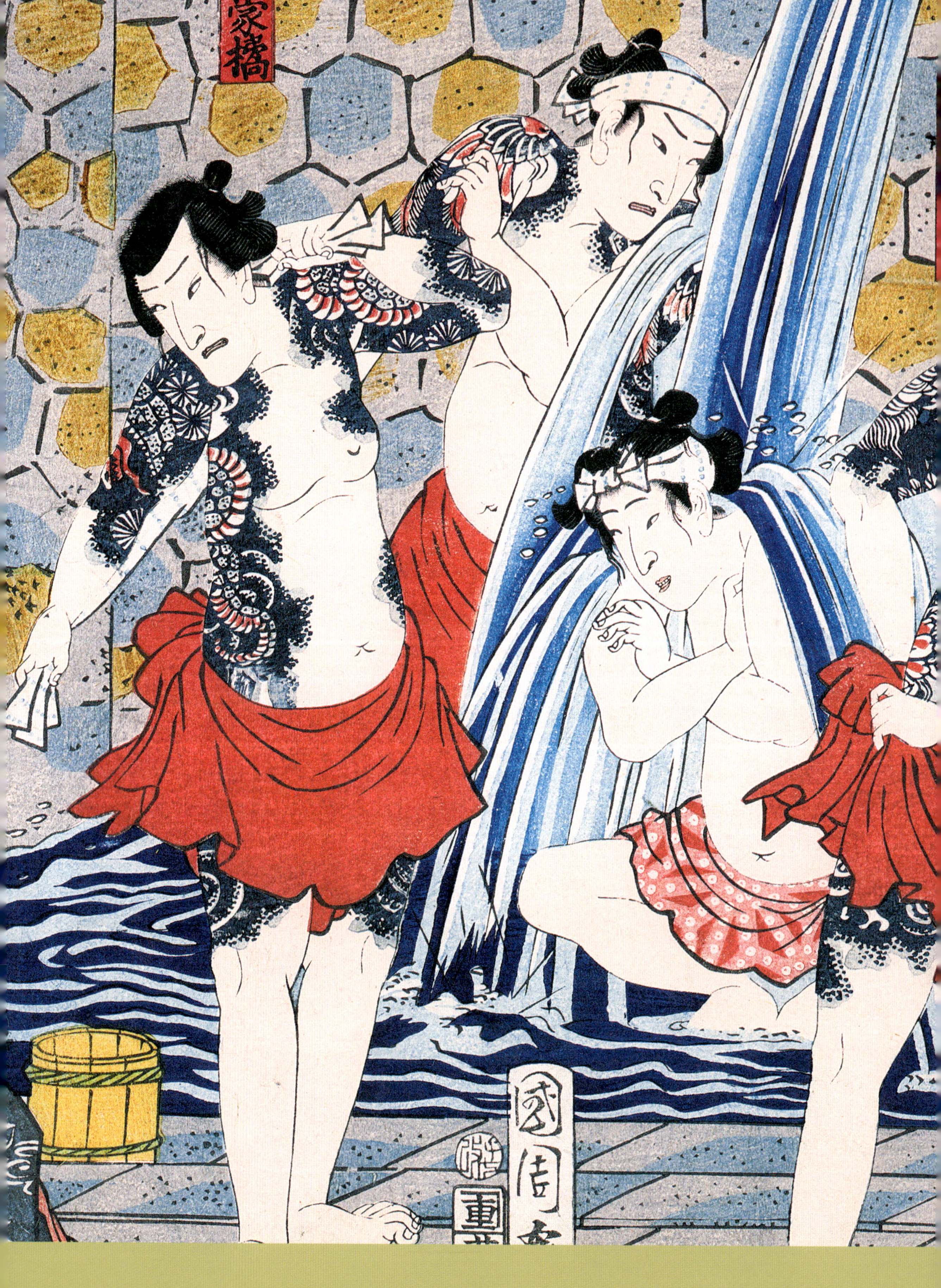
家橋
國周画

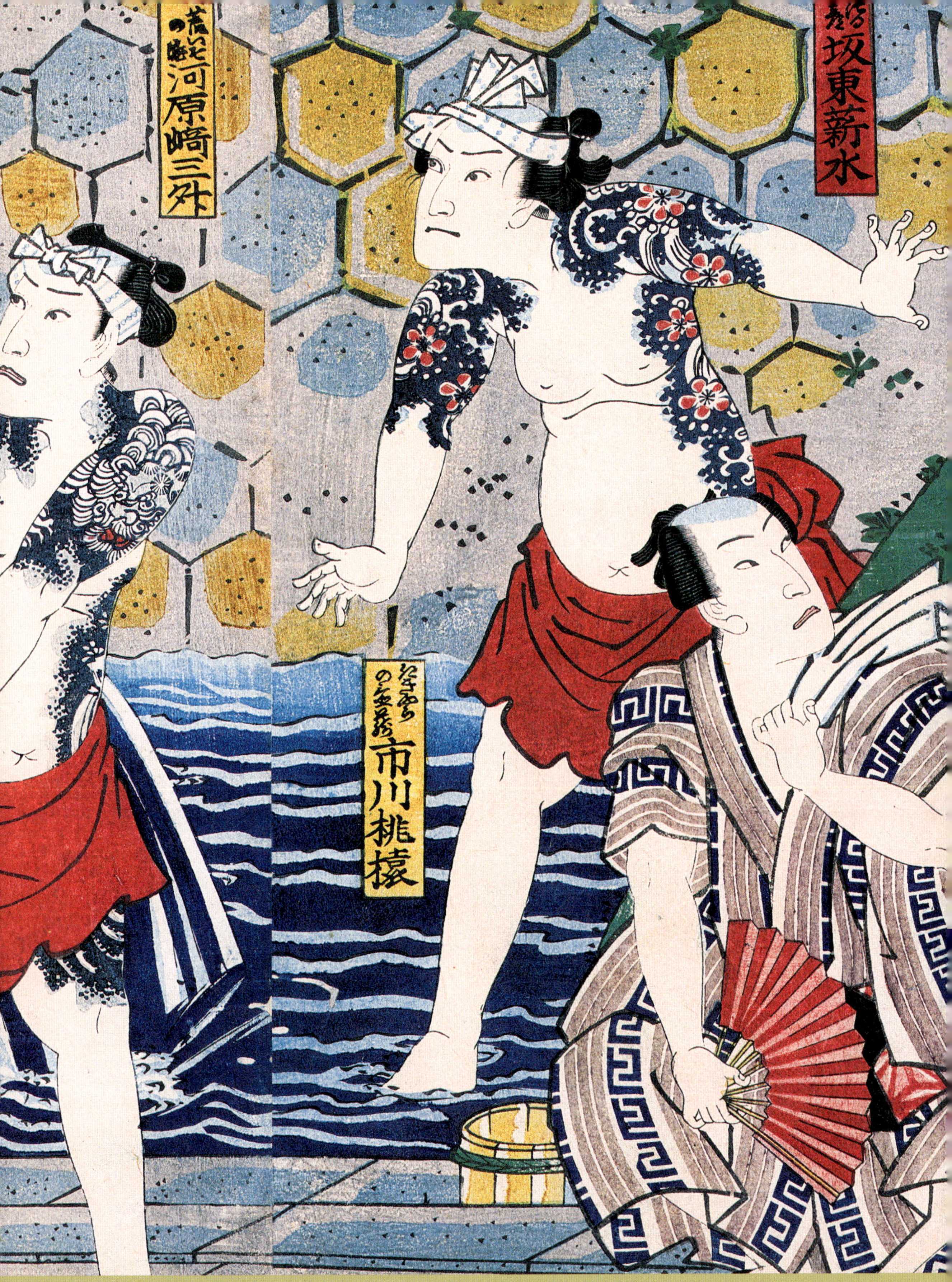

「俳優英雄王子の瀧催」「三ツ扇の粂吉　岩井燕子・舞づるの彦　坂東薪水・ききやうの□蔵　市川桃猿・荒いその瀧　河原崎三升・三ツ大吉　坂東しうか・うら梅の福　中村児雀・うす亀の市　市村家橘・□□□のお菊　沢村曙山・いびしの駒　中村芝翫・已引梅の国　沢村訥升」豊原国周（部分）

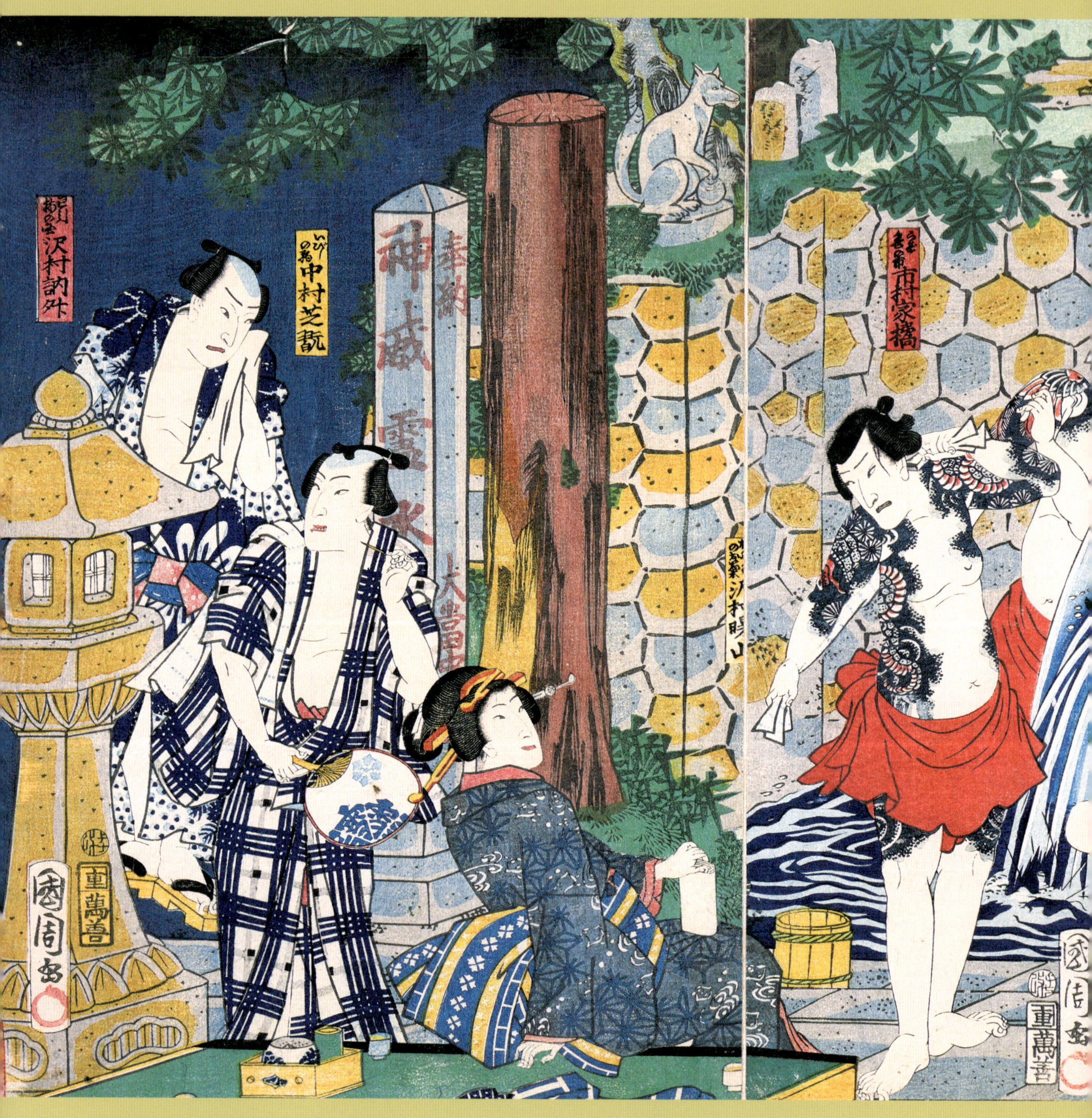

「俳優英雄王子の瀧催」「三ツ扇の粂吉　岩井燕子・舞づるの彦　坂東薪水・
ききやうの□蔵　市川桃猿・荒いその瀧　河原崎三升・三ツ大吉　坂東しうか・
うら梅の福　中村児雀・うす亀の市　市村家橘・□□□のお菊　沢村曙山・
いびしの駒　中村芝翫・巳引梅の国　沢村訥升」豊原国周

Actors Iwai Enshi as Mitsuou-no-Kumekichi, Bandō Shinsui as Maizulu-no-Hiko, Ichikawa Touen as Kikyō-no-□kura, Kawarazaki Sansho as Araiso-no-Taki, Bandō Shiuka as Mitsudaikichi, Nakamura Shijaku as Uraume-no-Fuku, Ichimura Kakitsu as Usukame-no-Ichi, Sawamura Shozan as □□□ -no-Okiku, Nakamura Shikan as Ibishi-no-Koma, Sawamura Totsushō as Ihikiume-no-Kuni, from the Kawatezoroi-Ouji-no-Kuwadate, Toyohara Kunichika

元治元年・1864　東京都立中央図書館特別文庫室蔵
1864, Tokyo Metropolitan Library

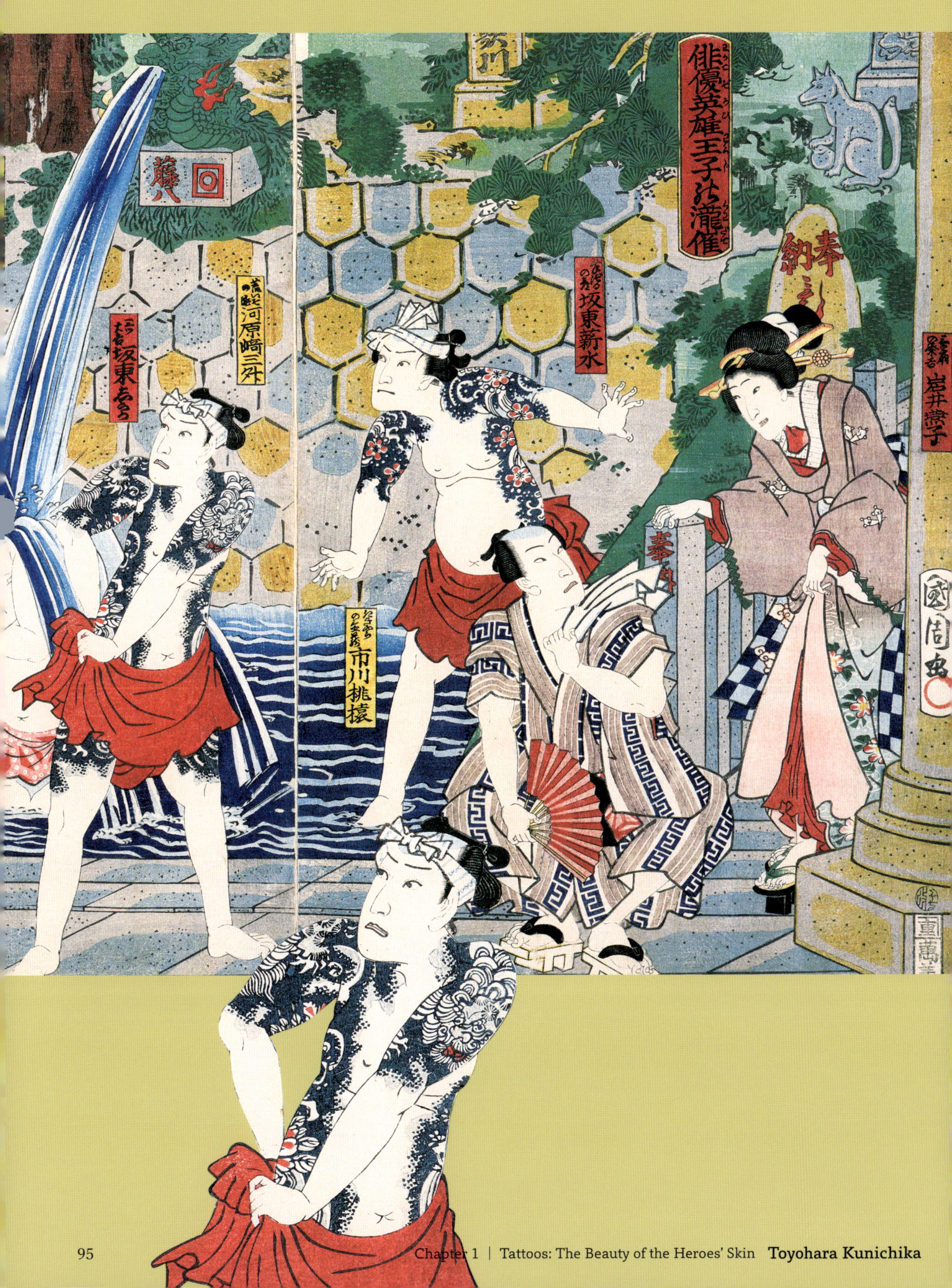

Chapter 1 | Tattoos: The Beauty of the Heroes' Skin **Toyohara Kunichika**

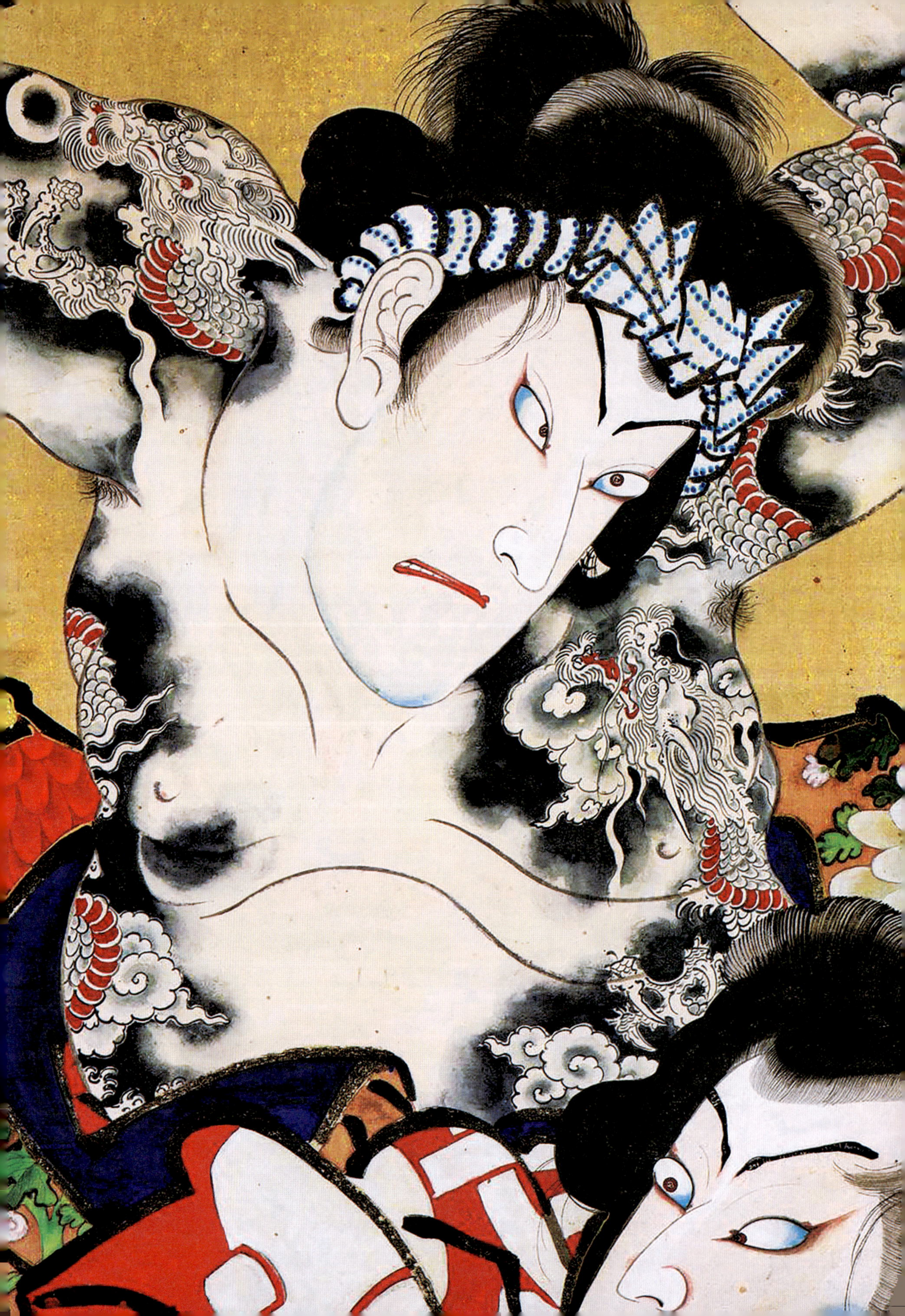

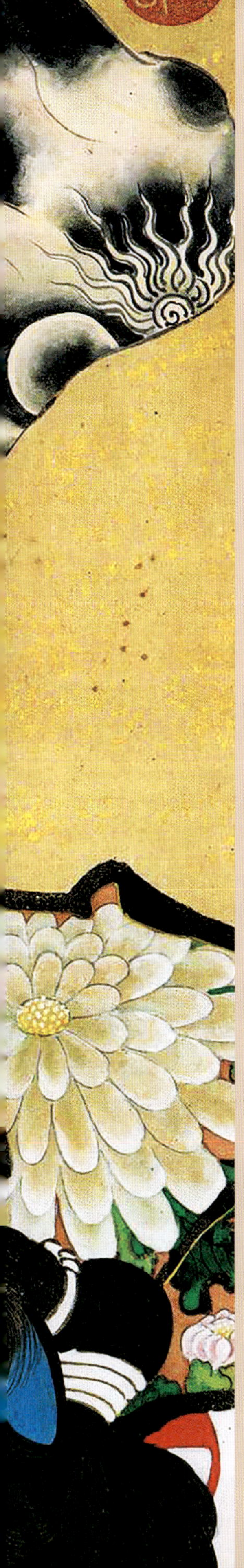

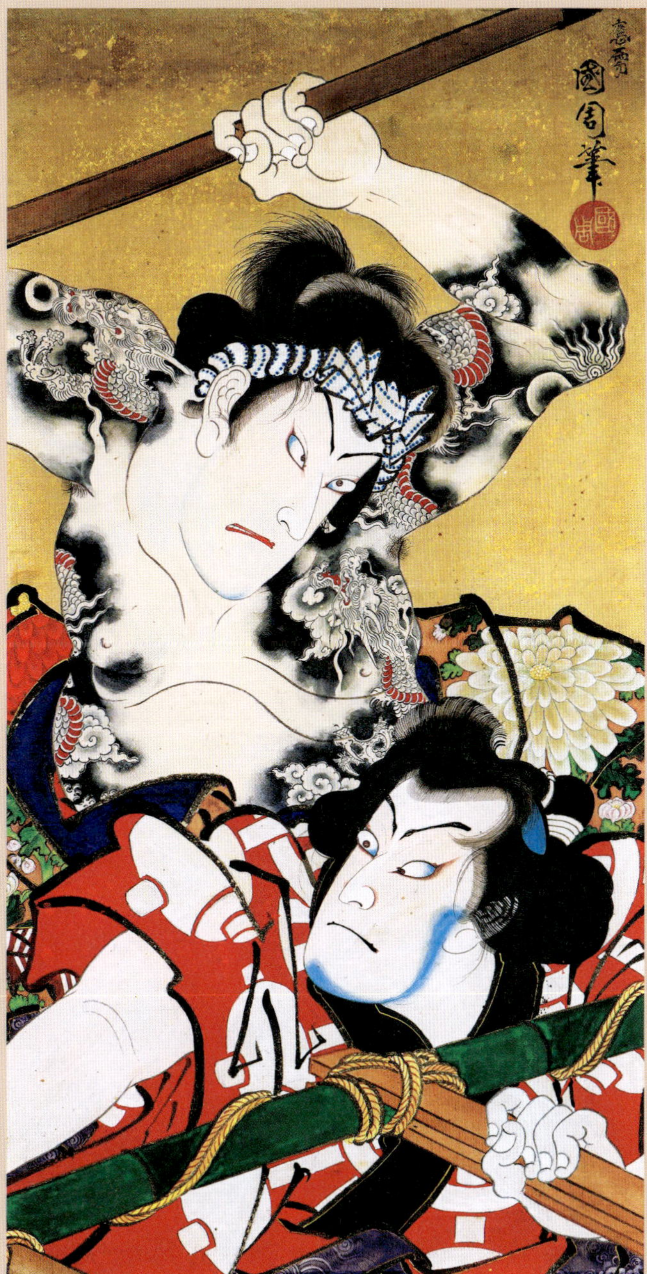

「め組の喧嘩」豊原国周
Megumi quarrel *(Megumi no-Kenka)*, Toyohara Kunichika
明治時代・19世紀　東京国立博物館蔵
出典：ColBase（https://colbase.nich.go.jp）
Meiji period, 19th century, Tokyo National Museum

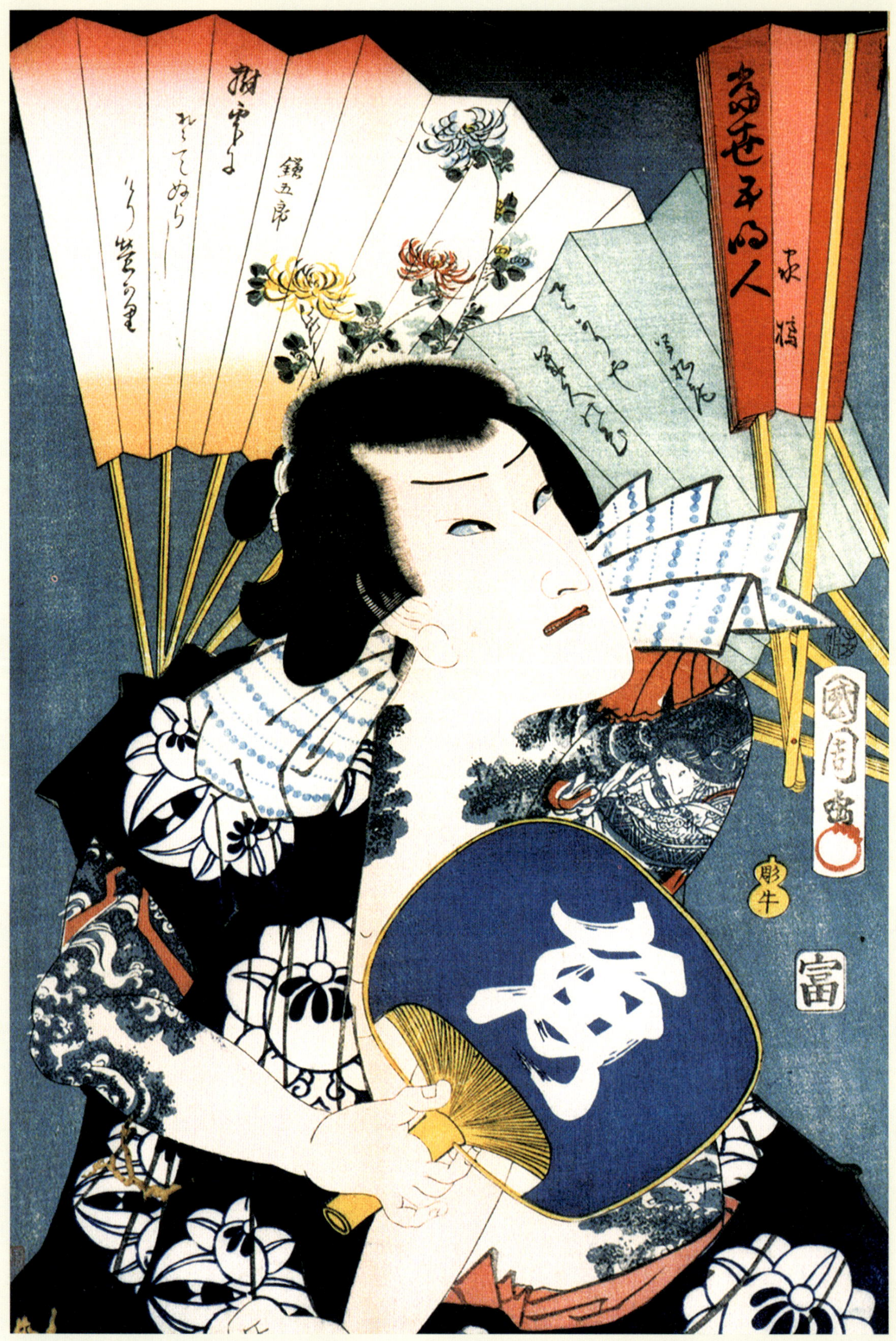

「當世五明人　家橘」豊原国周
Ichimura Kakitsu, from *the Tousei-Gomeijin*, Toyohara Kunichika

元治元年・1864　東京都立中央図書館特別文庫室蔵
1864, Tokyo Metropolitan Library

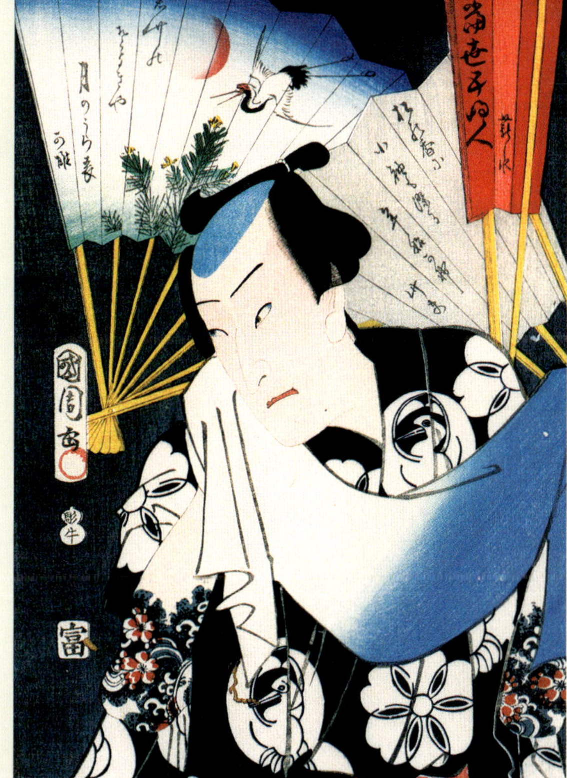

「當世五明人　薪水」豊原国周
Bando Shinsui , from the *Tousei-Gomeijin*,
Toyohara Kunichika
元治元年・1864
東京都立中央図書館特別文庫室蔵
1864, Tokyo Metropolitan Library

「當世五明人　芝翫」豊原国周
Nakamura Shikan, from the *Tousei-Gomeijin*,
Toyohara Kunichika
元治元年・1864　東京都立中央図書館特別文庫室蔵
1864, Tokyo Metropolitan Library

「當世五明人　三升」豊原国周
Kawarazaki Sanshou, from the *Tousei-Gomeijin*,
Toyohara Kunichika
元治元年・1864　東京都立中央図書館特別文庫室蔵
1864, Tokyo Metropolitan Library

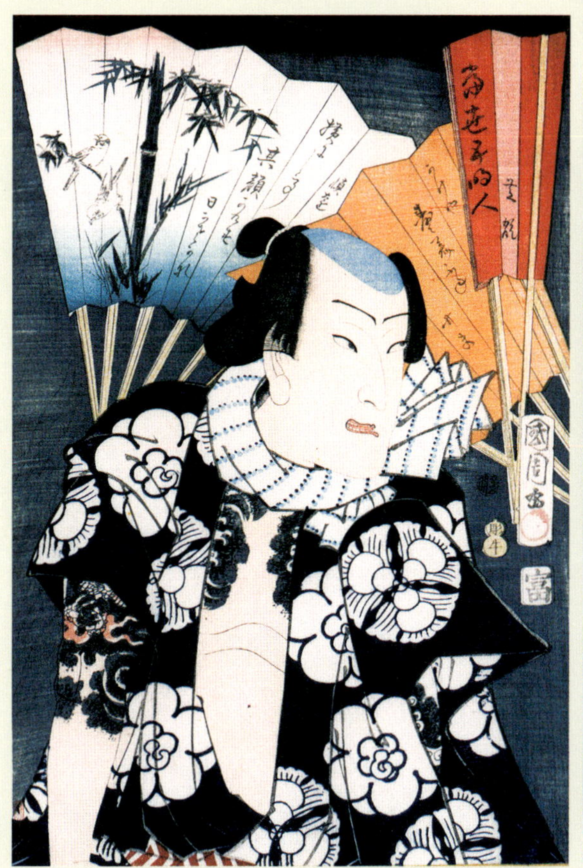

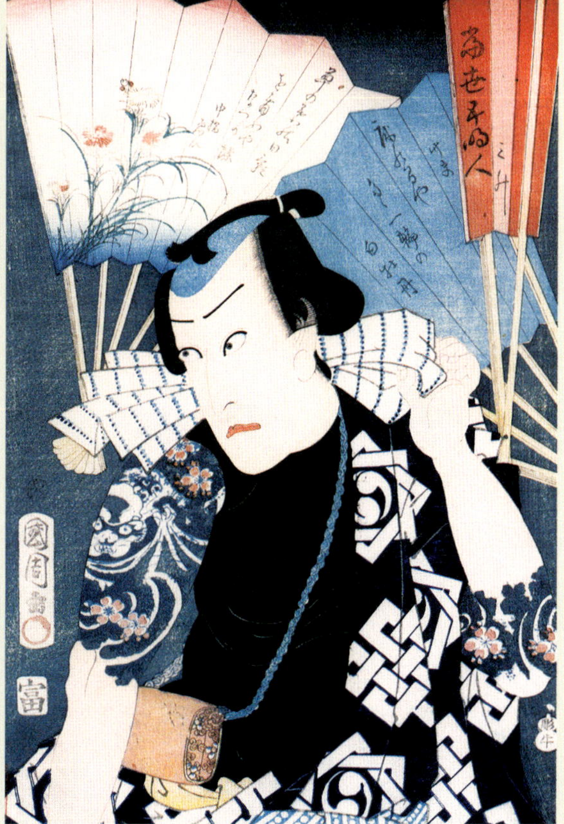

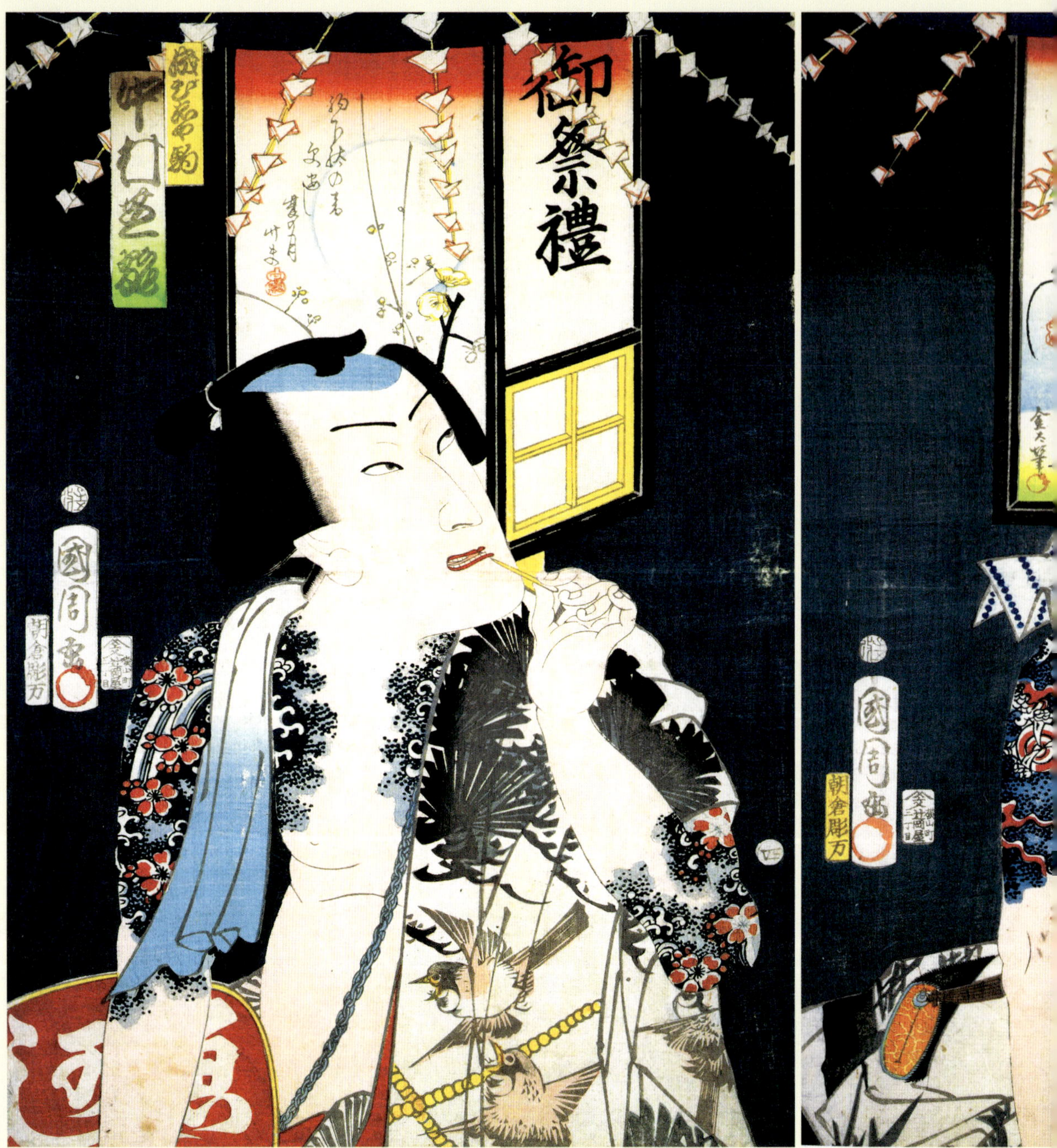

「成びしゃ駒　中村芝翫」豊原国周
Actors Nakamura Shikan as *Narubisha-Koma*, Toyohara Kunichika
元治元年・1864　国立国会図書館デジタルコレクション
1864, National Diet Library Digital Collections

「音羽屋瀧　坂東彦三郎」豊原国周
Actors Bandō Hikosaburō as *Otowaya-Taki*, Toyohara Kunichika
元治元年・1864　国立国会図書館デジタルコレクション
1864, National Diet Library Digital Collections

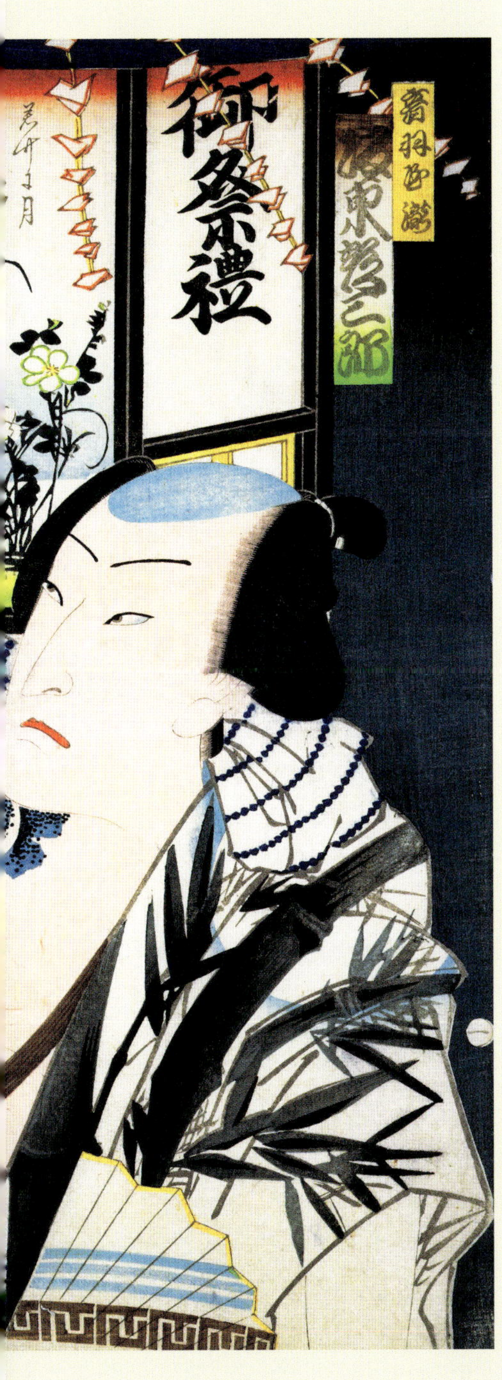

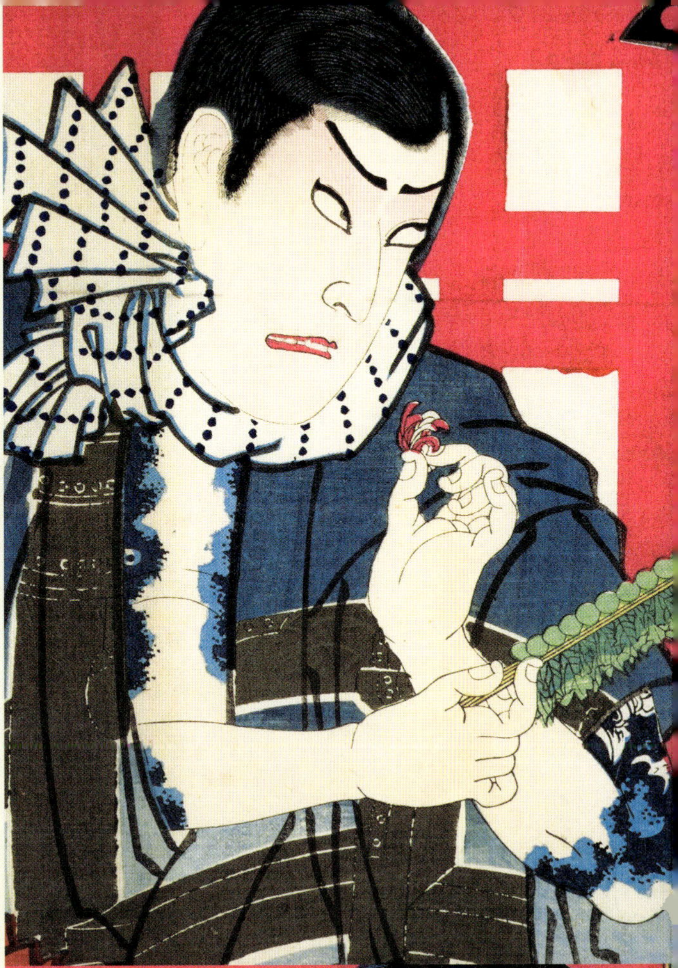

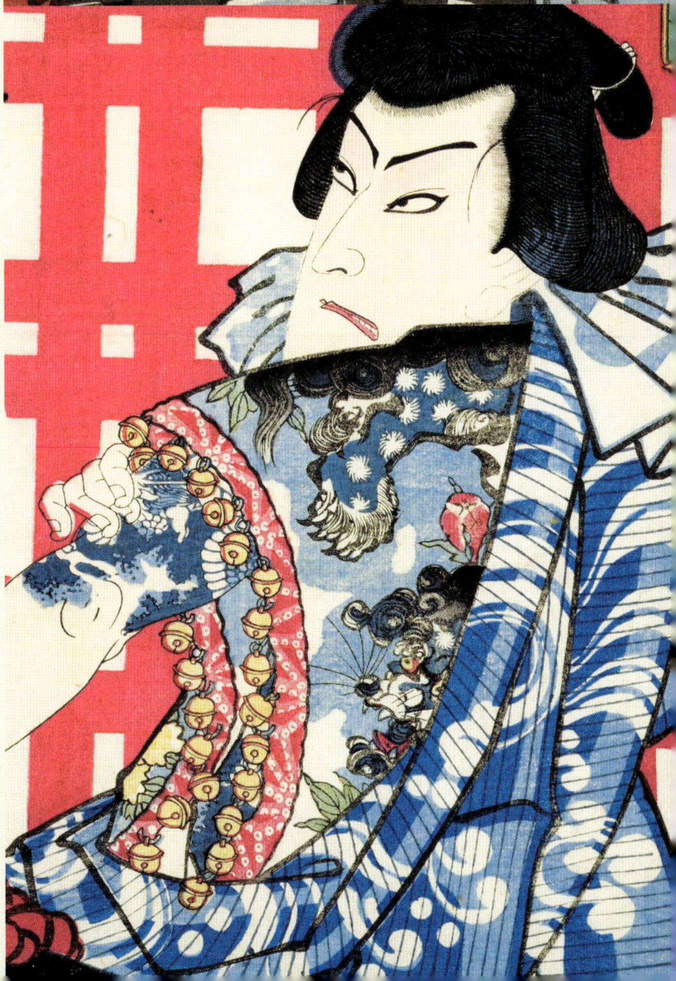

「見立弁慶揃　五条橋　市川左團次」
（部分）豊原国周
Actors Ichikawa Sadanji as *the Mitate-Benkeizoroi Gojōbashi*, Detail, Toyohara Kunichika
明治 5 年・1872　国立国会図書館デジタルコレクション
1872, National Diet Library Digital Collections

「見立弁慶揃　台物の浦　尾上菊五郎」
（部分）豊原国周
Actors Onoe Kikugorō as *the Mitate-Benkeizoroi Daimono-no-ura*, Detail, Toyohara Kunichika
明治 5 年・1872　国立国会図書館デジタルコレクション
1872, National Diet Library Digital Collections

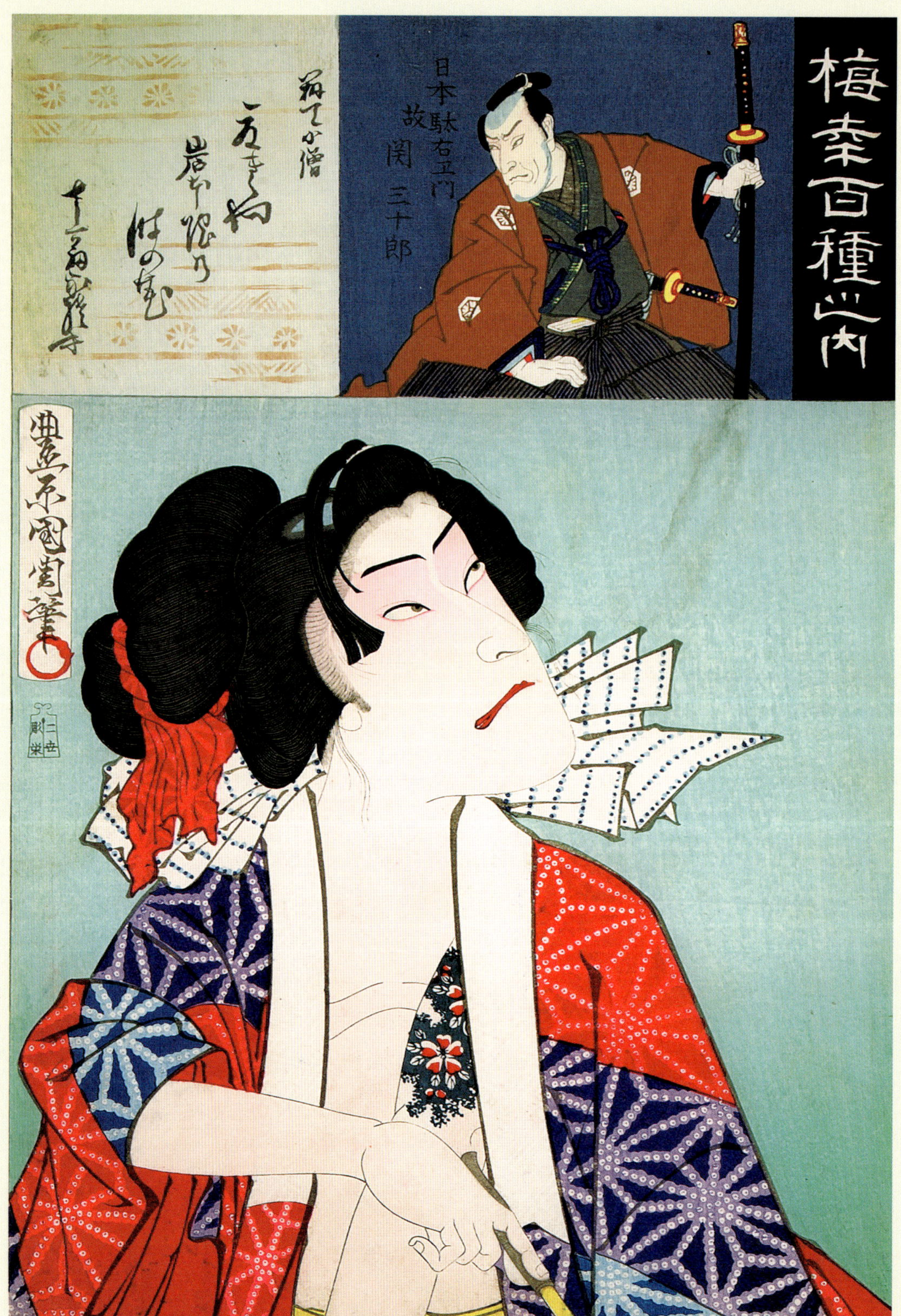

「梅幸百種之内　弁天小僧　尾上菊五郎」豊原国周
Actors Onoe Kikugorō as Bentenkozō, from the *Baiko Hyakusu-no-uchi*,
Toyohara Kunichika

明治 26 年・1893　東京都立中央図書館特別文庫室蔵
1893, Tokyo Metropolitan Library

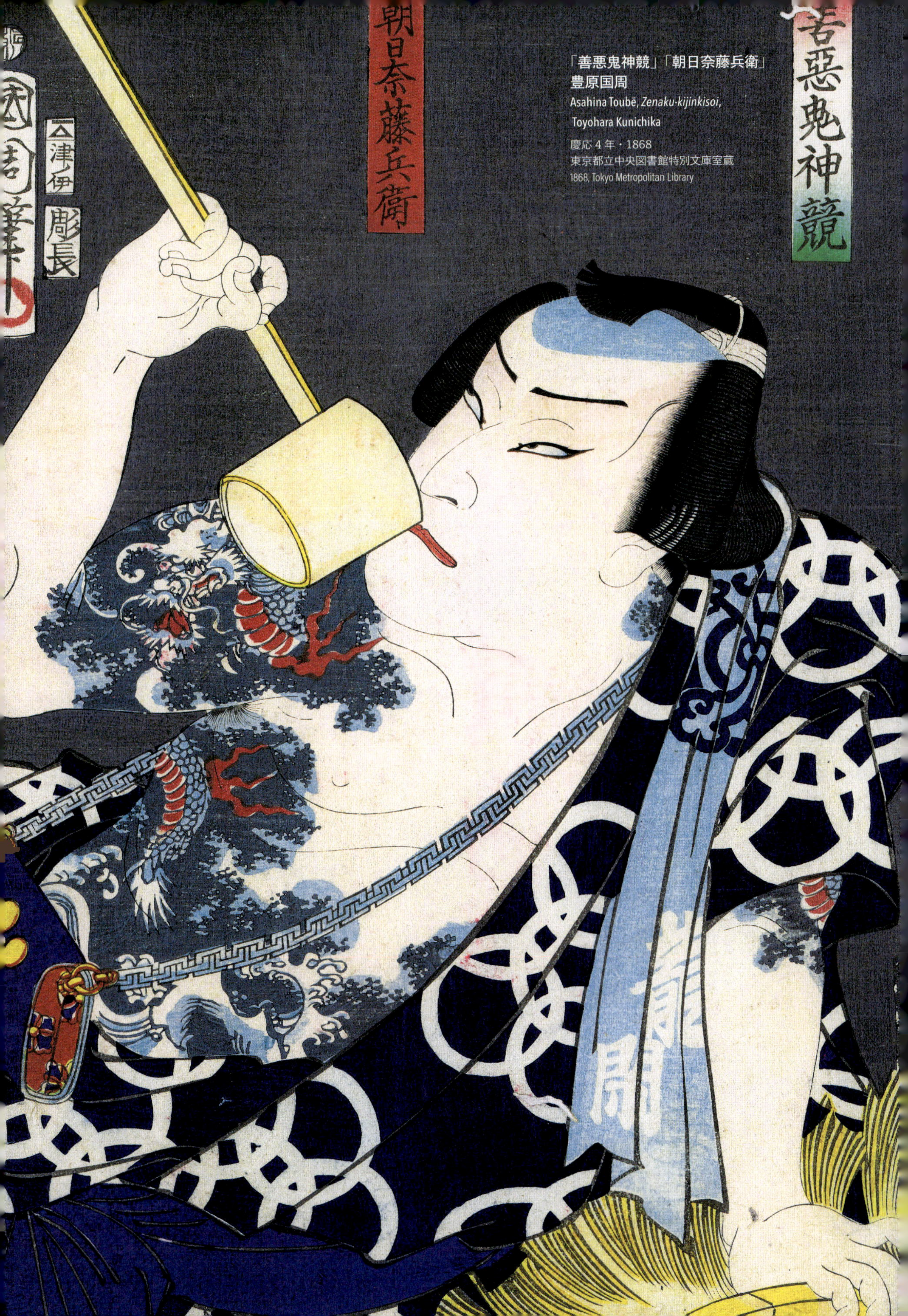

「善悪鬼神競」「朝日奈藤兵衛」
豊原国周

Asahina Toubē, *Zenaku-kijinkisoi*,
Toyohara Kunichika

慶応 4 年・1868
東京都立中央図書館特別文庫室蔵
1868, Tokyo Metropolitan Library

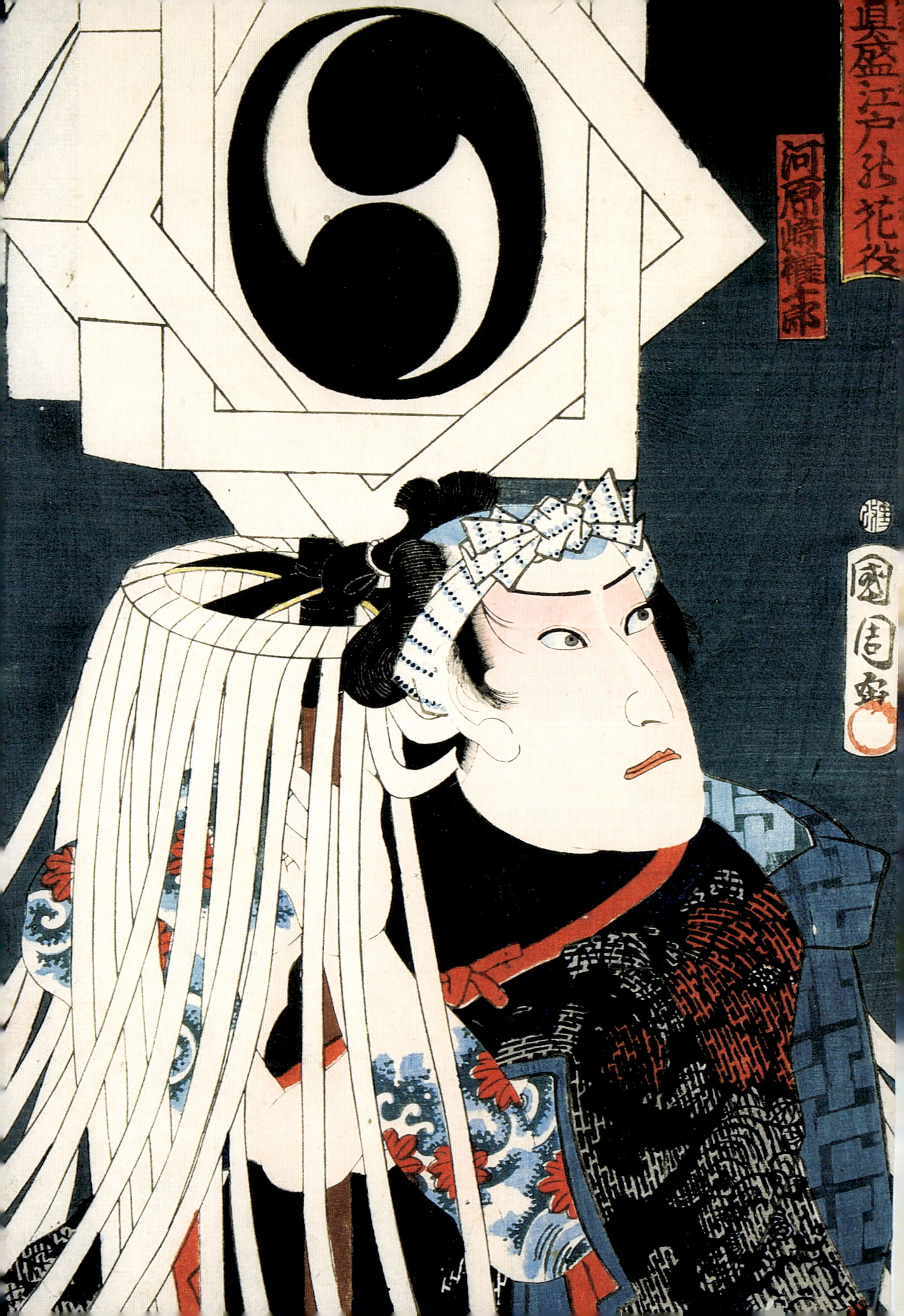
見盛江戸ノ花役
河原崎權十郎
國周画

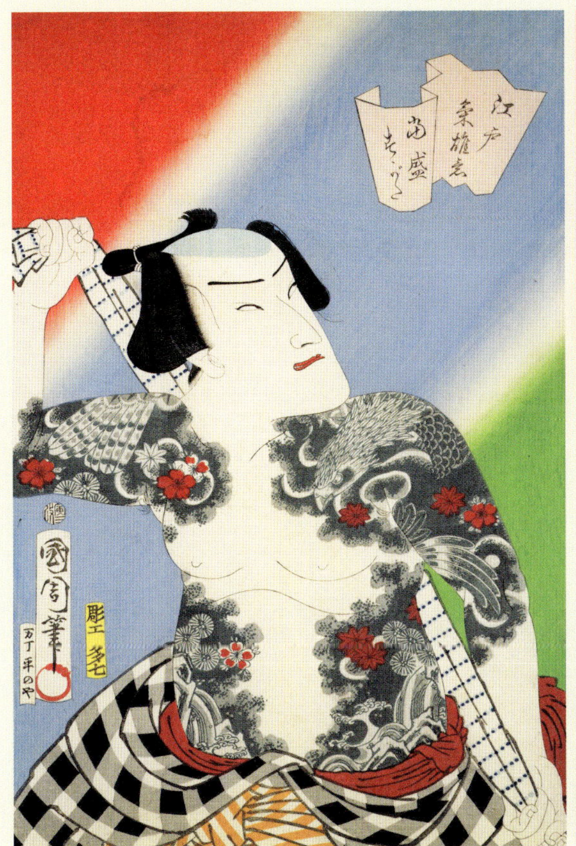

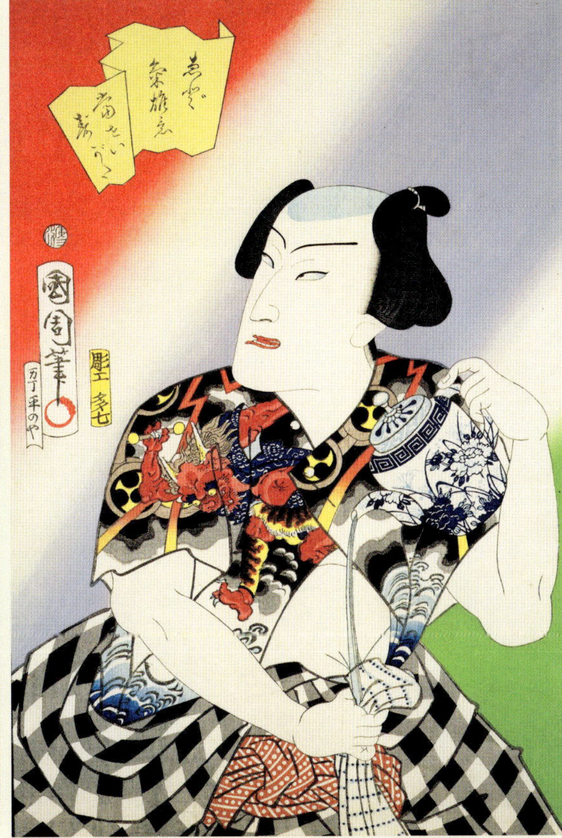

「江戸気雄意當盛すがた」（四代目市村家橘）
豊原国周

Actor Ichimura Kakitsu IV, from the series *Modern Figures with Edo Spirit (Edokioi-tōseisugata)*, Toyohara Kunichika

慶応２年・1866　国立国会図書館デジタルコレクション
1866, National Diet Library Digital Collections

「江戸気雄意當盛すがた」豊原国周

The series *Modern Figures with Edo Spirit (Edokioi-tōseisugata)*, Toyohara Kunichika

国立国会図書館デジタルコレクション
National Diet Library Digital Collections

「見立十二時之内　巳　弁天小僧
尾上菊五郎」豊原国周

Actors Onoe Kikugorō as the *Mitate-jūniji-no-uchi Mi Bentenkozō*, Toyohara Kunichika

明治７年・1874　山口県立萩美術館・浦上記念館蔵
1874, Hagi Uragami Museum

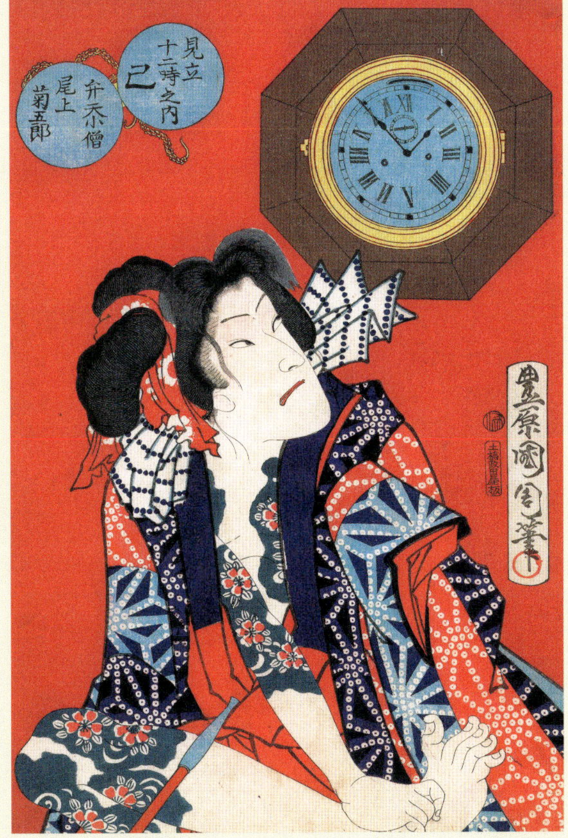

「真盛江戸の花役　河原崎権十郎」
豊原国周

Kawarazaki Gonjūrō, *Matsusakari-Edo-no-Hanagata*, Toyohara Kunichika

明治７年・1874　東京都立中央図書館特別文庫室
1874, Tokyo Metropolitan Library

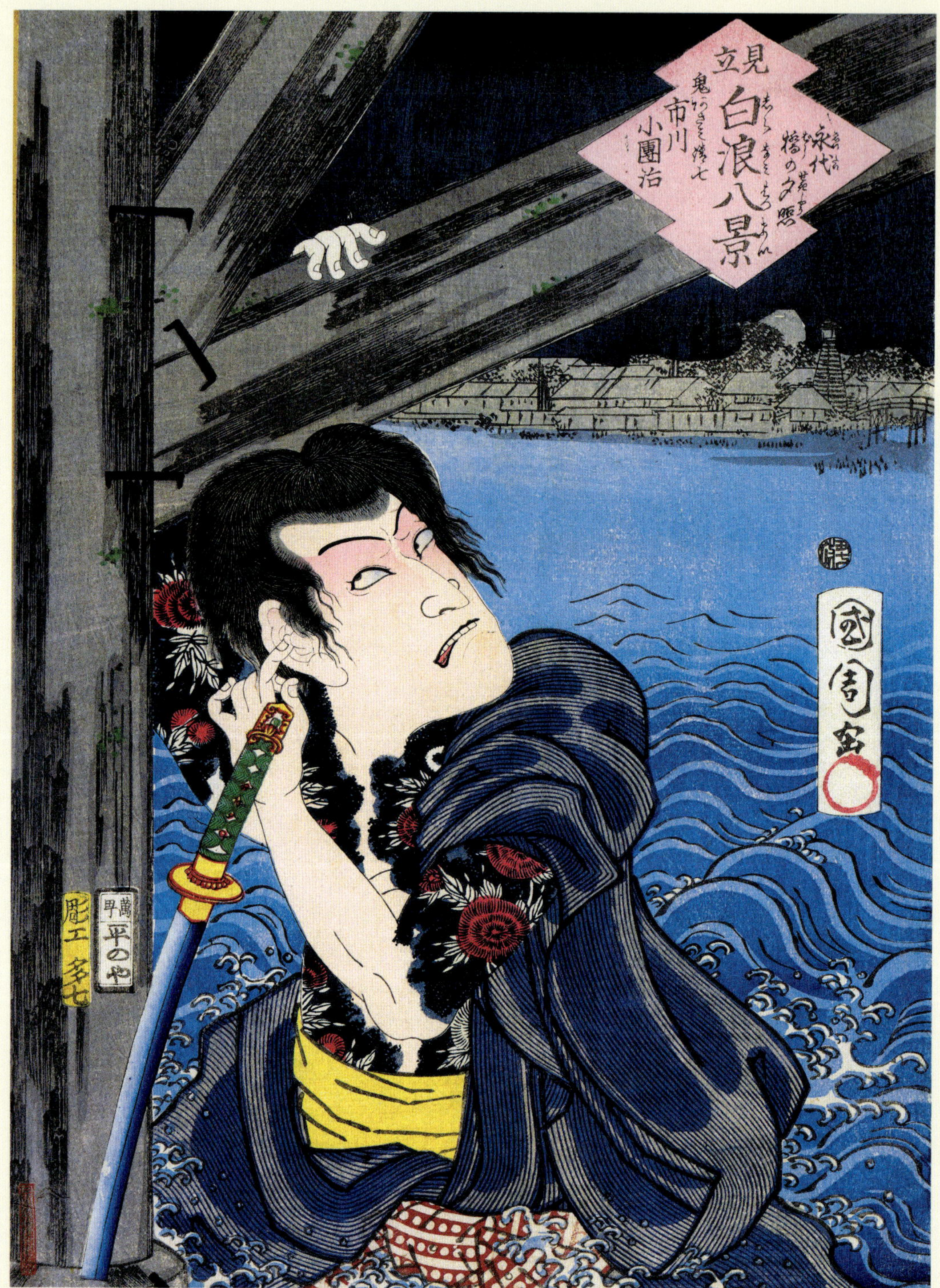

「見立白浪八景　永代橋の夕照・
鬼あざみ清七　市川小團次」豊原国周
Actors Ichikawa Kodanji as Oniazami Seishichi, Eitaibashi-no-
sekisho, from *Mitate-Shiranamihatsukei*, Toyohara Kunichika

慶応元年・1865　東京都立中央図書館特別文庫室蔵
1865, Tokyo Metropolitan Library

「鳶の伝吉　市村家橘」豊原国周
Actor Ichimura Kakitsu as Tobi-no-denkichi, Toyohara Kunichika

元治元年・1864　東京都立中央図書館特別文庫室蔵
1865, Tokyo Metropolitan Library

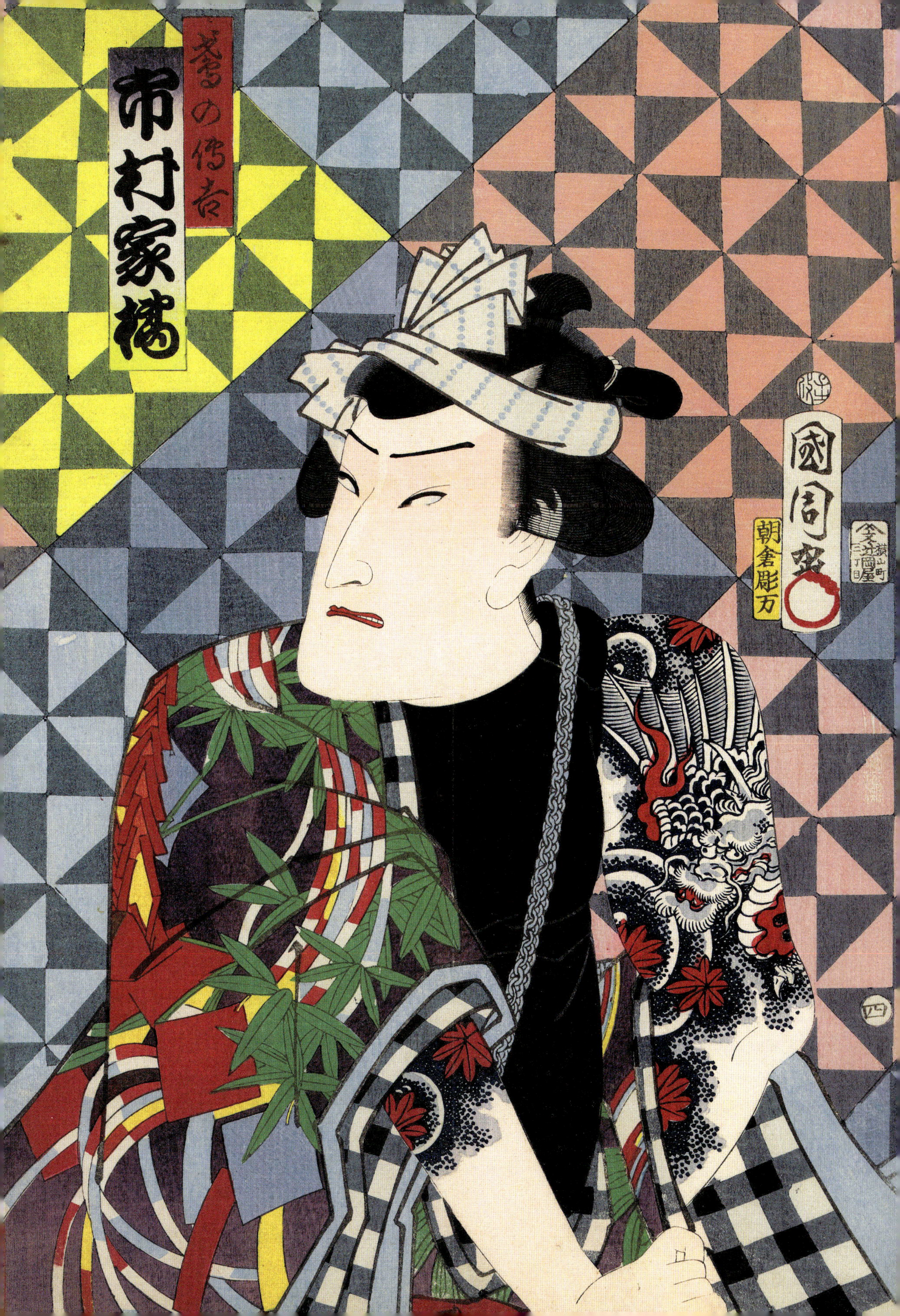

若の伊吾
市村家橘
國周画
朝倉彫万
横山町三丁目
和泉屋

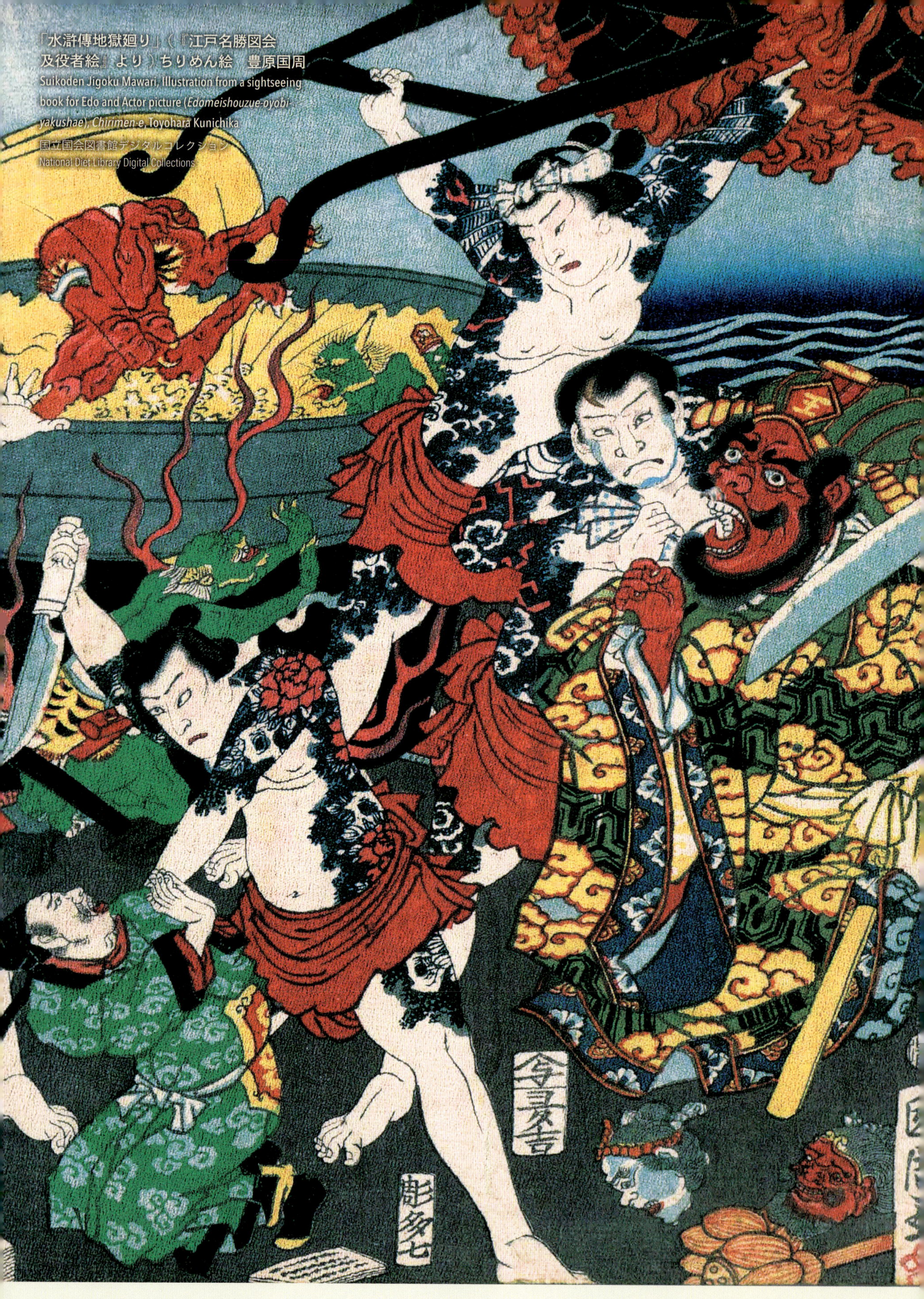
「水滸傳地獄廻り」（『江戸名勝図会
及役者絵』より）ちりめん絵　豊原国周
Suikoden Jigoku Mawari, Illustration from a sightseeing
book for Edo and Actor picture (Edomeishouzue-oyobi-
yakushae), Chirimen-e, Toyohara Kunichika
国立国会図書館デジタルコレクション
National Diet Library Digital Collections

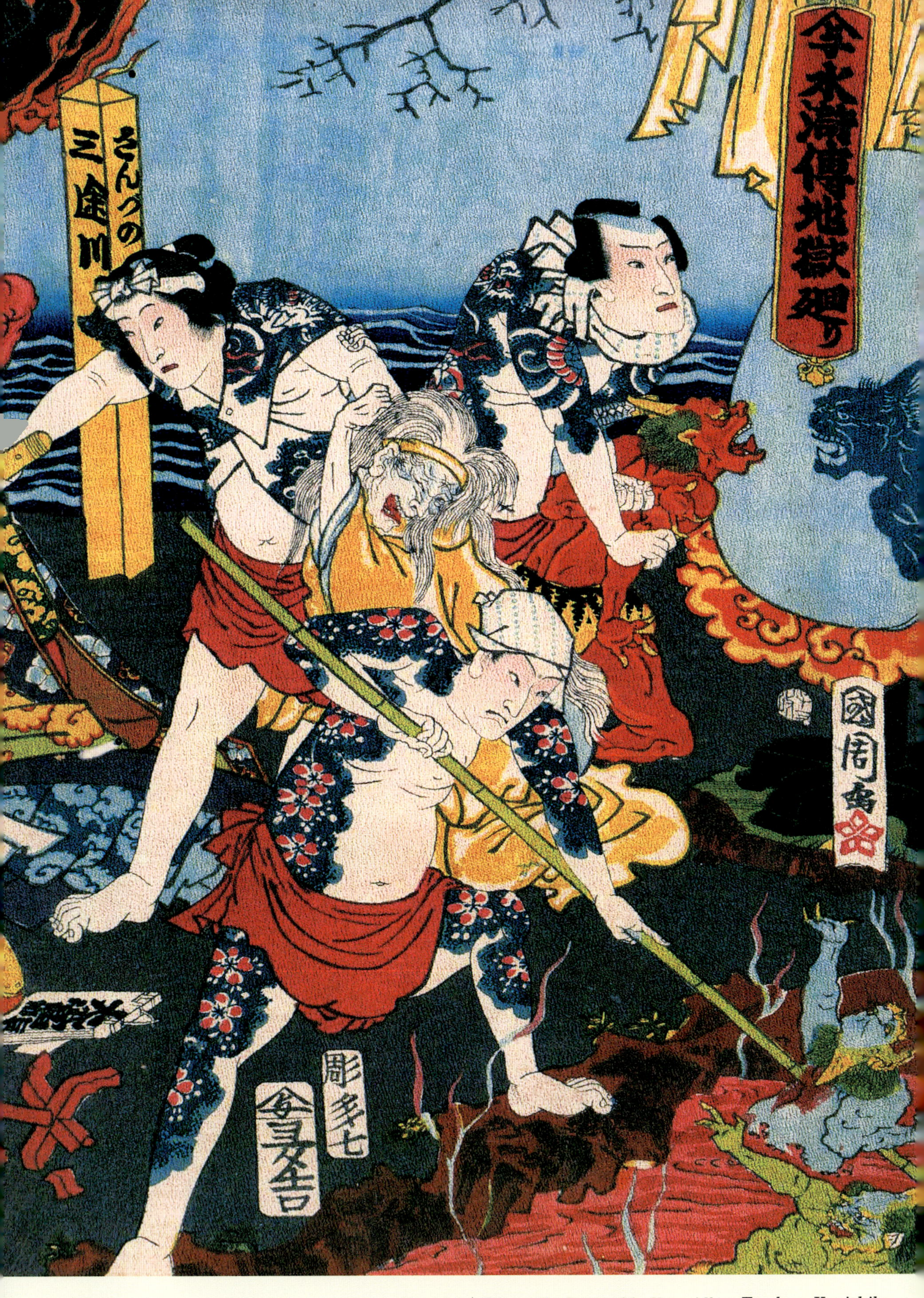

Chapter 1 | Tattoos: The Beauty of the Heroes' Skin **Toyohara Kunichika**

歌川芳艶

うたがわ よしつや
文政 5 年～慶応 2 年（1822-1866）

　江戸時代後期の浮世絵師。歌川国芳の門人。武者絵を得意とした。国芳の門弟の一人として活躍したが、月岡芳年や落合芳幾など並み居る才能ある同門たちの存在に隠れて、名前は殆ど知られていないが、国芳の武者絵を最もよく受け継いだ絵師である。刺青の下絵や江戸浅草奥山の生き人形の看板絵で知られた。

Utagawa Yoshitsuya 1822-1866

Late Edo-period Ukiyo-e Artist. A student of Utagawa Kuniyoshi, his forte was warrior pictures. While active as a member of Kuniyoshi's school, he was overshadowed by fellow members of that school, including Tsukioka Yoshitoshi and Ochiai Yoshiiku, and his name is hardly known. He was, however, the artist who most successfully carried on Kuniyoshi's warrior picture style. He was also known for producing underdrawings for tattoos and the signage for the *Iki Ningyo*, life-sized, hyperrealistic figures displayed at the popular Asakusa Okuyama recreation area in Edo.

「吉三　岡嶋屋　嵐　おかじま」
（江戸の花夜の賑）歌川芳艶
KIchizo Okajimaya, Flowers of Edo, Burning at night, (*Edo-no-hana, Yoru-no-nigiwai*), Detail, Utagawa Yoshitsuya

「澤村　きのくに」
（火消姿絵）歌川芳艶
Sawamura Kinokuni, Firefighter style (*Hikeshi-sugata*), Detail, Utagawa Yoshitsuya

「□嶋　市川　高　米升」
（江戸の花夜の賑）歌川芳艶
□shima Ichikawa, Flowers of Edo, Burning at night, (*Edo-no-hana, Yoru-no-nigiwai*), Detail, Utagawa Yoshitsuya

「権　かわら　佐木」
（江戸の花夜の賑）歌川芳艶
Gon Kawara, Flowers of Edo, Burning at night, (*Edo-no-hana, Yoru-no-nigiwai*), Detail, Utagawa Yoshitsuya

「浅田屋　浅尾　尾長　与六」
（火消姿絵）歌川芳艶
Asao Asadaya, Firefighter style (*Hikeshi-sugata*), Detail, Utagawa Yoshitsuya

「江戸花夜の賑　成駒
中むら　芝」歌川芳艶
Nakamura Narukoma, Flowers of Edo, Burning at night,(Edo-no-hana, Yoru-no-nigiwai), Detail, Utagawa Yoshitsuya

すべて（部分）　万延元年・1860　国立国会図書館デジタルコレクション　1860, National Diet Library Digital Collections

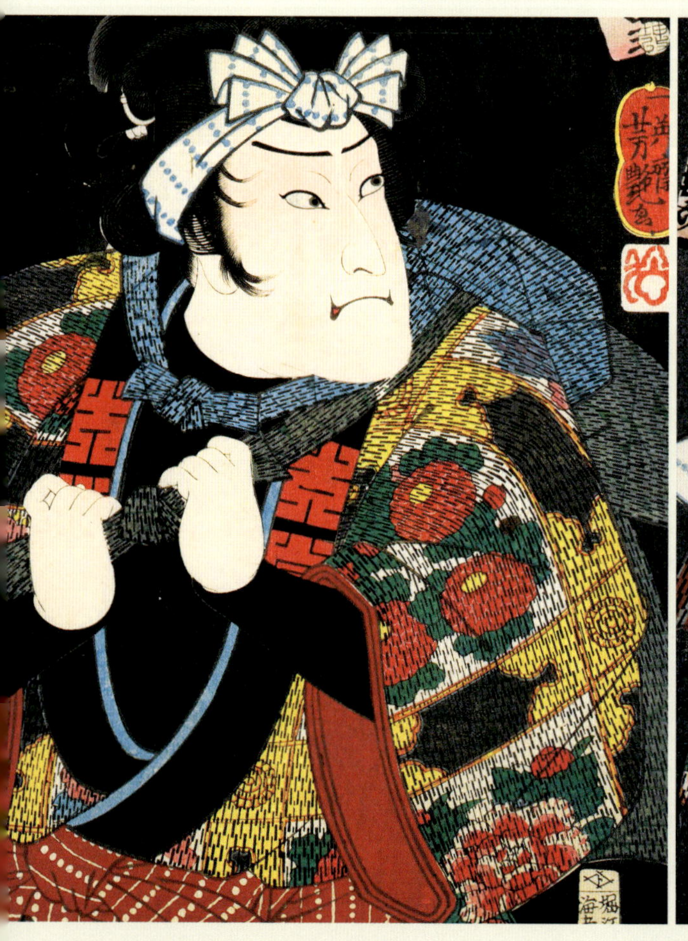

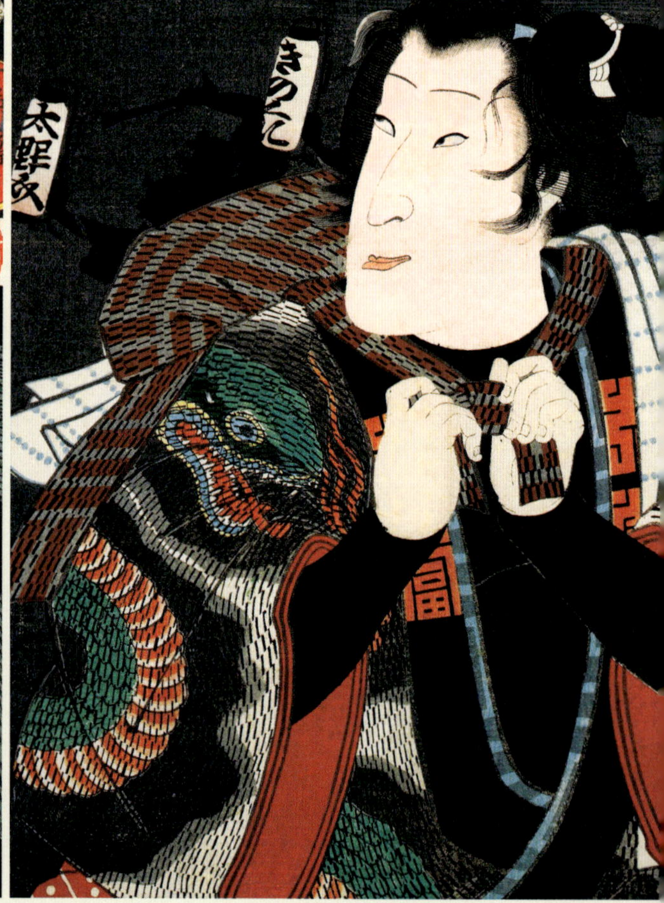

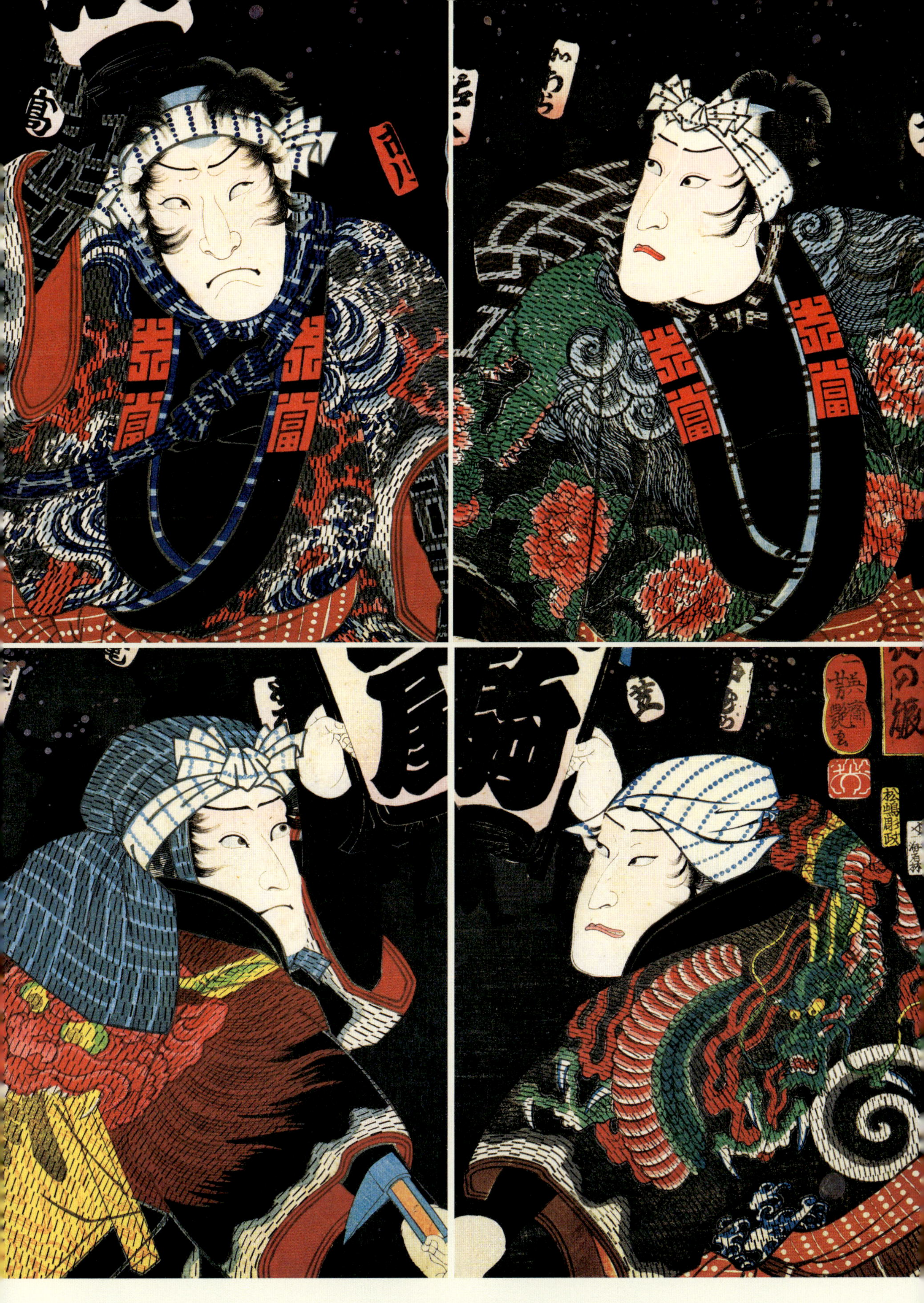

Chapter 1 | Tattoos: The Beauty of the Heroes' Skin   **Utagawa Yoshitsuya**

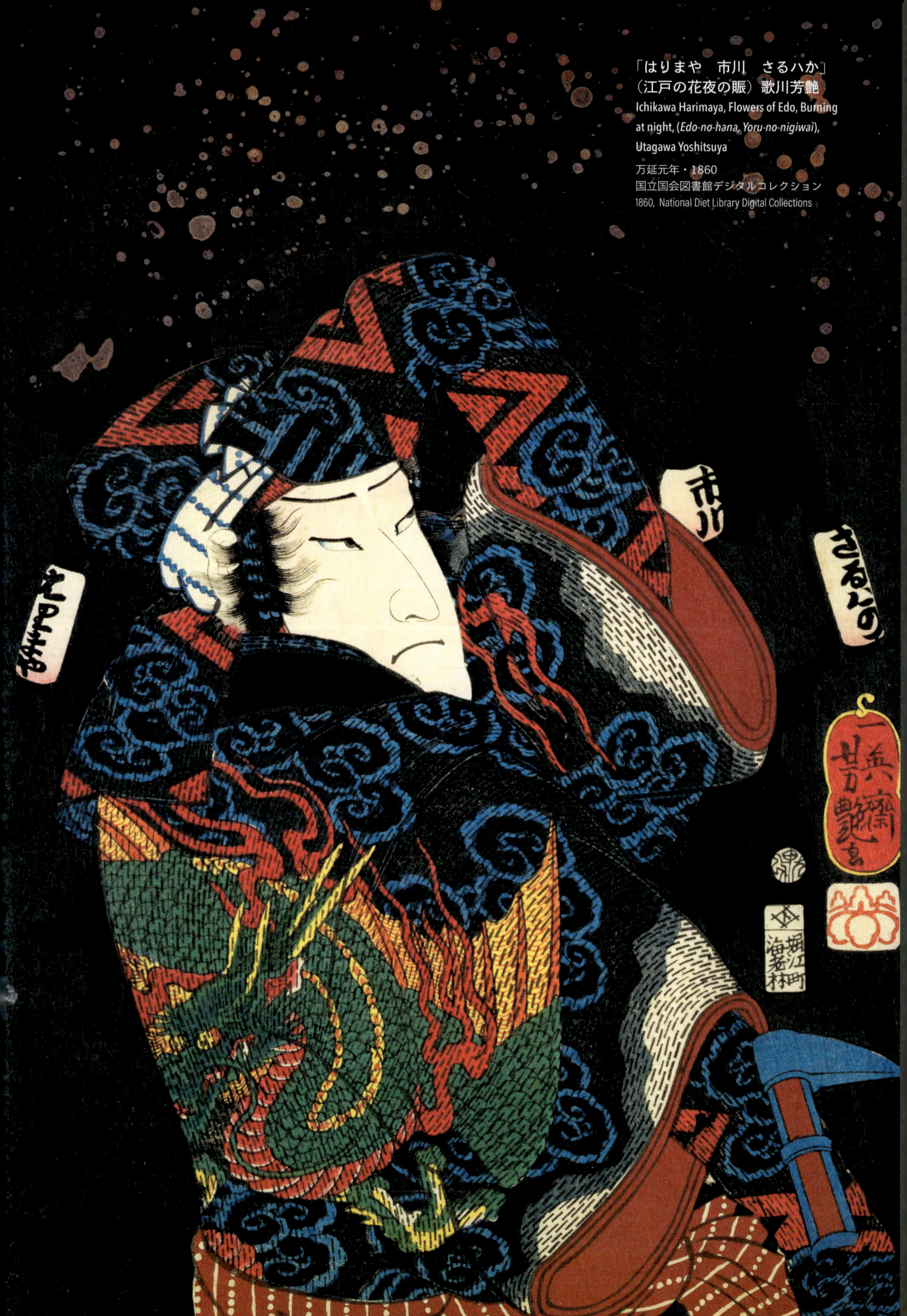

「はりまや　市川　さるハか」
（江戸の花夜の賑）歌川芳艶
Ichikawa Harimaya, Flowers of Edo, Burning
at night, (*Edo-no-hana, Yoru-no-nigiwai*),
Utagawa Yoshitsuya

万延元年・1860
国立国会図書館デジタルコレクション
1860, National Diet Library Digital Collections

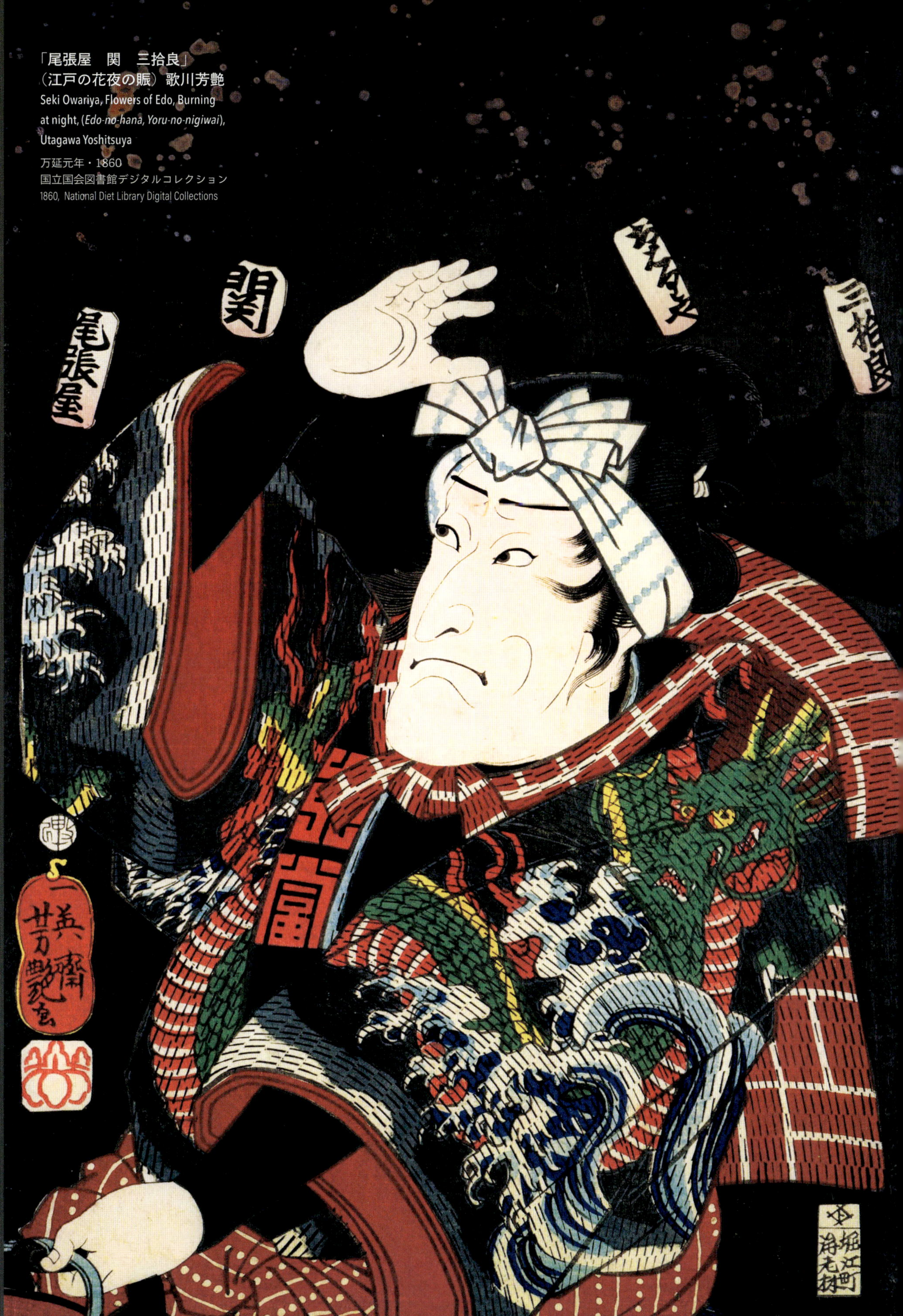

「尾張屋　関　三拾良」
（江戸の花夜の賑）歌川芳艶
Seki Owariya, Flowers of Edo, Burning
at night, (*Edo-no-hana, Yoru-no-nigiwai*),
Utagawa Yoshitsuya
万延元年・1860
国立国会図書館デジタルコレクション
1860, National Diet Library Digital Collections

うたがわ よしとら　生没年不詳

　幕末から明治期の浮世絵師。歌川国芳の門人。幕末期から作画、師の得意とした武者絵や役者大首絵を得意としたほか、横浜絵、開化絵を多く描いた。岡本勘蔵・綴『夜嵐阿衣花廼仇夢』など挿絵も多い。師の十三回忌のとき同門からしりぞけられ、以後永島姓で孟斎の号を用いたと伝えられる。明治以後も風俗画や時事画を描いた。

Utagawa Yoshitora n.d.

Ukiyo-e Artist in Bakumatsu and Meiji. A student of Utagawa Kuniyoshi, he was active from the Bakumatsu period (the closing years of the Tokugawa shogunate) as an artist whose fortes were warrior pictures and bust portraits of actors. He also produced many *Yokohama-e*, depictions of the strange foreigners and technical innovations in Yokohama, and images of modernizing Japan. He also illustrated many books, such as *Night-storm Okinu: Flower-Frail Dreams of Revenge* (*Yoarashi Okinu Hana no Adayume*) by Okamoto Kisen. At the twelfth anniversary of their master's death, his fellow Kuniyoshi-school artists rejected him. Thereafter, it is said, he used the surname Nagashima and the art name Mosai. He continued to produce genre paintings and pictures of current events.

「江戸の花子供遊び　十四組　北組」
歌川芳虎
Kita -Gumi Fourteen Gumi, Popular job in Edo, children's play
(*Edo-no-hana, Kodomo-asobi*), Utagawa Yoshitora

万延元年・1860　国立国会図書館デジタルコレクション
1860, National Diet Library Digital Collections

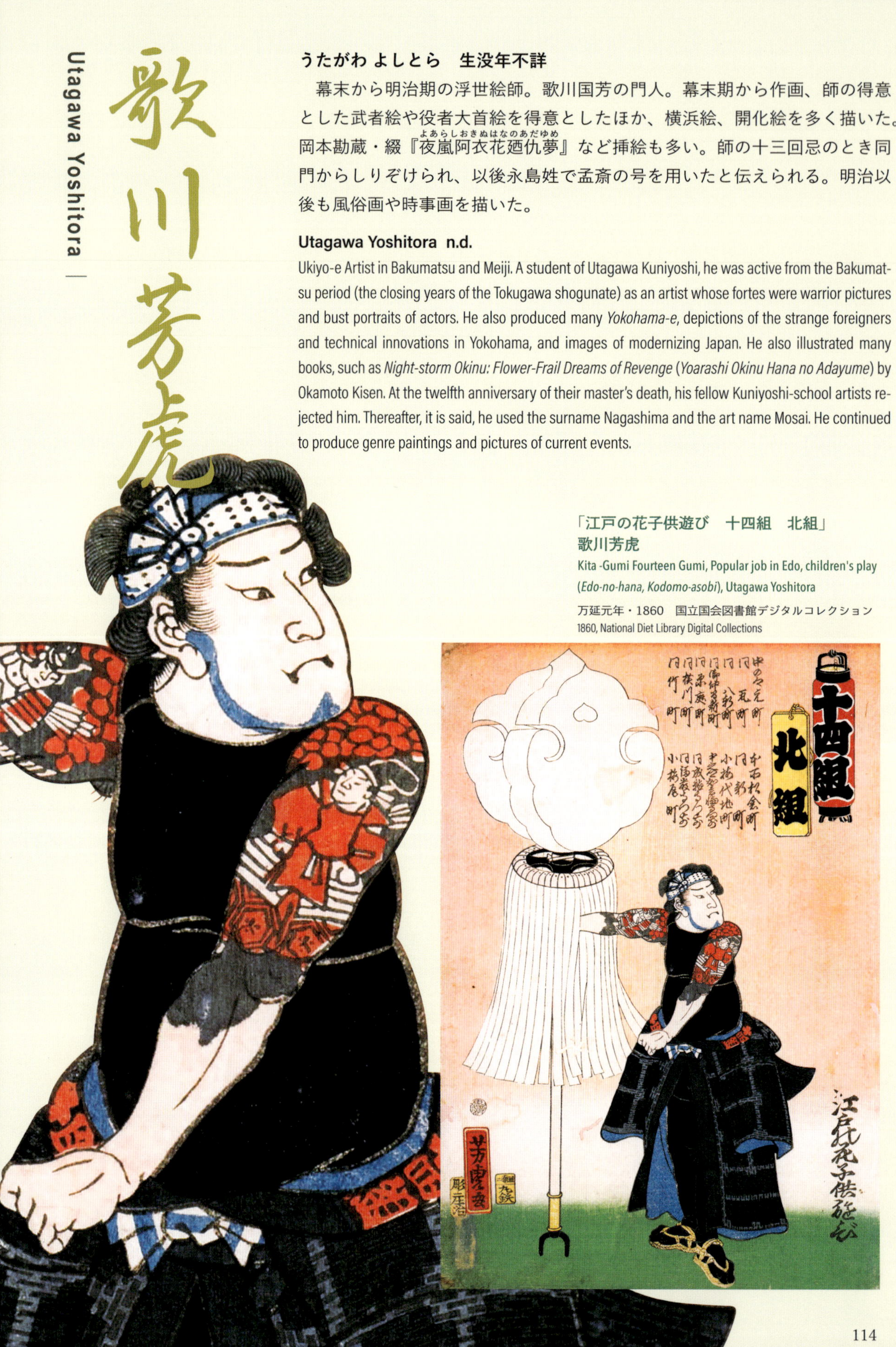

「江戸の花子供遊び　せ組　二番組」
歌川芳虎

Se-Gumi Second Gumi, Popular job in Edo, children's
play (*Edo-no-hana*, *Kodomo-asobi*), Utagawa Yoshitora

安政 5 年・1858
国立国会図書館デジタルコレクション
1858, National Diet Library Digital Collections

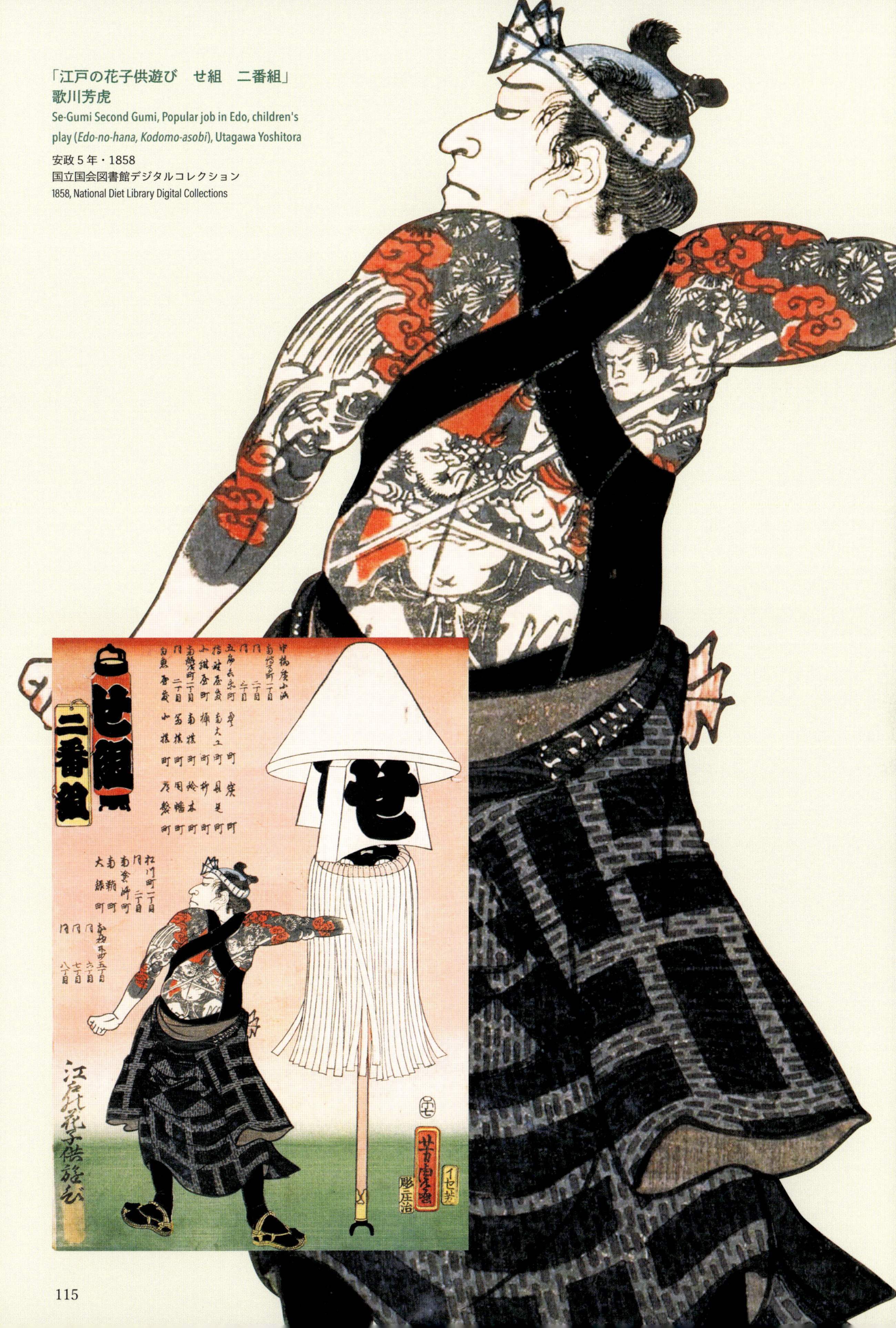

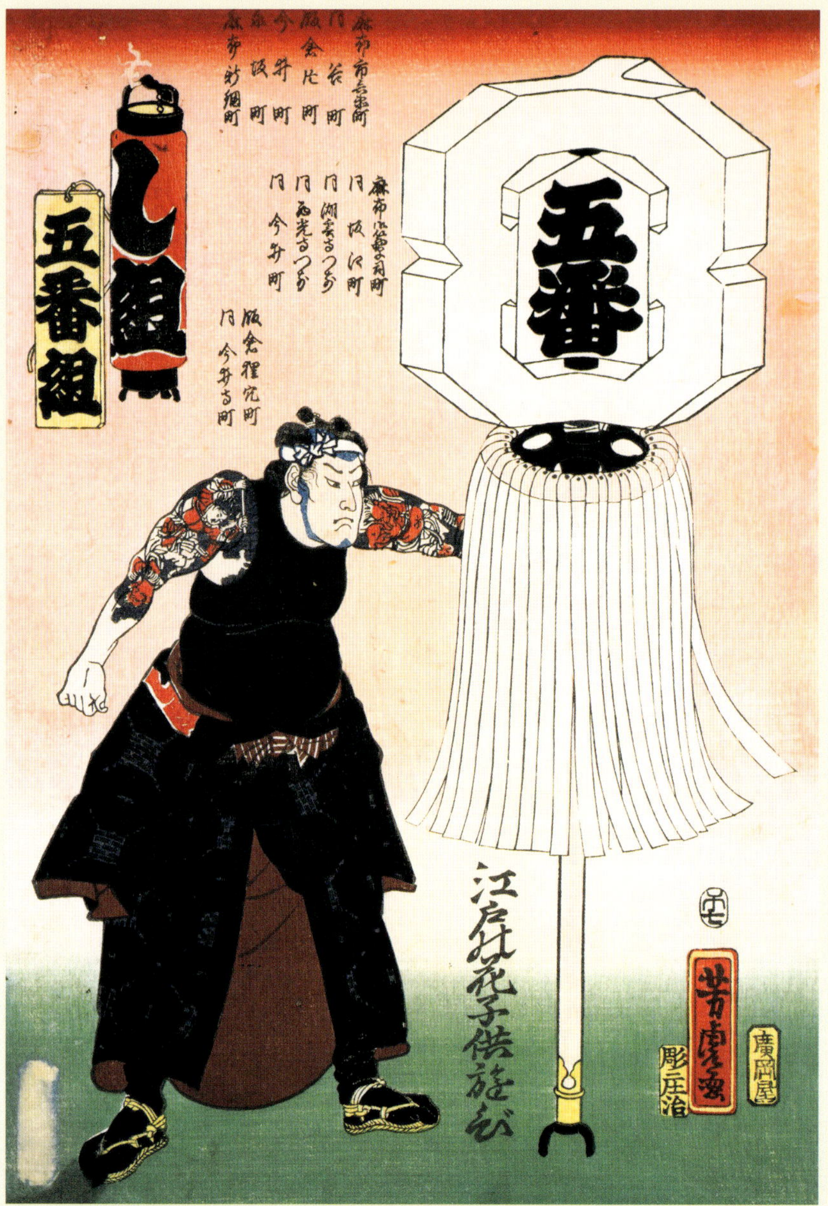

「江戸の花子供遊び　し組　五番組」
歌川芳虎
Si-Gumi Fifth Gumi, Popular job in Edo, children's play
(*Edo-no-hana, Kodomo-asobi*), Utagawa Yoshitora

安政 5 年・1858　国立国会図書館デジタルコレクション
1858, National Diet Library Digital Collections

「江戸の花子供遊び　る組　十番組」（部分）歌川芳虎
Ru-Gumi Ten Gumi, Popular job in Edo, children's play (*Edo-no-hana, Kodomo-asobi*), Detail, Utagawa Yoshitora

安政 6 年・1859　国立国会図書館デジタルコレクション
1859, National Diet Library Digital Collections

「江戸の花子供遊び　く組　五番組」（部分）歌川芳虎
Ku-Gumi Fifth Gumi, Popular job in Edo, children's play (*Edo-no-hana, Kodomo-asobi*), Detail, Utagawa Yoshitora

安政 5 年・1858　国立国会図書館デジタルコレクション
1858, National Diet Library Digital Collections

「江戸の花子供遊び　加組　八番組」（部分）歌川芳虎
Ka-Gumi Eighth Gumi, Popular job in Edo, children's play (*Edo-no-hana, Kodomo-asobi*), Detail, Utagawa Yoshitora

安政 5 年・1858　国立国会図書館デジタルコレクション
1858, National Diet Library Digital Collections

「江戸の花子供遊び　ね組　九番組」（部分）歌川芳虎
Ne Gumi Ninth Gumi, Popular job in Edo, children's play (*Edo-no-hana, Kodomo-asobi*), Detail, Utagawa Yoshitora

安政 6 年・1859　国立国会図書館デジタルコレクション
1859, National Diet Library Digital Collections

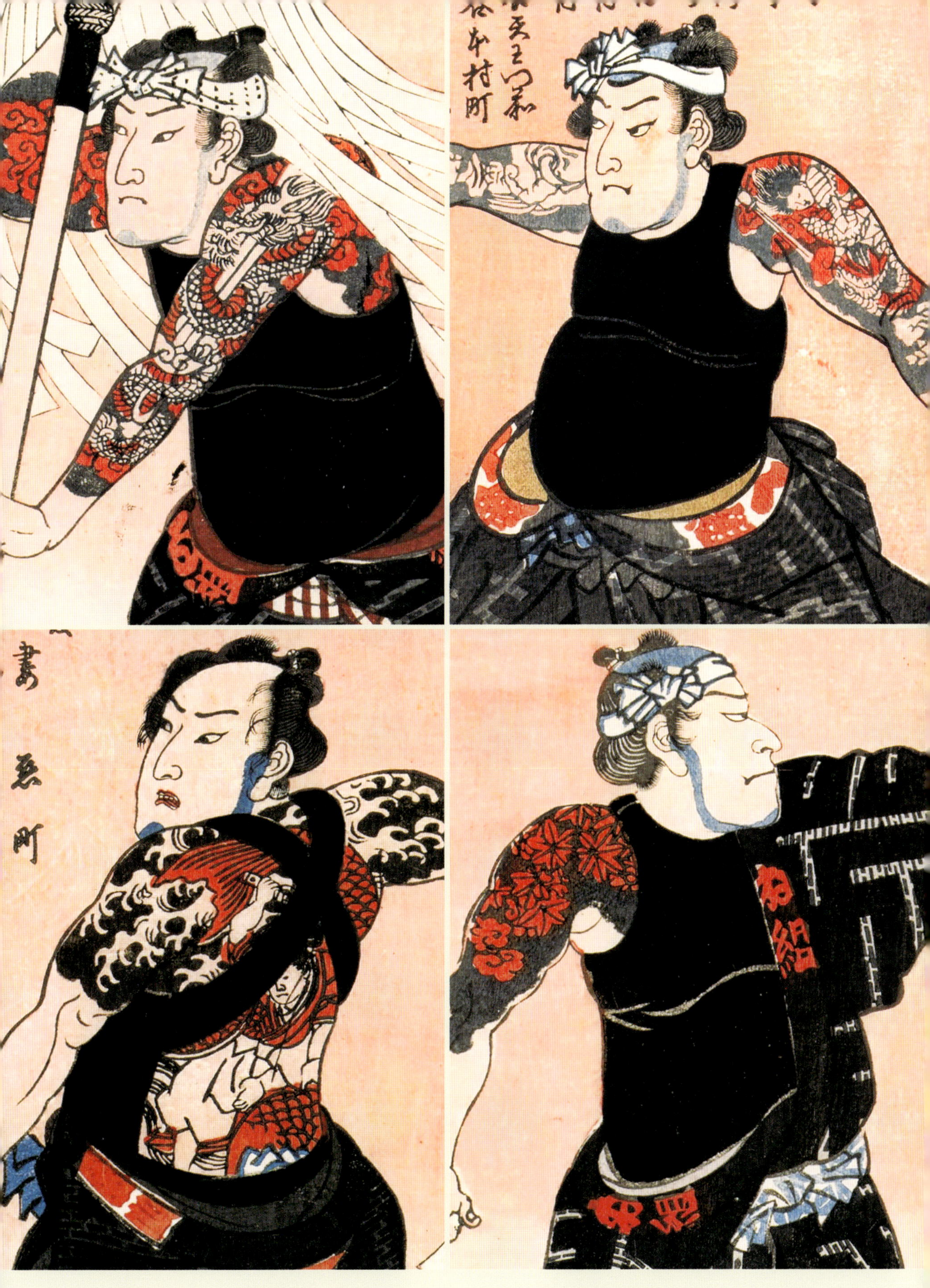

Chapter 1 | Tattoos: The Beauty of the Heroes' Skin **Utagawa Yoshitora**

梅堂小国政

ばいどう こくにまさ　生没年不詳

　作画期は明治20年代（1887-1896）
から明治（1868-1912）末ころ。梅堂、
楳堂、小国政、香朝楼、柳蛙と号す。
五世歌川国政が梅堂小国政と同一人物
とみられるが未詳である。

Baido Kokinimasa n.d.

Baido was active as an artist from about 1890 to 1912.
He used many art names, including Baido (two ver-
sions, using a different initial *Kanji*), Kokunimasa,
Kochoro, and Ryua. Utagawa Kunimasa V and Baido
Kunimasa may be the same artist, but that is not
confirmed.

「見立水滸傳」「九紋龍　市川團十郎・魯智深　市川
左團次・公孫勝　尾上菊五郎・扈三娘　中村福助・
武松　市川権十郎・関勝　中村芝翫」梅堂小国政
Actors Ichikawa Danjūrō as Kumonryū Shishin, Ichikawa Sadanji as
Kaoshō Rochishin, Onoe Kikugorō as Kouson Shō, Nakamura Fukusuke as
Ko Sanjō, Ichikawa Gonjūrō as Bushō, Nakamura Shikan as Kan Shō, from
Mitate-Suikoden, Baidō Kokunimasa
東京都立中央図書館特別文庫室蔵　Tokyo Metropolitan Library

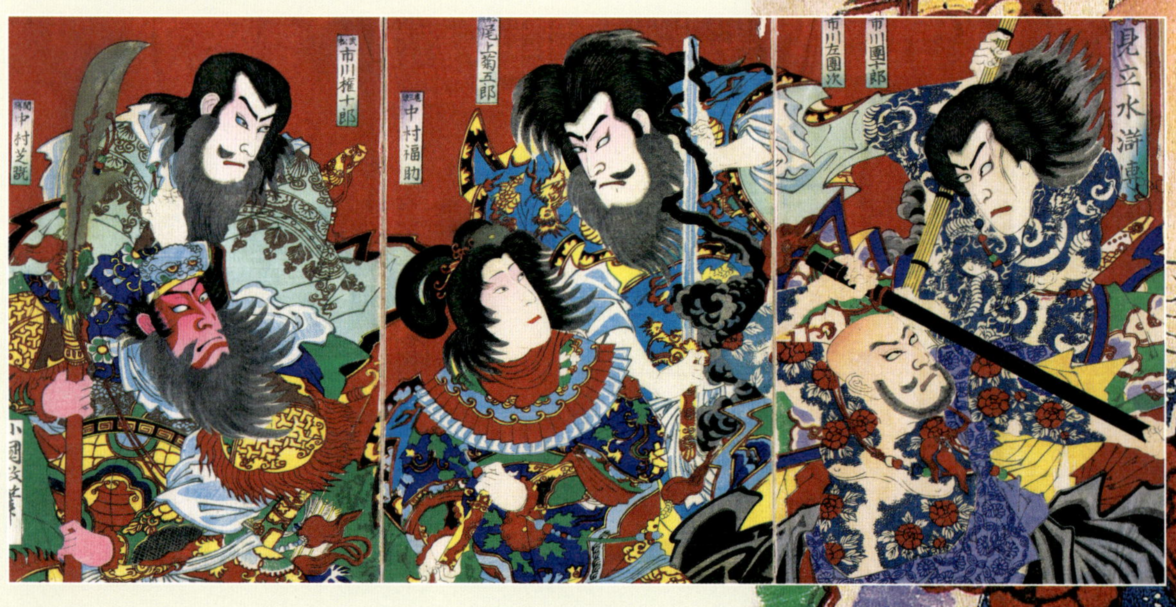

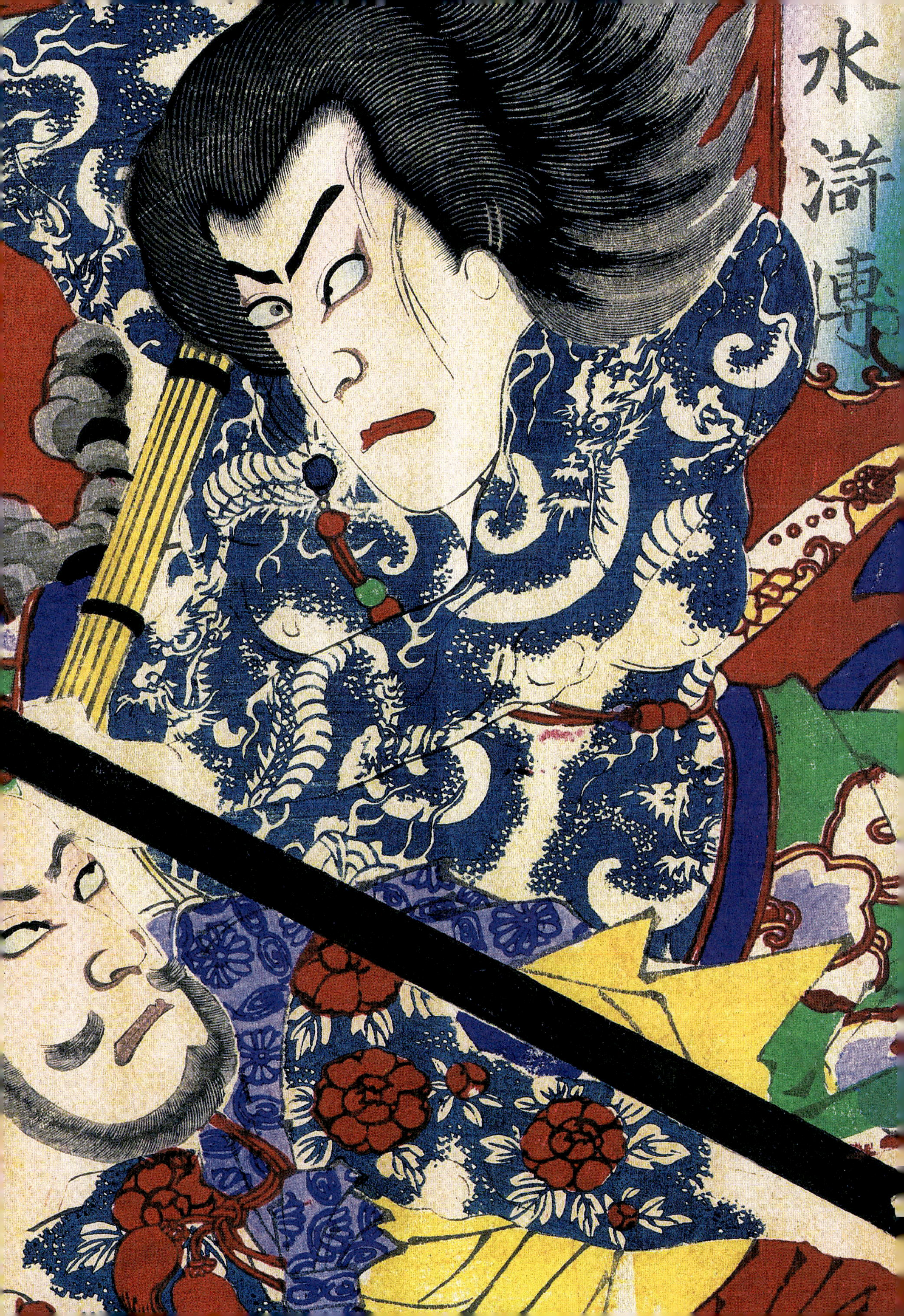

水滸傳

小林清親

こばやし きよちか　弘化 4 年〜大正 4 年（1847-1915）

　明治期の版画家。明治維新にあたり旧幕臣とともに静岡に下り、のち横浜に出て下岡蓮杖に写真術、西洋画法をワーグマンにまなぶ。浮世絵に洋画風の構図や光の強調を取り入れた連作「東京名所図」を出版、「光線画」の名で人気を博す。明治の風物や江戸の名所、静物などを描いて異彩を放った。のち諷刺画に一つの境地を開き、「清親ポンチ」とよばれる戯画・諷刺画を「団団珍聞」などにえがいた。

Kobayashi Kiyochika 1847-1915

Meiji-period print artist. After the Meiji Restoration, he moved with other former direct vassals of the Tokugawa shogunate to Shizuoka. He later appeared in Yokohama, where he studied photography with Shimooka Renjo and Western-style painting with Charles Wirgman. His *Famous Places in Tokyo* series, ukiyo-e prints in which he combined Western-style compositions with an emphasis on light, made him popular as the "light-beam artist." His depictions of Meiji scenes, famous Edo places, and still lifes stood out. He later developed new terrain in satirical pictures. His humorous and satirical works, known as "Kiyochika Punch," were published in *Marumaru Chinbun*, a political satire weekly.

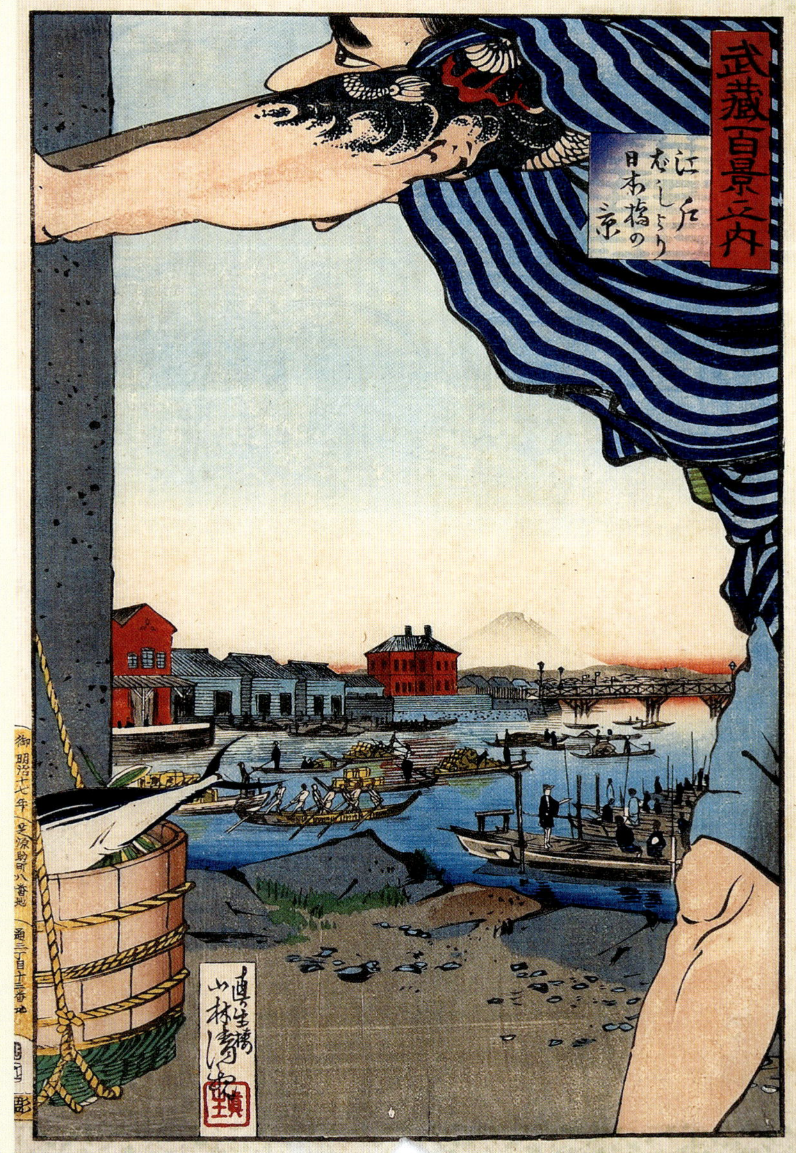

「武藏百景之内」「江戸ばしより日本橋の景」小林清親
View of Nihonbashi from Edo Bridge
(*Edobashi-yori-nihonnbashi-no-kei*),
from *Musashi-Hyakkei-no-uti*, Kobayashi Kiyochika

明治 17 年・1884
東京都立中央図書館特別文庫室蔵
1884, Tokyo Metropolitan Library

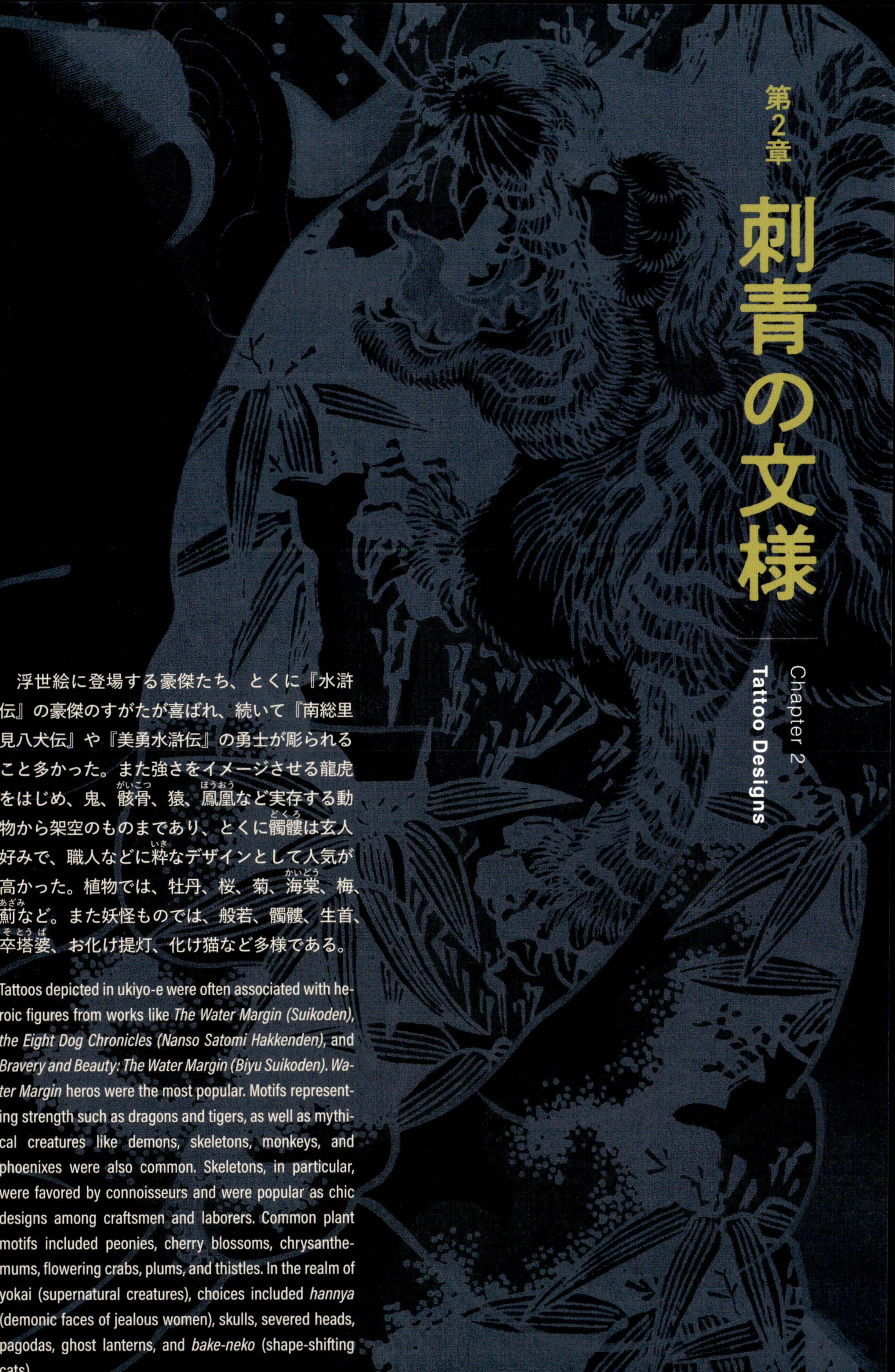

　浮世絵に登場する豪傑たち、とくに『水滸伝』の豪傑のすがたが喜ばれ、続いて『南総里見八犬伝』や『美勇水滸伝』の勇士が彫られること多かった。また強さをイメージさせる龍虎をはじめ、鬼、骸骨、猿、鳳凰など実存する動物から架空のものまであり、とくに髑髏は玄人好みで、職人などに粋なデザインとして人気が高かった。植物では、牡丹、桜、菊、海棠、梅、薊など。また妖怪ものでは、般若、髑髏、生首、卒塔婆、お化け提灯、化け猫など多様である。

Tattoos depicted in ukiyo-e were often associated with heroic figures from works like *The Water Margin (Suikoden)*, *the Eight Dog Chronicles (Nanso Satomi Hakkenden)*, and *Bravery and Beauty: The Water Margin (Biyu Suikoden)*. *Water Margin* heros were the most popular. Motifs representing strength such as dragons and tigers, as well as mythical creatures like demons, skeletons, monkeys, and phoenixes were also common. Skeletons, in particular, were favored by connoisseurs and were popular as chic designs among craftsmen and laborers. Common plant motifs included peonies, cherry blossoms, chrysanthemums, flowering crabs, plums, and thistles. In the realm of yokai (supernatural creatures), choices included *hannya* (demonic faces of jealous women), skulls, severed heads, pagodas, ghost lanterns, and *bake-neko* (shape-shifting cats).

Dragon

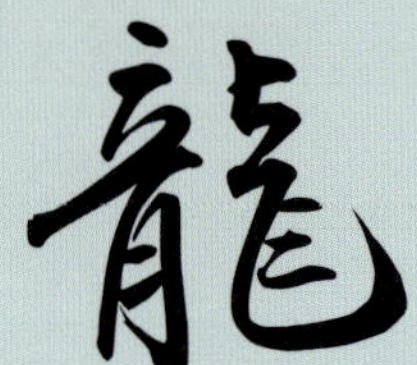

龍

りゅう

龍は九種の動物の部分からなる想像上の動物。体は大蛇に似て背に鱗があり、四足に五本の指、頭には角があり顔は長く耳があり、口辺に長い髭を持つ。神秘的で超自然的な威力をもつとされ、吉祥の文様などにも広く用いられている。文様は龍と唐花や龍に雲、龍虎文などがあり種類が多い。中国では麒麟、鳳凰、亀とともに四霊として尊ばれた。『水滸伝』に登場する史進は九匹の青龍を彫ったことから、九紋龍のニックネームで知られる。

The dragon is a creature imagined as made up of parts from nine types of animals. The body resembles a snake, and the back is covered with scales. The four legs each have five claws. There are horns jutting from the head, the face is long, and there are ears. There are long whiskers on the sides of the mouth. The dragon possesses mysterious supernatural powers signified by the extensive use of patterns symbolizing good luck In *The Water Margin*, Shijin is nicknamed Nine-tattoo Dragon because of the nine dragons tattooed on his body.

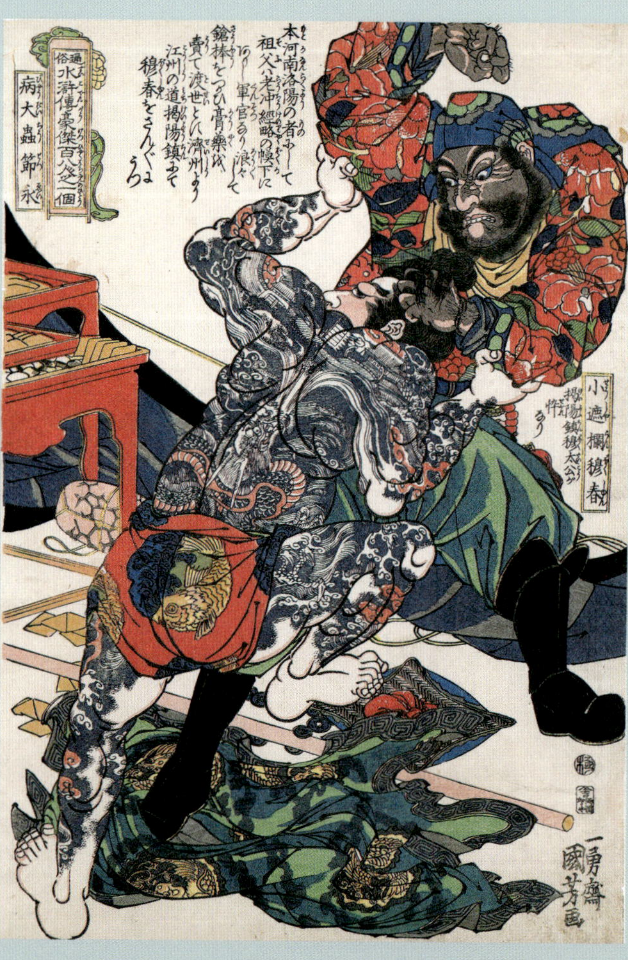

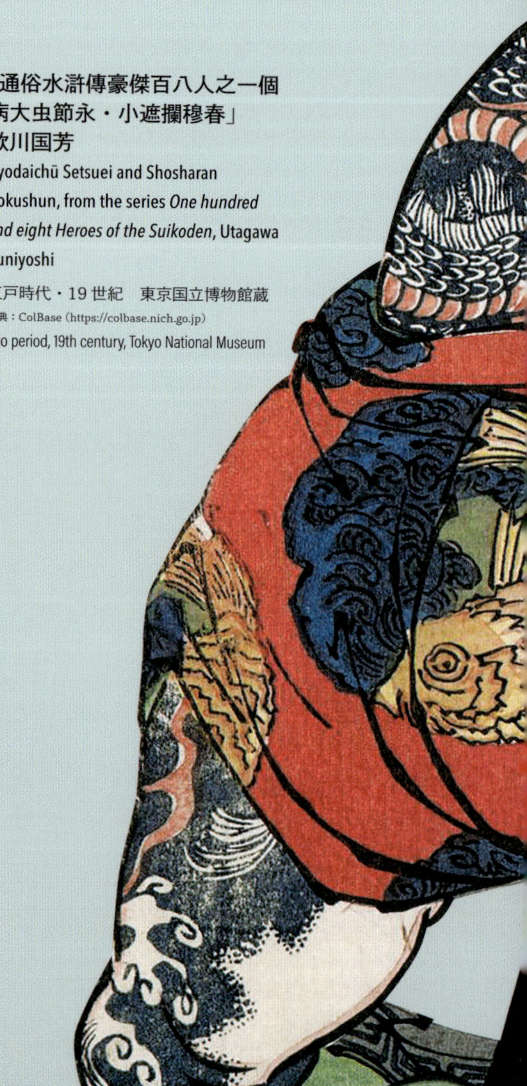

「通俗水滸傳豪傑百八人之一個
病大虫節永・小遮攔穆春」
歌川国芳
Byodaichū Setsuei and Shosharan Bokushun, from the series *One hundred and eight Heroes of the Suikoden*, Utagawa Kuniyoshi

江戸時代・19世紀　東京国立博物館蔵
出典：ColBase (https://colbase.nich.go.jp)
Edo period, 19th century, Tokyo National Museum

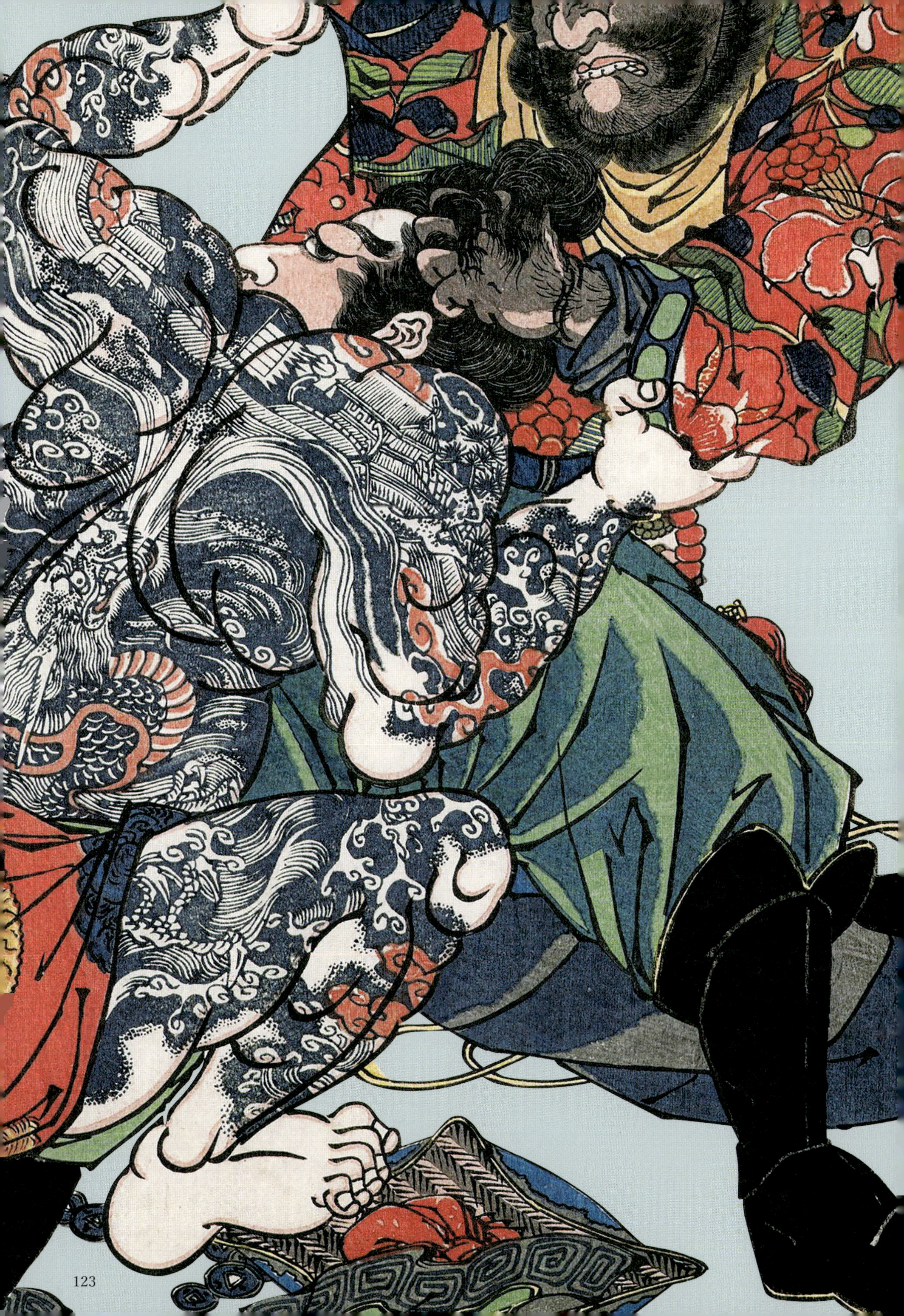

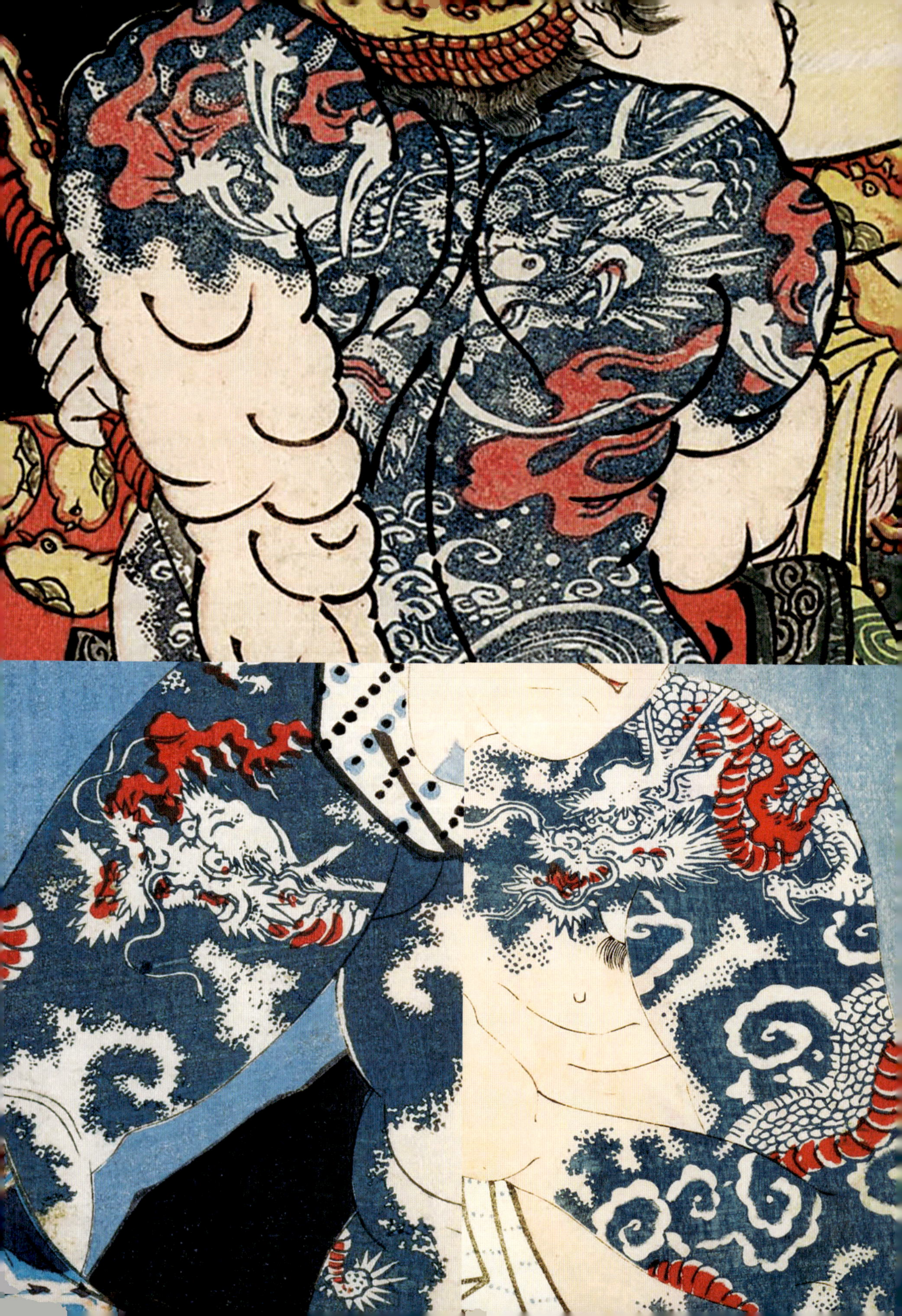

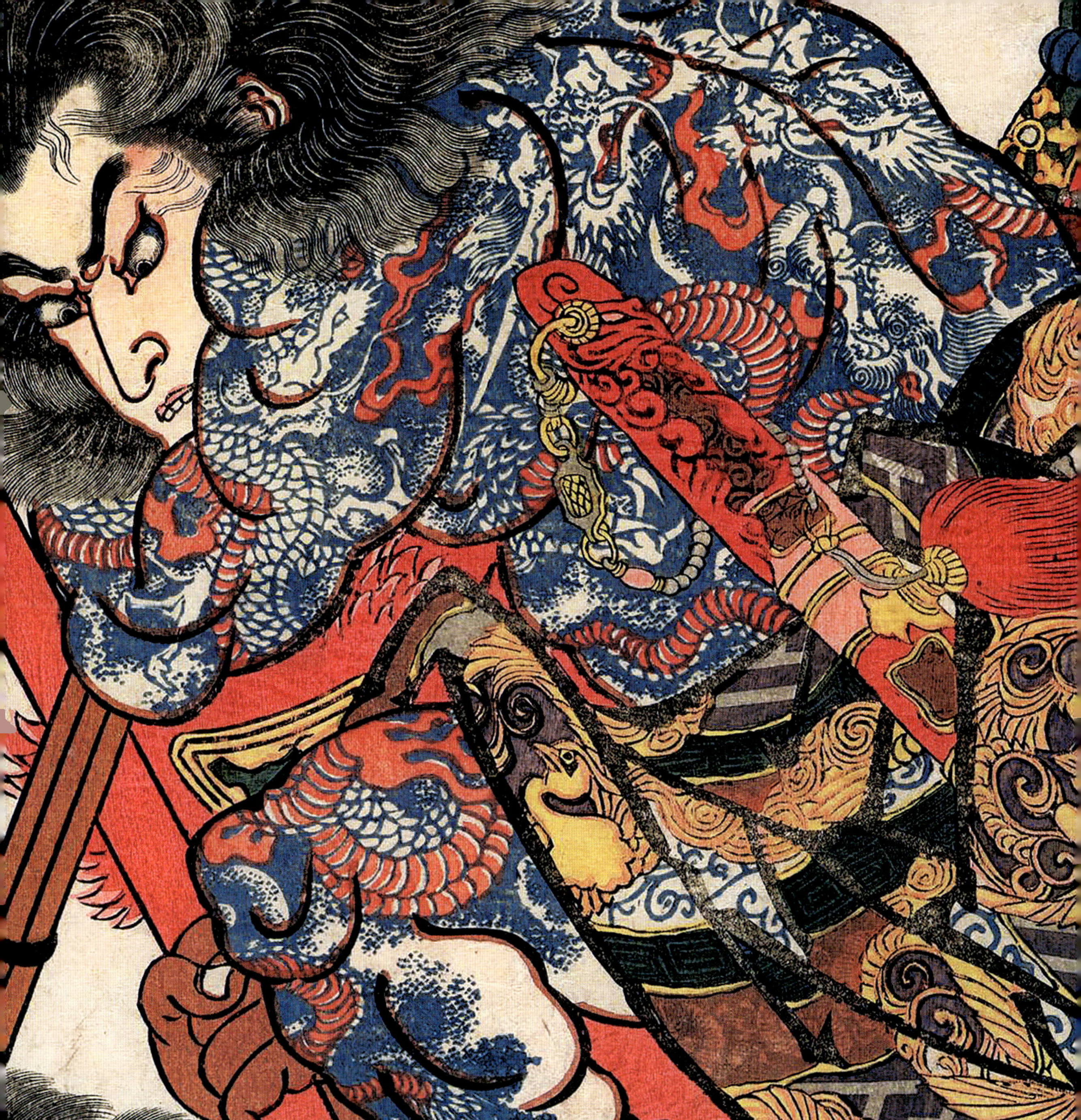

「通俗水滸傳豪傑百八人之一個　撲天鵰李應・没遮攔穆弘」
（部分）歌川国芳
Hakutenchō Rio and Bossharan Bokkō, from the series *One hundred and eight Heroes of the Suikoden*, Detail, Utagawa Kuniyoshi

江戸時代・19 世紀　東京国立博物館蔵　出典：ColBase (https://colbase.nich.go.jp)
Edo period, 19th century, Tokyo National Museum

「今様押絵鏡　出来ぼしの三吉」
（部分）歌川豊国
Dekiboshi no Sankichi, from the series *the Imayō Oshiekagami*, Detail, Utagawa Toyokuni III (Kunisada I)

安政 6 年・1859
国立国会図書館デジタルコレクション
1859, National Diet Library Digital Collections

「駕籠や市助　田舎侍・駕籠や和吉」
（部分）歌川豊国
Kagoya Ichisuke and Kagoya Wakichi, Detail, Utagawa Toyokuni III (Kunisada I)

万延元年・1860
国立国会図書館デジタルコレクション
1860, National Diet Library Digital Collections

「通俗水滸傳豪傑百八人之一個
九紋龍史進・跳澗虎陳達」（部分）
歌川国芳
Kumonryū Shishin and Chokankō Chintatsu, from the series *One hundred and eight Heroes of the Suikoden*, Detail, Utagawa Kuniyoshi

江戸時代・19 世紀　東京国立博物館蔵
出典：ColBase (https://colbase.nich.go.jp)
Edo period, 19th century, Tokyo National Museum

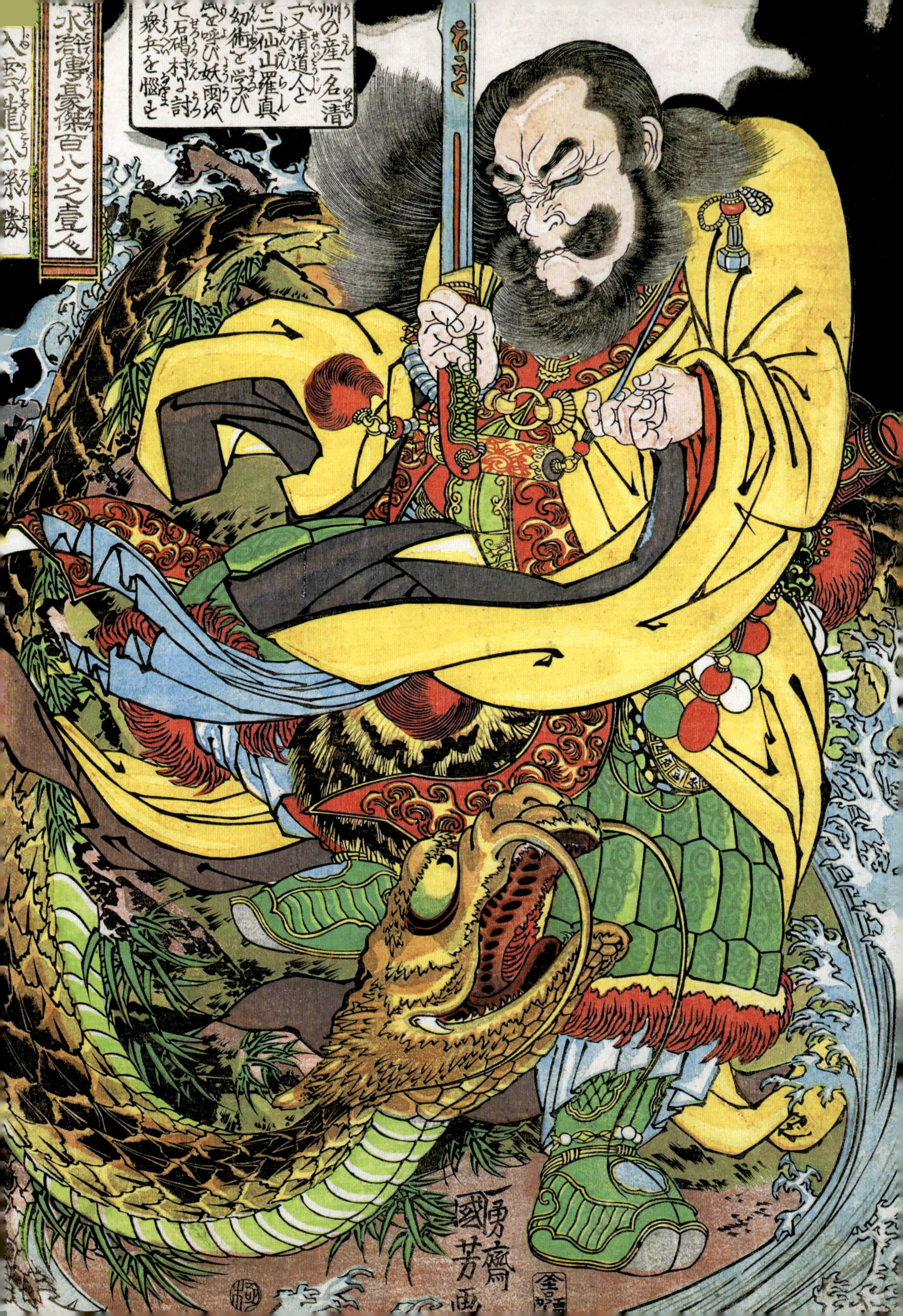

通俗水滸傳豪傑百八人之壹人
入雲龍公孫勝
うん州の産一名一清文清道人と云う三仙山羅真の幻術を学び風を呼び妖雨を呼て石碣村より討ろ衆兵を悩を

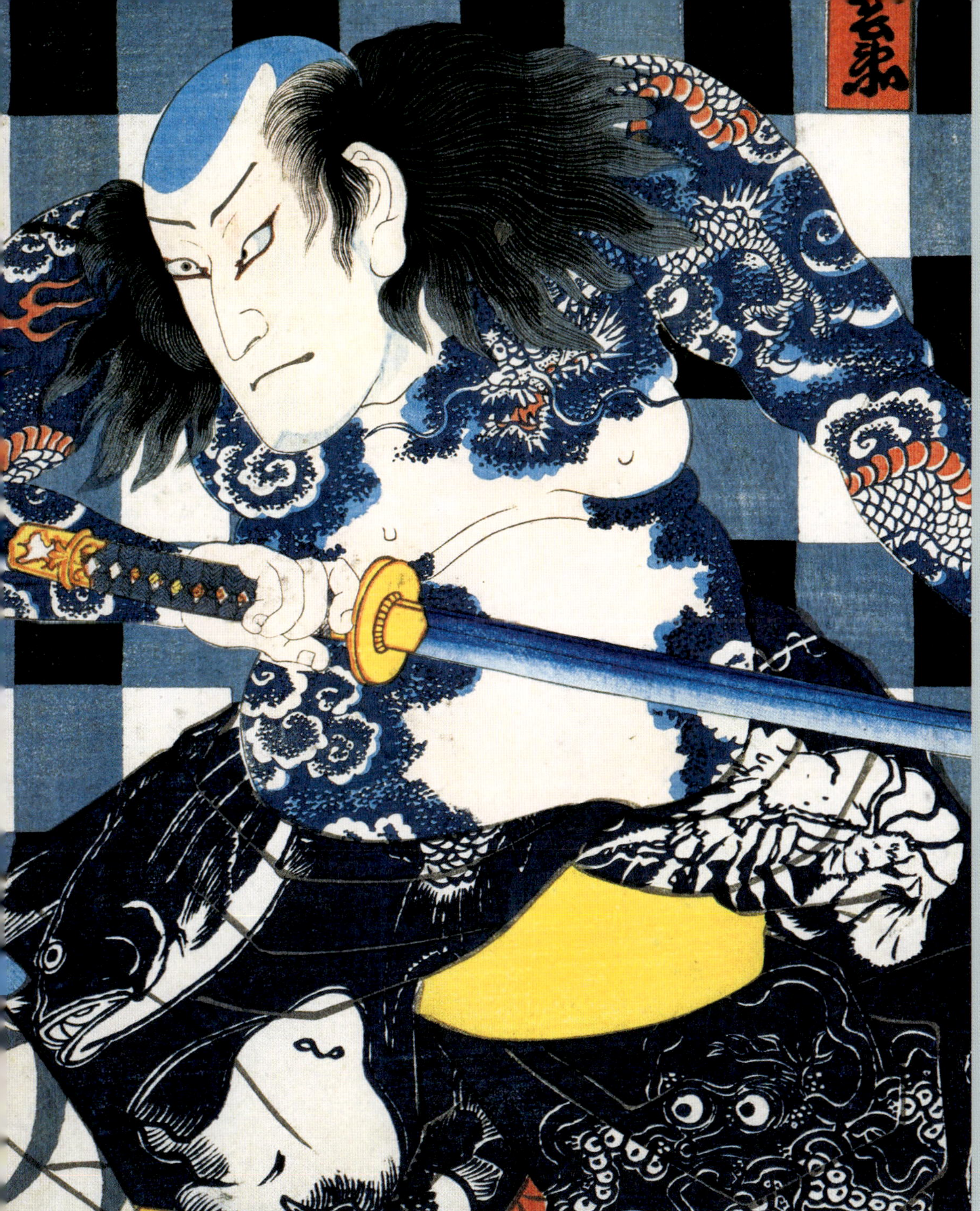

「團七九郎兵衛・夏祭意気地ノ江戸ッ子
一寸徳兵衛」（部分）歌川豊国
Danshichi Kurobei, *Natsumatsuri-ikijino-edokko*, Issun
Tokubei, Detail, Utagawa Toyokuni III (Kunisada I)
国立国会図書館デジタルコレクション
National Diet Library Digital Collections

「通俗水滸傳豪傑百八人之一個
入雲龍公孫勝」（部分）歌川国芳
Nyuunryu Kouson Shō, from the series *One hundred and
eight Heroes of the Suikoden*, Detail, Utagawa Kuniyoshi
江戸時代・19 世紀　東京国立博物館蔵
出典：ColBase (https://colbase.nich.go.jp)
Edo period, 19th century, Tokyo National Museum

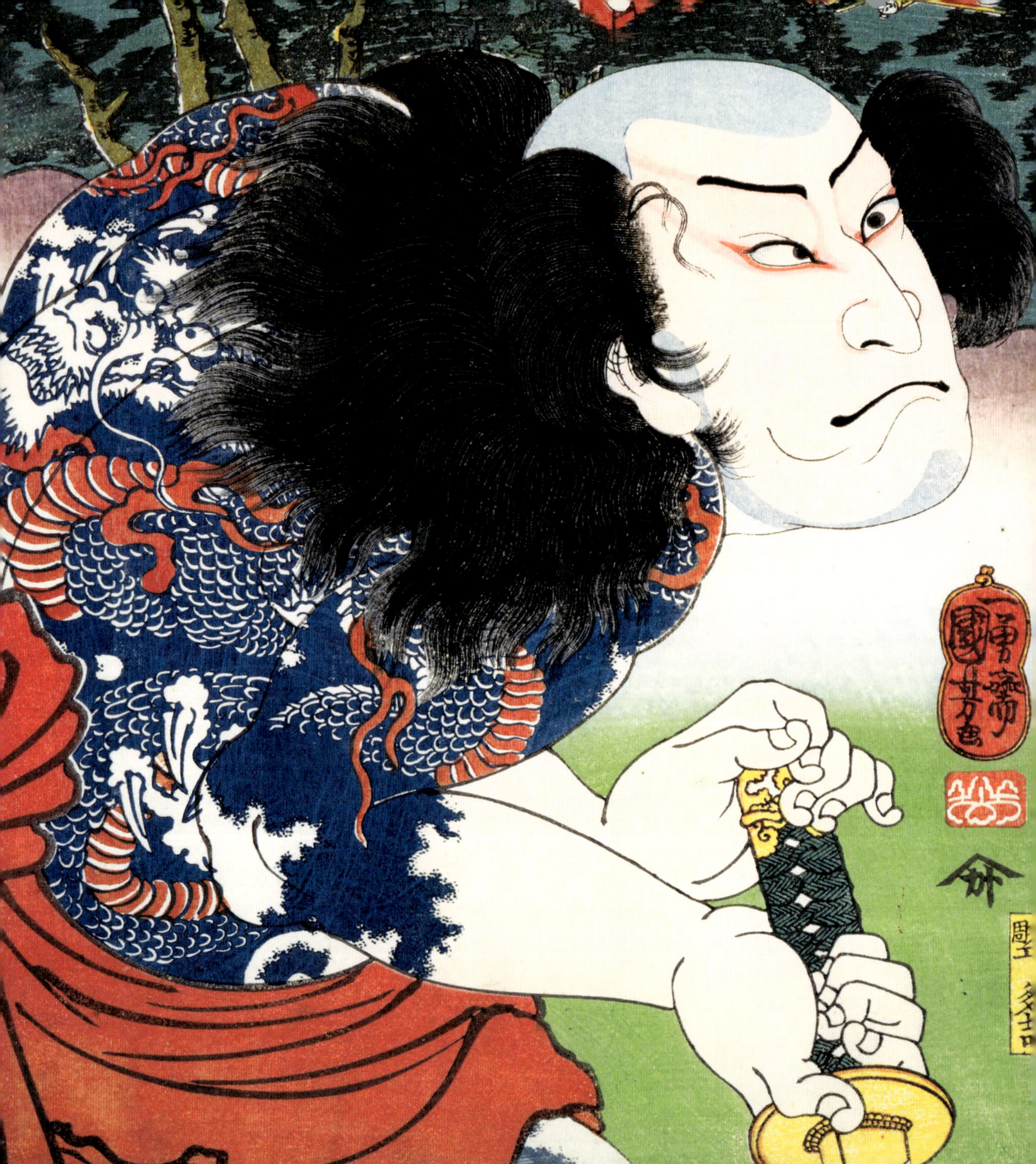

「江戸名所見立十二ケ月の内六月
山王御祭礼　團七九郎兵衛」（部分）
歌川国芳

Sannō Gosairei, Danshichi Kurobei, from the series
Edomeishō-mitate, June of 12 months, Detail,
Utagawa Kuniyoshi

国立国会図書館デジタルコレクション
National Diet Library Digital Collections

「當世好男子傳　九紋龍支進に比す
のざらし語助」（部分）歌川豊国

Nozarashi Gosuke, comparable to Kumonryū Shishin,
from the series *A Modern Shuihuzhuan* (*Tōsei suikoden*),
Detail, Utagawa Toyokuni III (Kunisada I)

安政5年・1858　国立国会図書館デジタルコレ
クション　1858, National Diet Library Digital Collections

「豊国漫画図絵　雲切仁左衛門」
（部分）歌川豊国

Kumokiri Nizaemon, from *The Heroes and Heroines
of the Popular Fiction* (*Toyokuni Manga Zue*), Detail,
Utagawa Toyokuni III (Kunisada I)

万延元年・1860　国立国会図書館デジタルコレ
クション　1860, National Diet Library Digital Collections

「蛍狩當風俗」（初代河原崎権十郎）（部分）歌川豊国
Actor Kawarazaki Gonjūrō I, from the set Fashionable Firefly-hunting
(*Hotaru-gari fūzoku*), Detail, Utagawa Toyokuni III (Kunisada I)

万延元年・1860
国立国会図書館デジタルコレクション
1860, National Diet Library Digital Collections

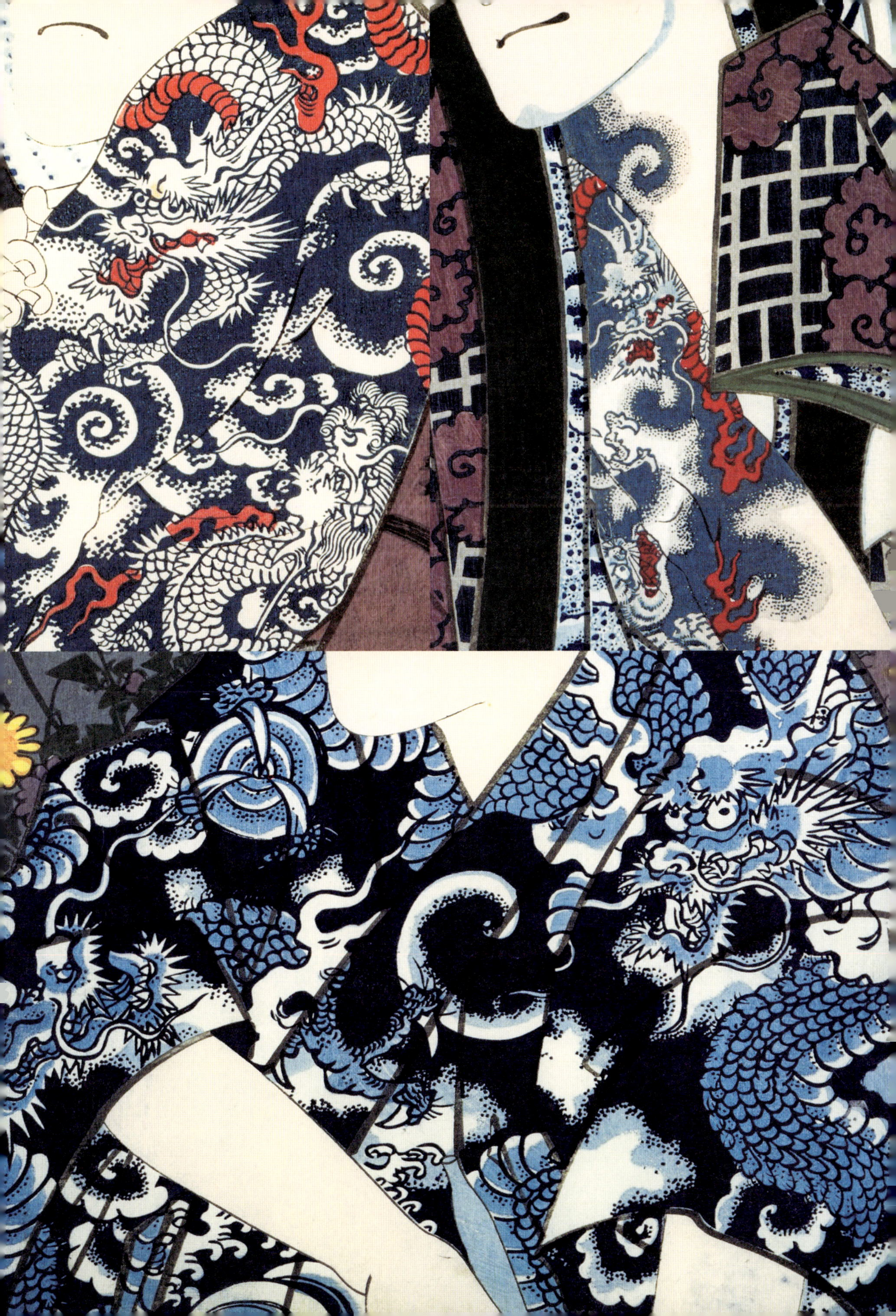

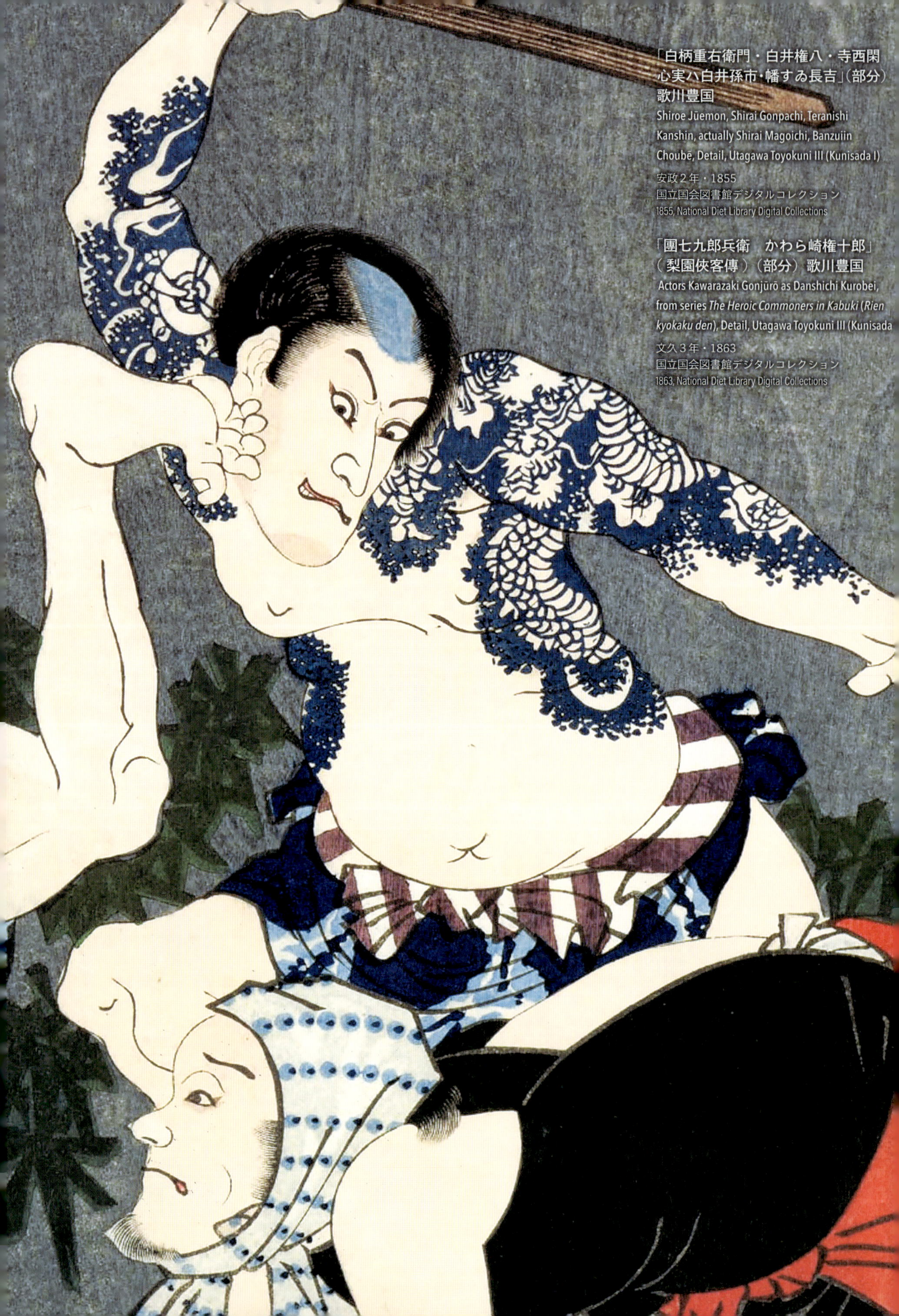

「白柄重右衛門・白井権八・寺西閑
心実ハ白井孫市・幡すゐ長吉」（部分）
歌川豊国
Shiroe Jūemon, Shirai Gonpachi, Teranishi
Kanshin, actually Shirai Magoichi, Banzuiin
Choube, Detail, Utagawa Toyokuni III (Kunisada I)

安政 2 年・1855
国立国会図書館デジタルコレクション
1855, National Diet Library Digital Collections

「團七九郎兵衛　かわら崎権十郎」
（梨園侠客傳）（部分）歌川豊国
Actors Kawarazaki Gonjūrō as Danshichi Kurobei,
from series *The Heroic Commoners in Kabuki* (*Rien
kyokaku den*), Detail, Utagawa Toyokuni III (Kunisada

文久 3 年・1863
国立国会図書館デジタルコレクション
1863, National Diet Library Digital Collections

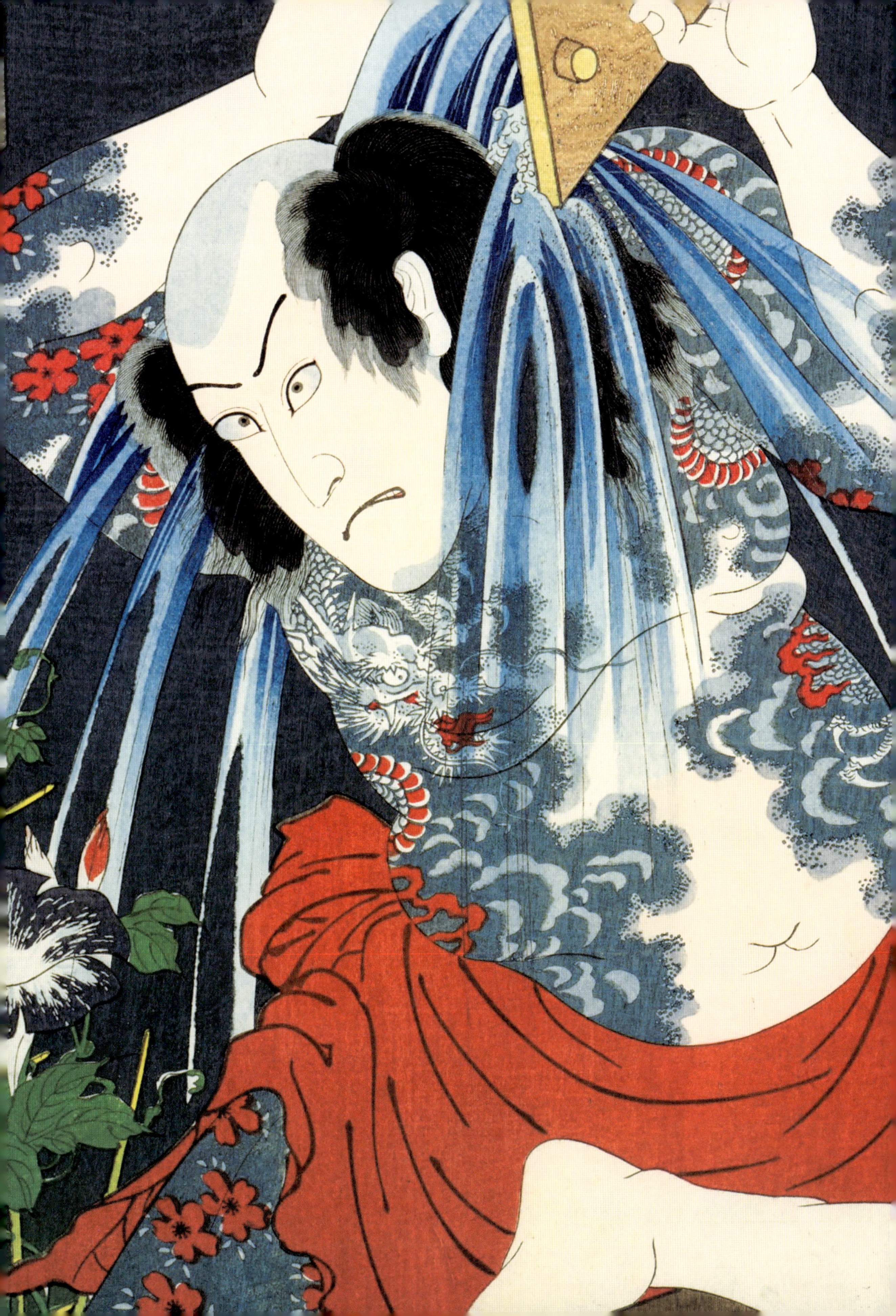

Lion and Tiger

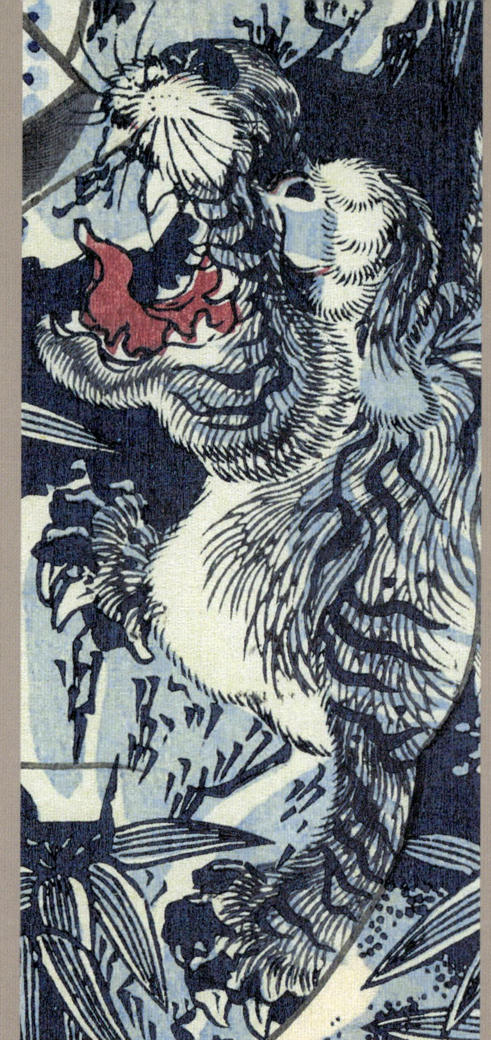

獅子・虎

獅子はライオンのことで、江戸時代末までは実物を見る機会がなかった。そのため渡来の絵画や文様を見て描かれた想像上の動物である。総身に彫られた百獣の王の獅子と、花の王の牡丹を取り合せた獅子に牡丹は豪華で艶やかである。

Japanese had no opportunity to see real lions until the last years of the Edo period. The lions in Japanese art were imaginary creatures seen in imported paintings and patterns. In this full-body-suit tattoo, the lion, the king of beasts, is combined with the tree peony, the king of flowers, to add magnificent, vivid color to the tattoo.

「近世水滸傳　竹垣の虎蔵　市村羽左衛門」歌川豊国
Actors Ichimura Uzaemon as Takegaki no Torazō, from the series A Modern Suikoden (*Kinsei Suikoden*), Utagawa Toyokuni III (Kunisada I),

文久 2 年・1862
東京都立中央図書館特別文庫室蔵
1862, Tokyo Metropolitan Central Library

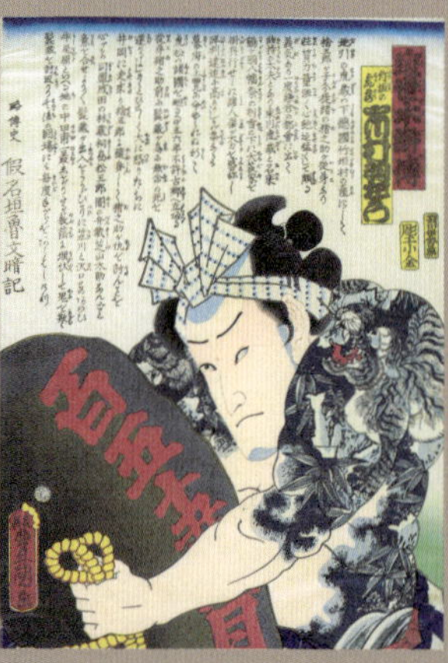

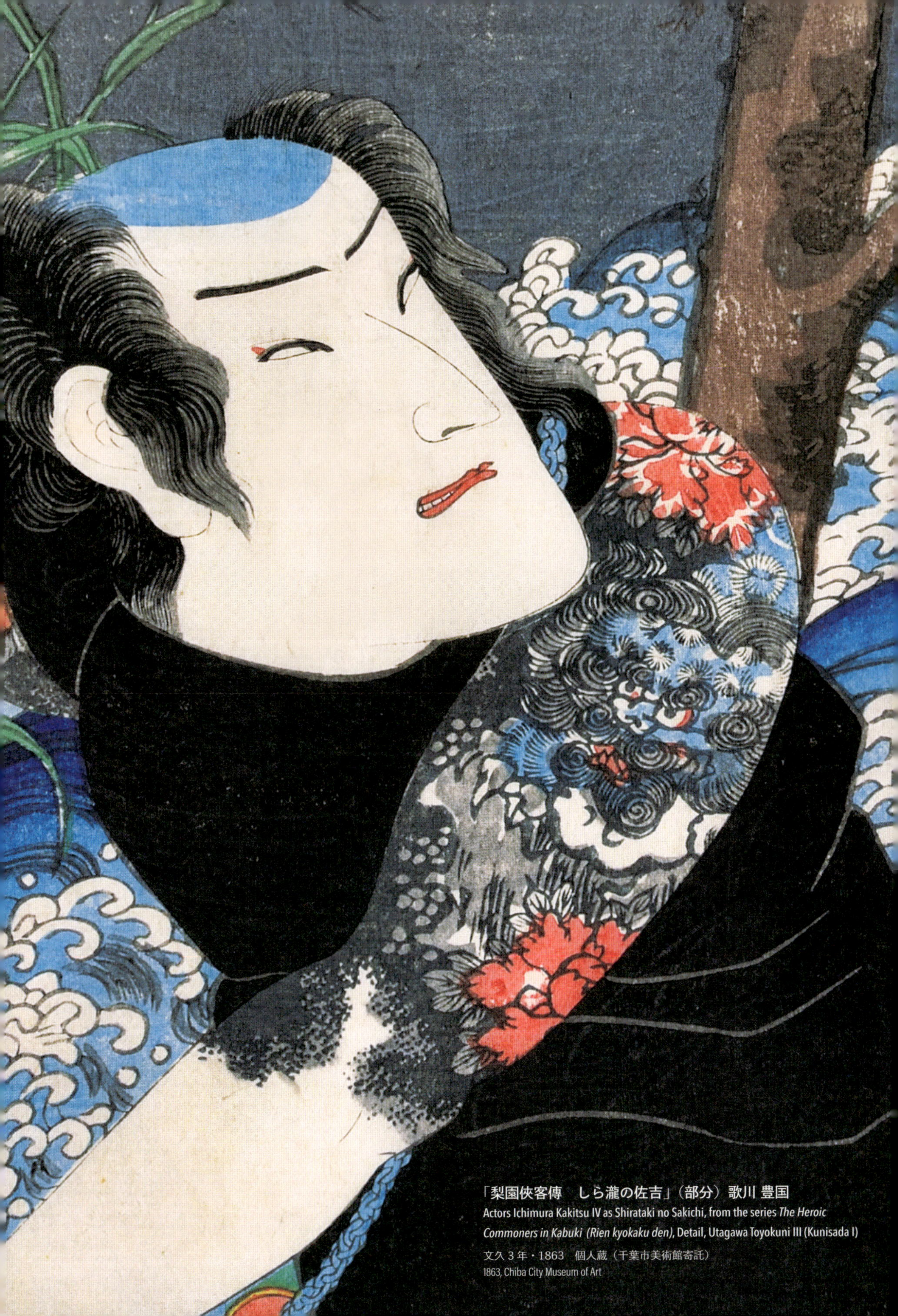

「梨園侠客傳　しら瀧の佐吉」（部分）歌川 豊国
Actors Ichimura Kakitsu IV as Shirataki no Sakichi, from the series *The Heroic Commoners in Kabuki (Rien kyokaku den)*, Detail, Utagawa Toyokuni III (Kunisada I)
文久 3 年・1863　個人蔵（千葉市美術館寄託）
1863, Chiba City Museum of Art

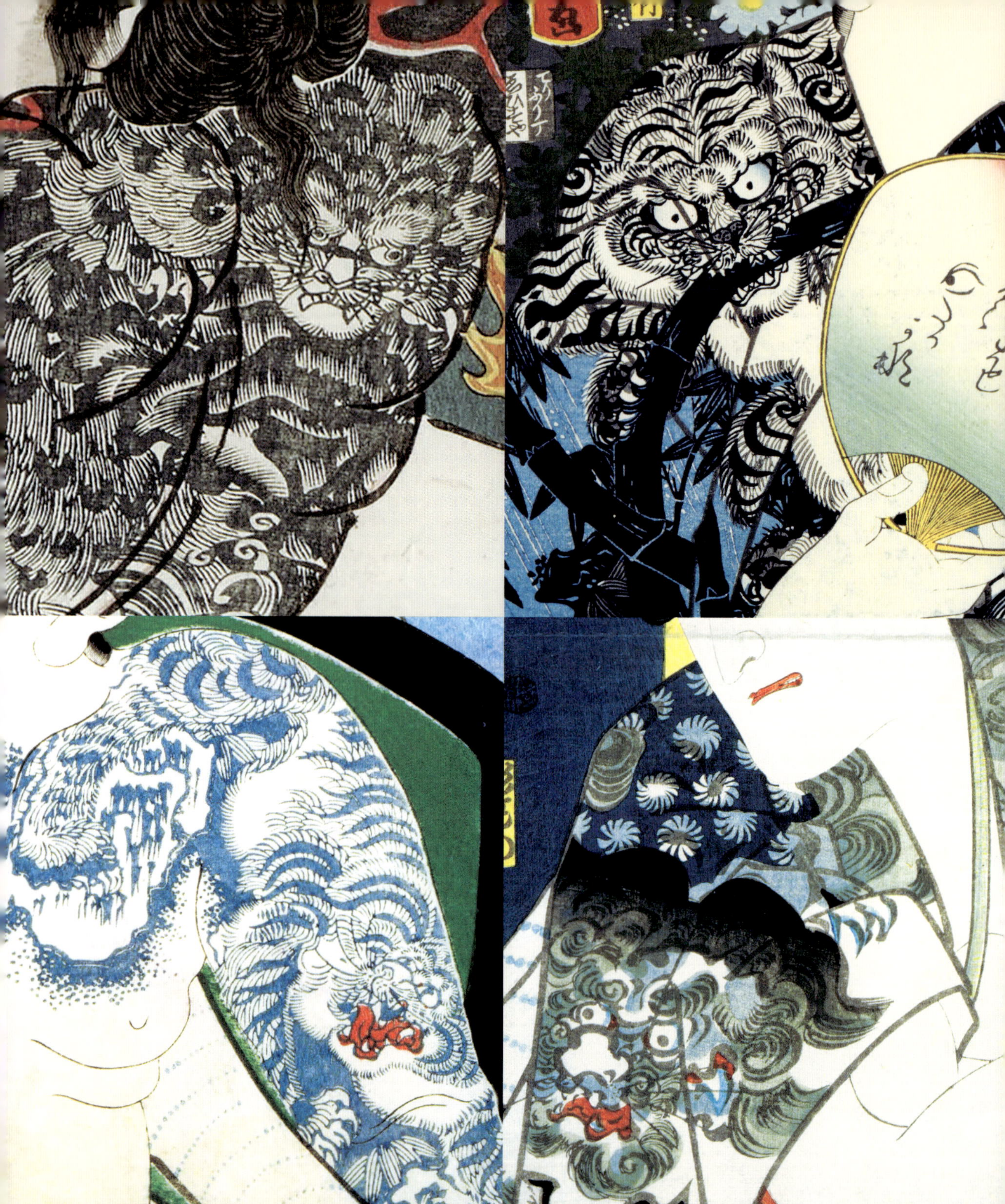

「通俗水滸傳豪傑百八人之一個　短命治郎阮小五」（部分）歌川国芳
Tanmei Jirō Gen Shōgo, from the series *One hundred and eight Heroes of the Suikoden*, Detail, Utagawa Kuniyoshi
江戸時代・19 世紀　東京国立博物館蔵
出典：ColBase（https://colbase.nich.go.jp）
Edo period, 19th century, Tokyo National Museum

「蛍狩當風俗」（初代河原崎権十郎）（部分）歌川豊国
Actor Kawarazaki Gonjūrō I, from the set Fashionable Firefly-hunting (*Hotaru-gari fūzoku*), Detail, Utagawa Toyokuni III (Kunisada I)
万延元年・1860
国立国会図書館デジタルコレクション
1860, National Diet Library Digital Collections

「駕籠や市助　田舎侍・駕籠や和吉」（部分）歌川豊国
Kagoya Ichisuke and Kagoya Wakichi, Detail, Utagawa Toyokuni III (Kunisada I)
万延元年・1860
国立国会図書館デジタルコレクション
1860, National Diet Library Digital Collections

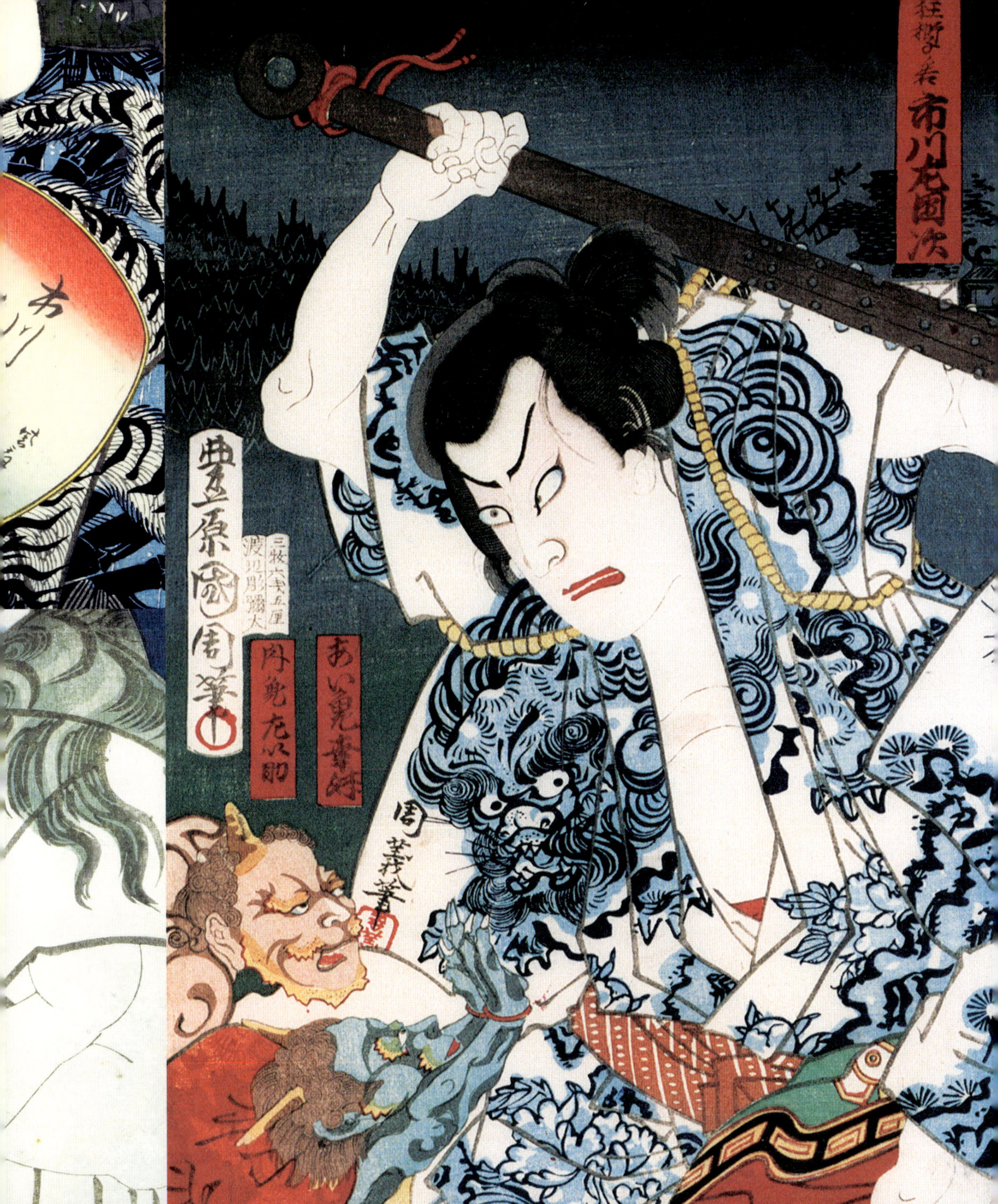

「二丁町市　市村羽左衛門」（部分）
豊原国周
Actors Ichimura Uzaemon as Nichōmachiichi,
Detail, Toyohara Kunichika

元治元年・1864
国立国会図書館デジタルコレクション
1864, National Diet Library

「當世見立地獄征罰」「狂獅子ノ若
市川左團次」豊原国周
Actors Ichikawa Sadanji as Kuruijishi-no-waka, from the series
Tousei-mitate-jigoku-seibatsu, Toyohara Kunichika

明治 9 年・1876　東京都立中央図書館特別文庫室蔵
1876, Tokyo Metropolitan Library

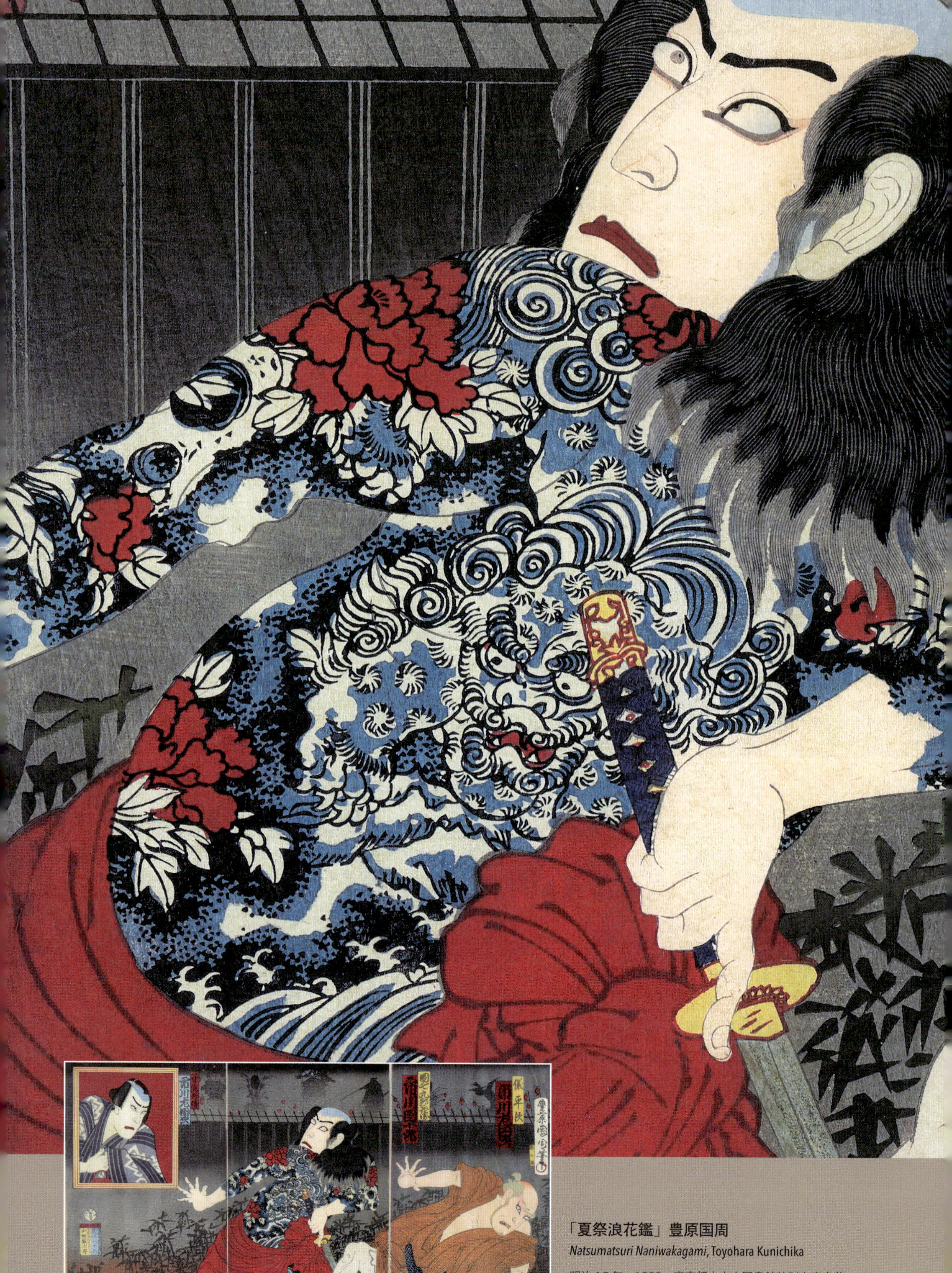

「夏祭浪花鑑」豊原国周
Natsumatsuri Naniwakagami, Toyohara Kunichika

明治 16 年・1883　東京都立中央図書館特別文庫室蔵
1883, Tokyo Metropolitan Library

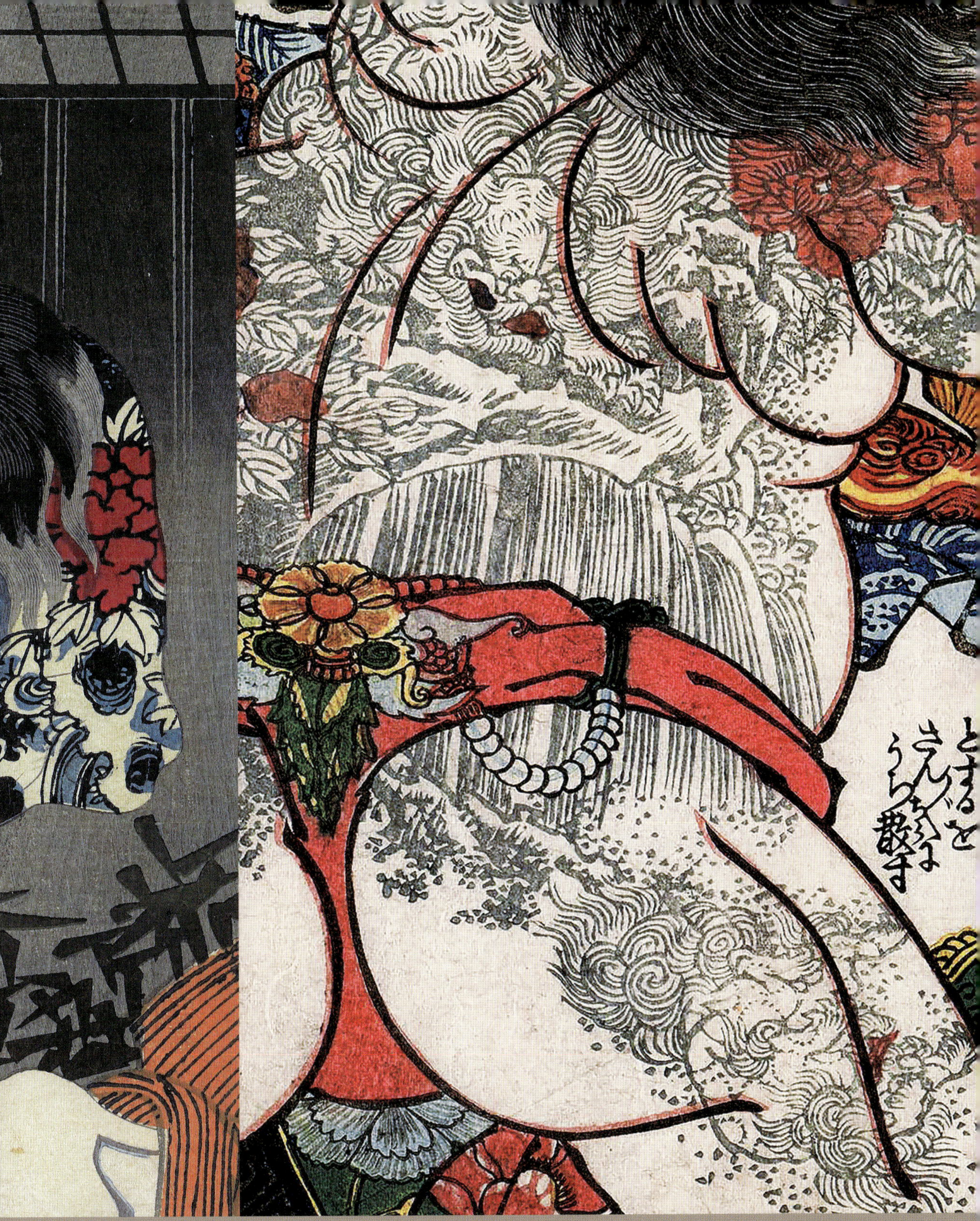

「通俗水滸傳豪傑百八人之一個　浪子燕青」（部分）歌川国芳
Roushi Ensei, from the series *One hundred and eight Heroes of the Suikoden*, Detail, Utagawa Kuniyoshi

江戸時代・19世紀　東京国立博物館蔵　出典：ColBase (https://colbase.nich.go.jp)
Edo period, 19th century, Tokyo National Museum

Tamatori-hime

海女の玉取り伝説で、龍神に奪われた「面向不背の玉」を取り戻す物語。藤原鎌足の子の不比等は玉を取り戻すため、海女と契り玉を奪い返すことを頼んだ。海女の手足は龍に食いちぎられたが、切り開かれた乳房のなかには玉が隠されていた。

The "Jewel-taking Princess" is a pearl diver who legend says recovered a beautiful jewel stolen by the dragon king who lives at the bottom of the sea. She had been asked by Fujiwara no Fumoto to recover the jewel, but while she accomplished her mission, her hands and feet were devoured by the dragon. The jewel was hidden in a cross-shaped wound under her breast.

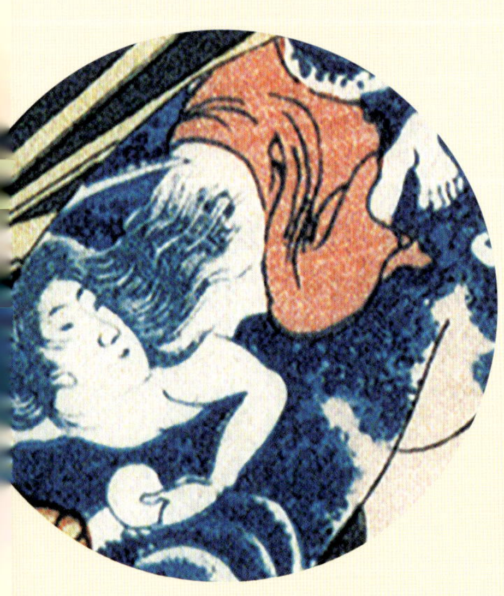

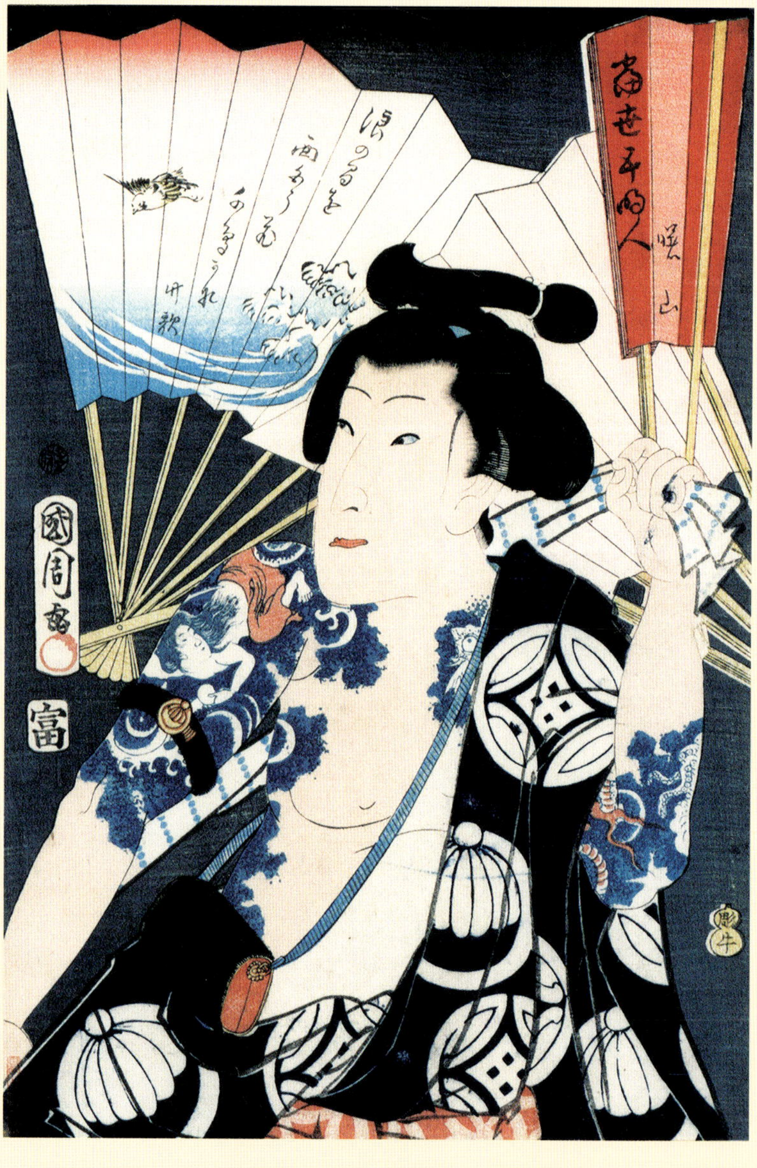

「當世五明人　曙山」豊原国周
Actors Sawamura Tanosuke III as Shōzan, from the series *Tousei-Gomeijin-Shōzan*, Toyohara Kunichika

元治元年・1864
東京都立中央図書館特別文庫室蔵
1864, Tokyo Metropolitan Library

制吒迦童子は八大童子の一つで、矜羯羅童子とともに不動明王に配される脇侍。幼い子どもの姿で緋衣をまとい、頭に五つの髻を結び、左に三鈷を握り、右に金剛棒を持って怒りの表情をしている。

One of the Eight Child Acolytes, *Seitaku-doji* is a Buddhist deity paired with *Kongara-doji* as an aide to Fudomyo, the Immovable Wisdom King. He is of depicted as a young child with his hair tied into five buns and an angry expression on his face.

制吒迦童子

せいたかどうじ

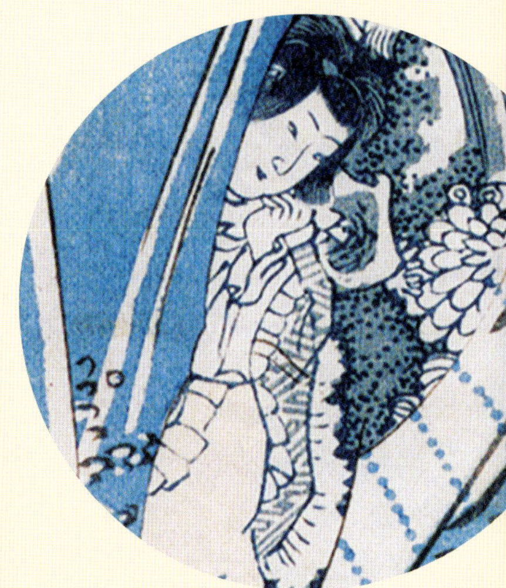

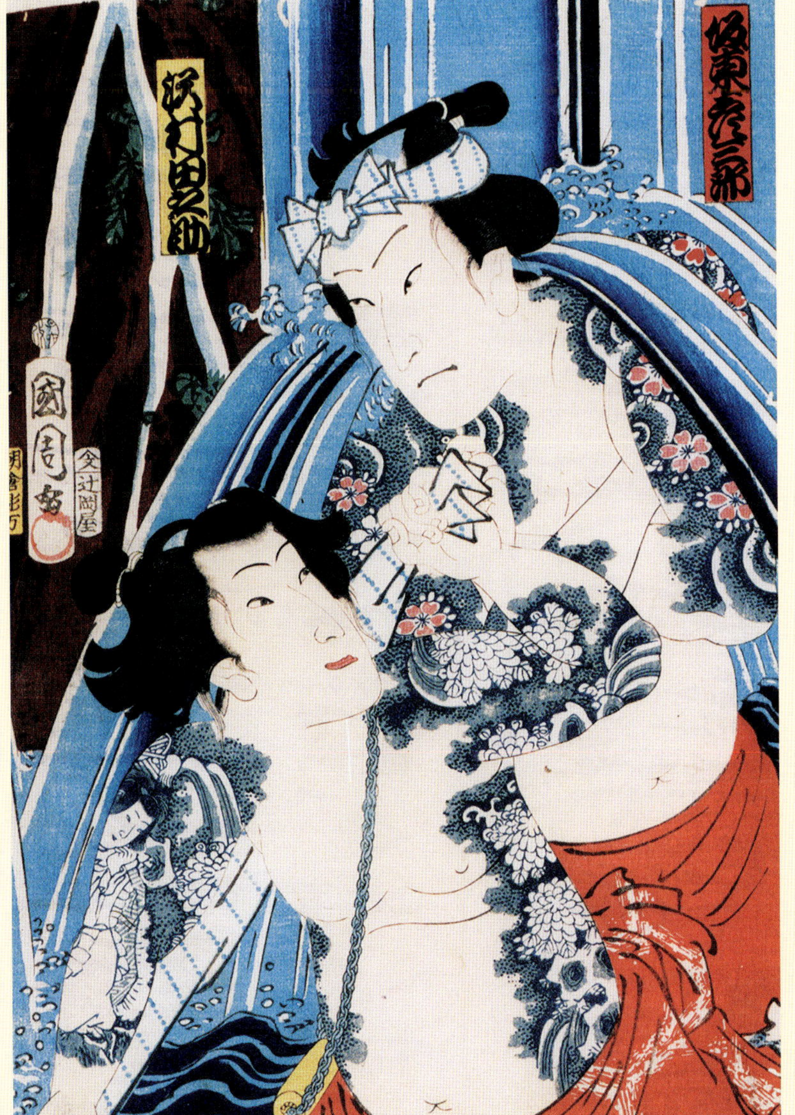

「當盛五人揃肌競」「市村家橘」
「中村芝翫」豊原国周
Ichimura Kakitsu , Nakamura Shikan, from the series
Tōsē-Goninsoroi-Hadakurabe, Toyohara Kunichika

元治元年・1864
東京都立中央図書館特別文庫室蔵
1864, Tokyo Metropolitan Library

鬼若丸

おにわかまる

鬼若丸は武蔵坊弁慶の幼名。母の胎内に十八ヶ月ものあいだいて、産まれたときには二・三歳の子供のように見えたことから、「鬼若」と名づけられ、七歳で天台宗の総本山である比叡山延暦寺に預けられた。右の図は、子供に害をなす暴れ巨鯉を短刀ひとつで退治し、僧達を驚かせたという話の一場面である。

"Oniwakamaru" was the childhood name of *Musashibo Benkei*, who said to have stayed in his mother's womb for eighteen months and resembled a two- or three-year-old child when he was born. That is why he was named *Oniwakamaru* (Little Demon).

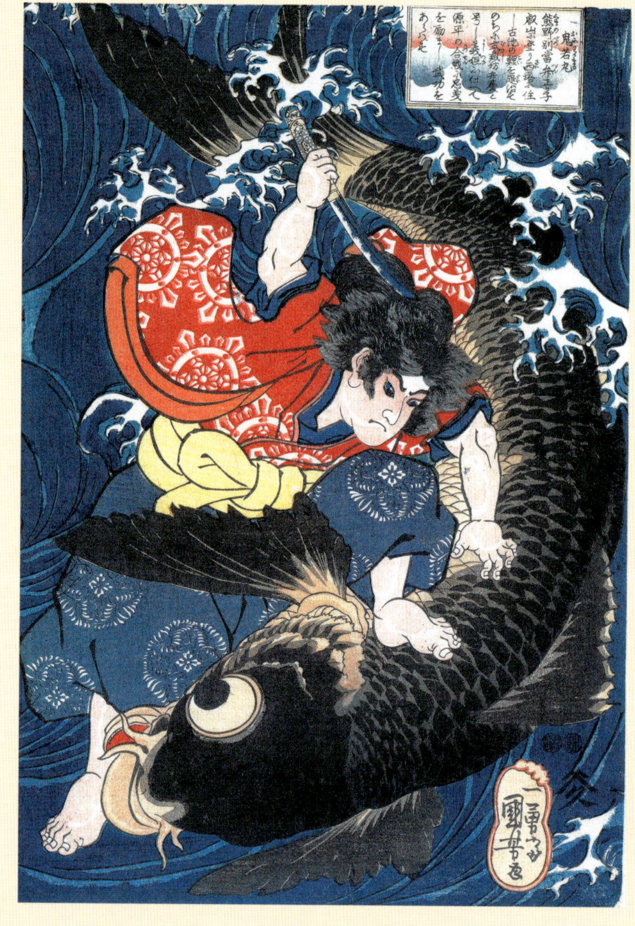

「鬼若丸」歌川国芳
Oniwakamaru, Utagawa Kuniyoshi

弘化末〜嘉永期・1847-52
山口県立萩美術館・浦上記念館蔵
Edo period, 1847-52, Hagi Uragami Museum

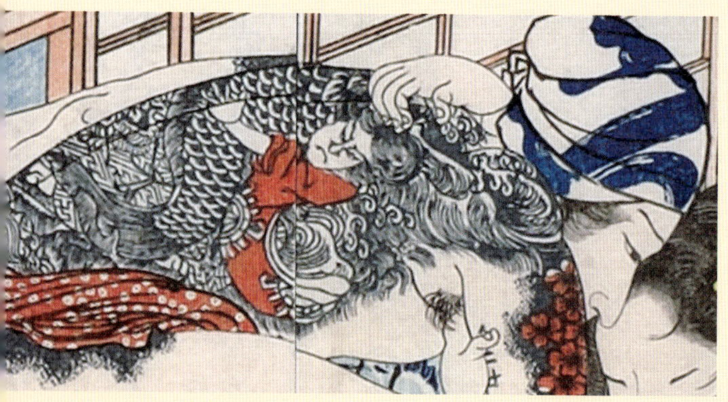

「華古与見」（部分）歌川国芳
Hanagoyomi: Calender for flower plucking, Detail, Utagawa Kuniyoshi

天保6年・1835
国際日本文化研究センター蔵
1835, International Research Center for Japanese Studies

「鬼若力之助　鯉つかみ」歌川国芳
Oniwaka Rikinosuke, Catch a carp (*Koitsukami*), Utagawa Kuniyoshi

嘉永3年・1850
山口県立萩美術館・浦上記念館蔵
1850, Hagi Uragami Museum

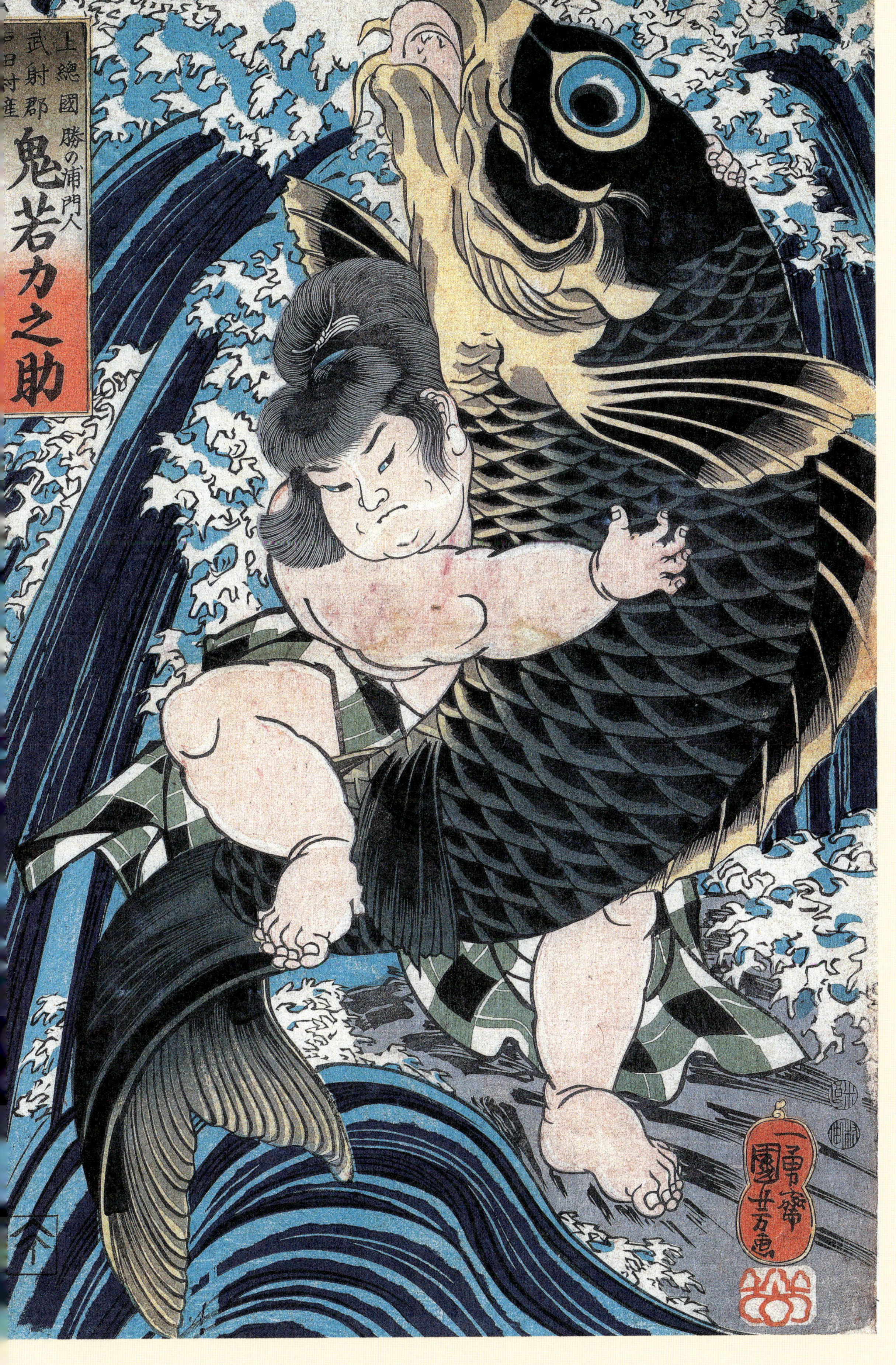

Chapter 2 │ Tattoo Designs **Oniwakamaru**

Oni (Demon)

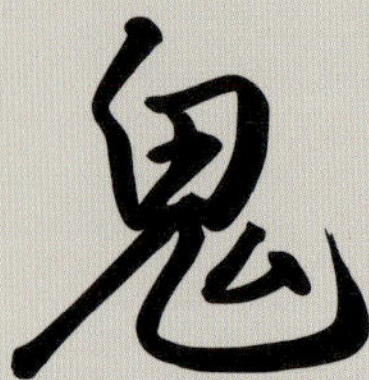

鬼

おに

鬼は想像上の怪物で、人間のかたちをして頭には角を生やし、口は横に裂けて鋭い牙をもっている。そして裸で腰には虎の皮の褌（ふんどし）を締めたすがたであらわれる。性質は荒々しく、手には金棒を握っている。地獄には赤鬼と青鬼が住むといわれている。

The *oni* is an imaginary monster in human form with horns growing on its head. The open mouth reveals sharp fangs. Naked to the waist, this *oni* wears a tiger pelt as a loincloth. His nature is violent, and he wields a metal staff.

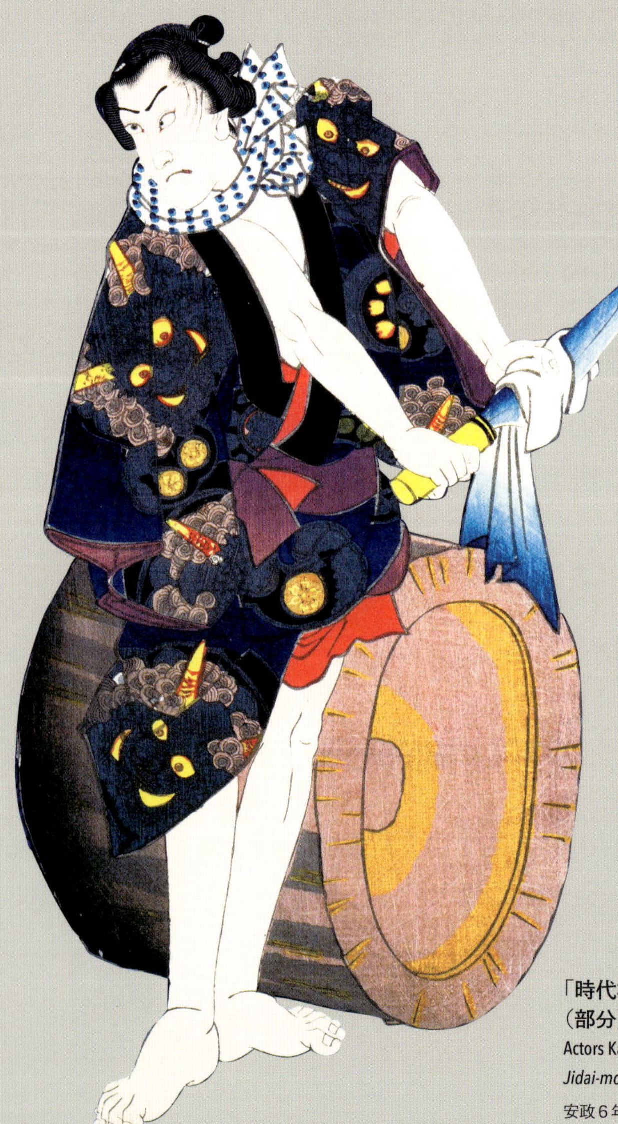

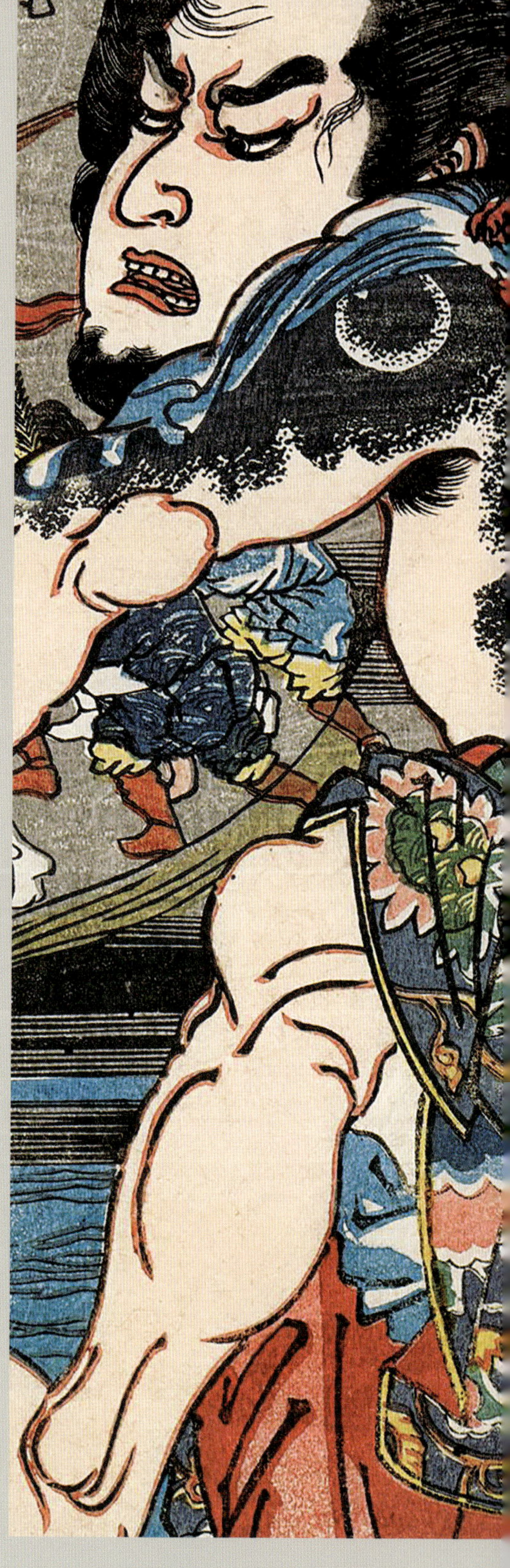

「時代模筆当白波　おさらば小僧傳次」
（部分）歌川豊国
Actors Kawarazaki Gonjūrō as Osarabakozō Denji, from the series
Jidai-moyō-ataru-shiranami, Detail, Utagawa Toyokuni III (Kunisada I)

安政６年・1859　国立国会図書館デジタルコレクション
1859, National Diet Library Digital Collections

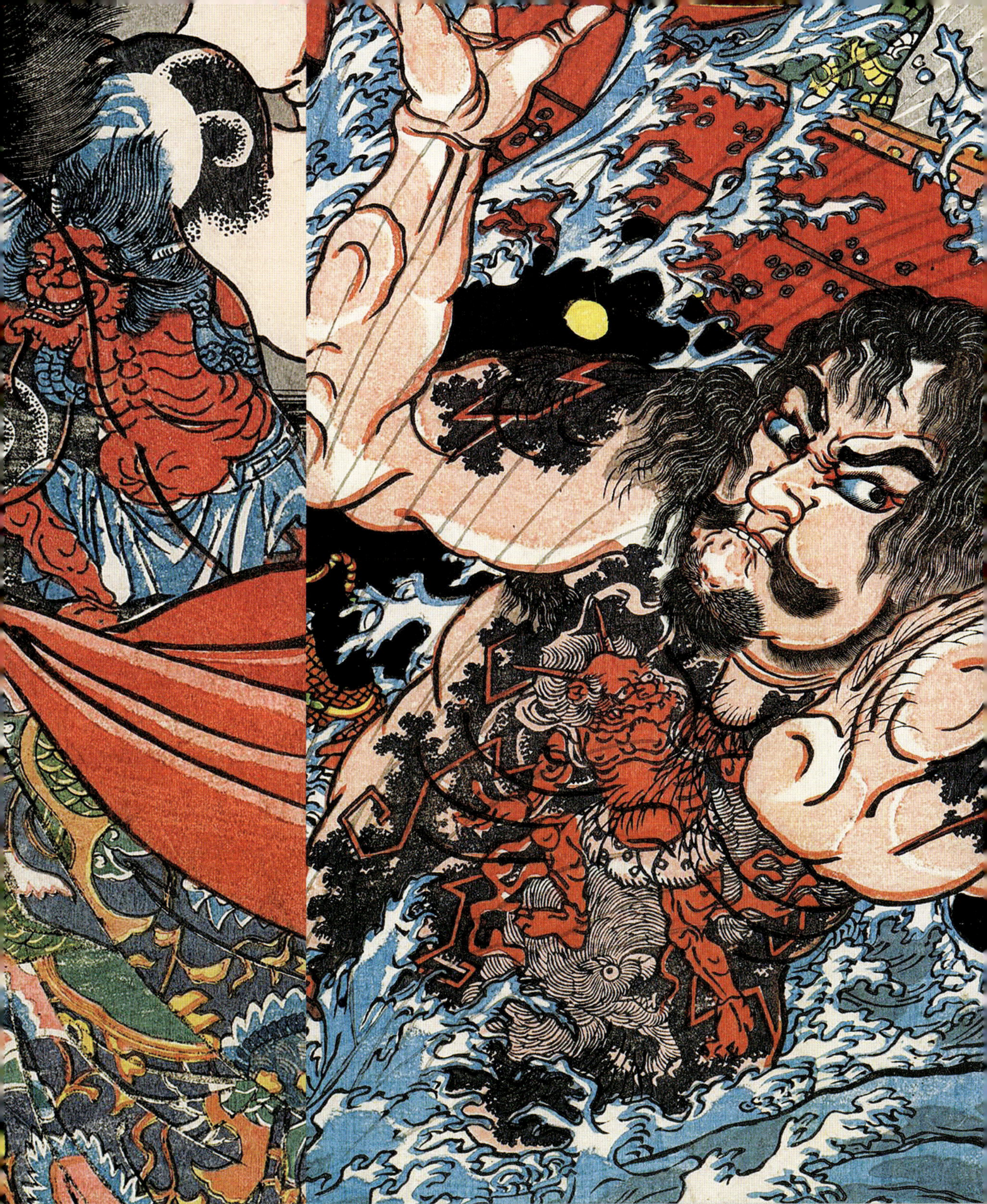

「通俗水滸傳豪傑百八人一個　金毛犬段景住」（部分）歌川国芳
Kinmōken Dan Keiju, from the series *One hundred and eight Heroes of the Suikoden*, Detail, Utagawa Kuniyoshi
江戸時代・19世紀　東京国立博物館蔵
出典：ColBase (https://colbase.nich.go.jp)
Edo period, 19th century, Tokyo National Museum

「通俗水滸傳豪傑百八人之一個　混江龍李俊」（部分）歌川国芳
Konkōryu Rishun, from the series *One hundred and eight Heroes of the Suikoden*, Detail, Utagawa Kuniyoshi
江戸時代・19世紀　東京国立博物館蔵
出典：ColBase (https://colbase.nich.go.jp)
Edo period, 19th century, Tokyo National Museum

Chapter 2　|　Tattoo Designs　**Oni**（Demon）

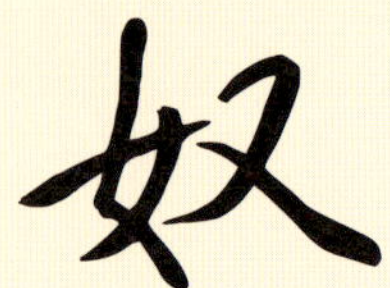

Yakko

奴
（やっこ）

奴は撥鬢とよばれる髪を結い、鎌髭をはやした威勢のいいすがたで知られる。江戸時代に武家に仕えた下男や中間のことで、大名行列の時などは槍を持ち、また長柄や挟み箱などを持って先頭に立った。奴詞ということばを使い、義侠的なおこないを誇った。その姿は奴凧として残っている。

Yakko are fellows known for tying their hair back and growing "sickle-shaped mustaches," for an imposing look. In the Edo period, *yakko* served warrior clans and marched, carrying lances, at the head of daimyo processions. They used their own rather rough argot, *yakko kotoba*, and took pride in behaving chivalrously.

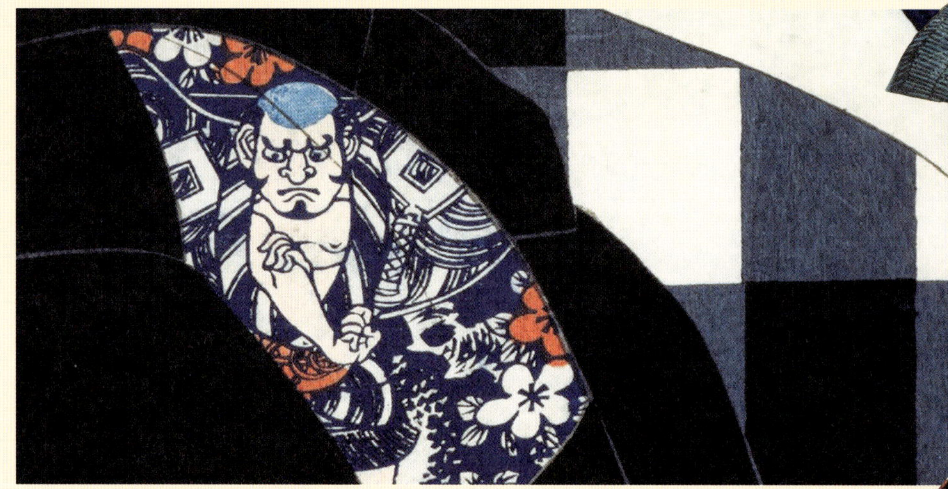

「深以仲意気地新倭羅　小糸佐七」（部分）歌川豊国
Actors Ichikawa Ichizō III as Sashichi and Nakamura Fukusuke I, Koito in the Play Koito and Sashichi (*Koito Sashichi*), Detail, Utagawa Toyokuni III (Kunisada I)

国立国会図書館デジタルコレクション
National Diet Library Digital Collections

Dogs

狗
（いぬ）

狗は古くから人とともに住み、猟犬や番犬とされた。神社や寺院、霊廟などには魔除けとして狛犬（こまいぬ）が置かれる。桃山から江戸時代にかけて狗は画題として取り上げられ、琳派の俵屋宗達の子狗図はよく知られる。

Dogs have long lived with people, serving as hunting dogs or guard dogs. Statues of guardian lion-dogs are often displayed at shrines and temples to ward off evil. In the Momoyama through the Edo periods (1574-1868), dogs became a painting subject, with the puppies painted by the Rimpa school's Tawaraya Sotatsu particularly famous.

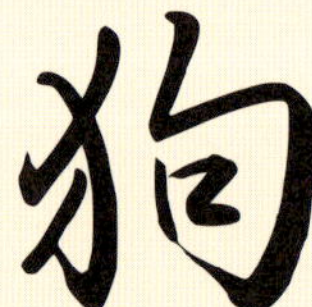

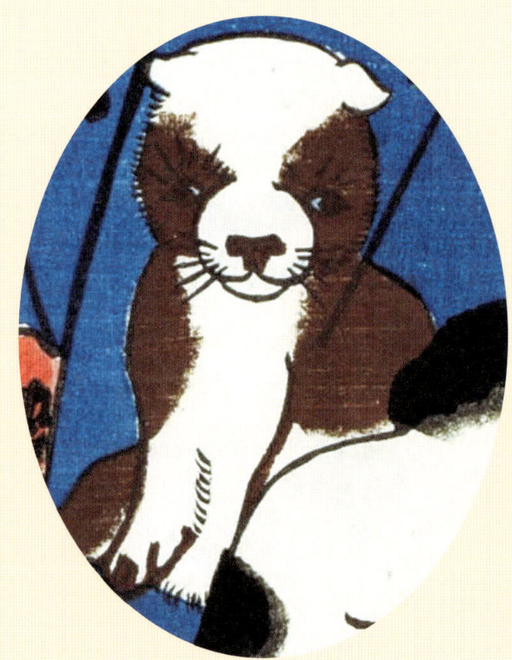

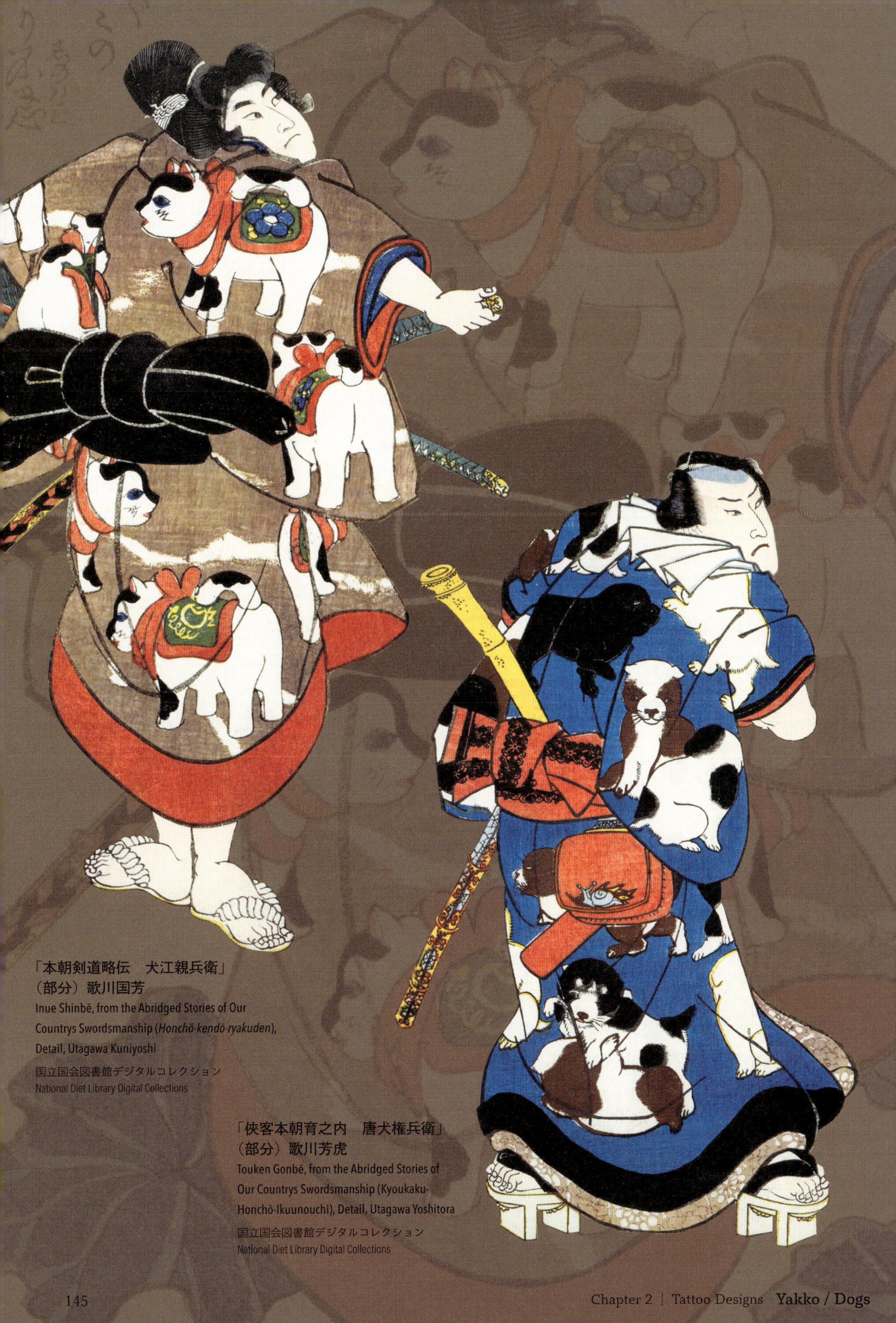

「本朝剣道略伝　犬江親兵衛」
（部分）歌川国芳
Inue Shinbē, from the Abridged Stories of Our
Countrys Swordsmanship (*Honchō-kendō-ryakuden*),
Detail, Utagawa Kuniyoshi
国立国会図書館デジタルコレクション
National Diet Library Digital Collections

「侠客本朝育之内　唐犬権兵衛」
（部分）歌川芳虎
Touken Gonbē, from the Abridged Stories of
Our Countrys Swordsmanship (*Kyoukaku-
Honchō-Ikuunouchi*), Detail, Utagawa Yoshitora
国立国会図書館デジタルコレクション
National Diet Library Digital Collections

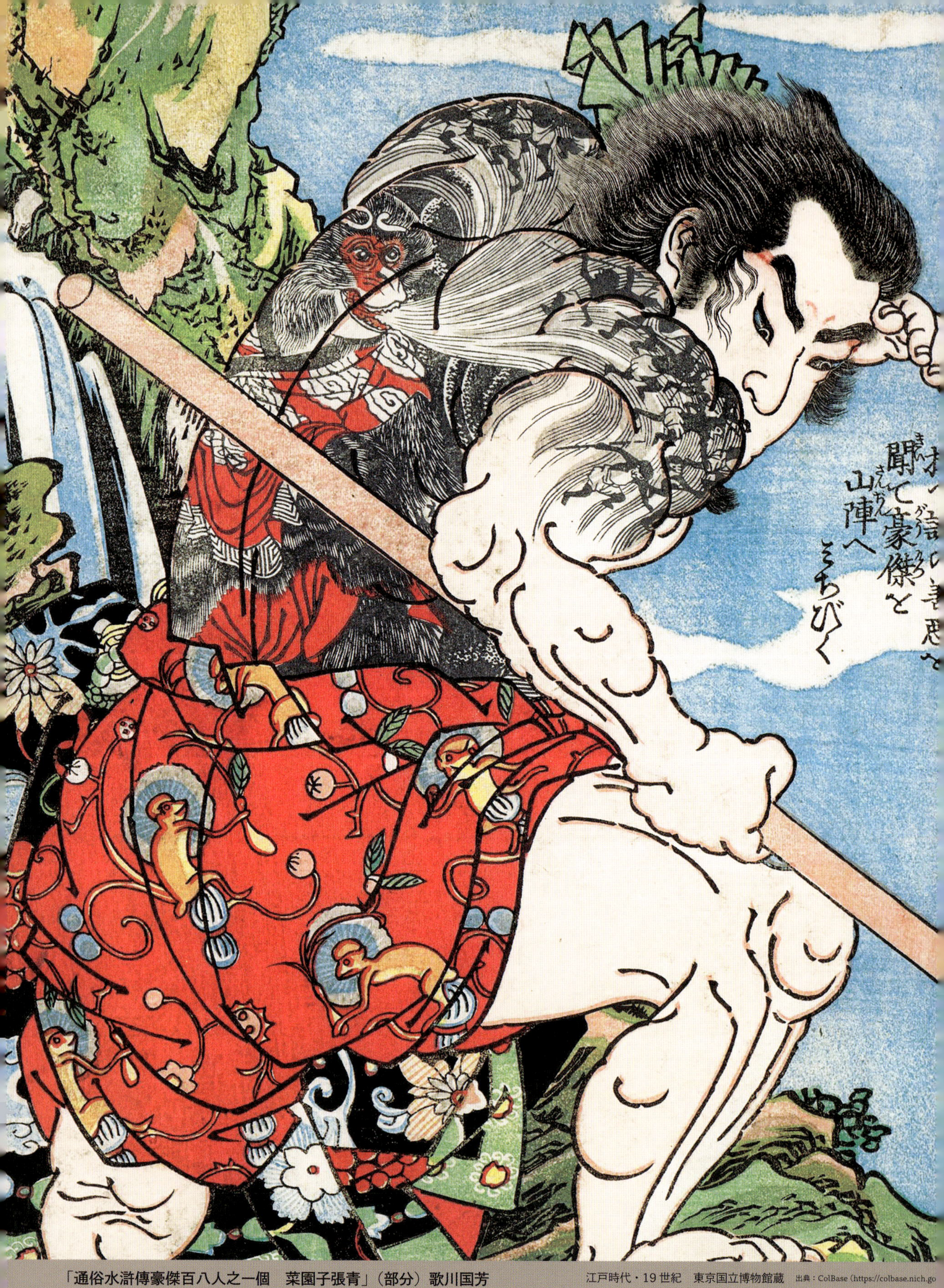

「通俗水滸傳豪傑百八人之一個　菜園子張青」（部分）歌川国芳
Saienshi Chousei, from the series *One hundred and eight Heroes of the Suikoden*, Detail, Utagawa Kuniyoshi

江戸時代・19世紀　東京国立博物館蔵　出典：ColBase (https://colbase.nich.go
Edo period, 19th century, Tokyo National Museum

猿

さる

中国では猿は古から神の使いと
され崇められている。比叡山ふも
との日吉神社では、神の使いとさ
れて尊ばれ、馬の守護神にもされ
ていた。また猿神信仰から「見ざ
る、聞かざる、言わざる」をあら
わした三猿を文様化したものが庚
申塔に刻み出されている。

In China, monkeys have long been revered as
divine messengers. At the *Hie* Shrine at the
foot of Mount *Hiei*, in Shiga, they are respected
as guardian deities for horses as well as divine messengers.

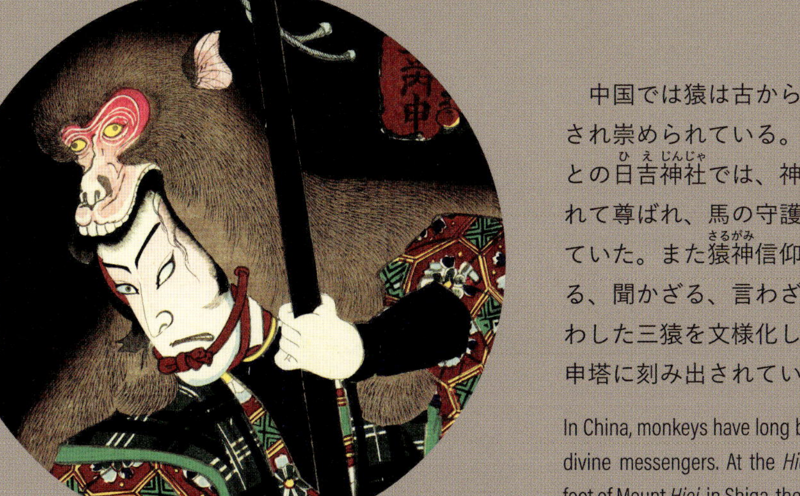

「奇術十二支之内　申　三生の小猿　尾上
菊五郎」（部分）豊原国周
Actors Onoe Kikugorō as Sanshō no Kozaru, from the series
Kijutsu-Jūnishi-no-uchi, Saru, Detail, Toyohara Kunichika
明治 10 年・1877　国立国会図書館デジタルコレクション
1877, National Diet Library Digital Collections

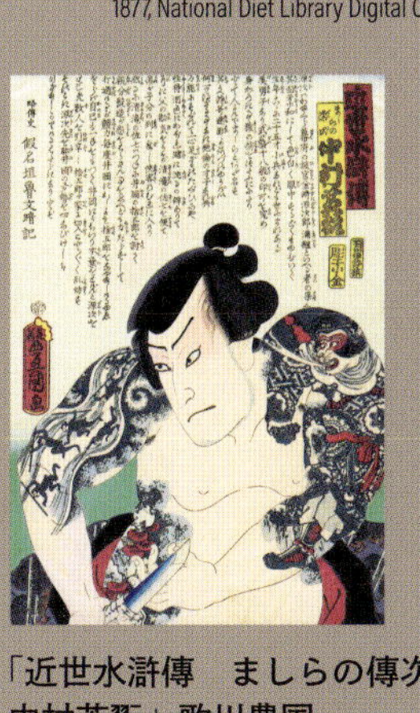

「近世水滸傳　ましらの傳次
中村芝翫」歌川豊国
Actors Nakamura Shikan IV as Mashira
no Denji, from the series *A Modern
Suikoden* (*Kinsei Suikoden*), Utagawa
Toyokuni III (Kunisada I)
文久 2 年・1862
東京都立中央図書館
特別文庫室蔵
1862, Tokyo Metropolitan Central
Library

狼

おおかみ

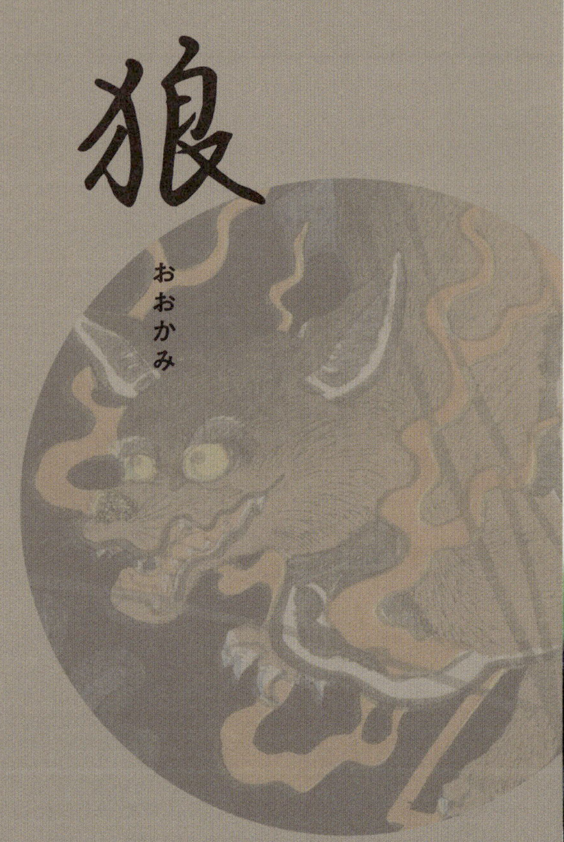

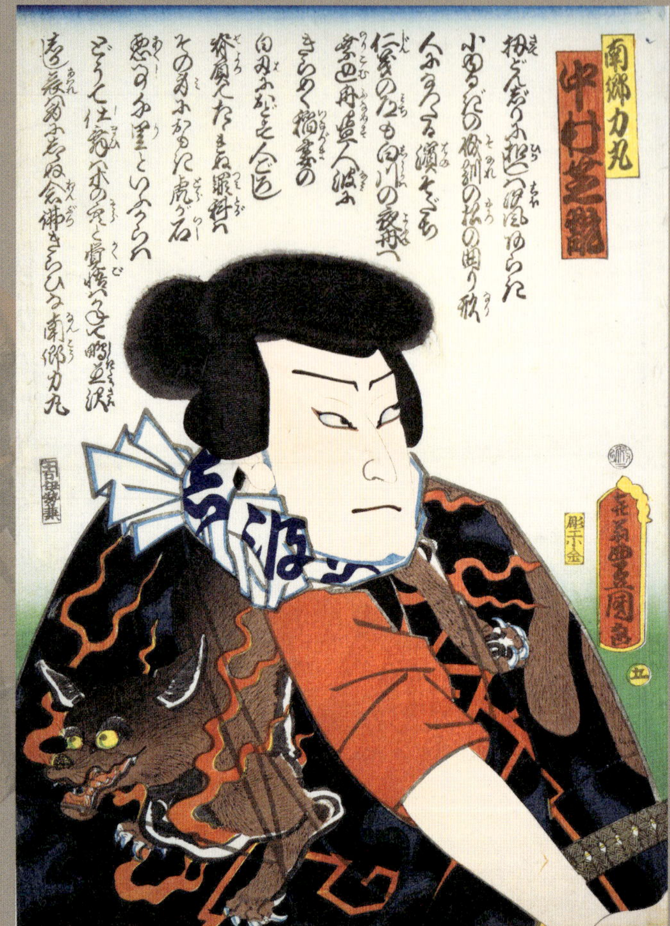

「南郷力丸　中村芝翫」歌川豊国
Actors Nakamura Shikan as Nangou Rikimaru,
Utagawa Toyokuni III (Kunisada I)

文久2年・1862　国立国会図書館
デジタルコレクション
1862, National Diet Library Digital Collections

　日本固有のニホンオオカミはかつて本州や四国、九州にいたが、明治の終わりに捕獲されたのを最後に絶滅したとみられる。狼は「大神」と当て字であらわしていた地域も多く、昔から山神の使いとして敬われた。江戸時代中期には眷属信仰の憑き物落としの霊験として盛んになった。

A species of wolf unique to Japan, the Japanese wolf was once found on Honshu, Shikoku, and Kyushu. By the end of the Meiji period, however, these wolves had been hunted to extinction. *Ookami*, the Japanese word for wolf, is a homonym for "great spirit," and in many regions was written with the kanji for "great spirit." Wolves had long been treated with respect as the messengers of mountain gods.

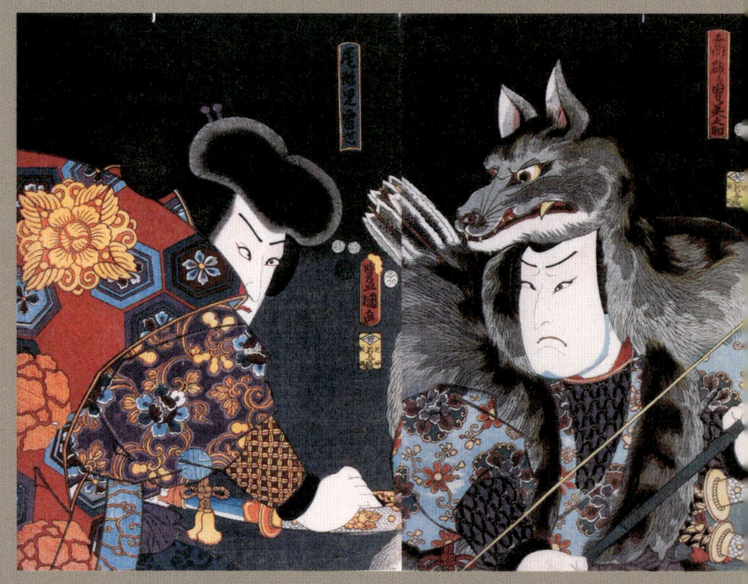

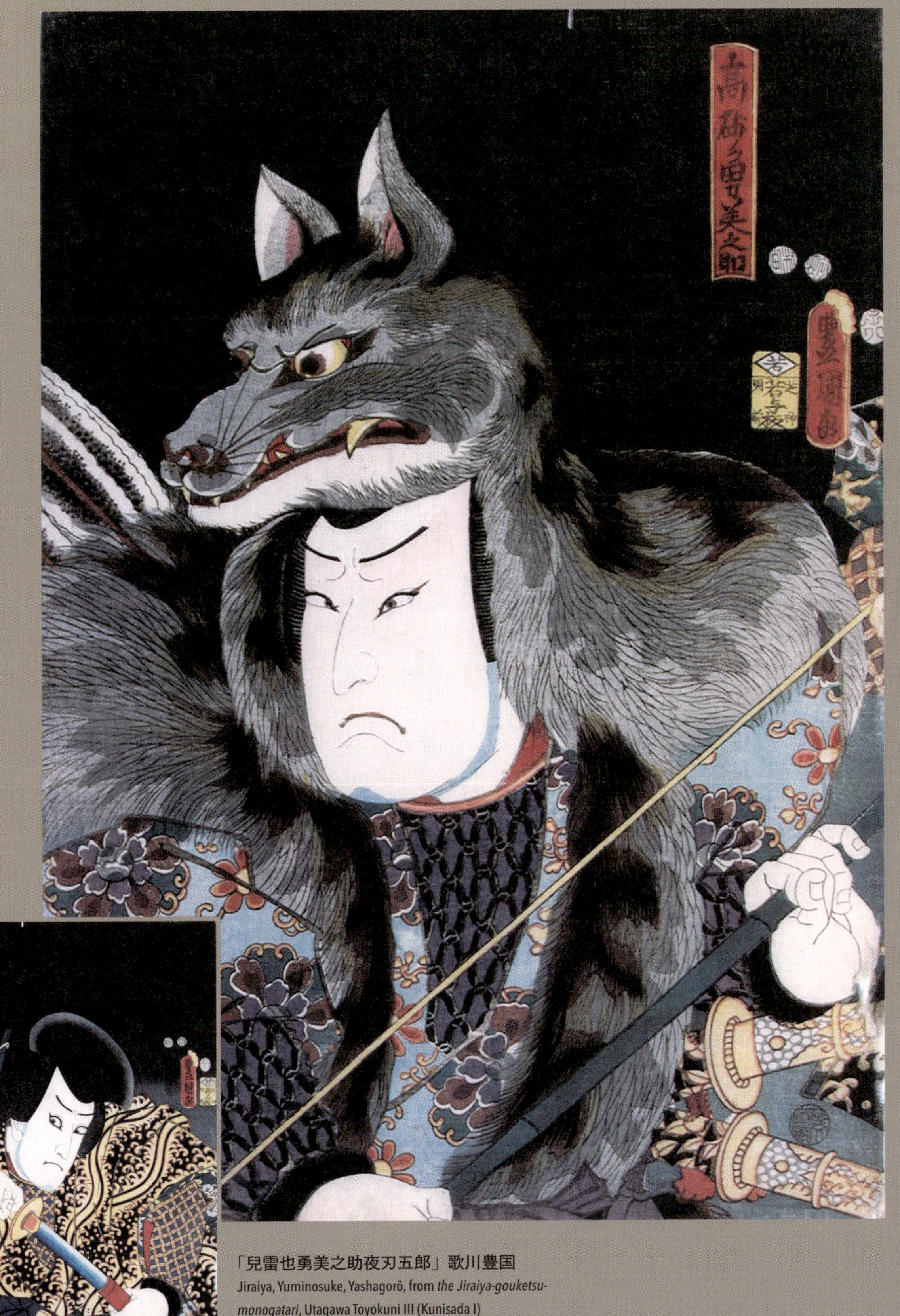

「兒雷也勇美之助夜刃五郎」歌川豊国
Jiraiya, Yuminosuke, Yashagorō, from *the Jiraiya-gouketsu-monogatari*, Utagawa Toyokuni III (Kunisada I)

嘉永 5 年・1852　静岡県立中央図書館蔵
1852, Shizuoka Prefectural Central Library

Shape-changing Cat

化け猫

ばけねこ

日本に家猫がやってきたのは、奈良時代に中国から仏教の経典を船で運ぶとき、鼠の害を防ぐために猫を乗せたのが最初といわれている。怪談で語られるのは三毛猫が多く、年を経た猫は尾が二つに割れて猫又になるといわれる。江戸時代には多くの化け猫の話が生まれ、講談や小説でひろく知られた。刺青に彫れば凄みが発揮される。

The first domesticated cats in Japan arrived during the Nara period (710-84) on ships transporting Buddhist sutras from China. Their job was to prevent the sutras from being damaged by rats. The cats who appear in ghost stories are usually tortoiseshells. As a cat grows older, its tail is said to split in two as it turns into a *neko-mata*, a two-tailed monster cat.

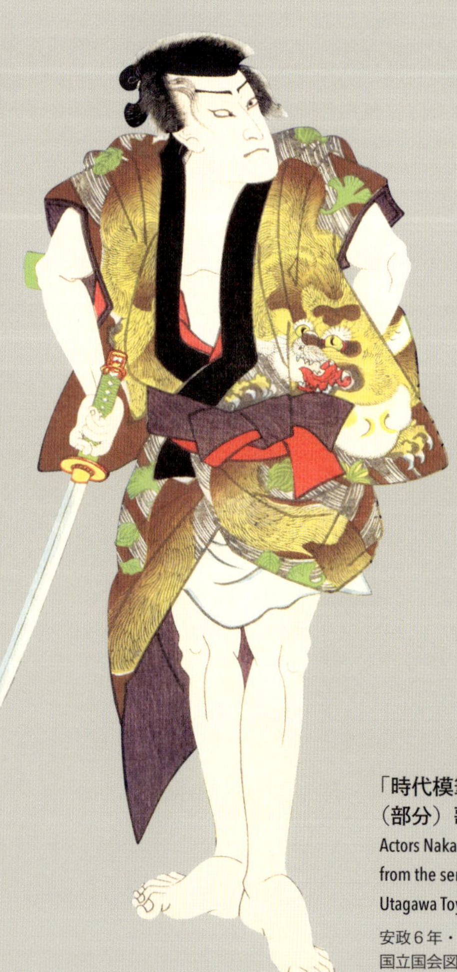

「時代模筆当白波　山猫三次」
（部分）歌川豊国
Actors Nakamura Fukusuke as Yamaneko Sanji, from the series *Jidai-moyō-ataru-shiranami*, Detail, Utagawa Toyokuni III (Kunisada I)

安政 6 年・1859
国立国会図書館デジタルコレクション
1859, National Diet Library Digital Collections

「江戸の花名勝会　ね　九番組」歌川豊国
Ne Ninth Gumi, from the *Edo-no-hana*, *Meishokai*, Utagawa Toyokuni III (Kunisada I)

元治元年・1865　国立国会図書館デジタルコレクション
1865, National Diet Library Digital Collections

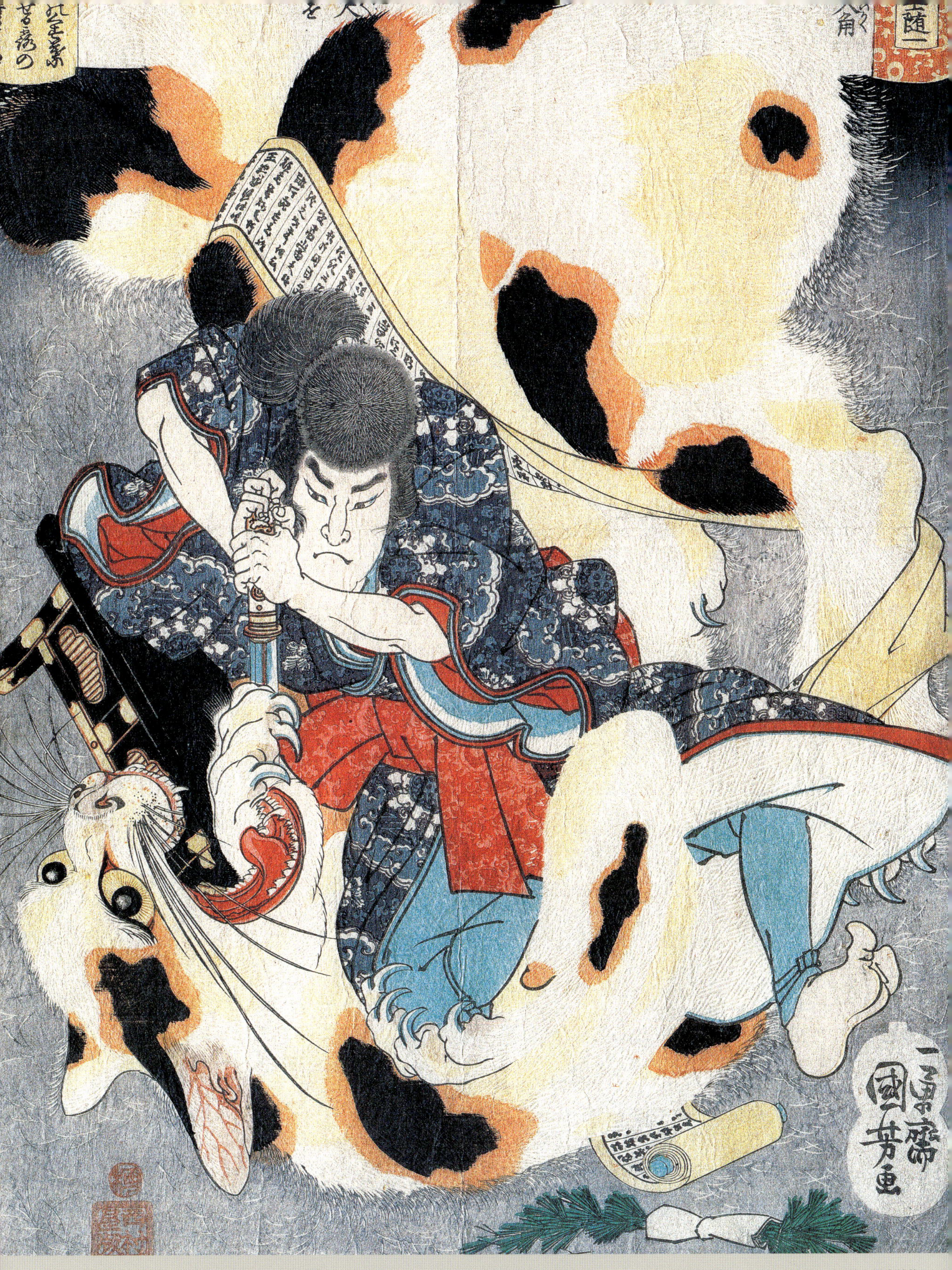

「曲亭翁精著八犬士随一　犬村大角妖猫退治」（部分）歌川国芳
Inumura Daikaku conquers monster cat, the best of Eight Dog Warriors written by
Kyokutei Bakin, Detail, Utagawa Kuniyoshi

天保末期頃・1842　山口県立萩美術館・浦上記念館蔵
Edo period, 1842, Hagi Uragami Museum

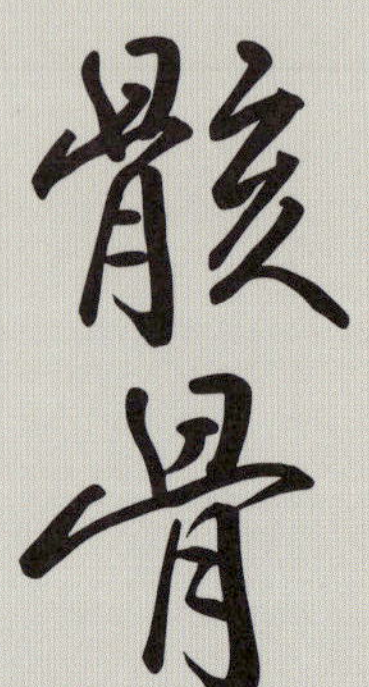

骸骨

（がいこつ）

骨だけになった死骸が骸骨で、全身の骨格をとどめているものをいう。また髑髏は野辺にさらされた人の頭蓋骨（されこうべ）のことで、野晒（のざらし）などともいわれる。江戸時代初期の侠客（きょうかく）である寺西閑心が羽織る着物には髑髏の絵が散りばめられ、不気味さが十分に漂っている。

When only the bones of a corpse remain, the full set of bones is called a skeleton or *gaikotsu*. The term *sarekobe* is used to refer to skulls left exposed in a field, to which the term *nozarashi* "abandoned in the field," is also applied.

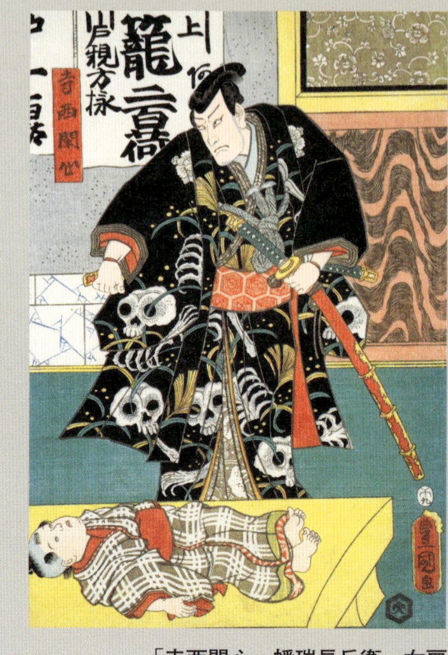

「寺西閑心・幡瑞長兵衛・女房おとき」歌川豊国

Teranishi Kanshin, Banzuiin Choubē, Nyōbo Otoki, Utagawa Toyokuni III (Kunisada I)

国立国会図書館デジタルコレクション
National Diet Library Digital Collections

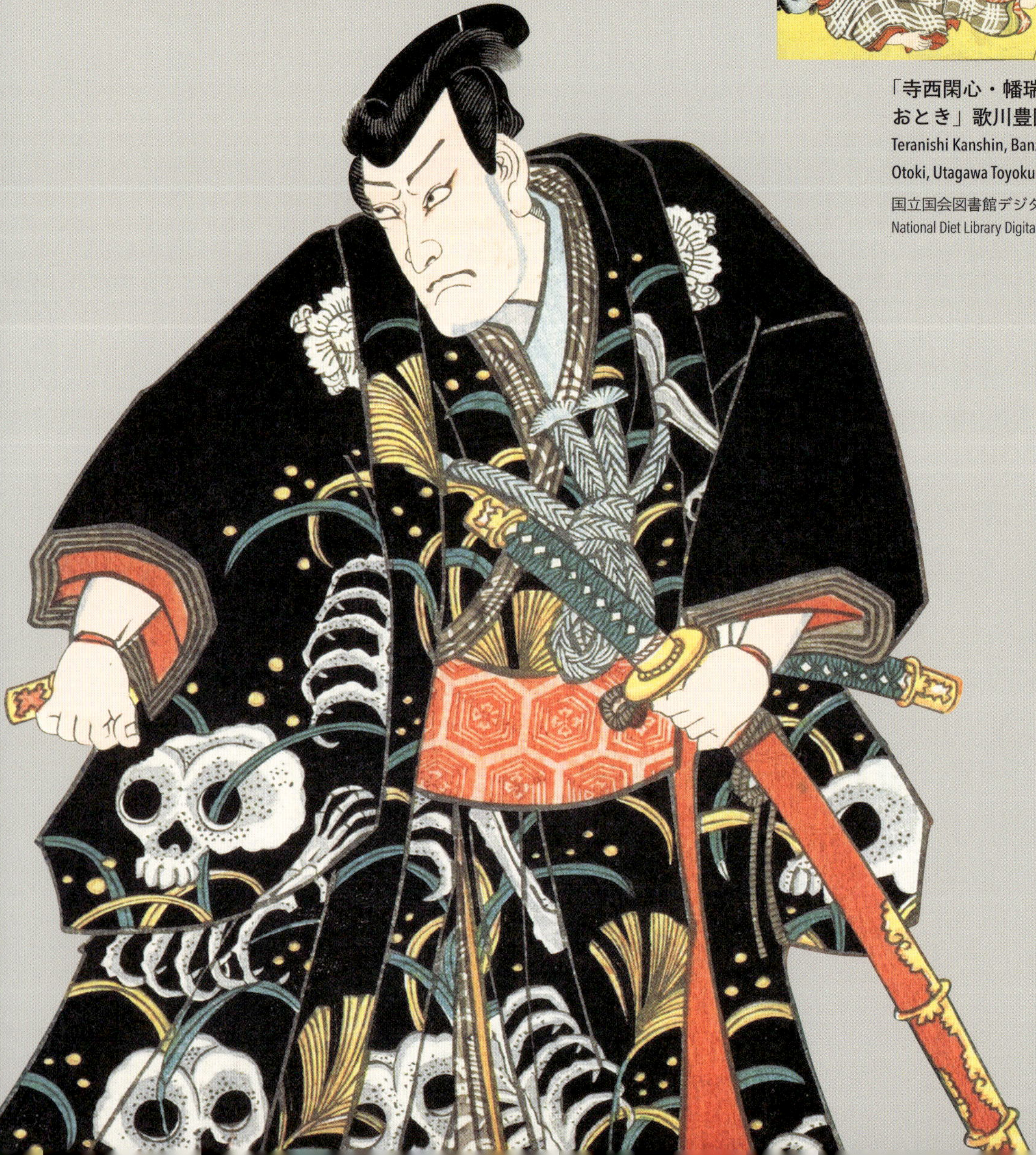

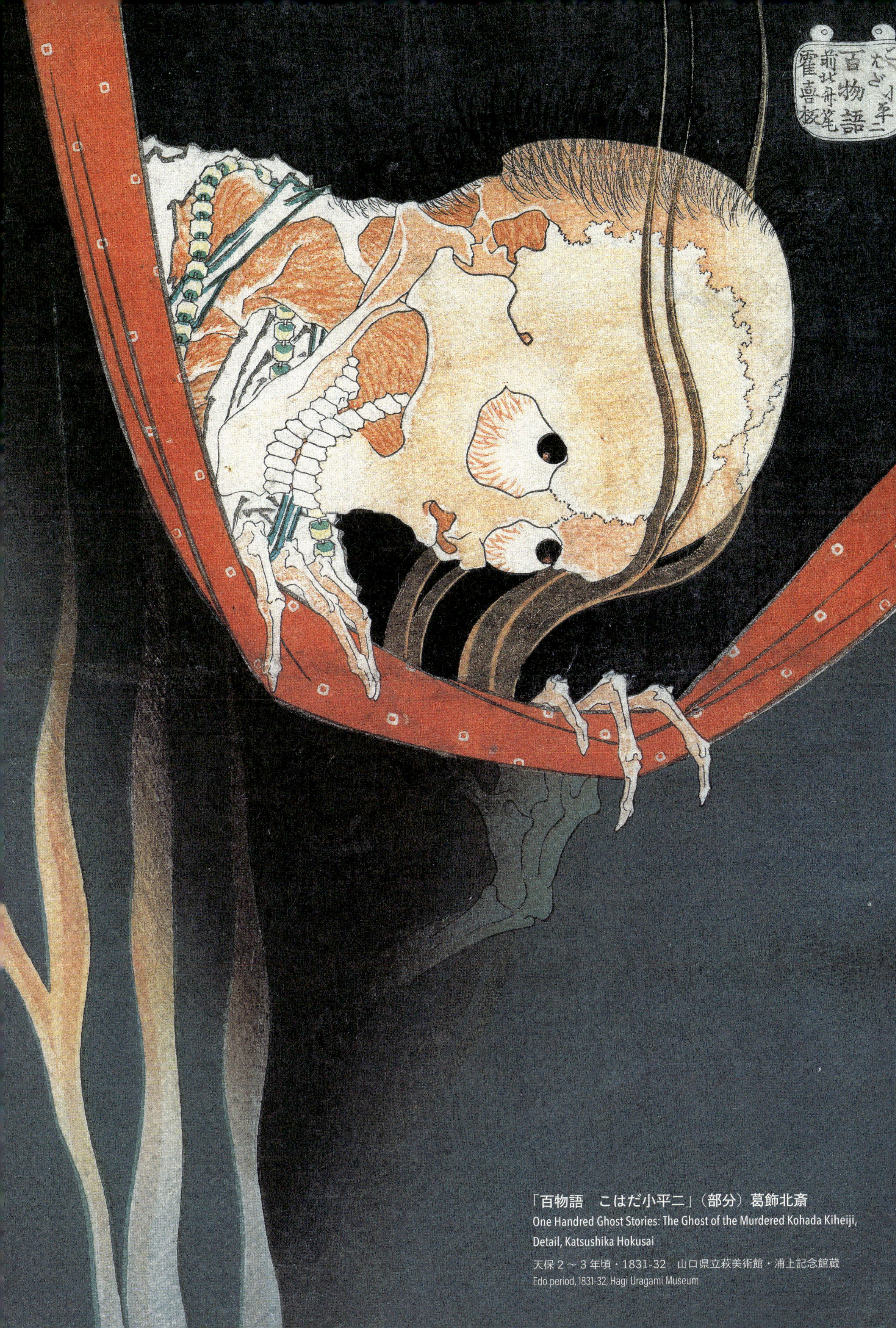

「百物語　こはだ小平二」（部分）葛飾北斎
One Handred Ghost Stories: The Ghost of the Murdered Kohada Kiheiji,
Detail, Katsushika Hokusai

天保 2 ～ 3 年頃・1831-32　山口県立萩美術館・浦上記念館蔵
Edo period, 1831-32, Hagi Uragami Museum

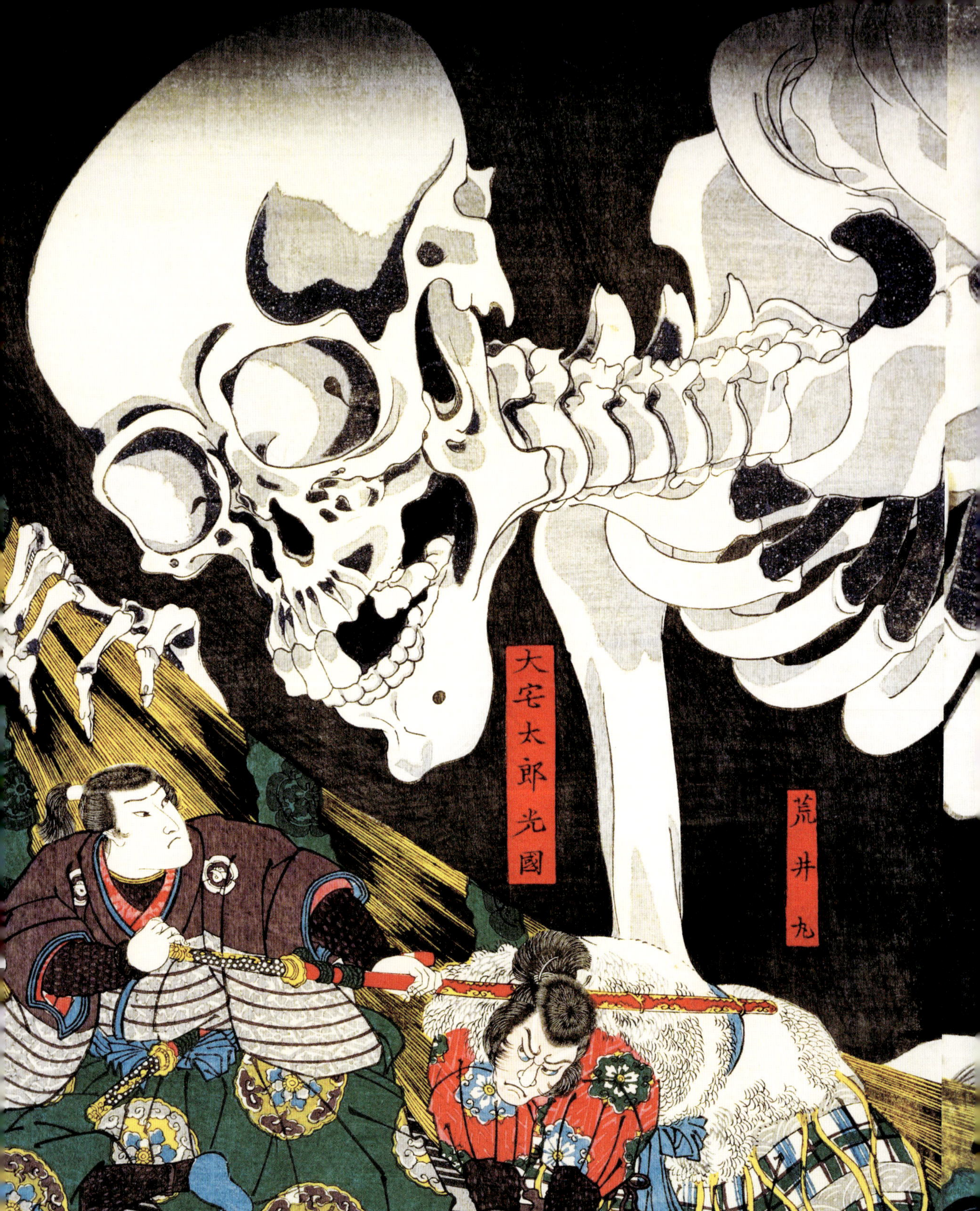

「瀧夜叉姫と骸骨の図」（部分）歌川国芳
Takiyasha Hime and Gaikotsu no Zu, Detail, Utagawa Kuniyoshi

国立国会図書館デジタルコレクション
National Diet Library Digital Collections

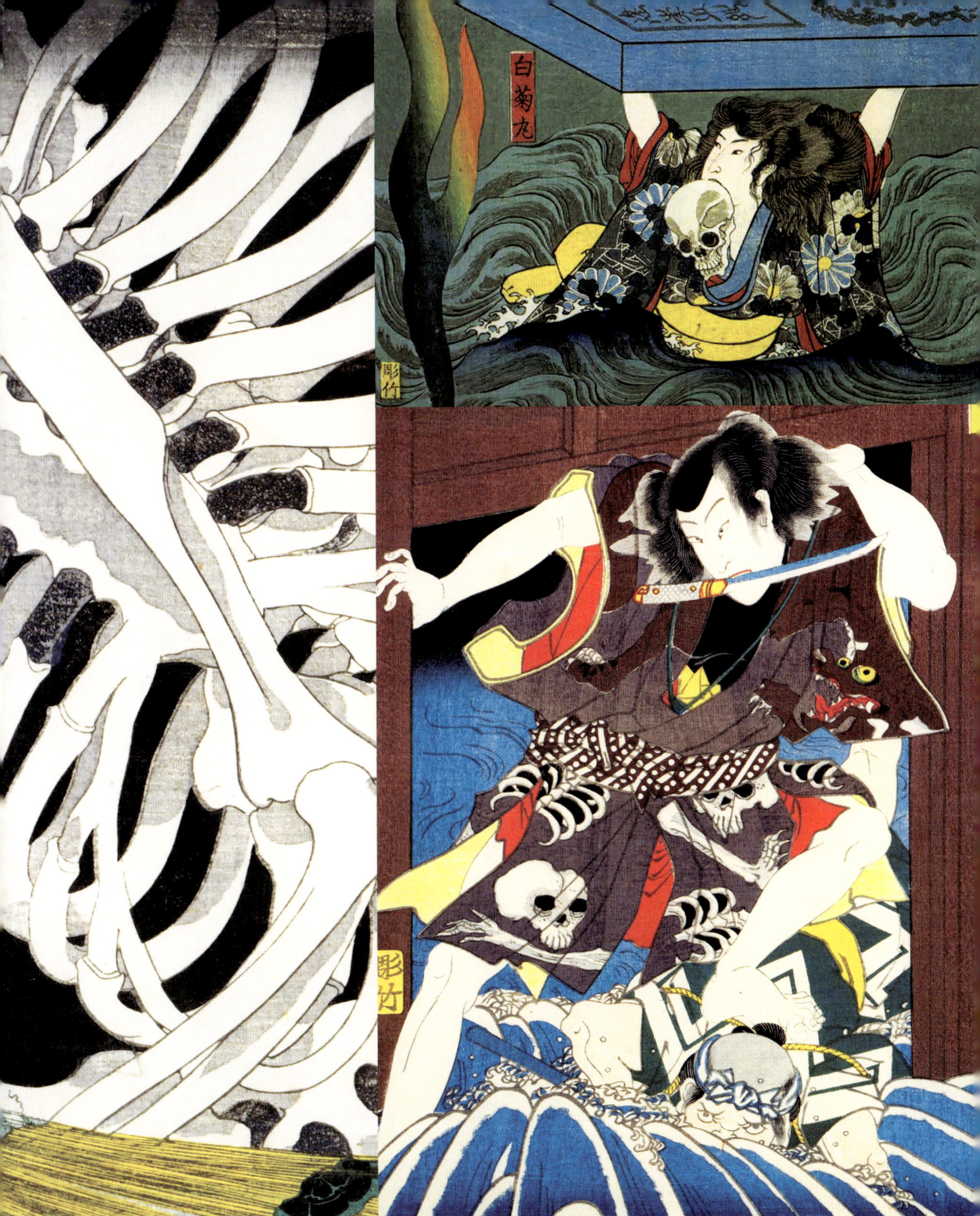

「小倉擬百人一首　凡河内躬恒　白菊丸」（部分）歌川国芳
Poem by Oshikōchi no Mitsune: Shiragikumaru, from the series *Ogura Imitations of One Hundred Poems by One Hundred Poets* (*Ogura nazorae hyakunin isshu*), Detail, Utagawa Kuniyoshi
国立国会図書館デジタルコレクション　National Diet Library Digital Collections

「豊国漫画図絵　狼ノ悪次郎」（部分）歌川豊国
Ookami no Akujirō, from *The Heroes and Heroines of the Popular Fiction* (*Toyokuni Manga Zue*), Detail, Utagawa Toyokuni III (Kunisada I)
万延元年・1860　国立国会図書館デジタルコレクション
1860, National Diet Library Digital Collections

鰐鮫

わにざめ

『古事記』に、大国主命が
因幡の海辺で、鰐にだまされて
皮をはがされ赤裸になった兎を
助ける話がある。鰐鮫は魚類
の鮫の俗称で、山陰地方では
いまでも大形の鮫を鰐とよ
ぶ。また『魏志倭人伝』には、
狗奴国の男子は鮫の害を防
ぐため刺青をすると記さ
れている。

In the *Kojiki* (Records of Ancient Mat-
ters, Japan's first official history),
there is a story in which the deity
Okuninushi rescues a rabbit that was
deceived by a crocodile on the Inaba
seacoast and was stripped of its skin. Wani
or *wanizame*, i.e. "crocodile," was a common term for fish resembling sharks, and
in the San'in region, large sharks are still
called *wani*.

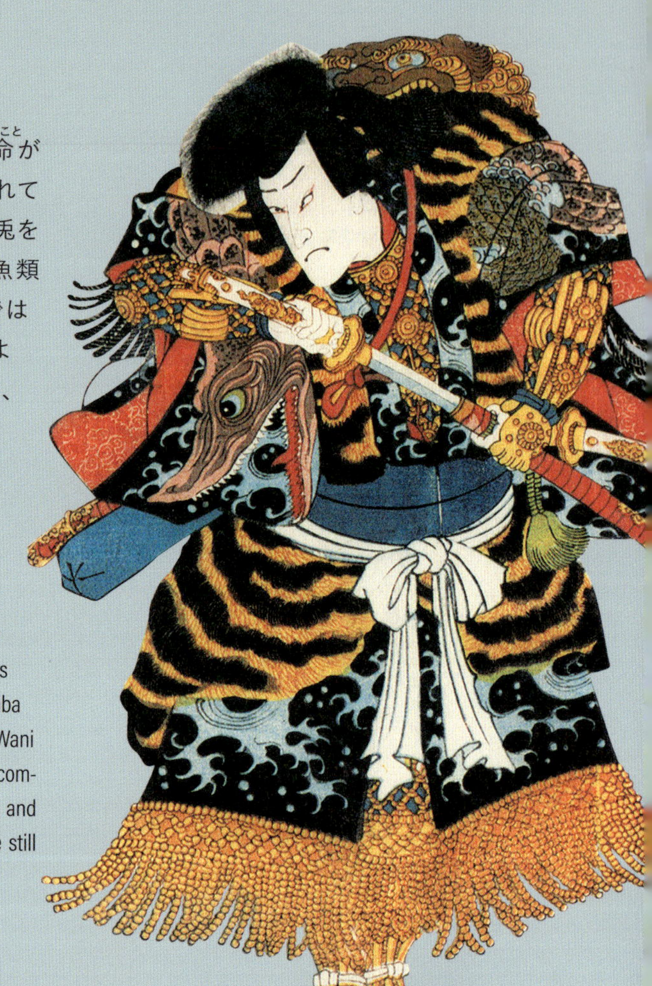

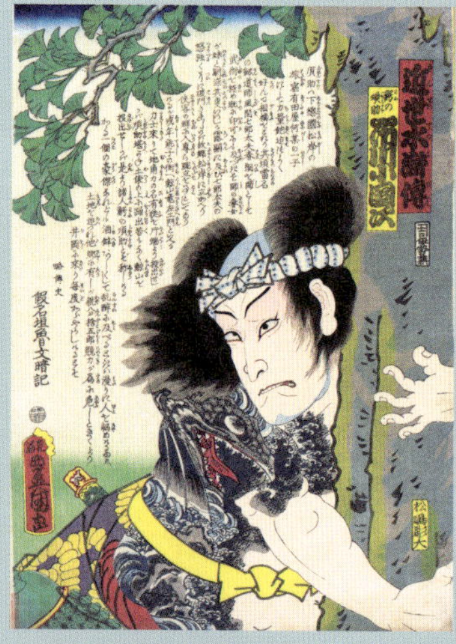

「近世水滸傳　鰐の順助
市川小團次」歌川豊国
Actors Ichikawa Kodanji as Wani no Junsuke, from
the series *A Modern Suikoden* (*Kinsei Suikoden*),
Utagawa Toyokuni III (Kunisada I)
文久 2 年・1862
東京都立中央図書館特別文庫室蔵
1862, Tokyo Metropolitan Central Library

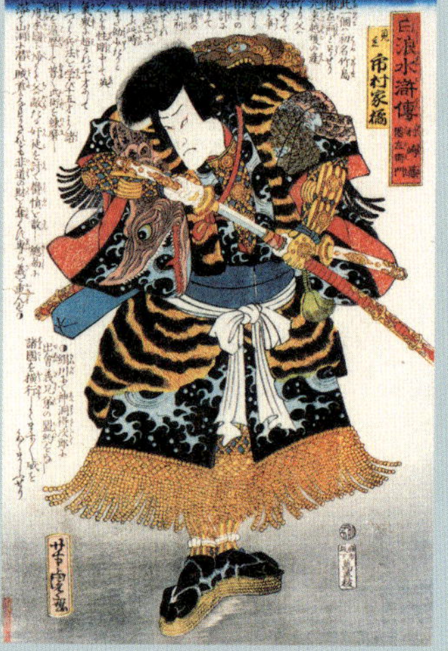

「白浪水滸傳　村崎篠團左衛門」
「見立　市村家橘」歌川芳虎
Actors Ichimura Kakitsu IV as Murasakishino
Danzaemon, from the series *Shiranami Suikoden*,
Utagawa Yoshitora
文久 3 年・1863
東京都立中央図書館特別文庫室蔵
1863, National Diet Library Digital Collections

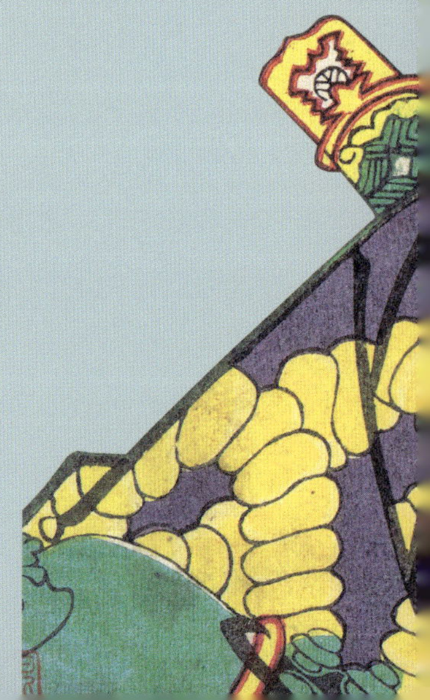

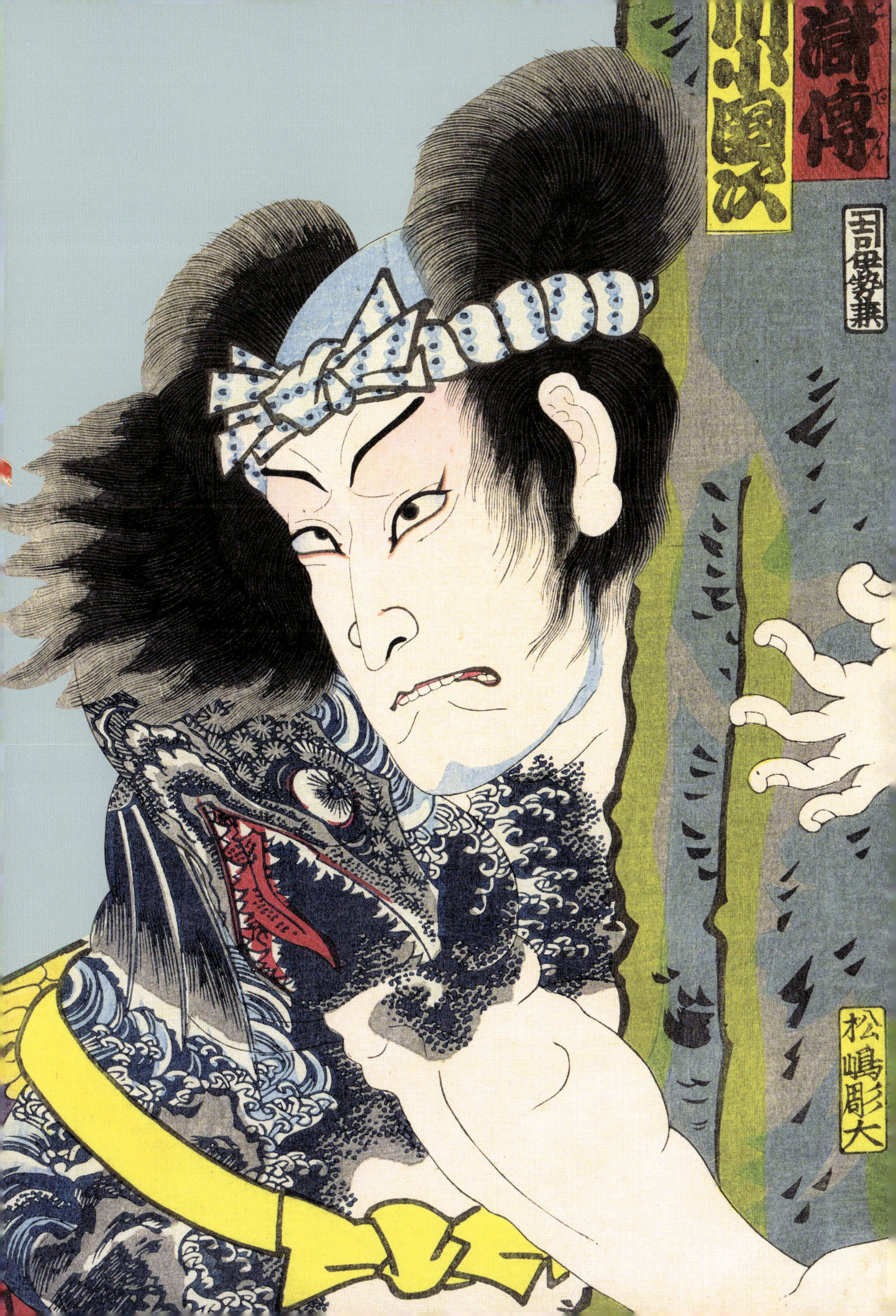

豪傑
司馬屋鷹兼
松嶋彫大

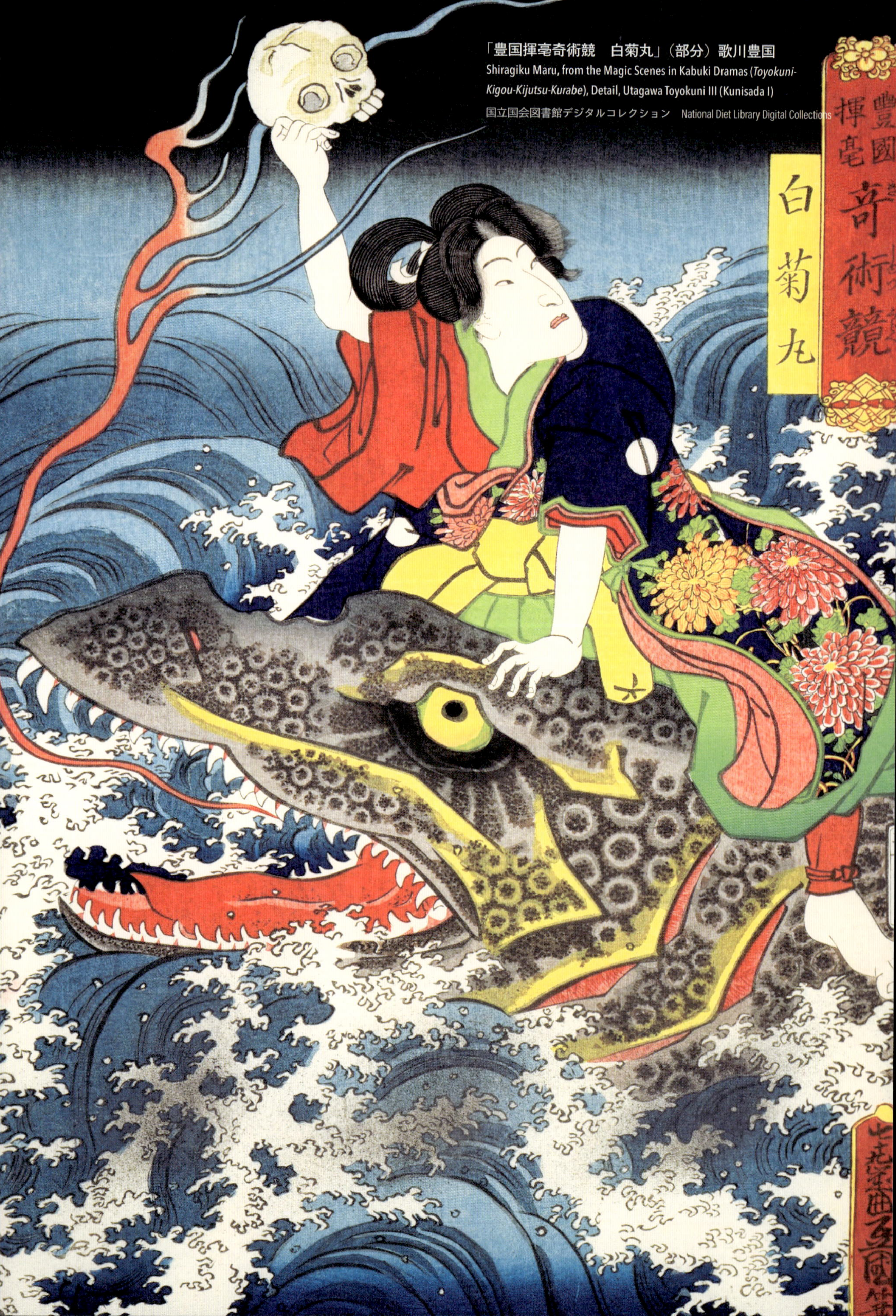

「豊国揮毫奇術競　白菊丸」（部分）歌川豊国
Shiragiku Maru, from the Magic Scenes in Kabuki Dramas (*Toyokuni-Kigou-Kijutsu-Kurabe*), Detail, Utagawa Toyokuni III (Kunisada I)
国立国会図書館デジタルコレクション　National Diet Library Digital Collections

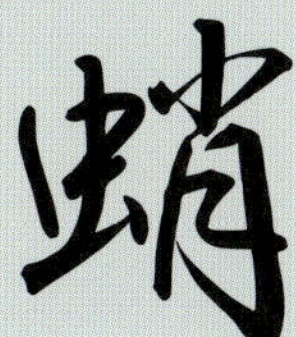

蛸

たこ

蛸は不気味で不思議なすがたのためか、西洋ではデビル・フィッシュ（悪魔の魚）とよばれ忌み嫌われている。日本でも古くは化け物として登場する説話や俗信も多い。賢くいたずら好きで、好奇心の強い生き物である。

Could it be the octopus's weird and uncanny form that has led to it being labeled a "devil fish" and loathed in the West? In Japan, too, it frequently appears as a monster in folktales and popular belief. That said, the octopus is a clever and very curious creature.

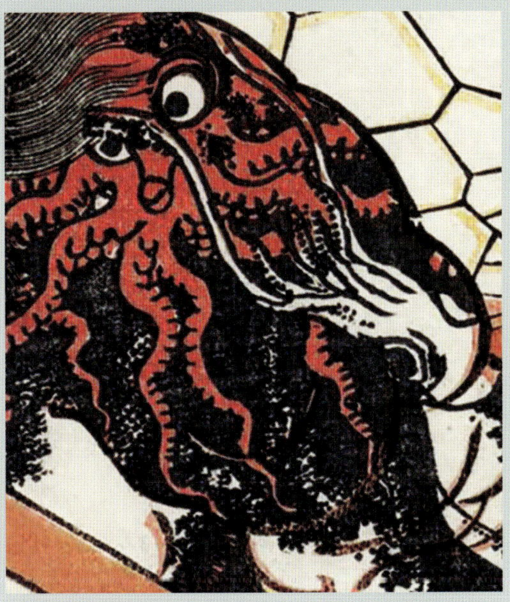

「通俗水滸傳豪傑百八人之一個　操刀鬼曹正」（部分）歌川国芳
Sotouki Sousei, from the series *One hundred and eight Heroes of the Suikoden*, Detail, Utagawa Kuniyoshi
江戸時代・19 世紀　東京国立博物館蔵
出典：ColBase (https://colbase.nich.go.jp)
Edo period, 19th century, Tokyo National Museum

海老

えび

正月の鏡餅に添える飾り海老は、長いひげをはやして腰の曲がった長寿の老人に似ることから、海の翁といって不老長寿の象徴とされた。すがたやかたちがおもしろいことから、網目に海老や、波に海老などの文様がある。

The shrimp that decorate *kagamimochi* at New Years are used because their long whiskers and curved backs evoke the image of long-lived elderly people. They are symbols of long life and referred to as the sea's grandfathers. Because their appearance is intriguing, there are motifs with shrimp caught in nets or tossed by the waves.

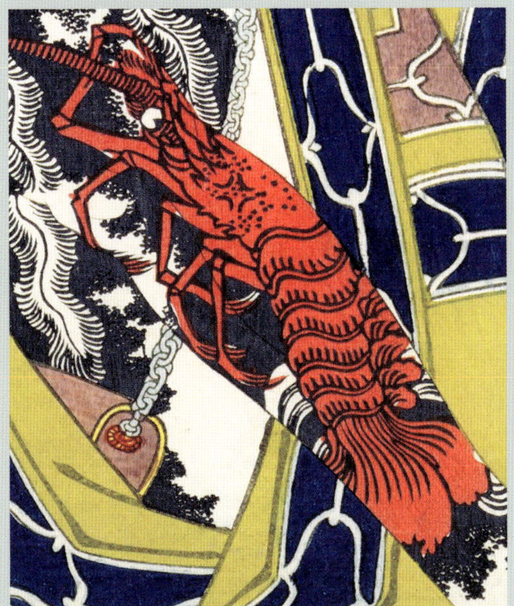

「當世好男子伝　憮小ニ比ス團七九郎兵衛」（市川小團次）（部分）歌川豊国
Actors Ichikawa Kodanji as Danshichi Kurobei, comparable to Ruǎn Xiǎowǔ (Genshogo ni hisu), from the series *A Modern Shuihuzhuan* (*Tōsei suikoden*), Detail, Utagawa Toyokuni III (Kunisada I)
国立国会図書館デジタルコレクション　National Diet Library Digital Collections

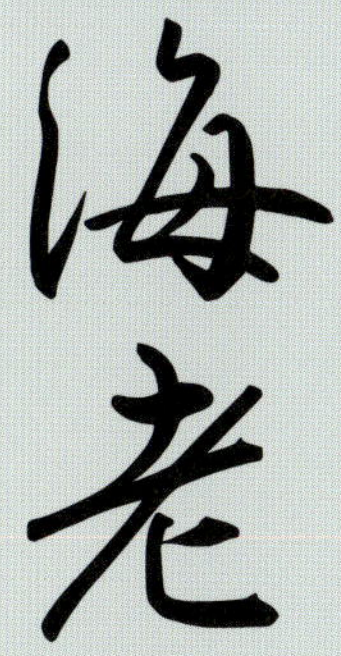

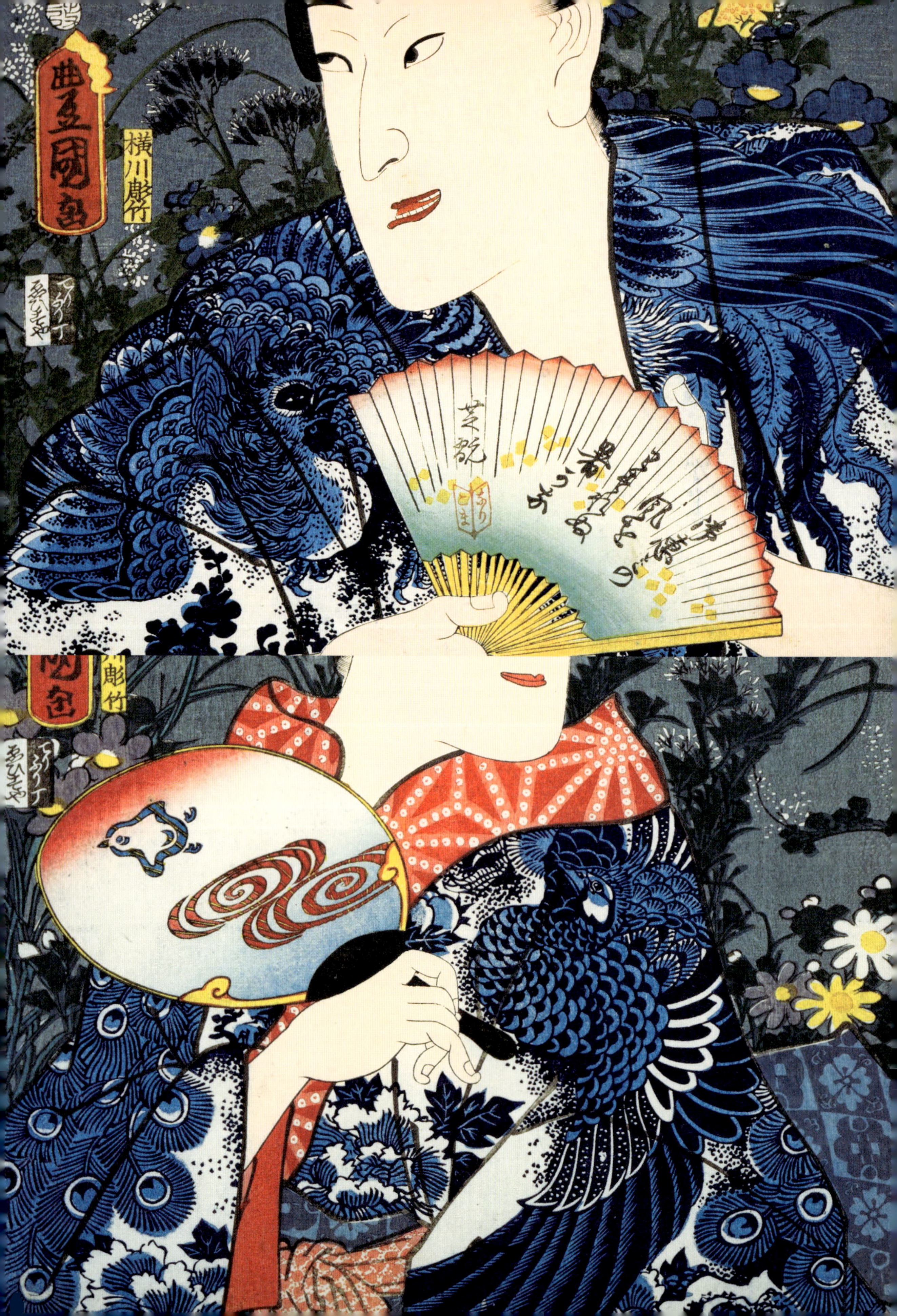

鳳凰

ほうおう

　中国の伝説による想像上の瑞鳥で、麒麟、亀、龍とともに四霊の一つに数えられる。徳の高い天子が生まれるめでたい前触れとしてあらわれると考えられた。古墳時代末期に中国六朝から鳳凰の文様が伝わり、吉祥文様として工芸品のデザインに用いられた。肩から胸にかけて羽を広げたすがたは神々しい限りである。

In Chinese legend, the imaginary bird known as the *zuichou* or phoenix is one of the Four Divine Beasts, along with the qilin (*kirin* in Japanese), turtle, and dragon. The appearance of a phoenix is believed to be an auspicious omen, heralding the birth of a virtuous emperor. The phoenix motif was transmitted from China and used in Japan as a propitious motif in designs for artisanal products.

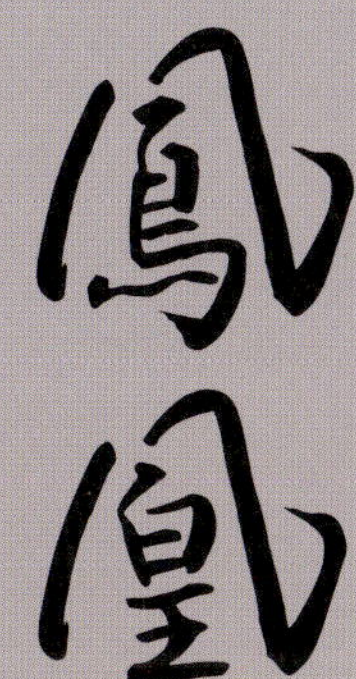

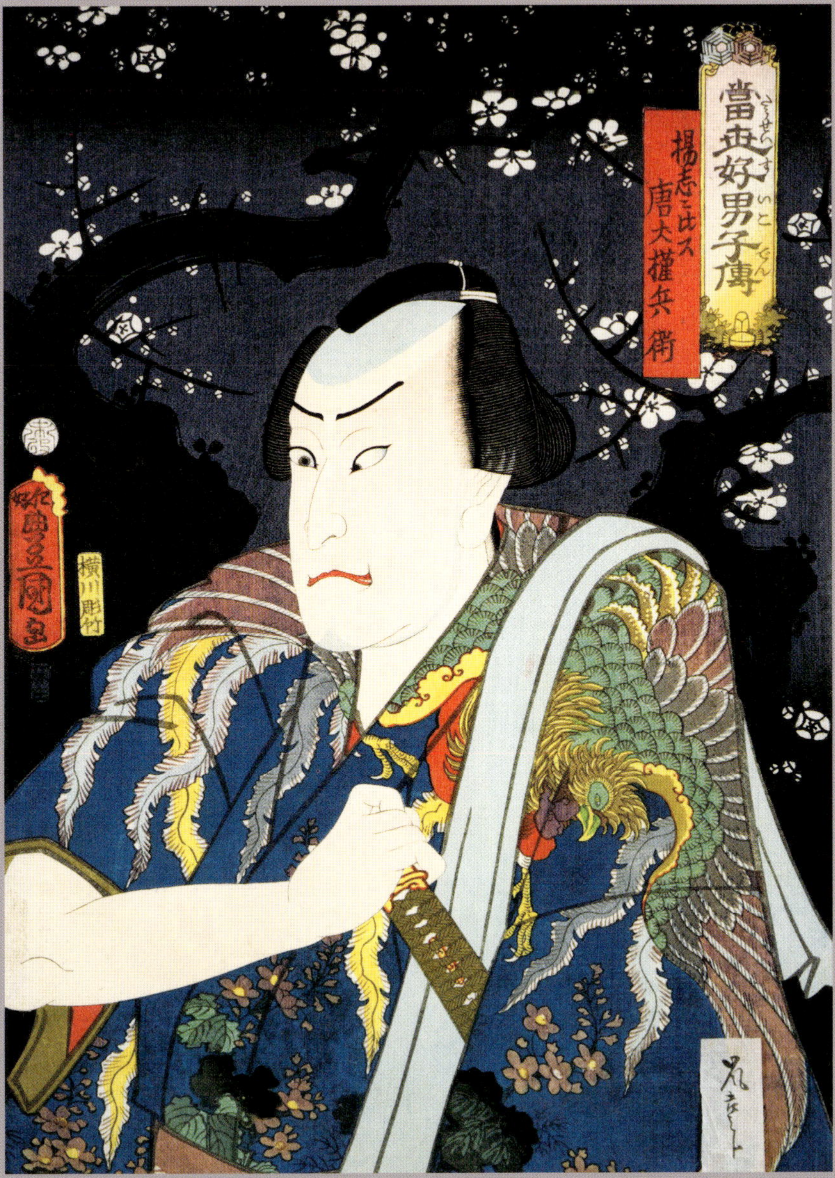

左頁・上下

「蛍狩當風俗」（初代河原崎権十郎）（部分）歌川豊国
Actor Kawarazaki Gonjūrō I, from the set Fashionable Firefly-hunting (*Hotarugari fūzoku*), Detail, Utagawa Toyokuni III (Kunisada I)

万延元年・1860
国立国会図書館デジタルコレクション
1860, National Diet Library Digital Collections

「當世好男子傳　揚志ニ比ス唐犬権兵衛」歌川豊国
Touken Gonbē, comparable to *Youzi* (*Youji ni hisu*), from the series *A Modern Shuihuzhuan* (*Tōsei suikoden*), Detail, Utagawa Toyokuni III (Kunisada I)

安政 6 年・1859
国立国会図書館デジタルコレクション
1859, National Diet Library Digital Collections

Hawk

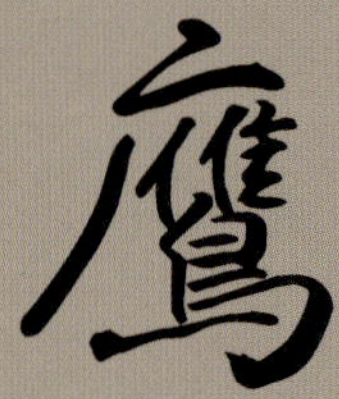

鷹

たか

鷹は鳥類の王であり狩猟神の使者とされ、守り札の牛王宝印に描かれた。古くから公家や武士に愛された鳥で、狩猟などに使われた。鷹狩りの様子、鋭い嘴や爪を持つすがたがデザインされ、武勇のすがたにあらわされている。

Considered the king of birds and a divine messenger representing the gods of hunting, the hawk appears on the seal of the Buffalo God. A bird adored by the nobility and warriors since ancient times, the hawk is used in hunting. In this falconry pattern, the design draws attention to the sharp beak and claws, treating the hawk as an expression of valor.

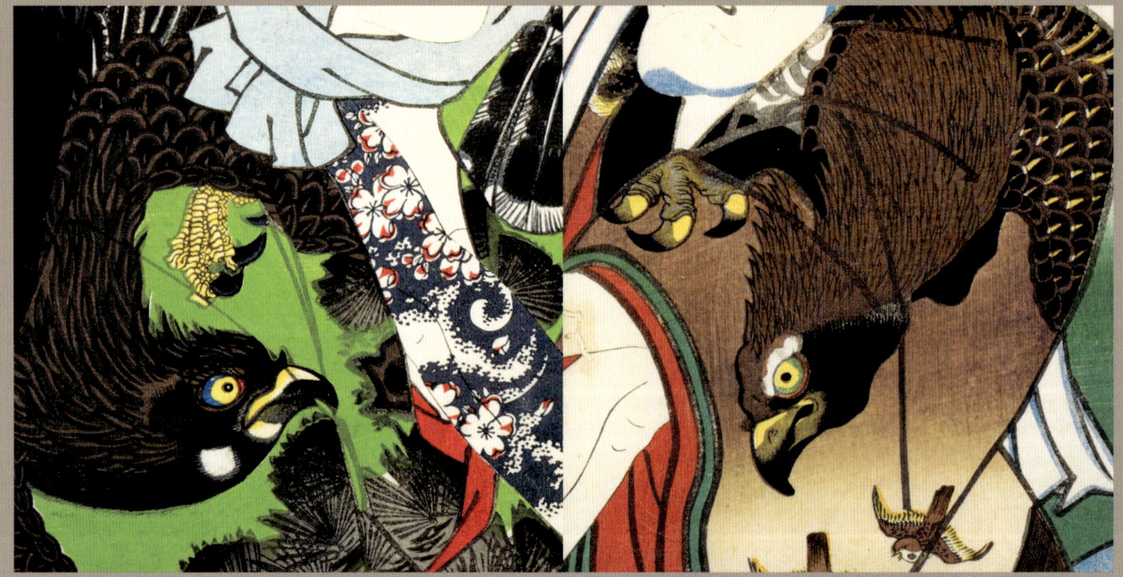

「當世好男子傳　林中に比す鮫鞘四郎三」（五代目坂東彦三郎）（部分）歌川豊国
Actors Bandō Hikosaburō V as Samezaya Shiroza, Comparable to Lin Zhong (Rinchū ni hisu), from the series *A Modern Shuihuzhuan* (*Tōsei suikoden*), Detail, Utagawa Toyokuni III (Kunisada I)
安政 6 年・1859　国立国会図書館デジタルコレクション
1859, National Diet Library Digital Collections

「日本駄右衛門　関三十郎」（部分）
歌川豊国
Actor Seki Sanjūrō III as Nippon Daemon, No. 1 from an untitled pentaptych, Detail, Utagawa Toyokuni III (Kunisada I)
文久 2 年・1862　国立国会図書館デジタルコレクション
1862, National Diet Library Digital Collections

「蛍狩當風俗」（初代河原崎権十郎）（部分）歌川豊国
Actor Kawarazaki Gonjūrō I, from the set Fashionable Firefly-hunting (*Hotarugari fūzoku*), Detail, Utagawa Toyokuni III (Kunisada I)
万延元年・1860
国立国会図書館デジタルコレクション
1860, National Diet Library Digital Collections

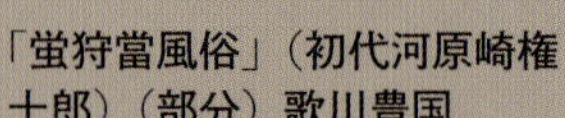

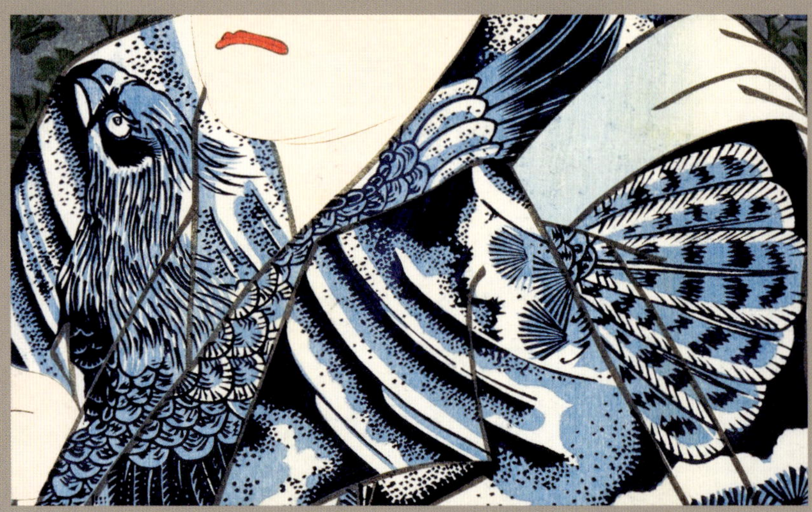

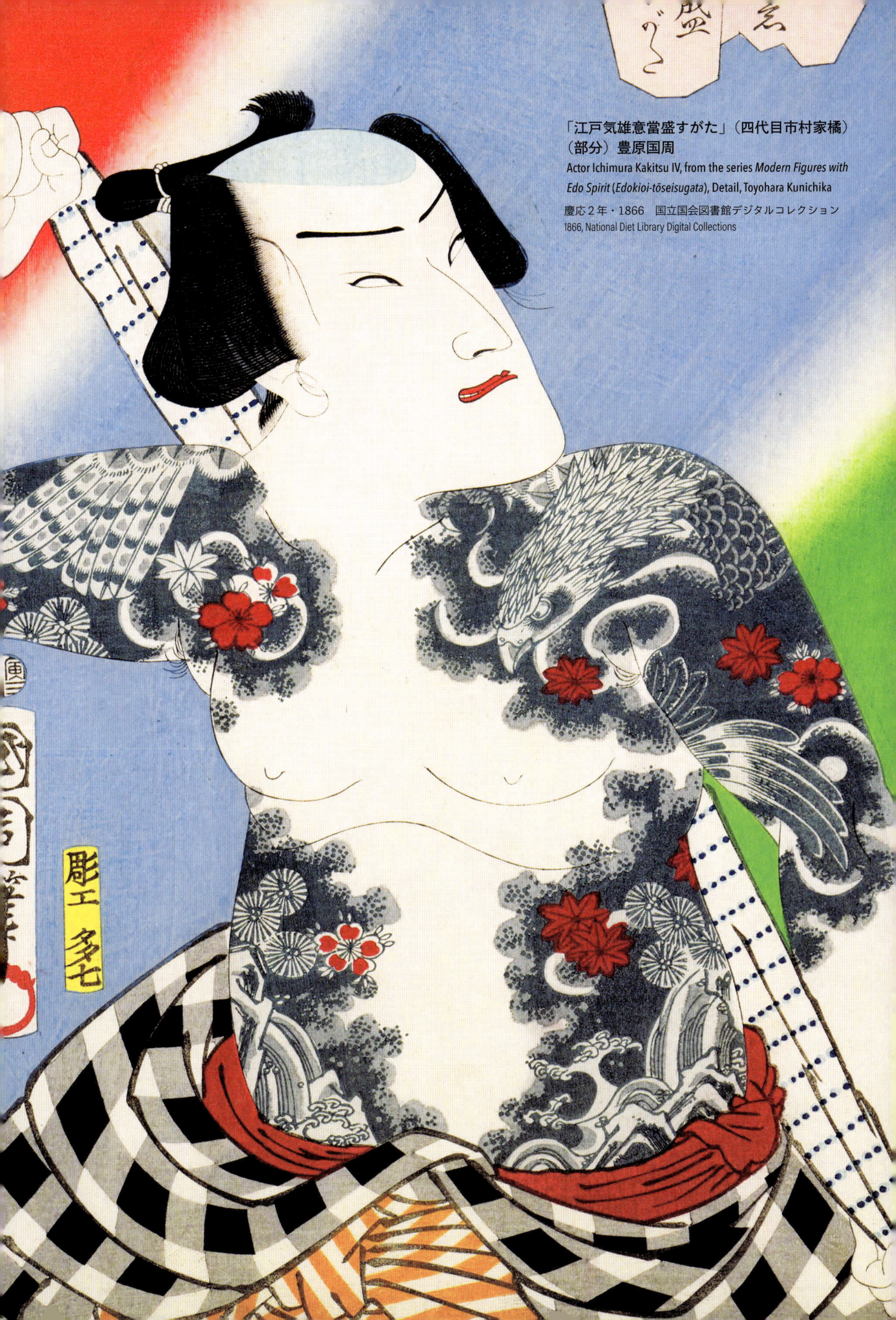

「江戸気雄意當盛すがた」（四代目市村家橘）
（部分）豊原国周

Actor Ichimura Kakitsu IV, from the series *Modern Figures with Edo Spirit (Edokioi-tōseisugata)*, Detail, Toyohara Kunichika

慶応2年・1866　国立国会図書館デジタルコレクション
1866, National Diet Library Digital Collections

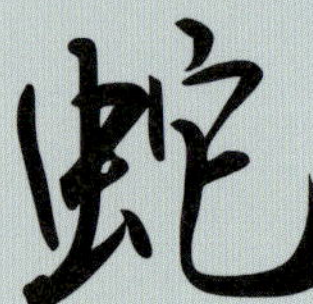

蛇

へび

古代から山の神や水の神、雷神として の蛇の信仰が伝えられ、八岐大蛇の 物語や、安珍清姫の伝説をはじめ、大 蛇にまつわる民話も少なくない。脱皮 によって成長するので生命力復活の象 徴として神聖視されている。

From ancient times snakes have been deified as gods of mountains, water, or lightning. They appear in many folktales, for example, *"Yamata no Orochi"* (the eight-legged, eight-headed serpent) or *"Anchin Kiyohime"* (the legend of a woman who is transformed by rage into a giant serpent and pursues and kills a monk who rejected her love).

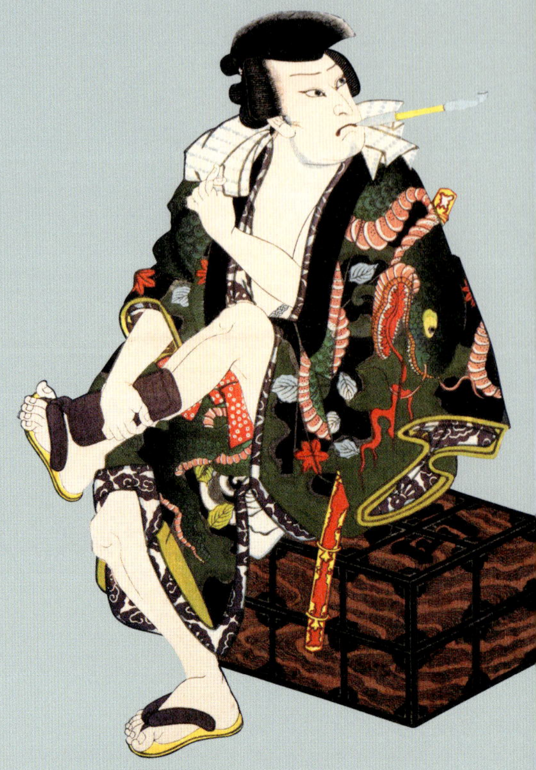

「時代模筆当白波　雲切仁左衛門」 （部分）歌川豊国
Kumokiri Nizaemon, from the series *Jidai-moyō-ataru-shiranami*, Detail, Utagawa Toyokuni III (Kunisada I)

安政6年・1859　国立国会図書館デジタルコレクション
1859, National Diet Library Digital Collections

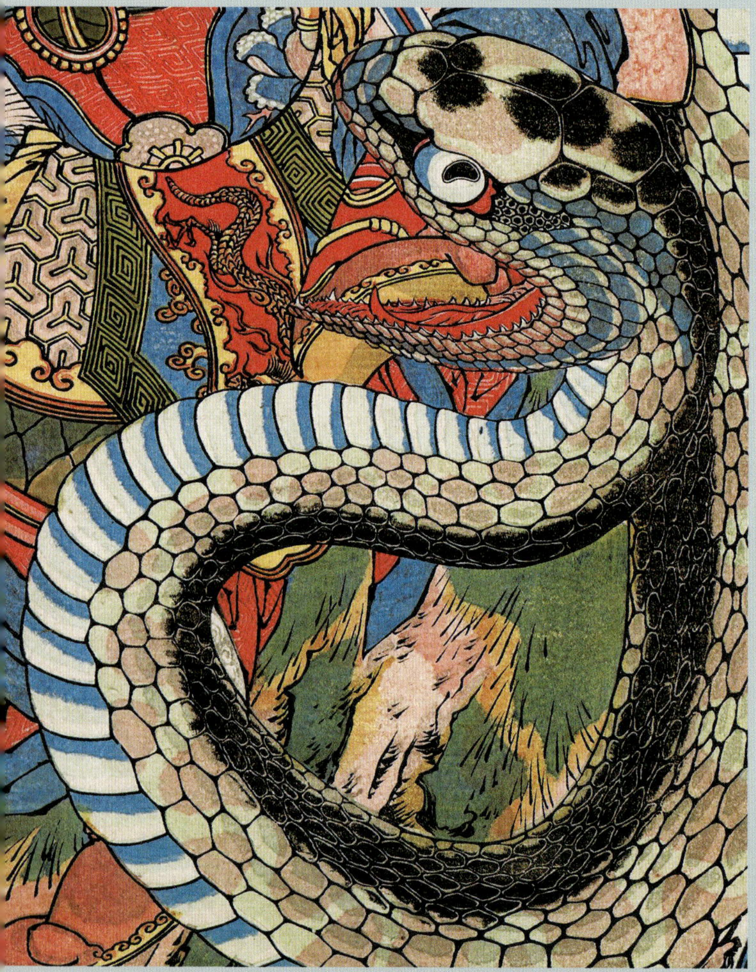

「通俗水滸傳豪傑百八人之一個 中箭虎丁得孫」（部分）歌川国芳
Chusenko Tei Tokuson (Ding Desun), from the series *One hundred and eight Heroes of the Suikoden*, Detail, Utagawa Kuniyoshi

江戸時代・19世紀 東京国立博物館蔵
出典：ColBase (https://colbase.nich.go.jp)
Edo period, 19th century, Tokyo National Museum

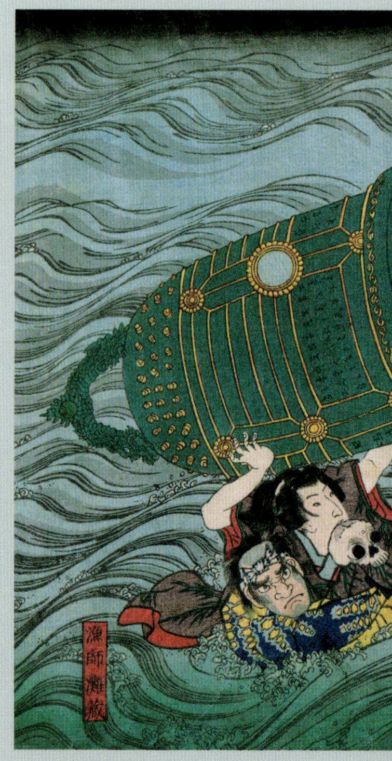

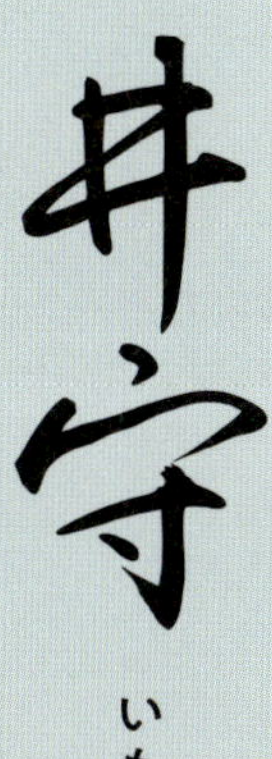

井守
（いもり）

日本の特産種で本州、四国、九州の池や沼などに棲み、アカハライモリの通称で知られる。背面は黒褐色で、腹面は赤色に黒い斑紋がある。鮮やかな赤と黒の化け物井守を岩沼吉六郎が体当たりで退治する場面は、不気味ですごみのある絵である。

This only-in-Japan type of newt lives in ponds and swamps in Honshu, Shikoku, and Kyushu. It is commonly called the Japanese fire-bellied newt. The back is dark brown, the belly red with black markings.

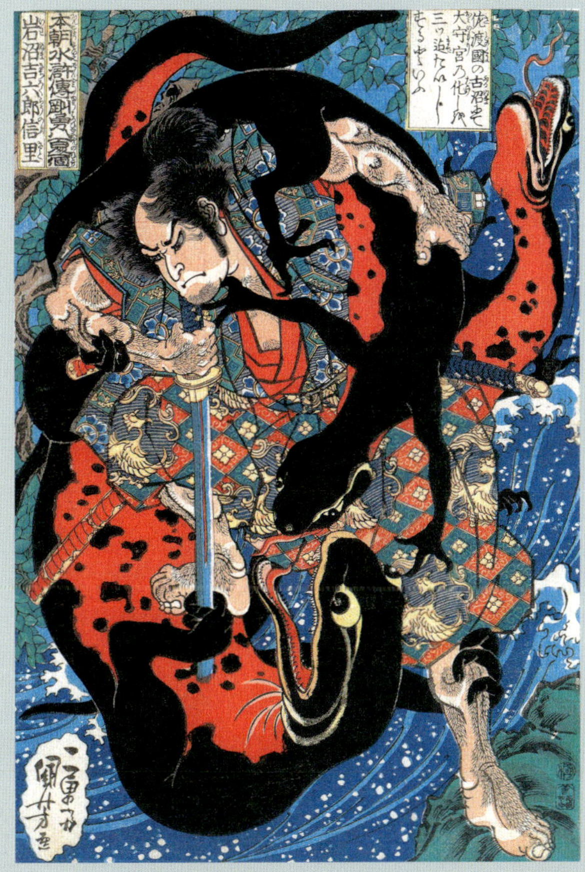

「本朝水滸傳剛勇八百人一個
岩沼吉六郎信里」歌川国芳
Iwanuma Kichirokurō Nobusato, from the series *One hundred and eight Heroes of the Suikoden*, Utagawa Kuniyoshi

天保前期・1830-35　山口県立萩美術館・浦上記念館蔵
c.1830-35, Hagi Uragami Museum

蜘蛛
（くも）

古くから蜘蛛は霊力を持つとされる。蜘蛛が巣をかけるのを、人の来訪の前兆とする俗信や、朝の蜘蛛を吉事の前兆とする俗信がある。大友宗麟の娘若菜姫（白縫）が蜘蛛の妖術で、仇敵菊地家をねらう『白縫譚』の一場面が描かれる。

From ancient times, the spider has been believed to possess magical powers. Folk beliefs assert that a spider building a nest is an omen foretelling the arrival of visitors and a spider in the morning foretells good fortune.

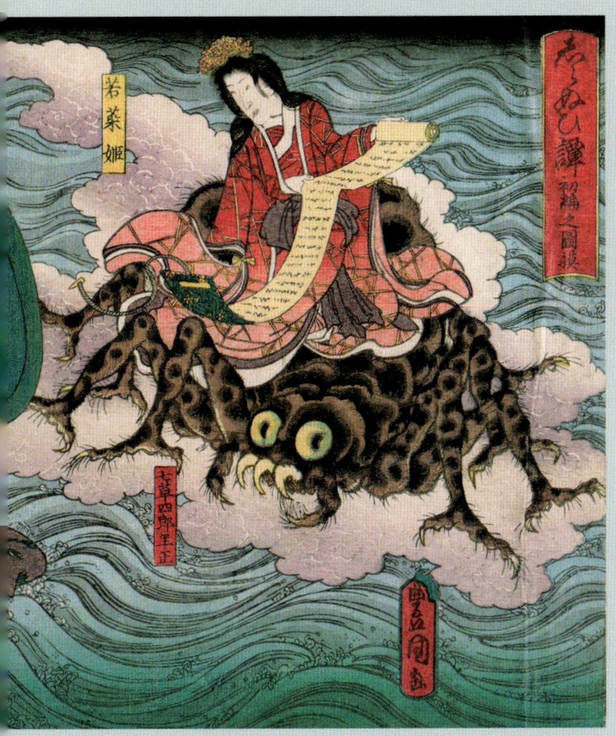

「志らぬひ譚　初編之図」「若菜姫」
「七草四郎年正」「漁師灘蔵」歌川豊国
The Tale of Shiranui, Part 1 (*Shiranui monogatari, shohen no zu*), Utagawa Toyokuni III (Kunisada I)

国立国会図書館デジタルコレクション
National Diet Library Digital Collections

Carp

鯉
こい

淡水魚の王といわれる鯉は、黄河の急流にある龍門という瀧を昇り龍になるという伝説から立身出世のシンボルとされた。波間におどる鯉の勢いあるすがたを織り出した荒磯緞子（ありそどんす）が知られる。鯉と波がよく調和したデザインである。

The carp is called the king of freshwater fish. Because carp swam upstream through the waterfall called the "Dragon Gate," against the Yellow River's swift current, they became symbols of worldly success. Damask with a carp in wave design (*ariso donsu*) is a type of textile with a pattern of a carp thrusting its way forward between the waves. The movements of the carp and the waves are beautifully harmonized in that design.

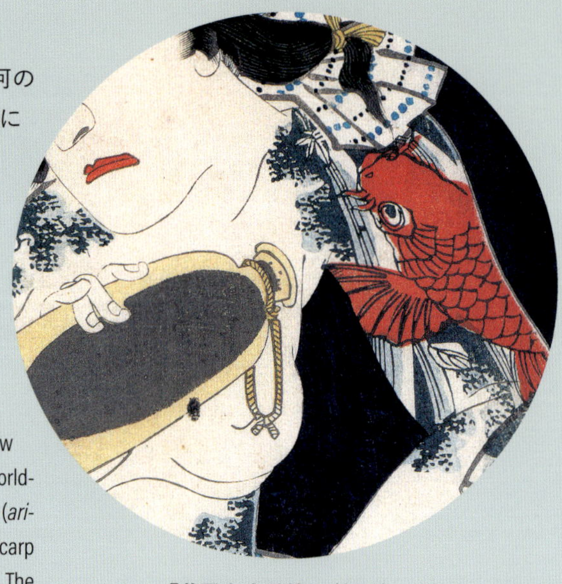

「花勇女水滸傳」（部分）
豊原国周
Hanayūjo Suikoden, Detail, Toyohara Kunichika

明治 2 年・1869
山口県立萩美術館・浦上記念館蔵
1869, Hagi Uragami Museum

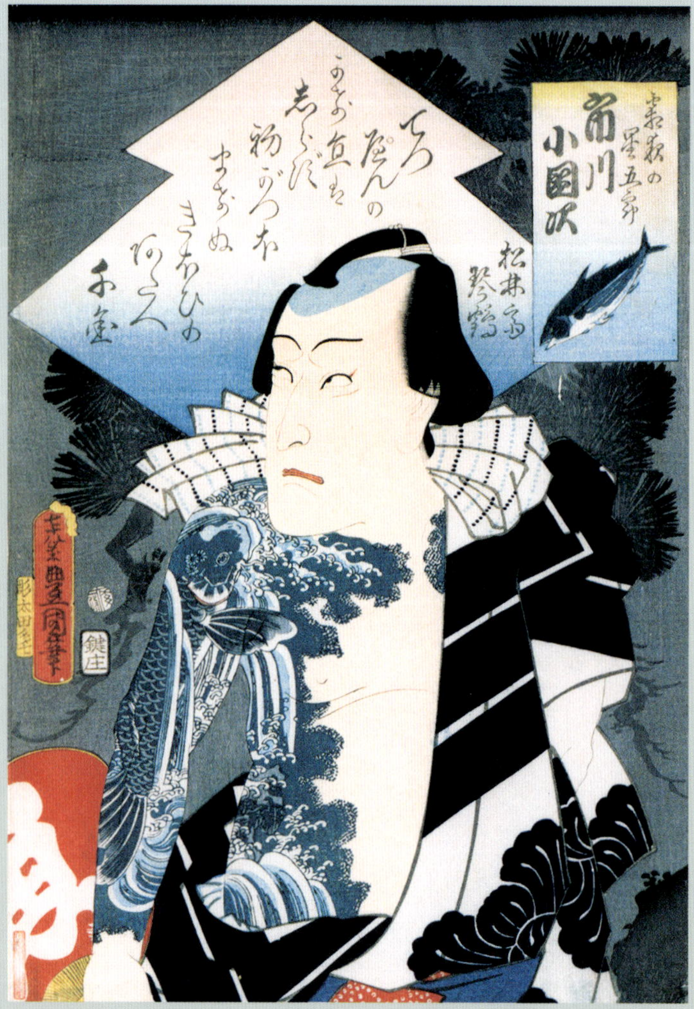

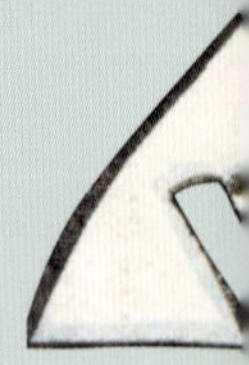

「霜夜の星五郎　市川小團次」
歌川豊国
**Actor Ichikawa Kodanji IV as Shimoyo no Seigorō,
Utagawa Toyokuni III (Kunisada I)**

文久 3 年・1863
東京都立中央図書館特別文庫室蔵
1863, National Diet Library Digital Collections

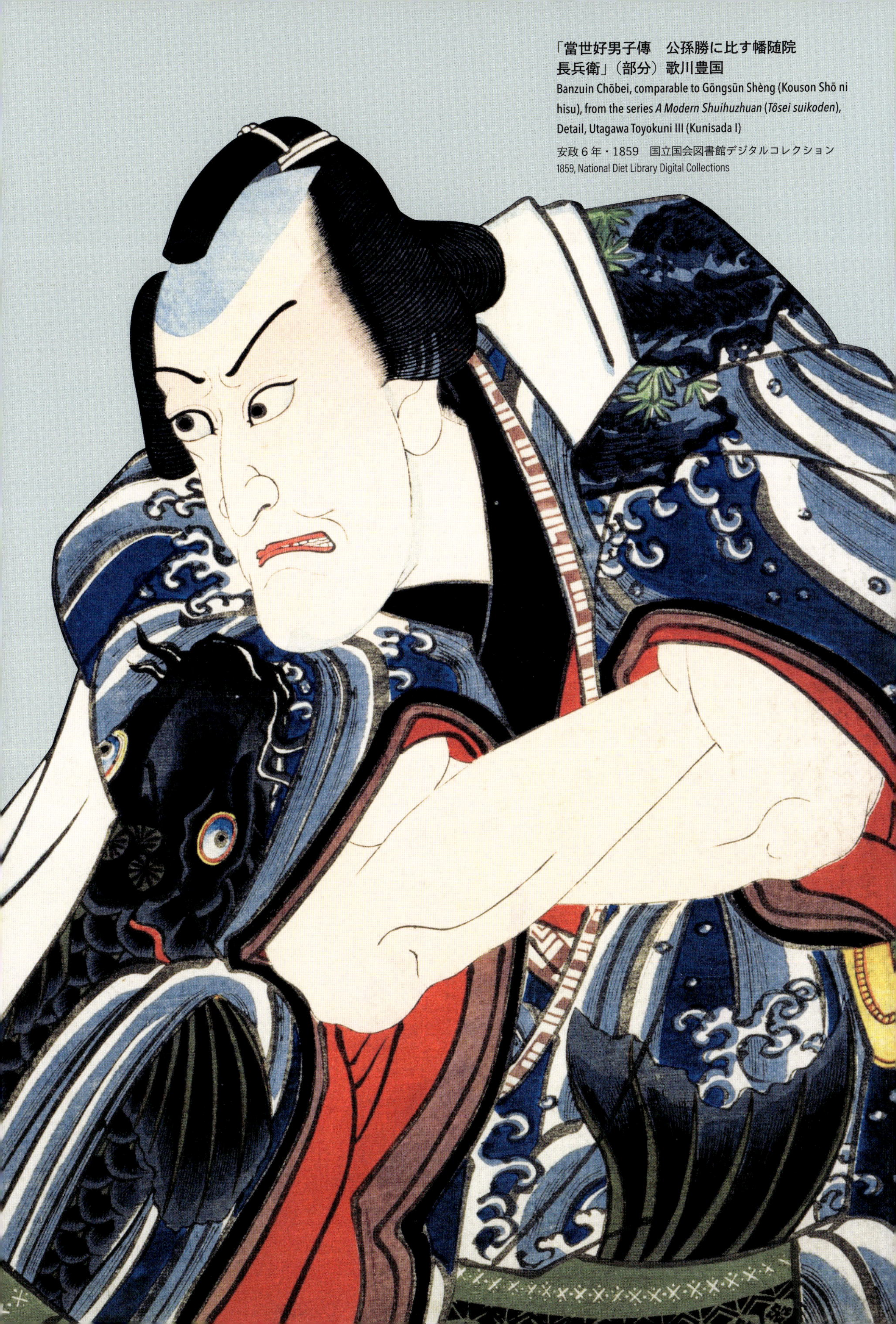

「當世好男子傳　公孫勝に比す幡随院
長兵衛」（部分）歌川豊国
Banzuin Chōbei, comparable to Gōngsūn Shèng (Kouson Shō ni
hisu), from the series *A Modern Shuihuzhuan* (*Tôsei suikoden*),
Detail, Utagawa Toyokuni III (Kunisada I)
安政6年・1859　国立国会図書館デジタルコレクション
1859, National Diet Library Digital Collections

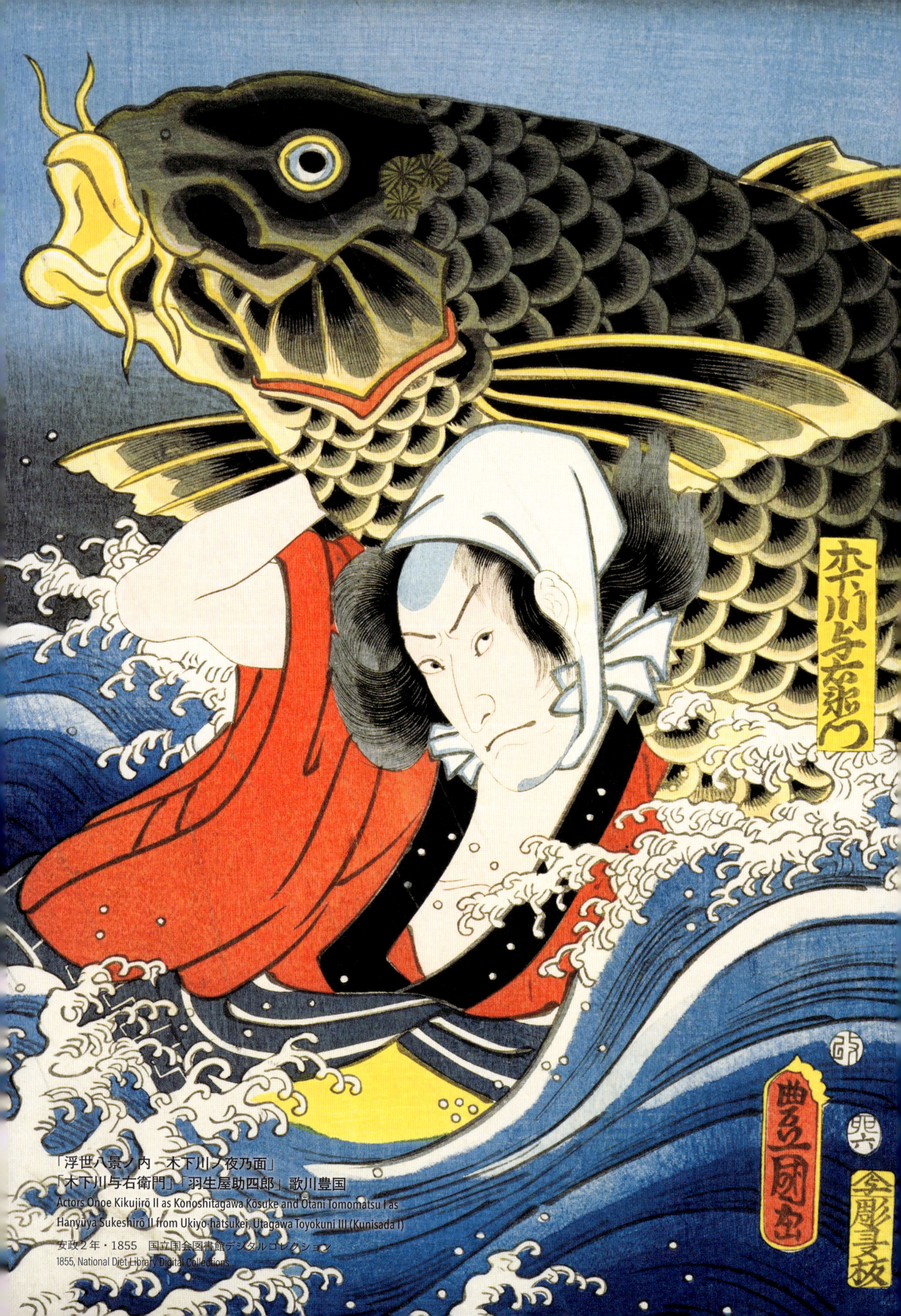

「浮世八景ノ内 木下川ノ夜乃面」
「木下川与右衛門」「羽生屋助四郎」歌川豊国
Actors Onoe Kikujirō II as Konoshitagawa Kōsuke and Otani Tomomatsu I as
Hanyūya Sukeshirō II from Ukiyo-hatsukei, Utagawa Toyokuni III (Kunisada I)
安政2年・1855　国立国会図書館デジタルコレクション
1855, National Diet Library Digital Collections

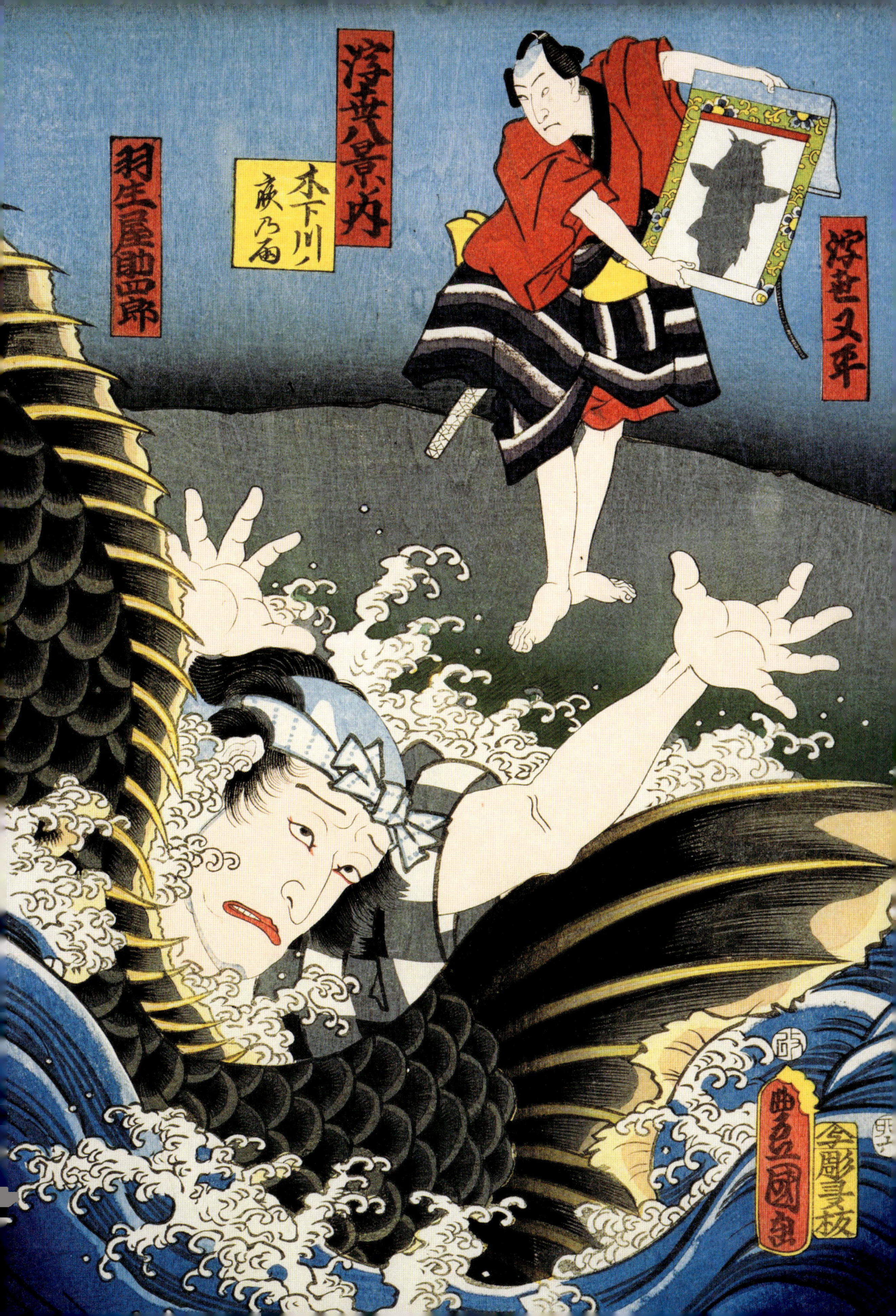
浮世八景ノ内
羽生屋助四郎
木下川
廓乃雨
浮世又平
豊国画
今彫重板

Thunder God

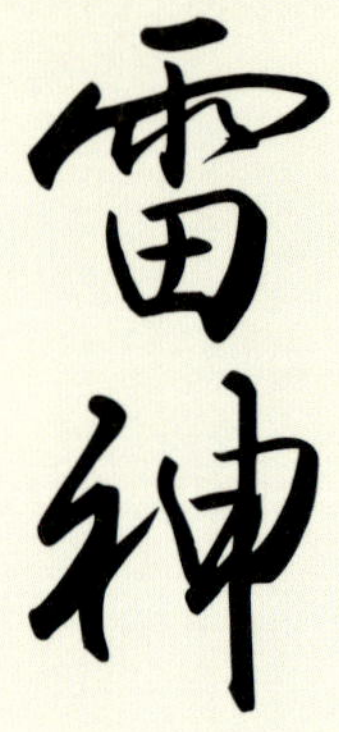

雷神
らいじん

雷神は雷鳴と稲妻を神格化したもので、わが国では古代から雷神信仰がみられ、『日本書紀』などでは神体は蛇体とされている。虎の皮の褌をした鬼が、輪形に連ねた蓮太鼓を負い、手に桴を持ったすがたで描かれる。絵画では風神と一対になって描かれることが多い。

The thunder god is the deification of thunder and lightning, and belief in the thunder god goes back to ancient times in Japan. The design often features an *oni* (demon) wearing a loincloth made of tiger skin, carrying a row of lotus-shaped drums on its back, and holding drumsticks in its hands.

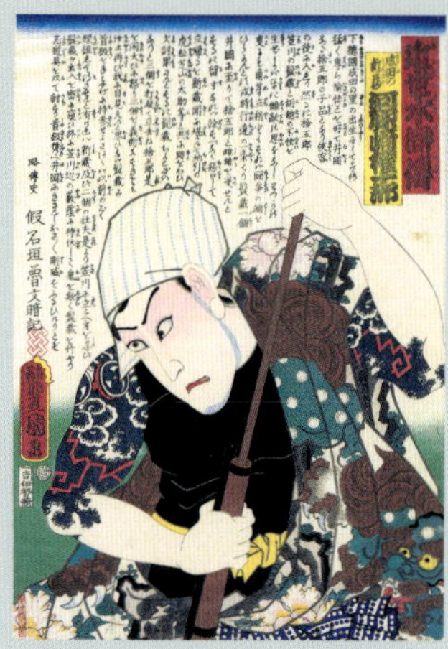

「近世水滸傳　成田の新蔵
河原崎権十郎」歌川豊国
Actors Kawarazaki Gonjūrō as Narita no Shinzou, from the series *A Modern Suikoden* (*Kinsei Suikoden*), Utagawa Toyokuni III (Kunisada I)

文久 2 年・1862
東京都立中央図書館特別文庫室蔵
1862, Tokyo Metropolitan Central Library

The term *inazuma* (literally, "rice wife") refers to lightning and can also be written with the kanji characters now used for lightning (雷) or electricity (電). Lightning has long been represented by jagged geometric forms: bent triangles, rectangles, rhombuses, or hexagonal forms.

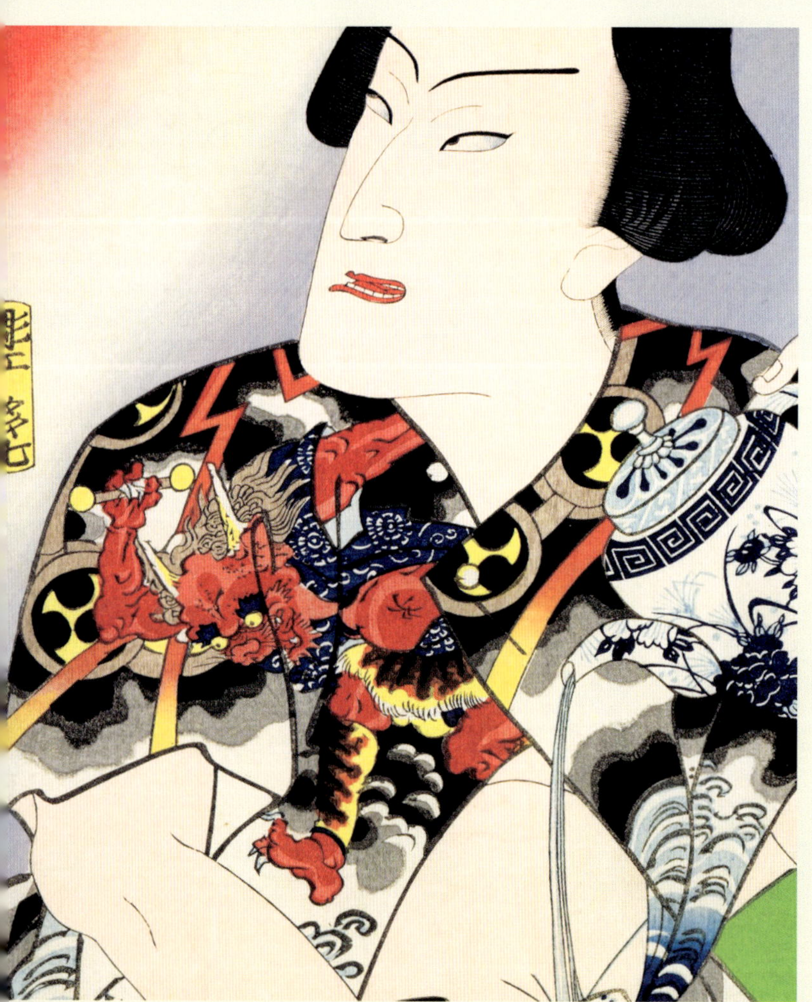

「江戸気雄意當盛すがた」（部分）豊原国周
Edokioi Tousei Sugata, Detail, Toyohara Kunichika

国立国会図書館デジタルコレクション
National Diet Library Digital Collections

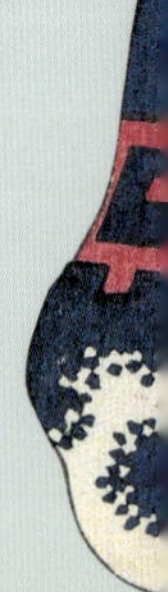

雲に稲妻
くもにいなづま

　稲妻は雷または電とも書き、空中での電気放電によっ
て閃く電光のこと。直線を曲折してあらわす幾何学文様
で古くからあった。中国では殷周の時代から好まれ、土
器や彩陶、銅器などに地紋として施された。三角形に
折り曲げたものや四角、　　　　　菱形、六角形などがある。

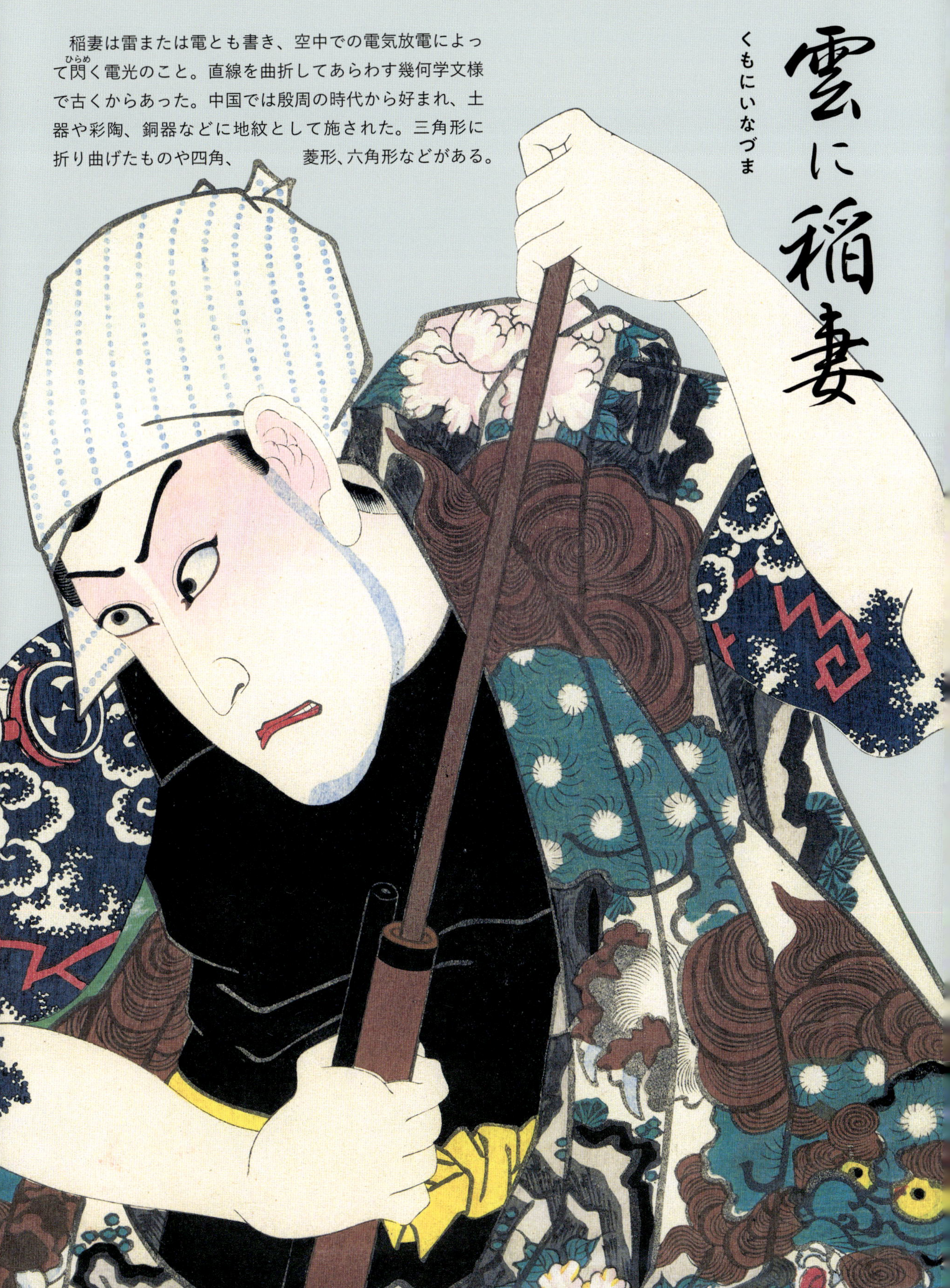

Cherry Blossom

桜

花は桜木、人は武士といわれ、武士社会でもっとも好まれた花である。鎌倉時代には武具のデザインに愛用され、小桜の花を染めた染革で小桜威の鎧や兜がつくられた。室町時代には蒔絵や刀の鐔などにも桜の文様が使われ、豪傑な武将のイメージとして用いられた。

"Among flowers, the cherry blossom; among men, the warrior": The cherry blossom was samurai society's most beloved flower. During the Kamakura period (1185-1333), cherry blossom designs were used on armor and helmets were made of leather dyed with cherry blossoms. These were used to project the image of formidable and valiant warriors.

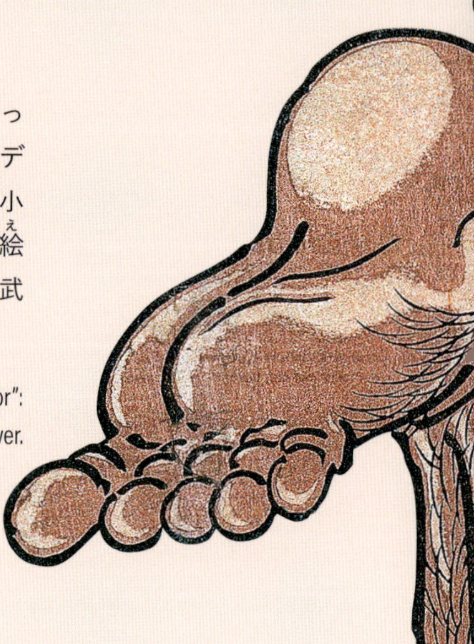

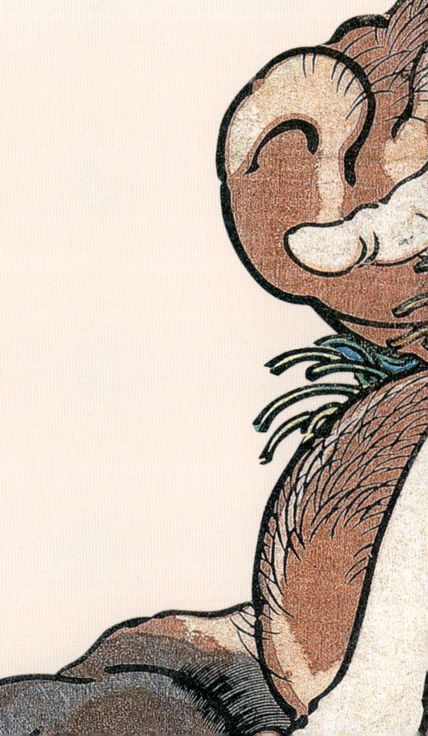

「本朝水滸傳豪傑八百人一個 天眼磯兵衛」歌川国芳
Tengan Isobē, from the series *One hundred and eight Heroes of the Suikoden*, Utagawa Kuniyoshi
天保2年頃・1831
山口県立萩美術館・浦上記念館蔵
c.1831, Hagi Uragami Museum

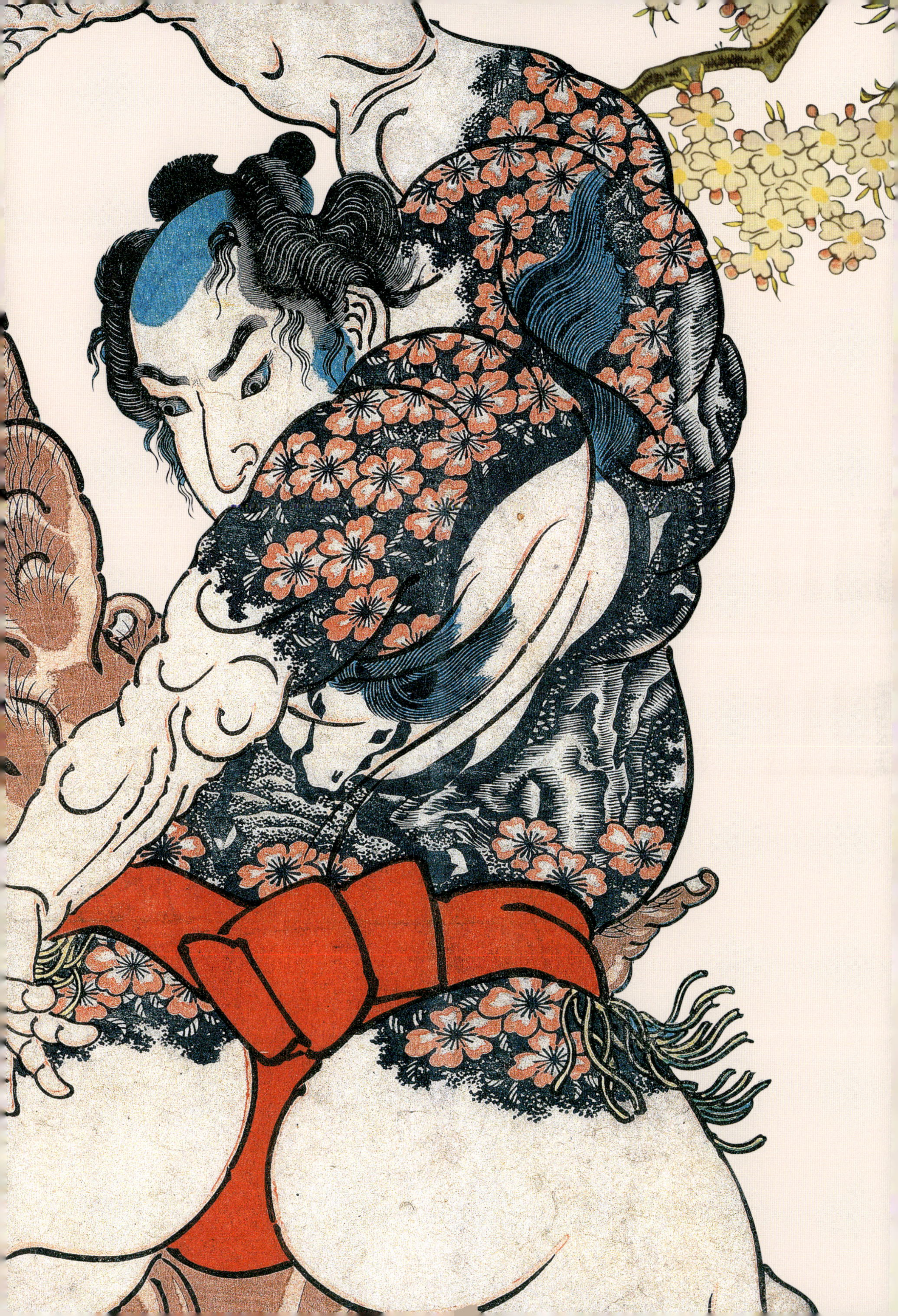

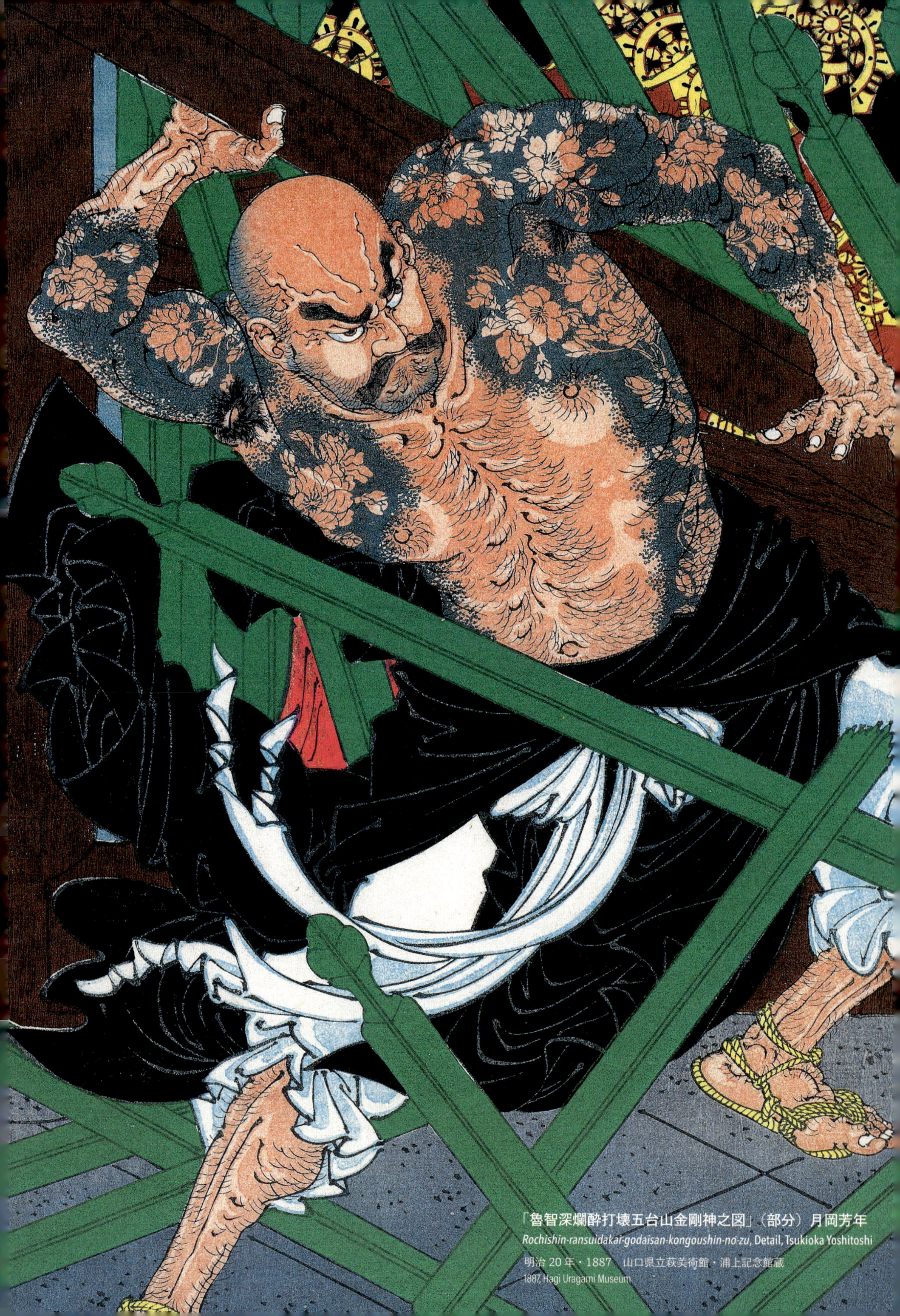

「魯智深爛酔打壊五台山金剛神之図」（部分）月岡芳年
Rochishin-ransuidakai-godaisan-kongoushin-no-zu, Detail, Tsukioka Yoshitoshi
明治20年・1887　山口県立萩美術館・浦上記念館蔵
1887, Hagi Uragami Museum

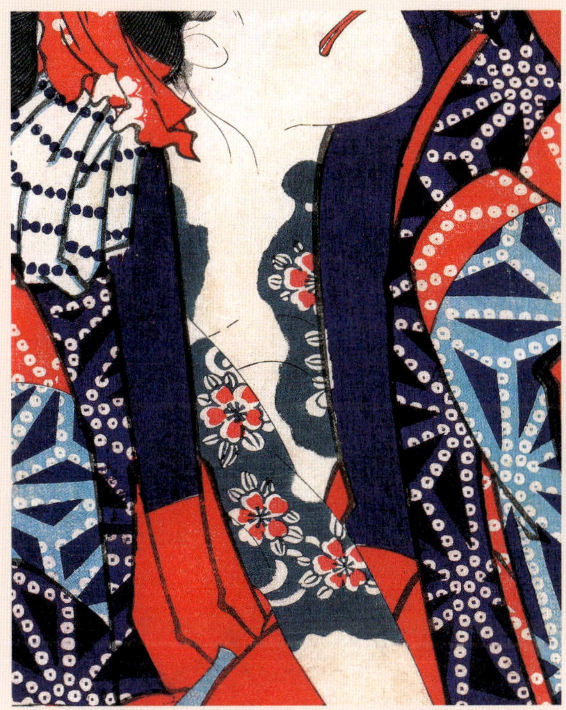

「見立十二時之内　巳　弁天小僧　尾上菊五郎」
（部分）豊原国周
Actors Onoe Kikugorō as *the Mitate-juniji-no-uchi Mi Bentenkozō*,
Detail, Toyohara Kunichika

明治 7 年・1874　山口県立萩美術館・浦上記念館蔵
1874, Hagi Uragami Museum

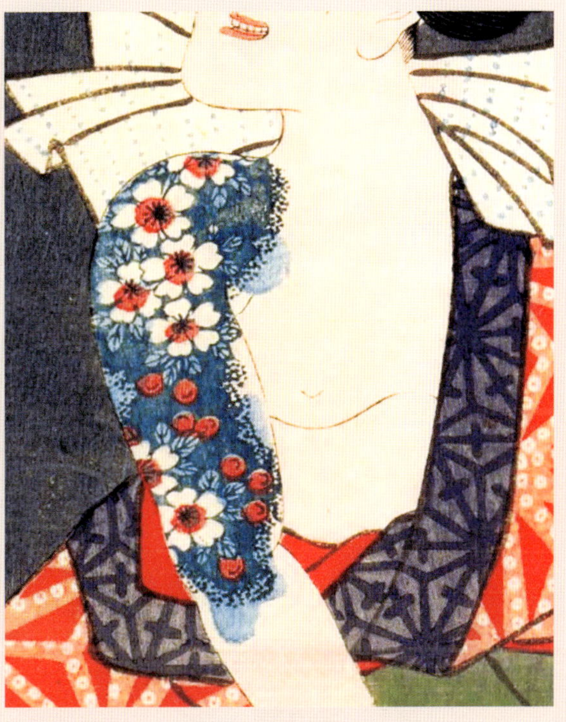

「豊国漫画図絵　弁天小僧菊之介」（部分）
歌川豊国
Bentenkozō Kikunosuke, from *The Heroes and Heroines of the Popular
Fiction* (*Toyokuni Manga Zue*), Detail, Utagawa Toyokuni III (Kunisada I)

万延元年・1860　国立国会図書館デジタルコレクション
1860, National Diet Library Digital Collections

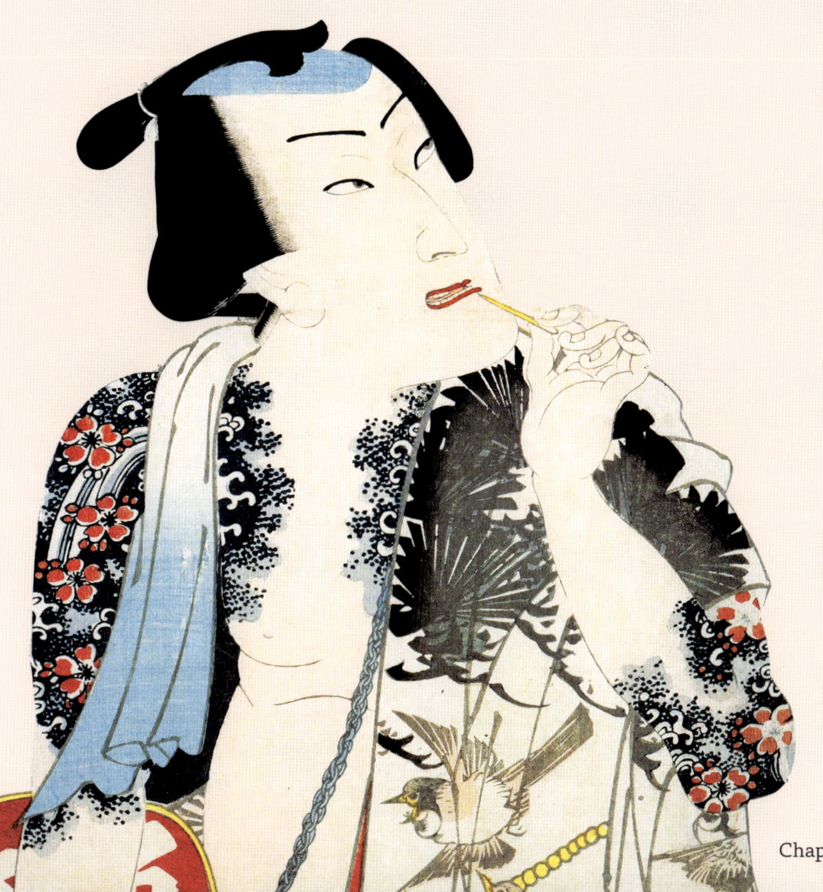

「成びしゃ駒　中村芝翫」（部分）
豊原国周
Actors Nakamura Shikan as *Narubisha-Koma*,
Detail, Toyohara Kunichika

元治元年・1864
国立国会図書館デジタルコレクション
1864, National Diet Library Digital Collections

牡丹

ぼたん

中国では牡丹を花王や百花王、神花とよび富貴の象徴とした。平安時代には宮廷や寺院で観賞用として栽培された。牡丹を美と権力の象徴とし、花王の牡丹と百獣の王である獅子とを組み合せた「牡丹に獅子」は、鎌倉・室町時代には武将の甲冑などに好まれ、刺青の図案になった。

In China, the tree peony was regarded as the king of flowers, a divine flower and symbol of wealth. The combination of the peony, symbolizing beauty and power, with the lion, known as the "King of Beasts," in the design called *botan ni shishi* (lions among peonies), was favored in the armor of warriors during the Kamakura and Muromachi periods (1185-1573). This design was favored as a powerful and majestic image, combining the elegance of the peony with the strength of the lion.

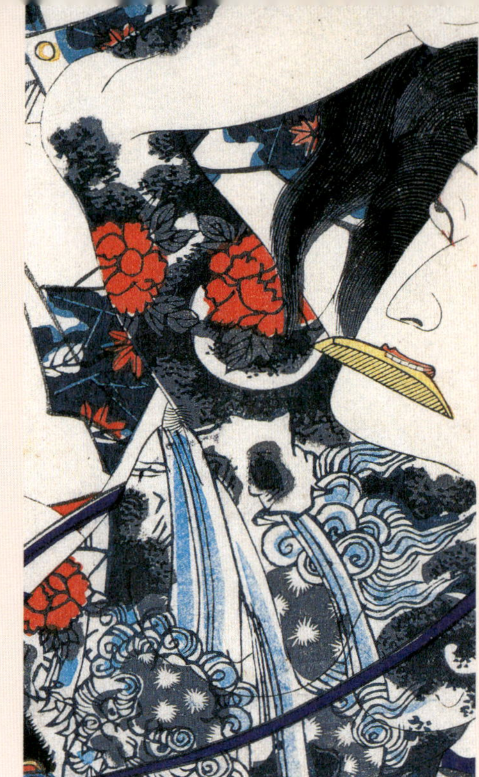

「花勇女水滸傳」（部分）豊原国周
Hanayūjo Suikoden, Detail, Toyohara Kunichika

明治 2 年・1869　山口県立萩美術館・浦上記念館蔵
1869, Hagi Uragami Museum

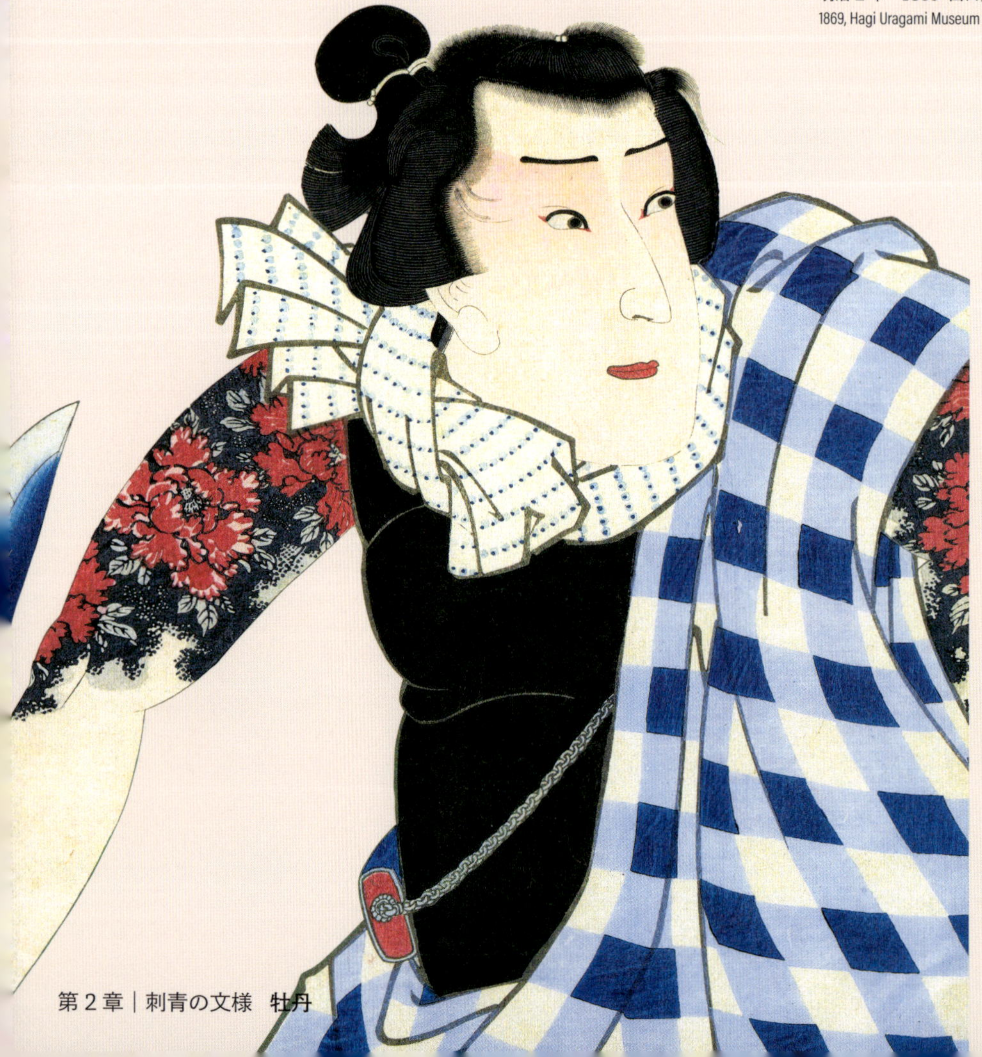

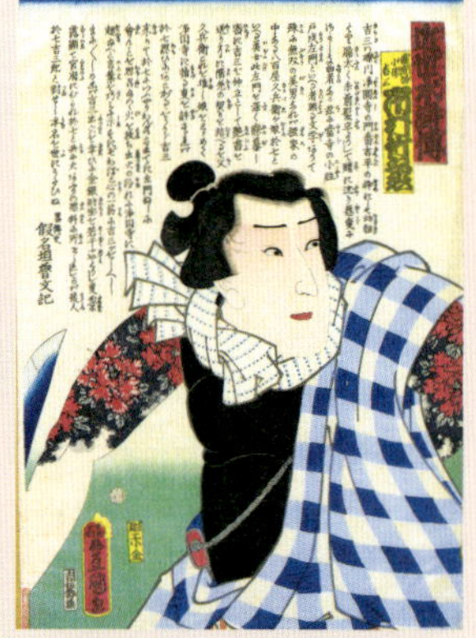

「近世水滸傳　湯灌場小僧吉三　市村竹之丞」歌川豊国
Actors Ichikawa Takenojō as Yukanba Kozo Kichisa, from the series *A Modern Suikoden* (*Kinsei Suikoden*), Utagawa Toyokuni III (Kunisada I)

文久 2 年・1862
東京都立中央図書館特別文庫室蔵
1862, Tokyo Metropolitan Central Library

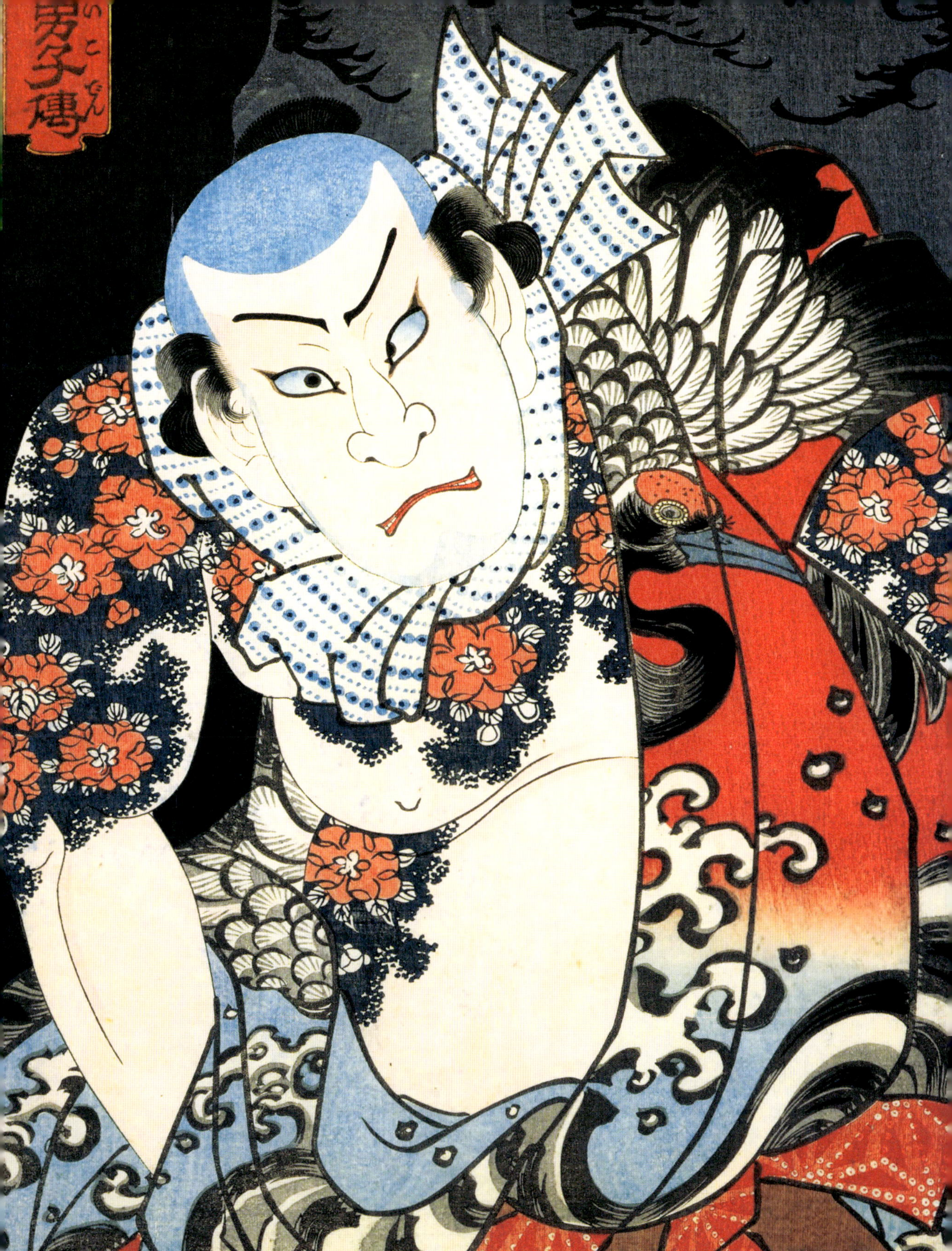

「當世好男子傳　花和尚魯智深に比す朝比奈藤兵衛」（部分）歌川豊国

Actors Nakamura Fukusuke I as Asahina Tōbei, comparable to Lu Zhishen the Tattooed Priest (Kaoshō Rochishin ni hisu) , from the series *A Modern Shuihuzhuan* (*Tōsei suikoden*), Detail, Utagawa Toyokuni III (Kunisada I)

安政 5 年・1858
国立国会図書館デジタルコレクション
1858, National Diet Library Digital Collections

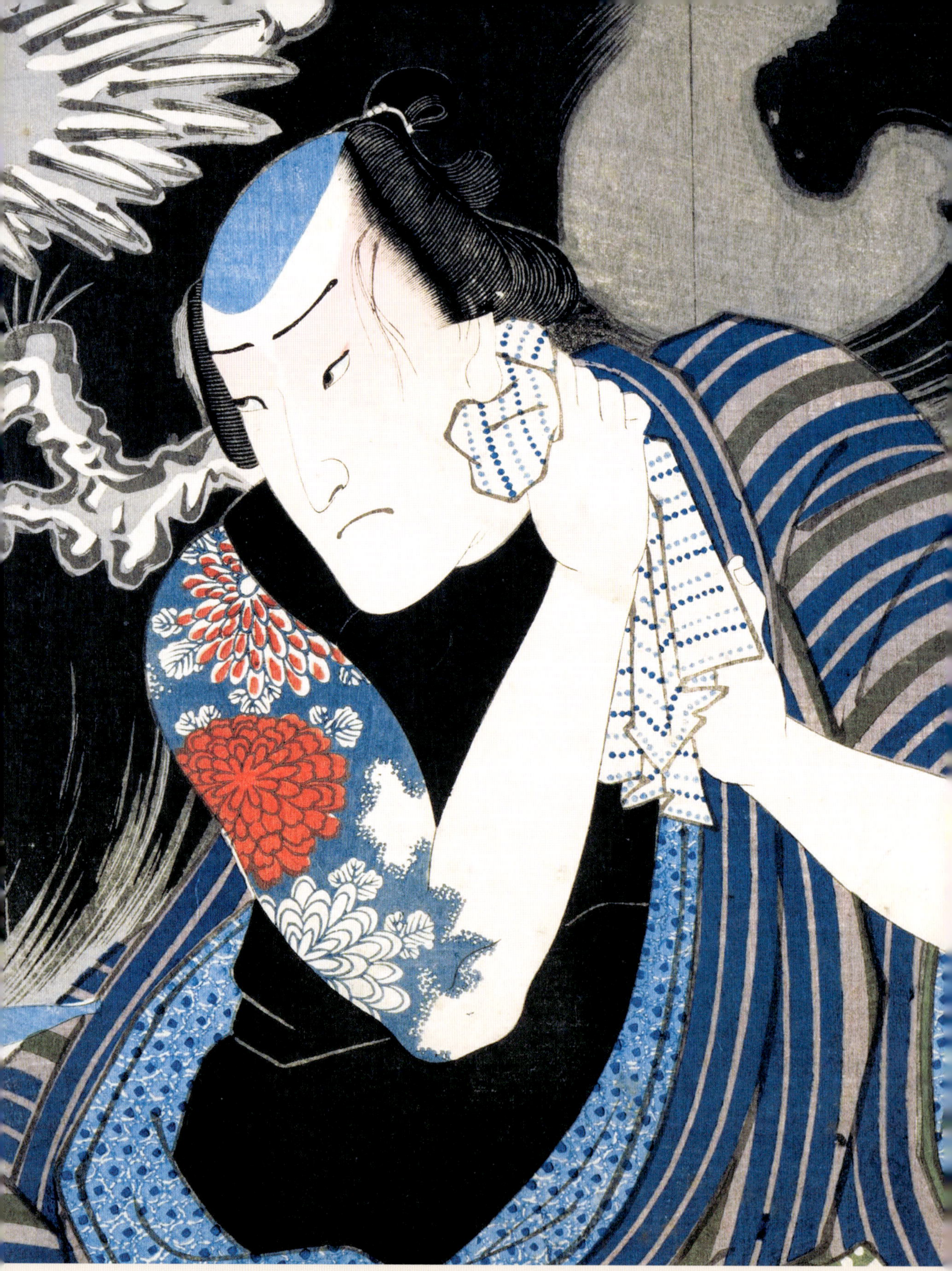

「かな屋金五郎・がくの小さん」（部分）歌川豊国
Kanaya Kingorou, Kosan'Ukinanogaku. Detail, Utagawa Toyokuni III (Kunisada I)

安政5年・1858　国立国会図書館デジタルコレクション
1858, National Diet Library Digital Collections

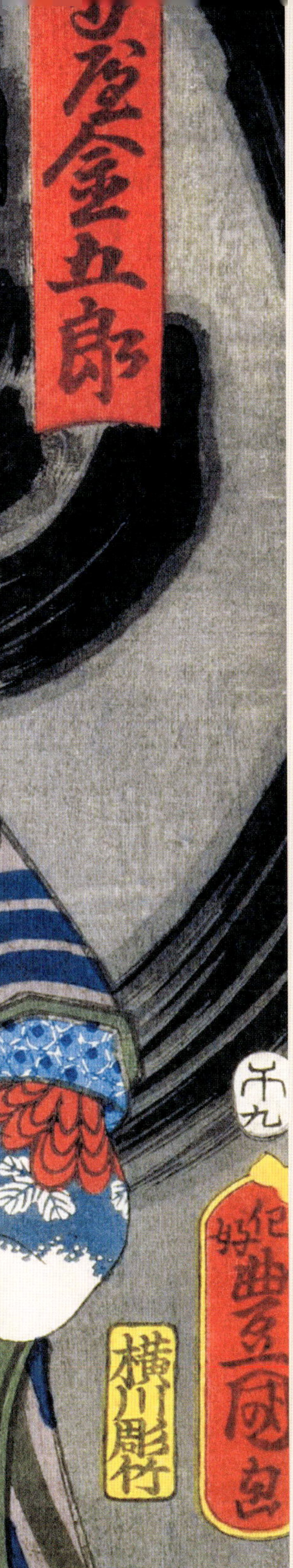

菊は中国では不老長寿の効き目があるとされ、奈良時代に大陸文化とともに薬草として渡来した。菊花文様は長寿吉祥としてデザインにも取り入れられ、鎌倉時代には大流行になった。また江戸時代の小袖や能装束には大胆に意匠化された図案が多い。歌舞伎役者の金屋金五郎の腕には菊花文様が冴えている。

In China, the chrysanthemum was seen as effective for prolonging life without aging. It was brought from China to Japan as a medicinal plant. Chrysanthemum flower patterns were incorporated in designs to signify long life and good fortune. These designs were enormously popular during the Kamakura period. During the Edo period they were used in bold designs for kimono (*kosode*) and Noh costumes.

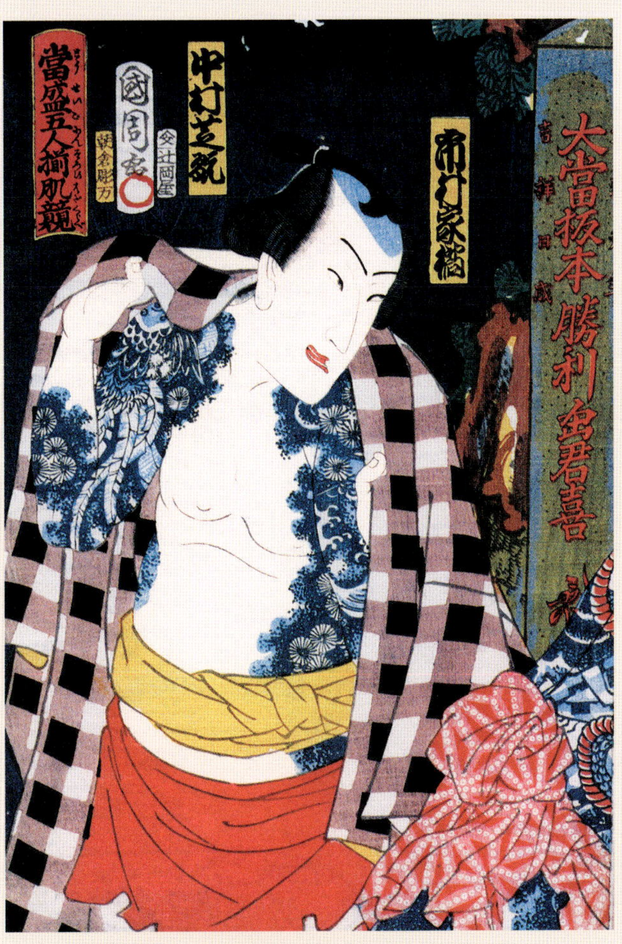

「當盛五人揃肌競」「市村家橘」「中村芝翫」豊原国周
Ichimura Kakitsu, Nakamura Shikan, from *the Tōsei-Goninsoroi-Hadakurabe*, Toyohara Kunichika

元治元年・1864　東京都立中央図書館特別文庫室蔵
1864, Tokyo Metropolitan Library

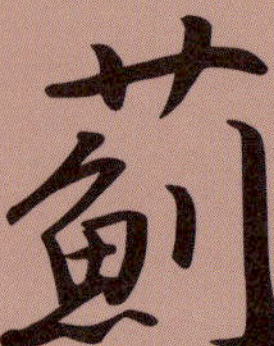

薊

あざみ

薊は厚い葉に多くの鋭い切れ込みがあり、先端には刺針がある。桃山時代までは文様として意匠化されず、江戸時代に着物の文様に用いられた。古くからのことばに「薊の花も一盛り」があり、地味でも盛りにはそれ相応に美しくなることをたとえている。僧から盗賊に身を落とした鬼桂助の背には、みごとな鬼薊が彫られている。

Thistles have thick leaves with numerous sharp incisions and spines at their tips. An old saying, "Even thistles can be glorious," suggests that even something as modest as a thistle can be beautiful in its own way when in full bloom. On the back of Oni Katsusuke, who went from being a monk to a bandit, we see a magnificent demon thistle tattoo.

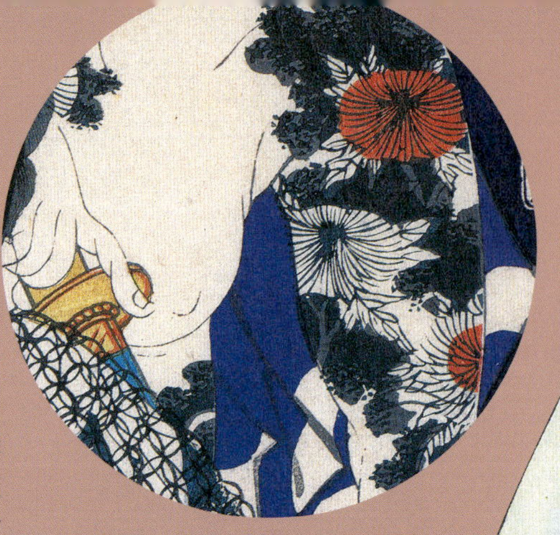

「花勇女水滸傳」（部分）
豊原国周
Hanayūjo Suikoden, Toyohara Kunichika

明治 2 年・1869
山口県立萩美術館・浦上記念館蔵
1869, Hagi Uragami Museum

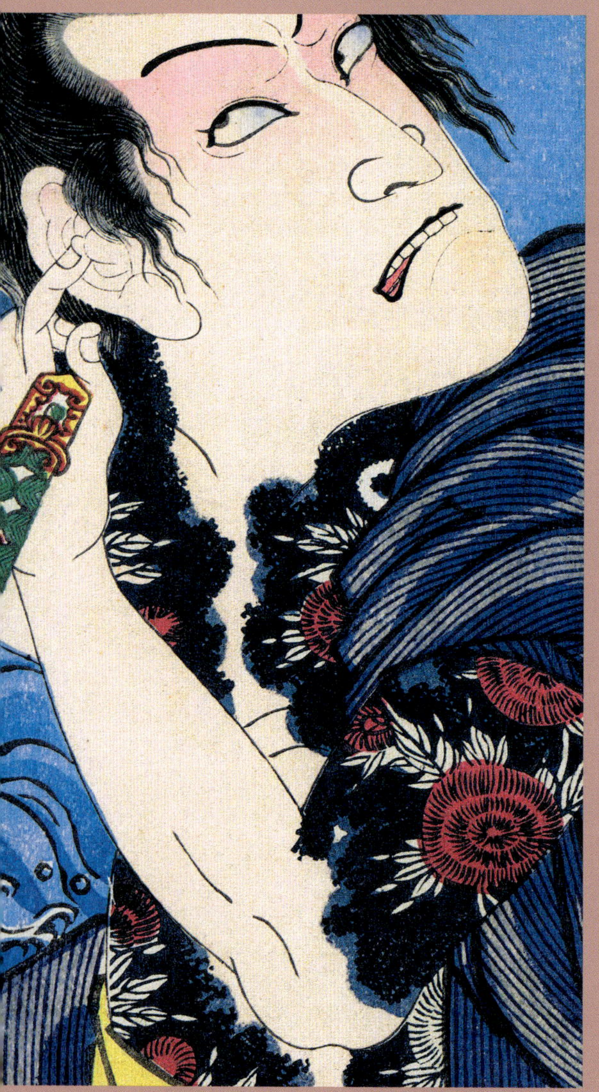

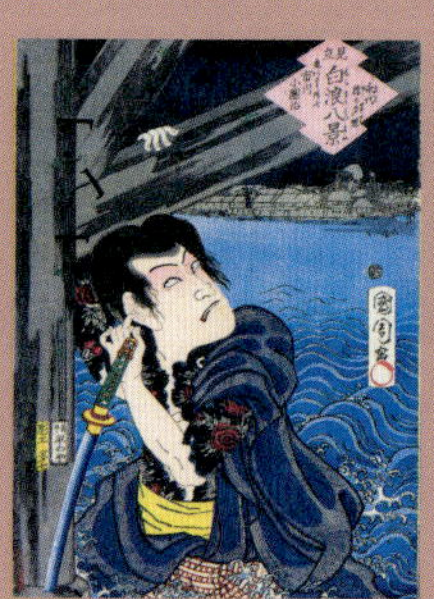

「見立白浪八景」「永代橋の夕照」
「鬼あざみ清七　市川小團次」
豊原国周
Actors Ichikawa Kodanji as Oniazami Seishichi, Eitaibashi-no-sekisho, from *Mitate-Shiranamihatsukei*, Toyohara Kunichika

慶応元年・1865
東京都立中央図書館特別文庫室蔵
1865, Tokyo Metropolitan Library

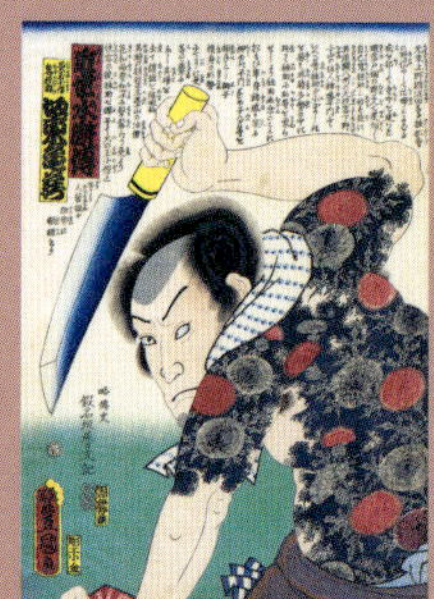

「近世水滸傳　炎玉小僧鬼桂助
坂東亀蔵」歌川豊国
Actors Bandō Kamezō as Hinotama Kozō Onikeisuke, from the series *A Modern Suikoden* (*Kinsei Suikoden*), Utagawa Toyokuni III (Kunisada I)

文久 2 年・1862
東京都立中央図書館特別文庫室蔵
1862, Tokyo Metropolitan Central Library

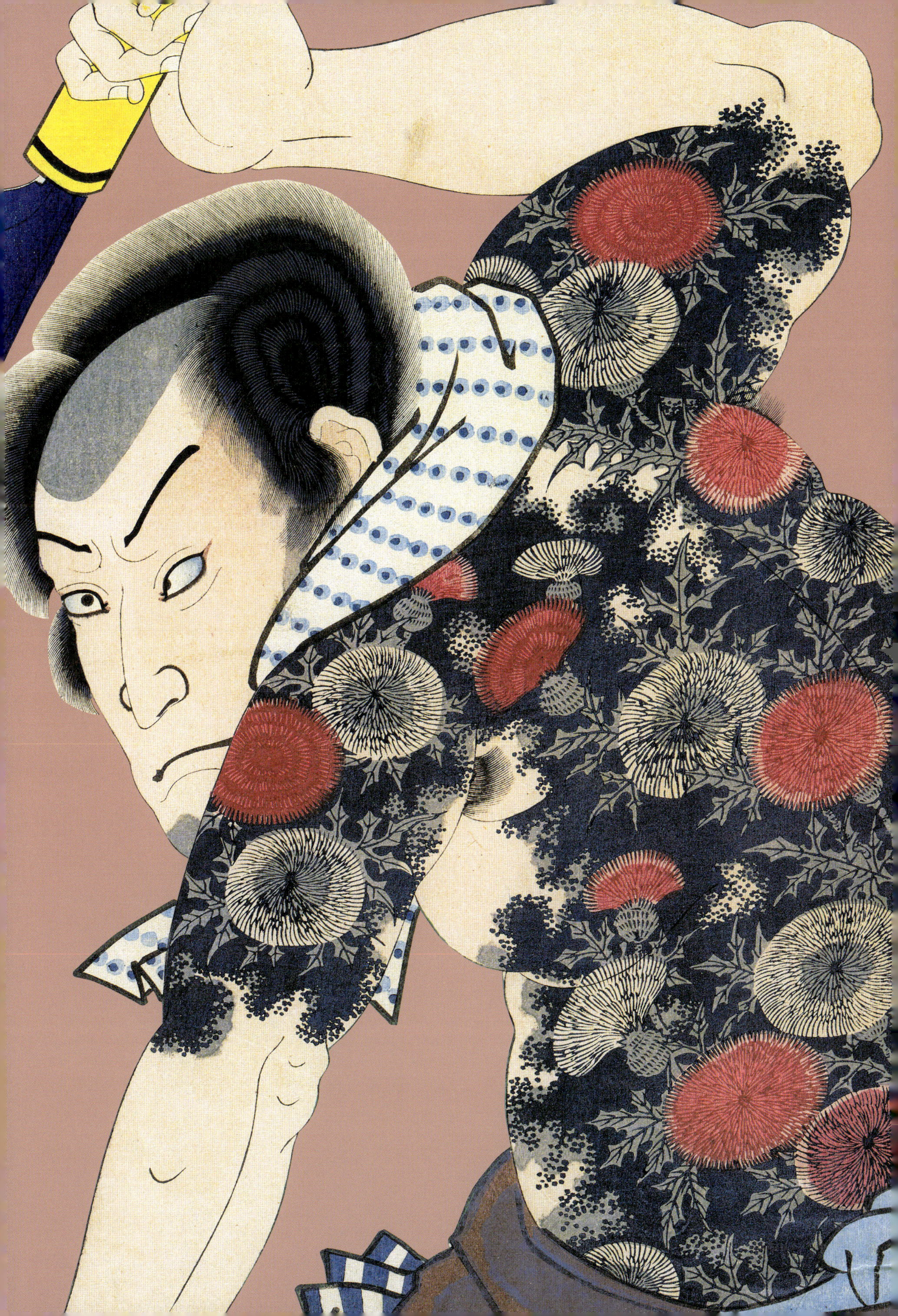

Plum

梅

うめ

早春に芳しい香りの五弁花をつけて咲く梅の高潔さは、常緑の松や雪にたえる竹とともに「歳寒の三友」とよばれ、東洋画の画題にもなった。また縁起を大切にした江戸の人々に好まれ、吉祥の文様として用いられた。梅の枝には邪気を払う霊力があるとする俗信がある。役者の両腕には鮮やかな梅の花弁がみごとに彫られている。

The purity of the plum tree, which produces fragrant five-petaled flowers in early spring, and its ability to bloom alongside evergreen pine and snow-resilient bamboo, made it one of the "Three Friends of Winter," a popular theme in Far Eastern painting. The people of Edo, who valued auspicious symbols, were fans of the plum tree and used it as a motif signifying good luck. It is also believed that plum branches ward off evil spirits.

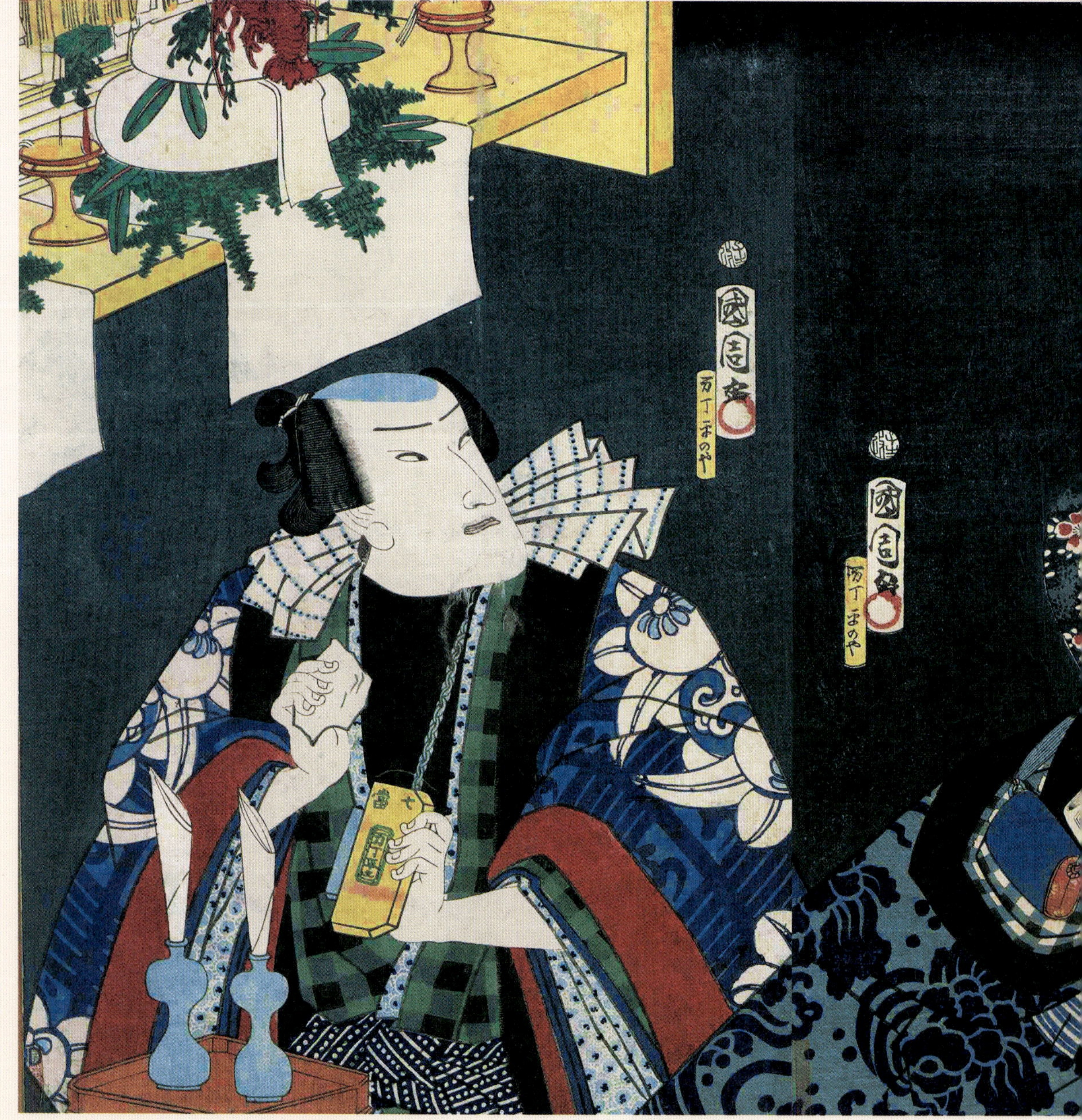

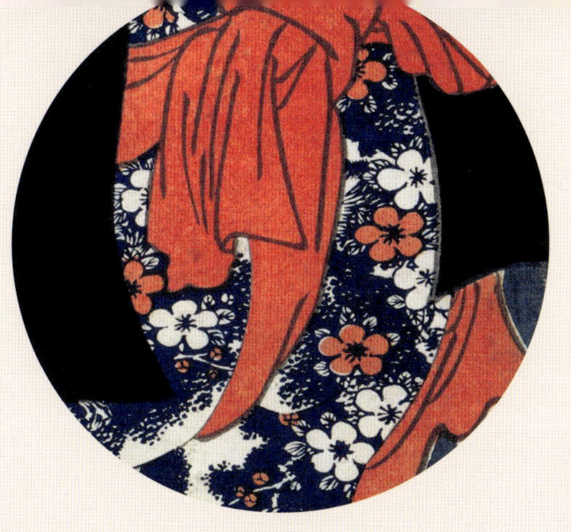

「深以仲意気地新倭羅　小糸佐七」
（部分）歌川豊国
Actors Ichikawa Ichizō III as Sashichi and
Nakamura Fukusuke I, Koito in the Play Koito
and Sashichi (Koito Sashichi), Detail, Utagawa
Toyokuni III (Kunisada I)
国立国会図書館デジタルコレクション
National Diet Library Digital Collections

「鬼ハ外福ハ内」豊原国周
Actor Sawamura Tanosuke III, Kawarazaki
Gonjūrō I, Ichimura Kakitsu IV, from the Oni-
wa-Soto, Fuku-wa-Uchi, Toyohara Kunichika

元治元年・1864
東京都立中央図書館特別文庫室蔵
1864, Tokyo Metropolitan Library

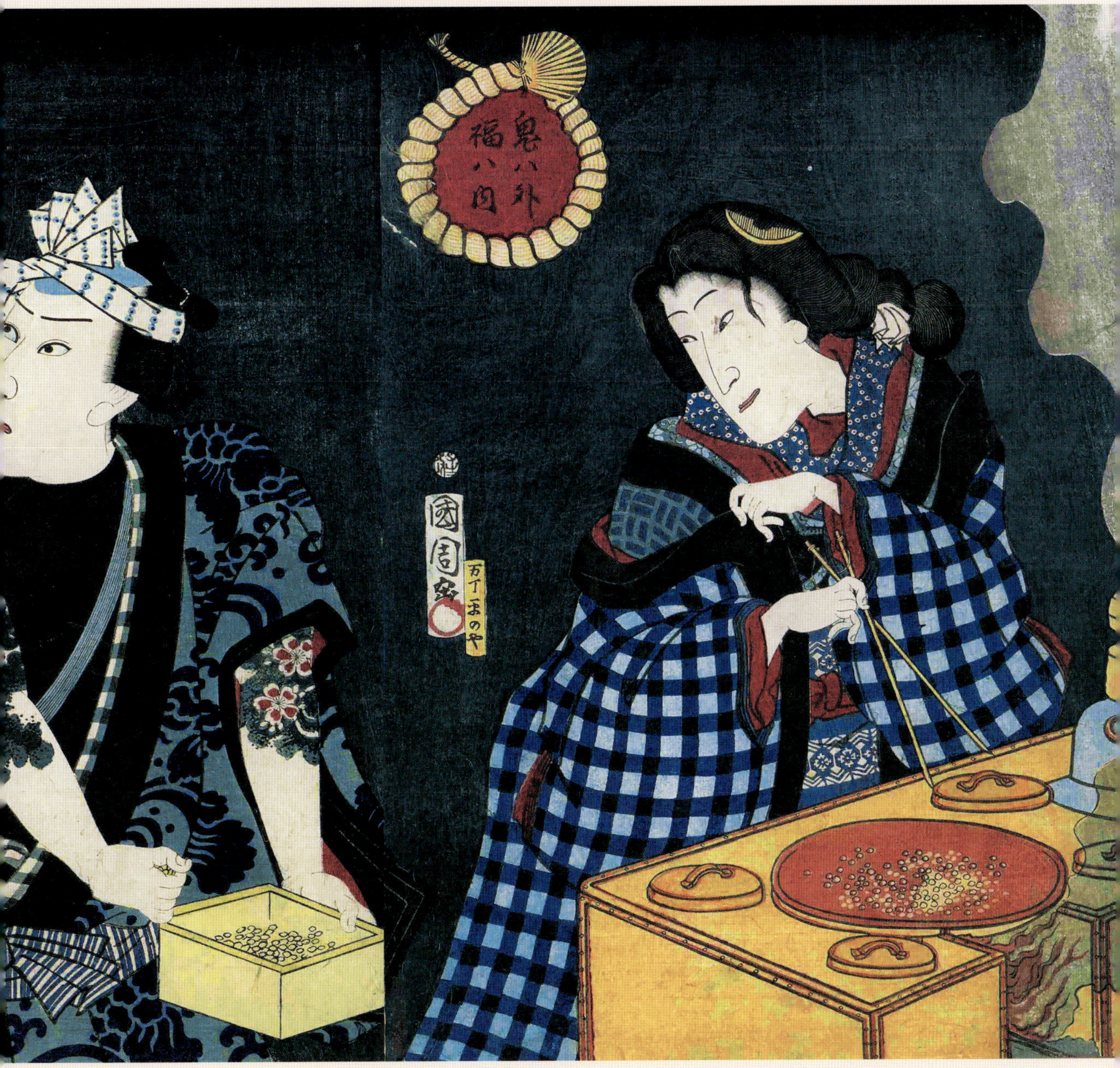

梵字入獅子、牡丹獅子、不動尊絵革など、甲冑の染革の図案集。編集の池田義信（溪斎英泉）は江戸時代後期の浮世絵師で、独力で浮世絵を学んだ。俗称を善次郎、名は茂義、のちに義信と改名した。画号には溪斎、国春楼などを用いた。浮世絵師としては珍しく幾種かの著述を残している。

This collection of designs for use on suits of armor includes Chinese lion-dogs with Sanskrit writing and Chinese lion dogs with peonies. The compiler of this collection, Ikeda Yoshinobu (Keisai Eisen), was a self-taught ukiyo-e artist active in the latter half of the Edo period. His childhood name was Zenjiro, his given name Shigeyoshi, and he later adopted the name Yoshinobu. His art names include Eisei and Kokushunro. Unusually for an ukiyo-e artist, he was also a writer, working in several genres.

好古集覧『革究図考』池田義信・編輯
Ikeda Yoshinobu, ed. *Kokoshuran kakuzenzuko*

弘化 2 年・1845　国立国会図書館デジタルコレクション
1845, National Diet Library Digital Collections

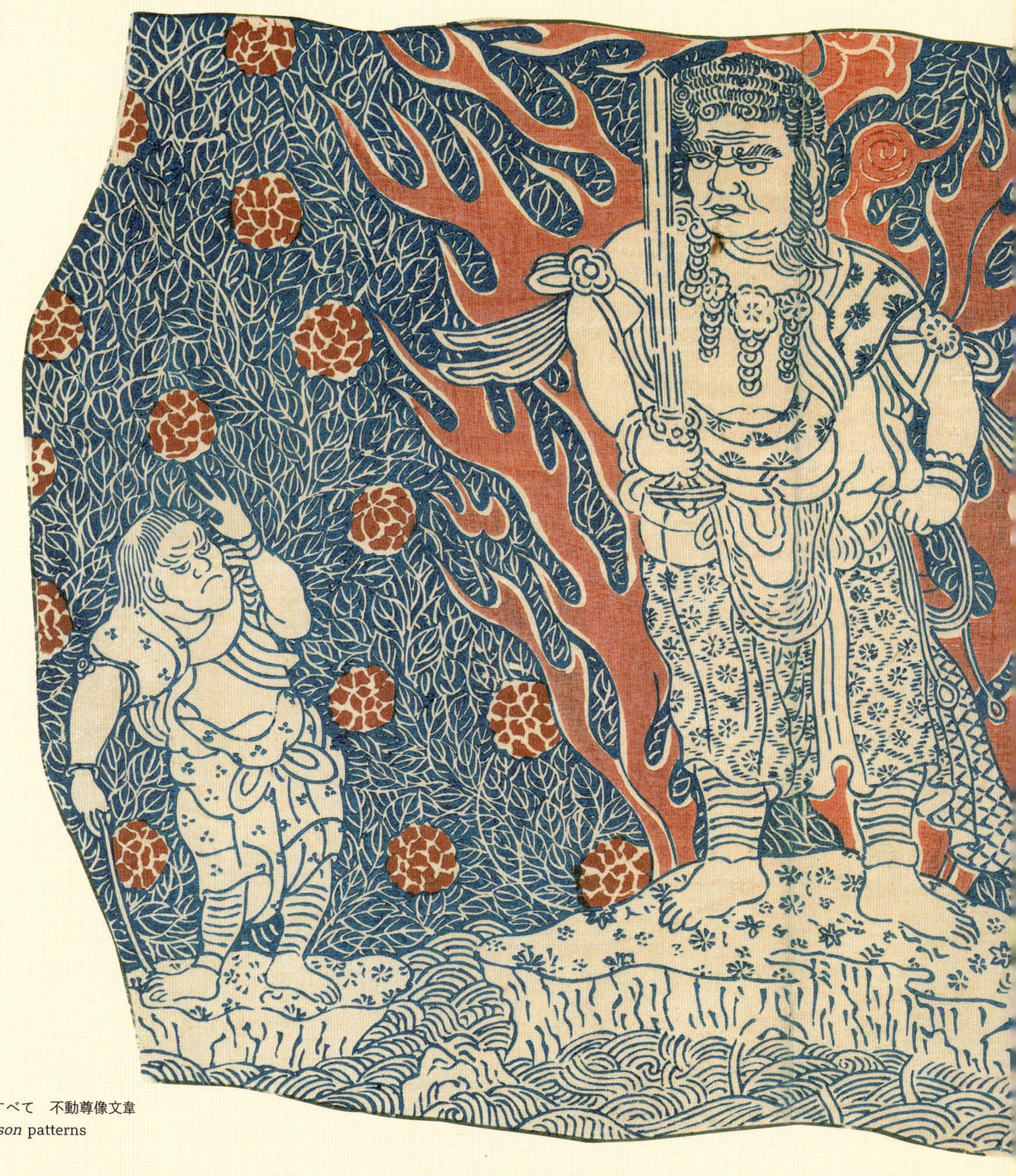

4 点すべて　不動尊像文章
Fudōson patterns

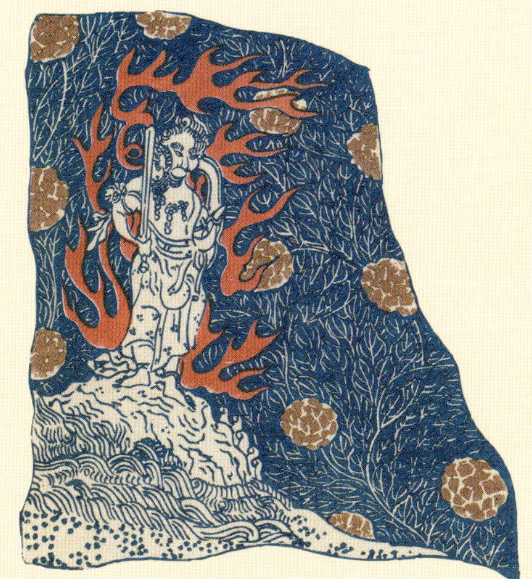

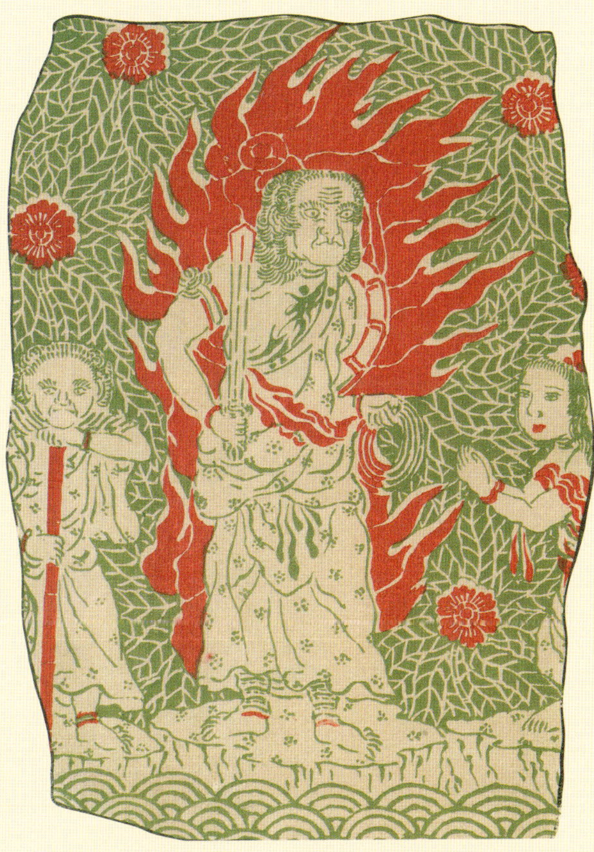

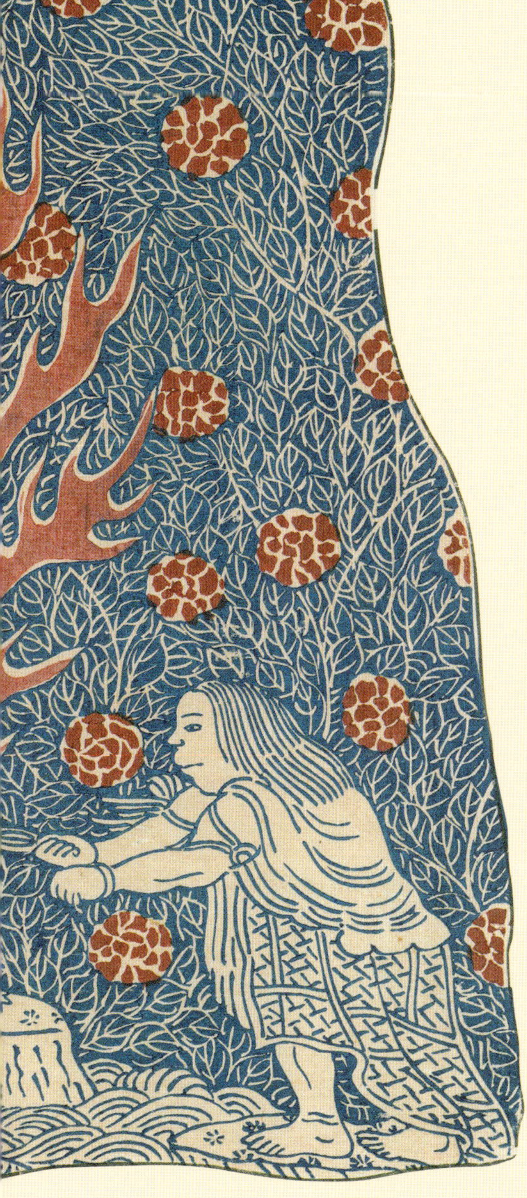

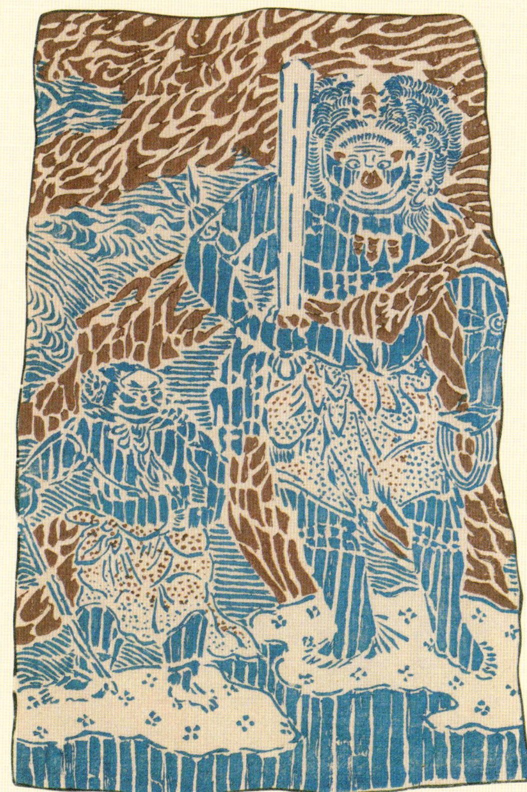

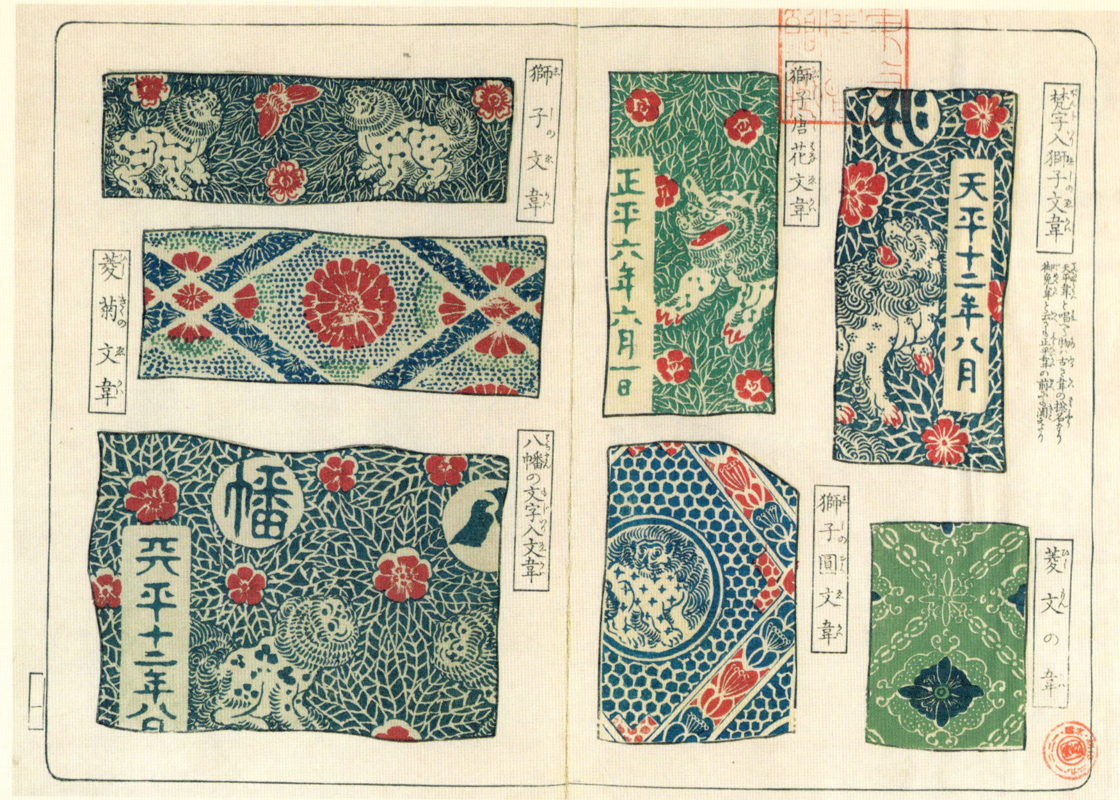

獅子文章・菱菊文章・八幡の文字入文章
Chinese lion-dogs pattern/Chrysanthemum pattern in diamond-shaped/*Hachiman* letter shape pattern

梵字入獅子文章・獅子唐花文章・菱文の章・獅子圓文章
Chinese lion-dogs with Sanskrit writing patterns/Chinese lion-dogs and *Karahana* patters/Diamond-shaped pattern/Round Chinese lion-dogs pattern

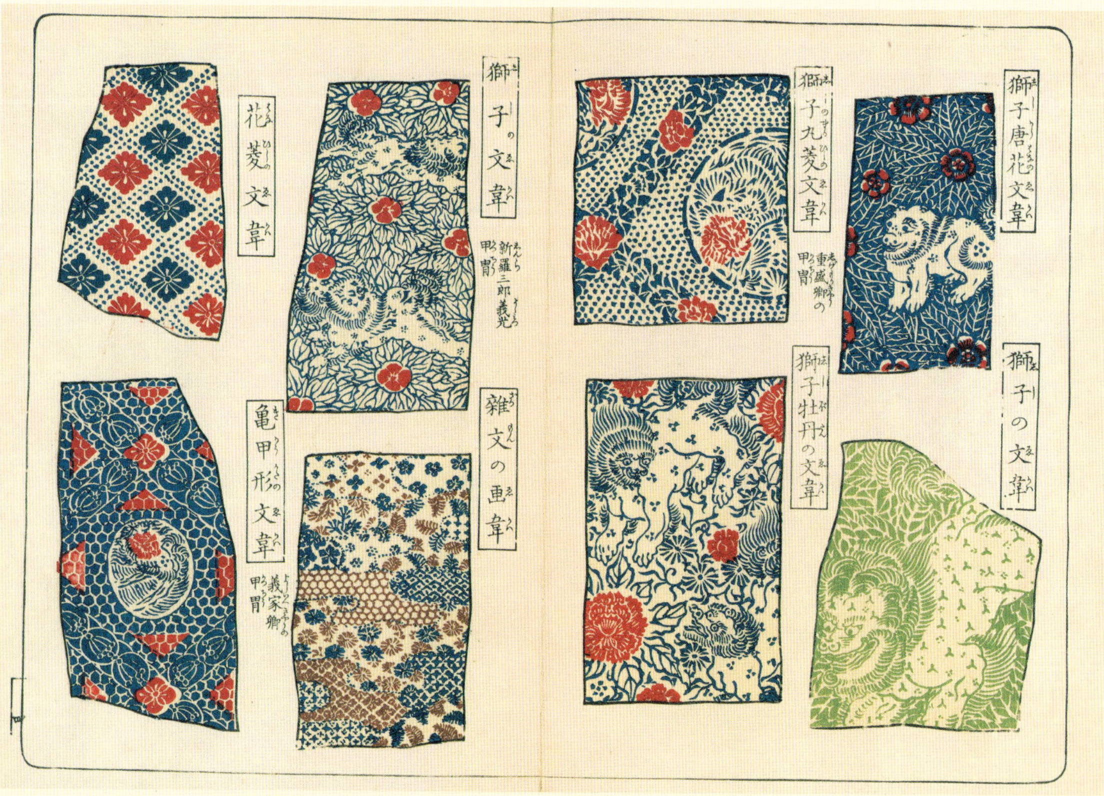

獅子文章・花菱文章・雑文の画章・亀甲形文章
Chinese lion-dogs pattern/Diamond-shaped flower patterns/Miscellaneous letter pattern/Tortoiseshell shape pattern

獅子唐花文章・獅子丸菱文章・獅子の文章・獅子牡丹の文章
Chinese lion-dogs and *Karahana* patterns/Chinese lion-dogs and Diamond-shaped patterns/Chinese lion-dogs pattern/Chinese lion dogs with peonies patterns

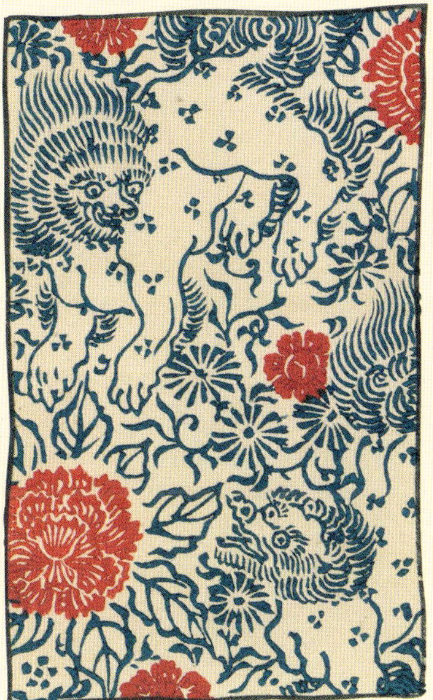

獅子牡丹の文章
Chinese lion dogs with
peonies patterns

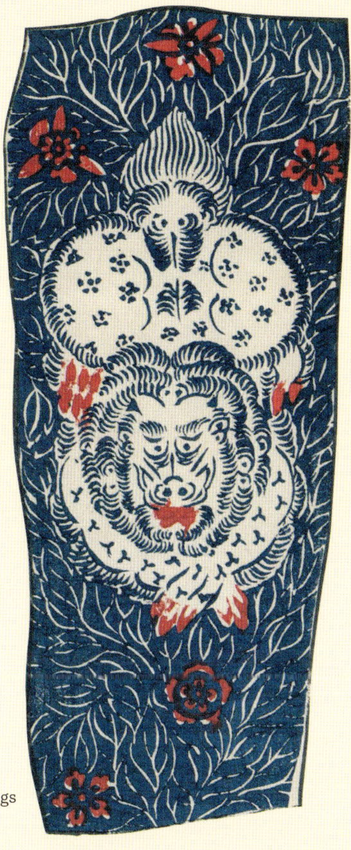

獅子文章
Chinese lion-dogs
pattern

獅子唐草文章
Chinese lion-dogs and
Karakusa patterns

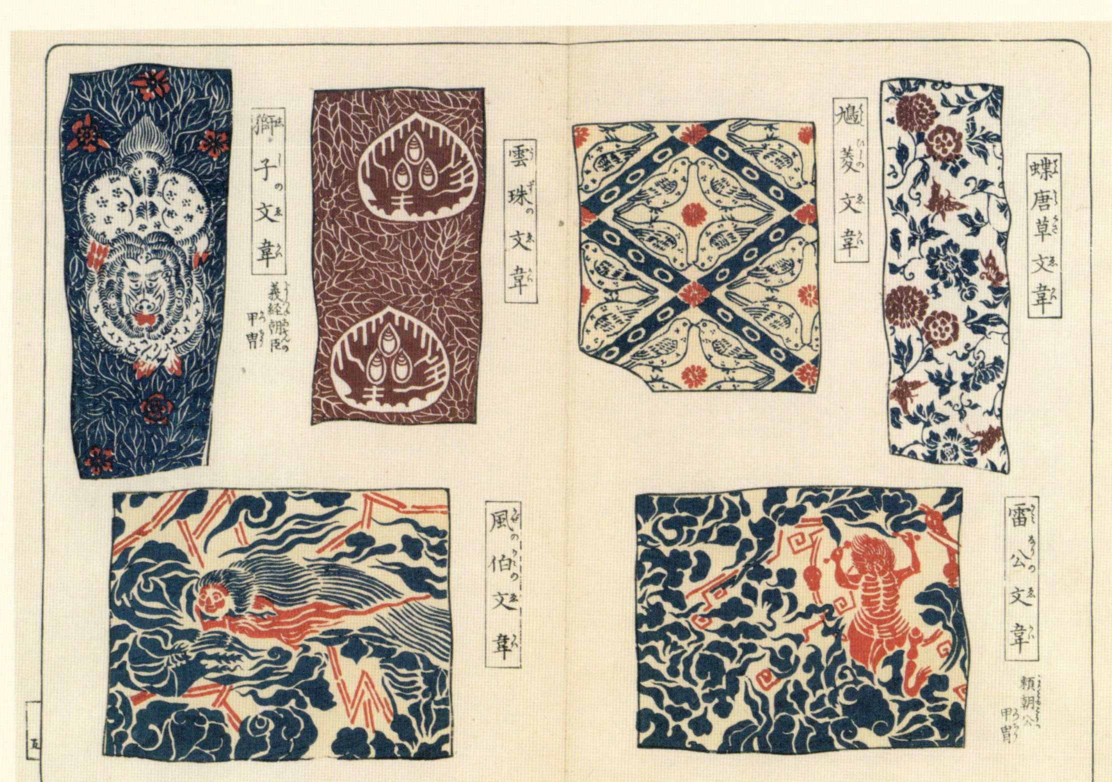

雲珠（うず）文章・獅子文章・風伯（ふうはく）文章
Uzu pattern/Chinese lion-dogs pattern/*Fūhaku* pattern

蝶唐草文章・鳩菱文章・雷公（らいこう）文章
Butterfly and *karakusa* patterns/Pigeon and diamond-
shaped patterns/*Raikō* pattern

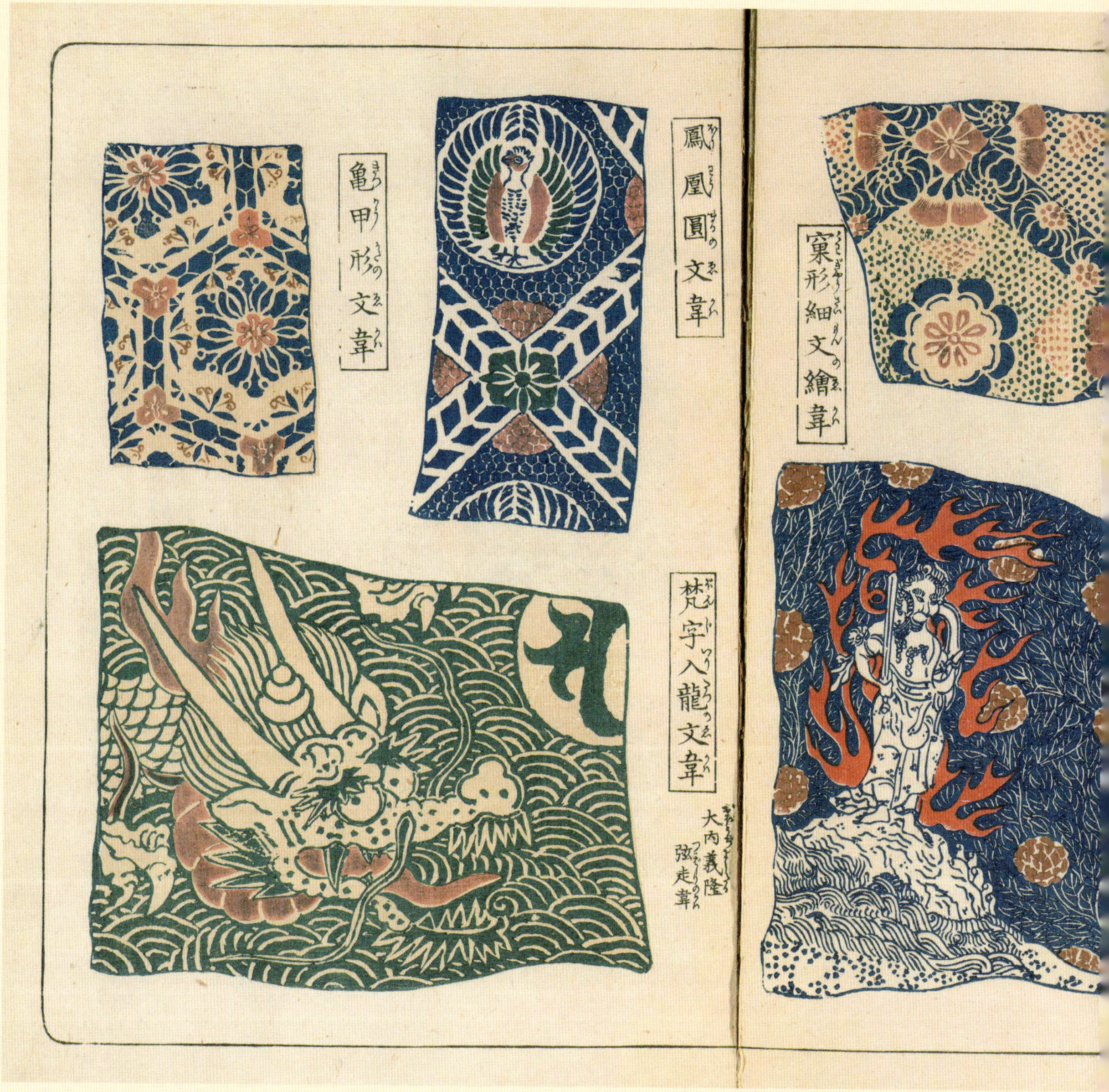

亀甲形文章

鳳凰圓文章

梵字入龍文章

大内義隆
弦走章

窠形細文繪章

鳳凰圓文章・亀甲形文章・梵字入龍文章
Phoenix round pattern/Tortoiseshell shape pattern/
Dragon with Sanskrit writing patterns

窠形細文繪章・六曜巴文章・不動尊像文章
Kanon pattern/*Rokuyō-tomoe* patterns/
Fudōson pattern

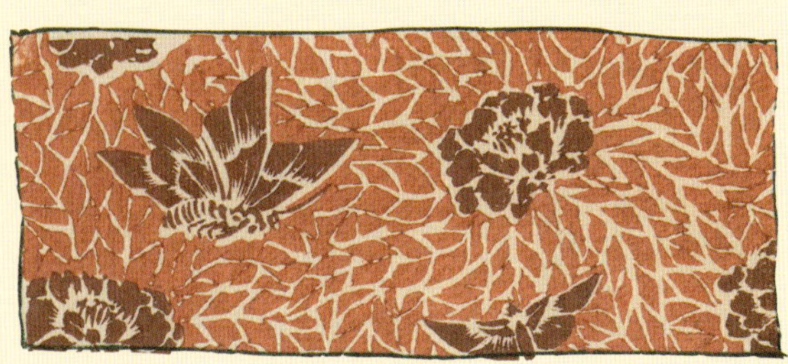

牡丹蝶文章
Peony and butterfly patterns

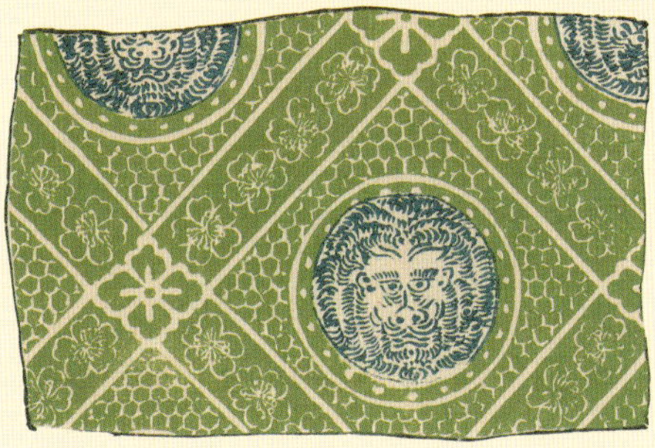

獅子面文章
Chinese lion-dogs face pattern

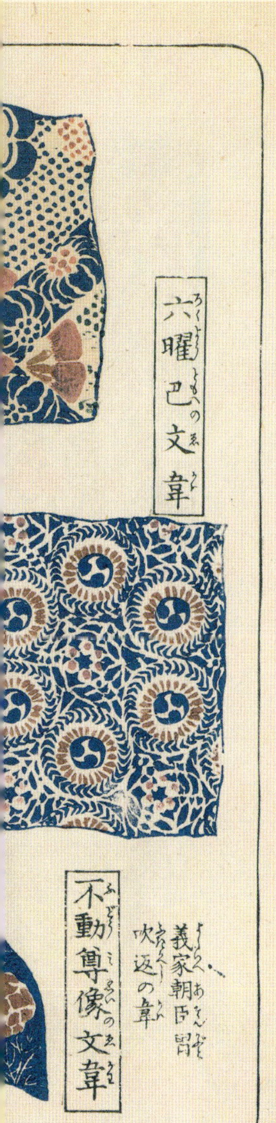

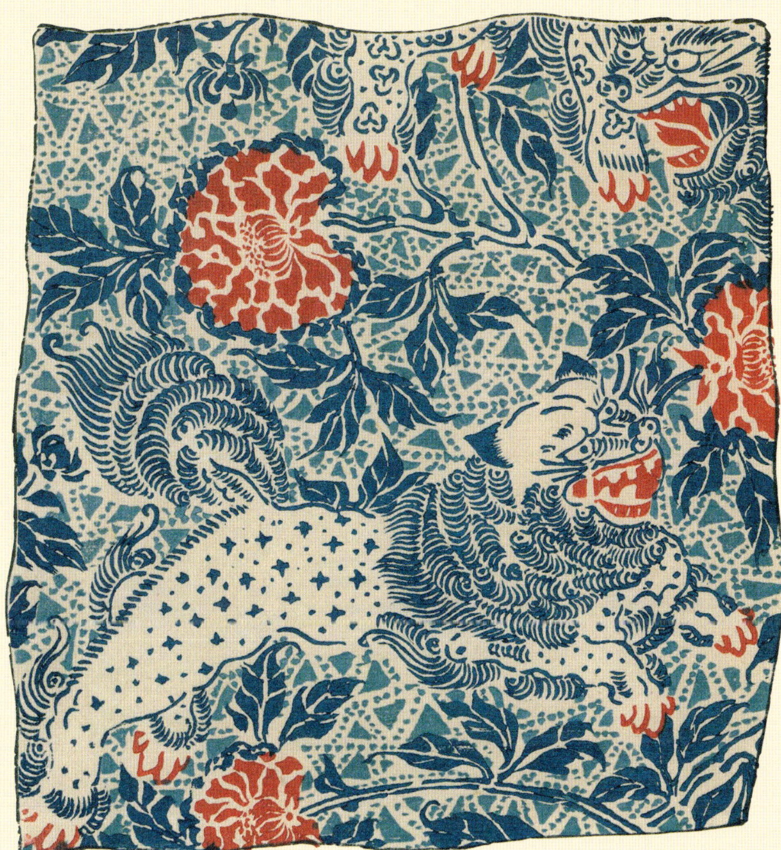
牡丹獅子文章
Chinese lion dogs with
peonies patterns

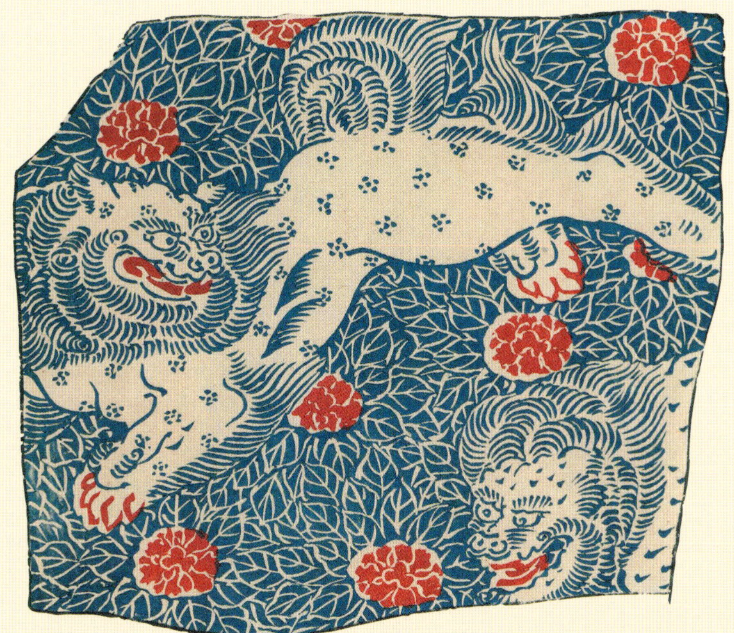
獅子牡丹文章
Peonies with Chinese
lion dogs patterns

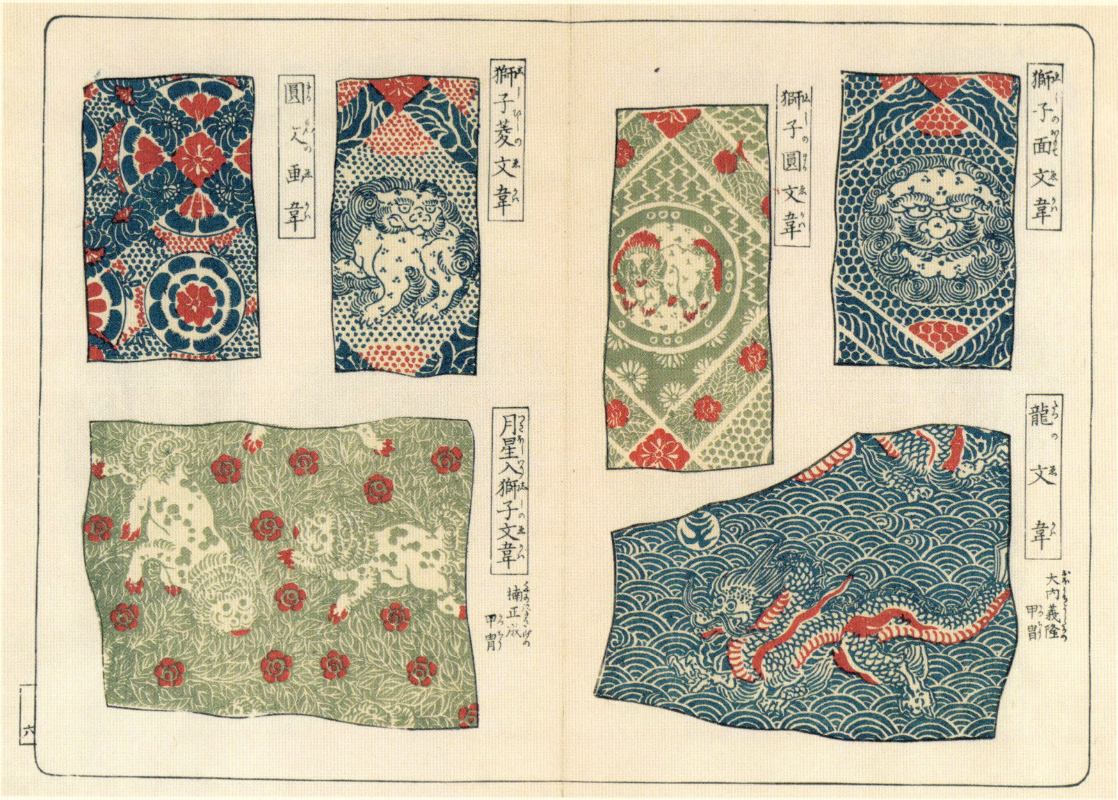

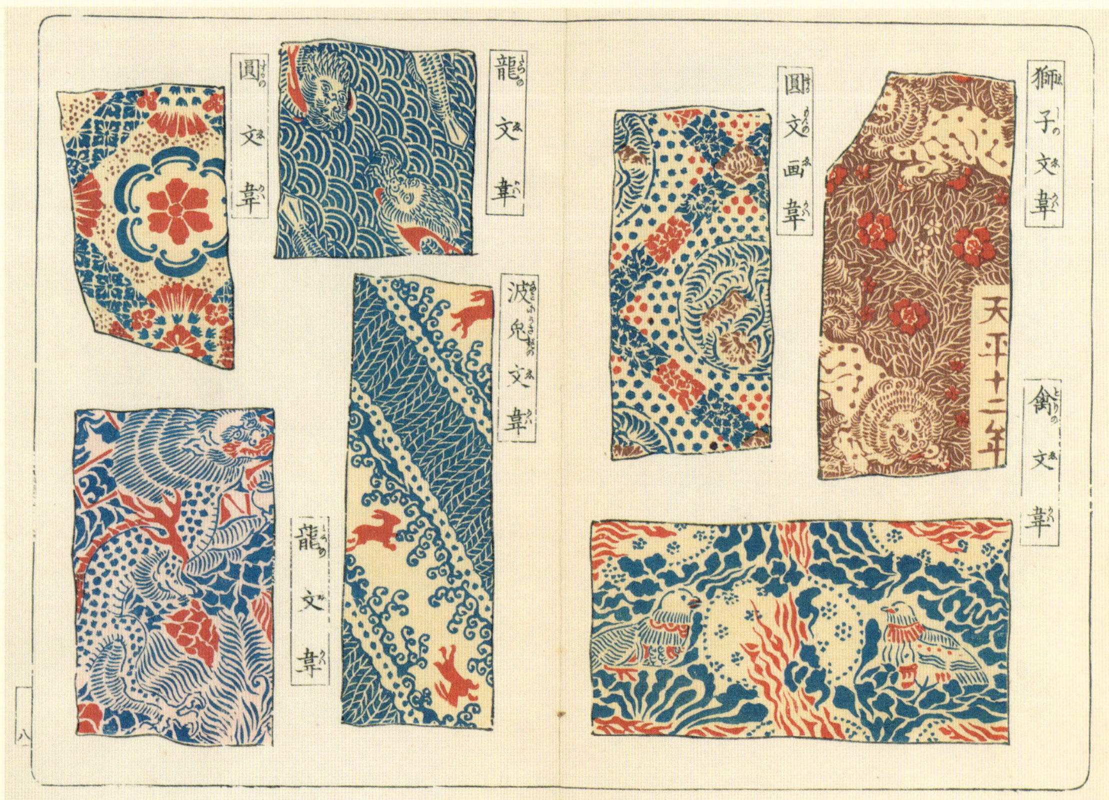

獅子菱文韋・圓文画韋・月星入獅子文韋
Chinese lion dogs and diamond-shaped patterns/Circular pattern/
Moon Star and lion patterns

獅子面文韋・龍文韋
Chinese lion-dogs face pattern/Dragon pattern

龍文韋・圓文画韋・波兎文韋・龍文韋
Dragon pattern/Circular pattern/Rabbit on the waves patterns/Dragon pattern

獅子文韋・圓文画韋・禽文韋
Chinese lion-dogs pattern/Circular pattern/Bird pattern

図版データ一覧・作品解説
List of Works / Description of Works

画像データ提供・資料掲載協力
Plates Cooperation

主要参考文献
Bibliography

［図版データ一覧・作品解説］
List of Works / Description of Works

○図版データは、作品名、作者名、制作年、判型、種類、版元、所蔵家の順に掲載する。制作年代は所蔵先のデータのため、不明なものは省略した。また解読不明な作品名は□で示した。

第1章 刺青　勇肌の美
Chapter 1 Tattoos: The Beauty of the Heroes' Skin

歌川国芳　Utagawa Kuniyoshi

18・19p

「**通俗水滸傳豪傑百八人之壹人　浪裡白跳張順**」歌川国芳　江戸時代・19世紀　大判　錦絵　加賀屋吉兵衛版　東京国立博物館蔵
Rōri Hakuchō Chōjun, from the series *One hundred and eight Heroes of the Suikoden*, Utagawa Kuniyoshi, Edo period, 19th century, Oban format, Tokyo National Museum
国芳の出世作としてよく知られる「通俗水滸傳豪傑百八人之壹人」は豪傑の勇猛な姿をえがき、浮世絵の武者絵というジャンルを確立したシリーズである。重複する人物図も含めると74図が確認されている。登場する豪傑たちの力動感あふれる描写と藍の刺青は、国芳錦絵の真骨頂である。この水門破りは手に汗を握る最大の見せ場で、総攻撃を開始した百八人の豪傑たちの運命と生死のすべてが、張順が水門を破れるかに賭けられている。両腕から胸にかけては大蛇退治の大模様が彫られている。動感の描写が力強く、魅力ある刺青である。

20p

「**通俗水滸傳豪傑百八人之一人　花和尚魯知深初名魯達**」歌川国芳　文政末期・1828-29　大判　錦絵　加賀屋吉右衛門版　山口県立萩美術館・浦上記念館蔵
Kaoshō Rochishin, from the series *One hundred and eight Heroes of the Suikoden*, Utagawa Kuniyoshi, Edo period, c.1828-29, Oban format, Hagi Uragami Museum
魯智深（ろちしん）は背中に海棠（かいどう）の花の彫物をしていたので、花（花繍・いれずみ）和尚とよばれた怪力無双の暴れ坊主。筋肉隆隆たる巨漢、髭面の坊主頭、精悍（せいかん）な顔、いかにも無頼な僧伽（そうぎゃ）の容貌である。手にした禅杖は、重さが10貫目(37kg)、長さが1.5メートルという鉄の棍棒である。いままさに松の大木を禅杖で打ち砕き、倒そうとする怪力のさまをえがいている。

21p

「**通俗水滸傳豪傑百八人之一個　撲天鵰李應・没遮攔穆弘**」歌川国芳　江戸時代・19世紀　大判　錦絵　東京国立博物館蔵
Hakutenchō Rio and Bossharan Bokkō, from the series *One hundred and eight Heroes of the Suikoden*, Utagawa Kuniyoshi, Edo period, 19th century, Oban format, Tokyo National Museum
背には虬龍（きゅうりゅう）が怒り、火焔を吐く力強い姿を彫った穆弘（ぼっこう）と、蛮人異風の容姿をした盗賊の頭目（とうもく）、李應（りおう）との雌雄を決する格闘の場面がえがかれる。李應は点鋼槍（てんこうそう）の名手であり、背中に隠した飛刀を使えば百歩の間を隔て、人を斬るほどの手練者（てだれもの）である。しかし穆弘の飛龍の剣の前では李應は形相を変えて奮戦した。

22p・125p

「**通俗水滸傳豪傑百八人之一個　九紋龍史進・跳澗虎陳達**」歌川国芳　江戸時代・19世紀　大判　錦絵　東京国立博物館蔵
Kumonryū Shishin and Chokankō Chintatsu, from the series *One hundred and eight Heroes of the Suikoden*, Utagawa Kuniyoshi, Edo period, 19th century, Oban format, Tokyo National Museum
九紋龍史進（くもんりゅうししん）は花和尚魯知深と並んで、水滸傳のなかでも人気のある英雄である。全身に九匹の龍を散らした刺青から九紋龍とよばれ、宋江麾下の部将として活躍した。史進の史家村に来た少華山の山賊、陳達（ちんたつ）と格闘する場面をえがく。双肩（もろはだ）をぬいで憤怒に駆られとびかかり、陳達を取りおさえ武人の荒々しさを如実に見せつけている。

23p

「**通俗水滸傳豪傑百八人之一個　九紋龍史進**」歌川国芳　江戸時代・19世紀　大判　錦絵　東京国立博物館蔵
Kumonryū Shishin, from the series *One hundred and eight Heroes of the Suikoden*, Utagawa Kuniyoshi, Edo period, 19th century, Oban format, Tokyo National Museum
史進は豪農の一人息子で、渾名（あだな）は九紋龍。総身（そうしん）には九匹の龍が怒ったごとく彫られその剛勇ぶりを発揮した。史家村や近郊の村々を掠奪してまわる山賊どもを少華山の山塞まで追いつめ、打ちすえて降伏させた。

24・143p

「**通俗水滸傳豪傑百八人之一個　混江龍李俊**」歌川国芳　江戸時代・19世紀　大判　錦絵　東京国立博物館蔵
Konkōryu Rishun, from the series *One hundred and eight Heroes of the Suikoden*, Utagawa Kuniyoshi, Edo period, 19th century, Oban format, Tokyo National Museum
渾名は混江龍（こんこうりゅう）で、長江を掻き回す龍という意味。長身で立派な風采の男である。張順と共に豪傑のなかでも水泳の達人で、その腕前を生かして敵の船底に鑿（のみ）を使って穴を空け、敵将が乗った船を怪力でひっくり返し溺れさせた。船が転覆する瞬間を鮮やかにとらえ、李俊の水中での勇壮ぶりをえがいた場面である。全身に水神である龍神の怒号する絵模様を飾っている。

25p

「**通俗水滸傳豪傑百八人之一個　舩火兒張横**」歌川国芳　江戸時代・19世紀　大判　錦絵　東京国立博物館蔵
Senkaji Chōou, from the series *One hundred and eight Heroes of the Suikoden*, Utagawa Kuniyoshi, Edo period, 19th century, Oban format, Tokyo National Museum
渾名は船頭を意味する、舩火兒（せんかじ）。張順は実弟で、李俊と穆弘は縄張りを接する兄弟分。敵将方天定を刺殺せんとする場面をえがく。激流を泳ぎ渡って捕えたのか、濡れ髪すがたの凛々しい裸身像である。その背には人魂か、それとも妖術の火焔が彫られている。張横（ちょうおう）は剣を持つ手を休めて振り返る。肩から胸もとにかけては荒鷲の勇猛さを神威、神勇とした彫物で飾っている。

26・137p
「通俗水滸傳豪傑百八人之一個　浪子燕青」歌川国芳
江戸時代・19 世紀　大判　錦絵　東京国立博物館蔵
Roushi Ensei, from the series *One hundred and eight Heroes of the Suikoden*, Utagawa Kuniyoshi, Edo period, 19th century, Oban format, Tokyo National Museum
渾名は伊達者を意味する浪子（ろうし）。燕青（えんせい）は小柄で細身、色白で絹のような肌を持ち、優美で勇壮な絶世の美青年である。足首から背先まで、全身に彫った唐獅子牡丹の刺青が映える。多芸多才な人物で、弩（いしゆみ）の腕は百発百中、小柄ながらも相撲の達人である。

27・134p
「通俗水滸傳豪傑百八人之一個　短命治郎阮小五」歌川国芳　江戸時代・19 世紀　大判　錦絵　東京国立博物館蔵
Tanmei Jirō Gen Shōgo, from the series *One hundred and eight Heroes of the Suikoden*, Utagawa Kuniyoshi, Edo period, 19th century, Oban format, Tokyo National Museum
渾名は短命治郎（たんめいじろう）、阮三兄弟の次兄で、長兄の阮小二、弟の阮小七とともに漁師をしている。眼光鋭く半裸の背には豹が閃光を放つ稲妻からあらわれ、獲物に飛びかかる瞬間をえがいた刺青が彫られている。敵兵を捕えその胸倉をひと突きにせんものと、剣を突き立てた勇ましいすがた。短命治郎という渾名は本人が短命ではなく、彼とかかわった相手の命が短くなってしまうためについたものである。

28p
「通俗水滸傳豪傑百八人一個　旱地忽律朱貴」歌川国芳
文政末期・1828-29 大判　錦絵　加賀屋吉右衛門版　山口県立萩美術館・浦上記念館蔵
Kanchi Kotsuritsu Shuki, from the series *One hundred and eight Heroes of the Suikoden*, Utagawa Kuniyoshi, Edo period, 1828-29, Oban format, Hagi Uragami Museum
朱貴（しゅき）は背が高く細身の体躯に口髭と顎鬚（あごひげ）を蓄え、梁山泊の古参のひとりである。双肩を脱ぎ、半裸になったその背には見事な九尾の狐の彫物がえがかれている。口から火焔を吐き、龍神の如き猛々しさである。王倫（おうりん）の命を受け湖のほとりに居酒屋を設け、往来の様子を偵察し、梁山泊に用のあるときは向かいの蘆の内に響矢を射込んで舟をよんだ。

29・142・143p
「通俗水滸傳豪傑百八人一個　金毛犬段景住」歌川国芳
大判　錦絵　江戸時代・19 世紀　東京国立博物館蔵
Kinmōken Dan Keijū, from the series *One hundred and eight Heroes of the Suikoden*, Utagawa Kuniyoshi, Edo period, 19th century, Oban format, Tokyo National Museum
背に仁王尊像を彫りつけた段景住（だんけいじゅう）が、乱暴をはたらき馬を強奪する悪漢どもを退治せんと、勇気を奮い立たせ急ぎ駆けつける場面をえがいている。馬の目利きには優れたが武術はまったく話にならず、馬を調達するたびに奪い取られていた。痩せた大男で、赤い髪と黄み掛った髭を持つことから金毛犬（きんもうけん）の渾名がついている。

30p
「通俗水滸傳豪傑百八人之壹人　短冥次郎阮小吾」歌川国芳　江戸時代・19 世紀　大判　錦絵　東京国立博物館蔵
Tanmei Jirō Gen Shōgo, from the series *One hundred and eight Heroes of the Suikoden*, Utagawa Kuniyoshi, Edo period, 19th century, Oban format, Tokyo National Museum
阮小吾（げんしょうご）は、梁山泊にほど近い石碣村（せきかつそん）の漁師の次男として生まれた。胸には豹の刺青を彫り、勇猛で水中に長く身を潜（かく）す術を持っていた。本図は、水中で敵将と格闘するすがたを交差させてえがき、斜めに走る水の動きや逃げる魚のようすがとらえられている。躍動感あふれる作品でシリーズのなかでも傑作とされる。

31・146p
「通俗水滸傳豪傑百八人之一個　菜園子張青」歌川国芳
江戸時代・19 世紀　大判　錦絵　東京国立博物館蔵
Saienshi Chousei, from the series *One hundred and eight Heroes of the Suikoden*, Utagawa Kuniyoshi, Edo period, 19th century, Oban format, Tokyo National Museum
渾名は菜園子（さいえんし）で、孟州の光明寺で野菜畑の番人をしていたことから名がついた。崖下を眺める張青の容姿は筋肉隆々とした肉体美で、その筋肉からは均整のとれた体躯のあとが見られる。珍しい刺青文様で、孫悟空が口から息とともに多くの猿たちを吹き出す図である。これは身外身（しんがいしん）とよぶ分身の術で、体毛を少し引き抜き、仙気とともに吹きつけると、無数の分身が口から飛び出してくる

31・159p
「通俗水滸傳豪傑百八人之一個　操刀鬼曹正」歌川国芳
江戸時代・19 世紀　大判　錦絵　東京国立博物館蔵
Soutouki Sousei, from the series *One hundred and eight Heroes of the Suikoden*, Utagawa Kuniyoshi, Edo period, 19th century, Oban format, Tokyo National Museum
渾名は操刀鬼（そうとうき）で、代々肉屋の生まれでその包丁さばきが見事なことからきている。総身には珍しい蛸（たこ）と烏賊（いか）と海老をあしらった刺青が彫られている。料理屋の食卓を思わせるような背後には、包丁が二丁置かれている。歌舞伎で演じる見得（みえ）のようで、六方（ろっぽう）を踏んだだんまりの勇姿である。張りのある力強い躍動感がみなぎっている。

32・33p
「木曾街道六十九次之内　四　浦和　魚屋團七」歌川国芳　嘉永 5 年・1852　大判　錦絵　住吉屋政五郎版　東京都立中央図書館特別文庫室蔵
Station IV Urawa, Sakanaya Danshichi, from the series *The Sixty-Nine Stations of the Kisokaidō Road*, Utagawa Kuniyoshi, 1852, Oban format, Tokyo Metropolitan Library
團七九郎兵衛は人形浄瑠璃『夏祭浪花鑑（なつまつりなにわかがみ）』の魚屋あがりの侠客。強欲な舅（しゅうと）義平次を殺めてしまった團七が、井戸から汲み上げた桶の水を頭からかぶり、返り血を流す長町裏の場面。透明感のある水の表現や、龍の彫物の細緻な描写が印象的である。

32・140p
「華古与見」歌川国芳　天保 6 年・1835　色摺　半紙本 3

冊　国際日本文化研究センター蔵
Hanagoyomi: Calender for flower plucking, Detail, Utagawa Kuniyoshi, 1835,Hanshi-bon, International Research Center for Japanese Studies
「華古与見（はなごよみ）」は、国芳の艶本の代表作。猫好きの国芳らしく猫が何匹もあらわれたり、料理茶屋の客室をえがいた大パノラマや火事場の大混乱ぶりなど、躍動感にあふれた絵が見ていて楽しい。鮮やかな色彩のなかでも藍色の表現が美しい。「神輿（みこし）が来たからゆかねばならん」「神輿よりこっちの（祭）が肝腎だよ」とは、画中の二人の会話。

歌川豊国 Utagawa Toyokuni III (Utagawa Kunisada I)

34・175p

「豊国漫画図絵　弁天小僧菊之介」歌川豊国　万延元年・1860　大判　錦絵　魚栄版　国立国会図書館デジタルコレクション
Bentenkozō Kikunosuke, from *The Heroes and Heroines of the Popular Fiction (Toyokuni Manga Zue)* ,Utagawa Toyokuni III (Kunisada I),1860, Oban format, National Diet Library Digital Collections
歌舞伎狂言『青砥稿花紅彩画（あおとぞうしはなのにしきえ）』、通称『白浪（しらなみ）五人男』の登場人物である弁天小僧は女装の盗賊である。浜松屋にあらわれゆすりをかけるが、一味の日本駄右衛門にわざと正体をみやぶられていなおる。娘姿から片肌をぬぎ大あぐらをかいて「知らざあ言って聞かせやしょう」と啖呵（たんか）をきる有名な場面。女物の着物をはだけ、肩には美しい桜の彫物が見える。

35p

「今四天王大山帰り　貞光ノ市・渡辺ノ福・季武ノ権・金時ノ米」『東錦絵』より　歌川豊国　安政5年・1858　大判　錦絵　2枚続　太田屋多吉版　国立国会図書館蔵デジタルコレクション
Ima Shitennō Ōyamagaeri, Sadamitsu no ichi, Watanabe no fuku, Kibu no gon, Kintoki no me, from the picture album *Azuma Nishiki-e* Utagawa Toyokuni III (Kunisada I), 1858, Oban format, National Diet Library Digital Collections
平安中期の武将である源頼光の四天王に見立てた、貞光ノ市（市川市蔵）、渡辺ノ福（中村福助）、季武ノ権（河原崎権十郎）、金時ノ米（市川小團次）の四人の鯔背（いなせ）な男たち。修験道場として知られる大山詣での帰りのため、纏（まとい）姿で勢揃いしている。貞光ノ市の右腕には正真正銘の倶利迦羅紋々（くりからもんもん）。黒龍の巻きつく模様の剣を呑む図で、不動明王の化身をかたどった彫物である。金時ノ米の背は蔦のからまる深山幽谷に、金時は松の古木で土蜘蛛を退治する図柄を彫った華やかな刺青である。

36・37p

「見立十人豊国一世一代　屋久ら水滸傳」歌川豊国　文久3年・1863　大判　錦絵　3枚続　太田屋多吉版　東京都立中央図書館特別文庫室蔵
Ten Imaginary Portraits, Toyokuni's Once-in-a-Lifetime Shuihuzhuan of the Stage (*Mitate jūnin Toyokuni issei ichidai yagura Suikoden*), Utagawa Toyokuni III (Kunisada I), 1863, Oban format, Tokyo Metropolitan Central Library
「近世水滸傳」の画巻のなかから侠客十人を選び『水滸傳』に似せてえがいた見立絵である。おもな人物は、右端のヒ首（あいくち）をくわえたのが夏目小僧、豆しぼりの鉢巻姿が成田の新蔵、法界坊姿の青髭が炎玉小僧である。役者は、右から河原崎権十郎、市川市蔵、市川團蔵、坂東彦三郎、市川小團次、市村羽左衛門、中村芝翫、沢村訥舛、沢村田之助、市川市蔵が演じている。

38・162p

「當世好男子傳　林中に比す鮫鞘四郎三」（五代目坂東彦三郎）歌川豊国　安政6年・1859　大判　錦絵　国立国会図書館デジタルコレクション
Actors Bandō Hikosaburō V as Samezaya Shiroza, comparable to Lin Zhong (Rinchū ni hisu), from the series *A Modern Shuihuzhuan (Tōsei suikoden)*, Utagawa Toyokuni III (Kunisada I),1859, Oban format, National Diet Library Digital Collections
幕末には人気役者を侠客に見立てた錦絵が数多く刊行され、「當世好男子傳」シリーズは安政5年（1858）から翌年にかけて3回売り出された。松竹梅を背景にえがいた3枚の揃いもので全9枚からなる。日本の侠客に扮した歌舞伎役者の肖像を、通俗小説『水滸傳』の登場人物に見立ててえがいている。坂東彦三郎が扮する鮫鞘四郎三は、「児雷也豪傑譚話（じらいやごうけつものがたり）」の児雷也が変装した侠客である。

38・39p

「當世好男子傳　張順に比す夢の市郎兵衛」（八代目片岡仁左衛門）歌川豊国　安政6年・1859　大判　錦絵　国立国会図書館デジタルコレクション
Actors Kataoka Nizaemon VIII as Yume no Ichirobei, comparable to Zhang Shun (Chōjun ni hisu), from the series *A Modern Shuihuzhuan (Tōsei suikoden)*, Utagawa Toyokuni III (Kunisada I), 1859, Oban format, National Diet Library Digital Collections
八代目片岡仁左衛門が扮する夢の市郎兵衛は寛永・正保年間の江戸の侠客。『水滸傳』に登場する泳ぎの名手である張順に見立てられた理由はわからない。雲龍の彫物をした左腕を襟もとから出しての大見得のポーズで決めている。

39p・159p

「當世好男子傳　憮小ニ比ス團七九郎兵衛」（市川小團次）歌川豊国　大判　錦絵　林庄版　国立国会図書館デジタルコレクション
Actors Ichikawa Kodanji as Danshichi Kurobei, comparable to Ruǎn Xiǎowǔ (Genshogo ni hisu), from the series *A Modern Shuihuzhuan (Tōsei suikoden)*, Utagawa Toyokuni III (Kunisada I), 1859, Oban format, National Diet Library Digital Collections
市川小團次が扮する團七九郎兵衛は、延享2年（1745）に初演された『夏祭浪花鑑』中の魚屋あがりの侠客。その衣装は柿色の弁慶縞で、團七縞とよばれ流行した。

40p

「當世好男子傳　行者武松に比す腕の袁三郎」歌川豊国　安政5年・1858　大判　錦絵　国立国会図書館デジタルコレクション
Ude no Kisaburō, comparable to Wu Song the Ascetic (Gyōja Bushō ni hisu), from the series *A Modern Shuihuzhuan (Tōsei suikoden)*, Utagawa Toyokuni III (Kunisada I), 1858, Oban format, National Diet Library Digi-

tal Collections
景陽岡で人食い虎を素手で打ち殺し、戦闘で片腕を切断したことで知られる『水滸傳』の武松に見立てられたのは、初代河原崎権十郎が扮する喧嘩で片腕を失った侠客・腕の喜三郎。腕に描かれた虎の彫物はこの二つのエピソードを重ねて暗示させている。

41・129p
「當世好男子傳　九紋龍支進に比すのざらし語助」歌川豊国　安政 5 年・1858　大判　錦絵　国立国会図書館デジタルコレクション
Nozarashi Gosuke, comparable to Kumonryū Shishin, from the series *A Modern Shuihuzhuan (Tōsei suikoden)*, Utagawa Toyokuni III (Kunisada I), 1858, Oban format, National Diet Library Digital Collections
薄（すすき）に髑髏（どくろ）模様がえがかれた衣装に、帯刀姿であらわれたのは三代目市川市蔵が扮する野晒語助。語助は歌舞伎『粋菩提悟道野晒』（すいぼだいさとりののざらし）に登場する大坂の侠客で、一休禅師の弟子だった。その奔放な性格のため破門され、浪花千日寺の近くで葬具造りを生業としていた。腕に龍の刺青を彫ることで、『水滸傳』の好漢のひとりである九紋龍史進に見立てられている。

42p
「當世好男子傳　恋青□久利加良傳七芝翫」歌川豊国　大判　錦絵　静岡県立中央図書館蔵
Actor Nakamura Shikan as Kurikara Denshichi, from the series *A Modern Shuihuzhuan (Tōsei suikoden)*, Utagawa Toyokuni III (Kunisada I), Oban format, Shizuoka Prefectural Central Library
燕青は『水滸傳』では体格は小柄で細身、色白で絹のような肌を持った絶世の美青年である。その燕青を、『夏祭浪花鑑』中の魚屋あがりの侠客である團七九郎兵衛に見立てている。

42p
「勇肌対弁慶」歌川豊国　万延元年・1860　大判　錦絵　太田屋多吉版　2 枚続　静岡県立中央図書館蔵
Isamihada vs.Benkei, Utagawa Toyokuni III (Kunisada I), 1860, Oban format, Shizuoka Prefectural Central Library
化政期から幕末にかけて、刺青を彫るものは侠客、鳶の者、臥煙（がえん）、駕籠（かご）かきなどが多かった。仕事柄つねに危険に身をさらす職業であり、上着をはだけてできる仕事だったからである。この見立絵はそんな駕籠かき人足の勇肌（いさみはだ）に、市川猿蔵（右）と市川市蔵（左）をえがいたものである。弁慶縞のゆかたに、桜ちらしと花魁道中の絵模様をさし、また牡丹総柄の刺青が彫られている。

43p
「あとヘハひかぬ男の木性　大工六三」（当見立五行相剋）歌川豊国　安政 5 年・1858　大判　錦絵　魚栄版　国立国会図書館デジタルコレクション
The temper of a man who does not pull back (*Atoehahikanu-otoko-no-kishō*), Daiku no Rokuzō, Utagawa Toyokuni III (Kunisada I), 1858, Oban format, National Diet Library Digital Collections
墨一色の背景をシルエットでえがき、闇夜に駕籠で帰るお園のあとを追ってきた大工の六三が、商売道具の鑿（のみ）を持ち殺意をみせて佇む。総身に雲龍の刺青を彫り、ゆかたにえがかれた定紋の蝶紋から役者紋であることがわかる。

この図は中国の五行説に似せた見立絵で、ほかに牛若傳次、八重桜の才三、寝津美幸蔵（ねずみこぞう）などがえがかれている。

44・45・144・183p
「深以仲意気地新倭羅　小糸佐七」歌川豊国　大判　錦絵　2 枚続　太田屋多吉版 国立国会図書館デジタルコレクション
Actors Ichikawa Ichizō III as Sashichi and Nakamura Fukusuke I, Koito in the Play Koito and Sashichi (*Koito Sashichi*), Utagawa Toyokuni III (Kunisada I), Oban format, National Diet Library Digital Collections
有名な世話物「お祭佐七」の舞台を借りての見立絵で、本名題は『江戸育御祭佐七（えどそだちおまつりさしち）』。柳橋の芸者小糸と恋仲の鳶のお祭佐七が、加賀家の武士倉田らの悪だくみで小糸を殺すが、のちに真相を知って敵を討つ物語。佐七は市川市蔵、小糸は市川新車である。佐七の総身には奴凧（やっこだこ）に桜散らし模様という、眼にも眩い刺青が彫られている。勇肌の美しさが萌えたつような錦絵である。

46p・127p
「團七九郎兵衛・夏祭意気地ノ江戸ッ子　一寸徳兵衛」歌川豊国　大判　錦絵　2 枚続　太田屋多吉版 国立国会図書館デジタルコレクション
Danshichi Kurobei, *Natsumatsuri-ikijino-edokko*, Issun Tokubei, Utagawa Toyokuni III (Kunisada I), Oban format, National Diet Library Digital Collections
世話物『夏祭浪花鑑』の團七九郎兵衛（中村芝翫）と一寸徳兵衛 (市川市蔵) の意地の張り合いの場面がえがかれる。背景は役者好みの弁慶格子縞で、團七の総身には曙ぼかしに縁どられた雲龍の絵模様が彫られ、まさに千両役者の醍醐味がある。團七が全身に刺青を入れたのは天保期の四代目中村歌右衛門の初役で、『夏祭浪花鑑』の團七九郎兵衛を演じて大当たりになった時からといわれている。

46・47p
「花菖蒲男鑑」歌川豊国　安政 2 年・1855　大判　錦絵　伊豆屋三吉版　東京都立中央図書館特別文庫室蔵
Hanashōbu Otokokagami, Utagawa Toyokuni III (Kunisada I), 1855, Oban format, Tokyo Metropolitan Central Library
延享元年の冬、堺の魚売りが長町裏で人を殺し、翌春に露顕して処刑された。この実話を題材とした『花菖蒲男鑑（はなしょうぶおとこかがみ）』の有名な場面、團七九郎兵衛が舅（しゅうと）三川屋義平次を殺す長町裏。演ずるのは團七九郎兵衛に四代目市川小團次、三川屋義平次には中山市蔵の顔ぶれである。

48p
「今様押絵鏡　白瀧の佐吉」歌川豊国　万延元年・1860　大判　錦絵　松林堂版 国立国会図書館デジタルコレクション
Shirataki no Sakichi, from the series *the Imayō Oshiekagami*, Utagawa Toyokuni III (Kunisada I), 1860, Oban format, National Diet Library Digital Collections
鏡をモチーフとした画面枠に、役者の大首絵を描いたシリーズ。このようなアイデアは豊国が以前から好んで用いてきたもので、天保期の蔦屋吉蔵版の役者大首絵揃物や嘉永期の「今昔忠孝家賀見」などに見られる。清瀧村の佐吉は上総国の生まれで、銚子港で人を殺して下野に潜んでいたが、3年を経て下総笹川（笠川）に赴き、笹川繁蔵の子分となった。実説では清瀧の「佐七」ではなく「佐吉」である。佐吉（市村羽左衛門）の腕には唐獅子牡丹が鮮やかに彫られている。

48p

「今様押絵鏡　出来ぼしの三吉」歌川豊国　安政6年・1859　大判　錦絵　松林堂版　国立国会図書館デジタルコレクション
Dekiboshi no Sankichi, from the series *the Imayō Oshiekagami*, Utagawa Toyokuni III (Kunisada I), 1859, Oban format, National Diet Library Digital Collections
安政6年初演の『頼三升曾我神垣（たのみますそがのかみがき）』より、出来ぼしの三吉（市川市蔵）には龍紋の勇肌が彫られた押絵鏡である。書入れにはそれぞれ自作の身体の句を掲げていて、新升は「おゑの露まつ蝶のちからかな」とある。押絵鏡は大首絵の変型で、美人画や役者似顔絵にこの形式をとったものが多い。

49p

「近世水滸傳　競力富五郎　中村芝翫」歌川豊国　文久元年・1861　大判　錦絵　伊勢屋兼吉版　東京都立中央図書館特別文庫室蔵
Actors Nakamura Shikan IV as Keiriki Tomigorō, from the series *A Modern Suikoden (Kinsei Suikoden)*, Utagawa Toyokuni III (Kunisada I), 1861, Oban format, Tokyo Metropolitan Central Library
「近世水滸傳」は、侠客たちの半身像を人気役者の似顔でえがき、幕末を代表する戯作者仮名垣魯文（かながきろぶん）が略伝を添えたシリーズ。組定重治（国定忠治）や縞の仁三郎（島村伊三郎）といった上州の侠客や、井岡の捨五郎（飯岡助五郎）や競力富五郎（勢力富五郎）ら天保水滸傳に関係する博徒たち、あるいは祐膳朝吉（祐典浅吉）のような甲州博徒などがえがかれている。

50・52p

「近世水滸傳　夏目子僧新助　岩井粂三郎」歌川豊国　文久元年・1861　大判　錦絵　伊勢屋兼吉版　東京都立中央図書館特別文庫室蔵
Actors Iwai Kumesaburō III as Natsume-kozō Shinsuke, from the series *A Modern Suikoden (Kinsei Suikoden)*, Utagawa Toyokuni III (Kunisada I),1861, Oban format, Tokyo Metropolitan Central Library
手ぬぐいを首に巻き、包丁を口に咥えたすがたで佇む。似顔は当時の人気女形である三代目岩井粂三郎。のちに八代目岩井半四郎となって、明治期まで活躍する。彫物は梅の模様で着物の図柄は竹に虎となっている。魯文の詞書によると、夏目子僧新助は葛飾の生まれで、容姿端麗の美少年であったという。幼くして父母を失い房州名古寺の小姓となるが、やがてやくざ者と付き合うようになり寺を追い出された。

51・52p

「近世水滸傳　清瀧の佐七　市村羽左衛門」歌川豊国　嘉永5年・1852　大判　錦絵　伊勢屋兼吉版　東京都立中央図書館特別文庫室蔵
Actors Ichimura Uzaemon XIII as Kiyotaki-no-Sashichi, from the series *A Modern Suikoden (Kinsei Suikoden)*, Utagawa Toyokuni III (Kunisada I), 1852, Oban format, Tokyo Metropolitan Central Library
似顔は小糸佐七を当り役とした、十三代目市村羽左衛門に見立てられている。総身の真っ白い肌には鷹の模様が彫ら

れ、鯉の瀧登りがえがかれた着物が派手で美しい。

52・53p

「近世水滸傳　笠川髭造　中村福助」歌川豊国　文久元年・1861　大判　錦絵　伊勢屋兼吉版　東京都立中央図書館特別文庫室蔵
Actors Nakamura Fukusuke II as Sasagawa Higezō, from the series *A Modern Suikoden (Kinsei Suikoden)*, Utagawa Toyokuni III (Kunisada I), 1861, Oban format, Tokyo Metropolitan Central Library
「近世水滸傳」は講談「天保水滸傳」に登場する侠客を中心とした揃物のシリーズ。笠川髭造とは笹川繁蔵のことで、実在の侠客。江戸時代後期の博徒で、江戸で力士となるが帰郷して常陸（ひたち）芝宿の親分文吉の跡目をつぐ。天保15年、縄張り争いから飯岡助五郎と大利根河原の決闘となり、助五郎の身内に暗殺された。似顔は歌舞伎役者の二代目中村福助。彫物は龍で着物の模様は蝙蝠（こうもり）である。

52p

「近世水滸傳　蟹の阿宅　岩井粂三郎」歌川豊国　文久3年・1863　大判　錦絵　伊勢屋兼吉版　東京都立中央図書館特別文庫室蔵
Actors Iwai Kumesaburō III as Kani-no-Otaku, from the series *A Modern Suikoden (Kinsei Suikoden)*, Utagawa Toyokuni III (Kunisada I), 1863, Oban format, Tokyo Metropolitan Central Library
世にも稀な毒婦、蟹の阿宅（おたく）の見立絵である。扮するは女形を演じては目をみはる岩井粂三郎。妖艶な美しさを感じさせる。この毒婦は股のところに蟹を彫り、大道で衆人に見せて嘲笑するものがいると、言いがかりをつけて金品をゆすったという。

54p

「梨園侠客傳　喧嘩屋五郎吉」歌川豊国　文久3年・1863　大判　錦絵　平野屋新蔵版　個人蔵（千葉市美術館寄託）
Kenkaya Gorokichi, from the series *The Heroic Commoners in Kabuki (Rien kyokaku den)*, Utagawa Toyokuni III (Kunisada I),1863, Oban format, Private collection (Chiba City Museum of Art)
「梨園侠客傳」は歌舞伎に登場する侠客をえがいたシリーズで、喧嘩屋五郎吉を演じるのは坂東彦三郎。侠客の肉体には滝に流れる鮮やかな花の刺青と、その背景に小鳥と草花がえがかれている。

54・55p・133p

「梨園侠客傳　しら瀧の佐吉」歌川豊国　文久3年・1863　大判　錦絵　平野屋新蔵版　個人蔵（千葉市美術館寄託）
Actors Ichimura Kakitsu IV as Shirataki no Sakichi, from the series *The Heroic Commoners in Kabuki (Rien kyokaku den)*, Utagawa Toyokuni III (Kunisada I), 1863, Oban format, Private collection (Chiba City Museum of Art)
しら瀧の佐吉を演じるのは四代目市村家橘。白く波打つ流れの杭にしがみつく佐吉。その腕には唐獅子に牡丹が彫られ、しかと見つめる眼差しが厳しさを感じさせる。侠客は、「弱きを助け、強きを挫く」ことを信条にして、任侠に生きる男たちのよび名である。単なるやくざ者や無法者とは異なり、「己の中の正義」を持つ者がこのようによばれる。

55p

「梨園侠客傳　釣ふねのさぶ」歌川豊国　文久３年・1863　大判　錦絵　平野屋新蔵版　個人蔵（千葉市美術館寄託）
Actors Nakamura Tsuruzō as Sampu of a fishing boat, from series *The Heroic Commoners in Kabuki (Rien kyokaku den)*, Utagawa Toyokuni III (Kunisada I), 1863, Oban format, Private collection (Chiba City Museum of Art)
釣ふねのさぶに扮するのは初代中村鶴蔵。『夏祭浪花鑑』に登場する團七九郎兵衛、一寸徳兵衛を加えた侠客三人の立引（たてひき）のひとりである釣船三婦（つりぶねのさぶ）のこと。腕組みをしてにらむその総身には龍の彫物が唸っている。

56・134p
「駕籠や市助　田舎侍・駕籠や和吉」歌川豊国　万延元年・1860　大判　錦絵　２枚続　辻岡屋文助版　国立国会図書館デジタルコレクション
Kagoya Ichisuke and Kagoya Wakichi, Utagawa Toyokuni III (Kunisada I), 1860, Oban format, National Diet Library Digital Collections
満開の桜の下で駕籠（かご）屋の市助と和吉が双肌を脱いで汗を拭う。市助の肌には牙をむく虎の図が彫られ、和吉の肩には渦巻く雲龍が見事である。江戸や京都、大坂に辻駕籠があり、街道には宿駕籠があった。庶民が乗ることは贅沢とされ制限令が出されたが次第に有名無実化し、江戸時代後期には各町に駕籠屋があり庶民に利用された。

57・129p
「豊国漫画図絵　雲切仁左衛門」歌川豊国　万延元年・1860　大判　錦絵　魚栄版　国立国会図書館デジタルコレクション
Kumokiri Nizaemon, from *The Heroes and Heroines of the Popular Fiction (Toyokuni Manga Zue)*, Utagawa Toyokuni III (Kunisada I), 1860, Oban format, National Diet Library Digital Collections
雲切仁左衛門は講談などで取り上げられる江戸時代の盗賊の頭目。手下の小頭には、因果小僧六之助（いんがこぞうろくのすけ）、素走り熊五郎（すばしりくまごろう）、木鼠吉五郎（きねずみごろう）、おさらば伝次、山猫三次らがいる。享保のころ関東一帯をあらしまわったとされ、これらの盗賊のことは大岡越前守の裁きぶりをえがいた『大岡政談』のひとつとなっている。渦巻雲の着物を羽織り、腕をぬっと出した肌には睨みあう龍虎の図が凄んでいる。

月岡芳年　Tsukioka Yoshitoshi

58・59p
「近世侠義傳　生魚長次郎」月岡芳年　慶応２年・1866　大判　錦絵　伊勢屋喜三郎版　東京都立中央図書館特別文庫室蔵
Namauo Chōjirō, from the series *A Biographies of Fine Modern Men (Kinsei Kyougiden)*, Tsukioka Yoshitoshi, 1866, Oban format, Tokyo Metropolitan Library
長次郎は鎌倉の谷七郷で魚を商っていたが、口論から人をあやめてしまい、身を置くところなく千葉の下総（しもうさ）に移り、銚子の五郎蔵の子分になる。振りかざした大出刃包丁に、あっけらかんと首が飛ぶ。「近世侠義傳」は、芳年が中国の古典『水滸傳』を、幕末の下総地方に起こった博徒間の闘争に見立ててえがいた36枚のシリーズ。江戸時代の

末期、東総を舞台にして展開した飯岡助五郎一家と岩瀬（笹川）繁蔵一家の争いをあつかった講談『天保水滸傳』の登場人物の略伝と画像である。

60p
「英名二十八衆句　團七九郎兵衛」月岡芳年　慶応２〜３年・1866-67　大判　錦絵　東京国立博物館蔵
Danshichi Kurobei, from the series *Eimei Nijuhasshuku*, Tsukioka Yoshitoshi, Edo period, 1866-67, Oban format, Tokyo National Museum
元禄11年（1698）冬、大坂長町裏で置きた魚屋による殺人事件を題材にした、歌舞伎『夏祭浪花鑑』の陰惨なシーン。三河屋義平次を泥沼のなかに組み伏せ、その上に團七が馬乗りになっている。團七の顔は描かれず背中の地獄の彫り物が際立つ。「英名二十八衆句」は月岡芳年と落合芳幾による連作で、それぞれが14図ずつ描いている。歌舞伎における殺しの残酷なシーンを描いたもので、残忍さを極めた血みどろの世界を活写する無惨絵の代表作である。

61p
「月百姿　史家村月夜　九紋龍」月岡芳年　明治18年・1885　大判　錦絵　秋山武右衛門版　山口県立萩美術館・浦上記念館蔵
Shikason Tsukiyo, Kumonryū Shishin, from the series the *One Hundred Aspects of the Moon (Tsuki Hyakushi)*, Tsukioka Yoshitoshi, 1885, Oban format, Hagi Uragami Museum
九紋龍史進は中国の四大奇書の一つである『水滸傳』の登場人物。華陰県史家村の豪農の生まれで武芸三昧に明け暮れる放蕩息子。宋の反乱軍の首領・史斌（しひん）をモデルとして創作されている。総身（そうしん）に九匹の龍の彫物をしていたところから九紋龍とよばれ、水滸傳百八人のなかでも人気が高い人物である。諸肌（もろはだ）を脱いで夕涼みする史進は思慮深げに遠くを眺める。

62・174p
「魯智深爛酔打壊五台山金剛神之図」月岡芳年　明治20年・1887　大判　錦絵　竪２枚続　松井栄吉版　山口県立萩美術館・浦上記念館蔵
Rochishin-ransuidakai-godaisan-kongoushin-no-zu, Tsukioka Yoshitoshi, 1887, Oban format, Hagi Uragami Museum
魯智深（ろちしん）は『水滸傳』の登場人物で豪傑のひとり。弱きを助けて強きを砕く、僧侶でありながら筋骨隆々たる巨漢で怪力の持ち主である。禅寺五台山が盗賊や破戒僧たちの巣窟となっていたことを知った魯智深は、その鉄杖を振って退治し、さらにその禅寺の金剛神まで木っ葉微塵（こっぱみじん）に打ち砕いてしまった。海棠の花模様を彫った刺青が、怒り狂った勇姿をいっそう異形なものにしている。

63p
「一魁随筆　朝比奈三郎義秀」月岡芳年　明治５〜６年・1872-73　大判　錦絵　千葉市美術館蔵
Asahina Saburou Yoshihide, from the series the *Ikkaii Zuihitsu*, Tsukioka Yoshitoshi, Meiji period, 1872-73, Oban format, Chiba City Museum of Art
朝比奈義秀は鎌倉時代前期の武将で、鎌倉幕府の御家人。和田義盛の子で、母は巴御前といわれる。勇猛かつ豪力無双の大力で、水泳が上手なことから将軍源頼家の前で鎌倉小坪の海に入り、三匹の鮫を抱いてあらわれ見物人を驚かせたという話が『吾妻鏡』にでている。妖怪絵の不気味さ

を残しながらも、人物の表情がユーモラスに描かれている。

64p
「勇の寿　二代目沢村訥升」月岡芳年　慶応元年・1865
大判　錦絵　大黒屋金之助版　山口県立萩美術館・浦上記
念館蔵
Sawamura Toshō II, from the series *Isami-no-Kotobuki,* Tsukioka Yoshitoshi, 1865, Oban format, Hagi Uragami Museum
65p
「勇の寿　河原崎権十郎」月岡芳年　慶応元年・1865　大
判　錦絵　大黒屋金之助版　山口県立萩美術館・浦上記念
館蔵
Kawarazaki Gonjūrō, from the series *Isami-no-Kotobuki,* Tsukioka Yoshitoshi, 1865, Oban format, Hagi Uragami Museum
66p
「勇の寿　沢村田之助」月岡芳年　慶応元年・1865　大判
錦絵　大黒屋金之助版　山口県立萩美術館・浦上記念館蔵
Sawamura Tanosuke, from the series *Isami-no-Kotobuki,* Tsukioka Yoshitoshi, 1865, Oban format, Hagi Uragami Museum
67p
「勇の寿　四代目中村芝翫」月岡芳年　慶応元年・1865
大判　錦絵　大黒屋金之助版　山口県立萩美術館・浦上記
念館蔵
Nakamura Shikan IV, from the series *Isami-no-Kotobuki,* Tsukioka Yoshitoshi, 1865, Oban format, Hagi Uragami Museum
67p
「勇の寿　四代目市村家橘」月岡芳年　慶応元年・1865
大判　錦絵　大黒屋金之助版　山口県立萩美術館・浦上
記念館蔵
Ichimura Kakitsu IV, from the series Isami-no-Kotobuki, Tsukioka Yoshitoshi, 1865, Oban format, Hagi Uragami Museum
この「勇の寿」は7枚揃いのシリーズで、当時人気の歌舞
伎役者が町火消しすがたで登場している。役者は江戸随一
の和事師（わごとし）とよばれ、女方もかねた二代目沢村
訥升（とっしょう）。錦絵のような立派な顔は、江戸歌舞伎
最後の名優のものであった四代目中村芝翫（しかん）。ほか
には四代目市村家橘（かきつ）、河原崎権十郎、十三代目市
村羽左衛門、五代目大谷友右衛門、三代目沢村田之助など
がえがかれる。田之助は優れた容貌と声で天才的な女形と
称されたが、病気のため33歳の若さで亡くなった。

落合芳幾　Ochiai Yoshiiku

68p
「當盛草子合　金鈴善悪譚」「魔陀羅丸」落合芳幾　慶応
2年・1866　大判　錦絵　加賀屋吉右衛門版　東京都立中
央図書館特別文庫室蔵
Madara Maru, *Kinrei Saga-Monogatari (Kinrei zen'aku monogatari), Tōsei Soshi Awase,* Ochiai Yoshiiku, 1866, Oban format, Tokyo Metropolitan Library
幕末・明治初期の戯作者・仮名垣魯文の読本『金鈴善悪譚
（きんれいさがものがたり）』の登場人物である魔陀羅丸は、
盗賊で猫術（みょうじゅつ）をつかう。同門の月岡芳年は、
巨大な猫に座り鉢から猫を出す怪しげなすがたをえがいて
いる。魔陀羅丸を演じているのは河原崎権十郎。見事な雲
龍の彫物すがたであらわれ、見得を切る様子に息をのむ場

面である。

69・70・71p
「弁天小僧菊之助　市村羽左衛門・玉島逸当実ハ日本駄
右衛門　関三十郎・浜松屋幸兵衛　市川團蔵・南郷力丸
中村芝翫」落合芳幾　文久2年・1862　大判　錦絵　3枚
続　辻岡屋文助版　国立国会図書館デジタルコレクション
Actors Ichimura Uzaemon as Benten Kozō Kikunosuke, Seki Sanjūrō as Nihon Daemon, Ichikawa Danjūrō as Hamamatsuya Kōbei, Nakamura Shikan as Nangou Rikimaru, Ochiai Yoshiiku, 1862, Oban format, National Diet Library Digital Collections
70・71p
「番頭与九郎 片岡十蔵・玉嶋逸当実ハ日本駄右衛門 関
三十郎・娘おなみ実ハ弁天小僧菊之助 市村羽左衛門・
鳶の者六吉 嵐吉六・若従四十八実ハ南郷力丸 中村芝翫」
落合芳幾　文久2年・1862　大判　錦絵　3枚続　近久屋
版　国立国会図書館デジタルコレクション
Actors Kataoka Jūzō as Bantō Yokurō, Seki Sanjūrō as Nihon Daemon, Ichimura Uzaemon as Benten Kozō Kikunosuke, Arashi Kichiroku as Tobi no Mono Rokukichi, Nakamura Shikan as Nangou Rikimaru, Ochiai Yoshiiku, 1862, Oban format, National Diet Library Digital Collections
『白浪五人男』は『青砥稿花紅彩画』の通称で知られる、五
世菊五郎の弁天小僧を中心に構成した白浪狂言。三世歌川
豊国の役者見立絵『白浪五人男』に想を得たもの。武家の
娘姿に化けた弁天が仲間の南郷力丸を供侍に仕立て、わざ
と万引きと見せかけて百両の金をゆすり取ろうとする「浜
松屋」店さきの場面である。黒頭巾の武士に桜の彫りもの
から男だと見破られ、本性をあらわして片肌をぬぎ大あぐ
らをかいて「知らざぁ言って聞かせやしょう」と啖呵（た
んか）をきる見せ場である。

72・73・74・75p
「天王御祭礼之図」落合芳幾　元治元年・1864　大判　錦
絵　3枚続　山本平吉版　東京都立中央図書館特別文庫室
蔵
Illustration of the Tenno Festival *(Tennou-Gosairei-no-Zu),* Ochiai Yoshiiku, 1864, Oban format, Tokyo Metropolitan Library
天王祭は悪疫よけの神とされる牛頭天王（ごずてんのう）
の夏祭りで、旧暦6月5日から14日にかけて神田明神の
境内にあった祇園三社の守護神を盛大に祀った。庶民の信
仰も厚く、錦絵をはじめ江戸の歳時記や名所案内にも数多
くえがかれ、天下祭といわれる山王祭や神田祭とならぶ大
きな祭礼であった。彫物すがたの若衆の熱気あふれる雰囲
気に刺青も映えている。

74・75p
「誠忠岳王図傳」落合芳幾　元治元年・1864　大判　錦絵
3枚続　伊場屋仙三郎版　山口県立萩美術館・浦上記念館
蔵
Illustrated biography of King Seichung Gakko *(Seichū-Gakuō-Zuden),* Ochiai Yoshiiku, 1864, Oban format, Hagi Uragami Museum
岳飛（がくひ）は中国南宋初期に活躍した武将で、女真族
の金と戦った英雄。母親の手によって背中に「盡忠報国」
の文字を刻まれた。北方から侵入して来る金軍と戦うため
に義勇軍に応募、たちまち頭角をあらわし幾度となく勝利
を収めた。しかしその名声を妬む宰相の秦檜（しんかい）
によって謀殺されてしまう。本図はどこの戦の場面をえが
いているのかわからない。兵隊たちの顔や衣服の陰影には

西洋画からの影響がうかがえる。

豊原国周　Toyohara Kunichika

76・77・78p
「花和尚魯知深　中村芝翫・九紋龍史進　尾上菊五郎」
豊原国周　明治 16 年・1883　大判　錦絵　3 枚続　鹿嶋松次郎版　東京都立中央図書館特別文庫室蔵
Actors Nakamura Shikan as Kaoshō Rochishin, Onoe Kikugorō as Kumonryū Shishin, Toyohara Kunichika, 1883, Oban format, Tokyo Metropolitan Library
九紋龍史進と花和尚魯智深がめぐり会う瓦罐寺（がかんじ）の場面を、だんまりに仕組んだもの。龍史進は尾上菊五郎、魯知深を中村芝翫が演じている。「だんまり」は歌舞伎の演出の一種。暗闇の場面のなかで何人かの人物が終始無言でものをさぐり合い、奪い合う立回りを様式化したものである。

78・79p
「水滸傳雪挑 夢物語廬生容画」「花和尚魯智深　市川左團次・九紋龍史進　市川團十郎」**豊原国周**　明治 19 年・1886　大判　錦絵　3 枚続　小宮山昇平版　東京都立中央図書館特別文庫室蔵
Suikoden Snow Battle (Suikoden-Yuki-no-Danmari, Yumemonogatari-Rosei-no-Sugata), Actors Ichikawa Sadanji as Kaoshō Rochishin, Ichikawa Danjūrō as Kumonryū Shishin, Toyohara Kunichika, 1886, Oban format, Tokyo Metropolitan Library
明治 19 年（1886）5 月新富座で上演された同名狂言の芝居絵である。評判記よれば人気上々で大喝采をあびたようである。描かれているのは魯智深と史進が勝負をかけて渡りあう瓦罐寺の場で、『水滸傳』のなかの初編前段の挿話を舞台化したものである。三代豊国の遺風を継いだ画法が一層の華麗さを演出している。刺青もまた衣装のように身体に溶け込み一体となっている。

79・80・81p
「水滸傳雪挑」**豊原国周**　明治 19 年・1886　大判　錦絵　3 枚続　福田熊次郎版　東京都立中央図書館特別文庫室蔵
Suikoden Snow Battle (Suikoden-Yuki-no-Danmari), Toyohara Kunichika, 1886, Oban format, Tokyo Metropolitan Library
えがかれているのは九紋龍史進と花和尚魯智深（かおしょうろちしん）が出逢う瓦罐寺の場面。河竹黙阿弥作の歌舞伎脚本『水滸傳雪挑（すいこでんゆきのだんまり）』は、東京の新富座で初演され、花和尚魯智深は初代市川左團次、九紋龍史進を九代目市川團十郎が演じている。史進は『水滸傳』の百八人の豪傑のなかで最初に登場する人物。崋山という山近くの庄屋の一人息子で、偉丈夫（いじょうぶ）な美青年である。総身に青龍の刺青をし、肩、腕、胸に九匹の龍が彫られている。魯智深は拳骨（げんこつ）三発で人を殺して和尚となったが、素行は悪く暴れもので五台山を追い出された豪傑である。

82・84p
「増補浪花鑑」**豊原国周**　明治 5 年・1872　大判　錦絵　3 枚続　東京都立中央図書館特別文庫室蔵
Zouho Naniwakagami, Toyohara Kunichika, 1872, Oban format, Tokyo Metropolitan Library

84・85p
「三河屋儀平治　尾上菊五郎・團七九郎兵衛　市川團十郎・一寸徳兵衛　市川左團次」豊原国周　明治 16 年・1883　3 枚続　大倉四郎兵衛版　国立国会図書館デジタルコレクション
Actors Onoe Kikugorō as Mikawaya Giheiji, Ichikawa Danjūrō as Danshichi Kurobei, Ichikawa Sadanji as Issun Tokubei, Toyohara Kunichika, 1883. Oban format, National Diet Library Digital Collections
『夏祭浪花鑑』は浪花の俠気の男たちとその妻の物語。堺の魚売りの團七が、喧嘩（けんか）がもとで入牢した。出牢の折には女房お梶と幼い息子、老俠客の三婦が出迎える。しかし團七は恩人につながる女を助けるため、強欲なお梶の父義平次を誤って殺害してしまう。ここにえがかれたのは團七が舅（しゅうと）を殺す「長町裏」の場面。陽気に流れる祭囃子を背景に、裸の團七が見せる美しいポーズの立回りが見どころで、「殺し場」の傑作である。團七九郎兵衛に中村芝翫、團七女房お梶に坂東三津五郎、お梶の父三河屋義平次を尾上菊五郎が演じている。

83・84・136・137p
「夏祭浪花鑑」**豊原国周**　明治 16 年・1883　大判　錦絵　3 枚続　山村鑛次郎版　東京都立中央図書館特別文庫室蔵
Natsumatsuri Naniwakagami, Toyohara Kunichika, 1883, Oban format, Tokyo Metropolitan Library
人形浄瑠璃『夏祭浪花鑑』は元禄 11 年（1698）、大坂で初世片岡仁左衛門が演じた歌舞伎狂言『宿無團七（やどなしだんしち）』で、俠客 3 人の立引（たてひき）に堺の魚売りが長町裏で人殺しをした事件を絡ませて脚色したもの。魚屋あがりの團七が舅を殺したあと、井戸から汲み上げた桶の水を頭からかぶり、返り血を流す場面をえがく。

86・87・88・89・166・176・180p
「花勇女水滸傳」**豊原国周**　明治 2 年・1869　大判　錦絵　3 枚続　具足屋嘉兵衛版　山口県立萩美術館・浦上記念館蔵
Hanayūjo Suikoden, Toyohara Kunichika, 1869, Oban format, Hagi Uragami Museum
歌舞伎の花形千両役者らの見立絵である。図の右から順に、坂東彦三郎、市村羽左衛門、沢村訥升。中央が大谷友右衛門、岩井粂三郎、沢村田之助、中村芝翫。左が河原崎権十郎、坂東三津五郎、市川小團次の役者たち。まことに豪華絢爛の美しさである。思い思いにその娟容（けんよう）を競い合い、妖艶美を湛えている。

88・89p
「しら浪六人小僧」「いんぐわ小僧六之介　市川團十郎・いなば小僧新介　中村宗十郎・鼠小僧次郎吉　尾上菊五郎・弁天小僧菊之介　岩井半四郎・天狗小僧忠力太郎　沢村訥升・火の玉小僧けい助　市川左團次」**豊原国周**　明治 11 年・1878　大判　錦絵　3 枚続　福田熊次郎版　東京都立中央図書館特別文庫室蔵
Actors Ichikawa Danjūrō as Ingakozō-Rokunosuke, Nakamura Sōjūrō as Inabakozō-Shinsuke, Onoe Kikugorō as Nezumikozou-Jirokichi, Iwaihanshirou as Bentenkozō-Kikunosuke, Sawamura Toshō as Tengukozō-Churikitarō, Ichikawa Sadanji as Hinotamakozō-Keisuke, from the Shiranamirokunin-Kozō, Toyohara Kunichika, 1878, Oban format, Tokyo Metropolitan Library
『白浪五人男』は、本外題を『青砥稿花紅彩画』といい、「浜松屋」「稲瀬川勢揃い」の二場だけの上演時には『弁天娘女男白波』（べんてんむすめめおのしらなみ）となり、通称「弁天小僧」とよばれる。盗賊を主人公とした出し物を「白浪物」とよぶのは、中国後漢の白波（浪）谷を隠れ家にした「白浪賊（はくはぞく）」からきている。白波五人男はその名の通り悪党だが、何となく憎めない五人の盗賊たちの物語である。

90・91・139・179p
「當盛五人揃肌競」「坂東彦三郎・沢村田之助・河原崎権十郎・市村家橘・中村芝翫」豊原国周　元治元年・1864　大判　錦絵　3枚続　辻岡屋文助版　東京都立中央図書館特別文庫室蔵
Bandou Hikosaburō, Sawamura Tanosuke, Kawarazaki Gonjurō, Ichimura Kakitsu , Nakamura Shikan, from the *Tose-Goninsoroi-Hadakurabe*, Toyohara Kunichika, 1864, Oban format, Tokyo Metropolitan Library
90・91p
「伍俳優時世大山」「浪花の米松　市川右團次・魁の梅吉　尾上菊五郎・打出のおつち　助高屋高助・松川の蔦蔵　市川左團次・翫すゝめの福右衛門　中村芝翫」豊原国周
明治 15 年・1882　大判　錦絵　3枚続　小林鉄次郎版　東京都立中央図書館特別文庫室蔵
Actors Ichikawa Udanji as Naniwa-no-Yonematsu, Onoe Kikugorō as Kai-no-Umekichi, Sukedakaya Takasuke as Uchide-no-Ozuchi, Ichikawa Sadanji as Matsukawa-no-Tsutazō, Nakamura Shikan as Kanjaku-no-Fukuemon, from the *Goninzure-Tokini-Ooyama*, Toyohara Kunichika, 1882, Oban format, Tokyo Metropolitan Library
92・93・94・95p
「俳優英雄王子の瀧催」「三ツ扇の粂吉　岩井燕子・舞づるの彦　坂東薪水・ききやうの□蔵　市川桃猿・荒いその瀧　河原崎三升・三ツ大吉　坂東しうか・うら梅の福　中村児雀・うす亀の市　市村家橘・□□□のお菊　沢村曙山・いびしの駒　中村芝翫・已引梅の国　沢村訥升」豊原国周　元治元年・1864　大判　錦絵　3枚続　万善版　東京都立中央図書館特別文庫室蔵
Actors Iwai Enshi as Mitsuou-no-Kumekichi, Bandō Shinsui as Maizulu-no-Hiko, Ichikawa Touen as Kikyō-no-□kura, Kawarazaki Sansho as Araiso-no-Taki, Bandō Shiuka as Mitsudaikichi, Nakamura Shijaku as Uraume-no-Fuku, Ichimura Kakitsu as Usukame-no-Ichi, Sawamura Shozan as □□□-no-Okiku, Nakamura Shikan as Ibishi-no-Koma, Sawamura Totsushō as Ihikiume-no-Kuni, from the *Kawatezoroi-Ouji-no-Kuwadate*, Toyohara Kunichika, 1864, Oban format, Tokyo Metropolitan Library
石尊権現は神奈川県伊勢原市、大山（おおやま）にある阿夫利神社が神仏習合により大山寺（たいさんじ）ともよばれたころの俗称。大山の信仰と修験道の信仰が融合した神である十一面観音を本地仏としている。江戸時代に大山詣が盛んになり、関東一円では大山講が組成され、源頼朝の戦勝祈願の故事にならい納め太刀が流行した。石尊権現の神名を記した大きな木刀を担いで大山に参詣し、瀧壺に打たれる姿がえがかれている。瀧に打たれ、総身の刺青が鮮やかに浮かび上がる。

96・97p
「め組の喧嘩」豊原国周　明治時代・19 世紀　絹本着色　軸 1 幅　東京国立博物館蔵
Megumi quarrel (*Megumi-no-Kenka*), Toyohara Kunichika, Meiji period, 19th century, Oban format, Tokyo National Museum
明治 23 年（1890）初演、竹柴其水（きすい）作の歌舞伎

『神明恵和合取組（かみのめぐみわごうのとりくみ）』の一場面。江戸の町火消のめ組の鳶（とび）の辰五郎（五代目尾上菊五郎）と力士四ツ車大八（四代目中村芝翫）の喧嘩を華やかにえがいたもので、通称「め組の喧嘩」とよばれる。上下に配置した役者のすがたが色鮮やかにえがかれている。ぐいっと睨みつける目や顔の緊張した表情、そして鳶口や竹梯子を持つ役者の動きが、大迫力をもって伝わってくる肉筆画である。

98p
「當世五明人　家橘」豊原国周　元治元年・1864　大判　錦絵　佐野屋富五郎版　東京都立中央図書館特別文庫室蔵
Ichimura Kakitsu, from the *Tousei-Gomeijin*, Toyohara Kunichika, 1864, Oban format, Tokyo Metropolitan Library
99p
「當世五明人　薪水」豊原国周　元治元年・1864　大判　錦絵　佐野屋富五郎版　東京都立中央図書館特別文庫室蔵
Bando Shinsui, from the *Tousei-Gomeijin*, Toyohara Kunichika, 1864, Oban format, Tokyo Metropolitan Library
99p
「當世五明人　芝翫」豊原国周　元治元年・1864　大判　錦絵　佐野屋富五郎版　東京都立中央図書館特別文庫室蔵
Nakamura Shikan, from the *Tousei-Gomeijin*, Toyohara Kunichika, 1864, Oban format, Tokyo Metropolitan Library
99p
「當世五明人　三升」豊原国周　元治元年・1864　大判　錦絵　佐野屋富五郎版　東京都立中央図書館特別文庫室蔵
Kawarazaki Sanshou, from the *Tousei-Gomeijin*, Toyohara Kunichika, 1864, Oban format, Tokyo Metropolitan Library
鯔背（いなせ）な五人の役者たちが、紺地に家紋模様を白く染め抜いた浴衣を羽織り、腕に彫られた刺青で見得を切る。五明とは、江戸の遊里などで客が夜五つ、現在の午後 8 時ごろで帰ることをいう。登場した役者は、四代目市村家橘（98p）・四代目中村芝翫（99p 上）・五代目坂東彦三郎（99p 右）・河原崎権十郎（99p 左）、残るは「當世五明人 曙山」（138p）の三代目沢村田之助の面々である。

100・175p
「成びしゃ駒　中村芝翫」豊原国周　元治元年・1864　大判　錦絵　辻岡屋文助版　国立国会図書館デジタルコレクション
Actors Nakamura Shikan as *Narubisha-Koma*, Toyohara Kunichika, 1864, Oban format, National Diet Library Digital Collections
100・101p
「音羽屋瀧　坂東彦三郎」豊原国周　元治元年・1864　大判　錦絵　辻岡屋文助版　国立国会図書館デジタルコレクション
Actors Bando Hikosaburo as *Otowaya-Taki*, Toyohara Kunichika, 1864, Oban format, National Diet Library Digital Collections
歌舞伎の屋号である成駒（なりこま）屋の四代目中村芝翫と、片や音羽屋の坂東彦三郎が御祭禮の行燈灯籠を背景に肩をはだけ威厳を持った表情で睨みを効かせている。芝翫の腕には龍田川、彦三郎は雲龍の彫物である。勇ましい立ちすがたにほれぼれする。

101p
「見立弁慶揃　五條橋　市川左團次」豊原国周　明治 5 年・1872　大判　錦絵　山崎屋清七版　国立国会図書館デジタルコレクション

Actors Ichikawa Sadanji as the *Mitate-Benkeizoroi Gojobashi*, Toyohara Kunichika, 1872, Oban format, National Diet Library Digital Collections
101p
「見立弁慶揃　台物の浦　尾上菊五郎」豊原国周　　明治
5 年・1872　大判　錦絵　山崎屋清七版　国立国会図書館デ
ジタルコレクション
Actors Onoe Kikugorō as the *Mitate-Benkeizoroi Daimono-no-ura*, Toyohara Kunichika, 1872, Oban format, National Diet Library Digital Collections
「見立弁慶揃」は、源義経の家来で武蔵坊と称した伝説色の
濃い豪勇の僧・弁慶に歌舞伎役者たちが扮したシリーズ。
千本の太刀を奪う悲願を立ててあと一本というときに義経
と出逢い、逆に義経に屈してしまう話が能の曲目『橋弁慶』
にでている。容姿とせりふに恵まれ、堅実な芸風で明治史
劇に本領を発揮した「五條橋」の市川左團次。いなせな江戸っ
子の主人公役に独自の境地を開いた五代目尾上菊五郎の「台
物の浦」にはじまり、河原崎三升の書写寺、中村芝翫の安宅、
沢村訥升の三井寺などがえがかれている。

102p
「梅幸百種之内　弁天小僧　尾上菊五郎」豊原国周　　明
治 26 年・1893　大判　錦絵　福田熊次郎版　東京都立中
央図書館特別文庫室蔵
Actors Onoe Kikugorō as Bentenkozō, from the *Baiko Hyakusu-no-uchi*, Toyohara Kunichika, 1893, Oban format, Tokyo National Museum
河竹黙阿弥作、通称「白浪五人男」「弁天小僧」で知られる
『青砥稿花紅彩画（あおとぞうしはなのにしきえ）』の三幕「浜
松屋店先」の場面。武家娘に変装した弁天小僧が、供侍に
化けた南郷とともに呉服商浜松屋で万引きしたとみせかけ、
強請（ゆすり）を働く。駄右衛門がわざと弁天小僧の正体
を見破ると本性をあらわし「知らざぁ言って聞かせやしょ
う」と啖呵（たんか）をきる一番の見せ場である。

103p
「善悪鬼神競」「朝日奈藤兵衛」豊原国周　　慶応 4 年・
1868　大判　錦絵　2 枚続　津ノ伊版　東京都立中央図書館
特別文庫室蔵
Asahina Toubē, *Zenaku-kijinkisoi*, Toyohara Kunichika, 1868, Oban format, Tokyo National Museum
「善悪鬼人鏡」は 2 枚続きの作品で、右に朝日奈藤兵衛（二
代目沢村訥升）、左に石川五右衛門（五代目大谷友右衛門）
が鏡合わせにえがかれている。石川五右衛門は安土桃山時
代の伝説的な盗賊。豊臣政権に反発する義賊につくり上げ
られるのは江戸時代の浄瑠璃や歌舞伎であり、『傾城吉岡
染』や『楼門五三桐』など戯曲や小説などの題材となった。
一方、朝日奈藤兵衛は江戸時代前期の侠客で大坂の生まれ。
大力であったことから鎌倉を舞台に、和田義盛と北条義時
の和田合戦に擬せられて朝比奈と称された。金輪紋の浴衣
から片肩を出し、柄杓で水を飲むすがたに凄みが感じられ
る。肩の龍文が吠えている。

104p
「真盛江戸の花役　河原崎権十郎」豊原国周　　明治 7 年・
1874　大判　錦絵　東京都立中央図書館特別文庫室蔵
Kawarazaki Gonjurō, *Matsusakari-Edo-no-Hanagata*, Toyohara Kunichika, 1874, Oban format, Tokyo Metropolitan Library
着込んだ黒い半纏（はんてん）には赤い花模様が浮かび上
がり、きりりと結んだ豆しぼりの手拭すがたが凛々しい。
河原崎権十郎が扮するのは町火消のすがた。腕には水の流

れに紅葉が散る龍田川の刺青である。右二つ巴の家紋の纏
（まとい）を担いだ美しい形が決まっている。纏は江戸時代
に町火消の各組が用いた旗印の一種で、各組により様々な
意匠が凝らしてある。

105・163p
「江戸気雄意當盛すがた」（四代目市村家橘）豊原国周
慶応 2 年・1866　大判　錦絵　平野屋新蔵版　国立国会図
書館デジタルコレクション
Actor Ichimura Kakitsu IV, from the series *Modern Figures with Edo Spirit (Edokioi-tōseisugata)*, Toyohara Kunichika, 1866, Oban format, National Diet Library Digital Collections
髪は栗髷（くりまげ）で小髷の鯔背な町鳶のすがた。弁慶
格子の浴衣に豆しぼりの手拭で背の汗をぬぐう。その千両
肌の双肩に彫られた鷲に松、紅葉に桜花ちらしの絵模様の
刺青が目をひく。役者似顔絵の魅力はなんといってもその
錦肌にある。さっと肩をはだけ、ぬいだ瞬間の華やいだ凄
味のあるかたちに、人は誰しも驚き恐れる。

105・170p
「江戸気雄意當盛すがた」豊原国周　　大判　錦絵　平野屋
新蔵版　国立国会図書館デジタルコレクション
The series *Modern Figures with Edo Spirit (Edokioi-tōseisugata)*, Toyohara Kunichika, Oban format, National Diet Library Digital Collections
この役者似顔絵も髪は栗髷で小髷の小粋なすがた。弁慶格
子の浴衣をはだけ、手に持った豆しぼりの手拭に茶瓶の水
をかけている。そしてその肌には、太鼓とバチを持った雷
神が稲妻を放つすがたの肉襦袢（にくじゅばん）を身につけ、
双肌を美しく飾っている。

105・175p
「見立十二時之内　巳　弁天小僧　尾上菊五郎」豊原国
周　　明治 7 年・1874　大判　錦絵　政田屋平吉版　山口県
立萩美術館・浦上記念館蔵
Actors Onoe Kikugorō as the *Mitate-Juniji-no-uchi Mi Bentenkozō*, Toyohara Kunichika, 1874, Oban format, Hagi Uragami Museum
『白浪五人男』に登場する女装の盗賊である弁天小僧が、浜
松屋で啖呵を切る有名な場面。延享 4 年（1747）に獄門になっ
た、日本左衛門こと浜島庄兵衛、中村左膳、岩淵弥七、中
島唯助らを題材とした架空の盗賊団。その後、講談で白浪
五人男として親しまれ、歌川豊国の役者見立絵となって市
井に知られた。この見立絵に想を得て脚色されたのが歌舞
伎『青砥稿花紅彩画』で、芝居が大評判となり日本駄右衛門、
弁天小僧菊之助、忠信利平、赤星十（重）三郎、南郷力丸
の五人男が定着した。

106・180p
「見立白浪八景」「永代橋の夕照」「鬼あざみ清七　市川
小團次」豊原国周　　慶応元年・1865　大判　錦絵　平野
屋新蔵版　東京都立中央図書館特別文庫室蔵
Actors Ichikawa Kodanji as Oniazami Seishichi, Eitaibashi-no-Sekisho, from *Mitate-Shiranamihatsukei*, Toyohara Kunichika, 1865, Oban format, Tokyo Metropolitan Library
河竹黙阿弥作の歌舞伎狂言「小袖曾我薊色縫（こそでそが
あざみのいろぬい）」の序幕に用いられた『十六夜清心（い
ざよいせいしん）』の役者絵。鬼あざみ清七を演じるのは
四代目市川小團次。大磯の遊女扇屋の十六夜と彼女になじ
んだ罪に問われ追放になった鎌倉極楽寺の所化（しょけ）
清心は稲瀬川で逢い、川へ身投げして心中を図る。しかし

十六夜は舟に助けられ、清心も死にきれず陸へ這いあがる。そして清心はのちに盗賊鬼薊清吉となるという物語。身投げ心中を図ったあと、死にきれず橋の橋脚にしがみつく清心の腕には真っ赤な薊の花が彫られている。

107p
「蔦の伝吉　市村家橘」豊原国周　元治元年・1864　大判　錦絵　辻岡屋文助版　東京都立中央図書館特別文庫室蔵
Actor Ichimura Kakitsu as Tobi-no-denkichi, Toyohara Kunichika, 1865, Oban format, Tokyo Metropolitan Library
歌舞伎脚本『心謎解色糸（こころのなぞとけたいろいと）』は、浄瑠璃『糸桜本町育』の書替えで、本町糸屋の姉娘小糸の許婚（いいなずけ）本庄綱五郎が妹娘おふさと結ばれる筋と、蔦の者お祭左七が芸者お糸を殺す筋とを組み合わせた作。本図は主役の五代目坂東彦三郎が演じた蔦の者お祭左七をえがいている。

108・109p
「水滸傳地獄廻り」（『江戸名勝図会及役者絵』より）ちりめん絵　豊原国周　国立国会図書館デジタルコレクション
Suikoden Jigoku Mawari, Illustration from a sightseeing book for Edo and Actor picture (Edomeishouzue-oyobi-yakushae), Chirimen-e, Toyohara Kunichika, National Diet Library Digital Collections
総身に刺青を彫った歌舞伎役者たちが地獄の世界に殴り込むという、荒っぽい様子がえがかれている。三途の川では亡者の衣服を剥ぎ取る奪衣婆（だつえば）が首根っこをつかまれ、側では閻魔大王も捕まり太刀を突きつけられている。大変な狼藉者たちに地獄の門番たちもなす術もなくお手上げの状態だ。

歌川芳艶　Utagawa Yoshitsuya

110p
「吉三　岡嶋屋　嵐　おかじま」（江戸の花夜の賑）歌川芳艶　万延元年・1860　大判　錦絵　海老屋林之助版　国立国会図書館デジタルコレクション
Kichizō Okajimaya, Flowers of Edo, Burning at night, (Edo-no-hana, Yoru-no-nigiwai), Utagawa Yoshitsuya, 1860, Oban format, National Diet Library Digital Collections
110p
「澤村　きのくに」（火消姿絵）歌川芳艶　万延元年・1860　大判　錦絵　海老屋林之助版　国立国会図書館デジタルコレクション
Sawamura Kinokuni, Firefighter style (Hikeshi-sugata), Utagawa Yoshitsuya, 1860, Oban format, National Diet Library Digital Collections
111p
「□嶋　市川　高　米升」（江戸の花夜の賑）歌川芳艶　万延元年・1860　大判　錦絵　海老屋林之助版　国立国会図書館デジタルコレクション
□shima Ichikawa, Flowers of Edo, Burning at night, (Edo-no-hana, Yoru-no-nigiwai), Utagawa Yoshitsuya, 1860, Oban format, National Diet Library Digital Collections
111p
「権　かわら　佐木」（江戸の花夜の賑）歌川芳艶　万延元年・1860　大判　錦絵　海老屋林之助版　国立国会図書

館デジタルコレクション
Gon Kawara, Flowers of Edo, Burning at night, (Edo-no-hana, Yoru-no-nigiwai), Utagawa Yoshitsuya, 1860, Oban format, National Diet Library Digital Collections
111p
「浅田屋　浅尾　尾長　与六」（火消姿絵）歌川芳艶　万延元年・1860　大判　錦絵　海老屋林之助版　国立国会図書館デジタルコレクション
Asao Asadaya, Firefighter style (Hikeshi-sugata), Utagawa Yoshitsuya, 1860, Oban format, National Diet Library Digital Collections
111p
「江戸花夜の賑　成駒　中むら　芝」歌川芳艶　万延元年・1860　大判　錦絵　海老屋林之助版　国立国会図書館デジタルコレクション
Nakamura Narukoma, Flowers of Edo, Burning at night, (Edo-no-hana, Yoru-no-nigiwai), Utagawa Yoshitsuya, 1860, Oban format, National Diet Library Digital Collections
112p
「はりまや　市川　さるハか」（江戸の花夜の賑）歌川芳艶　万延元年・1860　大判　錦絵　海老屋林之助版　国立国会図書館デジタルコレクション
Ichikawa Harimaya, Flowers of Edo, Burning at night, (Edo-no-hana, Yoru-no-nigiwai), Utagawa Yoshitsuya, 1860, Oban format, National Diet Library Digital Collections
113p
「尾張屋　関　三拾良」（江戸の花夜の賑）歌川芳艶　万延元年・1860　大判　錦絵　海老屋林之助版　国立国会図書館デジタルコレクション
Seki Owariya, Flowers of Edo, Burning at night, (Edo-no-hana, Yoru-no-nigiwai), Utagawa Yoshitsuya, 1860, Oban format, National Diet Library Digital Collections
江戸時代初期の江戸には消防組織はなく、武家屋敷の火災は大名や旗本が各自で消火に当たる。町屋の火災は町人自身が消火活動をするのが基本であった。しかし江戸の大半を焼失した明暦の大火では、大名火消程度では対応できないことがわかった幕府は、翌年の万治元年（1658）には、定（じょう）火消の制を成立させ、さらに享保年間には町火消の制が整えられ江戸の消防組織は確立した。火消の装束には、大名火消・定火消用と町火消用の二種があり、大名火消のものは定紋入りの火事羽織・胸当・当帯と野袴に、町火消のものは組別の半纏と釘目の股引や火消頭巾に特色がある。勇ましい姿の火消たちが纏うのは長半纏で鳶職（とびしょく）の火事場用、防寒用に着られたもの。裏に武者絵の描かれたものもある。ここにえがかれた火消たちの半纏は、火事場に水をよぶことから龍の模様や、力強さをあらわすために鬼や大蛇などがえがかれている。

歌川芳虎　Utagawa Yoshitora

114p
「江戸の花子供遊び　十四組　北組」歌川芳虎　万延元年・1860　丸鉄版　国立国会図書館デジタルコレクション
Kita -Gumi Fourth Gumi , Popular job in Edo, children's play (Edo-no-hana, Kodomo-asobi), Utagawa Yoshitora, 1860, Oban format, National Diet Library Digital Collections
115p

「兒雷也勇美之助夜刃五郎」歌川豊国　嘉永 5 年・1852
大判　錦絵　若狭屋与市版　静岡県立中央図書館蔵
Jiraiya, Yuminosuke, Yashagorō, from *the Jiraiya-gouketsu-monogatari*,
Utagawa Toyokuni III (Kunisada I), 1852, Oban format, Shizuoka Prefectural Central Library

150p
「時代模筆当白波　山猫三次」歌川豊国　安政 6 年・
1859　大判　錦絵　魚栄版　国立国会図書館デジタルコレ
クション
Actors Nakamura Fukusuke as Yamaneko Sanji, from the series *Jidai-moyō-ataru-shiranami*, Utagawa Toyokuni III (Kunisada I), 1859, Oban
format, National Diet Library Digital Collections

150p
「江戸の花名勝会　ね　九番組」歌川豊国　元治元年・
1865　大判　錦絵　加藤清版　国立国会図書館デジタ
レクション
Ne Ninth Gumi, from the *Edo-no-hana, Meishokai*, Utagawa Toyokuni III
(Kunisada I), 1865, Oban format, National Diet Library Digital Collections

151p
「曲亭翁精著八犬士随一　犬村大角妖猫退治」歌川国芳
天保末期頃・1842　大判　錦絵　西村屋与八版　山口県立
萩美術館・浦上記念館蔵
Inumura Daikaku conquers monster cat, the best of Eight Dog Warriors
written by Kyokutei Bakin, Utagawa Kuniyoshi, Edo period, c.1842, Oban
format, Hagi Uragami Museum

152p
「寺西閑心・幡瑞長兵衛・女房おとき」歌川豊国　大判
錦絵　国立国会図書館デジタルコレクション
Teranishi Kanshin, Banzuiin Chōnei, Nyōbo Otoki, Utagawa Toyokuni III
(Kunisada I), Oban format, National Diet Library Digital Collections

153p
「百物語　こはだ小平二」葛飾北斎　天保 2 〜 3 年頃・
1831-32　大判　錦絵　鶴屋喜右衛門版　山口県立萩美術
館・浦上記念館蔵
One Handred Ghost Stories: The Ghost of the Murdered Kohada Kiheiji,
Katsushika Hokusai, Edo period, 1831-32, Oban format, Hagi Uragami
Museum

154・155p
「瀧夜叉姫と骸骨の図」歌川国芳　大判　錦絵　国立国会
図書館デジタルコレクション
Takiyasha Hime and Gaikotsu no Zu, Utagawa Kuniyoshi, Oban format,
National Diet Library Digital Collections

155p
「小倉擬百人一首　凡河内躬恒　白菊丸」歌川国芳　大
判　錦絵　伊場仙版　国立国会図書館デジタルコレクショ
ン
Poem by Oshikōchi no Mitsune: Shiragikumaru, from the series Ogura
Imitations of One Hundred Poems by One Hundred Poets (*Ogura nazorae hyakunin isshu*), Utagawa Kuniyoshi, Oban format, National Diet Library Digital Collections

155p

「豊国漫画図絵　狼ノ悪次郎」歌川豊国　万延元年・
1860　大判　錦絵　魚栄版　国立国会図書館デジタルコレ
クション
Ookami no Akujirō, from *The Heroes and Heroines of the Popular Fiction
(Toyokuni Manga Zue)*, Utagawa Toyokuni III (Kunisada I),1860, Oban
format, National Diet Library Digital Collections

156・167p
「近世水滸傳　鰐の順助　市川小團次」歌川豊国　文久
2 年・1862　大判　錦絵　伊勢屋兼吉版　東京都立中央図
書館特別文庫室蔵
Actors Ichikawa Kodanji as Wani no Junsuke, from the series *A Modern
Suikoden (Kinsei Suikoden)*, Utagawa Toyokuni III (Kunisada I), 1862,
Oban format, Tokyo Metropolitan Central Library

156p
「白浪水滸傳　村崎篠團左衛門」「見立　市村家橘」歌川
芳虎　文久 3 年・1863　大判　錦絵　万善版　東京都立中
央図書館特別文庫室蔵
Actors Ichimura Kakitsu IV as Murasakishino Danzaemon, from the series
Shiranami Suikoden, Utagawa Yoshitora, 1863, Oban format, National
Diet Library Digital Collections

158p
「豊国揮毫奇術競　白菊丸」歌川豊国　大判　錦絵　平野
屋新蔵版　国立国会図書館デジタルコレクション
Shiragiku Maru, from the Magic Scenes in Kabuki Dramas (*Toyokuni-Kigou-Kijutsu-Kurabe*), Utagawa Toyokuni III (Kunisada I), Oban format,
National Diet Library Digital Collections

161p
「當世好男子傳　揚志ニ比ス唐犬権兵衛」歌川豊国　安
政 6 年・1859　大判　錦絵　林庄版　国立国会図書館デジ
タルコレクション
Touken Gonbē, comparable to *Youzi (Youji ni hisu)*, from the series *A
Modern Shuihuzhuan (Tōsei suikoden)*, Utagawa Toyokuni III (Kunisada
I), 1859, Oban format, National Diet Library Digital Collections

162p
「日本駄右衛門　関三十郎」歌川豊国　文久 2 年・1862
大判　錦絵　木屋版　国立国会図書館デジタルコレクショ
ン
Actor Seki Sanjūrō III as Nippon Daemon, No. 1 from an untitled pentaptych, Utagawa Toyokuni III (Kunisada I), 1862, Oban format, National Diet
Library Digital Collections

164p
「時代模筆当白波　雲切仁左衛門」歌川豊国　安政 6 年・
1859　大判　錦絵　魚栄版　国立国会図書館デジタルコレ
クション
Kumokiri Nizaemon, from the series *Jidai-moyō-ataru-shiranami*,
Utagawa Toyokuni III (Kunisada I), 1859, Oban format, National Diet Library Digital Collections
164p
「通俗水滸傳豪傑百八人之一個　中箭虎丁得孫」歌川国
芳　江戸時代・19 世紀　大判　錦絵　東京国立博物館蔵
Chusenko Tei Tokuson (Ding Desun), from the series *One hundred and
eight Heroes of the Suikoden*, Utagawa Kuniyoshi, Edo period, 19th cen-

tury, Oban format, Tokyo National Museum

165p
「本朝水滸傳剛勇八百人一個　岩沼吉六郎信里」歌川国芳　天保前期・1830-35　大判　錦絵　加賀屋吉右衛門版　山口県立萩美術館・浦上記念館蔵
Iwanuma Kichirokurō Nobusato, from the series *One hundred and eight Heroes of the Suikoden*, Utagawa Kuniyoshi, c.1830-35, Oban format, Hagi Uragami Museum

164・165p
「志らぬひ譚　初編之図」「若菜姫」「七草四郎年正」「漁師灘蔵」歌川豊国　大判　錦絵　国立国会図書館デジタルコレクション
The Tale of Shiranui, Part 1 *(Shiranui monogatari, shohen no zu)*, Utagawa Toyokuni III (Kunisada I), Oban format, National Diet Library Digital Collections

166p
「霜夜の星五郎　市川小團次」歌川豊国　文久 3 年・1863　大判　錦絵　鍵屋庄兵衛版　東京都立中央図書館特別文庫室蔵
Actor Ichikawa Kodanji IV as Shimoyo no Seigorō, Utagawa Toyokuni III (Kunisada I),1863, Oban format, National Diet Library Digital Collections

167p
「當世好男子傳　公孫勝に比す幡随院長兵衛」歌川豊国　安政 6 年・1859　大判　錦絵　国立国会図書館デジタルコレクション
Banzuin Chōbei, comparable to Gōngsūn Shèng (Kouson Shō ni hisu), from the series *A Modern Shuihuzhuan (Tôsei suikoden)*, Utagawa Toyokuni III (Kunisada I),1859, Oban format, National Diet Library Digital Collections

168・169p
「浮世八景ノ内　木下川ノ夜乃面」「木下川与右衛門」「羽生屋助四郎」歌川豊国　安政 2 年・1855　大判　錦絵　彫多版　国立国会図書館デジタルコレクション
Actors Onoe Kikujirō II as Konoshitagawa Kōsuke and Ōtani Tomomatsu I as Hanyūya Sukeshirō, from Ukiyo-hatsukei, Utagawa Toyokuni III (Kunisada I),1855, Oban format, National Diet Library Digital Collections

171p
「近世水滸傳　成田の新蔵　河原崎権十郎」歌川豊国　文久 2 年・1862　大判　錦絵　伊勢屋兼吉版　東京都立中央図書館特別文庫室蔵
Actors Kawarazaki Gonjūrō as Narita no Shinzou, from the series *A Modern Suikoden (Kinsei Suikoden)*, Utagawa Toyokuni III (Kunisada I), 1862, Oban format, Tokyo Metropolitan Central Library

172・173p
「本朝水滸傳豪傑八百人一個　天眼磯兵衛」歌川国芳　天保 2 年頃・1831　大判　錦絵　加賀屋吉右衛門版　山口県立萩美術館・浦上記念館蔵
Tengan Isobē, from the series *One hundred and eight Heroes of the Suikoden*, Utagawa Kuniyoshi, c.1831, Oban format, Hagi Uragami Museum

176p
「近世水滸傳　湯灌場小僧吉三　市村竹之丞」歌川豊国　文久 2 年・1862　大判　錦絵　伊勢屋兼吉版　東京都立中央図書館特別文庫室蔵
Actors Ichikawa Takenojō as Yukanba Kozo Kichisa, from the series *A Modern Suikoden (Kinsei Suikoden)*, Utagawa Toyokuni III (Kunisada I), 1862, Oban format, Tokyo Metropolitan Central Library

177p
「當世好男子傳　花和尚魯智深に比す朝比奈藤兵衛」歌川豊国　安政 5 年・1858　大判　錦絵　林庄版　国立国会図書館デジタルコレクション
Actors Nakamura Fukusuke I as Asahina Tōbei, comparable to Lu Zhishen the Tattooed Priest (Kaoshō Rochishin ni hisu), from the series *A Modern Shuihuzhuan (Tōsei suikoden)*, Utagawa Toyokuni III (Kunisada I),1858, Oban format, National Diet Library Digital Collections

178p
「かな屋金五郎・がくの小さん」歌川豊国　安政 5 年・1858　大判　錦絵　堀越版　国立国会図書館デジタルコレクション
Kanaya Kingorou, Kosan'Ukinanogaku. Utagawa Toyokuni III (Kunisada I), 1858, Oban format, National Diet Library Digital Collections

180・181p
「近世水滸傳　炎玉小僧鬼桂助　坂東亀蔵」歌川豊国　文久 2 年・1862　大判　錦絵　伊勢屋兼吉版　東京都立中央図書館特別文庫室蔵
Actors Bandō Kamezō as Hinotama Kozō Onikeisuke, from the series *A Modern Suikoden (Kinsei Suikoden)*, Utagawa Toyokuni III (Kunisada I), 1862, Oban format, Tokyo Metropolitan Central Library

182・183p
「鬼ハ外福ハ内」豊原国周　元治元年・1864　大判　錦絵　平野屋新蔵版　東京都立中央図書館特別文庫室蔵
Actor Sawamura Tanosuke III, Kawarazaki Gonjūrō I, Ichimura Kakitsu IV, from the Oni-wa-Soto, Fuku-wa-Uchi, Toyohara Kunichika, 1864, Oban format, Tokyo Metropolitan Library

[画像データ提供・資料掲載協力] **Plates Cooperation**

国際日本文化研究センター
国立国会図書館
埼玉県立近代美術館
静岡県立中央図書館
千葉市美術館
DNP アートコミュニケーションズ
東京国立博物館
東京都立中央図書館特別文庫室
山口県立萩美術館・浦上記念館

[**主要参考文献**] **Bibliography**

生誕 200 年記念「歌川国芳」監修・鈴木重三　日本経済新聞社　1996 年
江戸の華「歌舞伎絵展」監修・諏訪春雄　東武美術館　1999 年
「民衆文化とつくられたヒーローたち」国立歴史民俗博物館　2004 年
没後 150 年「歌川国芳展」監修・岩切友里子　日本経済新聞社　2011 年
没後 150 年記念「歌川国貞」太田記念美術館　2014 年
ボストン美術館蔵「俺たちの国芳 わたしの国貞」日本テレビ放送網　2016 年
「江戸の悪 PART II」太田記念美術館　2018 年
『文身百姿』玉林 繁著　文川堂書房　1936 年
『末期浮世絵師』その異常作品群　鈴木仁一著　東京美術　1971 年
『江戸のデザイン』草森紳一著　駸々堂出版株式会社　1972 年
歌舞伎・文楽・能『残酷の美』構成・解説　服部幸雄　芳賀書店　1974 年
『原色浮世絵刺青版画』監修・郡司正勝　芳賀書店　1977 年
『歌舞伎事典』服部幸雄・宮田鉄之助・廣末保 編　平凡社　1983 年
『江戸学事典』弘文堂　1984 年
江戸昭和競作『無惨絵』英名二十八衆句　花輪和一・丸尾末廣著
リブロポート　1988 年
『戯世の文』郡司正勝刪定集 第 5 巻　白水社　1991 年
傑作浮世絵コレクション『月岡芳年　血と怪奇の異才絵師』
企画・構成 青人社　河出書房新社　2014 年
傑作浮世絵コレクション『歌川国芳　遊戯と反骨の奇才絵師』
企画・構成 青人社　河出書房新社　2014 年
浮世絵に描かれた『刀剣と勇士の世界』監修・狩野博幸
企画・構成 青人社　河出書房新社　2019 年

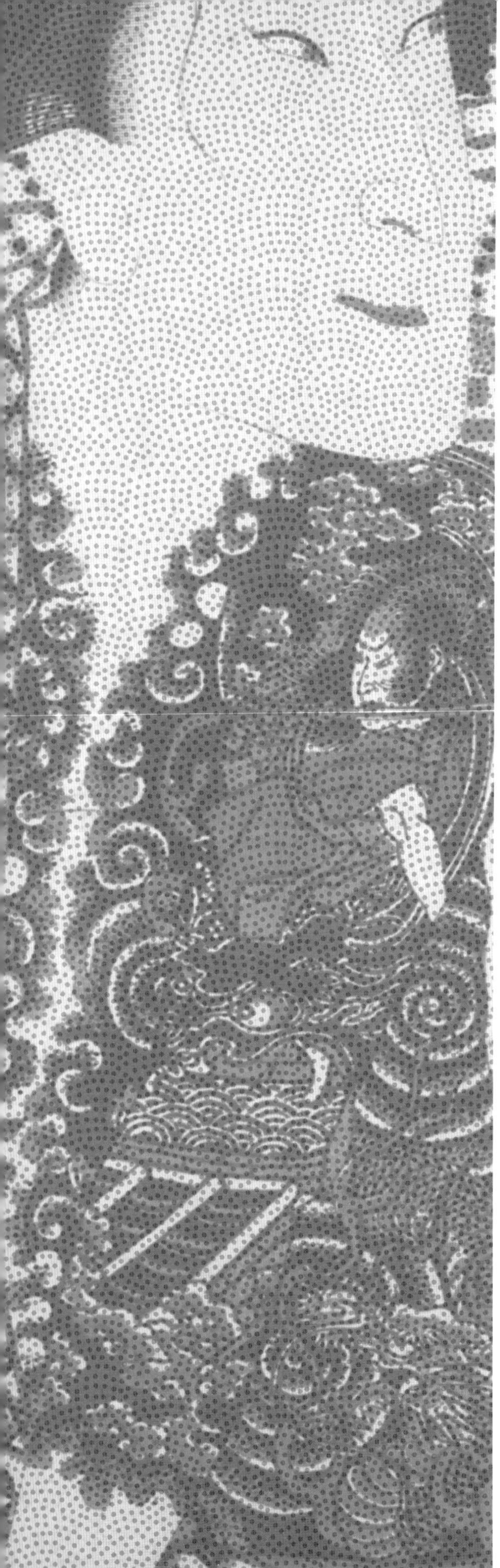

日本の図像　刺青
TATTOO: The Iconography of Japan

2023 年 12 月 25 日　初版第 1 刷発行
2025 年 5 月 5 日　　第 3 刷発行

企画・構成	編集室 青人社
序文	谷川 渥
編著	濱田信義
デザイン	谷平理映子（SPICE design）
翻訳	マクレリー ルシー（ザ・ワード・ワークス）
校閲	目黒ひかり
制作進行	宮城鈴香

発行人	三芳寛要
発行元	株式会社 パイ インターナショナル

〒 170-0005　東京都豊島区南大塚 2-32-4
TEL 03-3944-3981　FAX 03-5395-4830
sales@pie.co.jp

PIE International Inc.
2-32-4 Minami-Otsuka, Toshima-ku, Tokyo 170-0005 JAPAN
international@pie.co.jp

印刷・製本：シナノ印刷株式会社

© 2023 Nobuyoshi Hamada / PIE International
ISBN978-4-7562-5823-6 C0071
Printed in Japan

本書の収録内容の無断転載・複写・複製等を禁じます。
ご注文、乱丁・落丁本の交換等に関するお問い合わせは、小社までご連絡ください。
著作物の利用に関するお問い合わせはこちらをご覧ください。
https://pie.co.jp/contact/

TATTOO: The Iconography of Japan

Text by Nobuyoshi Hamada and Atsushi Tanigawa
Translated by The Word Works
Designed by Rieko Tanihira
Proofreading by Hikari Meguro

©2023 Nobuyoshi Hamada / PIE International
All rights reserved. No part of this publication may be reproduced,
stored in a retrieval system, or transmitted in any form or by any
means, graphic, electronic or mechanical, including photocopying
and recording, or otherwise, without prior permission in writing
from the publisher.

PIE International Inc.
2-32-4 Minami-Otsuka, Toshima-ku, Tokyo 170-0005 JAPAN
international@pie.co.jp
www.pie.co.jp/english

ISBN978-4-7562-5860-1（Outside Japan）
Printed in Japan

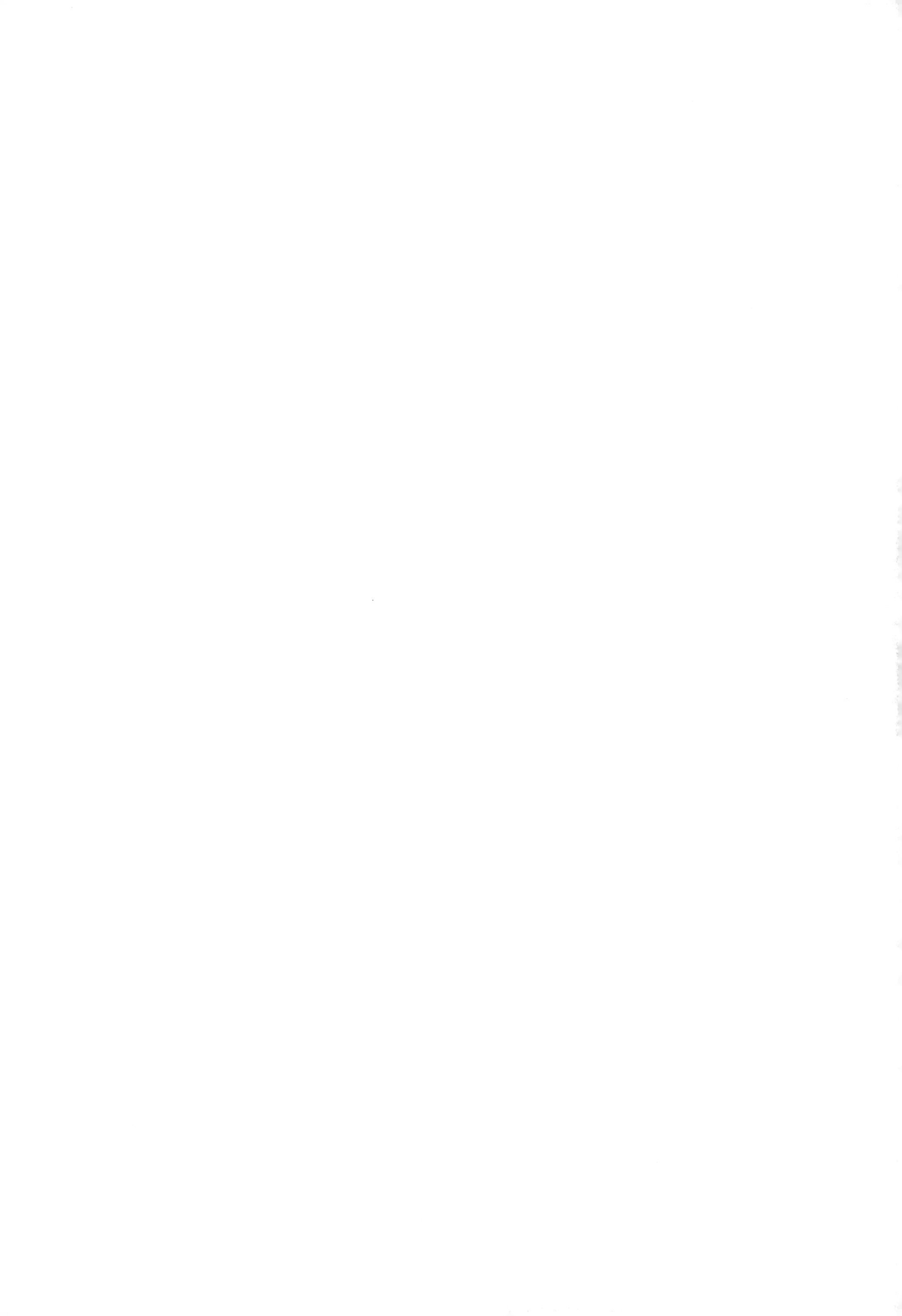

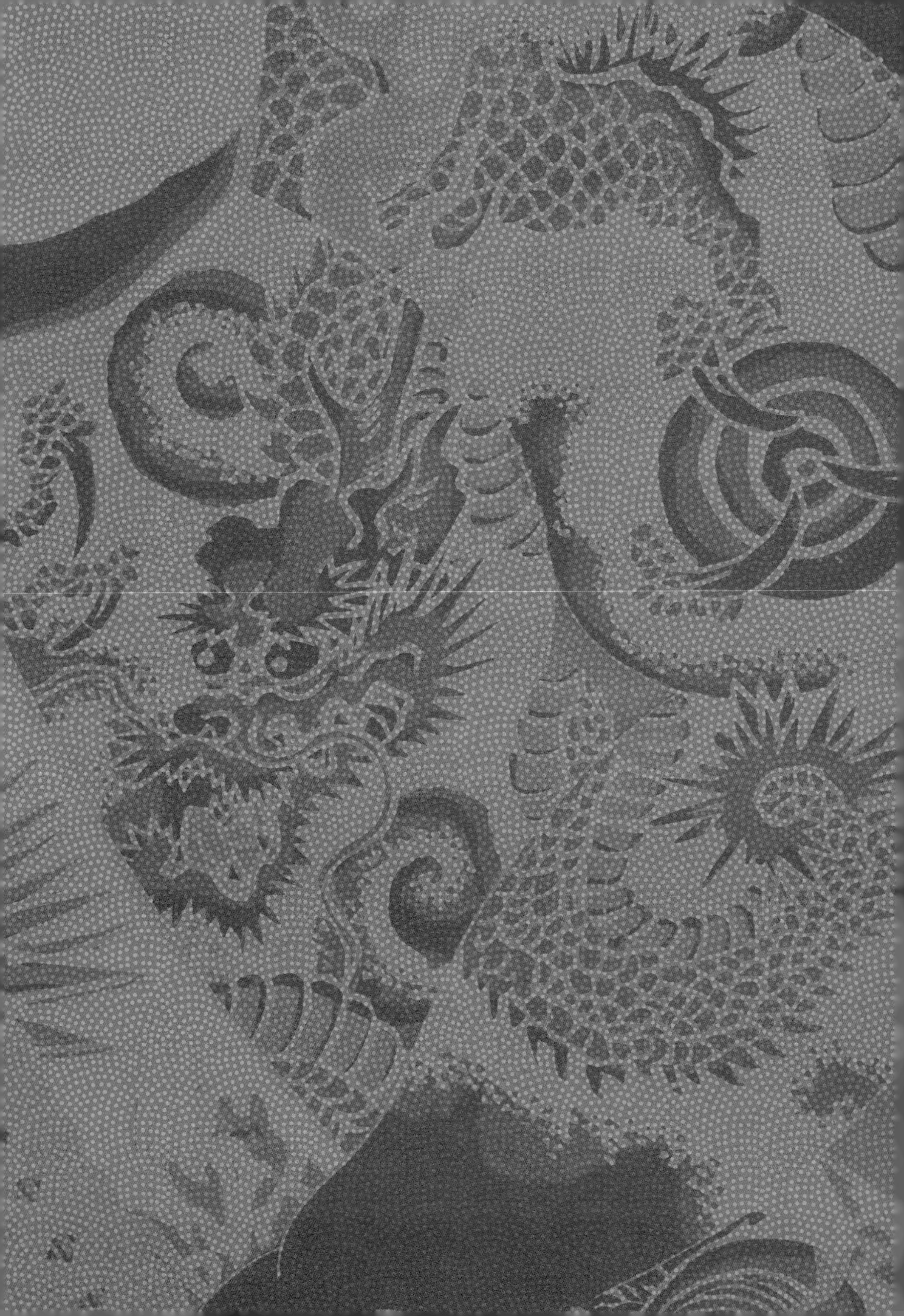

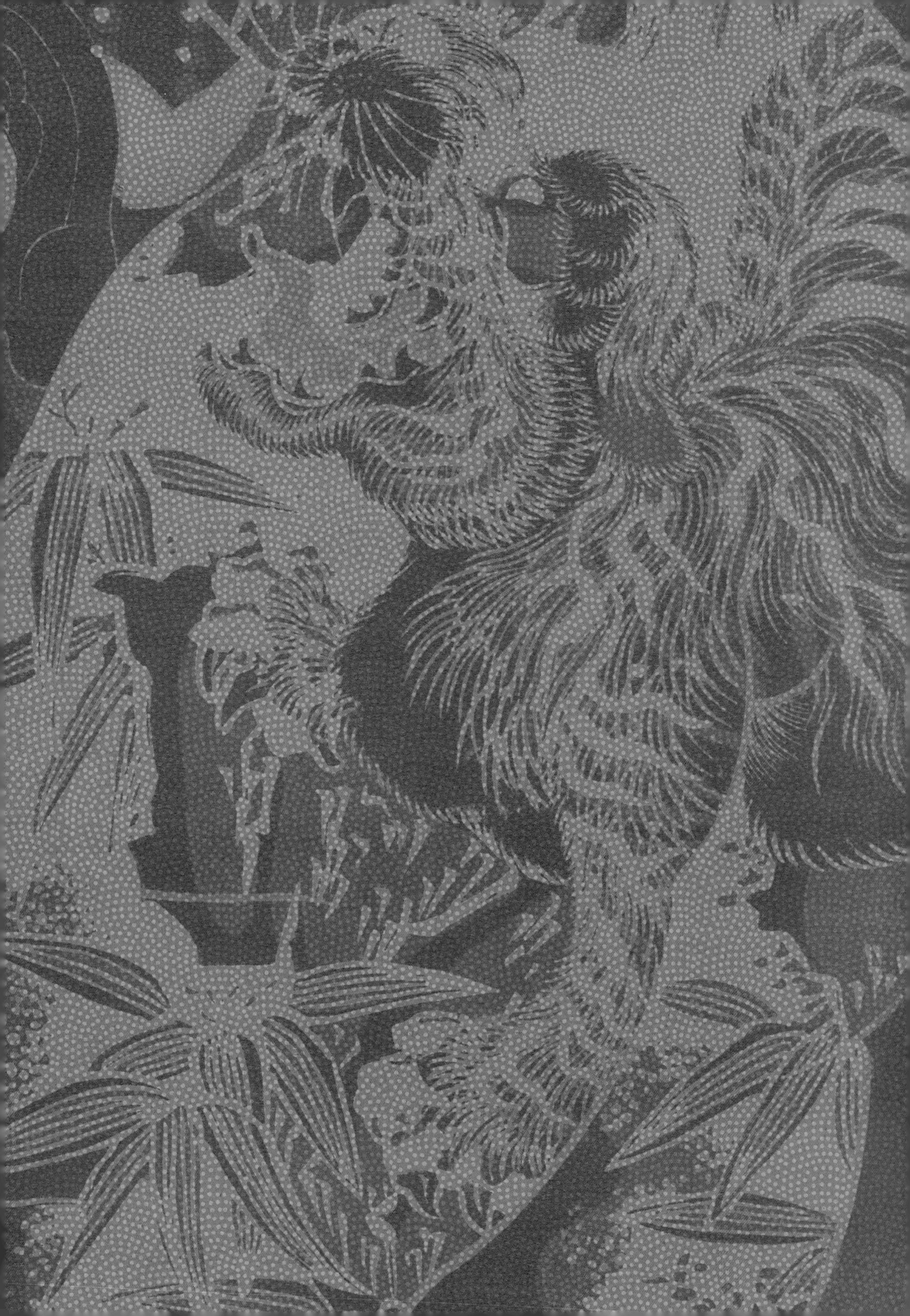

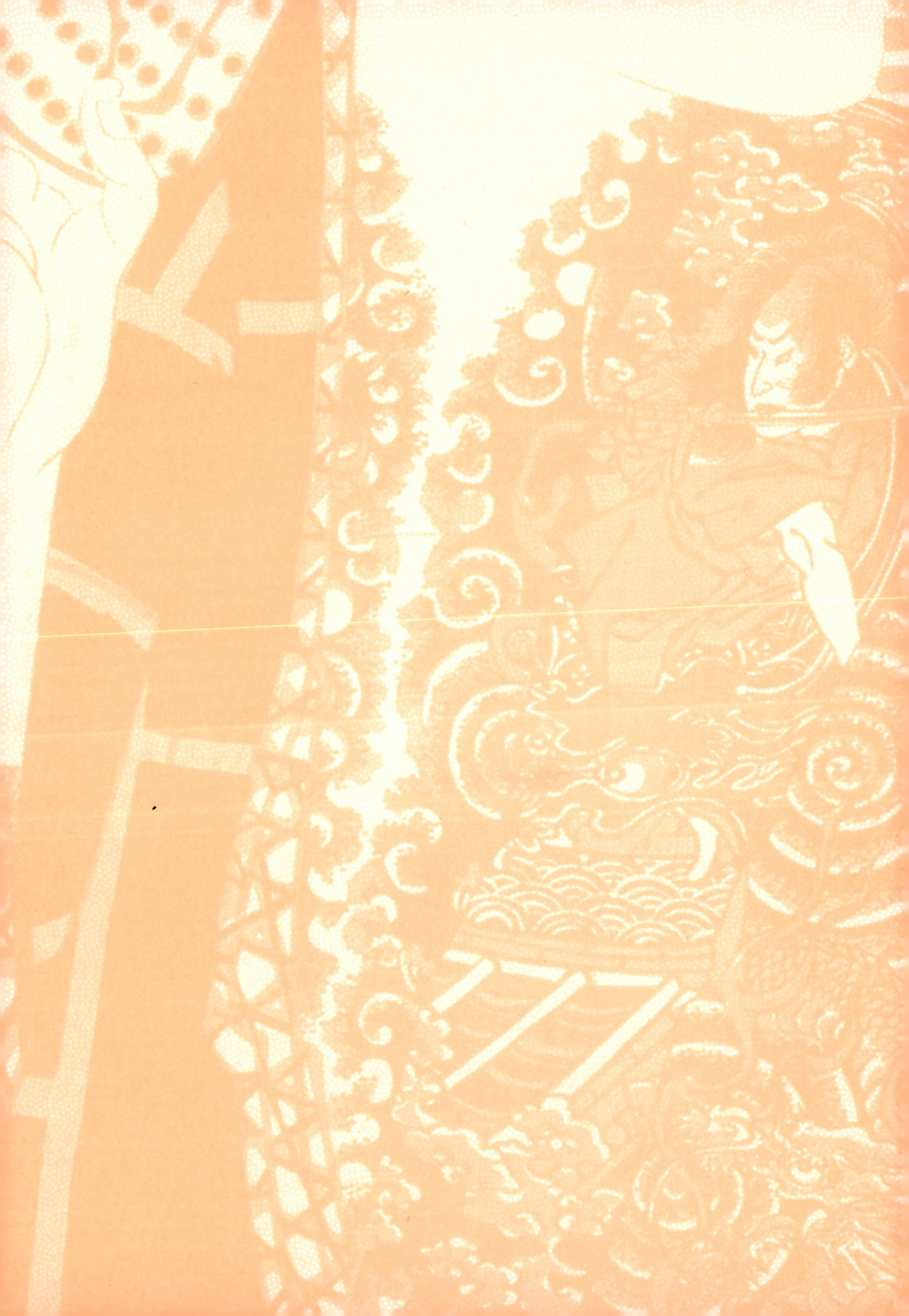